Semantic Web Information Management

Roberto De Virgilio · Fausto Giunchiglia ·
Letizia Tanca
Editors

Semantic Web Information Management

A Model-Based Perspective

Springer

Editors

Roberto De Virgilio
Dipto. Informatica e Automazione
Università Roma Tre
Via della Vasca Navale 79
00146 Rome
Italy
dvr@dia.uniroma3.it

Fausto Giunchiglia
Dipto. Ingegneria e Scienza dell'Informazione
Università di Trento
Via Sommarive 14
38100 Povo TN
Italy
fausto@dit.unitn.it

Letizia Tanca
Dipto. Elettronica e Informazione (DEI)
Politecnico di Milano
Via Ponzio 34/5
20133 Milan
Italy
tanca@elet.polimi.it

ISBN 978-3-642-42448-9 ISBN 978-3-642-04329-1 (eBook)
DOI 10.1007/978-3-642-04329-1
Springer Heidelberg Dordrecht London New York

ACM Computing Classification (1998): H.2, H.3, I.2

Cover design: KuenkelLopka GmbH, Heidelberg

Printed on acid-free paper

Springer is part of Springer Science+Business Media (www.springer.com)

Preface

The spread of daily increasing amounts of data, appropriately structured to be easily machine-processable on the Web according to semantics-oriented formats (e.g. RDF, RDFS, OWL), has inspired new research issues that can be summarized as (i) efficient and effective storage, (ii) feasible querying and reasoning, and (iii) practical usage of semantic data in real world scenarios. In this book, we lay the foundations to face such issues. The book ambition is to present and analyze the techniques for semantic information management, by taking advantage of the synergisms between the logical basis of the *Semantic Web* and the logical foundations of *Data Management*.

Rome	Roberto De Virgilio
Povo	Fausto Giunchiglia
Milan	Letizia Tanca

Contents

Contributors

Marcelo Arenas Pontificia Universidad Católica de Chile, Vicuña Mackenna 4860, 7820436 Macul, Santiago, Chile, marenas@ing.puc.cl

Paolo Atzeni Università Roma Tre, Via della Vasca Navale 79, 00146 Rome, Italy, atzeni@dia.uniroma3.it

Devis Bianchini University of Brescia, via Branze 38, 25123 Brescia, Italy, bianchin@ing.unibs.it

François Bry University of Munich, Oettingenstraße 67, 80538 Munich, Germany, bry@lmu.de

Andrea Calì University of Oxford, Eagle House, Walton Well Road, Oxford OX2 6ED, UK; University of Oxford, Wolfson Building, Parks Road, Oxford OX1 3QD, UK, andrea.cali@oxford-man.ox.ac.uk

Diego Calvanese Free University of Bozen-Bolzano, Piazza Domenicani 3, 39100 Bolzano, Italy, calvanese@inf.unibz.it

Michele Catasta National University of Ireland, Galway, Ireland, michele.catasta@deri.org

Simona Colucci Politecnico di Bari, via E. Orabona 4, 70125 Bari, Italy; Data Over Ontological Models—D.O.O.M. srl, via N. Paganini 7, 75100 Matera, Italy, s.colucci@poliba.it

Valeria De Antonellis University of Brescia, via Branze 38, 25123 Brescia, Italy, deantone@ing.unibs.it

Giuseppe De Giacomo SAPIENZA Università di Roma, Via Ariosto 25, 00185 Rome, Italy, degiacomo@dis.uniroma1.it

Roberto De Virgilio Università Roma Tre, Via della Vasca Navale 79, 00146 Rome, Italy, dvr@dia.uniroma3.it

Pierluigi Del Nostro Università Roma Tre, Via della Vasca Navale 79, 00146 Rome, Italy, pdn@dia.uniroma3.it

Renaud Delbru National University of Ireland, Galway, Ireland, renaud.delbru@deri.org

Tommaso Di Noia Politecnico di Bari, via E. Orabona 4, 70125 Bari, Italy, t.dinoia@poliba.it

Orri Erling OpenLink Software, 10 Burlington Mall Road, Suite 265, Burlington, MA 01803, USA, oerling@openlinksw.com

Feroz Farazi University of Trento, Trento, Italy, farazi@disi.unitn.it

Florian Fischer University of Innsbruck, Innsbruck, Austria, florian.fischer@sti2.at

Flavius Frasincar Erasmus University Rotterdam, Burgemeester Oudlaan 50, 3062 PA Rotterdam, The Netherlands, frasincar@ese.eur.nl

Tim Furche University of Munich, Oettingenstraße 67, 80538 Munich, Germany, tim@furche.net

Giorgio Gianforme Università Roma Tre, Via della Vasca Navale 79, 00146 Rome, Italy, giorgio.gianforme@gmail.com

Fausto Giunchiglia Università di Trento, Via Sommarive 14, 38100 Povo TN, Italy, fausto@dit.unitn.it

Georg Gottlob University of Oxford, Wolfson Building, Parks Road, Oxford OX1 3QD, UK; University of Oxford, Blue Boar Court, 9 Alfred Street, Oxford OX1 4EH, UK, georg.gottlob@comlab.ox.ac.uk

Claudio Gutierrez Universidad de Chile, Blanco Encalada 2120, 8370459 Santiago, Santiago, Chile, cgutierr@dcc.uchile.cl

Jan Hidders Delft University of Technology, P.O. Box 5031, 2600 GA Delft, The Netherlands, a.j.h.hidders@tudelft.nl

Martin Homola Fondazione Bruno Kessler, Via Sommarive 18, 38123 Trento, Italy; Comenius University, 84248 Bratislava, Slovakia, homola@fmph.uniba.sk

Thomas Hornung Albert-Ludwigs-Universität Freiburg, Georges-Köhler-Allee, Geb. 51, 79110 Freiburg, Germany, hornungt@informatik.uni-freiburg.de

Geert-Jan Houben Delft University of Technology, P.O. Box 5031, 2600 GA Delft, The Netherlands, g.j.p.m.houben@tudelft.nl

Uzay Kaymak Erasmus University Rotterdam, Burgemeester Oudlaan 50, 3062 PA Rotterdam, The Netherlands, kaymak@ese.eur.nl

Georg Lausen Albert-Ludwigs-Universität Freiburg, Georges-Köhler-Allee, Geb. 51, 79110 Freiburg, Germany, lausen@informatik.uni-freiburg.de

Domenico Lembo SAPIENZA Università di Roma, Via Ariosto 25, 00185 Rome, Italy, lembo@dis.uniroma1.it

Maurizio Lenzerini SAPIENZA Università di Roma, Via Ariosto 25, 00185 Rome, Italy, lenzerini@dis.uniroma1.it

Erwin Leonardi Delft University of Technology, P.O. Box 5031, 2600 GA Delft, The Netherlands, e.leonardi@tudelft.nl

Clemens Ley Oxford University, Wolfson Building, Parks Road, Oxford OX1 3QD, UK, Clemens.Ley@comlab.ox.ac.uk

Benedikt Linse University of Munich, Oettingenstraße 67, 80538 Munich, Germany, Benedikt.Linse@ifi.lmu.de

Thomas Lukasiewicz University of Oxford, Wolfson Building, Parks Road, Oxford OX1 3QD, UK; Technische Universität Wien, Favoritenstraße 9-11, 1040 Wien, Austria, thomas.lukasiewicz@comlab.ox.ac.uk

Bruno Marnette Oxford University, Wolfson Building, Parks Road, Oxford OX1 3QD, UK, Bruno.Marnette@comlab.ox.ac.uk

Michael Meier Albert-Ludwigs-Universität Freiburg, Georges-Köhler-Allee, Geb. 51, 79110 Freiburg, Germany, meierm@informatik.uni-freiburg.de

Michele Melchiori University of Brescia, via Branze 38, 25123 Brescia, Italy, melchior@ing.unibs.it

Ivan Mikhailov OpenLink Software, 10 Burlington Mall Road, Suite 265, Burlington, MA 01803, USA, imikhailov@openlinksw.com

Viorel Milea Erasmus University Rotterdam, Burgemeester Oudlaan 50, 3062 PA Rotterdam, The Netherlands, milea@ese.eur.nl

Giorgio Orsi Politecnico di Milano, Via Ponzio 34/5, Milan, Italy, orsi@elet.polimi.it

Jorge Pérez Pontificia Universidad Católica de Chile, Vicuña Mackenna 4860, 7820436 Macul, Santiago, Chile, jperez@ing.puc.cl

Stefano Paolozzi Università Roma Tre, Via della Vasca Navale 79, 00146 Rome, Italy, stefano.paolozzi@gmail.com

Christoph Pinkel MTC Infomedia OHG, Kaiserstr. 26, 66121 Saarbrücken, Germany, c.pinkel@mtc-infomedia.de

Olga Poppe University of Munich, Oettingenstraße 67, 80538 Munich, Germany, olga.poppe@pms.ifi.lmu.de

Azzurra Ragone Politecnico di Bari, via E. Orabona 4, 70125 Bari, Italy, a.ragone@poliba.it

Riccardo Rosati SAPIENZA Università di Roma, Via Ariosto 25, 00185 Rome, Italy, rosati@dis.uniroma1.it

Michele Ruta Politecnico di Bari, via E. Orabona 4, 70125 Bari, Italy, m.ruta@poliba.it

Marco Ruzzi SAPIENZA Università di Roma, Via Ariosto 25, 00185 Rome, Italy, ruzzi@dis.uniroma1.it

Michael Schmidt Albert-Ludwigs-Universität Freiburg, Georges-Köhler-Allee, Geb. 51, 79110 Freiburg, Germany, mschmidt@informatik.uni-freiburg.de

Luciano Serafini Fondazione Bruno Kessler, Via Sommarive 18, 38123 Trento, Italy, serafini@fbk.eu

Pavel Shvaiko TasLab, Informatica Trentina S.p.A., Trento, Italy, pavel.shvaiko@infotn.it

Umberto Straccia ISTI-CNR, Via G. Moruzzi 1, 56124 Pisa, Italy, straccia@isti.cnr.it

Letizia Tanca Politecnico di Milano, Via Ponzio 34/5, 20133 Milan, Italy, tanca@elet.polimi.it

Eufemia Tinelli Politecnico di Bari, via E. Orabona 4, 70125 Bari, Italy, e.tinelli@poliba.it

Riccardo Torlone Università Roma Tre, Via della Vasca Navale 79, 00146 Rome, Italy, torlone@dia.uniroma3.it

Nickolai Toupikov National University of Ireland, Galway, Ireland, nickolai.toupikov@deri.org

Giovanni Tummarello National University of Ireland, Galway, Ireland, giovanni.tummarello@deri.org

Gulay Unel University of Innsbruck, Innsbruck, Austria, gulay.unel@sti2.at

Kees van der Sluijs Eindhoven University of Technology, P.O. Box 513, 5600 MB Eindhoven, The Netherlands, k.a.m.sluijs@tue.nl

Yannis Velegrakis University of Trento, Via Sommarive 14, 38100 Trento, Italy, velgias@disi.unitn.eu

Antonius Weinzierl Technische Universität Wien, Favoritenstraße 9-11, 1040 Wien, Austria, aweinz@kr.tuwien.ac.at

Mikalai Yatskevich Université Rennes 1, Rennes, France, mikalai.yatskevich@univ-rennes1.fr

Chapter 1
Introduction

Roberto De Virgilio, Fausto Giunchiglia, and Letizia Tanca

In the most recent years, the Semantic Web has become a promising research field, which tries to automate and support sharing and reuse of the data and metadata representing the growing amount of digital information available to our society. The underlying idea of having a description of the data on the Web, in such a way that it can be employed by machines for automation, integration and reuse across various applications, has been exploited in several research fields. However, the gigantic amount of such useful information makes more and more difficult its efficient management, undermining the possibility to transform it into useful *knowledge*.

Databases have been designed to store high volumes of data and to provide an efficient query interface. Semantic Web formats are geared towards capturing domain knowledge, annotations, and offering a high-level, machine-processable view of information. The complementary strengths and weaknesses of these data models motivate the research we present in this book, trying to bridge the two worlds in order to leverage the efficiency and scalability of database-oriented technologies to support an ontological, high level view of data and metadata. The book ambition is to present and analyze the techniques for semantic information management, by taking advantage of the synergisms between the logical basis of the Semantic Web and the logical foundations of Data Management.

R. De Virgilio (✉)
Dipto. Informatica e Automazione, Università Roma Tre, Via della Vasca Navale 79, 00146 Rome, Italy
e-mail: dvr@dia.uniroma3.it

F. Giunchiglia
Dipto. Ingegneria e Scienza dell'Informazione, Università di Trento, Via Sommarive 14, 38100 Povo TN, Italy
e-mail: fausto@dit.unitn.it

L. Tanca
Dipto. Elettronica e Informazione (DEI), Politecnico di Milano, Via Ponzio 34/5, 20133 Milan, Italy
e-mail: tanca@elet.polimi.it

R. De Virgilio et al. (eds.), *Semantic Web Information Management*,
DOI 10.1007/978-3-642-04329-1_1, © Springer-Verlag Berlin Heidelberg 2010

This book is neither a primer nor a survey: rather, it is a handbook which prospects novel solutions for the Semantic Web. In particular, it presents and analyzes the most recent (and qualified) techniques for semantic information management. The leitmotif of this research is the proposal of models and methods especially fit to represent and manage data appropriately structured to be easily machine-processable on the Web.

The overture of the book is organized in two chapters, introducing the two fundamental concepts of Data Management and Semantic Web, respectively. *Data management* is a key point for every information system and involves many challenging tasks such as data storage, migration, integration, extraction, and normalization. The *Semantic Web*, as first proposed by Tim Berners-Lee,[1] represents the new generation of Web, in which information will no longer be meant for human perusal only, but also for being processed by machines, enabling intelligent information services, personalized Web-sites, and semantically empowered search-engines. The rest of the book is organized into five parts, briefly described in the following paragraphs.

PART 1. Semantic Web Data Storage Different storage models can be proposed, at different levels of abstraction, to support semantic data storage. Maybe the simplest model defined to properly represent semantic information is RDF, Resource Description Framework. The RDF model is based on the concept of triple, which relates two concepts (resources) by means of a predicate. A natural way to make persistent RDF data is the triple model, which suggests to directly store the triples as "basic bricks"; however, several more models and techniques have been proposed. Part I is devoted to reviewing some of these formalisms, also trying to compare and discuss their strengths and weaknesses.

Chapter 4 provides a comprehensive description of some relational RDF storage schemes and will discuss their advantages and limitations. Indeed, instead of designing RDF storage solutions from scratch, it is possible to invest on existing relational technologies, which can offer efficient storage and high performance querying at relatively low cost; it is thus possible to obtain systems that support the full power of RDF while achieving high performance results.

Chapter 5 presents another approach for storing, managing, and processing RDF data, based on the notion of construct, that represents a concept of the domain of interest. This makes the approach easily extensible and independent of the specific knowledge representation language. The chapter is completed by the description of real world scenarios where complex data management operations, which go beyond simple selections or projections and involve the navigation of huge portions of RDF data sources, are in order.

Finally, Chap. 6 presents the experience of Sindice.com, where a general model for the Web of Data is reflected in the architecture and components of a large-scale infrastructure. Aspects such as data collection, processing, indexing, ranking are touched, and an application built on top of the said infrastructure is described.

[1] Tim Berners-Lee. The Semantic Web, In *Scientific American*, 2001.

PART 2. Reasoning in the Semantic Web The utility of storing semantic data certainly depends on the possibility of *reasoning* on it. Since its earliest times, one of the most important tasks of Artificial Intelligence, and in particular of Knowledge Representation, was that of deriving logical consequences from a set of asserted facts or axioms. The notion of reasoning somehow generalizes that of deduction, by also requiring a rich conceptual structure as a support for inference. The challenge of the Semantic Web is the provision of distributed information with well-defined meaning, understandable for different parties, thus *ontologies*, defined as explicit models of conceptualizations with a well-defined semantics, are discussed as appropriate tools for Semantic Web data representation and reasoning.

In Chap. 7, we introduce the basics of formal languages and reasoning in a Web context. As noticed above, reasoning in the context of Web-based systems has a distinct set of requirements in terms of quality and quantity of the information it has to cope with. Thus this chapter focuses on reasoning on Semantic Web-oriented data, by discussing the basic different paradigms forming the background for knowledge representation in Web-based Systems and then examining how these paradigms are reflected in current standards and trends on the Web. Initially, the relevant background, including fundamentals of Logic Programming and Description Logics, are introduced along with the most common reasoning techniques. In particular, in the realm of Logic Programming, the Datalog language was developed in the 80s as a database query and rule language, and a wealth of results and optimizations from the area of deductive database research are now available. On the other hand, Description Logics (DLs) have played a crucial role in the last decade as a (family of) formalisms for representing ontologies. Currently, much research on DLs is directed towards scalable and efficient query answering over ontologies. The chapter also provides some of the relevant standards of the Semantic Web, namely OWL 2 and WSML.

The increasing complexity of the ontologies and the domains they represent makes ontology engineering extremely complex: an approach inspired by software engineering, where modularization is a widely acknowledged feature, suggests the construction of modular ontologies to conquer such complexity. Distributed reasoning is the other side of the coin of modular ontologies: given an ontology comprising of a set of modules, it is desired to perform reasoning by combination of multiple reasoning processes performed locally on each of the modules. Chapter 8 surveys and compares the main formalisms for modular ontologies and distributed reasoning in the Semantic Web, also discussing reasoning capabilities of each framework.

In an open world, such as the Web, one of the most challenging tasks is ontology alignment (also called matching or mapping) which is the process of finding relationships among the elements (e.g., concepts, roles and individuals) of two ontologies. In the context of Chap. 9, *matching* is an operation that takes two graph-like structures (e.g., lightweight ontologies) and produces an alignment between the nodes of these graphs that correspond semantically to each other. Semantic matching is based on two ideas: (i) discovering an alignment by computing semantic relations (e.g., equivalence, more general); (ii) determining semantic relations by analyzing the meaning (concepts, not labels) which is codified in the entities and the structures of ontologies. Chapter 9 first overviews the state of the art in the ontology matching field and then presents basic and optimized algorithms for semantic matching as well as their implementation within the S-Match system, also evaluating S-Match against state of the art systems.

Relating and integrating ontologies is a arduous task because of the difficulty of finding high quality matchings between different ontologies, and because possible mismatches can arise during the alignment process. Despite the numerous solutions proposed for the ontology matching problem, ontology matching tools produce, up to now, results with a significant amount of wrong alignments (lack of precision) and they are unable to retrieve all the correct ones (lack of recall). Thus, in most situations, automatically-created ontology alignments need to be revised by a human expert and, since this process is extremely time-consuming, many research efforts have been put in the definition of automated support for their analysis and repairing. Chapter 10 proposes an overview of the most interesting approaches to automatic ontology mapping revision, taking into account that interontology consistency must be achieved in such a way that as little information as possible is lost during the process, especially because in some cases only the mappings can be accessed while the input ontologies cannot be modified.

Chapter 11, the last of Part II, deals with a tOWL, a temporal extension of the OWL DL language. In its role as reference system, time is, beyond any doubt, one of the most encountered dimensions in a variety of domains, thus dealing with time is one of the major concerns in different fields, including knowledge representation. Rather than representing time- and change-extensions of RDF—which are able to cope only to a limited extent with the semantics of temporal representations, and moreover do not have an RDF/XML serialization—or proposing OWL ontologies for modeling time and/or change, tOWL *builds upon OWL*, thus extending its expressivity. The current contribution is focused around employing the tOWL language for the representation of business processes, showing the example of a Leveraged Buyout process, which shows the tOWL applicability in a business context.

PART 3. Semantic Web Data Querying The popularity gained by the relational model for databases is clearly not independent of the effectiveness of the SQL query language. It is fundamental to achieve similarly adequate means to query the Semantic Web, were a new issue arises: since it is also possible to reason over data, querying and reasoning should be combined in order to let the underlying systems produce the best possible results.

Chapter 12 presents *Datalog*$^{\pm}$, a family of expressive extensions of Datalog which, by progressively adding the possibility to express certain constraints (TGD's, EGD's and negative constraints), allows forms of ontological knowledge beyond plain Datalog and allows query answering over ontologies. All the works on TGD's and the other mentioned constraints make use of a technique called *chase*, which amounts to repairing violations of TGDs and EGDs starting from a database, until a fixpoint is reached. One of the main difficulties behind all these approaches is the fact that such a fixpoint may be infinite. Several works in the literature consider classes of TGDs for which the chase terminates and therefore generates a finite instance; *Datalog*$^{\pm}$ deals with these constraints as rules for which the chase does not terminate, but for which query answering is nonetheless decidable in general and tractable in many cases in the data complexity.

In January 2008, W3C recommended a query language called SPARQL for querying RDF data. Chapter 13 gives a detailed description of the semantics of this language, starting with the definition of a formal semantics for the core part of SPARQL, and then moving to the semantics of the entire language, including a number of delicate features such as blank nodes in graph patterns and bag semantics for solutions. The definition of a formal semantics for SPARQL has played a key role in the standardization process of this query language. Although taken one by one the features of SPARQL are intuitive and simple to describe and understand, it turns out that the combination of them makes SPARQL a complex language. Reaching a consensus in the W3C standardization process about a formal semantics for SPARQL was not an easy task. However, the official specification of SPARQL, endorsed by the W3C, formalizes a semantics based on the one specified in Chap. 13.

Rather than relying on a fixed schema, web data have widely varied, constantly changing schemata. Thus, storage and access methods that rely on fixed, pre-established schemata are highly inefficient for querying, and new methods specifically tailored to these properties of relationships on the web are needed. For XML (eXtensible Markup Language), where data is mostly considered tree shaped, such methods are mainly based on labeling schemes, which assign labels to nodes in a tree or graph in such a way that various relations between nodes can be decided given just the labels of two nodes. Labeling schemes are particularly effective if queries are mostly concerned with the relationships between entities in a query, e.g., the existence of a certain relation, the reachability between two entities, etc. However, the existing indexing and labeling schemes for RDF (and graph data in general) sacrifice one of the most attractive properties of XML labeling schemes, the constant time (and per-node space) test for adjacency (child) and reachability (descendant). After presenting existing indexing and labeling schemes for RDF and other graph data, Chap. 14 introduces the first labeling scheme for RDF data that retains this property. Moreover, this labeling scheme is applied to (acyclic) SPARQL queries to obtain an evaluation algorithm with time and space complexity linear in the number of resources in the queried RDF graph.

Observing the two main querying paradigms presented in Part III, we realize that there is much room for improving Semantin Web query languages. In particular, Chap. 15 investigates the addition of rules and quantifier alternation to SPARQL. This extension, called SPARQLog, augments previous RDF query languages by arbitrary quantifier alternation: blank nodes may occur in the scope of all, some, or none of the universal variables of a rule. In addition SPARQLog is aware of important RDF features such as the distinction between blank nodes, literals and IRIs or the RDFS vocabulary. A sound and complete operational semantics, that can be implemented using existing logic programming techniques, is defined, and a number of expressivity and complexity results are proven which apply similarly also in the more general setting of data exchange.

As the conclusion of Part III, Chap. 16 discusses requirements and desiderata for SPARQL benchmarks and presents SP2Bench, a publicly available, language-specific performance benchmark for SPARQL. SP2Bench provides a meaningful analysis and comparison benchmark platform for existing storage schemes for RDF data as well as for SPARQL queries. With the SP2Bench framework, the chapter presents its data generator, benchmark queries, and performance metrics. SP2Bench is settled in the DBLP scenario and comprises a data generator for creating arbitrarily large DBLP-like documents and a set of carefully designed benchmark queries. The generated documents mirror vital key characteristics and socialworld distributions encountered in the original DBLP data set, while the queries implement meaningful requests on top of this data, covering a variety of SPARQL operator constellations and RDF access patterns.

PART 4. Semantic Web Applications This part illustrates how Semantic Web concepts, methods and techniques can be employed to provide the means for resource interpretation and sharing in modern, open knowledge spaces.

Chapter 17 carefully discusses the application of Semantic Web techniques for data integration. Data integration is the problem of combining data from different sources providing a single interface for the information users. In the framework where a global schema, the source schemata, and the mapping between the source and the global schema are specified, with the global schema specified in OWL, a number of interesting questions arise as for computational complexity of query answering under different instantiations of the framework in terms of query language and form and interpretation of the mapping. Since query answering in the considered setting is computationally complex, the various sources of complexity are analyzed and discussed, and in order to achieve efficient query answering, OWL 2 QL is adopted as the ontology language used to express the global schema. OWL 2 QL essentially corresponds to a member of the DL-Lite family, a family of Description Logics designed to have a good trade-off between expressive power of the language and computational complexity of reasoning.

Recently, the adoption of service-oriented technologies has improved interoperability at the application level by exporting systems functionalities as Web services. Service discovery has been applied to collaborative environments where independent partners cooperate through resource sharing without a stable network configuration, possibly adopting different semantic models. In Chap. 18, we present model-based techniques that generate semantic service descriptions, allowing collaborative partners to export their functionalities in a semantic way. Semantic-based service matchmaking is employed to evaluate similarity between service requests and service offers, in an evolving service knowledge space where collaborative partners that provide similar services are semantically related and constitute synergic service centres in a given domain.

Finally, Chap. 19 presents a knowledge-based framework for skills and talent management based on an advanced matchmaking between profiles of candidates and available job positions. Interestingly, informative content of top-k retrieval is enriched through semantic capabilities. Top-k retrieval allows to select most promising candidates according to an ontology formalizing the domain knowledge. Such a knowledge is further exploited to provide a semantic-based explanation of missing or conflicting features in retrieved profiles, along with additional profile characteristics emerging from the retrieval procedure and not specified in the original request.

The chapter also provides a concrete case study, followed by an exhaustive experimental campaign.

PART 5. Engineering Semantic Web Systems The novelty introduced by the Semantic Web affects every stage of the software lifecycle, thus leading to new approaches to the design and engineering of modern, open and heterogeneous Web-based systems.

In the last years, data model interoperability has received a lot of attention. In contrast with most of the work, which has concentrated on interoperability problems related to specific data models, Chap. 20 proposes a model-independent approach, which works for different ontological dialects and for various database models. Also, it supports translations in both directions (ontologies to databases and vice versa) and allows for flexibility in the translations, so that customization is possible. The proposal extends recent work for schema and data translation within the MIDST project, which implements the ModelGen operator we have seen in the Data Management chapter.

In Part I, we discussed models and techniques for RDF data storage. As a natural follow-up, Chap. 21 discusses how OpenLink Virtuoso, a general-purpose Relational Database Management System, has been effectively adapted for storing such kind of data. Virtuoso's relational engine has been endowed with native RDF support with dedicated data types, bitmap indexing and SQL optimizer techniques. We discuss scaling out by running on a cluster of commodity servers, each with local memory and disk, and look at how this impacts query planning and execution and how we achieve high parallel utilization of multiple CPU cores on multiple servers. We present comparisons with other RDF storage models as well as other approaches to scaling out on server clusters. We present conclusions and metrics as well as a number of use cases, from DBpedia to bio informatics and collaborative web applications.

Chapter 22 considers the contribution of model-driven approaches based on the Semantic Web for the development of Web applications. The model-driven web engineering approach, that separates concerns on different abstraction level in the application design process, allows for more robust and structural design of web applications. This is illustrated by the use of Hera, an approach from the class of Web engineering methods that relies on models expressed using RDF(S) and an RDF(S) query language. Besides other features of Hera, adaptation and personalization are discussed as a main aspect, and it is illustrated how they are expressed using semantic data models and languages.

We now leave the stage to the two introductory chapters, which present the fundamentals of database models and of the most common semantic models (e.g., RDF, RDFS, OWL), also briefly highlighting the most important differences between the two modeling paradigms.

Chapter 2
Data and Metadata Management

Paolo Atzeni and Riccardo Torlone

Abstract In this chapter, we illustrate fundamental notions of Data Management. We start from the basic concepts of database schema and instance, illustrating how they are handled within dictionaries in relational databases. We then address, from a general point of view, the notion of data model as a means for the representation of information at different levels of details, and show how dictionaries can be used to manage schemas of different data models. A further level of abstraction, called metamodel, is then introduced with the aim of supporting the interoperability between model based applications. Finally, we discuss a methodology for schema translation that makes use of the metamodel as an intermediate level.

2.1 Introduction

A fundamental requirement in the whole life cycle of any database application is the ability of looking and managing data at different levels of abstractions. According to a widely accepted vision in the field of databases, at the lowest level of abstraction, we have raw data, which cannot provide any information without suitable interpretation. At a higher level we have *schemas*, which describe the structure of the instances and provide a basic tool for the interpretation of data. Actually, at this level we can have further forms of *metadata*, that is, information that describes or supplements actual data. Notable examples are the *constraints*, which allow the specification of properties that must be satisfied by actual data. Then we have a third level of abstraction which involves precise formalisms for the description of schemas called *data models*. A data model is a fundamental ingredient of database applications as it provides the designer with the basic means for the representation of reality in terms of schemas.

Unfortunately, a large variety of data models are used in practical applications and, for this reason, the interoperability of database applications is historically one of the most complex and time-consuming data management problems. In order to alleviate this problem, it is useful to add to the picture a further level of abstraction

P. Atzeni (✉) · R. Torlone
Università Roma Tre, Via della Vasca Navale 79, 00146 Rome, Italy
e-mail: atzeni@dia.uniroma3.it

R. Torlone
e-mail: torlone@dia.uniroma3.it

R. De Virgilio et al. (eds.), *Semantic Web Information Management*,
DOI 10.1007/978-3-642-04329-1_2, © Springer-Verlag Berlin Heidelberg 2010

providing a unified formalism, which we call *metamodel*, for the representation of different models. The definition of a metamodel able to describe all the data models of interest has two main advantages. On the one hand, it provides a framework in which database schemas of heterogeneous models can be handled in a uniform way and, on the other hand, it allows the definition of model-independent transformations that can be used in multiple translations between different models.

The goal of this chapter is to discuss these fundamental issues related to the management of data and metadata. We start from the notion of database schema and show how schemas are handled in practice by relational systems through special tables of the *dictionary*, a portion of the database used by the system to store any kind of metadata. We then illustrate various logical and conceptual data models, showing that it is possible to manage schemas of different models by just adding new tables to the dictionary, one for each new construct of the model at hand. This approach leads to a metamodel made of a collection of model-independent construct types, which we call *metaconstructs*, used in models to build schemas and corresponding to the tables of the extended dictionary. Interestingly, it comes out a rather compact metamodel, coherently with the observation that the constructs of most known models fall into a rather limited set of generic types of constructs: lexical, abstract, aggregation, generalization, function [25]. This approach can greatly simplify the translations of schemas between heterogeneous models since we can use the metamodel as a "lingua franca" in which schemas are converted and transformed to suit the features of the target model. The availability of a repository of basic transformations defined at the metamodel level, and so model-independent, can further simplify the whole translation process.

The rest of the chapter is devoted to a more detailed treatment of this matter and is organized as follows. Database schemas and models are discussed in Sects. 2.2 and 2.3, respectively. In Sect. 2.4, we illustrate the metamodel approach to the management of multiple models and, in Sect. 2.5, we present the translation methodology based on such a metamodel. In Sect. 2.6, we discuss related work and finally, in Sect. 2.7, we sketch some conclusions.

2.2 Databases, Schemas and Dictionaries

The notion of *database* as a large, shared, persistent collection of data to be managed effectively and efficiently is now well accepted and described in textbooks [7, 19, 23, 33]. Among the major features in database management, the most relevant here is the use of structures that allow for the high-level, synthetic description of the content of a database: a database has a *schema*, which describes the features of data, and an *instance* (sometimes called *database*), which includes the actual content. The schema is rather stable over time (it can vary, but usually in a very slow manner), whereas the instance changes continuously. For example, in a relational database we have the database schema that contains a number of relation schemas, each defined by means of an SQL `CREATE TABLE` statement, which specifies the name of the

EMPLOYEE		
EmpNo	LastName	Dept
1001	Rossi	IT
1002	Sagan	FR
1003	Petit	FR
1004	Grand	FR

DEPARTMENT		
DeptID	Name	City
IT	Italy	Rome
FR	France	Paris
DE	Germany	Hamburg

Fig. 2.1 A simple relational database

table,[1] its columns (each with the respective type), and the constraints defined over it (for example, its primary key). Then, the actual content of tables is the result of INSERT (and also, UPDATE and DELETE) statements, which refer to the actual rows. Database schemas are a form of *metadata*, that is, data that describes actual data.

In the usual graphical representation for the relational model (Fig. 2.1), relations are shown in tabular form, with the headings that essentially correspond to the schema (types are omitted, but can be easily guessed or understood) and the bodies that contain the data in the instance.

The major benefit of the distinction between schemas and instances is the fact that most of the actions over the database refer to the schema. In particular, if we want to extract data from a database (usually we say that we *query* the database), we need only mention schema elements, and just a few values (if any) that are relevant to the specific operation. For example, if (with respect to the database in Fig. 2.1), we are interested in finding the list of the employees, each with the city of the corresponding department, we can write an expression that contains only the names of the tables and of the columns, and no specific data. Schemas are also fundamental in the choice of the appropriate physical structures for the database, an aspect that is essential for pursuing efficiency. Physical structures are defined in the final phase of database design, and refer to the database schema alone.

In relational databases, a description of schemas is usually handled within the database itself. Indeed, a portion of the database, called the *dictionary* or the *catalog*, is composed of tables that describe all the tables in the database. In this way, data and metadata are managed in an uniform way. Figure 2.2 shows the idea of the dictionary, with its main tables (a real one contains dozens of them), which refers to the database in Fig. 2.1. Let us briefly comment on it. A database environment usually handles various schemas, here we assume that there is the *system* schema, which describes the dictionary itself, and a *user* one (called Sample), which refers to the database in Fig. 2.1. They are listed in the SCHEMA relation. The relations of interest are both those in the *user* schema and those in the *system* schema. So, we have five of them, listed in the TABLE relation. Finally, the COLUMN relation has one tuple for each attribute in each of the relations in the database. In the dictionary, we have used numerical identifiers (SchemaID, TableID, ColumnID) over

[1] Following SQL terminology, we use *relation* and *table* as synonyms. Similarly for *column* and *attribute*.

SCHEMA		
SchemaID	SchemaName	Owner
1	System	System
2	Sample	Paolo

TABLE		
TableID	TableName	Schema
11	Schema	1
12	Table	1
13	Column	1
21	Employee	2
22	Department	2

COLUMN				
ColumnID	ColumnName	Schema	Table	Type
101	SchemaID	1	11	int
102	SchemaName	1	11	string
103	TableID	1	12	int
104	TableName	1	12	string
105	Schema	1	12	string
106	ColumnID	1	13	int
107	ColumnName	1	13	string
...	...	...	...	...
201	EmpNo	2	21	int
202	LastName	2	21	string
203	Dept	2	21	string
204	DeptID	2	22	string
205	Name	2	22	string
206	City	2	22	string

Fig. 2.2 A simplified dictionary for a relational database

which cross references have been built (so that, for example, the value 22 in the last row of COLUMN means that City is an attribute of the relation whose identifier is 22, namely DEPARTMENT).

2.3 Data Models

The notion of *data model* has been considered for decades in the database field (see for example the book by Tsichritzis and Lochovsky [36] for an early but still current discussion). A synthesis, useful for our goals, is the following: "a data model defines the rules according to which data are structured" [36, p. 10]. Specifically, we can say that a model includes a set of structures (or better, types of structures), called constructs, together with the rules that can be used to combine them to form schemas. Other features can be important for models, including *constraints* (that is, rules that specify properties that must be satisfied by instances) and *operations* (which specify the dynamic aspects of databases, that is, how they evolve over time). Here, for the sake of space, we concentrate on structures which allow for synthetic and effective arguments, omitting operations and devoting only limited attention to constraints.

It is common to classify data models according to two main categories (indeed, the distinction is useful, but not so sharp as it might appear at first): *logical* models are those used for the organization of data in databases;[2] *conceptual* models are

[2]The term *logical* is used in contrast to *physical*: the latter refer to lower level representation, which takes into account features of secondary storage organization, such as blocks, addresses and allocation, whereas the former refers to the structures that can be seen by users and programs.

	EMPLOYEE		
	EmpNo	LastName	Dept
e#1	1001	Rossi	d#1
e#2	1002	Sagan	d#2
e#3	1003	Petit	d#2
e#4	1004	Grand	d#2

	DEPARTMENT		
	DeptID	Name	City
d#1	IT	Italy	Rome
d#2	FR	France	Paris
d#3	DE	Germany	Hamburg

Fig. 2.3 A simple object-relational database

used in the early steps of design, mainly to produce a description of the concepts of the application world whose data are to be stored in the database.

The most popular logical model nowadays is the relational one, used in the previous section to illustrate the main ideas at the basis of the organization of data in current databases. Various extensions exist for the relational model, mainly under the generic name of *object-relational*, which however includes many variations. Growing interest is being devoted to the management of XML documents in databases, which has lead to the idea that *DTD* and *XSD*, languages for specifying schemas of XML documents, can be seen as data models. Each of these models has a number of constructs. For example, a simple[3] version of the object-relational model could have:

- relations and attributes as in the relational model;
- *typed tables*, another construct for handling sets of elements, where each element beside attribute values (as in traditional relations) has a system-handled identifier;
- *references* between typed tables, implemented by means of the system-handled identifiers;
- *subclass* relationships between typed tables, used to specify that the elements of a typed table refine those in another one.

A tabular representation for an object-relational database is shown in Fig. 2.3: here we emphasize only two new constructs, typed tables, with system-managed identifiers associated with elements (put outside the borders of tables, to suggest that their values are not really visible), and references, implemented by using identifiers in the Dept column to correlate each employee with the department he or she belongs to.

Within the category of conceptual models, there is probably even a greater variety, as the various methodologies and design tools use different models. However, we have again a few well known representatives, each with variants. Let us comment on two of the models.

The most common conceptual model in the database world is the *entity-relationship* (*ER*) model [17]. It is based on three major constructs: (i) *entity*, used to represent sets of things, facts, people of the real world that are of interest for the application at hand; (ii) *relationship*, a logical association between entities, where

[3] As we said, there are many implementations of the idea of an object-relational model, and here we are only interested in the key points rather than the details.

Fig. 2.4 A simple ER schema

Fig. 2.5 A simple object-oriented schema

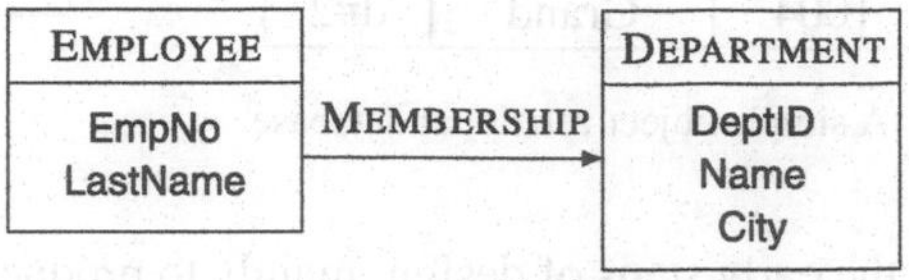

an occurrence of a relationship is a pair[4] of occurrences of entities; (iii) *attribute*, a function that associates a value with each occurrence of an entity or of a relationship. Schemas in the ER model have an effective graphical representation, as shown in Fig. 2.4, where we have a schema with two entities, a relationship and a few attributes, which correspond to the same application domain as the examples shown earlier for the relational and object-relational model.

Other conceptual models are based on the object-oriented paradigm. In particular, we consider a model similar to *UML class diagrams*, but with many simplifications and some variations, useful for our discussion. From our perspective, and adapting the notation, the constructs of this model are: (i) *class*, very similar to the notion of entity discussed above; (ii) *reference*, a directed one-to-many relationship whose occurrences connect one occurrence of a class with an occurrence of another; (iii) *field*, essentially an attribute for a class. Figure 2.5 shows a schema in this model, according to a suitable notation.

It is worth noting that we could define dictionaries for describing schemas in each of the models. Obviously, we could use any of the models for each dictionary. In order to prepare for a discussion to be carried out in the next section, we show in Figs. 2.6 and 2.7 portions of the relational dictionary for the entity-relationship and for the object-oriented model, with data that describe the schemas in Figs. 2.4 and 2.5, respectively. With respect to Fig. 2.4, let us observe that, while we have omitted some columns, we have shown without explanation a few of them, to give the idea that a number of details can be easily modeled in this way, concerning the identifiers of entities (the IsKey column of ATTRIBUTEOFENTITY) and cardinalities of relationships (IsOpt1, IsFunctional1).

2.4 Management of Multiple Models

The existence of a variety of models, discussed and exemplified in the previous section, suggests the need for a unified management of them. This has various goals, the most important of which is the support to the integration of heterogeneous schemas and their translation from a model to another.

---

[4]Relationships can be n-ary, but here we refer to binary ones for the sake of simplicity.

SCHEMA		
SchemaID	SchemaName	...
3	SchemaER1	...

ENTITY		
EntityID	EntityName	Schema
61	Employee	3
62	Department	3

ATTRIBUTEOFENTITY					
AttrID	AttrName	Schema	Entity	IsKey	...
301	EmpNo	3	61	true	...
302	LastName	3	61	false	...
303	DeptID	3	62	true	...
304	Name	3	62	false	...
305	City	3	62	false	...

BINARYRELATIONSHIP							
RelID	RelName	Schema	Entity1	IsOpt1	IsFunctional1	Entity2	...
401	Membership	3	61	false	true	62	...

Fig. 2.6 The dictionary for a simple ER model

SCHEMA		
SchemaID	SchemaName	...
4	SchemaOO1	...

CLASS		
ClassID	ClassName	Schema
71	Employee	4
72	Department	4

FIELD					
FieldID	FieldName	Schema	Class	IsID	...
501	EmpNo	4	71	true	...
502	LastName	4	71	false	...
503	DeptID	4	72	true	...
504	Name	4	72	false	...
505	City	4	72	false	...

REFERENCEFIELD					
RefID	RefName	Schema	Class	ClassTo	isOpt
801	Membership	4	71	72	false

Fig. 2.7 The dictionary for a simple object-oriented model

In this section, we illustrate an approach to the unified management of schemas (and data as well, but we do not discuss this issue here), based on the idea of a metamodel, which we have developed in the last few years [6, 8].

We use the term *metamodel* to refer to a set of *metaconstructs*, which are basically construct types used to define models. The approach is based on Hull and King's observation [25] that the constructs used in most known models can be expressed by a limited set of generic (i.e., model-independent) types of constructs: lexical, abstract, aggregation, generalization, function. Our metamodel is defined by a set of generic metaconstructs, one for each construct type. Each model is defined by its constructs and the metaconstructs they refer to. With this approach, the models discussed in the previous sections could be defined as follows (with a few more details than those we noted):

- the relational model has (i) aggregations of lexicals (the tables), with the indication, for each component (a column), of whether it is part of the key or whether nulls are allowed; (ii) foreign keys defined over components of aggregations;

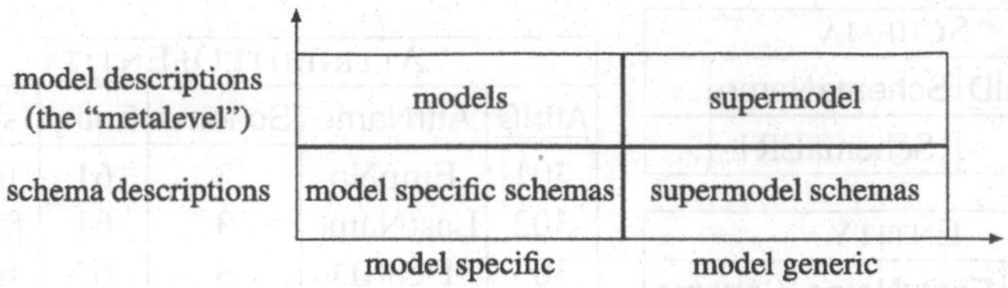

Fig. 2.8 The four parts of the dictionary

- a simplified object-relational model has (i) abstracts (tables with system-managed identifiers); (ii) lexical attributes of abstracts (for example, EmpNo and LastName), each of which can be specified as part of the key; (iii) reference attributes for abstracts, which are essentially functions from abstracts to abstracts (in the example, in Fig. 2.3, the Dept attribute in table EMPLOYEE);
- a binary entity relationship model has (i) abstracts (entities); (ii) lexical attributes of abstracts, each of which can be specified as part of the key; (iii) binary aggregations of abstracts (relationships);
- an object-oriented model has (i) abstracts (classes), (ii) reference attributes for abstracts, which are essentially functions from abstracts to abstracts, (iii) lexicals (fields or properties of classes).

A major concept in this approach is the *supermodel*, a model that has constructs corresponding to all the metaconstructs known to the system. Thus, each model is a specialization of the supermodel and a schema in any model is also a schema in the supermodel, apart from the specific names used for constructs. It is important to observe that the supermodel is rather stable but not frozen: in fact, the set of models that can be represented depends on the richness of the supermodel. Given a supermodel, should a wider class of models be needed, with "new" constructs, then the supermodel could be extended.

The approach can be synthesized and implemented by means of a complex dictionary [4], capable of handling information on the supermodel, on the various models, and on schemas. The dictionary has four parts, as shown in Fig. 2.8. The core of the dictionary is the upper right portion: it contains a description of the supermodel, with all the constructs it includes, usually a rather limited number. Figure 2.9 shows the relational implementation of such a portion. It includes three tables: SMCONSTRUCT, which lists the constructs in the supermodel, SMREFERENCE, which specifies how the constructs are related to one another, and SMPROPERTY, which indicates the features of interest for each construct. For example, we can see that each AttributeOfAbstract is related to an Abstract and has an IsId property (to specify whether it is part of the identifier).

The various models are defined in the "models" part (the upper left part of Fig. 2.8) with respect to the supermodel. We show a portion of this part in Fig. 2.10: tables are similar to those in Fig. 2.9, the main difference being the fact that constructs, references and properties have names that are specific to the various models and that there is a table for representing models. Each construct, reference, property is also related to a corresponding item in the supermodel (via smConstruct,

SMCONSTRUCT	
ConstructID	ConstructName
1001	Abstract
1002	AttributeOfAbstract
1003	BinaryAggregationOfAbstracts
1004	AbstractAttribute
...	...

SMREFERENCE			
RefID	RefName	Construct	ConstructTo
2001	Abstract	1002	1001
2002	Abstract1	1003	1001
2003	Abstract2	1003	1001
...	...	...	...

SMPROPERTY			
PropID	PropertyName	Construct	Type
3001	AbstractName	1001	string
3002	AttributeName	1002	string
3003	IsId	1002	bool
3004	IsFunctional1	1003	bool
3005	IsFunctional2	1003	bool
...	...	...	...

Fig. 2.9 The description of the supermodel in the metalevel dictionary

smRef, smProperty, respectively). We omit further discussion as the figure is self-explanatory.

The metalevel dictionary in Fig. 2.10 describes the structure of the various dictionaries we have seen in the previous section. In fact, the rows in the CONSTRUCT table correspond to the tables in the various dictionaries, specifically those in Figs. 2.6 and 2.7. Also, the rows in tables REFERENCE and PROPERTY describe the various columns of the tables in Figs. 2.6 and 2.7. These tables constitute the "model specific schema" component of the multilevel dictionary (lower left part in Fig. 2.8).

We have described so far three of the components of the dictionary sketched in Fig. 2.8. The fourth, the lower right part, is probably the most interesting for the management of schemas in different models and for supporting their translations. In fact, it describes schemas in supermodel terms. An example is in Fig. 2.11. Two observations are important. First, we can see that here we have a table for each construct in the supermodel (so for each row in table SMCONSTRUCT in Fig. 2.9), and contains the descriptions of schema in the various models, according to supermodel terminology. Second, the content of the table is essentially the union of the contents of the respective tables in the model-specific dictionaries, when the two models both have a construct for a given supermodel construct. For example, table ABSTRACT is basically the union of tables ENTITY (in Fig. 2.6) and CLASS (in Fig. 2.7).

MODEL	
ModelID	ModelName
5001	ER
5002	OODB
…	…

CONSTRUCT			
ConstructID	ConstructName	Model	smConstruct
6001	Entity	5001	1001
6002	AttributeOfEntity	5001	1002
6003	BinaryRelationship	5001	1003
6004	Class	5002	1001
6005	Field	5002	1002
6006	ReferenceField	5002	1004
…	…	…	…

REFERENCE				
RefID	RefName	smRef	Constr	ConstrTo
7001	Entity	2001	6002	6001
7002	Entity1	2002	6003	6001
7003	Entity2	2003	6003	6001

PROPERTY			
PropID	PropertyName	smProperty	…
8001	EntityName	6001	…
8002	AttributeName	6002	…
8003	IsKey	6002	…
8004	IsFunctional1	6003	…
8005	IsFunctional2	6003	…
…	…	…	…
8011	ClassName	6011	…
8012	FieldName	6012	…
8013	IsId	6013	…
…	…	…	…

Fig. 2.10 The description of some models in the dictionary

2.5 Model-generic Schema Translation

The dictionary we have illustrated in the previous section is interesting as it allows for a model-generic description of schemas which is also *model-aware*, in the sense that it specifies the features of the various models and the model each schema belongs to. We have been experimenting, with a number of applications, a platform that includes such a dictionary towards a more general model management system [3]. The most interesting results we have obtained concern a model-generic approach to schema translation [6, 8]. The problem can be stated as follows: given two data models M_1 and M_2 and a schema S_1 of M_1, find a schema S_2 of M_2 that properly represents S_1. A possible extension of the problem considers also the data level: given a database instance I_1 of S_1, find also an instance I_2 of S_2 that has the same information content as I_1.

SCHEMA		
SchemaID	SchemaName	...
3	SchemaER1	...
4	SchemaOO1	...

ATTRIBUTEOFABSTRACT					
AttrID	AttrName	Schema	Abstract	IsKey	...
301	EmpNo	3	61	true	...
302	LastName	3	61	false	...
303	DeptID	3	62	true	...
304	Name	3	62	false	...
305	City	3	62	false	...
501	EmpNo	4	71	true	...
502	LastName	4	71	false	...
503	DeptID	4	72	true	...
504	Name	4	72	false	...
505	City	4	72	false	...

ABSTRACT		
AbstractID	EntityName	Schema
61	Employee	3
62	Department	3
71	Employee	4
72	Department	4

BINARYAGGREGATIONOFABSTRACT							
AggID	AggName	Schema	Abstract1	IsOpt1	IsFunctional1	Abstract2	...
401	Membership	3	61	false	true	62	...

ABSTRACTATTRIBUTE					
AbsAttID	AbsAttName	Schema	Abstract	AbstractTo	...
801	Membership	4	71	72	...

Fig. 2.11 A model-generic dictionary based on the supermodel

Since, as we saw in the previous sections, many different data models exist, what we need is an approach that handles the various models in an effective and efficient way. Indeed, with many constructs and variants thereof, the number of different models grow. Indeed, each of the models we have mentioned in the previous sections has many variants, which, in the translation process, require attention. For example, if we just consider the object-relational model, we have a number of features that can appear in different ways, including the following:

- keys may be specifiable or not;
- generalizations may be allowed or not;
- foreign keys may be used or not;
- nested attributes may be allowed or not.

As these features are mainly independent from one another, it is clear that we can easily have hundreds or even thousands of models. Therefore, it would be impossible to have a specific translation for each pair of models, as, for n models, we would need n^2 translations. The supermodel, as we have discussed it in the previous section, can give a significant contribution to this issue: as every schema, in every model, is also a schema in the supermodel (modulo construct renaming), we can use the supermodel as a "pivot" model: we can think of translations as composed of first a "copy" from the source model to the supermodel, then an actual translation within the supermodel, and finally a "copy" back to the target model. This would drastically reduce the needed number of translations, from a quadratic number to a linear one.

However, even a linear number of translations can be too big, if we have hundreds or thousands of models. However, as we said, the size of the space of models is due to the combination of independent variants of constructs. Then, it is possible to define simple translation operations each concerned with a specific transformation concerning a feature of a construct, so that a translation is composed of a sequence of simple steps. For example, if we want to translate an object-relational schema (in a model that does not allow for keys but has generalizations) into the relational model, then we can proceed with four steps:

1. eliminate generalizations;
2. add keys;
3. replace references with foreign keys;
4. replace objects with tables.

The interesting thing is that if we have other variants of the object-relational model, we probably need another combination of elementary steps, but with significant reuse. Let us comment this with the help of Fig. 2.12 in which we show some of the models of interest and a number of elementary translations between them. In the

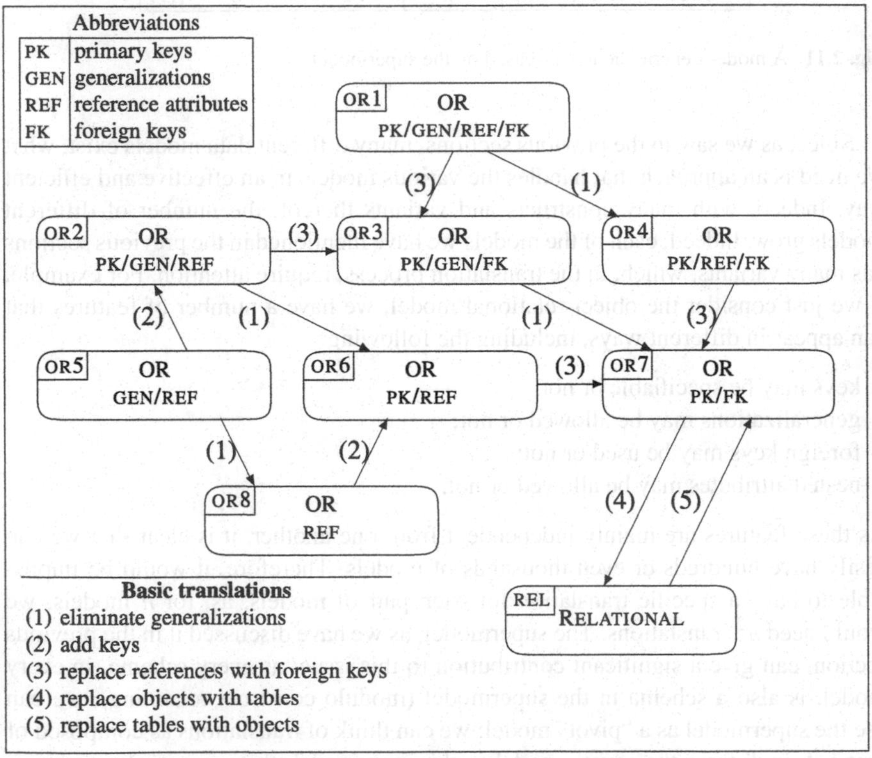

Fig. 2.12 Some models and translations between them

case above, the source model would be OR5 and we would reach the target one (REL) by means of the application of elementary translations (1)–(4). Other translations over models in the same picture could be implemented by means of other sequences of the same elementary translations.

This approach can become very effective if a library of elementary transformations is defined and complex transformations are built by sequences of elementary ones. We have also developed techniques for the automatic selection of translations in the library [6]. In principle, elementary translations could be developed by using any language. We have developed a complete prototype [5] that uses a Datalog with OID invention and handles a significant number of models within various families, namely relational, object-relational, object-oriented, entity-relationship and XSD-based.

2.6 Related Work

Data models are extensively discussed in every database textbook [7, 19, 23, 33] and have always been one of the most investigated database research areas: in the last thirty years, we have witnessed a huge list of proposals for data models, at different levels of abstraction. Early, but still current, comparisons of the main features of various data models can be found in the book by Tsichritzis and Lochovsky [36] and in the survey by Hull and King [25].

On the practical side, even if the ER model is still often used in conceptual database design [9], many variants exists and recently new models which better capture the requirements of novel application domains have emerged [16]. At the logical level we have a similar situation: even if the relational model has imposed itself as a de-facto standard, a large variety of data models (in many cases just extensions of the relational model) are actually used to represent, store, and process data [1]. It follows that sharing and exchange of information between heterogeneous data sources have always been one of the most time-consuming data management problems. Indeed, work on database interoperability dates back to the early 1970s [35] and various aspects of this general problem, such as database federation [34], database integration [10, 26], schema matching [32], schema merging [30], and data exchange [20, 21], have been deeply investigated in the literature.

Recently, Bernstein set the various problems within a very general framework that he called *model management* [11–13]. Its value as a methodology for approaching several meta-data related problems with a significant reduction of programming effort has been widely accepted (see [14] for a number of practical examples).

According to Bernstein [11], model management is based on five basic operators that, suitably combined, can be used to address the vast majority of problems related to database interoperability: (i) *Match*, which takes as input two schemas and returns a mapping between them, (ii) *Compose*, which takes as input two mappings between schemas and returns a mapping that combines them, (iii) *Merge*, which takes as input two schemas and returns a schema that corresponds to their "union" together with two mappings between the original schemas and the output schema,

(iv) *Diff*, which takes as input two schemas and a mapping between them and returns the portion of the first schema not involved in the mapping, and (v) *ModelGen*, which takes as input a schema in a source model and a target model and returns the translation of the schema into the target model.

Several studies have been conducted on model management, basically by focusing on some of the above operators. The Compose operator has been investigated in [27]. Rondo [28] is a rather complete framework for Model Management, but it does not address the problem of model translation, corresponding to the ModelGen operator. Cupid [27] focuses on the Match operator, whereas Clio [24, 29] provides, in a sense, an implementation of both the Match and of the Merge operators. The latter operator has also been studied in [30].

In this chapter, we have discussed a metamodel approach to the management of multiple models that corresponds to an implementation of the ModelGen operator [6]. It should be said that many studies have been done on issues related to model translation: some of them have focused on specific problem (e.g., the XML-relational mapping [22]) or on specific data models (survey papers on this subject can be found in [37]); others have studied the problem from a more general perspective [2, 15, 18, 31]. The main difference between our approach and these works relies on our notion of metamodel that introduces a higher level of abstraction with two main benefits. On the one hand, it provides a very natural way to describe heterogeneous models and, on the other hand, it allows us to define generic transformations between primitives that are independent of the specific models involved in a translation.

2.7 Conclusion

In this chapter, we have addressed some issues at the basis of the management of data and metadata. In particular, we have considered schemas and models, the fundamental ingredients of database applications, and have shown how schemas of different models can be represented in a unified way by suitably extending the dictionary of a database management system. We have then introduced the notion of metamodel, a tool for the uniform representation of different models, to support the translation of heterogeneous schema from one model to another.

References

1. Abiteboul, S., Buneman, P., Suciu, D.: Data on the Web: From Relations to Semistructured Data and XML. Morgan Kauffman, San Mateo (1999)
2. Abiteboul, S., Cluet, S., Milo, T.: Correspondence and translation for heterogeneous data. Theor. Comput. Sci. **275**(1–2), 179–213 (2002)
3. Atzeni, P., Bellomarini, L., Bugiotti, F., Gianforme, G.: From schema and model translation to a model management system. In: Sharing Data, Information and Knowledge, BNCOD 25. LNCS, vol. 5071, pp. 227–240. Springer, Berlin (2008)

4. Atzeni, P., Cappellari, P., Bernstein, P.A.: A multilevel dictionary for model management. In: ER Conference. LNCS, vol. 3716, pp. 160–175. Springer, Berlin (2005)
5. Atzeni, P., Cappellari, P., Gianforme, G.: MIDST: model independent schema and data translation. In: SIGMOD Conference, pp. 1134–1136. ACM, New York (2007)
6. Atzeni, P., Cappellari, P., Torlone, R., Bernstein, P.A., Gianforme, G.: Model-independent schema translation. VLDB J. **17**(6), 1347–1370 (2008)
7. Atzeni, P., Ceri, S., Paraboschi, S., Torlone, R.: Databases: Concepts, Languages and Architectures. McGraw-Hill, New York (1999)
8. Atzeni, P., Torlone, R.: Management of multiple models in an extensible database design tool. In: EDBT Conference. LNCS, vol. 1057, pp. 79–95. Springer, Berlin (1996)
9. Batini, C., Ceri, S., Navathe, S.: Database Design with the Entity-Relationship Model. Benjamin and Cummings, Redwood City (1991)
10. Batini, C., Lenzerini, M., Navathe, S.B.: A comparative analysis of methodologies for database schema integration. ACM Comput. Surv. **18**(4), 323–364 (1986)
11. Bernstein, P.A.: Applying model management to classical meta data problems. In: CIDR Conference, pp. 209–220 (2003)
12. Bernstein, P.A., Halevy, A.Y., Pottinger, R.: A vision of management of complex models. SIGMOD Rec. **29**(4), 55–63 (2000)
13. Bernstein, P.A., Melnik, S.: Model management 2.0: manipulating richer mappings. In: SIGMOD Conference, pp. 1–12 (2007)
14. Bernstein, P.A., Rahm, E.: Data warehouse scenarios for model management. In: ER, pp. 1–15 (2000)
15. Bowers, S., Delcambre, L.M.L.: The Uni-Level Description: A uniform framework for representing information in multiple data models. In: ER Conference. LNCS, vol. 2813, pp. 45–58. Springer, Berlin (2003)
16. Ceri, S., Fraternali, P., Bongio, A., Brambilla, M., Comai, S., Matera, M.: Designing Data-Intensive Web Applications. Morgan Kauffman, San Mateo (2003)
17. Chen, P.: The entity-relationship model: Toward a unified view of data. ACM Trans. Database Syst. **1**(1), 9–36 (1976)
18. Cluet, S., Delobel, C., Siméon, J., Smaga, K.: Your mediators need data conversion! In: SIGMOD Conference, pp. 177–188 (1998)
19. ElMasri, R., Navathe, S.: Fundamentals of Database Systems, 5th edn. Addison-Wesley, Reading (2007)
20. Fagin, R., Kolaitis, P.G., Miller, R.J., Popa, L.: Data exchange: semantics and query answering. Theor. Comput. Sci. **336**(1), 89–124 (2005)
21. Fagin, R., Kolaitis, P.G., Popa, L.: Data exchange: getting to the core. ACM Trans. Database Syst. **30**(1), 174–210 (2005)
22. Florescu, D., Kossmann, D.: Storing and querying XML data using an rdmbs. IEEE Data Eng. Bull. **22**(3), 27–34 (1999)
23. Garcia-Molina, H., Ullman, J.D., Widom, J.: Database Systems: The Complete Book, 2nd edn. Prentice-Hall, Englewood Cliffs (2008)
24. Haas, L.M., Hernández, M.A., Ho, H., Popa, L., Roth, M.: Clio grows up: from research prototype to industrial tool. In: Proceedings of the ACM SIGMOD International Conference on Management of Data, Baltimore, Maryland, USA, June 14–16, 2005, pp. 805–810. ACM, New York (2005)
25. Hull, R., King, R.: Semantic database modelling: Survey, applications and research issues. ACM Comput. Surv. **19**(3), 201–260 (1987)
26. Lenzerini, M.: Data integration: A theoretical perspective. In: PODS, pp. 233–246 (2002)
27. Madhavan, J., Halevy, A.Y.: Composing mappings among data sources. In: VLDB, pp. 572–583 (2003)
28. Melnik, S., Rahm, E., Bernstein, P.A.: Rondo: A programming platform for generic model management. In: Halevy, A.Y., Ives, Z.G., Doan, A. (eds.) SIGMOD Conference, pp. 193–204. ACM, New York (2003)
29. Miller, R.J., Haas, L.M., Hernández, M.A.: Schema mapping as query discovery. In: VLDB, pp. 77–88 (2000)

30. Pottinger, R., Bernstein, P.A.: Merging models based on given correspondences. In: VLDB, pp. 826–873 (2003)
31. Poulovassilis, A., McBrien, P.: A general formal framework for schema transformation. Data Knowl. Eng. **28**(1), 47–71 (1998)
32. Rahm, E., Bernstein, P.A.: A survey of approaches to automatic schema matching. VLDB J. **10**(4), 334–350 (2001)
33. Ramakrishnan, R., Gehrke, J.: Database Management Systems, 3rd edn. McGraw-Hill, New York (2003)
34. Sheth, A., Larson, J.: Federated database systems for managing distributed database systems for production and use. ACM Comput. Surv. **22**(3), 183–236 (1990)
35. Shu, N.C., Housel, B.C., Taylor, R.W., Ghosh, S.P., Lum, V.Y.: Express: A data extraction, processing, and restructuring system. ACM Trans. Database Syst. **2**(2), 134–174 (1977)
36. Tsichritzis, D., Lochovski, F.: Data Models. Prentice-Hall, Englewood Cliffs (1982)
37. Zaniolo, C. (ed.): Special issue on Data Transformations. Data Eng. **22**(1) (1999). IEEE Computer Society

Chapter 3
The Semantic Web Languages

Fausto Giunchiglia, Feroz Farazi, Letizia Tanca, and Roberto De Virgilio

Abstract The Semantic Web is basically an extension of the Web and of the Web-enabling database and Internet technology, and, as a consequence, the Semantic Web methodologies, representation mechanisms and logics strongly rely on those developed in databases. This is the motivation for many attempts to, more or less loosely, merge the two worlds like, for instance, the various proposals to use relational technology for storing web data or the use of ontologies for data integration. This chapter comes after one on data management, in order to first complete the picture with the description of the languages that can be used to represent information on the Semantic Web, and then highlight a few fundamental differences which make the database and Semantic Web paradigms complementary, but somehow difficult to integrate.

3.1 Introduction

The *World Wide Web* (Web from now on) is an enormous collection of data and documents of any kind, mixed and integrated in all possible ways, that keeps growing not monotonically. The Web is an open environment, where users can add or delete documents and data as they prefer, without any restriction. Some documents stay

---

F. Giunchiglia (✉)
Dipto. Ingegneria e Scienza dell'Informazione, Università di Trento, Via Sommarive 14, 38100 Povo TN, Italy
e-mail: fausto@disi.unitn.it

F. Farazi
Department of Information Engineering and Computer Science, University of Trento, Trento, Italy
e-mail: farazi@disi.unitn.it

L. Tanca
Dipto. Elettronica e Informazione (DEI), Politecnico di Milano, Via Ponzio 34/5, 20133 Milan, Italy
e-mail: tanca@elet.polimi.it

R. De Virgilio
Dipto. Informatica e Automazione, Università Roma Tre, Via della Vasca Navale 79, 00146 Rome, Italy
e-mail: dvr@dia.uniroma3.it

R. De Virgilio et al. (eds.), *Semantic Web Information Management*,
DOI 10.1007/978-3-642-04329-1_3,

in time, some change, some appear and disappear and this process is completely unpredictable. And this applies not only to the Web but virtually to any repository of data (e.g., text, media, sensor data), also within company intranets. As a further complication, these data are highly *semantically heterogeneous*, in other words, we have, as a widespread common phenomenon, that the same information is represented in many different ways (e.g., the same amount of amount of money can be represented in dollars, in euros, in pounds).

The *Semantic Web* [5, 6] was originally proposed by its inventor as the way to solve the problem of semantic heterogeneity in the Web. The proposed solution is to add, as an extra abstraction layer, a so-called *semantic layer*, to be built on top of the Web, which makes data not only human processable but also machine processable. In the research in data and knowledge management, the word semantics has been used and abused many times. In the Semantic Web, this word assumes a rather precise connotation and it amounts to assuming that the meaning of data and documents is codified as *metadata*, namely, data about data. The key idea is, therefore, to incrementally add new (meta)data whose only purpose is to explicitly codify the intended meaning of Web data. As a trivial example, the fact that a photo contains the face of Fausto can be codified into a data structure (a triple) whose contents can be represented, using a logical notation, as $about(photo1, Fausto)$ where $photo1$ and $Fausto$ are unique identifiers for the involved resources.

The Semantic Web, as clearly shown in Parts I, II of this book, is therefore an extension of the Web and of the Web enabling database and Internet technology, and, as a consequence, the Semantic Web methodologies, representation mechanisms and logics strongly rely on those developed in databases. And, this is the motivation for the many attempts to (more or less loosely) merge the two worlds like, for instance, the various proposals to use relational technology for storing web data (e.g., Chap. 4) or the use of ontologies for data integration (Chap. 17), just to name a few. And, this is also why this article comes second in this book after an article on data management.

At the same time, this is also the place to highlight a few fundamental differences which make the database and Semantic Web paradigms complementary but very different and somehow difficult to integrate. The crucial distinction is between the "closed" nature of the first vs. the "open" nature of the second. For instance, since incompleteness is inherent in the nature of Web data, in the Web no assumption is made about information which has not been explicitly stated, while in the database realm what has not been asserted or inferred is considered as false. In an analogous way, no uniqueness hypothesis is made as for the identifiers of web objects (this is why the Web had to recover this notion via Unique Resource Identifiers (URI)), while one strong requirement of database objects is that they be uniquely identified. Confronting the strengths and weaknesses of both paradigms, in order to be able to build new systems that are able to encompass the strengths of both, is thus worthwhile: the lessons learned from Classical Logic, which is the logical paradigm disciplining the Semantic Web, can be used to extend the expressive power of database query languages and to deal with incomplete information in databases; on the other hand, the introduction of some restrictions to the logics adopted for the Semantic Web may help retain the good complexity results typical of database querying. This book should be read exactly in this perspective, keeping in mind that each chapter relates research which is ongoing in one of these two general directions.

The rest of the chapter is structured as follows. In Sect. 3.2, we describe the hierarchy of the languages that can be used to represent information on the Semantic Web. Section 3.3 presents the data model used in RDF and an example of how simple statements can be represented in RDF. Section 3.4 describes OWL, its sublanguages and an example representing the same statements represented in RDF. In Sect. 3.5, we describe C-OWL (Context OWL) namely OWL extended to take into account context via mappings across multiple ontologies. In Sect. 3.6, after the introduction to the most important Web Languages, we dig a little deeper in the connections between the Semantic Web and databases briefly discussed above. We conclude the chapter in Sect. 3.7.

3.2 The Hierarchy of Languages

We stated above that the Semantic Web is just metadata explicitly encoding the implicit semantics of Web data. But which kinds of metadata? According to the Semantic Web approach, data are organized in (at least) four levels of increased expressibility, each corresponding to a specific representation need, namely: XML [8] and XML Schema [13], RDF [3] and RDF Schema [9], OWL [26] and C-OWL [7]. Notice that, strictly speaking, XML is not a semantic Web language as it codifies no semantics. Its presentation is however very relevant as all the Semantic Web languages are defined as extensions of XML and, anyhow, XML is a first important step, with respect to HTML,[1] towards semantic interoperability as it provides a way to standardize the use of tags, thus enabling syntactic interoperability.

XML: Raw Data—No Semantics XML is designed to represent information by using customized tags. Because of the customizable tag support, it is used to exchange a wide variety of information on the Web and elsewhere. Statements like "GeoNames has coverage of all countries" and "It was modified on April 25, 2009" can be represented in XML using tags 'GeoNames', 'coverage' and 'modified' along with a leading statement saying that the following information is in a specific XML version:

```
<?xml version="1.0" ?>
  < GeoNames >
  <coverage>Countries</coverage>
  <modified>April 25, 2009</modified>
  </GeoNames>
```

[1] http://www.w3.org/html/.

The purpose of XML Schema is to define a set of rules to which an XML document conforms. An XML Schema is similar to a class in an object oriented programming language and an XML document is similar to an instance of that class. XML Schema is used for exchanging information between interested parties who have agreed to a predefined set of rules, but the absence of meaning of the vocabulary terms used in XML Schema makes it difficult for machines to accomplish communication between them when new XML vocabulary terms are used. On one hand machines can not differentiate between polysemous terms, and on the other hand they can not combine the synonymous terms.

RDF(S): Representing Objects and Relations Among Them RDFS is an acronym for RDF Schema. We use RDF(S) meaning both RDF and RDFS. The goal of RDF(S) is to provide meaning to data therefore overcoming the drawback (absence of meaning) of XML. The simplest forms of RDF metadata are tags of single resources, e.g., photo tags in Flickr. One such metadata could state, for instance, that a specific Web page is the homepage of a specific user, or that a photo is about a specific location, or that a document is about a specific topic.

RDF is used to (i) describe information about Web resources and the systems that use these resources; (ii) make information machine processable; (iii) provide internetworking among applications; (iv) provide automated processing of Web information by intelligent agents. It is designed to provide flexibility in representing information. Its specification is given in [3, 9, 18, 20, 23, 25].

RDF Schema is an extension of RDF. It provides a vocabulary for RDF to represent classes of the resources, subclasses of the classes, properties of the classes and relations between properties. The capability of representing classes and subclasses allows users to publish ontologies on the Web, but these ontologies have limited use as RDFS can not represent information containing disjointness and specific cardinality values.

OWL: Ontologies—Representing Classes and Relations Among Them OWL is a quite expressive representation language. It provides the syntax to specify classes (sets of objects, also called concepts), various operations on classes such as, for instance, that two or more classes are disjoint. However, OWL does not have built-in primitives for the (very important) part-whole relations [28]. The simplest metadata expressing properties of classes are tags which encode properties of sets of resources, e.g., del.ic.ious tags. One such metadata could state that a set of web pages is about a specific topic, or that a set of photos is about the same person. In most common uses, however, the OWL metadata are organized in graph structures encoding complex relations among classes, i.e., ontologies [19], where each node is associated to a concept (represented as a natural language label) and where links codify semantic (logical) relations between the labels of the two nodes involved. As a very important example, in the case of lightweight ontologies [14, 17], schematic metadata are organized as trees where the labels of nodes lower in the tree are more specific than the labels of the nodes above.

The details of the OWL specification are described in [4, 10, 21, 26, 27, 31].

C-OWL: Contextual Ontologies—Representing Context Mappings OWL allows to represent one ontology at a time. In practice, the Semantic Web is plenty of ontologies developed independently, each modeling a specific subdomain. OWL has an import operation which allows to import an ontology as a part of the specification of a more complex ontology. However, in most cases, the import operation is far too strong. One would simply like to relate the concept in one ontology with the concept of another ontology. Furthermore, OWL cannot natively deal with the fact that the meaning of certain words (class names) is context dependent [7], in other words, that the same word in different ontologies may represent a different concept. One trivial example of context dependency is that the meaning of the word *car* as codified in the FIAT database means, e.g., the set of FIAT cars, and is therefore different from the meaning of this same word inside the BMW database. Context OWL (C-OWL) [7] is a proposed extension of OWL (but not a Web Standard) which allows to represent multiple OWL ontologies and the mappings (relations) between these ontologies, where each ontology represents a localized view of a domain.

Two of the papers in Part II describe how reasoning about ontologies can be exploited in order to automatically compute context mappings.

The step from XML to RDF is key as the encoding of semantics is the basis for *achieving semantic interoperability*. Once the semantics are explicitly represented, the meaning of a given data can be normalized with respect to all its syntactic variations. Or, viceversa, the multiple meanings (also called senses) of a word can be made explicit. For instance, it is possible to distinguish between the three possible meanings of the word *Java* (a kind of coffee bean, a programming language, and an island name) and, dually, it is possible to say that *automobile* and *car*, which are synonyms, mean actually the same thing. The step from RDF to OWL is key for allowing complex *reasoning about documents*, sets of documents and their relations. Of course, it is also possible to perform reasoning with RDF only. Reasoning about instances amounts to propositional reasoning. At this level, it is possible to reason about single instances (documents), for instance to derive, given the proper background knowledge [15, 16], that the content of a document which talks about *animals* is more general than the content of another document which talks about *cats*. Reasoning in OWL is much more powerful and it allows to reason about complex properties of sets of instances. It allows, for instance, to derive, given the proper background knowledge, that any *professor* in a given university *teaches at least one course*.

3.3 RDF(S)

RDF is a language for representing data in the Semantic Web. RDF is designed (i) to provide a simple data model so that users can make statements about Web resources; (ii) to provide the capability to perform inference on the statements represented by users.

The data model in RDF is a graph data model. The graph used in RDF is a directed graph. A graph consists of nodes and edges. Statements about resources can

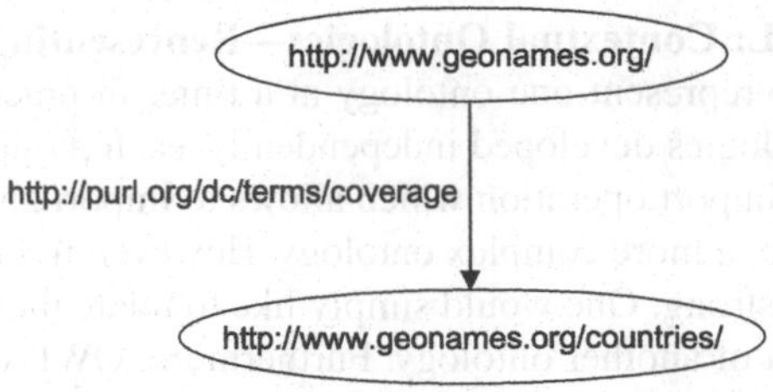

Fig. 3.1 Graph data model of a statement representing subject, object and predicate as URIs

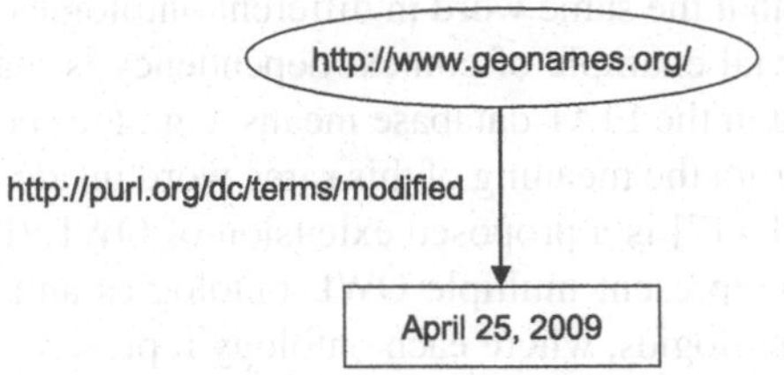

Fig. 3.2 Graph data model of a statement representing subject and predicate as URIs and the object as a literal

be represented by using graph nodes and edges. Edges in RDF graphs are labeled. An edge with two connecting nodes form a triple. One of the two nodes represents the subject, the other node represents the object and the edge represents a predicate of the statement. As the graph is a directed graph, the edge is a directed edge and the direction of the edge is from the subject to the object. The predicate is also called as property of the subject or a relationship between subject and object.

RDF uses URI references to identify subjects, objects and predicates. The statement "GeoNames has coverage of all countries" can be represented in RDF, where 'GeoNames' is a subject, 'countries' is an object and 'coverage' is a predicate. The URIs of the subject 'GeoNames', object 'countries' and predicate 'coverage' are "http://www.geonames.org", "http://www.geonames.org/countries" and "http://purl.org/dc/terms/cove-rage", respectively. Figure 3.1 provides a graphical representation of this RDF statement.

Objects in RDF statements can be literals. In the statement "GeoNames was modified on April 25, 2009", 'GeoNames' is a subject, 'modified' is an object and 'April 25, 2009' is a predicate, which is a literal. The URIs of the subject 'GeoNames' and predicate 'modified' are "http://www.geonames.org" and "http://purl.org/dc/terms/modified" respectively and the object 'April 25, 2009' can be represented as is without a URI. Figure 3.2 provides a graphical representation of this RDF statement.

Statements about GeoNames can be described in RDF using constructs rdf:Description, rdf:resource, rdf:about and rdfs:label as follows:

```
<?xml version="1.0"?>
    <rdf:RDF
        xmlns:rdf="http://www.w3.org/1999/02/22-rdf-syntax-ns#"
        xmlns:rdfs="http://www.w3.org/2000/01/rdf-schema#"
        xmlns:dc="http://purl.org/dc/terms#">
```

```
    <rdf:Description rdf:about="http://www.geonames.org">
      <rdfs:label>GeoNames</rdfs:label>
      <dc:coverage rdf:resource="http://www.geonames.org/countries"/>
      <dc:modified>April 25, 2009</dc:modified>
    </rdf:Description>
  </rdf:RDF>
```

3.4 OWL

Similarly, to what happens with RDF, OWL data are represented as triples subject, object and predicate. As it turns out, there are (at least) three OWL languages of increasing logical expressivity, namely: *OWL Lite*, *OWL DL*, *OWL Full*. As a matter of fact, there are many variants and extensions of OWL each corresponding to a Logic and associated expressivity levels. C-OWL itself is an extension of OWL, one of the papers in Part II in this book describes an extension of OWL to account for time, and similarly for the work on modular ontologies again in Part II of this book.

Concentrating on the three basic OWL languages, the most important is OWL DL, where DL stands for *Description Logic* and owns its name to the fact that it is a notational variant, tuned to Web use, of Description Logics [2]. The key feature is that reasoning in OWL DL can be implemented by exploiting the many state-of-the-art DL reasoners, e.g., Pellet [30].

More detailed descriptions of all three sub-languages of OWL—OWL Lite, OWL DL and OWL Full, are provided below.

OWL Lite OWL Lite allows the use of a subset of the OWL and RDF(S) vocabulary. The main goal is to trade expressivity for efficiency (and guaranteed termination) of reasoning. In particular, it is possible to use thirty-five out of forty OWL constructs and eleven out of thirty-three RDF(S) constructs (not including the subproperties of the property `rdfs:member`). The lists of the thirty-three RDF(S) constructs, of the forty OWL constructs and of the eleven RDF(S) constructs that can be used in OWL are provided in Appendixes A and B at the end of this chapter.

To define a class in OWL Lite, one must use the OWL construct `owl:Class` rather than the RDF(S) construct `rdfs:Class` which is not allowed. Other five OWL constructs, namely: `complementOf`, `disjointWith`, `hasValue`, `oneOf` and `unionOf` are not allowed in OWL Lite. Other OWL Constructs are allowed to use in OWL Lite but their use is limited. Thus, all three cardinality constructs—`cardinality`, `maxCardinality` and `minCardinality`, can only have 0 or 1 in their value fields. Furthermore, `equivalentClass` and `intersectionOf` cannot be used in a triple if the subject or object represents an anonymous class.

OWL DL OWL DL can use all eleven RDF(S) constructs used by OWL Lite. Similarly, to OWL Lite, it uses only the `owl:Class` construct to define a class. OWL DL allows to use all forty OWL constructs. However, some of these constructs have restricted use. In particular, classes cannot be used as individuals, and vice versa. Each individual must be an extension of a class. Even if an individual cannot be classified under any user defined class, it must be classified under the general `owl:Thing` class. Individuals can not be used as properties, and vice versa. Moreover, properties can not be used as classes, and vice versa.

Properties in OWL DL are differentiated into data type properties and object properties. Object properties connect class instances and data type properties connect instances to literals. OWL DL allows the use of the `intersectionOf` construct with any number of classes and of any non negative integer in the cardinality restrictions value fields.

The restrictions provided in OWL DL allow to maintain a balance between expressivity and computational completeness. Even though its computational complexity is higher than that of OWL Lite, reasoning in OWL DL remains decidable (of the same complexity of the corresponding Description Logic).

OWL Full OWL Full can use all forty OWL constructs and eleven RDF(S) constructs without any of the restrictions imposed on OWL-DL. Moreover, the constructs `rdfs:Class` as well as `owl:Class` can be used to define a class. The key difference with respect to OWL DL is that in OWL Full what we can say, e.g., classes, properties and even bits of syntax can be used as individuals. The price for this increased expressivity is that reasoning in OWL Full is undecidable, i.e., it may not terminate on certain inputs.

To provide an example of OWL full the GeoNames statement, can be repressented on OWL using the constructs owl:Ontology, owl:Thing, rdfs:labels and rdf:resource as follows:

```
<?xml version="1.0"?>
  <rdf:RDF
     xmlns:rdf="http://www.w3.org/1999/02/22-rdf-syntax-ns#"
     xmlns:rdfs="http://www.w3.org/2000/01/rdf-schema#"
     xmlns:owl="http://www.w3.org/2002/07/owl#"
     xmlns:dc="http://purl.org/dc/terms#">
   <owl:Ontology rdf:about=""/>
   <owl:Thing rdf:about="http://www.geonames.org">
    <rdfs:label>GeoNames</rdfs:label>
    <dc:coverage rdf:resource="http://www.geonames.org/countries"/>
    <dc:modified>April 25, 2009</dc:modified>
   </owl:Thing>
  </rdf:RDF>
```

3.5 C-OWL

The key addition that C-OWL provides on top of OWL is the possibility to represent multiple ontologies and context mappings, namely triples subject relation object between two concepts, or between two instances or between two properties in two different ontologies. The mapping relations in the triple can be one of more specific, more general, equivalent, disjoint and compatible. C-OWL allows for the use of any of the OWL sub-languages but the two ontologies involved in a mapping must belong to the same sub-language.

C-OWL mappings are also called bridge rules. An ontology plus the set of bridge rules where the subject concept belongs to the ontology itself is called a contextual ontology. To provide an example of contextual ontology, we provide below the simple Wine ontology originally described in [7]. In this contextual ontology, two ontologies Wine and Vino are mapped. For the detailed description, we refer to the C-OWL paper.

```
<?xml version="1.0"?>
<rdf:RDF
    xmlns:rdf="http://www.w3.org/1999/02/22-rdf-syntax-ns#"
    xmlns:rdfs="http://www.w3.org/2000/01/rdf-schema#"
    xmlns:cowl="http://www.example.org/wine-to-vino.map#">
<cowl:mapping>
  <rdfs:comment>Example of a mapping of wine into vino</rdfs:comment>
  <cowl:srcOntology rdf:resource="http://www.ex.org/wine.owl"/>
  <cowl:tgtOntology rdf:resource="http://www.ex.org/vino.owl"/>
 <cowl:bridgRule cowl:br-type="equiv">
   <cowl:srcC rdf:resource="http://www.ex.org/wine.owl#wine"/>
   <cowl:tgtC rdf:resource="http://www.ex.org/vino.owl#vino"/>
 </cowl:bridgRule>
 <cowl:bridgRule cowl:br-type="onto">
   <cowl:srcC rdf:resource="http://www.ex.org/wine.owl#RedWine"/>
   <cowl:tgtC rdf:resource="http://www.ex.org/vino.owl#VinoRosso"/>
 </cowl:bridgRule>
 <cowl:bridgRule cowl:br-type="into">
   <cowl:srcC rdf:resource="http://www.ex.org/wine.owl#Teroldego"/>
   <cowl:tgtC rdf:resource="http://www.ex.org/vino.owl#VinoRosso"/>
 </cowl:bridgRule>
 <cowl:bridgRule cowl:br-type="compat">
   <cowl:srcC rdf:resource="http://www.ex.org/wine.owl#WhiteWine"/>
   <cowl:tgtC rdf:resource="http://www.ex.org/vino.owl#Passito"/>
 </cowl:bridgRule>
 <cowl:bridgRule cowl:br-type="incompat">
   <cowl:srcC rdf:resource="http://www.ex.org/wine.owl#WhiteWine"/>
   <cowl:tgtC rdf:resource="http://www.ex.org/vino.owl#VinoNero"/>
 </cowl:bridgRule>
</cowl:mapping> </rdf:RDF>
```

As it can be noticed, a mapping is defined by source and target ontology and a set of bridge rules, where each bridge rule is defined by the source and target concepts selected from the respective ontologies, and the semantic relation which holds between the two concepts.

3.6 Semantic Web and Databases

As announced by the book subtitle, we are analyzing data management in the Semantic Web in a *model-based perspective*. Indeed, both in databases and in the web, good modeling is crucial, since good modeling is key of having efficient representation and reasoning [1]. Thus, many of the most interesting efforts of the two research communities have been devoted to finding and refining appropriate representation formalisms, each with the aim to capture the distinguishing characters of the context they wish to model. This paper and the previous one in this book try to present these efforts from the two communities. However, since the goal of this book is to bridge the two worlds, and since the appropriate management of data in the Semantic Web is crucial, some brief considerations on the differences between the basic modeling assumptions of the two areas are in order.

As will also be seen in Chap. 7, the most famous approach to deduction and reasoning in databases is based on Datalog [11]. Thus, when referring to the differences between inference in the Semantic Web and inference in the database domain we will mostly refer to the underlying deduction frameworks, namely Classical Logic (mainly Description Logic and its variations) and Datalog.

One of the most important differences between the two worlds is the "open" nature of the Web, vs. the "closed" nature of databases. In Classical Logic, unstated information does not assume a truth value: that is, when an assertion is not found as a known fact, nothing can be said about its truth value. On the other hand, in the database realm the facts that have neither been asserted nor inferred are considered as false. The first attitude is known as the *Open World Assumption* (*OWA*), while the second is the *Closed World Assumption* (*CWA*), and each of them is perfectly coherent with the framework in which it is assumed.

The CWA [29] can be seen as an inference rule that, given a set of sentences S and an atom A, if A does not follow from S (i.e., cannot be inferred from S), derives $\neg A$. The CWA accounts for the way database people see the database as a mirror of the real world. Indeed, though we can reasonably allow for a database to be incomplete, that is, not to contain *all* the facts which are true in the world, most database applications can perfectly accommodate the much more restrictive hypothesis that *what is not recorded must be considered as false*. Indeed, in information systems—where databases are most used—it is reasonable to assume that all relevant information is actually available. The result of this assumption allows for a much simpler treatment of negation, in that not only what is explicitly asserted as false is so.

An important consequence of the CWA is the so-called *minimal model semantics* of databases. Since, from a proof-theoretic point of view, the CWA implies that facts that cannot be proven must be considered as false, then *the* model of the database consists of all the facts that are true in *all* the worlds satisfying S, that is, a minimal model.

On the other hand, in the Semantic Web, there is no need to assume that a certain (although ample) collection of information sources should contain all information which is true; thus the Classical paradigm is more appropriate for web modeling since, when a fact F is not inferrable from S, it does not exclude interpretations of S which contain F. This allows for the possibility that, coming into play another information source which entails F, we should not fall into contradiction.

Some sort of reconciliation is possible between the two attitudes by taking an *epistemic* view of the database content: in [24], the epistemic operators provide a clean way to express the difference between the description of the external world, and that of the database itself, that is, *what the database knows*. Thus, of a certain fact we can ask whether it is *known to the database*, mimicking the semantics of a database query. Within this view, a clear model-theoretic semantics can be given to databases which is no longer incompatible with the classical paradigm underlying the semantic web. Including these operators in the various adopted logics may increase their computational complexity, and various researchers have engaged in solving this problem [12].

The "closed" view adopted in the database world also has two more aspects, namely the *unique name assumption*, which states that individuals with different names are different, and the *domain closure assumption*, which comes in different flavors but basically states that there are no other individuals than those in the database. Both assumptions do not favor the richness of expressivity needed for the web, and thus are to be rejected in that context. By contrast, they prove to be very practical in the database domain, where unambiguous answers to "for all" queries and queries involving negation can be provided, based on the three assumptions above.

The above problems are part of the wider question of *incomplete information*: for instance, in the open perspective of the web we would like to be able to assert that an employee belongs to a department, without being obliged to name this department explicitly. One way to (partially) solve the problem in relational databases is the introduction of null values, whose treatment still produces a lot of research because as yet considered unsatisfactory; using different models, like the object-oriented one or semistructured data models helps a little in this direction, though introducing new problems related to a lower efficiency as to data manipulation.

Another example of incomplete information is given by disjunction: we might want to state that John has gone out either with Jane or with Sara, but asserting such disjunctive information is impossible in the relational database model, and requires appropriate extensions. Disjunctive information management is also a difficult task in relation to negation and the CWA. Indeed, suppose that a disjunctive sentence $P \vee Q$ holds in a database: then by the CWA we will be able to derive $\neg P$ and also $\neg Q$, which obviously leads to inconsistency.

Among other important differences of the two approaches, we mention the question of infinity, which in its turn is strictly related to the meaning of database instances. In the traditional context of relational databases, a database (instance) is a finite set of finite relations, i.e., the totality of all tuples that can appear in a database is finite. Thus, since a database instance can be viewed as an interpretation of the first-order theory defined by the database schema (plus possibly a deductive program) and the integrity constraints, only finite models for the database schema are admissible. In the Classical paradigm, no assumption is made as to the interpretations that are acceptable for a theory, thus infinite models are not ruled out. Moreover, the idea that an instance is an interpretation leads to identification between information and interpretation (which is the basis of the so-called Herbrand model semantics of datalog), whereas an ontology is seen as a theory which admits many possible interpretations.

More differences between the two paradigms reside in the use and treatment of constraints and restrictions. An interesting and detailed discussion on these topics can be found in [22].

3.7 Conclusion

In this chapter, we have presented a short introduction to the Semantic Web, to its underlying motivations and ideas and to the main languages used to implement it. The main goal of this chapter is to integrate the contents of the previous chapter on database technology and to provide the necessary basic notions needed in order to properly read the contents of the rest of the book.

Appendix A: RDF(S) Constructs

This appendix provides a list of the thirty-three RDF(S)constructs excluding the sub-properties of rdfs:member.

The RDF(S) constructs are rdf:about, rdf:Alt, rdf:Bag, rdf:Description, rdf:first, rdf:ID, rdf:List, rdf:nil, rdf:Object, rdf:predicate, rdf:Property, rdf:resource, rdf:rest, rdf:Seq, rdf:Statement, rdf:subject, rdf:type, rdf:value, rdf:XMLLiter-al, rdfs:Class, rdfs:comment, rdfs:Container, rdfs:ContainerMembershipProp-erty, rdfs:Datatype, rdfs:domain, rdfs:isDefinedBy, rdfs:label, rdfs:Literal, rdfs:member, rdfs:range, rdfs:seeAlso, rdfs:subClassOf, and rdfs:subProperty-Of.

Details of the meaning of the above constructs can be found in the RDF(S) manuals. To provide a few examples, rdfs:Class allows to represent a concept, rdfs:subClassOf to state that a concept is more specific than another, rdf:resource to represent a resource (an instance of a concept), rdfs:label to represent a human readable label (for a concept or resource or property), rdfs:comment to provide a human readable description of a concept or resource or property.

Appendix B: OWL Constructs

This appendix provides the lists of the forty OWL constructs and eleven RDF(S) constructs that can be used in an OWL representation.

The OWL constructs are owl:AllDifferent, owl:allValuesFrom, owl:AnnotationProperty, owl:backwardCompatibleWith, owl:cardinality, owl:Class, owl:complementOf, owl:DataRange, owl:DatatypeProperty, owl:DeprecatedClass, owl:DeprecatedProperty, owl:differentFrom, owl:disjointWith, owl:distinctMembers, owl:equivalentClass, owl:equivalentProperty, owl:FunctionalProperty, owl:hasValue, owl:imports, owl:incompatibleWith, owl:intersectionOf, owl: InverseFunctionalProperty, owl:inverseOf, owl:maxCardinality, owl:minCardinality, owl:Nothing, owl:ObjectProperty, owl:oneOf, owl:onProperty, owl:Ontology, owl:OntologyProperty, owl:priorVersion, owl:Restriction, owl:sameAs, owl:someValuesFrom, owl:SymmetricProperty, owl:Thing, owl:TransitiveProperty, owl:unionOf, and owl:versionInfo.

The RDF(S) constructs are rdf:about, rdf:ID, rdf:resource, rdf:type, rdfs:comment, rdfs:domain, rdfs:label, rdfs:Literal, rdfs:range, rdfs:subClassOf, and rdfs:subPropertyOf.

To provide a few examples of the meaning of the constructs above, owl:Class can be used to represent a concept, owl:equivalentClass to state that a concept is equivalent to another, owl:Thing to represent an instance of a concept, owl:sameAs to state that two instances refer the same thing.

References

1. Amarel, S.: On representations of problems of reasoning about actions. In: Machine Intelligence 3, pp. 131–171. Elsevier, Amsterdam (1968)
2. Baader, F., Calvanese, D., McGuinness, D.L., Nardi, D., Patel-Schneider, P.F. (eds.): The Description Logic Handbook: Theory, Implementation, and Applications. Cambridge University Press, Cambridge (2003)
3. Beckett, D.: RDF/XML Syntax Specification (Revised). Technical Report, World Wide Web Consortium (W3C), Recommendation, February 10 (2004)
4. Bechhofer, S., Harmelen, F.V., Hendler, J., Horrocks, I., McGuinness, D.L., Patel-Schneider, P.F., Stein, L.A.: OWL Web Ontology Language Reference. Technical Report, World Wide Web Consortium (W3C), Recommendation, February 10 (2004)
5. Berners-Lee, T.: Weaving the Web. Orion Business Books (1999)
6. Berners-Lee, T., Hendler, J.A., Lassila, O.: The Semantic Web. Sci Am. J. **284**(5), 34–43 (2001)
7. Bouquet, P., Giunchiglia, F., Harmelen, F.V., Serafini, L., Stuckenschmidt, H.: C-OWL: Contextualizing ontologies. In: International Semantic Web Conference, pp. 164–179 (2003)
8. Bray, T., Paoli, J., Sperberg-McQueen, C.M., Maler, E., Yergeau, F.: Extensible Markup Language (XML) 1.0 (Fourth Edition). Technical Report, World Wide Web Consortium (W3C), Recommendation, February 10 (2004)
9. Brickley, D., Guha, R.V.: RDF Vocabulary Description Language 1.0: RDF Schema. Technical Report, World WideWeb Consortium (W3C), Recommendation, February 10 (2004)
10. Carroll, J.J., Roo, J.D.: OWL Web Ontology Language Test Cases. Technical Report, World Wide Web Consortium (W3C), Recommendation, February 10 (2004)
11. Ceri, S., Gottlob, G., Tanca, L.: Logic Programming and Databases. Springer, Berlin (1990)
12. Donini, F.M., Lenzerini, M., Nardi, D., Schaerf, A., Nutt, W.: Adding epistemic operators to concept languages. In: 3th International Conference on Principles of Knowledge Representation and Reasoning (KR'92), Cambridge, MA (1992)
13. Fallside, D.C., Walmsley, P.: XML Schema Part 0: Primer Second Edition. Technical Report, World Wide Web Consortium (W3C), Recommendation, October 28 (2004)

14. Giunchiglia, F., Marchese, M., Zaihrayeu, I.: Encoding classifications into lightweight ontologies. In: Journal on Data Semantics VIII. LNCS, vol. 4380, pp. 57–81. Springer, Berlin (2007)
15. Giunchiglia, F., Shvaiko, P., Yatskevich, M.: Discovering missing background knowledge in onology matching. In: Proceedings: 17th European Conference on Artificial Intelligence (ECAI), pp. 382–386 (2006)
16. Giunchiglia, F., Dutta, B., Maltese, V.: Faceted lightweight ontologies. In: Borgida, A., Chaudhri, V., Giorgini, P., Yu, E. (eds.) Conceptual Modeling: Foundations and Applications. LNCS, vol. 5600. Springer, Berlin (2009)
17. Giunchiglia, F., Zaihrayeu, I.: Lightweight ontologies. In: The Encyclopedia of Database Systems. Springer, Berlin (2008, to appear)
18. Grant, J., Beckett, D.: RDF Test Cases. Technical Report, World Wide Web Consortium (W3C), Recommendation, February 10 (2004)
19. Guarino, N., Giaretta, P.: Ontologies and knowledge bases: towards a terminological clarification. In: Mars, N. (ed.) Towards Very Large Knowledge Bases: Knowledge Building and Knowledge Sharing. IOS Press, Amsterdam (1995)
20. Hayes, P.: RDF Semantics. Technical Report, World Wide Web Consortium (W3C), Recommendation, February 10 (2004)
21. Hefflin, J.: OWL Web Ontology Language Use Cases and Requirements. Technical Report, World Wide Web Consortium (W3C), Recommendation, February 10 (2004)
22. Patel-Schneider, P.F., Horrocks, I.: A comparison of two modelling paradigms in the Semantic Web. J. Web Semant. **5**(4), 240–250 (2007)
23. Klyne, G., Carroll, J.J.: Resource Description Framework (RDF): Concepts and Abstract Syntax. Technical Report, World Wide Web Consortium (W3C), Recommendation, February 10 (2004)
24. Lifschitz, V.: Nonmonotonic databases and epistemic queries. In: 12th International Joint Conference on Artificial Intelligence (IJCAI'91), Sydney, Australia (1991)
25. Manola, F., Miller, M.: RDF Primer. Technical Report, World Wide Web Consortium (W3C), Recommendation, February 10 (2004)
26. McGuinness, D.L., Harmelen, F.V.: OWL Web Ontology Language Overview. Technical Report, World Wide Web Consortium (W3C), Recommendation, February 10 (2004)
27. Patel-Schneider, P.F., Hayes, P., Horrocks, I.: OWL Web Ontology Language Guide Semantics and Abstract Syntax. Technical Report, World Wide Web Consortium (W3C), Recommendation, February 10 (2004)
28. Rector, A., Welty, C.: Simple part-whole relations in OWL Ontologies, W3C Working Draft, August 11 (2005)
29. Reiter, R.: On closed world data bases. In: Symposium on Logic and Data Bases (1977)
30. Sirin, E., Parsia, B., Grau, B.C., Kalyanpur, A., Katz, Y.: Pellet: a practical owl-dl reasoner. J. Web Semant. (2003)
31. Smith, M.K., Welty, C., McGuinness, D.L.: OWL Web Ontology Language Guide. Technical Report, World Wide Web Consortium (W3C), Recommendation, February 10 (2004)

Part I
Semantic Web Data Storage

Chapter 4
Relational Technologies, Metadata and RDF

Yannis Velegrakis

Abstract Metadata plays an important role in successfully understanding and querying data on the web. A number of metadata management solutions have already been developed but each is tailored to specific kinds of metadata. The Resource Description Framework (RDF) is a generic, flexible and powerful model which is becoming the de-facto standard for metadata representation on the Web. Its adoption has created an exponential growth of the amount of available RDF data calling for efficient management solutions. Instead of designing such solutions from scratch, it is possible to invest on existing relational technologies by exploiting their long presence and maturity. Relational technologies can offer efficient storage and high performance querying at relatively low cost. Unfortunately, the principles of the relational model are fundamentally different from those of RDF. This difference means that specialized storage and querying schemes need to be put in place in order to use relational technologies for RDF data. In this work, we provide a comprehensive description of these relational RDF storage schemes and discuss their advantages and limitations. We believe that through carefully designed schemes, it is possible to achieve sophisticated high performance systems that support the full power of RDF and bring one step closer the materialization of the Semantic Web vision.

4.1 Introduction

Recent years have shown a tremendous proliferation of systems that make available on the web data and information from almost every field of human activity, i.e., from corporate environments and scientific domains to personal media and social activities. Interaction with these systems is becoming increasingly complex, mainly due to the fact that their internal data has dramatically increased in size, structural complexity, semantic heterogeneity and interaction intricacy. To cope with this issue, and successfully query, discover, retrieve, integrate and maintain this data, metadata plays an important role. The term metadata is used to refer to any secondary piece of information that is separate in some way from the primary data. In corporate environments, for instance, metadata regarding data quality [28, 44, 46] can help in detecting erroneous, inaccurate, out-of-date or incomplete values and can have significant impact on the quality of query results [16]. In scientific domains, whenever

Y. Velegrakis (✉)
University of Trento, Via Sommarive 14, 38100 Trento, Italy
e-mail: velgias@disi.unitn.eu

R. De Virgilio et al. (eds.), *Semantic Web Information Management*,
DOI 10.1007/978-3-642-04329-1_4,

data is collected from various sources, cleansed, integrated and analyzed to produce new forms of data [36], any provenance [8], superimposed information [26], different forms of annotations [11, 21] or information on the performed transformations [4, 41], can be important in order to allow users to apply their own judgment to assess the credibility of the query results.

The relational model provides a clear separation between data values and metadata information. The metadata of a relational database concerns the structure of the data (i.e., the schema), constraints that may exist on the data, statistics that are of use by query optimizers, and information about time and permissions on the various schema components. Additional types of metadata cannot be easily incorporated in this model, and query languages, such as SQL, have no provision for metadata based queries, i.e., queries involving metadata terms. Over the years, there have been numerous research efforts to cope with this limitation. Table 4.1 illustrates some of these efforts along-side the way they have approached the problem. A common de-

Table 4.1 Metadata management approaches in relational and semi-structured data systems

Metadata	Approach
Annotations [21]	Atomic value annotations attached to a block of values within a tuple. They accompany the values as retrieved. Relational algebra query language.
Provenance [11]	Atomic data values carry their provenance, which propagates with them as they are retrieved. Query language supports predicates on provenance.
Quality Parameters [28]	Data values are associated with quality parameters (accuracy, freshness, etc.). SQL is extended to retrieve data using these parameters.
Schema & Mappings [41, 47]	Explicit modeling of schema and mapping information, and associations of it with portions of the data. SQL extension to retrieve data and metadata that satisfy certain metadata properties.
Security [7]	Credential-based access control. System reads complex security profiles and returns data results accordingly.
Super-imposed Information [26]	Loosely-coupled model of information elements, marks and links used to represent superimposed information. It has no specific schema, but is in relational model and can be queried using SQL.
Time [13]	Creation and modification time is recorded with the data and used in query answering. Query language supports predicates on time values.

nominator of these efforts is the extension of the data model with special structures to store the metadata of interest and the extension of the query language with additional operators that are specifically designed for a specific kind of metadata.

A closer look of the works in Table 4.1 can also reveal the high heterogeneity of the kinds of metadata that have been considered and the high degree of specialization of each solution towards the specific metadata it is targeting. In particular, it can be observed that some metadata is expressed as single atomic values, e.g., the creation time of an element in a database [13], while others have a more complex structure, e.g., the schema mapping [41] or security [7] specification. Furthermore, metadata may be associated either to individual data values [11, 13, 28] or to groups of values, i.e., set of attributes in a tuple [21]. As far as it concerns the query language, it can be noticed that there is a clear distinction between data and metadata. Either there are queries that return only metadata information, i.e., the relations of a database schema, or data-only queries, or queries returning data accompanied by their associated metadata. However, in many real-world scenarios, the distinction between data and metadata is blurred. The same piece of information may be seen by some as data and by others as metadata which means that a clear distinction between the kind of arguments (data or metadata) that a query operator can accept may not be desired. It can also be observed that each solution is not directly applicable to other forms of metadata, at least not without some major modifications. Past attempts on building generic metadata stores (e.g., [6, 23]) have employed complex modeling tools for this purpose: [23] explicitly represented the various artifacts using Telos [30], while the Microsoft Repository [6] employed data repositories (intended for shared databases of engineering artifacts). A simple, elegant approach to uniformly model and query data, arbitrary metadata and their association has been elusive.

In parallel to the database community, the Web community faced a similar need. More than ever before, a model for the uniform representation and querying of metadata on the Web had been apparent. The model had to be machine readable, flexible and easily integrateable with existing web technologies and tools. This led to the introduction of RDF that is currently emerging as the dominant standard for representing interlinked metadata on the Web. It is a representation language based on directed labeled graphs in which nodes are called resources and edges are called properties. The graph structure is expressed through a series of triples, each representing an edge between two resources (the first and third component of the triple) with the second component of the triple being the identifier of the edge. RDF has an XML syntax, which means that it is humanly and machine readable. It allows the representation of many different kinds of metadata with highly heterogeneous structures. Its wide adoption by organizations and individuals as the format for web metadata publishing, brings the web one step closer to the realization of the Semantic Web vision [37].

The increased amount of RDF data has naturally called for efficient storage and querying solutions, that has led to the development of a number of different systems, typically referred to as *triple stores* [3, 5, 10, 12, 22, 33]. Unfortunately, the flexibility that RDF offered, came at a price. Its triple-based nature required special storage, indexing, retrieval and update techniques. Early RDF systems stored triples in giant three-column tables that were efficient for simple triple-based queries, especially in the presence of the right index structures, but had serious scalability issues in complex graph-based queries.

In order to avoid building new native RDF solutions from scratch, it seemed logical to invest on the many years of research and development that has taken place in the area of relational data management. Relational systems have matured enough and are prevalent, thus they can be easily adopted in real world application scenarios. Many popular systems such as Jena [12], Oracle [14], Sesame [10] and 3Store [22], are based on this idea. Of course, the tabular nature of the relational model cannot directly serve the graph-based query expressions and data traversal functionality that RDF requires. As such, special schemas need to be designed in order to alleviate that issue and improve query performance.

In this work, we provide an overview of the ways that the database and the web communities have dealt with the issue of metadata management. Section 4.2 is an introduction to the relational model. Section 4.3 presents a rough categorization of the metadata management techniques in the relational data management community. A quick overview of RDF and its basic modeling principles is made in Sect. 4.4. Finally, Sect. 4.5 presents different modeling schemes for storing RDF data in relational data management systems.

4.2 The Relational Model

Assume an infinite set of attribute names $\mathcal{L}$ and a set of atomic types, e.g., **Integer**, **String**, etc., with pairwise disjoint domains. The name of an atomic type is used to represent both the type and its domain.

A relational database (or relational instance) [15] consists of a set of relations (or relational tables). A relational table is a named set of tuples. A tuple is an ordered set of $\langle a, v\rangle$ pairs, called attributes, with $a \in \mathcal{L}$ and $v \in \mathbf{Integer} \cup \mathbf{String} \cup \dots$ The cardinality of a tuple is the number of attributes it contains. All the tuples in the same relation must have the same cardinality, and all the attributes in the same position of each tuple must have the same attribute name and values of the same type. The schema of a relational table, denoted as $R(A_1{:}T_1, A_2{:}T_2, \dots, A_n{:}T_n)$, describes the structure of its tuples. In particular, R is the name of the table, n is the cardinality of its tuples, and $A_k{:}T_k$ is the name and type of the attributes in the kth position of each tuple in the table. The schema of a relational database is the set of the schemas of its relational tables.

A number of different languages have been proposed over the last three decades for querying relational data. The most popular is without a doubt SQL [19]. An SQL query is formed by a select, a from and a where clause. The from clause consists of a set of variables, each associated to a relational table. Each variable is bound to the tuples of the table with which it is associated. The where clause contains a set of conditions. Given a binding of the variables of a query, if the conditions in the where clause are satisfied by the tuples to which the variables are bound, the binding is said to be a *true* binding. For each true binding, a tuple is generated in the answer set according to the expressions in the select clause. Each select clause expression is defined by the following grammar:

$$exp ::= constant \mid variable.attributeName \mid f(exp_1, \ldots, exp_n)$$

Since the output of an SQL query is a set of homogeneous tuples, i.e., a relational table, queries can be composed to form more complex queries. SQL supports a number of additional constructs for grouping, sorting and set operations and others, but we will not elaborate further on those since they are out of the scope of the current work.

The tabular form of the relational model makes it ideal for representation of sets of data with homogeneous structures and the appropriate index structures can provide efficient tuple selection operations based on attribute values.

4.3 Modeling Metadata in Relational Systems

There have been numerous efforts for storing metadata in relational databases. These efforts boil down to three main categories. The first is the use of separate specialized structures that represent the metadata. The second is the use of intermixed structures in which the same table contains both data and metadata. The third kind is the use of intensional associations that allows metadata to be associated to data without the need for the latter to be aware of that.

4.3.1 Separate Structures

This approach involved specially designed tables whose semantics are known in advance and are not considered part of the database schema or instance. They contain meta-information about the stored data, and they can be queried using the relational query language supported by the system. However, they cannot be used for associating generic kinds of metadata to the data values. A classical example of this case are the catalog tables of the relational DBMS.

4.3.2 Intermixed Context

In the case in which different kinds of metadata need to be associated to specific data values, a different mechanism is needed. Data annotations are classical examples of such metadata. An annotation may vary from security information to data quality parameters, with the simplest and most prevalent kind of annotation being the user comments.

(a)

Restaurants

Name	**Name$_c$**	**City**	**City$_c$**
Chinatown		N.Y.	*in USA*
Pizza Roma	*very nice*	L.A.	
Pizza Roma	*expensive*	L.A.	
Pizza Roma	*from citySearch*	L.A.	*from citySearch*

(b)

Restaurants

Name	**City**
Chinatown	N.Y.
Pizza Roma	L.A.

Restaurants$_c$

Key	**Name$_c$**	**City$_c$**
Chinatown		*in USA*
Pizza Roma	*very nice*	
Pizza Roma	*expensive*	
Pizza Roma	*from citySearch*	*from citySearch*

(c)

Restaurants

Name	**City**	**Name$_c$**	**City$_c$**	**value**
Chinatown	N.Y.		1	*in USA*
Pizza Roma	L.A.	1		*very nice*
Pizza Roma	L.A.	1		*expensive*
Pizza Roma	L.A.	1	1	*from citySearch*

Fig. 4.1 Schemes for storing annotations in relational data

A possible scheme for data annotations is used in the DBNotes system [8]. For every attribute A, in a data table, a second attribute A_c is introduced to keep the annotation of the value in A. An example of this scheme is illustrated in Fig. 4.1(a). Attributes Name$_c$ and City$_c$ contain the annotations of the values in attributes Name and City, respectively. A limitation of the scheme is that in the case in which a value has more than one annotation, the whole tuple needs to be repeated, once for every annotation. This is the case of the `Pizza Roma` restaurant in the example. Note how the tuple `[Pizza Roma, L.A.]` has to be repeated three times to accommodate the three different annotations of the value `Pizza Roma`. Furthermore, if an annotation is referring to more than one attributes of a tuple, the annotation has to be repeated for every attribute. For instance, the annotation `from citySearch` in the Restaurants table is repeated in both columns Name$_c$ and City$_c$.

To avoid the redundancy a variation of the described scheme can be used. The variation is based on the existence of keys or of row identifiers. In particular, the scheme assumes that for every table T there is a table T_c that stores the annotations. The attributes of the table T_c are basically the attributes A_c of the previous scheme, with one additional attribute, used to reference the key (or row id) of the respective data tuple. This variation is illustrated in Fig. 4.1(b). Tuple repetition may still be required in case of multiple annotations on a value, but in this case the wasted space is only for the repetition of the row identifier (or the key) and not for the whole data tuple values.

In certain practical scenarios, an annotation may need to be assigned to more than one tuple attributes as a block and not to each attribute individually. The Mondrian system [21] uses a different variation of the previous scheme to achieve this. It assumes a column A_c of type **bit** for every attribute A of the data table, and a column value, in each data table. When an annotation needs to be placed on a group of attributes in a tuple, the annotation value is inserted in the value column, and the bit columns of the respective attributes are set to 1. An example is illustrated in Fig. 4.1(c) in which the annotation `from citySearch` is assigned to both values `Pizza Roma` and `L.A.`.

4.3.3 Intensional Associations

The two schemes presented have three main limitations. First, they require explicit association of every metadata entry with its respective data entries. This is not practical in cases in which multiple data elements share the same metadata information. For instance, assume the existence of a table Restaurants with information about restaurants as illustrated in Fig. 4.2, and a user that needs to annotate all the restaurants in N.Y. city with some comment about them. After finding all the tuples in the Restaurant table for which city="N.Y.", an explicit association will have to be made between each such tuple and the respective comment. The second limitation is that future data cannot be handled automatically. For instance, assume that ten

Restaurants

Name	Type	City	Price
Chinatown	Chinese	N.Y.	8
Pizza Roma	Italian	L.A.	30
The India	Indian	San Jose	25
Yo-Min	Chinese	N.Y.	22
Spicy Home	Indian	L.A.	25
Noodle plate	Chinese	N.Y.	15
Curry	Indian	San Jose	20

Comments

References	Comment	Date	Author
select * from Restaurants where city="L.A."	It has 7% tax	03/06	John
select * from Restaurants where city="N.Y."	Tip is 15%	06/06	Mary
select city from Restaurants where city="L.A."	Is in the US	01/04	Kathy
select * from Comments where author="John"	Not to trust	06/05	Nick

Fig. 4.2 A database instance with intensional associations

new New York restaurants are inserted in the Restaurants table and that the comment the user needs to add is generic and applies to every New York restaurant. An association between the user comment and each of these new restaurants will again have to be explicitly made. The third limitation of the schemes described in the previous subsections is that the data table is fully aware of the existence of the metadata. Any metadata value change to be implemented requires access to the table that the data values are also stored. This is something that may not always be possible since owners of data and metadata may be different entities with different privileges.

To overcome these limitations, an intensional association framework [34] can be put in place. The idea is to replace the traditional value-based association between tables with associations based on queries. An example is illustrated in Fig. 4.2. Table Comments contains comments that various users have made over time. Column References is of a special type that contains, instead of a regular atomic value referring to the key of the data table, a query expression. The evaluation of this query expression determines the data values that the respective comment is about. For instance, the first tuple in the Comments table is about all the restaurants in Los Angeles (L.A.). Note that one metadata tuple is enough to cover all the restaurants on which the comment applies. In real systems where the same metadata value may have to be assigned to multiple data tuples, this scheme can lead to significant saving in terms of space. Furthermore, assuming that a new restaurant opens in L.A. and the respective tuple is inserted in the Restaurants table. The tuple will be automatically associated to the first entry in the Comments table, since it will satisfy the specifications of the query in the References column of the metadata tuple.

By using queries as attributes, one can assign metadata to data without any modification on the data tables. Furthermore, the select clause of the query can be used to assign the metadata information to a subset of the columns of the data tuple, as is the case with the third tuple in the Comments table in Fig. 4.2. An additional feature is that the queries used as values can reference tuples in any table in the database, even in their own. One such example, is the fourth tuple of the Comments table that represents a comment that applies on the first tuple of the same table. The modeling of this scheme allows for a uniform management of data and metadata and facilitates the construction of metadata hierarchies, i.e., metadata assigned to other metadata.

Of course, the presence of queries as values require modifications of the query evaluation engine. Some first steps have already been done towards evaluation techniques [32, 39], and index structures [38].

4.4 RDF

RDF (Resource Description Framework) [43] has been introduced as a mean to represent metadata on the web. It views web data as a set of *resources*, that may also be related to each other. Any web entity is considered a resource, uniquely identified by its *Unique Resource Identifier* (*URI*). Information about web entities is expressed through *RDF statements*. An *RDF statement* specifies a relationship between two resources. It is a triple of the form $\langle subject, predicate, object \rangle$. The *subject* is a URI representing a web artifact, *statement* is a label, and *object* is either another URI or a literal. The information, for instance, that W3C is the owner of the web page http://www.w3.org/RDF, can be expressed through the statement

⟨http://www.w3.org/RDF, "owner", http://www.w3.org⟩

assuming that the URI of the W3C is http://www.w3.org.

Web metadata may not always be about web entities but about other metadata. To facilitate this kind of information, statements themselves are considered resources, thus, they can be used in statements like any other resource.

By representing every statement as an edge that connects the resources that appear in its subject and object and is labeled with its predicate, one can generate a graph representation of any RDF data. Since statements are also resources, an edge can connect not only nodes but also edges, thus, the generated graph structure is actually a hypergraph.

A set of RDF triple statements form an *RDF base*. More formally, we assume the existence of an infinite set of *resources* $\mathcal{U}$, each with a *unique resource identifier* (URI), an infinite set of labels $\mathcal{A}$, and an infinite set of *literals* $\mathcal{L}$. Each literal can be considered a resource having itself as its actual URI. A *property* is an association between two resources which is also a resource. A property is represented by a triple $\langle s, p, o \rangle$, where p is the URI of the property while s and o the URIs of the resources it associates. The URI p of a property $\langle s, p, o \rangle$ is denoted by $URI(p)$ or simply p.

Definition 4.1 A *RDF base* Σ is a tuple $\langle I, P \rangle$, where $I \subseteq \mathcal{U}$ is a set of individuals, $P \subseteq I \times \mathcal{U} \times I$ is a set of properties and $I \cap \{URI(p) \mid p \in P\} = \emptyset$.

To describe and/or control the structure or RDF data, W3C has introduced *RDF Schema* (RDFS) [42]. RDFS is a set of constructs that allows the definition of schematic, i.e., typing, information about RDF data. It defines classes as a way to group together RDF resources that have common structures, differentiates between a property and a nonproperty resources, allows the definition of inheritance and enables the definition of constraints on the resources that a property is allowed to associate.

RDFS assumes that set $\mathcal{U}$ contains the following special resources:[1] **rdfs:Literal**, **rdfs:Property**, **rdfs:Class**, **rdf:Thing**, **rdfs:type**, **rdfs:domain**, **rdfs:range**, the **rdfs:subClassOf** and the **rdfs:subPropertyOf**.

Typing information is modeled through the **rdfs:type** property. All the resources associated to a resource C through the **rdfs:type** property are said to be *instances* of C. Every resource is an instance of the resource **rdf:Thing**. Each resource C that can have instances is itself an instance of the resource **rdfs:Class**. All such instances are referred to as *classes*. Resources **rdfs:Property**, **rdfs:Literal**, **rdfs:Class** and

[1] The names of the properties are their URIs. For simplicity, name-spaces have been omitted from the discussion.

rdf:Thing are classes. The instances of the class **rdfs:Literal** are all the literal values. Every instance of a class that is not an instance of class **rdfs:Property** is referred to as *individual*. A partial order can be defined among classes, through properties that are instances of **rdfs:subClassOf**. If a class is a subclass of another, then the set of instances of the first is a subset of the set of instance of the second. The subclass relationship forms a lattice hierarchy among the classes, with class **rdf:Thing** being at the top of the lattice.

Every property resource is an instance of a *property class*. Property classes are used to restrict the resources properties can associate. A *property class* is an instance of class **rdfs:Property** and is associated through properties **rdfs:domain** and **rdfs:range** to two other classes. When a property is an instance of a property class, the resources it associates must be instances of the domain and range classes of its property class.

A partial order subproperty relationship can be defined between the property classes, similarly to the subclass relationship that can be defined among classes. The subproperty relationship is defined through the **rdfs:subPropertyOf**. When a property is a subproperty of another, then the domain and range classes of the first must be subclasses of the domain and range of the second.

Definition 4.2 A *RDF/RDFS base* Σ is a tuple $\langle I, P, C, P_c, \tau, \tau_c, \dot{\preceq}_c, \dot{\preceq}_p\rangle$, where $I \subseteq \mathcal{U}$ is a set of individuals, and P is a set of properties with $P \subseteq I \times \mathcal{U} \times I$ and $I \cap \{URI(p) \mid p \in P\} = \emptyset$. C is a set of classes that includes **rdfs:Class**, P_c is a set of property classes that includes **rdfs:Property**, $\tau | I \to C$ and $\tau_p | P \to P_c$ are typing function, $\dot{\preceq}_c$ is a partial order relationship[2] on C with **rdfs:Class** as the root, and $\dot{\preceq}_p$ is a partial order relationship[3] on P with **rdfs:Property** as root.

4.5 Using Relational Systems for RDF Storage

The current RDF storage and retrieval landscape reminisces XML. Although there are proposals for native RDF storage, a great majority has opted towards the use of relational data management systems. This trend comes at no surprise. Development of new solutions from scratch requires significant amount of effort, time and money. Relational technologies, on the other hand, have been around for more than three decades, have great achievements to demonstrate and are dominating the market. They can offer numerous of-the-shelf solutions with great query performance and good scalability. Unfortunately, using a relational system for that purpose is not a straight forward task, mainly due to the different foundational principles between the RDF and the relational model. Special schema design and RDF-tailored query answering techniques need to be put in place for such a coupling to work. The following sections provide an overview of the different schemes that can be

[2]Representing the subclass relationships.

[3]Representing the sub-property relationships.

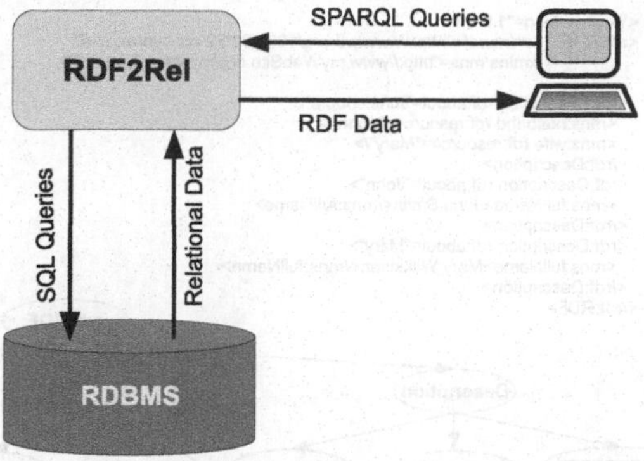

Fig. 4.3 The generic architecture of systems that employee relational data management solutions for storing, querying and retrieving RDF data

used for that purpose. Many of them are already adopted by major RDF stores, such as Jena [12], Oracle [14], RDFStore [3], Sesame [10], 3Store [22], DLDB [33] or Hexastore [45]. A typical architecture consists of a relational system with an additional layer that stands between the relational repository and the user or application interface. The layer is aware of the storage scheme used in the relational repository and is responsible for translating the RDF queries posed by users or applications to queries on the relational structures. The architecture is graphically depicted in Fig. 4.3.

The length of the URIs is one of the first issues faced in relational RDF storage. A URI typically consists of a web address followed by some directory path and the name of the intended resource. Although storing and retrieving long strings is not an issue in modern DBMS, it is becoming an issue in indexing. Many indexing mechanisms use a maximum of 256 or 512 characters as key values, thus, only the first 256 or 512 characters of the URIs will be used in the index. Truncating URIs makes the index useless since the truncated URIs may become non-unique. To avoid this issue, URIs can be stored in a reverse form, so that any possible truncation occurs only on its head. Alternatively, URIs can be mapped to unique system generated identifiers, preferably of numerical nature. Comparisons on numerical values are more efficient than string comparisons, thus, such a mapping offers significant performance improvements. In what follows, we assume that such a mapping is always possible and we will treat URIs and their respective system generated identifiers as synonyms.

A similar technique based on hash encoding is used by 3Store [22]. In particular, for every URI or atomic value that exists in the database, a hash key is computed and used instead of a URI or a literal. The selection of the right hash functions can significantly reduce the time required to compare two values/URIs, and can lead to considerable query performance improvements.

4.5.1 Storing RDF as XML

Since RDF has an XML syntax, any XML storage mechanism can be used to store RDF data. Currently, there is a rich literature addressing the issue of storing and

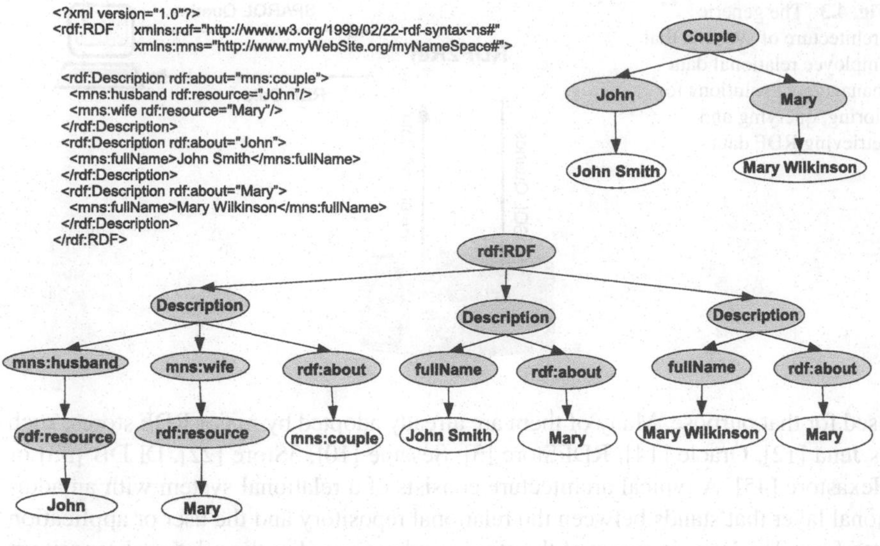

Fig. 4.4 XML syntax (*top left*) of some RDF structure (*top right*) and the tree representation of its XML syntax (*bottom*)

querying XML data in relational databases. Several mapping strategies have been proposed, and many systems have already been developed, such as, Stored [18], Edge [20], Interval [17], XRel [49], XPERANTO [40] or LegoDB [9]. Furthermore, most major commercial relational DBMSs, e.g., IBM DB2 [48], Oracle [24] and Microsoft SQL Server [29], are currently supporting the shredding, storing, querying and retrieving of XML documents.

There are two main drawbacks in following such a strategy. The first is the mismatch between the syntactic variations of the XML representation and the RDF data model. In particular, the tree representation of the XML syntax of some RDF structure may involve additional elements that may not correspond to any of the RDF structures. For instance, Fig. 4.4 illustrates an RDF model representing a couple where John Smith is the husband and Mary Wilkinson the wife. The top left-hand side of the figure is the XML syntax of the RDF model, while the top right-hand side is its graph representation. The lower part of the figure is the tree representation of the XML data of the top left-hand side. It can easily be noticed the differences between the two graph representations, which means that queries on the RDF structure will have to be translated accordingly if the RDF structures are stored according to the XML representation.

A second drawback of the strategy is the mismatch between the XML and the RDF query patterns. XML queries are based on the tree structure of XML and typically involve root-to-element paths or subtree selections. RDF resources, on the other hand, lack such a hierarchy. They are structured as directed graphs, and naturally, RDF queries typically involve random graph traversals.

Statements

subject	predicate	object
1	type	article
1	title	LAURIN
1	author	Catarci
1	author	Santucci
1	author	Calvanese
1	journal	WWW
1	year	2001
1	file	CSC01.pdf
2	type	book
2	author	Codd
2	title	The Relational Model
2	year	1990
2	publisher	Addison-Wesley
3	type	book
3	title	Principles of DB Systems
3	author	Vianu
3	author	Hull
3	author	Abiteboul
3	year	1995
3	publisher	Addison-Wesley
4	type	article
4	title	Web-Based Data
4	author	Atzeni
4	author	Merialdo
4	author	Mecca
4	journal	IEEE Int. Comp.
4	file	AMM02.pdf

Fig. 4.5 A vertical table

4.5.2 Vertical Table

Since an RDF base is expressed as a set of triple statements of the form ⟨subject, predicate, object⟩, a straightforward solution is to use a 3-attribute table for storing the statements. This schema is referred to as the *vertical table* scheme. Each tuple in a vertical table represents a triple statement, with its three attributes corresponding to the subject, the predicate and the object part of the triple, respectively. Figure 4.5 illustrates a vertical table that models a part of an RDF base.

Assume that a user is interested in finding whether `Calvanese` has any publications and poses the SPARQL query:

select ?subject **where** {?subject `author Calvanese`}

To retrieve the answer, the SPARQL query is translated to the following SQL expression:

```
select subject
from Statements
where predicate="author" and object="Calvanese"
```

which can be efficiently answered in the presence of indexes on the attributes of the table Statements.

On the other hand, to answer queries like, for instance, the one that looks for the journals in which Mecca and Atzeni have sent a publication together, requires multiple self-joins over the Statements table which leads to significant performance issues. The particular query, for instance, can be answered through the relational query:

```
select s3.object from Statements s1, Statements s2, Statements s3
    where s1.predicate="author" and s1.object="Mecca" and
          s2.predicate="author" and s1.object="Atzeni" and
          s3.predicate="journal" and s1.subject=s2.subject and
          s1.subject=s3.subject
```

The advantage of the vertical table scheme is that it is suitable for storing highly heterogeneous data. It can easily model resources with any number of properties. The scheme facilitates statement-based queries, i.e., queries consisting of a triple statement that lacks one or two parts and returns the resources of the triples complementing the missing parts, like, the example query about Calvanese above. This is because statement-based queries get translated to selectivity relational queries which can be efficiently answered in the presence of the right index structures. On the other hand, due to the joins that need to be performed, data browsing and path queries on the RDF structures are costly to implement.

In the presence of schema information, the vertical table can be used to answer schema queries, i.e., queries related to RDF metadata. The scheme stores the schema information in triples as it does with the rest of the data [27]. Thus, it is easy, for instance, to answer whether a class is a direct subclass of another. It will be hard, however, to answer whether a class is a subclass of another in the general case, since the system will have to search and combine many triple statements.

4.5.3 Graph-based Storage

Since the RDF model is basically a directed graph, a large number of queries are about detecting subgraphs satisfying some path expressions. The vertical table scheme has poor performance for this type of queries because they require multiple join operations.

To overcome this problem, the design of the relational tables can be based on the paths that are most likely to be used [27]. To cover all the possible cases, one can extract for each resource e all the path expressions to every other resource reachable from e and explicitly store them. This precomputation avoids expensive joins during

Class(classname, pre, post, depth)
Property(propertyName, domain, range, pre, post, depth)
Resource(resourceName, ppathID, datatype)
Triple(subject, predicate, object)
Path(pathID, pathexp)
Type(resourceName, className)

Fig. 4.6 Relational schema for a graph-based RDF storage

query answering and improves significantly the query response time. An important requirement, however, is that the data contains no cyclic paths.

To reduce the size of the tables, an idea is to use different tables to represent different parts on the RDF graph [27]. In particular, one can extract different subgraphs based on the class hierarchy, the properties, etc., and store each one of them in its own table. That way, depending on their kind, queries will be directed and answered on the respective tables. The extraction of the subgraphs can be based on the special RDF properties. For instance, the *class*, *inheritance*, *property*, *type*, *domain-range* and generic subgraphs can be extracted from the RDF graph based on the properties rdf:subclassOf, rdfs:subPropertyOf, rdf:type, rdfs:domain/range and rdfs:seeAlso/isDefinedBy relationships. Clearly, the structure of each such graph is much less complex that the structure of the whole RDF graph which leads to better response times. Furthermore, based on the characteristics of each such graph, different techniques can be used for the representation of the different graphs in the relational tables.

A possible schema of the relational tables for a graph-based RDF storage is illustrated in Fig. 4.6. Relations Class and Property are used to store the classes and properties of the RDF Schema. Attributes pre, pos and depth represent the Li and Moon [25] encoding of each class/property in the RDF graph. The Li and Moon encoding is a numbering scheme that has been extensively used in the XML literature to check ancestor/decedent relationships. It assigns to each node three numbers. The first and the second, represent the preorder and the postorder position of each node in the XML tree. The third determines the depth of each node, computed as the length of the path from the root to the specific node. Trying to apply the specific numbering scheme on an RDF graph gives rise to two main issues. First, since RDF graphs are directed acyclic graphs and not trees, it is not clear what node should serve as the root from which the numbering should start. Second, multiple different paths may have a common start and end nodes, and choosing one over another may have consequences. To overcome these issues, nodes with in-degree equal to 0 can be characterized as "*roots*" and paths can be computed from each such node to any other. Furthermore, in the case of multiple paths to a node, multiple copies of that node can be created, one for each different path.

In the relational schema of Fig. 4.6, table Triple is used to model all the RDF statements and is used to efficiently answer predicate queries. Table Type is used to record for every resource instance the RDF schema class it belongs. The attributes of these two tables are self-explanatory.

Materializing the different paths from the roots to the nodes is also an issue, since the paths can be of variable size. To avoid expensive join operations, every path can be encoded as a string of labels and resource names separated through some special character, i.e., "/". The role of table Path and Resource is to materialize this encoding. The former encodes every path along with a unique identifier. The latter, associates every node, i.e., resource, in the RDF graph with its paths in the Path table.

Finding the resources reachable through a path can be answered by selecting from the Path table those tuples for which the pathexp attribute is equal to the path specified in the query. This selection can be performed fast if a Hash or B+ tree index is available. Since the paths recorded in pathexp are all paths starting from a root, the specific selection can work only if the path specified in the query also starts from a root. If it starts from a non-root node, then the table Path needs to be searched for the tuples with a pathexpr attribute value ending with the requested path. Such an operation cannot exploit the index, and is based on sequential scan. To avoid sequential scan, paths can be stored in pathexp in reverse order, i.e., starting from the ending node and ending with the root. That way, the index can be exploited to improve searching for paths ending to a node.

4.5.4 Graph Schema–Vertical Data

An approach similar to the graph-based storage has been used in RDFSuite [3], but with further improvements and features. The general idea is to exploit to the maximum the RDF Schema information whenever this is available. Two sets of relational tables are needed. The first is used to represent the RDF Schema information and the second the actual RDF data.

To represent the RDF schema information, and in particular the class and property hierarchies, four tables are used, namely the Class, Property, SubClass and SubProperty. The Class and Property tables hold the classes and properties defined in the RDF Schema, respectively. The SubClass and the SubProperty tables, store the `rdfs:subClass` and `rdfs:subProperty` relationships that exist between the classes and the properties, respectively. A special table Type is used in which the build-in classes defined in RDF Schema [42], i.e., `rdfs:Class` or `rdfs:Property`, and the literals, i.e., `string` or `integer`, are hard-coded into its contents. The schema of the tables along with a small fraction of the table contents are illustrated in Fig. 4.7. Note that table Class is a unary table, while tables SubClass and SubProperty are binary since they store the relationship between the classes and properties that exist in the tables Class and Property, respectively. The Property table on the other hand is a ternary relationship since it provides for every property, the domain and range classes. B^+-tree indexes are required on every attribute in these tables to achieve satisfactory performance.

For representing the RDF data, an idea similar to the vertical table scheme can be used. In particular, a table Instance with two attributes is required. The first attribute of a tuple in that table keeps the URI of an instance resource and the second the

Class

URI	about
1	Vehicle
2	Truck
3	Car
4	License
5	Private
6	Business

Property

URI	about	domain	range
11	licence	1	4
22	privateLicence	2	6
33	businessLicence	3	5

Subclass

URI	super
2	1
3	1

Subproperty

URI	super
22	11
33	11

Instance

URI	classid
100	2
200	3
300	5
301	6

PropertyInstance

from	name	to
100	brand	500
200	brand	501
200	privateLicence	300
100	businessLicence	301

Type

URI	value
500	MAN
501	VW
600	rdfs:Class
601	rdfs:Property

3

URI
200

5

URI
300

brand

from	to
100	500
200	501

privateLicence

from	to
200	300

2

URI
100

6

URI
301

businessLicence

from	to
100	301

Fig. 4.7 A Graph Schema Vertical Data encoding example

URI of the class that the instance belongs. A similar approach is used to represent the properties of the instances, through a Property table with three columns: two for keeping the URIs of the instances that the property relates, and one for storing the name of the property. A fraction of the Instance and PropertyInstance tables is illustrated in Fig. 4.7. As before, B^+-tree indexes are constructed for every attribute in these tables.

The Instance and the PropertyInstance tables may get too large and affect performance. An alternative modeling is to use one table for the instances of each different class. The name of each such table is the name of the class, and the tuples it contains are the URIs of the instances of the respective class. The tables in Fig. 4.7 that have a number as a name are examples of this variation. The same applies for the property instances, but this time the table is labeled with the name of the property and it must have two columns that record the two resources that the property instance associates.

Having separate tables for instances and properties of different classes may lead to more efficient query answering since fewer tuples may have to be scanned. However, this option is not applicable in cases that the number of classes are extremely large, since this will require the definition of an extremely large number of tables. Although the number of tables supported by the majority of modern relational systems is large enough, there are RDF bases that require the creation of more than

300.000 tables, which even if supported by the relational system, it will have serious performance and management issues.

4.5.5 Property Table

An alternative to the vertical table schema that aims at reducing the number of joins required during query answering is to cluster the properties of the resources and find groups of entities that share the same set of properties. The common properties can then be modeled as attributes of the same table, referred to as a *property table*. This modeling makes explicit the association of the different properties, eliminating the need for joins. A property table consists of N attributes. The first functions as a key and is typically a URI. The remaining $N-1$ attributes represent a set of $N-1$ properties that are commonly found to all the resources, or at least the majority of them. For instance, by studying the RDF data of Fig. 4.5, one can notice that properties type and title appear to all the four resources, while the property year appears in the majority of them, i.e., it appears in all resources apart from 4. Thus, we can construct a relational table with four attributes, the first corresponding to the resource URI and the rest to the attributes type, title and year. The table is illustrated on the left-hand side of Fig. 4.8.

Note that resource 4 in Fig. 4.5 has no year property, and this is reflected in the Property table of Fig. 4.8 through a NULL value on the respective attribute. The property table could have also included attributes journal and file for storing the data of the respective properties. However, since these properties appear to only few resources, they would have required the respective columns to be padded with a lot of nulls, resulting to an unjustified waste of space. To avoid this, a different table, referred to as the *excess table*, is instead introduced. Its schema and functionality is the same as the table in Fig. 4.5. The context of this table are shown on the right-hand side of Fig. 4.8.

A requirement of the property table scheme is that the properties used in the property table are not multi-valued. In the RDF example of Fig. 4.5, certain resources have more than one author. Since the relational model is in First Normal Form [2], such multi-values attributes cannot be modeled in the property table, and unavoidably will be included in the excess table.

A variation of the property table scheme is one that considers multiple property tables. How many such tables and with what attributes is something that is determined by the property clustering technique. For instance, by noticing that although there is no journal property for every resource in the RDF data, for those resources that exist, property file is also present. Thus, a second property table can be created for only the properties journal and file.

The advantage of the property table scheme is that queries involving popular attributes in the cluster, can be answered without joins. For instance, asking for the article with the title "LAURIN" published in 2001, can be answered with a selection query on the property table. Of course, queries involving attributes that

Property Table

URI	type	title	year
1	article	LAURIN	2001
2	book	The Relational Model	1990
3	book	Principles of DB Systems	1995
4	article	Web-Based Data	NULL

Excess Table

URI	predicate	object
1	author	Catarci
1	author	Santucci
1	author	Calvanese
1	journal	WWW
1	file	CSC01.pdf
2	author	Codd
2	publisher	Addison-Wesley
3	author	Vianu
3	author	Hull
3	author	Abiteboul
3	publisher	Addison-Wesley
4	author	Atzeni
4	author	Merialdo
4	author	Mecca
4	journal	IEEE Int. Comp.
4	file	AMM02.pdf

Fig. 4.8 A property table scheme

have not been modeled in the property table and are located in the excess table will unavoidably require joins.

The property table scheme makes no use of schema information, thus it can be used for schema-less data. However, the existence of RDF schema can offer new opportunities for optimizing the encoding. In particular, since classes are used to cluster together resources with the same structure, one could use the classes as a guide for generating multiple property tables, for instance, one for each class. The properties encoded in each such table will be the properties of the respective class, and the table will be referred to as a *class property table*. For example, assuming that for the RDF data of Fig. 4.5 there are two main classes, one for articles and one for books. The data can then be represented into two class property tables as illustrated in Fig. 4.9. Note that even in this case, the multi-valued properties continue to be an issue and still require an excess table in order to be stored. On the other hand, all the other properties will be accommodated to one or more property tables. The case in which a property is modeled in more than one property tables, is the one in which the property is shared by more than one classes. For instance, the property title appears in both property tables of Fig. 4.9. This is a fundamental difference between the property tables based on the RDF Schema and the property tables based on property clustering. In the latter case, no property gets repeated in more than one table.

Article Property Table

URI	type	title	year	file	journal
1	article	LAURIN	2001	CSC01.pdf	WWW
4	article	Web-Based Data	NULL	AMM02.pdf	IEEE Int. Comp.

Book Property Table

URI	type	title	year	publisher
2	book	The Relational Model	1990	Addison-Wesley
3	book	Principles of DB Systems	1995	Addison-Wesley

Excess Table

URI	predicate	object
1	author	Catarci
1	author	Santucci
1	author	Calvanese
2	author	Codd
3	author	Vianu
3	author	Hull
3	author	Abiteboul
4	author	Atzeni
4	author	Merialdo
4	author	Mecca

Fig. 4.9 A property table scheme with class property tables

Although the property table scheme may be proved to be efficient for many applications, there are cases in which it may underperform. One of these cases is the one in which the data from different class property tables needs to be combined. For instance, assume that one is interested in finding the years in which publications have taken place. In the case of class property tables, this will translate to the union query that selects the years from the two class property tables. The scheme performs well if the data is highly structured data, i.e., conforms to some schema. This minimizes, and in the best case eliminates, the number of properties that are recorded in the excess table. However, we should not forget that one of the main reasons of the RDF popularity is its ability to model highly heterogeneous data, which means that a large majority of the data of interest is of such nature.

4.5.6 Vertical Partitioning

The property table clusters together properties that are common to a group of resources, but those properties that cannot be accommodated in any cluster will have all to be stored in the excess table. A different scheme that aims at tackling this limitation is the vertical partitioning. The idea of the vertical partitioning scheme [1] is similar to the idea of column-store in databases. It groups together properties of the same type and store each such group in a separate table. These tables can be linked type

URI	value
1	article
2	book
3	book
4	article

title

URI	value
1	LAURIN
2	The Relational Model
3	Principles of DB Systems
4	Web-Based Data

year

URI	value
1	2001
2	1990
3	1995

author

URI	value
1	Catarci
1	Santucci
1	Calvanese
2	Codd
3	Vianu
3	Hull
3	Abiteboul
4	Atzeni
4	Merialdo
4	Mecca

journal

URI	value
1	WWW
4	IEEE Int. Comp.

publisher

URI	value
2	Addison-Wesley
3	Addison-Wesley

file

URI	value
1	CSC01.pdf
4	AMM02.pdf

Fig. 4.10 A vertical partitioning scheme example

together based on the resource URIs. More specifically, all the subject-predicate-object triples that have the same predicate value form a group stored under a two-column relational table named after the name of the predicate. The first column is the URI of the resource, i.e., the subject, and the second is the value of the property, i.e., the object. In total, there will be k such tables, where k is the number of different properties that the RDF data contains. A vertical partitioning example for the RDF data of Fig. 4.5 is illustrated in Fig. 4.10.

URI attributes cannot be keys for the tables in the vertical partitioning scheme, unless the represented property is not a multi-valued property. However, since joins are based on the URIs, the existence of indexes on all the URI attributes is required. Furthermore, indexes can also be constructed on the value attribute for facilitating selection based on property values. If the tuples in each table are sorted by the URI attribute, then joins between two tables can be performed in an efficient manner using merge-joins [35]. This also means efficient handling of multi-valued properties since all the entries of a multi-valued property will be stored consecutively in the respective property tables.

The defragmentation of the set of triples into sets that are stored into separate tables can significantly improve query answering for queries that require searching to only few properties, since the data access is needed to only the tables of interest.

Despite its advantages, the vertical partitioning scheme is not free of limitations. The most critical one is that queries with conditions on several properties will require joins of multiple tables, which although can be speed-up with the right indexing and join technique, it is not as efficient as sequential access to tables that contain all the attributes of interest. Another limitation is that the names of the properties are not recorded as data, but as metadata in the names of the individual tables. This means that the data can be access only if the names of the respective properties are known. Thus, queries requiring the discovery of all the properties that a specific resource may have, cannot be directly answered. A solution is to use the metadata information offered by relational DBMSs, in particular the catalog tables, in order to obtain a list of the available tables. Even with such a knowledge though, to find all the properties that a particular resource may have, will require a separate query to be sent to every table in the database in order to discover whether it contains a tuple for the specific resource of interest.

4.5.7 Smart Indexing

In recent years, a new query model has emerged on the web. Users may not have complete knowledge of the data they are querying since it is highly heterogeneous and its structure difficult to communicated. In such an environment, queries are mainly of exploratory nature and, in some cases, underspecified. For this kind of queries, schema-based approaches like the vertical partitioning or the property tables may not be the preferable solution.

For efficiently answering queries that look for properties of a given resource, the triple nature of RDF can be exploited to build specialized indexes [45]. Since RDF data is described by a list of triples of the form ⟨*subject*, *predicate*, *object*⟩, there are 6 different ways one can retrieve that data, each corresponding to one of the 3! different ways that the components *subject*, *predicate* and *object*, can be combined. For example, one combination is to first provide a *subject*, retrieve all the *predicates* of that *subject*, and for each such *predicate* retrieve the *objects* of the triples that have the specific *subject* and *predicate*. Given the six different ways the three components can be combined, there are six different indexes that can be constructed, one for each combination. Each such index, consists of a list of lists of resources. A graphical illustration of such a structure is depicted in Fig. 4.11. Assume that this figure is the index for the combination *subject-predicate-object*. Since the *subject* is first, the first horizontal list has as many elements as the different *subject* values that can be found in the RDF data triples. Each element corresponds to one such value *s* and points to another list. Since *predicate* is the second component in the *subject-predicate-*

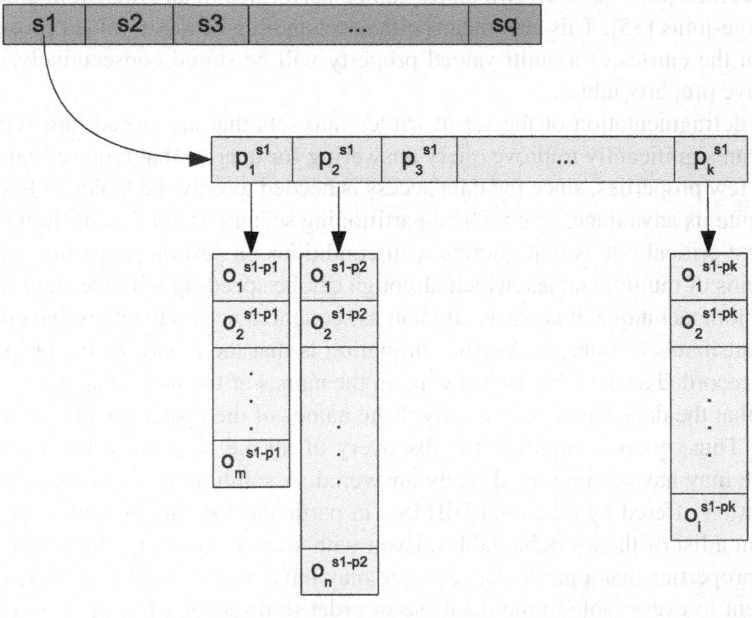

Fig. 4.11 One of the six triple-based indexing structures

object combination, the pointed list consists of as many elements as the number of different *predicate* values that are found in the RDF data triples with *s* as a *subject*. Each of these elements corresponds to one *predicate* value *p* and points also to a list. That list contains all the *object* values that can be found in the RDF data triples that have *s* as a *subject* and *p* as a *predicate*. This kind of lists are those depicted vertically in Fig. 4.11.

An index structure like the one described above is constructed for each of the six different combinations of *subject*, *predicate* and *object*, in order to cover all the possible orders they may be queried. Each index has all the information that can be found in the list of triples, thus no additional storage is required. Since each index hold all the triple information, one would expect the total required space to be six times the size of the set of triples. This is not actually true. The reason is that the lists of the third component in a combination are the same independently of the order of the first two components, thus, there is no need for storing them twice. For instance, the lists for the *object* values in the combination *predicate-subject-object* is the same as the list of *object* values in the combination *subject-predicate-object*.

The materialization of a specific combination of the index structure in a relational system requires a number of two-column and a number of single-column tables. In particular, a two-column table is needed to model the list for the first component of the combination, i.e., the top horizontal list in Fig. 4.11. The first column of the table contains the values of the component that the list represents, and the second column contains the reference to the table that models the respective list of the second component. The latter has also a two-column structure. The first column contains the values of the second component in the combination. In each tuple of that table, the second attribute is a reference pointer to a table materializing the list with the respective values of the third component, i.e., the materialization of the vertical lists depicted in Fig. 4.11.

Among the advantages of this scheme is its natural support for multi-valued properties, the lack of any need for nulls, and the reduced number of I/O operations to access the data of interest. The main limitation, however, is the space. Every value in the triples is indexed twice. For instance, an *object* value of a triple is indexed by the *subject-predicate-object* and by the *predicate-subject-object* combination structure.

The RDF-3X [31] system is following a similar approach for the management of RDF data. RDF-3X is not based on relational technology. It has been built from scratch, and is tailored specifically to RDF data. It stores RDF data as a list of triples, as in the case of a vertical table (ref. Sect. 4.5.2), and builds on top of it a series of specialized indexes for the various query operators. The list of triples, however, can easily be stored in a relational database if needed. Like hexastore, it builds indexes for all the six different permutations of the three dimensions that constitute an RDF triple, but it goes beyond this by constructed additional indexes oven aggregation operators on them. The constructed indexes can be compressed in an efficient way and can lead into a space requirement that is less than the one of the actual triple data. Query answering in RDF-3X is also based on merge-join operators performed over sorted index lists.

4.6 Conclusion

The goal of this chapter was to explore the links between metadata management, RDF and relational technologies. The first part introduced relational systems and presented the main directions that have been followed in storing and querying metadata in such systems. The second part introduced RDF which is the emerging standard for metadata representation on the web. It presented the rational of its introduction, the reasons for its success and its main modeling principles. It was recognized that building native RDF solutions from scratch requires a lot of effort and under the current rate that the web evolves, any delay is a luxury the community cannot afford. Efficient and effective solutions are needed right now. The exploitation of the relational technology appears as a promising option. Relational systems have been around for decades. They are mature enough, easily accessing and offer great performance and scalability. However, the different principles between the RDF and the relational model makes the use of relational systems for RDF storage and retrieval a complicated task. We presented alternative schemes that have been proposed in the scientific literature, and we have described the advantages and disadvantages of each one. From the descriptions, it is becoming clear that there is no such thing as golden rule or best solution. Each technique is best suited for certain cases. The decision on which technique one could use, highly depends on the characteristics of the RDF data to be stored and the kind of queries that are to be asked.

References

1. Abadi, D.J., Marcus, A., Madden, S., Hollenbach, K.J.: Scalable Semantic Web data management using vertical partitioning. In: Proceedings of the International Conference on Very Large Data Bases (VLDB), pp. 411–422 (2007)
2. Abiteboul, S., Hull, R., Vianu, V.: Foundations of Databases. Addison-Wesley, Reading (1995)
3. Alexaki, S., Christophides, V., Karvounarakis, G., Plexousakis, D.: On storing voluminous RDF descriptions: the case of web portal catalogs. In: Proceedings of the International Workshop on the Web and Databases (WebDB), pp. 43–48 (2001)
4. Alexe, B., Tan, W.C., Velegrakis, Y.: STBenchmark: towards a benchmark for mapping systems. In: Proceedings of VLDB Journal, vol. 1(1), pp. 230–244 (2008)
5. Beckett, D.: The design and implementation of the Redland RDF application framework. Comput. Networks **39**(5), 577–588 (2002)
6. Bernstein, P.A.: Repositories and object oriented databases. ACM SIGMOD Rec. **27**(1), 88–96 (1998)
7. Bertino, E., Castano, S., Ferrari, E.: On specifying security policies for web documents with an XML-based language. In: Proceedings of the Symposium on Access Control Models and Technologies (SACMAT), pp. 57–65 (2001)
8. Bhagwat, D., Chiticariu, L., Tan, W.C., Vijayvargiya, G.: An annotation management system for relational databases. In: Proceedings of the International Conference on Very Large Data Bases (VLDB), pp. 900–911 (2004)
9. Bohannon, P., Freire, J., Roy, P., Siméon, J.: From XML schema to relations: a cost-based approach to XML storage. In: Proceedings of the International Conference on Data Engineering (ICDE), p. 64 (2002)

10. Broekstra, J., Kampman, A., van Harmelen, F.: Sesame: an architecture for storin gand querying RDF data and schema information. In: Proceedings of the Spinning the Semantic Web Conference, pp. 197–222 (2003)
11. Buneman, P., Khanna, S., Tan, W.: On propagation and deletion of annotations through views. In: Proceedings of the Symposium on Principles of Database Systems (PODS) (2002)
12. Carroll, J.J., Dickinson, I., Dollin, C., Reynolds, D., Seaborne, A., Wilkinson, K.: Jena: implementing the Semantic Web recommendations. In: Proceedings of the International World Wide Web Conference (WWW), pp. 74–83 (2004)
13. Chawathe, S., Abiteboul, S., Widom, J.: Representing and querying changes in semistructured data. In: Proceedings of the International Conference on Data Engineering (ICDE), pp. 4–19 (1998)
14. Chong, E.I., Das, S., Eadon, G., Srinivasan, J.: An efficient SQL-based RDF querying scheme. In: Proceedings of the International Conference on Very Large Data Bases (VLDB), pp. 1216–1227 (2005)
15. Codd, E.F.: A relational model of data for large shared data banks. Commun. ACM **13**(6), 377–387 (1970)
16. Dasu, T., Johnson, T.: Exploratory Data Mining and Data Cleaning. Wiley, New York (2003)
17. DeHaan, D., Toman, D., Consens, M.P., Özsu, M.T.: A comprehensive XQuery to SQL translation using dynamic interval encoding. In: Proceedings of the ACM International Conference on Management of Data (SIGMOD), pp. 623–634 (2003)
18. Deutsch, A., Fernández, M.F., Suciu, D.: Storing semistructured data with STORED. In: Proceedings of the ACM International Conference on Management of Data (SIGMOD), pp. 431–442 (1999)
19. Eisenberg, A., Melton, J., Kulkarni, K.G., Michels, J.E., Zemke, F.: SQL: 2003 has been published. ACM SIGMOD Rec. **33**(1), 119–126 (2004)
20. Florescu, D., Kossmann, D.: A performance evaluation of alternative mapping schemes for storing XML in a relational database. Tech. Rep., INRIA (1999)
21. Geerts, F., Kementsietsidis, A., Milano, D.: MONDRIAN: annotating and querying databases through colors and blocks. In: Proceedings of the International Conference on Data Engineering (ICDE) (2006)
22. Harris, S., Shadbolt, N.: SPARQL query processing with conventional relational database systems. In: Proceedings of the International Conference on Web Information Systems Engineering (WISE), pp. 235–244 (2005)
23. Jarke, M., Gallersdorfer, R., Jeusfeld, M.A., Staudt, M.: ConceptBase—a deductive object base for meta data management. J. Intell. Inf. Syst. **4**(2), 167–192 (1995)
24. Krishnamurthy, R., Kaushik, R., Naughton, J.F.: XML-SQL query translation literature: the state of the art and open problems. In: Proceedings of the XML Database Symposium (XSym), pp. 1–18 (2003)
25. Li, Q., Moon, B.: Indexing and querying XML data for regular path expressions. In: Proceedings of the International Conference on Very Large Data Bases (VLDB), pp. 361–370 (2001)
26. Maier, D., Delcambre, L.M.L.: Superimposed information for the Internet. In: International Workshop on the Web and Databases (WebDB), pp. 1–9 (1999)
27. Matono, A., Amagasa, T., Yoshikawa, M., Uemura, S.: A Path-based relational RDF database. In: Proceedings of the Australasian Database Conference (ADC), pp. 95–103 (2005)
28. Mihaila, G., Raschid, L., Vidal, M.E.: Querying "quality of data" metadata. In: Proceedings of the IEEE META-DATA Conference (1999)
29. Microsoft support for XML. http://msdn.microsoft.com/sqlxml
30. Mylopoulos, J., Borgida, A., Jarke, M., Koubarakis, M.: Telos: representing knowledge about information systems. ACM Trans. Database Syst. (TODS) **8**(4), 325–362 (1990)
31. Neumann, T., Weikum, G.: RDF-3X: a RISC-style engine for RDF. In: Proceedings of VLDB Journal, vol. 1(1), pp. 647–659 (2008)
32. Neven, F., Bussche, J.V., Gucht, D.V., Vossen, G.: Typed query languages for databases containing queries. In: Proceedings of the Symposium on Principles of Database Systems (PODS), pp. 189–196 (1998)

33. Pan, Z., Heflin, J.: DLDB: extending relational databases to support Semantic Web queries. In: Proceedings of the International Workshop on Practical and Scalable Semantic Systems (PSSS) (2003)
34. Presa, A., Velegrakis, Y., Rizzolo, F., Bykau, S.: Modelling associations through intensional attributes. In: Proceedings of the International Conference on Conceptual Modeling (ER) (2009)
35. Ramakrishnan, R., Gehrke, J.: Database Management Systems. McGraw-Hill, New York (2007)
36. Rose, R., Frew, J.: Lineage retrieval for scientific data processing: a survey. ACM Comput. Surv. **37**(1), 1–28 (2005)
37. Shadbolt, N., Berners-Lee, T., Hall, W.: The Semantic Web revisited. IEEE Intell. Syst. **21**(3), 96–101 (2006)
38. Srivastava, D., Velegrakis, Y.: Intensional associations between data and metadata. In: Proceedings of the ACM International Conference on Management of Data (SIGMOD), pp. 401–412 (2007)
39. Stonebraker, M., Anton, J., Hanson, E.N.: Extending a database system with procedures. ACM Trans. Database Syst. (TODS) **12**(3), 350–376 (1987)
40. Tatarinov, I., Viglas, S., Beyer, K.S., Shanmugasundaram, J., Shekita, E.J., Zhang, C.: Storing and querying ordered XML using a relational database system. In: Proceedings of the ACM International Conference on Management of Data (SIGMOD), pp. 204–215 (2002)
41. Velegrakis, Y., Miller, R.J., Mylopoulos, J.: Representing and querying data transformations. In: Proceedings of the International Conference on Data Engineering (ICDE), pp. 81–92 (2005)
42. W3C: RDF vocabulary description language 1.0: RDF Schema (2004). http://www.w3.org/TR/rdf-schema/
43. W3C: Resource Description Framework (RDF) (2004). http://www.w3.org/TR/rdf-concepts/
44. Wang, R., Reddy, M.P., Kon, H.B.: Toward quality data: an attribute-based approach **13**(3–4), 349–372 (1995)
45. Weiss, C., Karras, P., Bernstein, A.: Hexastore: sextuple indexing for Semantic Web data management. In: Proceedings of VLDB Journal, vol. 1(1), pp. 1008–1019 (2008)
46. Widom, J.: Trio: A system for integrated management of data, accuracy, and lineage. In: Proceedings of the Biennial Conference on Innovative Data Systems Research (CIDR), pp. 262–276 (2005)
47. Wyss, C.M., Robertson, E.L.: Relational languages for metadata integration. ACM Trans. Database Syst. (TODS) **30**(2), 624–660 (2005)
48. IBM Db2 XML Extender. http://www4.ibm.com/software/data/db2/extenders/xmlext.html
49. Yoshikawa, M., Amagasa, T., Shimura, T., Uemura, S.: XRel: a path-based approach to storage and retrieval of XML documents using relational databases. ACM Trans. Int. Technol. **1**(1), 110–141 (2001)

Chapter 5
A Metamodel Approach to Semantic Web Data Management

Roberto De Virgilio, Pierluigi Del Nostro, Giorgio Gianforme, and Stefano Paolozzi

Abstract The Semantic Web is gaining increasing interest to fulfill the need of sharing, retrieving and reusing information. In this context, the Resource Description Framework (RDF) has been conceived to provide an easy way to represent any kind of data and metadata, according to a lightweight model and syntaxes for serialization (RDF/XML, N3, etc.). Despite RDF has the advantage of being general and simple, it cannot be used as a storage model as it is, since it can be easily shown that even simple management operations involve serious performance limitations. In this paper, we present a novel approach for storing, managing and processing RDF data in an effective and efficient way. The approach is based on the notion of construct, that represents a concept of the domain of interest. This makes the approach easily extensible and independent from the specific knowledge representation language. We refer to real world scenarios in which we consider complex data management operations, which go beyond simple selections or projections and involve the navigation of huge portions of RDF data sources.

5.1 Introduction

From the origin of the World Wide Web, the publication of information has been an uninterrupted activity, so that a huge amount of data is currently available over the Internet. This information is often (always) incomplete and requires a human

R. De Virgilio (✉)
Dipto. Informatica e Automazione, Università Roma Tre, Via della Vasca Navale 79, 00146 Rome, Italy
e-mail: dvr@dia.uniroma3.it

P. Del Nostro · G. Gianforme · S. Paolozzi
Università Roma Tre, Via della Vasca Navale 79, 00146 Rome, Italy

P. Del Nostro
e-mail: pdn@dia.uniroma3.it

G. Gianforme
e-mail: giorgio.gianforme@gmail.com

S. Paolozzi
e-mail: stefano.paolozzi@gmail.com

R. De Virgilio et al. (eds.), *Semantic Web Information Management*,
DOI 10.1007/978-3-642-04329-1_5,

intervention to be interpreted and completed with the right semantics, that is implicit in the context. This implies that actual technologies and consequently software agents, in general, are not able to understand the meaning of data or perform advanced searches and retrievals. Moreover, even human interaction can not assure the absence of misunderstanding. These drawbacks forced the scientific community to reconsider the initial approach that does not meet the growing needs for sharing, retrieving, and reusing information.

In 2001, Tim Berners Lee [8] proposed the concept of Semantic Web, a world where information is processable by machines other than humans, opening new interesting perspectives. In order to let a rough data be unambiguously interpreted by a computer, it is necessary to describe it by means of metadata that associate a well defined meaning. For this purpose, the W3C developed the Resource Description Framework (RDF) [22] that is commonly used as data model for the Semantic Web. It is a family of specifications used to express statements on Web resources, uniquely identified by an Uniform Resource Identifier (URI). A statement is a triple $\langle$*Subject*, *Predicate*, *Object*$\rangle$ expressing that a resource (Subject) is related to another resource or a value (Object) through a property (Predicate).

This structure can be profitably represented as a directed labeled graph where nodes are resources or literals and edges represent predicates, also called properties in RDF terminology. Nodes without content (blank nodes) are used in order to express incomplete information, queries or resources with a complex structure (specified via other triples). Many serializations of the abstract RDF model exist. They are designed to allow the exchange of metadata across applications. The most popular are RDF/XML and Notation 3.

According to the database nomenclature, an RDF document can be seen as an instance of a database without a fixed schema, in the sense that when creating or editing an RDF document, there are no constraints on the structure of the statements (e.g., resource types, domain and range of predicates). In order to define a schema (again according to database nomenclature) for RDF documents, the W3C defined RDFS (RDF Schema). In other words, an RDFS is useful to specify common structural constraints for data contained in an RDF document (e.g., classes or types of resources, subclasses, domain and range of predicates and subpredicates). In general, an RDF document is not forced to be conform to some RDFS, but, without loss of generality, we can assume this is always the case.

Due to its simplicity, RDF is easily manageable by applications and increasingly used over the Web. Let us consider the online Semantic Web search engine Swoogle[1] reporting more than 2,868,760 indexed Semantic Web documents. Then the rise of Semantic Web technologies imply a growing number of meta-information to be stored, managed and queried. As we will detail in Sect. 5.4, many proposals exist for the storage of RDF data. Most of the repositories are based on a triple storage model in which a single table for storing RDF triples is used. The table is made of three columns corresponding to the subject, predicate and object of the

[1] http://swoogle.umbc.edu/.

RDF statement. A variant of this approach is the quad storage model where a column represents the name of the RDF graph where triples comes from. On top of this two common storage models, tuning operations are performed by means of indexes or partitions in order to enhance query response time.

Differently from the approaches in literature, that provide implementation solutions, we follow a process that starts with the definition of a representation of the RDF data model at a conceptual level. In this phase, we find out the structural aspects of interest of RDF. At logical level, we define a mapping between our metamodel and the relational model that allows us to store semantic data in tables and take advantage from the relational DBMS technology. Moreover, at physical level, we adopt special optimization techniques for the storage model that increase greatly the performance of query processing.

Here, we concentrate on RDF and RDFS but we remark extensibility of our representation technique: the model can be enriched to refine our RDF representation as well as to represent structural aspects of more complex models like OWL.

Our goals and contributions are the following:

- the definition of a high level, easy-to-extend metamodel for the representation of Semantic Web data, expressed in various formats;
- a logical organization of data, obtained as a relational implementation of our metamodel;
- the adoption of optimizations based on indexing and partitioning of relational implementation to allow high performance querying.

We compare performance and scalability of our approach with SDB Jena,[2] Sesame [9] and Openlink Virtuoso [12] systems. The aspects that we have measured are the scalability of the approaches on importing RDF data and query performance over a representative query space for RDF.

5.2 Motivating Example

The most trivial strategy to store an RDF document is to use a relational schema with only one three columns table. This is depicted in Fig. 5.1. In the left side, there is graphical representation of RDF classes (of resources) and predicates between them; in the right side there is a relational table suitable for storing RDF data, filled with some sample data. We distinguish between relations between two resources (called predicates in the following) and relations between a resource and a literal (called properties in the following). In detail, each *Person* may have a property, *Name*, and two predicates, *Child* and *Brother*, representing family relationships between persons. There are four instances of the class *Person* (with *URI1*, *URI2*, *URI3* and *URI4* as URIs,[3] respectively), each one with a corresponding instance of the

[2] http://jena.hpl.hp.com/wiki/SDB.

[3] RDF exploits Universal Resource Identifiers (URIs), which appear as URLs that often use sequences of numbers as identifiers. In this paper, our examples will use more intuitive names.

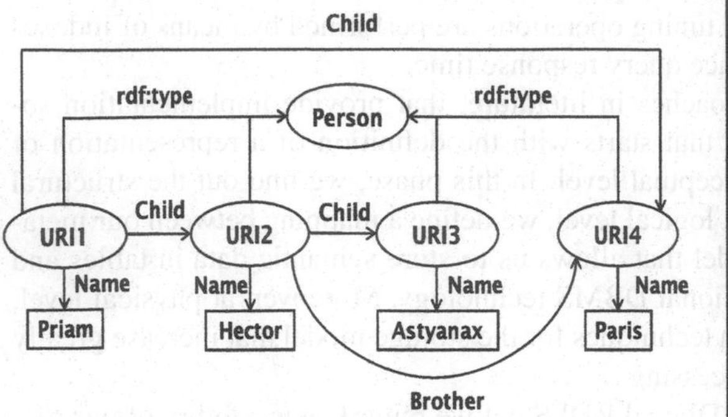

people

Subject	Property/ Predicate	Object
URI1	rdf:type	Person
URI2	rdf:type	Person
URI3	rdf:type	Person
URI4	rdf:type	Person
URI1	Name	Priam
URI2	Name	Hector
URI3	Name	Astyanax
URI4	Name	Paris
URI1	Child	URI2
URI1	Child	URI4
URI2	Child	URI3
URI2	Brother	URI4

Fig. 5.1 RDF classes and triple instances

property *Name* (with values *Priam*, *Hector*, *Astyanax* and *Paris*, respectively) and related by three instances of the predicate *Child* and one instance of the predicate *Brother* representing that *Hector* and *Paris* are brothers because sons of *Priam*, and *Astyanax* is son of *Hector*.

As an example, we can formulate the SQL query to find all of the persons that have a child whose name is '*Paris*' as follows:

```
SELECT p4.obj
FROM people AS p1, people AS p2, people AS p3, people AS p4
WHERE p1.prop="Child" AND p1.obj=p2.subj AND p2.prop="rdf:type"
      AND p2.obj="Person" AND p1.obj=p3.subj AND p3.prop="Name"
      AND p3.obj="Paris" AND p4.subj=p1.subj AND p4.prop="Name"
```

This query performs many self-joins over the same table. Since the table `people` could contain a relevant amount of rows (i.e., statements), the entire process can be computationally unfeasible. Indeed, the execution time increases as the number of triples scales, because each filtering or join condition will require a scan or index lookup.

5.3 Management of RDF Data

Figure 5.2 shows the basic architecture of our system called SWIM (Semantic Web Information Management), which includes three main components: (i) the *Importer*, (ii) the *Storage System* and (iii) the *Query Front-end*. The flow of data and metadata in this framework and their management can be summarized as follows.

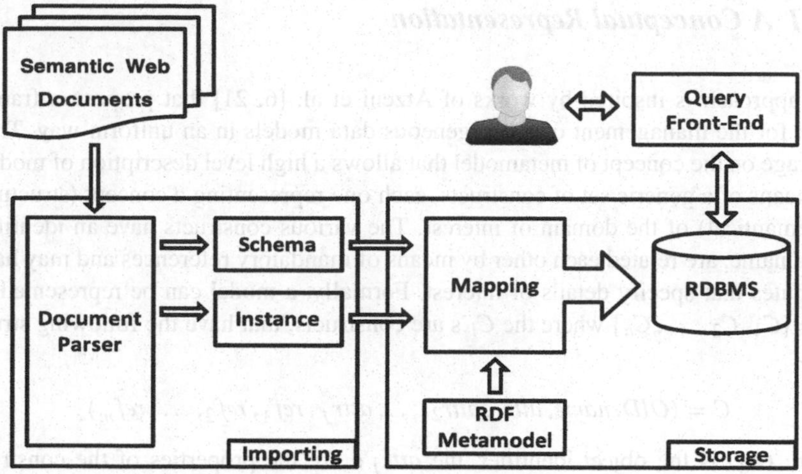

Fig. 5.2 The basic architecture of the system

- **The Importer:** A collection of Semantic Web documents is captured by the `Importer`. We assume that these documents are expressed in RDF according to a domain ontology but we will show that, in principle, the approach does not depend on the specific format of data source. The module parses each document extracting the schema describing intensional knowledge, and the instance, describing extensional properties and relations among data.
- **The Storage System:** The back-end database is populated with the incoming statements. All the elements are stored in a relational database, that implements a metamodel for semantic languages. This metamodel is made of a set of primitives, each of which represents an element of the RDF model. Thus, each primitive is used to gather elements of the knowledge source modeled in the same way. A relational DBMS is used to actually store all the imported elements. The main advantage of this storage model is that different and possibly heterogeneous formats of semantic data can be managed. The `Mapping` module is in charge of associating each element of the source model with the corresponding primitive of the metamodel and storing the elements accordingly. The storage model is supported by special optimization methods that increase the performance of the system in accessing data and answering queries.
- **Query Front-end:** The user poses queries to the system through a front-end user interface. The idea here is that different users with different expertise can specify queries in different languages: final user can take advantage from a high level user interface in which queries are expressed in a Query-By-Example fashion. Then the queries are executed by the storage system to retrieve all the elements included in the answer.

The rest of the paper is devoted to a more detailed description of our proposal for the efficient and scalable processing of RDF data.

5.3.1 A Conceptual Representation

Our approach is inspired by works of Atzeni et al. [6, 21] that propose a framework for the management of heterogeneous data models in an uniform way. They leverage on the concept of metamodel that allows a high level description of models by means of a generic set of constructs, each one representing a concept (structural or semantical) of the domain of interest. The various constructs have an identifier and a name, are related each other by means of mandatory references and may have attributes that specify details of interest. Formally, a model can be represented as $M = \{C_1, C_2, \ldots, C_n\}$ where the C_i's are constructs, that have the following structure:

$$C = (OID, name, attr_1, attr_2, \ldots, attr_f, ref_1, ref_2, \ldots, ref_m)$$

where *OID* is the object identifier, the $attr_j$'s are the properties of the construct and the ref_k's are the references of the construct. For example, the simplest version of the entity-relationship model with entities, attributes of entities and binary relationships could involve three constructs, one for each of these concepts: ENTITY, ATTRIBUTE and RELATIONSHIP. In detail, ENTITY would have no attributes and no references; ATTRIBUTE would have a reference toward the ENTITY it belongs to and an attribute to specify whether it is an identifier of such ENTITY; RELATIONSHIP would have two references toward involved entities and a set of properties to represent its cardinalities.

Following this idea, we propose a simple model where a set of constructs properly represent concepts expressible with RDF. The goals of such construct-based representations of data models are clearly different. Atzeni et al. exploit this uniform representation in order to perform transformations of schemas from a model to another; they consider a set of constructs able to represent several data models, factoring out the common concepts in different data models. We want to manage (i.e., importing, storing, querying, and updating) the RDF model only and define a reduced set of constructs for the sake of making explicit and typing the different implicit facets of the main RDF concepts, namely resource and predicate. The rationale behind our approach is that the distribution of the information, when well defined and organized, can lead to a better management of the information themselves.

Another difference is that they consider a well marked distinction between schema and instance level. Constructs and transformation rules for the instance level are automatically derived from corresponding structures at schema level. For our purposes, we need to manage schemas and instances at the same time, since typical operations on RDF documents (such as queries or updates) generally involve both the levels. Hence our model is designed to properly represent RDFS (i.e., schema level) and RDF documents (i.e., instance level) in a uniform way.

In order to represent the basic concept of an RDF statement at schema level, with no further abstraction, two constructs should be enough, one to represent classes (of resources) and one to represent predicates involving two classes. The concept of class is atomic and clearly defined and cannot be subsequently specified, while the concept of statement allows for a more precise modeling. In fact, as we informally anticipated in Sect. 5.2 we can distinguish between two kinds of statement on the basis of their objects, that can be a literal with a primitive type value or a resource with its own URI. We named these constructs PROPERTY and PREDICATE, respectively.

Hence, for the schema level (i.e., RDFS), we have three basic constructs: CLASS, PROPERTY and PREDICATE. More in detail, the CLASS construct has only the mandatory fields, *OID* and *name*; the PROPERTY construct has a reference to the CLASS it belongs to and has a *type* attribute to specify the datatype for that property at instance level; the PREDICATE construct has two references toward CLASSes to represent the subject and the object of a statement. Moreover, the PREDICATE construct has three properties to specify notably features (`isTransitive`, `isSymmetric`, `isFunctional`).

At instance level (i.e., RDF), there is one construct for each of these schema constructs, called RESOURCE, I-PROPERTY, and I-PREDICATE, respectively. Each instance construct has a reference to the construct of schema level it corresponds to and inherits from it the same references, toward instance level constructs corresponding to schema level constructs pointed by those references. They do not inherit the properties of schema level constructs, but can have other properties. In fact, I-PROPERTY has a *value* property to store the actual value of the property and RESOURCE has a *URI* property to store the URI of a resource. The *OID* identifier supports the management of blank nodes, whereas the attribute *URI* has a unique anonymous ID. In order to simplify the notation and reduce redundancy, we omit the field *name* for instance level constructs.

Formally, we define:

$$M_{\text{RDFbasic}} = \{\text{CLASS}, \text{PROPERTY}, \text{PREDICATE}, \text{RESOURCE}, \text{I-PROPERTY}, \text{I-PREDICATE}\}$$

where the constructs have the following structure:

$$\text{CLASS} = (\mathit{OID}, \mathit{name})$$

$$\text{PROPERTY} = (\mathit{OID}, \mathit{name}, \mathit{type}, \mathit{ClassOID})$$

$$\text{PREDICATE} = (\mathit{OID}, \mathit{name}, \mathit{SubjectClassOID}, \mathit{ObjectClassOID}, \mathit{isTransitive}, \mathit{isSymmetric}, \mathit{isFunctional})$$

$$\text{RESOURCE} = (\mathit{OID}, \mathit{URI}, \mathit{ClassOID})$$

$$\text{I-PROPERTY} = (\mathit{OID}, \mathit{value}, \mathit{ResourceOID}, \mathit{PropertyOID})$$

$$\text{I-PREDICATE} = (\mathit{OID}, \mathit{i\text{-}SubjectOID}, \mathit{i\text{-}ObjectOID}, \mathit{PredicateOID})$$

In order to obtain a suitable RDFS representation, we have to properly represent two more structural concepts: subclasses and subpredicates. This is done in a straightforward way, simply adding two new constructs, namely SUBCLASS and

SUBPREDICATE. They have the same structure with two references but, obviously, those of the first construct are toward classes and those of the second one toward predicates. Their complete signature are, respectively:

$$\text{SUBCLASS} = (\mathit{OID}, \mathit{name}, \mathit{classOID}, \mathit{subClassOID})$$

$$\text{SUBPREDICATE} = (\mathit{OID}, \mathit{name}, \mathit{predicateOID}, \mathit{subPredicateOID})$$

These constructs do not have corresponding instance level constructs, since they just represent structural relationships between classes or predicates that are implicitly inherited (i.e., can be inferred) by resources of those classes and instances of those predicates, respectively. Hence, the complete model for RDF M_{RDF} can be defined as M_{RDFbasic} plus these two extra constructs.

Another advantage of this construct-based approach is extendibility. This simple model can be extended in order to manage other RDF concepts, simply adding constructs. For example, in order to represent containers we could add three new constructs. They are *Container*, *SimpleElement* and *ResourceElement*. We use the first one to specify that a blank node (represented with a class as well) represents a container (in practice, this is done by means of the reference *ResourceOID* of the construct toward a resource). The construct *Container* has also a property *type* to denote the container type (i.e., `Seq`, `Alt`, or `Bag`). The other constructs represent elements of a container that can be, respectively, literals, or resources; a resource element has a reference toward a class (to specify to which class the element of the container belongs to) and both the kind of elements have a reference to the container to which they belong to. Again, these constructs have corresponding instance level constructs, called *i-Container*, *i-SimpleEl* and *ResourceElement*, respectively. The references of those instance level constructs can be trivially derived from the schema. Moreover, *i-SimpleEl* and *ResourceElement* have a property *name* for sorting purposes, and *i-SimpleEl* has a property *value* in order to store the actual value of the element. The new constructs have the following structures:

$$\text{CONTAINER} = (\mathit{OID}, \mathit{type}, \mathit{classOID})$$

$$\text{SIMPLEELEMENT} = (\mathit{OID}, \mathit{type}, \mathit{containerOID})$$

$$\text{CLASSELEMENT} = (\mathit{OID}, \mathit{containerOID}, \mathit{classOID})$$

$$\text{I-CONTAINER} = (\mathit{OID}, \mathit{i\text{-}classOID}, \mathit{containerOID})$$

$$\text{I-SIMPLEEL} = (\mathit{OID}, \mathit{name}, \mathit{value}, \mathit{i\text{-}containerOID}, \mathit{simpleElementOID})$$

$$\text{RESOURCEELEMENT} = (\mathit{OID}, \mathit{name}, \mathit{i\text{-}containerOID}, \mathit{ClassElementOID}, \mathit{resourceOID})$$

Hence, an extended model for RDF $M_{\text{RDFextended}}$ can be defined as M_{RDF} plus this six extra constructs. Since containers are not so used in practice (this is the case for all the large RDF repositories available online, including the one we decided to use for our experiments), in the following we consider the M_{RDF} model.

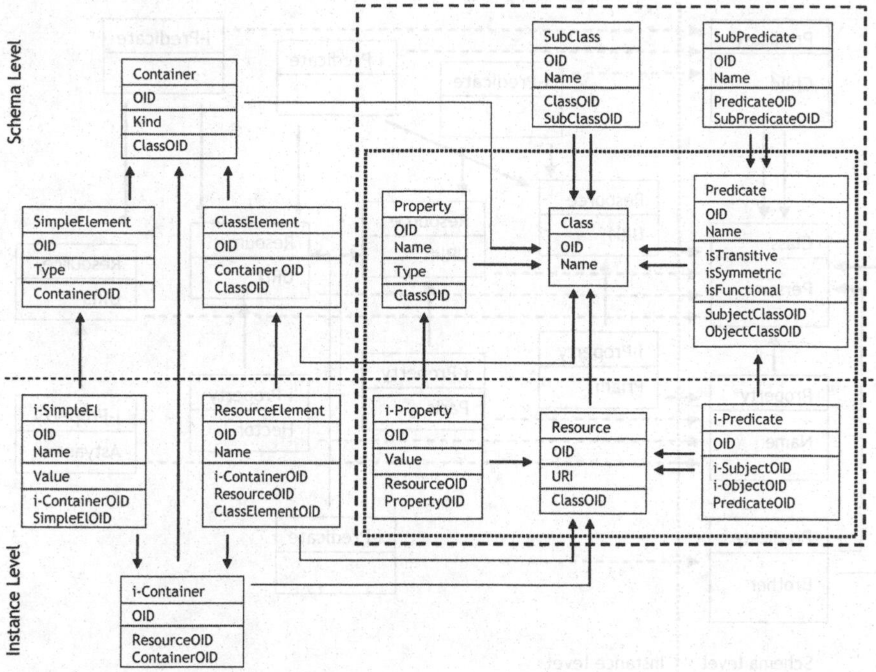

Fig. 5.3 The M_{RDF} model with extensions

In Fig. 5.3, an UML-like diagram of the various version of the RDF model we have presented so far. The whole figure represents $M_{\text{RDFextended}}$; enclosed in the dashed box there is M_{RDF}; enclosed in the dotted box there is M_{RDFbasic}.

For instance, through our approach, we can represent the RDF document, presented in Sect. 5.2, as depicted in Fig. 5.4. For the sake of simplicity, we indicate the name of the schema level constructs while at the instance level we show values and URIs. Moreover, we represent references only by arrows (dashed lines correspond to references from instance to schema level).

5.3.2 Logical Level

We use a relational implementation of such model. For each construct, we create a table, and for each field of a construct we add a column to the table corresponding to such construct.

The OID attribute is the primary key for each table, and we add an integrity constraint for each reference, from the pointer construct to the pointed one (i.e., from the column corresponding to the reference field toward the OID column of the referenced construct).

In Fig. 5.5, some tables of our logical organization are depicted. The value of the rows are those corresponding to our running example. Notice that, since we exploit

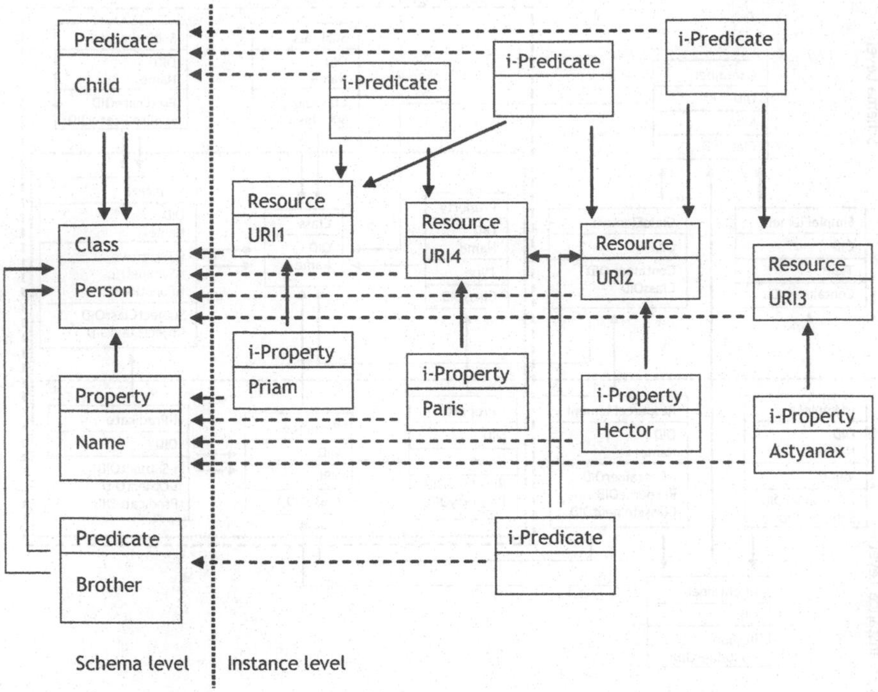

Fig. 5.4 Conceptual representation of the running example

Schema Level

SCHEMA	
OID	Schema Name
s1	Greece

Class	
OID	Name
c1	Person

Property			
OID	Name	Type	ClassOID
prop1	Name	String	c1

Predicate						
OID	Name	isTransitive	isSymmetric	isFunctional	SubjectClassOID	ObjectClassOID
pred1	Child	false	false	false	c1	c1
pred2	Brother	true	true	false	c1	c1

Instance Level

INSTANCE		
OID	Instance Name	Schema OID
i1	GreeceInstance	s1

i-Property			
OID	Value	ResourceOID	PropertyOID
i-prop1	Priam	r1	prop1
i-prop2	Hector	r2	prop1
i-prop3	Astyanax	r3	prop1
i-prop4	Paris	r4	Prop1

Resource		
OID	URI	ClassOID
r1	URI1	c1
r2	URI2	c1
r3	URI3	c1
r4	URI4	c1

i-Predicate			
OID	i-SubjectOID	i-ObjectOID	PredicateOID
i-pred1	r1	r4	pred1
i-pred2	r1	r2	pred1
i-pred3	r2	r3	pred1
i-pred4	r2	r4	pred2

Fig. 5.5 Logical implementation of our running example

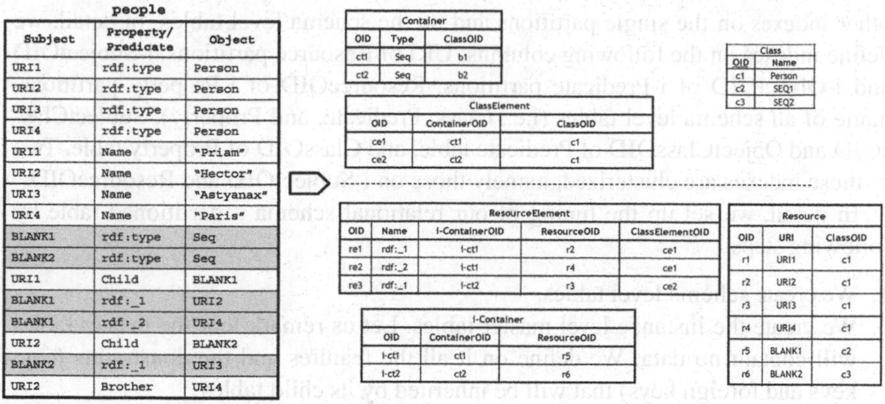
people
Subject Property/Predicate Object
URI1 rdf:type Person
URI2 rdf:type Person
URI3 rdf:type Person
URI4 rdf:type Person
URI1 Name "Priam"
URI2 Name "Hector"
URI3 Name "Astyanax"
URI4 Name "Paris"
BLANK1 rdf:type Seq
BLANK2 rdf:type Seq
URI1 Child BLANK1
BLANK1 rdf:_1 URI2
BLANK1 rdf:_2 URI4
URI2 Child BLANK2
BLANK2 rdf:_1 URI3
URI2 Brother URI4
Container
OID Type ClassOID
ct1 Seq b1
ct2 Seq b2
Class
OID Name
c1 Person
c2 SEQ1
c3 SEQ2
ClassElement
OID ContainerOID ClassOID
ce1 ct1 c1
ce2 ct2 c1
ResourceElement
OID Name i-ContainerOID ResourceOID ClassElementOID
re1 rdf:_1 i-ct1 r2 ce1
re2 rdf:_2 i-ct1 r4 ce1
re3 rdf:_1 i-ct2 r3 ce2
i-Container
OID ContainerOID ResourceOID
i-ct1 ct1 r5
i-ct2 ct2 r6
Resource
OID URI ClassOID
r1 URI1 c1
r2 URI2 c1
r3 URI3 c1
r4 URI4 c1
r5 BLANK1 c2
r6 BLANK2 c3

Fig. 5.6 Logical representation of containers

different levels of abstraction, the logical level could be implemented also by other storage model (e.g., an object oriented model).

To demonstrate the flexibility of our approach, let us show how the logical level is affected by the insertion of new constructs at the conceptual level. Let us consider a variant of the example of Sect. 5.2, where we represent the children of a person with an RDF container (namely a `Seq` container). This situation is depicted in Fig. 5.6.

In our representation, we can address RDF containers exploiting the constructs `Container`, `ClassElement` and `Class` at schema level, and, at instance level, `ResourceElement`, `i-Container`, and `Resource`. In particular, we represent a container with an instance of `Resource` construct (a blank node) and each element of the container with an instance of `ResourceElement` construct. The logical representation is presented in the right side of Fig. 5.6 (where we omit not relevant constructs).

5.3.3 *Physical Level*

The resulting tables of logical level could be very large. We exploit potentialities offered by relational DBMS, tuning our schema in order to obtain better performances. The first step is the horizontal partitioning of the logical and potentially huge instance level tables into smaller physical tables, called partitions. Each partition inherits the same structure (e.g., columns and datatypes) of the original table, called master. Partitioning is performed row by row and is based on the value of a column, called range. For instance, we use as range the column classOID for the table Resource, predicateOID for i-Predicate, and propertyOID for i-Property at instance level. If it were necessary, we can partition constructs at schema level too. This step is completely transparent to the user.

The second step is the definition of indexes on the whole set of tables. Clearly, we define an index for each range column used for the partitioning. Moreover, we define other indexes on the single partitions and on the schema level tables. In detail, we define indexes on the following columns: URI of Resource partitions, i-SubjectOID and i-ObjectOID of i-Predicate partitions, ResourceOID of i-Property partitions, name of all schema level tables (i.e., Class, Predicate, and Property), SubjectClassOID and ObjectClassOID of Predicate table, and ClassOID of Property table. Two of these indexes are clusterized, namely those on i-SubjectOID and ResourceOID.

In detail, we set up the tuning of our relational schema a partitioned table by following steps:

1. We create schema level tables.
2. We create the instance level master tables. Let us remark that the master tables will contain no data. We define on it all the features and the constraints (e.g., keys and foreign keys) that will be inherited by its child tables.
3. We choose the range from the master tables (a single column or a set). Then, on the base of this range, we create several partition tables that inherit the structure (i.e., attributes and constraints) from the corresponding master table. These tables will not add any columns to the set inherited from the parent.
4. We add table's *check* constraints to the partition tables to define the allowed key values in each partition.
5. We create an index on the key column(s) in each partition and the other aforementioned useful indexes.
6. Finally, we define a trigger (or rule) to redirect data inserted into a master table to the appropriate partition.
7. Optionally, we can iterate partitioning on the resulting partition tables.

Let us consider the example depicted in Fig. 5.7.

It shows the physical design of the running example, described in Sect. 5.2. For instance, the PREDICATE table is partitioned into two tables respect to the two values of `Name` (i.e., `Child` and `Brother`).

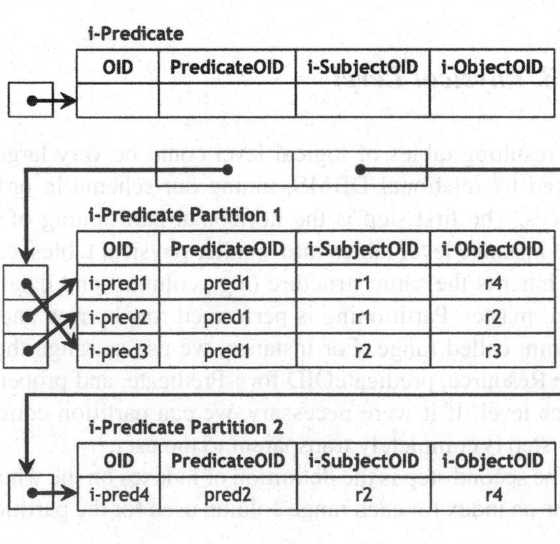

Fig. 5.7 Physical organization of the running example

5.3.4 *Query Processing*

The relational implementation of our conceptual model has a direct influence on the choice of the query language to be adopted: we use SQL.

Let us briefly comment on our queries. We can have an higher number of joins, with respect to other approaches, since we distribute the information across several tables. Moreover, our joins are lighter in terms of computational cost, because they involve smaller tables (i.e., with a lower number of rows) and, in some cases, they can operate directly on partitions of tables (thus reducing further on the number of involved rows).

5.4 Related Work

Managing RDF(S) data represents an important and wide area of research, as demonstrated by a number of methodologies and techniques and tools developed in the last years [11]. In this section, we briefly discuss some widely-used or representative RDF storage systems, summarizing the current researches concerning the management of RDF documents.

We distinguish between two main directions in RDF management studies, namely: (i) *storing*, that can be a complex activity, due to the fact that some storage systems requiring fixed schemas may be unable to handle general data such as that from RDF, where the schema is not known in advance; (ii) *querying*, that might be seen as more complex than "conventional" querying, because the meaning conveyed by RDF data has to be properly "understood" and processed.

RDF storing approaches can be divided into two main areas: the first one is based on a native storage system development while the second one focuses on the use of relational (or object-relational) databases to store RDF data [15] (see Fig. 5.8).

Comparing the two approaches, native storage systems (such as AllegroGraph[4] or OWLLIM [16]) are more efficient in terms of load and update time. On the con-

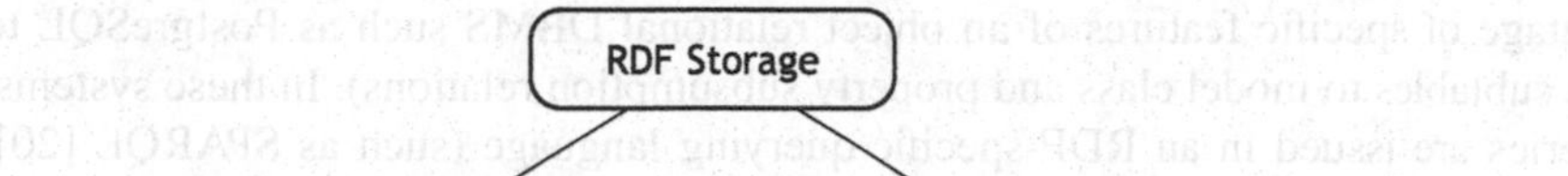

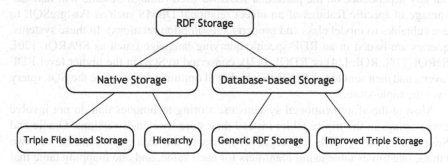

Fig. 5.8 Native storage systems vs. database-based storage systems

[4] AllegroGraph RDF-Store, available at http://www.franz.com/products/allegrograph/.

trary, database-based approaches are more efficient in querying due to the availability of many query management features. However, native approaches have the drawback of having to redefine important database features such as: query optimization, transaction processing, and so on.

The efficiency of querying RDF documents depends on the logical and physical organization of such data and on the adopted query language.

Some interesting studies have been focused on the physical organization of RDF Data. Indeed it seems that a relational model is a natural fit for RDF. RDF model is a set of statements about Web resources, identified by URIs. The statements have the form ⟨*subject*, *predicate*, *object*⟩, then an RDF model can be easily implemented as a relational table with three columns. Many RDF storage systems have used this kind of approach such as the ICSFORTH RDFSuite [3], the Sesame schema-based repository and querying system [9], the KAON[5] Project, the TAP[6] suite, Jena [24], Oracle [10] and many others.

The most common systems for triple approach are Jena and Sesame. Jena is a Java Semantic Web toolkit that provides a rich API for manipulating RDF and persistent storage of triples using either Sleepycat/Berkeley DB or via JDBC to talk to a variety of RDBMSs including MySQL, PostgreSQL, Oracle, Interbase and others. Jena has been used with millions of triples in memory (if rather slow) and is limited mostly only by system resources. Jena depends on a selection of standard Java APIs which are widely portable and the large range of storage options allow it to be deployed on many systems.

Sesame is a Java system which defines a Storage And Inference Layer (SAIL) to use over lower level storage layers such as RDBMSs so to abstract from individual storage system detail. The DBMS backing store supports RDFS class and property subsumption over PostgreSQL, MySQL and Oracle databases, with different functionality depending on database features. The DBMS backend also supports and optimizes RDF schemas and RDF Semantics inferencing.

Each of the aforementioned RDF storage solutions implements a multi-layered architecture, where RDF-specific functionality (for example, query translation) is performed in a layer above the RDBMS. In this way it is possible to operate without any dependence on the particular RDBMS used (though Sesame will take advantage of specific features of an object relational DBMS such as PostgreSQL to use subtables to model class and property subsumption relations). In these systems, queries are issued in an RDF-specific querying language (such as SPARQL [20], SeRQL [18], RQL [14] or RDQL [17]), converted to SQL in the higher level RDF layers, and then sent to the RDBMS which will optimize and execute the SQL query over the triple-store.

Most of the aforementioned systems use storing techniques that do not involve entire strings in the triples table; instead they store shortened versions. Oracle and Sesame map string URIs to integer identifiers so the data is normalized into two tables, one triples table using identifiers for each value, and one mapping table that

[5] KAON—the Karlsruhe Ontology and Semantic Web Tool Suite. http://kaon.semanticweb.org/.

[6] TAP project, 2002. http://tap.stanford.edu/.

maps the identifiers to their corresponding strings. 3store [13] uses a similar approach, with the only difference that the identifiers are created by applying a hash function to each string.

Both Jena and Oracle propose changes to the schema to reduce the number of self-joins introducing the concept of *property tables*. They proposed two types of property tables. The first type, contains clusters of properties that tend to be defined together. The second type of property table, exploits the type property of subjects to cluster similar sets of subjects together in the same table [23]. Moreover, these schemas do not perform well for queries that cannot be answered from a single property table, but need to combine data from several tables [1, 2]. Moreover, such systems impose a relational-like structure on semi-structured RDF data. However, imposing structure where it does not naturally exist results into sparse representation with many NULL values in the formed property tables. Indeed, considering the NULL values management in case of blank nodes or the awkward expression of multi-valued attributes in a flattened representation, we have a significant computational overhead [7].

In order to overcome some of the aforementioned hindrances, our approach can take into account also blank nodes.

Some authors [4, 5] propose to store RDF data as a graph. However, these solutions do not provide the scalability necessary for query processing over large amounts of RDF data. For scalability and performance issues, we believe that the aforementioned approaches must be augmented by other storage strategies that can be efficient and sufficiently general.

Recently, Abadi et al. [1] have proposed the *Vertical Partitioning* approach. They propose a triple table split into *n* two-column tables, one table per property, where *n* is the number of unique properties in the data. In these tables, the first column contains the subjects that define one of the properties and the second column contains the object values for those subjects. Multi-valued subjects, i.e., those subjects related to multiple objects by the same property, are represented by multiple rows in the table with the same subject and different object values. Each table is sorted by subject, in this way it is possible to quickly locate particular subjects. Moreover, it is possible to exploit fast merge-joins in order to reconstruct information about multiple properties for subsets of subjects. However, Sidirourgos et al. [19] deeply analyze the Vertical Partitioning, concluding that its hard-coded nature makes it difficult to use.

Another relevant tool for the management of RDF data is Virtuoso [12]. Despite it becomes a commercial product, an open-source version, called Openlink Virtuoso, is also available, we have been evaluating this version in this paper. The architecture of the system includes a native object relational repository, a Web Server that can run pages in different languages (e.g., VSP,[7] PHP and ASP) and data access interfaces (e.g., ODBC, JDBC, ADO.NET and OLE/DB). The repository, implemented in a native database, is based on a classical storage model of quads $\langle graph, subject, predicate, object \rangle$. The quad repository however, has been

[7] Virtuoso Server Pages: http://docs.openlinksw.com/virtuoso/vsp1.html.

improved with optimization techniques to (i) enhance performance and (ii) reduce disk space occupation. With respect to point (i), two covering indexes GSPO, OGPS (i.e., G for graph, S for subject, P for predicate and O for object) are defined to improve the efficiency of a large portion of possible queries; in order to use these indexes the user should specify the graph in the query, otherwise the indexes are not exploited. With respect to point (ii), Virtuoso stores distinct values eliminating common prefixes reducing the disk space occupation by 66%. SPARQL queries are translated to SQL by an internal query engine. Virtuoso offers a variety of functionality for the management of RDF data, for the purpose of this paper, we specifically concentrate on loading and querying performances.

To overcome some of the aforementioned problems, we develop an approach which main characteristics can be summarized as follows: strong flexibility and extendibility. The proposed approach represents concepts of RDF pointing out semantics of elements. In this way, information stored in an RDF document are properly grouped making more effective the querying process.

5.5 Experimental Results

Several experiments have been done to evaluate the performance of our framework. In this section, we relate on them. We compare performance and scalability of our approach with the popular full triple-store implementations: SDB Jena, Sesame and Openlink Virtuoso systems.

5.5.1 RDF Benchmark

We used the public available Wikipedia3 monthly updated dataset,[8] based on the Wikimedia dump of the English Wikipedia (enwiki, currently from March 26, 2006). It is a conversion of the English Wikipedia into RDF and consists of roughly 47 million triples. Therefore, it provides a good (real) sample of the unstructured nature of Semantic Web data. The Wikipedia3 data structure is based on a custom ontology[9] which is closely modeled after WikiOnt.[10] We split the Wikipedia3 dataset into 7843 smaller chunks and converted them to triples using the Jena parser. The dataset contains two main classes *Article* and *Category*, where Category is subClass of *Article*, four properties (i.e., *text, dc:title, dc:modified, dc:contributor*) and seven predicates (i.e., *skos:subject, skos:narrower*, *link* with subPredicates *internalLink, externalLink, interwikiLink and redirectsTo*). We counted about 5 million

[8] Available at http://labs.systemone.net/wikipedia3.

[9] Available at www.systemone.at/2006/03/wikipedia.

[10] http://meta.wikimedia.org/wiki/Transwiki:Wikimania05/Paper-IM1.

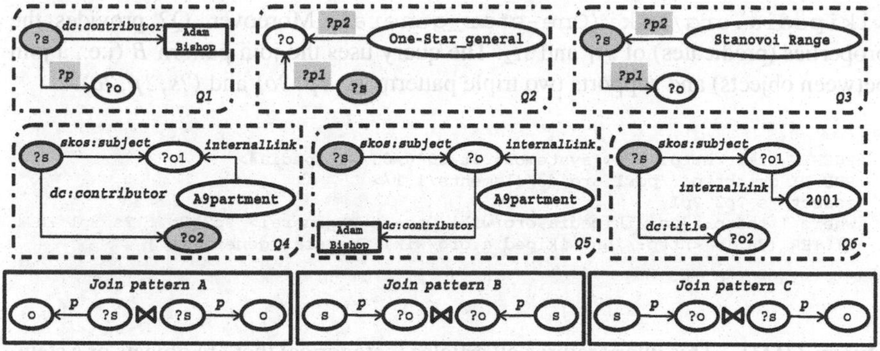

Fig. 5.9 Graphical sketch of the six representative queries

articles (of which one million categories), one million triples where the four properties occur, and 41 million triples where the predicates occur (of which 35 million internalLink). Most of properties and predicates are multi-valued: they appear more than once for a given subject. Moreover, most of the triples have a multi-valued property (predicate).

The goal of our experiments is the comparison between SWIM methodology and the most common RDF storage system: SDB Jena, Sesame and Openlink Virtuoso. Therefore, we implemented six representative queries, sketched in Fig. 5.9. Most of the common RDF query languages are based on *triple query pattern matching*. A pattern is a triple $\langle subject, property/predicate, object\rangle$ $\langle s, p, o\rangle$ where any s, p or o can be constant or variable (denoted, in the latter case, by $?s$, $?p$ and $?o$). We can combine these basic patterns into more complex ones through join conditions. As in [19], we identify three different *join patterns*, denoted by A, B and C shown in the bottom of Fig. 5.9. Our queries results are by different combinations of A, B and C (A, B; A, C; B, C). Therefore, we performed experiments on a complete query space. Later, we will discuss how these queries are executed by the different approaches. More in detail, the full queries are described in the following paragraphs.

Query 1 (Q1) This query returns all articles (categories), of which *Adam Bishop* is a contributor, and properties (predicates) coming out. This query uses the join pattern A (i.e., a join between subjects). Here, we support two triple patterns $(?s, p, o)$ and $(?s, ?p, ?o)$.

```
PREFIX wiki:<http://www.systemone.at/2006/03/wikipedia#>
PREFIX dc:<http://purl.org/dc/elements/1.1/>
select ?s ?p
where { ?s dc:contributor 'Adam Bishop'. ?s ?p ?o .
FILTER (?p != dc:contributor) }
```

Query 2 (Q2) This query returns all articles (categories) involved in a statement st_1 sharing the same object with a statement st_2, and whose subject is `http://en.`

wikipedia.org/wiki/One-star_general. Moreover, Q2 provides the properties (predicates) of st_1 and st_2. The query uses the join pattern *B* (i.e., a join between objects) and supports two triple patterns (*s*, ?*p*, ?*o*) and (?*s*, ?*p*, ?*o*).

```
PREFIX wiki:<http://www.systemone.at/2006/03/wikipedia#>
PREFIX dc:<http://purl.org/dc/elements/1.1/>
select ?s ?p2 ?p1
where { <http://en.wikipedia.org/wiki/One-star_general> ?p2 ?o . ?s ?p1 ?o .
FILTER (?s != <http://en.wikipedia.org/wiki/One-star_general>) }
```

Query 3 (Q3) This query returns all articles (categories) that are objects of a statement st_1 having http://en.wikipedia.org/wiki/Stanovoi_Range as subject. Moreover, Q3 returns properties (predicates) of st_1 and st_2, where the latter represents all statements of which the resulting articles (categories) are subjects. Q3 uses the last join patterns *C* (i.e., a join condition between subjects and objects) and consider two triple patterns (*s*, ?*p*, ?*o*) and (?*s*, ?*p*, ?*o*).

```
PREFIX wiki:<http://www.systemone.at/2006/03/wikipedia#>
PREFIX dc:<http://purl.org/dc/elements/1.1/>
select ?s ?p2 ?p1
where  {<http://en.wikipedia.org/wiki/Stanovoi_Range> ?p2 ?s .  ?s ?p1 ?o .}
```

Query 4 (Q4) This query provides all articles (categories) with respective contributors such that they are *skos:subject* (i.e., we refer to the *skos:subject* predicate) of others articles (categories), which are internal links of the article http://en.wikipedia.org/wiki/DC3A9partment.

In other words, the resulting items are subjects in statements (?*s*, *skos:subject*, ?*o*) having the objects in common with statements http://en.wikipedia.org/wiki/D%C3%A9partment, *wiki:internalLink*, ?*o*).

Q4 uses a combination of the join patterns *A* and *B* (i.e., two join conditions subject-subject and object-object at the same time), supporting the triple patterns (?*s*, *p*, ?*o*) and (*s*, *p*, ?*o*). This combination can make Q4 hardly computable and, thereby, time-expensive.

```
PREFIX wiki:<http://www.systemone.at/2006/03/wikipedia#>
PREFIX dc:<http://purl.org/dc/elements/1.1/>
select ?s ?o2
where { ?s <http://www.w3.org/2004/02/skos/core#subject> ?o1.
   ?s dc:contributor ?o2.
   <http://en.wikipedia.org/wiki/D\%C3\%A9partment> wiki:internalLink ?o1 .}
```

Query 5 (Q5) Following Q4, this query returns all articles (categories) that are *skos:subjects* of others articles (categories), of which *Adam Bishop* is a contributor and which are internal links of the article http://en.wikipedia.org/

wiki/D%C3%A9partment. Q5 uses a combination between the join patterns *B* and *C* and provides the triple patterns (?*s*, *p*, ?*o*), (?*s*, *p*, *o*) and (*s*, *p*, ?*o*).

```
PREFIX wiki:<http://www.systemone.at/2006/03/wikipedia#>
PREFIX dc:<http://purl.org/dc/elements/1.1/>
select ?s
where { ?s <http://www.w3.org/2004/02/skos/core#subject> ?o.
    ?o dc:contributor 'Adam Bishop'.
    <http://en.wikipedia.org/wiki/D\%C3\%A9partment> wiki:internalLink ?o .}
```

Query 6 (Q6) The last query provides all articles (categories) with referring titles that are *skos:subjects* of others articles (categories), linked to articles published in 2001. Q6 uses a combination between the join patterns *A* and *C* and presents the triple patterns (?*s*, *p*, ?*o*) and (?*s*, *p*, *o*).

```
PREFIX wiki:<http://www.systemone.at/2006/03/wikipedia#>
PREFIX dc:<http://purl.org/dc/elements/1.1/>
select ?s ?o2
where { ?s <http://www.w3.org/2004/02/skos/core#subject> ?o1.
?o1 wiki:internalLink <http://en.wikipedia.org/wiki/2001>. ?s dc:title ?o2.}
```

5.5.2 *Platform Environment*

Our benchmarking system is a dual quad core 2.66 GHz Intel Xeon, running Linux Gentoo, with 8 GB of memory, 6 MB cache, and a 2-disk 1 Tbyte striped RAID array. We implemented our experiments using PostgreSQL 8.3. As Beckmann et al. [7] experimentally showed, it is relevantly more efficient in respect with commercial database products. We used the default Postgres configuration: we preferred to not calibrate the system for specific needs.

SDB was tested on PostgreSQL. This implementation provides the main table `triples` containing three columns: s (i.e., subject), p (i.e., property) and o (i.e., object). It defines a primary key on the columns triple (s, p, o) and uses two unclustered B+ tree indices. One index is on (s, o), one is on (p, o). The table contains hashing values coming from URIs and property names, stored into the table `nodes`.

Sesame was tested with stable 2.2.4 version on a PostgreSQL store that utilizes B+ tree indices on any combination of subjects, properties and objects. We will show that scalability on Sesame is still an issue as it must perform many self-joins like all triple-stores.

We tested Openlink Virtuoso with its repository implementation in a native database, relying on the classical storage model of quads ⟨*graph*, *subject*, *predicate*, *object*⟩ and optimized by covering indexes. We used the Sesame API of Openlink Virtuoso to data access.

We submitted the six queries to all above systems in SPARQL. The SPARQL queries are translated to SQL by internal query engines of those systems.

The SWIM storage exploits the native partitioning technique of PostgreSQL. We use the M_{RDF} set of constructs implemented as described in Sects. 5.3.2 and 5.3.3. At instance level, on the Resource table (and relative partitions), we used a constraint of unique value on the *URI* attribute. On the i-Property and i-Predicate tables, we used an unclustered B+ tree index on the *Name* attribute and for each partitions we used clustered B+ tree indexes on the *SubjectResourceOID* and *ResourceOID* attributes, and unclustered B+ tree indexes on the *ObjectResourceOID* and *Value* attributes. Each partition has a check constraint and a trigger to redirect data inserted into the parent table and query processing into the children. In our implementation, we generate OIDs and translated textual data (e.g., *value* of i-Property) by MD5[11] coding to gain more performance.

5.5.3 Evaluating Results

Performance Results The six queries have been tested on all systems and the resulting query execution times are shown in Fig. 5.10. Times are expressed in logarithmic scale (i.e., base 10 and times in centiseconds). Each number is the average of three runs of the query. Internal database cache and operating system cache can

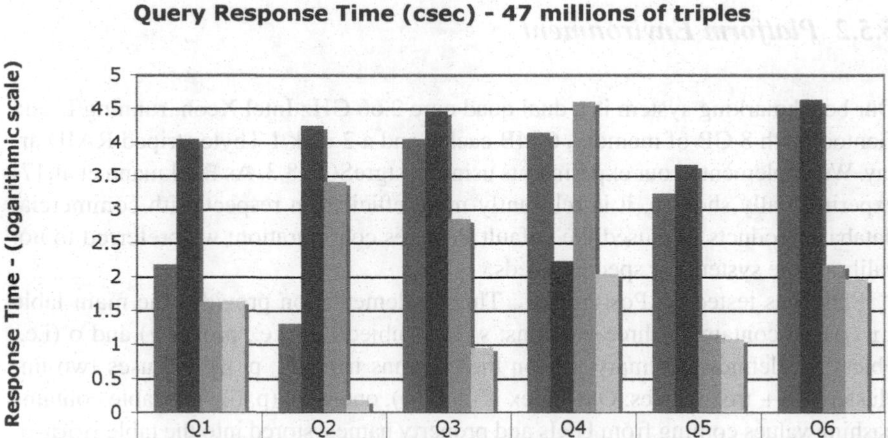

	Q1	Q2	Q3	Q4	Q5	Q6
Jena	2.17609126	1.30103	4.03941412	4.14072796	3.23299611	4.48131361
Sesame	4.04170842	4.24278981	4.45759429	2.23044892	3.66001122	4.62820495
Virtuoso	1.62324929	3.40483372	2.85491302	4.59648713	1.14612804	2.17026172
SWIM	1.63346846	0.17609126	0.95424251	2.0374265	1.07918125	1.95904139

Fig. 5.10 Performance comparison between the different approaches

[11] http://tools.ietf.org/html/rfc1321.

cause false measurements then before each query execution we have restarted the database and cleaned any cache.

Let us consider the Geometric Mean[12] of query response times (i.e., in seconds) since it provides a more accurate reflection of the global speedup factor. SDB presents 16.9 seconds, Sesame 75.3 seconds, Openlink Virtuoso 4.3 seconds, and SWIM 0.2 seconds. Therefore, our approach performs factors of 16 and 75 faster than the approaches from SDB and Sesame, respectively, and a factor of 4 faster than Openlink Virtuoso.

In the following, we will explain the obtained results for the execution of each query.

Q1 In Wikipedia3 dataset, Adam Bishop is contributor of significant amount of articles that are linked to others articles (categories) in different way. SDB exploits the index on (p, o) and the property table to access all resulting properties (i.e., $?p$ in Q1). Sesame exploits the same index to extract all subjects $?s$ but the join condition on all resulting subjects increases dramatically the computation time. The join condition is on the triple pattern $(?s, ?p, ?o)$ that doesn't activate any index optimization. SWIM and Openlink Virtuoso times are quite identical. Virtuoso uses the quad indexes to access all $(?s, ?p, ?o)$ triples efficiently and SWIM is supported by the partitioning and clustered indexes to access the *contributor* property instantly and to select the triples $(?s, ?p, ?o)$ with the subject $?s$ in common.

Q2 This query presents high selectivity. The article *One-Star_general* occur only in triples $(?s, ?p, ?o)$ where $?p$ is a property, and then all $?p2$ in Q2 will be properties. We remind the smaller percentage of properties with respect the amount of predicates in Wikipedia3. SDB exploits the property table technique to execute Q2 in an efficient way, while Sesame and Openlink Virtuoso can't use efficiently their indexing since the join condition is over Literals. Sesame and Openlink Virtuoso has to scan also the relevant amount of predicates that don't contribute to the final results. SWIM exploits the partitioning again and, moreover, the subdivision in constructs reduces relevantly research space and guide the query to i-Property construct directly.

Q3 Despite of Q2, a huge portion of data is involved into the processing since the article *Stanovoi_Range* presents many *internalLink* occurrences. We remind 31 millions of occurrences of *internalLink* in Wikipedia3. Q3 shows that the expensive object-subject joins of the triple-store approach is crucial since it performs much more slowly than our system. SDB and Jena has to operate expensive joins (i.e., self and merge joins, respectively) between huge amount of data. The respective optimizations do not support that systems. Openlink Virtuoso presents a similar computational complexity however showing a better indexing usage. SWIM exhibits again effectiveness of the construct-based approach, supported by efficiency of the partitioning optimization.

[12] The nth root of the product of n numbers.

Q4 Following Q1, Q2 and Q3, this query combines different join patterns. In particular, Q4 performs join conditions subject-subject and object-object at the same time. The join condition object-object is between occurrences of *shos:subject* and *internalLink*. This makes computationally complex the query execution (i.e., maybe the most complex computation). SDB and Virtuoso shows dramatic response times due to reasons expressed above. Sesame exploits indices on any combination of subjects, properties and objects. SWIM confirms the efficiency of the approach reducing relevantly the query search space and join complexity through the partitioning on *skos:subject* and *contributor*.

Q5 Following Q4, this query performs join conditions object-object and subject-object presenting similar join complexity. Q5 introduces higher selectivity on *contributor* expressing the object constant *Adam Bishop*. As in Q4, SDB can't exploit the property table technique while Sesame is not well supported by indexing. Instead, the triple pattern (s, p, o) reduces the computation of Openlink Virtuoso that can exploit its indexing. As in Q1, SWIM is quite comparable with Openlink Virtuoso.

Q6 This last query performs a combination between the join conditions subject-subject and subject-object introducing the selectivity on *internalLink* with the constant object *2001*. Also in this case, the heavy self and merge joins relevantly increases the response time in SDB and Jena. Openlink Virtuoso faces with the high complexity of Q6 too, but answering in a more efficient way. Finally, SWIM confirms its strength with fast responsiveness.

Summarizing, the triple-store approach presents relevant performing issue. SDB and Sesame presents the worst results, due to its unprofitable storage model. Openlink Virtuoso obtains best results in the queries where there aren't combinations of join conditions or where these combinations are alleviate by triple patterns (s, p, o) that introduce helpful selectivity. The results of SWIM are better in the most of cases due to its internal data organization at each level of abstractions (i.e., construct-based aggregations and partitioning). This demonstrates the effectiveness of the approach against the complete query space. However, in Q1, Q5, Q6 SWIM response times are comparable with Openlink Virtuoso.

Scalability Results A relevant important factor to consider is how performance scales with the increasing size of data. To measure the scalability of each approach, we have performed an incremental import of data. Each Wikipedia3 file has been imported separately, each of which containing around 6000 triples. The import of a single file corresponds to add new knowledge to the RDF storage. Query scalability is tested using the six queries. After the import of each Wikipedia3 file, a query is executed for all the approaches, measuring the query answer time. Figure 5.11 shows the scalability performance of all queries. The diagrams illustrate and prove the behavior of the triple-store approach (i.e., in particular SDB and Sesame) that scales super-linearly. Openlink Virtuoso grows linearly in Q1, Q3, Q5 and Q6. SWIM grows with a linear factor in all queries. This is because all joins for these queries are quite linear due to our internal data organization.

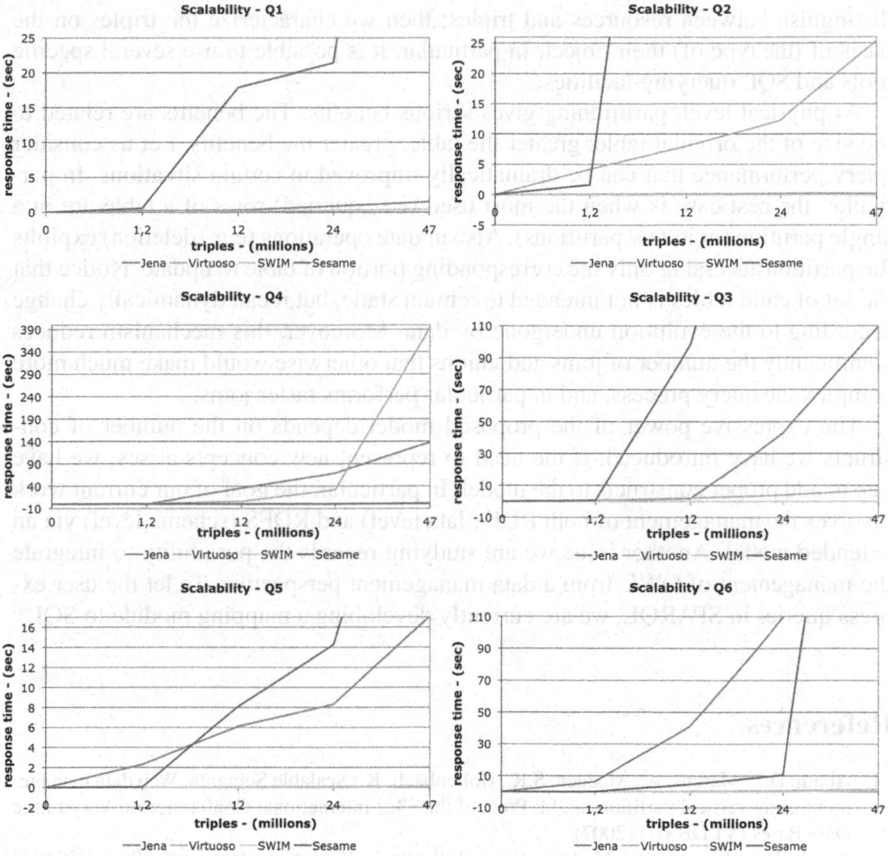

Fig. 5.11 Query performance as number of triples scale

5.6 Conclusion

Due to the growing importance of Semantic Web, several applications that use RDF data have been developed. This large amount of data must be rapidly accessed in order to be effectively used. Storing and maintaining RDF data represent crucial activities to achieve this complex purpose. The classical "triple-store" approaches are not good enough because most of the queries require a high number of self-joins on the triples table.

In order to overcome these problems, we proposed a model-based approach to store and maintain large amount of RDF data and showed that it achieves performance results similar to other well-known approaches.

We have described our idea of modeling RDF data at different levels: conceptual, logical and physical. Each level provides relevant benefits. The novelty introduced at conceptual level is the characterization of RDF elements. Whatever is the syntax used in an RDF document, all the elements are represented in a uniform way. We distinguish between resources and triples; then we characterize the triples on the basis of (the type of) their object. In particular, it is possible to use several specific tools and SQL querying facilities.

At physical level, partitioning gives serious benefits. The benefits are related to the size of the original table: greater the table, greater the benefits. Let us consider query performance that can be dramatically improved in certain situations. In particular, the best case is when the most used (i.e., queried) rows of a table are in a single partition (or in few partitions). Also update operations (e.g., deletion) exploits the partition accessing only the corresponding portion of table to update. Notice that the set of child tables is not intended to remain static, but it can dynamically change according to the evolution undergone by data. Moreover, this mechanism reduces significantly the number of joins and unions that otherwise would make much more complex the query process, and in particular performs faster joins.

The expressive power of the proposed model depends on the number of constructs we have introduced. If the need to represent new concepts arises, we have just to add proper constructs to the model. In particular, the goal of our current work involves the management of both RDF (data level) and RDFS (schema level) via an extended model. Another issue we are studying regards the possibility to integrate the management of OWL from a data management perspective. To let the user express queries in SPARQL, we are currently developing a mapping module to SQL.

References

1. Abadi, D.J., Marcus, A., Madden, S.R., Hollenbach, K.: Scalable Semantic Web data management using vertical partitioning. In: Proc. of the 33rd International Conference on Very Large Data Bases (VLDB'07) (2007)
2. Abadi, D.J., Marcus, A., Madden, S.R., Hollenbach, K.: Sw-store: a vertically partitioned dbms for Semantic Web data management. VLDB J. **18**(2), 385–406 (2009)
3. Alexaki, S., Christophides, V., Karvounarakis, G., Plexousakis, D., Tolle, K.: The ICS-FORTH RDFSuite: managing voluminous RDF description bases. In: 2nd Intl. Workshop on the Semantic Web (SemWeb'01, with WWW10), Hong Kong (2001)
4. Angles, R., Gutiérrez, C.: Querying RDF data from a graph database perspective. In: Proc. of the 2nd European Semantic Web Conference (ESWC 2005), Heraklion, Crete, Greece, pp. 346–360 (2005)
5. Bönström, V., Hinze, A., Schweppe, H.: Storing RDF as a graph. In: LA-WEB (2003)
6. Atzeni, P., Cappellari, P., Bernstein, P.A.: Model-independent schema and data translation. In: Proc. of the 10th Int. Conference on Extending Database Technology (EDBT'06), Munich, Germany (2006)
7. Beckmann, J., Halverson, A., Krishnamurthy, R., Naughton, J.: Extending RDBMSs to support sparse datasets using an interpreted attribute storage format. In: Proc. of the 22rd Int. Conference on Data Engineering (ICDE'06), Atlanta, USA (2006)
8. Berners-Lee, T., Hendler, J.A., Lassila, O.: The Semantic Web. Sci. Am. J. **284**(5), 34–43 (2001)
9. Broekstra, J., Kampman, A., van Harmelen, F.: Sesame: a generic architecture for storing and querying RDF and RDF schema. In: Proc. of the First Internation Conference on Semantic Web (ISWC'02), Sardinia, Italy (2002)
10. Chong, E.I., Das, S., Eadon, G., Srinivasan, J.: An efficient SQL-based RDF querying scheme. In: Proc. of the 31th International Conference on Very Large Data Bases (VLDB'05), Trondheim, Norway (2005)

11. Furche, T., Linse, B., Bry, F., Plexousakis, D., Gottlob, G.: RDF querying: language constructs and evaluation methods compared. In: Proc. of Int. Summer School on Reasoning Web, Lisbon, Portugal (2006)
12. Erling, O., Mikhailov, I.: RDF support in the virtuoso DBMS. In: Proc. of the Conference on Social Semantic Web (CSSW 2007), pp. 59–68 (2007)
13. Harris, S., Gibbins, N.: 3store: efficient bulk RDF storage. In: Proc. of the First International Workshop on Practical and Scalable Semantic Systems (PSSS'03) (2003)
14. Karvounarakis, G., Magkanaraki, A., Alexaki, S., Christophides, V., Plexousakis, D., Scholl, M., Tolle, K.: Querying the Semantic Web with RQL. Comput. Networks **42**(5), 617–640 (2003)
15. Li, M., Wang, C., Jing, L., Feng, C., Pan, P., Yu, Y.: Effective and efficient Semantic Web data management over DB2. In: Proc. of ACM SIGMOD International Conference on Management of Data (SIGMOD'08), Vancouver, BC, Canada (2008)
16. Kiryakov, A., Ognyanov, D., Manovand, D.: OWLIM—a pragmatic semantic repository for OWL. In: Proc. of Int. Workshop on Scalable Semantic Web Web Knowledge Base Systems (SSWS'05), New York City, USA (2005)
17. RDQL: A Query Language for RDF. W3C Member Submission 9 January 2004. http://www.w3.org/Submission/RDQL/ (2004)
18. The SeRQL query language (revision 1.2), http://www.openrdf.org/doc/sesame/users/ch06.html
19. Sidirourgos, L., Goncalves, R., Kersten, M.L., Nes, N., Manegold, S.: Column-store support for RDF data management: not all swans are white. In: Proc. of the Int. Conf. on Very Large Database (VLDB'08) (2008)
20. SPARQLQuery Language for RDF. W3C Working Draft 4 October 2006. http://www.w3.org/TR/rdf-sparql-query/ (2006)
21. Torlone, R., Atzeni, P.: A unified framework for data translation over the Web. In: Proc. of the 2th Int. Conf. of Web Information System (WISE'01), Japan (2001)
22. W3C. The Resource Description Framework. Available at http://www.w3.org/RDF/
23. Wilkinson, K.: Jena property table implementation. In: Proc. of the International Workshop on Scalable Semantic Web Knowledge Base, pp. 35–46 (2006)
24. Wilkinson, K., Sayers, C., Kuno, H., Reynolds, D.: Efficient RDF storage and retrieval in Jena2. In: Proc. of the first International Workshop on Semantic Web and Databases (SWDB'03), Berlin, Germany (2003)

Chapter 6
Managing Terabytes of Web Semantics Data

**Michele Catasta, Renaud Delbru,
Nickolai Toupikov, and Giovanni Tummarello**

Abstract A large amount of semi structured data is now made available on the Web in form of RDF, RDFa and Microformats. In this chapter, we discuss a general model for the Web of Data and, based on our experience in Sindice.com, we discuss how this is reflected in the architecture and components of a large scale infrastructure. Aspects such as data collection, processing, indexing, ranking are touched, and we give an ample example of an applications built on top of said infrastructure.

6.1 Introduction

The amount of Resource Description Framework (RDF) documents and HTML pages which have entities marked up using Microformats,[1] have grown tremendously in the past years. On the one hand, the Linked Open Data[2] (LOD) community has made available several billion triples equivalent of information, driven by the idea of open access to semi structured data. On the other hand, an increasing number of relevant Web 2.0 players (LinkedIn, Yahoo Locals, Eventful, Digg, Youtube, Wordpress to name just a few) have also added some form of semi-structured data markups. Precise measurements of this growth are not available, but partial reports allow an educated guess of the current size in billions of RDF triples and approximately half a billion of semantically marked up web pages, likely totalling several billion triples equivalent.

[1]http://microformats.org.

[2]Linked Data: http://linkeddata.org/.

The authors' names are listed in alphabetical order for convenience. This was a fully collaborative effort.

M. Catasta (✉) · R. Delbru · N. Toupikov · G. Tummarello
Digital Enterprise Research Institute, National University of Ireland, Galway, Ireland
e-mail: michele.catasta@deri.org

R. Delbru
e-mail: renaud.delbru@deri.org

N. Toupikov
e-mail: nickolai.toupikov@deri.org

G. Tummarello
e-mail: giovanni.tummarello@deri.org

R. De Virgilio et al. (eds.), *Semantic Web Information Management*,
DOI 10.1007/978-3-642-04329-1_6, © Springer-Verlag Berlin Heidelberg 2010

Also given the support now available in Yahoo! with the Searchmonkey project, and in Google with its recently added support for RDFa[3] semi-structured snippets, more and more data is expected to be made available calling for solutions in the same scale of that of classic web search engines.

In this chapter, we first discuss a general model for the Web of Data, which allows multiple forms of web semantics to be seen as a uniform space. Then inspired by the work in the Sindice.com project, we will discuss a high level overview of the elements that allow providing services and building applications leveraging the Web of Data as a whole.

6.1.1 Definition and Model for the Web of Data

For the purpose of this chapter, we define the Web of Data as the part of the HTTP accessible web which returns entities described semantically using standard interchange formats and practices. These include pages which embed microformats as well as RDF models using different standards. The LOD community, for example, advocates the use of HTTP content negotiation and redirect[4] to provide either machine or human readable versions of the RDF data. RDFa, on the other hand, is a standard that enables embedding of RDF directly within HTML documents. In each case, it is possible to abstract the following core elements in semi-structured data web publishing:

A dataset is a collection of entity descriptions. One dataset is usually the content of a database which powers a web application exposing metadata, be this dynamic web site with just partial semantic markups (e.g., Web 2.0 sites) or a Semantic Web database which exposes its content such as the LOD datasets. Datasets however can also come in the form of a single RDF document, e.g., an individual FOAF file posted on a user's homepage. A dataset is said to be a RDF *Named Graph* [4] which is uniquely identified by an URI. This name, or URI, is often mapped to a *context*.

An entity description is a set of assertions about the entity which is contained within a dataset. Assertions can be solely regarding the entity (e.g., properties such as its name or type) or connecting one or more entities either inside or outside the dataset, using resolvable URIs. Thanks to the flexibility of the semi-structured RDF model, it is always possible to map assertions to RDF *statements*. When RDF is used natively by a website to describe entities, it is possible to furthermore distinguish between *authoritative statements* and *authoritative descriptions*, those that are made within the context where the URI name is minted, and *nonauthoritative*

[3] A serialization format for RDF which allows triples to be embedded in XML documents in a way comparable with Microformats.

[4] URL redirection is a directive that allows to indicate that further action, e.g. fetch a second URL, needs to be taken by the user agent in order to fulfil the request.

statements and *nonauthoritative descriptions*, those that are made outside the context where the URI name is minted such as in third parties web sites. For example, the authoritative description about http://dbpedia.org/resource/Galway is the set of statements that is obtained when resolving the URI itself.

Keeping in mind that we do want to keep statements from different contexts separated, we can see the collection of all the datasets as follow. Given three infinite sets U, B and L called, respectively, URI references, blank nodes and literals, a contextualized RDF statement or quad $(\mathrm{s}, \mathrm{p}, \mathrm{o}, \mathrm{c})$ is an element q of $Q = (U \cup B) \times U \times (U \cup B \cup L) \times (U)$. Here, s is called the subject, p the predicate, o the object and c the context of the statement. The context is generally, as explained above, the identifier of the dataset.

A View represents a single HTTP accessible document, retrieved by resolving an URI, that points to a full or partial view of the knowledge contained in the dataset. A view can be seen as a function $v : U \rightarrow Q$ that, given an URI $u \in U$, returns a semi-structured representation of the entity denoted by u that is a set of quads $Q_u \subseteq Q$. In case of LOD, a typical view is the RDF model returned by a LOD dataset when one dereferences the URI of a resource. For example, when dereferencing http://dbpedia.org/resource/Galway, a view of the information about this URI is created by the underlying database of DBPedia and it is returned as RDF model. LOD views are 1 to 1 mapping from the URI to the complete entity description. This however is more the exception than the rule for other kind of web data publishing where most often only partial entity descriptions are provided in the views. For example, in the case of microformats or RDFa, views are pages that talk about different aspects of the entity, e.g., a page listing social contacts for a person, a separate page listing personal data as well as a page containing all the posts by a user. The union of all the views provided within a context, e.g., a website, might enable an agent, e.g., a crawler, to reconstruct the entire dataset, but there is no guarantee on this.

This three layer model, which is graphically represented in Fig. 6.1, forms the base for the infrastructure we will describe in the following sections.

6.2 Providing Services on the Web of Data: A Model for a Large Scale Semantic Data Processing Infrastructure

Developed by DERI's Data Intensive Infrastructures group,[5] the Sindice project aims at building scalable APIs to locate and make use of Semantic Web data. By using the Sindice API, for example, it is possible to use keywords and semantic pattern queries to search for people, places, events and connections among these based on the semi-structured content of documents found on the web.

Technically, Sindice is designed to provide these services fulfilling three main nonfunctional requirements: scalability, run time performance and ability to cope

[5]http://di2.deri.ie.

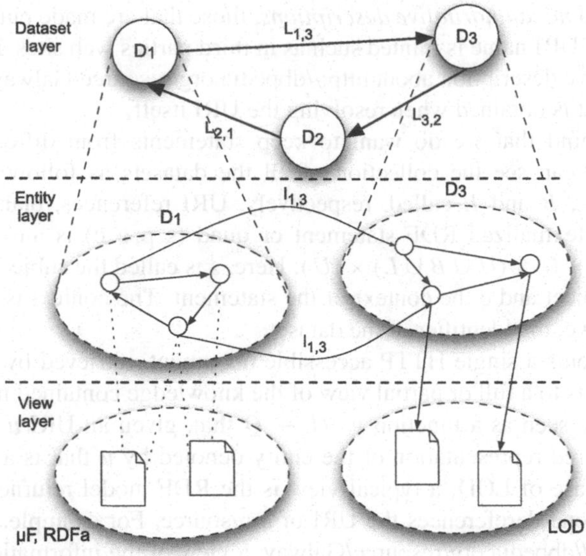

Fig. 6.1 The three-layer model of the Web of Data

with the many changes in standards and usage practices on the Web of Data. We begin our description in Sect. 6.3, describing a data collection publishing strategy (Semantic Sitemap) which is peculiar to the LOD scenario and employed to harvest very large datasets.

The data collected in this way, along with the data collected in other methods similar to those of conventional web search engines is then preprocessed. In this phase, the raw content harvested, e.g. the semantically annotated HTML, is analysed by a set of parsers which we are currently publishing as open source under the name *any23*.[6] These parsers are used to extract RDF data from various formats. Different RDF serialization formats (RDF/XML, Notation 3, Turtle, N-Triples, RDFa) are supported, as well as several microformats (hCard, hEvent, hListing, hResume and others).

At this point, the semantics of the document (the complete or partial view over an entity), regardless of the original format, is represented in RDF. Information then reaches the "context-dependent" reasoning engine, discussed in Sect. 6.4, which is a part of the preprocessing step where inference is performed for each single document to be indexed.

Indexing is performed by our Semantic Information Retrieval Engine (SIREn), discussed in Sect. 6.5, and enables answering both textual and semantic queries and forms the core of the Sindice public APIs. To be able to provide high quality top-k results, a dataset-centric ranking strategy is employed, described in Sect. 6.6. These elements and their interrelations are depicted in a high level view in Fig. 6.2.

[6]http://code.google.com/p/any23/.

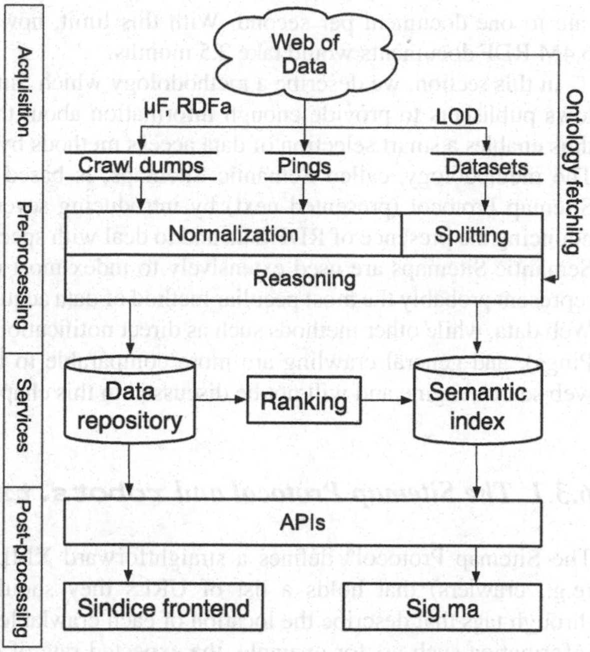

Fig. 6.2 Overview graph

Finally, these services can be leveraged as API to create advanced applications which make use of Web of Data. This is the case of Sig.ma, an end user targeted application that enables visual "entity based search and information mashups", described in Sect. 6.7.

6.3 Semantic Sitemap: A Dataset Publishing Model

There are many ways to make information available on the Web of Data. Even restricting to the RDF world, for example, an online database might be published as one single RDF dump. Alternatively, the LOD paradigm is based on using resolvable URIs to offer access to individual descriptions of resources. Other datasets might offer access to its data via a SPARQL endpoint that allows clients to submit queries using the SPARQL RDF query language and protocol[7] or might expose HTML views that embed RDFa.

If several of these options are offered simultaneously for the same database, the choice of access method can have significant effects on the amount of networking and computing resources consumed on the client and the server side. Such choices can have serious implications. Considering that results are generated from semantic queries, which tend to be resource intensive, it might be sensible to limit the query

[7] SPARQL: http://www.w3.org/TR/rdf-sparql-query/.

rate to one document per second. With this limit, however, crawling Geonames' 6.4M RDF documents would take 2.5 months.

In this section, we describe a methodology which Sindice supports fully that allows publishers to provide enough information about their publishing model, and thus enables a smart selection of data access methods by clients and crawlers alike. The methodology, called Semantic Sitemaps, is based on extending the existing Sitemap Protocol (presented next) by introducing several new XML tags for announcing the presence of RDF data and to deal with specific RDF publishing needs. Semantic Sitemaps are used extensively to index most of the LOD datasets. They represent probably the most peculiar method of data acquisition targeted at Semantic Web data, while other methods such as direct notifications of URLs to index (called Pings), and general crawling are more comparable to those used in conventional web search engine and will not be discussed in this chapter.

6.3.1 The Sitemap Protocol and `robots.txt`

The Sitemap Protocol[8] defines a straightforward XML file for automatic agents (e.g., crawlers) that holds a list of URLs they should index. This is possible through tags that describe the location of each crawlable resource along with meta-information such as, for example, the expected rate of change for each individual URL or the date when this was last modified. An example of a sitemap is shown in the following listing:

Listing 6.1 Example of sitemap

```
<?xml version="1.0" encoding="UTF-8"?>
<urlset xmlns="http://www.sitemaps.org/schemas/sitemap/0.9">
  <url>
    <loc>http://www.example.com/</loc>
    <lastmod>2005-01-01</lastmod>
    <changefreq>monthly</changefreq>
    <priority>0.8</priority>
  </url>
</urlset>
```

Once a sitemap has been created, it must be saved in a file on the server. The protocol defines a way to extend the `robot.txt` file, so that a robot can find the location of the sitemap file on a given site.

6.3.2 The Semantic Sitemaps Extension

This section introduces the Semantic Sitemaps proposal. We will start by clarifying the notion of a *dataset*, then list the key pieces of information that can be provided

[8] Sitemap Protocol: http://www.sitemaps.org/protocol.php.

in a Semantic Sitemap, and finally look at two specific issues: obtaining individual resource descriptions from a large dump; and the topic of authority on the Semantic Web.

6.3.2.1 Datasets

The Semantic Sitemap extension has the concept of dataset at its core: datasets are well defined resources which can have one or more access methods. It is well defined what properties apply to a certain access method and what properties apply to a given dataset. Therefore, properties that apply to that dataset will be directly related to all the data that can be obtained, independently from the access method. A publisher can host multiple datasets on the same site and can describe them independently using different sections of the Semantic Sitemap. While there is nothing that prevents information overlap or contradictions between different datasets, it is expected that this is not the case.

6.3.2.2 Adding Dataset Descriptions to the Sitemap Protocol

The Semantic Sitemap extension allows the description of a dataset via the tag `<sc:dataset>`, to be used at the same level as `<url>` tags in a regular sitemap. Access options for the datasets are given by additional tags such as `<sc:dataDump>`, `<sc:sparqlEndpoint>` and `<sc:linkedDataPrefix>`. If a sitemap contains several dataset definitions, they are treated independently. The following example shows a sitemap file applying the extension.

Listing 6.2 Example of semantic sitemap

```
<?xml version="1.0" encoding="UTF-8"?>
<urlset xmlns="http://www.sitemaps.org/schemas/sitemap/0.9"
    xmlns:sc="http://sw.deri.org/2007/07/sitemapextension">
  <sc:dataset>
    <sc:datasetLabel>
      Example Corp. Product Catalog
    </sc:datasetLabel>
    <sc:datasetURI>
      http://example.com/catalog.rdf#catalog
    </sc:datasetURI>
    <sc:linkedDataPrefix sc:slicing="subject-object">
      http://example.com/products/
    </sc:linkedDataPrefix>
    <sc:sampleURI>
      http://example.com/products/widgets/X42
    </sc:sampleURI>
    <sc:sampleURI>
      http://example.com/products/categories/all
```

```
    </sc:sampleURI>
    <sc:sparqlEndpoint sc:slicing="subject-object">
      http://example.com/sparql
    </sc:sparqlEndpoint>
    <sc:dataDump>
      http://example.com/data/catalogdump.rdf.gz
    </sc:dataDump>
    <sc:dataDump>
      http://example.org/data/catalog_archive.rdf.gz
    </sc:dataDump>
    <changefreq>weekly</changefreq>
  </sc:dataset>
</urlset>
```

The dataset is labelled as the *Example Corp. Product Catalog* and identified by `http://example.com/catalog.rdf#catalog`. Hence it is reasonable to expect further RDF annotations about the dataset `http://example.com/catalog.rdf`.

The resources described in the dataset all have identifiers starting with `http://example.com/products/`, and their descriptions are served as Linked Data. A dump of the entire dataset is available, split into two parts and the publisher states that dataset updates can be expected weekly.

RDF dataset dumps can be provided in formats such as RDF/XML, N-Triples and N-Quads[9] (similar to N-Triples with a fourth element specifying the URI of the RDF document containing the triple; the same triple might be contained in several different documents). Optionally, dump files may be compressed in GZIP, ZIP or BZIP2 format.

6.4 Pre-processing: Context-dependent Reasoning

After having created from the views a complete or partial entity description, the information is pushed into the indexing pipeline. The main component of the indexing pipeline is the "context-dependent" reasoning engine. Reasoning over semi-structured entity description enables to make explicit what would otherwise be implicit knowledge: it adds value to the information and enables an entity-centric search engine to ultimately be much more competitive in terms of precision and recall [14]. The drawback is that inference can be computationally expensive, and therefore drastically slow down the process of indexing large amounts of information.

Our work is specifically concerned on how to efficiently reason over very large collections of entity description which have been published on the Web. To reason on such descriptions, we assume that the ontologies that these descriptions refer to are either included explicitly with `owl:imports` declarations or implicitly by

[9] N-Quads: http://sw.deri.org/2008/07/n-quads/.

using property and class URIs that link directly to the data describing the ontology itself. This later case should be the standard if the W3C best practices [15] for publishing ontologies and the Linked Data principles [2] are followed by ontology creators. As ontologies might refer to other ontologies, the import process then needs to be recursively iterated (see Sect. 6.4.2 for a detailed formalisation).

A naive approach would be to execute such recursive fetching for each entity description and create a single RDF model composed by the original description plus the ontologies. At this point, the deductive closure (see Sect. 6.4.3 for a detailed formalisation) of the RDF model can be computed and the entity description—including ontologically inferred information—can be indexed.

Such a naive procedure is however obviously inefficient since a lot of processing time will be used to recalculate deductions which, as we will see, could be instead reused for possibly large classes of other entity descriptions during the indexing procedure.

To reuse previous inference results, a simple strategy has been traditionally to put several (if not all) the ontologies together compute and reuse their deductive closures across all the entity description to be indexed. While this simple approach is computationally convenient, it turns out to be sometimes inappropriate, since data publishers can reuse or extend ontology terms with divergent points of view.

For example, if an ontology other than the FOAF vocabulary itself extends `foaf:knows` as a symmetric property, an inferencing agent should not consider this axiom outside the scope of the entity description that references this particular ontology. Not doing so would severely decrease the precision of semantic querying, by diluting the results with many false positives.

For this reason, a fundamental requirement of the procedure that we developed has been to confine ontological assertions and reasoning tasks into contexts in order to track provenance of inference results. By tracking provenance of each single assertion, we are able to prevent one ontology to alter the semantics of other ontologies on a global scale.

6.4.1 Contexts on the Semantic Web

As discussed previously, the dataset URI provides a natural way to define its context. Naming an RDF graph has multiple benefits. It helps tracking the provenance of each statement. In addition, since named graphs are treated as first class objects, it enables the description and manipulation of a set of statements just as for any other resource. However, in this section, the notion of context refers to the entity URI at which the entity description is retrievable. For our purposes, it is sufficient to understand, in this section, that by *context* we identify the set of statements of an entity description.

Guha [10] proposed a context mechanism for the Semantic Web which provides a formal basis to specify the aggregation of contexts. Within his framework, a context denotes the scope of validity of a statement. This scope is defined by the symbol *ist* ("is true in context"), introduced by Guha in [9]. The notation $ist(c, \varphi)$ states that a proposition φ is true in the context c.

The notion of context presented in this section is based on Guha's context mechanism. Its aim is to enable the control of integration of ontologies and ultimately avoid the aggregation of ontologies that may result in undesirable inferred assertions.

6.4.1.1 Aggregate Context

An *Aggregate Context* is a subclass of *Context*. Its content is composed by the content retrieved by resolving its URI, and by the contents lifted from other contexts. An aggregate context must contain the full specification of what it imports. In our case, each entity description is considered an *Aggregate Context*, since it always contains the specification of what it imports through explicit or implicit import declarations, described next.

6.4.1.2 Lifting Rules

Since contexts are first class objects, it becomes possible to define expressive formulae whose domains and ranges are contexts. An example are so called *Lifting Rules* that enable to *lift* axioms from one context to another. In Guha's context mechanism, a lifting rule is a property type whose domain is an *Aggregate Context* and range a *Context*. A lifting rule can simply import all of the statements from a context to another, but can also be defined to select precisely which statements have to be imported.

6.4.2 Import Closure of RDF Models

On the Semantic Web, ontologies are meant to be published so to be easily reused by third parties. OWL provides the `owl:imports` primitive to indicate the inclusion of a target ontology inside an RDF nodel. Conceptually, importing an ontology brings the content of that ontology into the RDF model.

The `owl:imports` primitive is transitive. That is, an import declaration states that, when reasoning with an ontology O, one should consider not only the axioms of O, but the entire import closure of O. The imports closure of an ontology O is the smallest set containing the axioms of O and of all the axioms of the ontologies that O imports. For example, if ontology O_A imports O_B, and O_B imports O_C, then O_A imports both O_B and O_C.

The declaration of `owl:imports` primitives is a not a common practice in Semantic Web documents, most published RDF models do not contain explicit `owl:imports` declarations. For example, among the 50 million of documents in Sindice, only 66.38 thousand are declaring at least one `owl:imports`.

Instead, RDF models generally refer to classes and properties of existing ontologies by their URIs. For example, most FOAF profile documents don't explicitly import the FOAF ontology, but instead just refer to classes and properties of the FOAF vocabulary. Following the W3C best practices [15] and Linked Data principles [2], the URIs of the classes and properties defined in an ontology should be resolvable and provide the machine-processable content of the vocabulary.

In the presence of such dereferenceable class or property URIs, we perform what we call an *implicit import*. By dereferencing the URI, we attempt to retrieve a document containing the ontological description of the entity and to include its content inside the source RDF model.

Also implicit import is considered transitive. For example, if a RDF model refers to an entity E_A from an ontology O_A, and if O_A refers to an entity E_B in an ontology O_B, then the model imports two ontologies O_A and O_B.

6.4.3 Deductive Closure of RDF Models

In Sindice, we consider for indexing inferred statements from the deductive closure of each entity description we index. What we call here the "deductive closure" of a RDF model is the set of assertions entailed in the aggregate context composed of the entity description itself and of its ontology import closure.

When reasoning with Web data, we cannot expect to deal with a level of expressiveness of OWL-DL [5], but would need to consider OWL Full. Since under such circumstances, we cannot strive for complete reasoning anyway, we therefore content with an incomplete but finite entailment regime based on a subset of RDFS and OWL, namely the Horst fragment [13] as implemented by off-the-shelf rule-based materialisation engines such as for instance OWLIM.[10] Such an incomplete deductive closure is sufficient with respect to increasing the precision and recall of the search engine, and provides useful RDF(S) and OWL inferences such as class hierarchy, equalities, property characteristics such as inverse functional properties or annotation properties.

A rule-based inference engine is currently used to compute full materialisation of the entailed statements with respect to this finite entailment regime. In fact, is it in such a setting a requirement that deduction to be finite, which in terms of OWL Full can only be possible if the entailment regime is incomplete (as widely known the RDF container vocabulary alone is infinite already [12]). This is deliberate and we consider a higher level of completeness hardly achievable on the Web of Data: in a setting where the target ontology to be imported may not be accessible at the time of the processing, for instance, we just ignore the imports primitives and are thus anyway incomplete from the start.

One can see that the deductive closure of an aggregate context can lead to inferred statements that are not true in any of the source contexts alone.

---

[10] http://www.ontotext.com/owlim/.

Definition 6.1 Let c_1 and c_2 be two contexts with, respectively, two propositions φ_1 and φ_2, $ist(c_1, \varphi_1)$ and $ist(c_2, \varphi_2)$, and $\varphi_1 \wedge \varphi_2 \models \varphi_3$, such that $\varphi_2 \not\models \varphi_3$, $\varphi_1 \not\models \varphi_3$, then we call φ_3 a *newly entailed proposition* in the aggregate context $c_1 \wedge c_2$. We denote the set of all newly defined propositions Δ_{c_1,c_2}:

$$\Delta_{c_1,c_2} = \bigl\{ist(c_1, \varphi_1) \wedge ist(c_2, \varphi_2) \models ist(c_1 \wedge c_2, \varphi_3) \\ \text{and } \neg\bigl(ist(c_1, \varphi_3) \vee ist(c_2, \varphi_3)\bigr)\bigr\}$$

For example, if a context c_1 contains an instance x of the class *Person*, and a context c_2 contains a proposition stating that *Person* is a subclass of *Human*, then the entailed conclusion that x is a human is only true in the aggregate context $c_1 \wedge c_2$:

$$ist\bigl(c_1, Person(x)\bigr) \wedge ist\bigl(c_2, subClass(Person, Human)\bigr) \\ \rightarrow ist\bigl(c_1 \wedge c_2, Human(x)\bigr)$$

Note that, by considering (in our case (Horn) rule-based) RDFS/OWL inferences only, aggregate contexts enjoy the following monotonicity property:[11] if aggregate context $c_1 \subseteq c_2$ then $ist(c_2, \phi)$ implies $ist(c_1, \phi)$, or respectively, for overlapping contexts, if $ist(c_1 \cap c_2, \phi)$ implies both $ist(c_1, \phi)$ and $ist(c_2, \phi)$.

Such property is exploited in a distributed ABox reasoning procedure based on an persistent TBox, called an ontology base. The ontology base is in charge of storing any ontology discovered on the Web of Data with the import relations between them. The ontology base also stores inference results that has been performed in order to reuse such computation later. More information about the implementation issues of such reasoning procedure can be found in [6].

6.4.4 Technical Overview

In Sindice, reasoning is performed for every entity description at indexing time. This is possible with the help of a distributed architecture based on Hadoop.[12] Each Hadoop node has its own ontology base which support the linked ontology and inference model described in the previous section. A single ontology base is shared across several Hadoop worker jobs. This architecture can be seen as a distributed ABox reasoning with a shared persistent TBox.

Each hadoop worker job acts as a reasoning agent processing a n entity description at a time. It first analyses the description in order to discover the explicit `owl:imports` declarations or the implicit ones by resolving each class and property URIs. Then, the reasoning agent lift the content of the referred ontologies inside

[11] We remark here that under the addition of possibly non-monotonic rules to the Semantic Web architecture, this context monotonicity only holds under certain circumstances [18].

[12] Hadoop: http://hadoop.apache.org/core/.

the RDF model by querying the ontology base with the URIs of the ontologies. The ontology base responds by providing the set of ontological assertions. As none of the triple-stores available today support context aware reasoning, our implementation required considerable low level modifications to the Aduna Sesame framework.[13]

6.4.5 Performance Overview

Using a three nodes Hadoop cluster on commodity server machines, we are able to process[14] an average of 40 documents per second when building the 50 million documents index currently available in the Sindice index.

The processing speed varies depending on the type of RDF model. On models with a simple and concise representation, such as the ones found in the Geonames' dataset, the prototype is able to process up to 80 entity descriptions per second. It is to be noticed however that these results come from a prototypical implementation, still to be subject to many possible technical optimizations.

It is interesting to make a few observation based on the large corpus of documents processed by Sindice. We observe that on a snapshoot of the index containing 6 million of documents, the original size of the corpus was 18 GB whereas the total size after inference was 46 GB, thus a ratio of 2.5. As a result of inference, we can then observe that in Sindice we are indexing twice as many statements as we would by just indexing explicit semantics. Also, we find that the number of ontologies, defined as documents which define new classes or properties, in our knowledge base is around 95.000, most of which are fragments coming from projects such as OpenCyc, Yago and DBpedia. The ratio of ontologies to semantic documents is nevertheless low, currently 1 to 335.

6.4.6 Discussion

Reasoning of the Web of Data enables the Sindice search engine to be more effective in term of precision and recall for Semantic Web information retrieval. As an example, it would not be possible to answer a query on FOAF social networking files asking for entities which have label "giovanni" unless reasoning is performed to infer `rdfs:labels` from the property `foaf:name`.

The context mechanism allows Sindice to avoid the deduction of undesirable assertions in RDF models, a common risk when working with the Web of Data. However, this context mechanism does not restrict the freedom of expression of data publisher. Data publisher are still allowed to reuse and extend ontologies in any manner, but the consequences of their modifications will be confined in their own

[13]OpenRDF Sesame: http://www.openrdf.org/.

[14]Including document pre-processing and post-processing (metadata extraction, indexing, etc.).

context, and will not alter the intended semantics of the other RDF models published on the Web.

6.5 Indexing: The SIREn Model

In developing the Semantic Information Retrieval Engine (SIREn), the goal has been to be able to index the entire "Web of Data". The requirements have therefore been:

1. Support for the multiple formats which are used on the Web of Data.
2. Support for entity centric search.
3. Support for context (provenance) of information: entity descriptions are given in the context of a website or dataset.
4. Support for semi-structural full text search, top-k query, scalability via shard over clusters of commodity machines, efficient caching strategy and real-time dynamic index maintenance.

With respect to point 1, the problem is solved as we normalize everything to RDF as previously explained. With respect to points 2 and 3, the main use case for which SIREn is developed is entity search: given a description of an entity, i.e., a star-shaped queries such as the one in Fig. 6.3(b), locate the most suitable entities and datasets. This means that, in terms of granularity, the search needs to move from "page" (as per normal web search) to a "dataset-entity". The Fig. 6.3(a) shows an RDF graph and how it can be split into three entities *renaud*, *giovanni* and *DERI*. Each entity description forms a subgraph containing the incoming and outgoing relations of the entity node.

6.5.1 SIREn Data Model

SIREn, similarly to XML information retrieval engine, adopts a tree data structure and orderings of tree nodes to model datasets, entities and their RDF descriptions. The data tree model is pictured in Fig. 6.4(a). This model has a hierarchical structure with four different kinds of nodes: context (dataset), subject (entity), predicate and object. Each node can refer to one or more terms. In case of RDF, a term is not necessarily a word (as in part of an RDF Literal), but can be an URI or a local blank node identifier.

Inverted indexes based on tree data structure enable to efficiently establish relationships between tree nodes. There are two main types of relations: *Parent-Child* and *Ancestor-Descendant*. To support these relations, the requirement is to assign unique identifiers (node labels) that encodes relationships between the tree nodes. Several node labelling schemes have been developed and the reader can refer to [19] for an overview of them. In the rest of the paper, we will use a simple prefix scheme, the *Dewey Order* encoding [3].

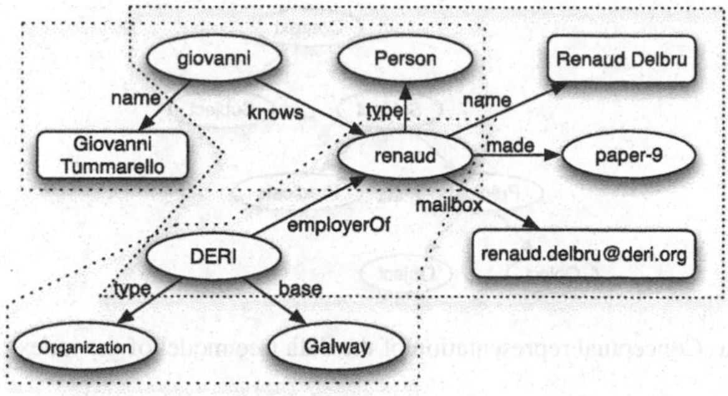

(a) Visual representation of an RDF graph. The RDF graph is divided (*dashed lines*) into three entities identified by the node *renaud*, *giovanni* and *DERI*

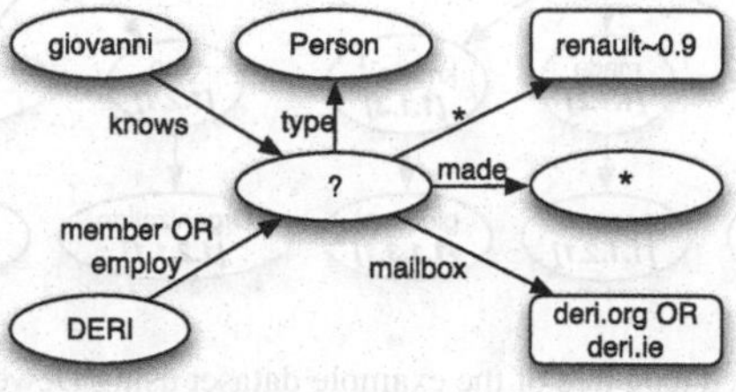

(b) Star-shaped query matching the entity *renaud* where *?* is the bound variable and ⋆ a wildcard

Fig. 6.3 In these graphs, oval nodes represent resources and rectangular ones represent literals. For space consideration, URIs have been replaced by their local names

Using this labelling scheme, structural relationships between elements can be determined efficiently. An element u is an ancestor of an element v if label(u) is a prefix of label(v). Figure 6.4(b) presents a data tree where nodes have been labelled using Dewey's encoding. Given the label $\langle 1.2.1.1 \rangle$ for the term `Organization`, we can efficiently find that its parent is the predicate `rdf:type`, labelled with $\langle 1.2.1 \rangle$.

The data tree structure covers the quad relations CSPO (outgoing relations) and COPS (incoming relations). Incoming relations are symbolized by a predicate node with a $^{-1}$ tag in Fig. 6.4(b). The tree data structure is not limited to quad relations, and could in theory be used to encode longer paths such as 2-hop outgoing and incoming relations.

In SIREn, the node labelled tree is embedded into an inverted list. Each term occurrence is stored with its node label, i.e., the path of elements from the root node (context) to the node (predicate or object) that contains the term. A detailed description of how this tree data structure is encoded in the inverted index is given in [7].

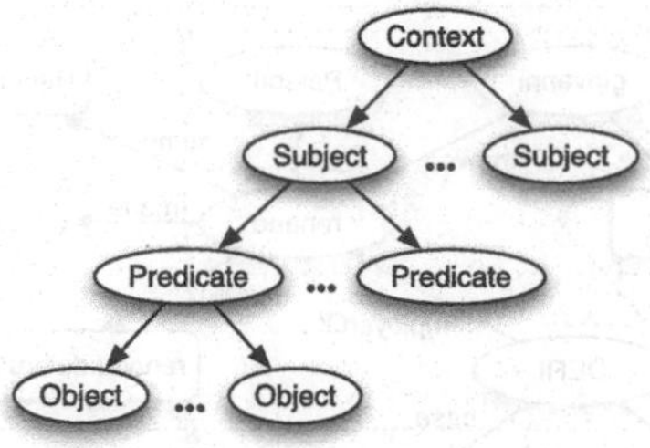

(a) Conceptual representation of the data tree model of the index

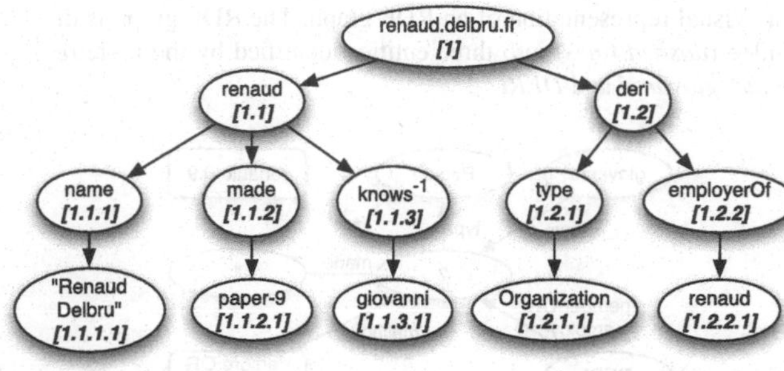

(b) Node-labelled data tree of the example dataset using Dewey's encoding

Fig. 6.4 The SIREn data model

6.5.2 SIREn Query Model

Since RDF is semi-structured data, we expect three types of queries: 1. full-text search (keyword based), 2. semi-structural queries (complex queries specified in a star-shaped structure), 3. or a combination of the two (where full-text search can be used on any part of the star-shaped query). We present in this section a set of query operators over the content and structure of the data tree that cover the three types of queries.

6.5.2.1 SIREn Operators

Content Operators The content query operators are the only ones that access the content of a node, and are orthogonal to the structure operators. They include extended boolean operations such as boolean operators (intersection, union, difference), proximity operators (phrase, near, before, after, etc.) and fuzzy or wildcard operators.

These operations allow to express complex keyword queries for each node of the tree. Interestingly, it is possible to apply these operators not only on literals, but also on URIs (subject, predicate and object), if URIs are normalized (i.e., tokenized). For

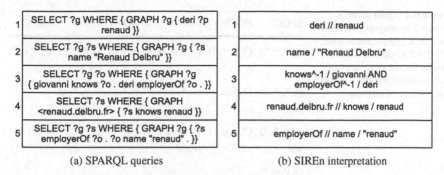

	(a) SPARQL queries		(b) SIREn interpretation
1	SELECT ?g WHERE { GRAPH ?g { deri ?p renaud }}	1	deri // renaud
2	SELECT ?g ?s WHERE { GRAPH ?g { ?s name "Renaud Delbru" }}	2	name / "Renaud Delbru"
3	SELECT ?g ?o WHERE { GRAPH ?g { giovanni knows ?o . deri employerOf ?o . }}	3	knows^-1 / giovanni AND employerOf^-1 / deri
4	SELECT ?s WHERE { GRAPH <renaud.delbru.fr> { ?s knows renaud }}	4	renaud.delbru.fr // knows / renaud
5	SELECT ?g ?s WHERE { GRAPH ?g { ?s employerOf ?o . ?o name "renaud" . }}	5	employerOf // name / "renaud"

(a) SPARQL queries (b) SIREn interpretation

Fig. 6.5 SPARQL queries and their SIREn interpretation

example, one could just use an RDF local name, e.g., `name`, to match `foaf:name` ignoring the namespace. Structure operators

In the following, we define a set of operations over the structure of the data tree. Thanks to these operations, we are able to search content to limited tree nodes, to query node relationships and to retrieve paths of nodes matching a given pattern. Joins over paths are possible using set operators, enabling the computation of entities and datasets matching a given star-shaped query.

Ancestor-Descendant: A//D A node A is the ancestor of a node D if it exists a path between A and D. For example, the SPARQL query, in Fig. 6.5(a) line 1, can be interpreted as an Ancestor-Descendant operator, as shown in Fig. 6.5(b) line 1, and will return the path ⟨1.2.2.1⟩.

Parent-Child: P/C A node P is the parent of a node C if P is an ancestor of C and C is exactly one level above P. For example, the SPARQL query, in Fig. 6.5(a) line 2, can be translated into a Parent-Child operator, as shown in Fig. 6.5(b) line 2, and will return the path ⟨1.1.1.1⟩.

Set manipulation operators These operators allow to manipulate nodes of the tree (context, subject, predicate and object) as sets, implementing union (∪), difference (\) and intersection (∩). For example, in Fig. 6.5(a) the SPARQL query, line 3, can be interpreted as two Parent-Child operators with the intersection operator (AND), as shown in Fig. 6.5(b) line 3.

In addition, operators can be nested to express longer path as shown in Fig. 6.5(a), line 4 and 5. However, the later query is possible only if deeper trees have been indexed, i.e., 2-hop outgoing and incoming relations of an entity.

6.5.2.2 SPARQL Interpretation

In this section, we discuss the extension by which, given the above discussed operators, it is possible to support a subset of the standard SPARQL query language.

By indexing outgoing relations alone, we can show to cover the quad access patterns listed in Table 6.1. A quad lookup is performed using the AC or PC operators. Join operations over these patterns are also feasible. Intersection, union and

Table 6.1 Quad patterns covered by outgoing relations and their interpretation with the SIREn operators. The *?* stands for the elements that are retrieved and the * stands for a wildcard element

SPOC	POCS	OCSP	CPSO	CSPO	OSPC
(?, *, *, ?)	(?, p, *, ?) *p*	(?, *, o, ?) *o*	(?, *, *, c) *c*	(s, *, *, c) *c/s*	(s, *, o, ?) *s//o*
(s, *, *, ?) *s*	(?, p, o, ?) *p/o*	(?, *, o, c) *c//o*	(?, p, *, c) *c//p*	(s, p, *, c) *c/s/p*	
(s, p, *, ?) *s/p*	(?, p, o, c) *c//p/o*	(s, *, o, c) *c/s//o*			
(s, p, o, ?) *s/p/o*					

difference between two or more quad patterns can be achieved efficiently using set manipulations over tree nodes.

The covered quad patterns are a subset of the quad patterns covered by conventional RDF data management systems [11]. In fact, they give the ability to retrieve information about variables that are restricted to be at the subject, object or context position.

It is important to underline, however, that we are restricting the search of an entity inside a dataset, i.e., SIREn does not allow the use of joins over different contexts, and the intersection of quad patterns within an entity, i.e., SIREn does not allow the use of chains of joins among multiples entities. This limits the query expressiveness to a star-shaped query, e.g., in Fig. 6.3(b).

6.5.3 Experimental Benchmark

We compared the performance of our approach to native quad and triple stores using two large datasets having different characteristics. We assess the space requirements, the performance of compression, the index creation time and the query evaluation speed.

Our first comparison system is the native store backend (based on b+-trees) of Sesame 2.0, a very popular open-source system which is commonly used as baseline for comparing quad store performances (e.g., in [16, 20]). The second system we compare against is the state-of-the-art triple store RDF-3X [16].

For our experiments, we used two datasets. The first one, called "Real-World" dataset has been obtained by random sampling the content of the Sindice.com semantic search engine. The real world dataset consists of 10M triples (approximately 2 Gb in size), and contains a balanced representation of triples coming from the Web of Data, e.g., from RDF and Microformats datasets published online. The second dataset is the MIT Barton dataset that consists of 50M triples (approximatively 6 Gb in size).

Table 6.2 Indexing time in minutes per dataset and system

	SIREn10	SIREn100	Sesame	RDF-3X
Barton	3	1.5	266	11
Real-World	1	0.5	47	3.6

The machine that served for the experiment was equipped with 8 GB ram, 2 quad core Intel processors running at 2.23 GHz, 7200 RPM SATA disks, Linux 2.6.24-19, Java Version 1.6.0.06 and GCC 4.2.4. The following benchmarks were performed with cold-cache by using the `/proc/sys/vm/drop_caches` interface to flush the kernel cache and by reloading the application after each query to bypass the application cache.

In Table 6.2, the index creation time for the two datasets is reported. For SIREn, we report two cases: SIREn10 is the time it takes to construct the index committing 10.000 triples at a time while SIREn100 is the time it takes when the batch is composed by 100.000 triples. Concerning RDF-3X, it is important to notice that it does not support context, therefore it indexes triples and not quads and does not support incremental indexing; RDF-3X needs the full dataset beforehand in order to construct the indexes in one batch process, as opposed to Sesame whose data structures support incremental updates. We can see from the results in Table 6.2 that SIREn is 50 to 100 times faster than Sesame and 3 to 6 times faster than RDF-3X.

In the next test, we plot the performance of SIREn and Sesame in an incremental update benchmark. The Fig. 6.6(a) shows the commit times for an incremental 10.000 triples batch on the two systems. As the time scales are greatly different, the graph is reported in Log scale. While the absolute time is significant, the most important result is the constant time exhibited by SIREn for incremental updates, as compared to the Sesame performance which progressively decreases as the index size increases.

We continue the test, with SIREn only, in Fig. 6.6(b), where the commit time is plotted for a synthetic dataset constructed by replicating Barton 20 times so to reach 1 billion triples. The total indexing creation time is 31 minutes. We can notice that SIREn keeps a constant update time during the entire indexing. Outliers are due to periodic merges of the index segments.

Finally, we evaluate SIREn scalability by indexing a dataset composed by 1 billion entities described in approximately 10 billion triples. The dataset is derived from the billion triple challenge dataset.[15] To avoid hitting the limit of 2 billion entities due to the current implementation, we remove entities which have only one or two triples of description and duplicate the remaining triples to reach 10 billion. The set of queries is provided at http://siren.sindice.com. The performance is given in the Table 6.3.

[15]Semantic Web Challenge: http://challenge.semanticweb.org/.

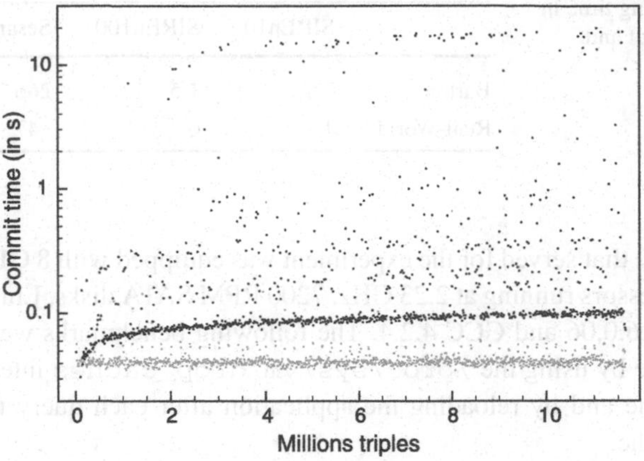

(a) Plots showing the commit time every 10.000 triples during the index creation on Real-World

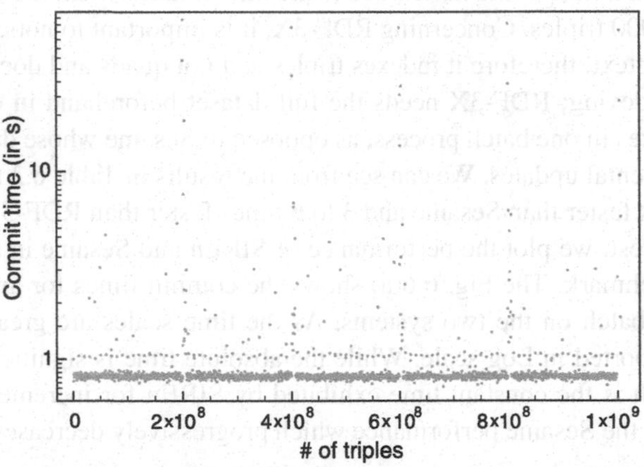

(b) Plots showing the commit time every 500.000 triples during the index creation on the billion triples dataset

Fig. 6.6 *Dark dots* are Sesame commit time records while *gray dots* are SIREn commit time records

Table 6.3 Querying time in seconds and number of hits for the 10 billion triples benchmark

	Q1	Q2	Q3	Q4	Q5	Q6	Q7	Q8
Time (s)	0.75	1.3	1.4	0.5	1.5	1.6	4	0.35
Hits	7552	9344	3.5M	57K	448	8.2M	20.7M	672

6.6 Ranking: The DING Model

Effective processing of top-k queries is a crucial requirement in an environment that involves such massive amount of data. End-users are more interested in the most relevant top-k query answers from the potentially huge answer space. One solution is based on link analysis algorithms for determining the "popularity" of a resource on the Web, and has become a central technique in web search. A static "popularity score" is computed for each resource, giving the possibility to rank and select the most relevant top-k results. As the Web of Data graph is becoming very large, containing over billions of nodes and edges, it is clear that link analysis algorithms for computing popularity score on web-scale graph is becoming an important requirement.

Current link analysis algorithms for the Web of Data generally work on a flat link graph of entities. In addition to their high computation complexity, they suffer from biased ranking since they do not take into consideration the structure of the Web of Data. Based on previous observations, we derive a two-layer model that both considers the hierarchical structure and the link structure, and propose a novel ranking algorithm called DING (for Dataset rankING). DING first aggregates entities into datasets before performing link analysis on the dataset graph. Then, for each dataset, a ranking is computed for the local entity collection. As a final step, the popularity of the dataset is propagated to its entities and combined with their local ranks in order to compute a global rank for each entity.

6.6.1 A Two-layer Model for Web Data

In this section, we introduce the two layer model for the Web of Data that is at the core of the DING algorithm. The two model layer is in fact the model pictured in Fig. 6.1, but without the view layer. The top layer (dataset layer) is composed of a collection of interconnected datasets whereas the lower layer (entity layer) is composed of independent graphs of entities. We first define the graph model on which DING performed link analysis. The graph model is a subset of the one defined in Sect. 6.1.1. We finally present the two types of links that are used in the two-layer model.

In this section, we see the Web of Data as a set of datasets $\mathcal{D}$. A dataset $D_i \in \mathcal{D}$ is a named graph where nodes are strictly URIs, i.e., where each statement (s, p, o, c) is an element of U^4. We discard deliberately all the other statements, i.e., the ones containing a blank node or a literal, since they are not of interest for DING. In addition, all nonauthoritative statements are discarded.

A statement is interpreted as a link between two entities. We consider two types of links. The "intra-dataset" links are links from one authoritative entity to another authoritative entity in a same dataset. The "inter-dataset" links are links from one authoritative entity to an nonauthoritative entity. While the later type of links indicates a link between two resources, we interpret this as a link from a dataset D_i named c_i to a dataset D_j named c_j. Furthermore, inter-links are aggregated into *linksets*. A linkset $L_{i \to j}$ is defined as a subset of D_i and contains the links from D_i to D_j.

Intra-dataset links form a local graph of entities while inter-dataset links form a global graph of datasets. We derive from this final observation the two-layer model for the Web of Data, shown in Fig. 6.1 where the top layer (dataset layer) is a collection of interconnected datasets and the lower layer (entity layer) is composed of independent local graphs of entities.

6.6.2 DING Algorithm

The DING algorithm is an adaptation of the PageRank's random surfer to the two-layer graph structure presented in the previous section. Instead of visiting web pages, the random surfer now browses datasets. The random walk model is as follows:

1. At the beginning of each browsing session, a user randomly selects a dataset node.
2. Then the user may choose one of the following actions:
   a. Selecting randomly an entity in the current dataset.
   b. Jumping to another datasets that is linked by the current dataset.
   c. Ending the browsing.

According to this hierarchical random walk model, we can apply a two-stage computation. In the first stage, we calculate the importance of the dataset nodes which is explained next. The second stage calculates the importance of entities inside a dataset. We argue that local entity ranking is strongly dependent of the nature (graph structure) of the dataset. The datasets on the web of data may come in a variety of graph structures, such as generic graphs coming from user input, hierarchical graphs, pattern-based graphs like citation datasets, etc. An approach which takes into account the peculiar properties of each dataset could give better results. We explain in Sect. 6.6.3 how to combine the importance of datasets and entities.

The dataset surfing behaviour is the same as the page surfing behavior in PageRank. We can obtain the importance of the dataset nodes by applying a PageRank algorithm on the dataset-level weighted graph.

The rank score $r(D_i)$ of a dataset is composed of a part $\sum_{j \in O(i)} r(D_j) p_{j \to i}$ corresponding to the votes from the datasets linking to D_i and of a part corresponding to the probability pr_i of a random jump to D_i from any dataset in the collection. The probability pr_i is defined as:

$$pr_i = \frac{n(D_i)}{\sum_{D_j \in D} n(D_j)} \tag{6.1}$$

Although the algorithm only examines the dataset level of browsing, we still assume that the browsing is done on a URI level. As a consequence, the probability pr_i of selecting a dataset during a random jump is proportional to its size, $n(D_i)$. Similarly, the probability $p_{j \to i}$ of following a linkset from D_j to D_i is proportional to the size of the linkset $L_{j \to i}$. The final DING rank formula is given below. As in PageRank, the two parts are combined using the teleportation factor α. We set α the recommended [17] value of 0.85, since we found that this value provides also good results for the DING use case.

$$r(D_i) = (1-\alpha)pr_i + \alpha \sum_j r(D_j) p_{j \to i} \tag{6.2}$$

A method used in layered ranking algorithms is to assign to the page the importance of the supernode [8]. In our case, this would correspond to assign the DING rank of the dataset to all its entities. In large datasets, such as DBPedia, this approach does not hold. Any query is likely to return many entities having the same importance from one dataset. This unnecessarily pushes part of the ranking problem to query-time. Instead, we should assign a score combining both the importance of a dataset and the importance of an entity within its dataset.

6.6.3 Combining DING and Entity Rank

The combination of dataset and local entity ranks is a key part of the DING approach to ranking. One is to adopt a purely probabilistic point of view, interpreting the dataset rank score as the probability of selecting the dataset and the local rank score as the probability of selecting an entity in the dataset. Hence, we would have the global score of the entity e from dataset D defined as

$$r(e) = P(e \cap D) = P(e) * P(D) \tag{6.3}$$

This approach has however one practical issue, it favors smaller datasets. Indeed, their local ranking scores will be much higher than the ones in larger datasets, since in the probabilistic model all scores in a dataset sum to 1. As a consequence any small dataset receiving even a single link from a larger one will likely have its top entities score way above many of the ones from the larger dataset, and opens a spamming possibility. One solution is to normalize, based on the dataset size, the local ranks to a same *average*. In our experiments, we used the following formula for ranking an entity e in a dataset D:

$$r(e) = P(D) * P(e) * \frac{n(D)}{\sum_{D' \in \mathcal{D}} n(D')}$$

where $n(D)$ is the size of the dataset D in terms of entities and $\mathcal{D}$ the set of datasets.

6.7 Leveraging Sindice in SIGMA

In this section, we present Sig.ma, an application, with a matching developer API, that leverages the Sindice Semantic Web index as well as other services to automatically integrate and make use of information coming from multiple web sources.

Sig.ma, which can be tried online at http://sig.ma, can be used for multiple purposes:

Browsing the Web of Data starting from a textual search, the user is presented with a rich aggregate of information about the entity likely identified with the query. Links can be followed to get more aggregate pages, thus effectively navigating the Web of Data as a whole.

Live views on the Web of Data integrated data views have persistent URLs and can be embedded in HTML pages using a concise JS tag. These views are "Live" new data will appear on these views exclusively coming from the sources that the mashup creator has selected at creation time.

Property search for multiple entities A user, but more interestingly an application, can make a request to Sig.ma for a list of properties and a list of entities. For example requesting "affiliation, picture, email, telephone number, [...] @ Giovanni Tummarello, Michele Catasta [...]" Sig.ma will do its best to find the specified properties and return an array (raw JSON or in a rendered page) with the requested values.

6.7.1 Sig.ma: Processing Dataflow and Interaction with Sindice

Sig.ma revolves around the creation of *Entity Profiles*. An entity profile—which in the Sig.ma dataflow is represented by the "data cache" storage (Fig. 6.7)—is a

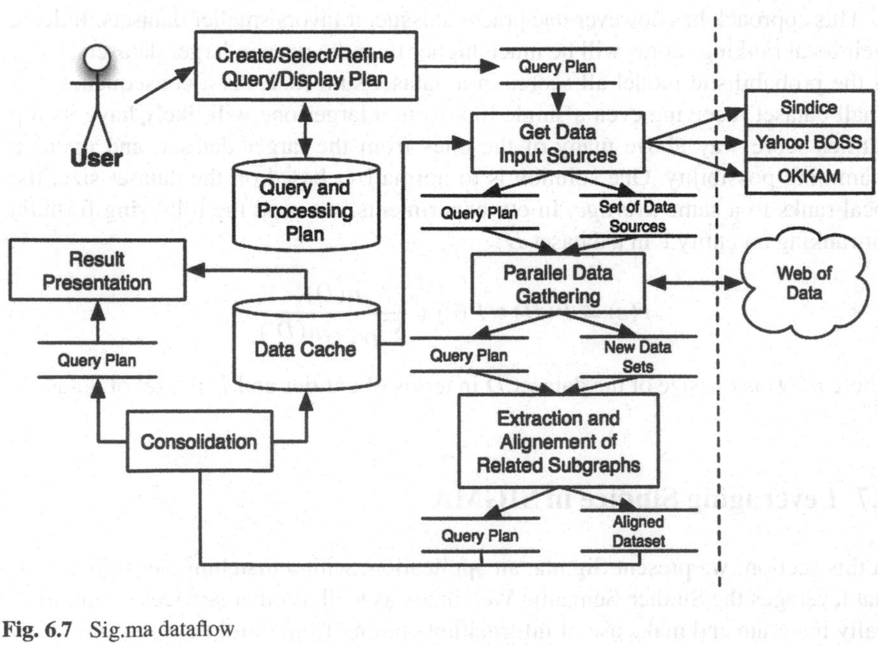

Fig. 6.7 Sig.ma dataflow

summary of an entity that is presented to the user in a visual interface, or which can be returned by the API as a rich JSON object or a RDF document. Entity profiles usually include information that is aggregated from more than one source. The basic structure of an entity profile is a set of key-value pairs that describe the entity. Entity profiles often refer to other entities, for example the profile of a person might refer to their publications.

A *data source*, in our terminology, is a view, e.g., a document that contains semi-structured data, or a complete entity description. The role of Sindice in Sigma is to retrieve data sources using a combination of keywords and structured queries. The process of creating an entity profile involves the following main steps, which are described in detail later in this section:

Creation of the Sig.ma query plan: The keyword and structured queries provided by the user form the initial "Query Plan" in Sig.ma.

Data Sources Selection: The query plan is sent to Sindice and possibly other services which returns a list of related data sources.

Parallel Data Gathering: All the candidate data sources are retrieved from the Sindice internal data repository or fetched from the Web if necessary.

Extraction and Alignment of Entity Descriptions: The RDF sources are broken down into entity descriptions when necessary. Then, the set of sources is expanded based on `owl:sameAs` links and inverse functional properties found in the descriptions.

Consolidation: All the descriptions are then merged into a single entity profile, by means of various heuristics.

Result Presentation: The result is presented to the user through a Web user interface, or to a machine through a JSON object or RDF model.

Source List Refinement: After the entity profile is presented to the user, it can be refined by modifying the sources list. This final step generates a closed loop in the Sig.ma dataflow, which actually represent an "expansion-refinement" loop which is driven by the user input.

6.7.1.1 Creation of a Sig.ma Query Plan

The process of creating a Sig.ma query plan takes three inputs, each of which is optional:

1. A keyword search phrase
2. A number of source URLs
3. A number of resource identifiers (URIs)

The difference between the last two items is that a source URL names a document, which is accessible on the Web, and might contain descriptions of any number of entities. A resource identifier names a specific entity, but may or may not be resolvable to a web document.

The initial user interface shown to a Sig.ma user presents an input box that allows entry of either a search phrase, or a single resource identifier. Other combinations of inputs are accessed through hyperlinks either from within Sig.ma or from a permalink.

6.7.1.2 Data Sources Selection

The first challenge is to identify a set of initial sources that describe the entity sought for by the user. This is performed via textual or URI search on the Sindice index and yields a top-k source list, ranked thanks to DING, and are added to the input source URL set.

Next, a search for each resource identifier is performed in the Sindice index. As we have seen, the Sindice index does not only allow search for keywords, but also for URIs mentioned in documents or entity descriptions. This allows us to find data sources that mention a certain identifier, and thus are likely to contribute useful structured information to the description of the entity named by the identifier. Likewise, in later phases, the Sindice semantic query language is used in multiple occasions to find more sources based on star-shaped queries, classes and more either alone or in combination with textual queries.

Now, we have a list of sources that potentially describe the entity signified by the user query. The list is naturally ranked: sources directly specified in the input come first, and the other sources are ranked as returned by the Sindice index. Also sources that come from less structured queries, i.e., full text queries in Sindice, are ranked lower than those coming from more potentially accurate semantic queries, e.g. queries for inverse functional properties. Results coming from other search engines, e.g., the Yahoo! BOSS API,[16] are also processed by extracting the structured content from the pages returned from the service.

If the source list is long, it is trimmed. The desired length is still subject to experimentation, but 25 sources seems to be a good compromise between response time and data variety and it is still manageable in the user interface. The user interface has then a control for requesting more resources, which repeats the process with a higher source cutoff limit.

6.7.1.3 Extraction and Alignment of Related Subgraphs

The RDF model extracted from each data source can be either a complete entity description or a view, e.g., a document with one or more partial entity descriptions. In the latter case, we proceed by dividing it into entity descriptions when necessary.

As an example of a decomposition into entity descriptions, consider the case of a typical FOAF[17] file that describes a person. It will be decomposed into one entity description for the file's owner, one small description for each of their friends listed

[16] http://developer.yahoo.com/search/boss/.

[17] http://www.foaf-project.org/.

in the profile, and possibly one description for the FOAF document itself, containing statements about its `foaf:maker` and `foaf:primaryTopic`.

Each description will be matched and scored against the keyword phrase, considering both RDF literals and URIs. This helps to pick out the correct resource in cases such as FOAF files, which talk about multiple people, but it is easy to select the right one given a name. Entity descriptions below a certain threshold are removed from consideration.

We now have a ranked list of descriptions, coming from different sources, that are believed to describe the same entity. Of course, since fuzzy keyword matching is used in several places in the process, the result can contain false positives.

If the number of highly-scoring resource descriptions is low at this point, then an attempt is made to discover additional sources, based on the RDF data we have already retrieved and established to likely describe the target entity. We obtain new resource identifiers for the target entity using four methods:

1. If the selected entity descriptions are centred on a URI, then this URI is considered.
2. If the entity descriptions include any `owl:sameAs` links, then the target URIs are considered.
3. If the entity descriptions include any OWL inverse functional properties (IFPs) from a hardcoded list (e.g., `foaf:mbox` and `foaf:homepage`), then a Sindice index search for other resources having the same IFP value is performed—resources having the same value for an IFP are considered equivalent under OWL inference rules.
4. By means of a query to the OKKAM service. OKKAM is an experimental service which assigns names to entities on the web [1]. OKKAM returns resource identifiers along with a confidence value. Any resource identifiers whose confidence value exceed a certain threshold are added to the set of input resource identifiers. We observe that currently the number of entities that are reliably recognized by the OKKAM service is still low, as not many OKKAM ids can be found out in the web, so this step will often not produce a result. In the case where it returns results however, it is a high-quality identifier that is likely to contribute relevant results to the next steps.

Any resource identifier discovered using these methods will be added into the *Query Plan*, which will be then examined in the *refinement* step.

6.7.1.4 Consolidation

All selected resource descriptions are merged into a single entity profile. This simply means that all key-value pairs from all resource descriptions are combined into a single description. A reference to the original source is kept for each value.

Several techniques are employed, both empirical and following the ontology description as well as best practices and heuristics to extract property names. Next, we apply a manually-compiled list of approximately 50 preferred terms. For example, we replace all of the following property names with the preferred term "web page": work info homepage, workplace homepage, page, school homepage, weblog, website, public home page, url, web.

After consolidation, properties are ranked. We use a simple ranking metric: the frequency of the property, i.e., the number of sources that mentions the property. This will push generic properties such as "label" and "type" to the top. The cardinality of a property, i.e., the number of distinct values for the property, is also factored in: properties where many sources agree on one or a few values (as observable e.g., with a person's name or homepage) receive a boost.

Value Labelling, Consolidation and Source List Refinement For key-value pairs where the value is not a literal value (such as a name or a date), but a reference to another resource (usually by URI), a best-effort attempt is made to retrieve a good label for the resource using methods such as fetching the remote RDF resource and looking for properties, such as `foaf:name` or `dc:title` or `rdfs:label` or treating the URI as a text and cleaning it accordingly.

If a property has several values with identical or very similar labels, then they are collapsed into one value to improve the visual presentation. For example, several sources that describe a scientist can state that they have authored a certain paper, using different identifiers for the paper. Without label-based consolidation, the paper would appear several times because the identifiers are not the same. After label consolidation, it appears only once. Both identifiers are retained internally. A click on the paper link will cause a new Sig.ma search that has the label and both of the URIs as input. Since labels are retrieved and displayed incrementally, the value consolidation has to be performed in the same fashion.

After the entity profile is presented to the user, e.g., see as an example Fig. 6.8, the result can be refined by adding or removing sources. Almost any entity profile initially includes some poor sources that add noise to the results. The user can however correct the results. For example, if the profile shows a poor label or unrelated depiction for the entity, a click will remove the offending source, and the next-best label or depiction will automatically take its place if present. Confirming sources has also an important role. When the user asks for more data sources, priority is specific semantic queries for the URIs or other properties specified in the explicitly confirmed sources.

6.8 Conclusion

In this chapter, we presented a model for the Web of Data and then illustrated how this is reflected in the building blocks of Sindice, an infrastructure for large scale processing of Semantic Data.

The structure of a Semantic search engine is still to be consolidated in literature, so in developing Sindice we explored several trade offs.

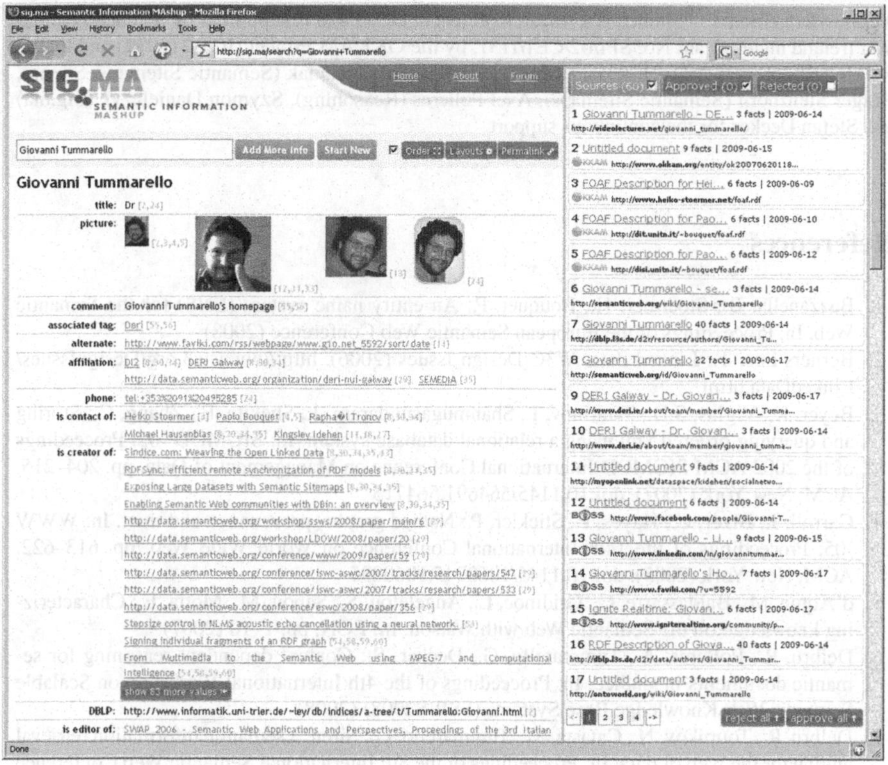

Fig. 6.8 Screenshot of Sig.ma for Giovanni Tummarello

For example, with respect to DBMS and IR systems, SIREn positions itself somewhere in the middle as it allows semi-structural queries while retaining many desirable IR features: single inverted index, effective caching, top-k queries and efficient index distribution over shards.

In SIREn, the tradeoff is query complexity vs. scalability. It might be arguable that an indexing approach that limits itself to relatively simple queries, as opposed to the full SPARQL expressiveness for example, can still be sufficient to solve interesting use cases and enabling useful applications.

Similarly, the reasoning model that we propose seems to offer useful inference capabilities for Web published RDF data but is currently limited to the expressiveness of RDFS plus certain OWL Lite rules.

Developing credible Semantic Web applications on top of these functionalities is probably the only way to prove that the above choices have been satisfactory.

To do so, and also as an inspiration for others, we explored ourself the actual usefulness of the APIs by building demonstrators. One such project, Sig.ma, seems to indicate that in fact simple semantic queries and services, when driven by an appropriate logic, can already bring interesting and useful results.

Acknowledgements Sindice is a research project at DERI and is supported by Science Foundation Ireland under Grant No. SFI/02/CE1/I131, by the OKKAM Project (ICT-215032) and by the ROMULUS project (ICT-217031). Thanks go to Richard Cyganiak (Semantic Sitemaps, Sigma), Holger Stenzhorn (Semantic Sitemaps), Axel Polleres (Reasoning), Szymon Danielczyk (Sig.ma) and Stefan Decker for the continuous support.

References

1. Bazzanella, B., Stoermer, H., Bouquet, P.: An entity name system (ENS) for the Semantic Web. In: Proceedings of the European Semantic Web Conference (2008)
2. Berners-Lee, T.: Linked data. W3C Design Issues (2006). http://www.w3.org/DesignIssues/LinkedData.html
3. Beyer, K., Viglas, S.D., Tatarinov, I., Shanmugasundaram, J., Shekita, E., Zhang, C.: Storing and querying ordered xml using a relational database system. In: SIGMOD '02: Proceedings of the 2002 ACM SIGMOD International Conference on Management of Data, pp. 204–215. ACM, New York (2002). doi:10.1145/564691.564715
4. Carroll, J., Bizer, C., Hayes, P., Stickler, P.: Named graphs, provenance and trust. In: WWW '05: Proceedings of the 14th International Conference on World Wide Web, pp. 613–622. ACM, New York (2005). doi:10.1145/1060745.1060835
5. d'Aquin, M., Baldassarre, C., Gridinoc, L., Angeletou, S., Sabou, M., Motta, E.: Characterizing knowledge on the Semantic Web with Watson. In: EON, pp. 1–10 (2007)
6. Delbru, R., Polleres, A., Tummarello, G., Decker, S.: Context dependent reasoning for semantic documents in sindice. In: Proceedings of the 4th International Workshop on Scalable Semantic Web Knowledge Base Systems (SSWS2008) (2008)
7. Delbru, R., Toupikov, N., Catasta, M., Tummarello, G.: Siren: a semantic information retrieval engine for the web of data. In: Proceedings of the 8th International Semantic Web Conference (ISWC 2009) (2009)
8. Eiron, N., McCurley, K.S., Tomlin, J.A.: Ranking the web frontier. In: WWW '04: Proceedings of the 13th International Conference on World Wide Web, pp. 309–318. ACM, New York (2004). doi:10.1145/988672.988714
9. Guha, R.V.: Contexts: a formalization and some applications. Ph.D. Thesis, Stanford, CA, USA (1992)
10. Guha, R.V., McCool, R., Fikes, R.: Contexts for the Semantic Web. In: International Semantic Web Conference, pp. 32–46 (2004)
11. Harth, A., Decker, S.: Optimized index structures for querying rdf from the web. In: LA-WEB, pp. 71–80 (2005)
12. Hayes, P.: RDF Semantics. W3C Recommendation, World Wide Web Consortium (2004)
13. ter Horst, H.J.: Completeness, decidability and complexity of entailment for RDF Schema and a semantic extension involving the OWL vocabulary. J. Web Semant. 3(2–3), 79–115 (2005)
14. Mayfield, J., Finin, T.: Information retrieval on the Semantic Web: Integrating inference and retrieval. In: Proceedings of the SIGIR Workshop on the Semantic Web (2003)
15. Miles, A., Baker, T., Swick, R.: Best Practice Recipes for Publishing RDF Vocabularies. Tech. Rep. (2006). http://www.w3.org/TR/swbp-vocab-pub/
16. Neumann, T., Weikum, G.: RDF-3X—a RISC-style engine for RDF. In: Proceedings of the VLDB Endowment, vol. 1(1), pp. 647–659 (2008). doi:10.1145/1453856.1453927
17. Page, L., Brin, S., Motwani, R., Winograd, T.: The pagerank citation ranking: Bringing order to the web. Technical Report 1999-66, Stanford InfoLab (1999)
18. Polleres, A., Feier, C., Harth, A.: Rules with contextually scoped negation. In: 3rd European Semantic Web Conference (ESWC2006). LNCS, vol. 4011. Springer, Berlin (2006). http://www.polleres.net/publications/poll-etal-2006b.pdf

19. Su-Cheng, H., Chien-Sing, L.: Node labeling schemes in XML query optimization: a survey and trends. IETE Tech. Rev. **26**(2), 88 (2009). doi:10.4103/0256-4602.49086
20. Zhang, L., Liu, Q., Zhang, J., Wang, H., Pan, Y., Yu, Y.: Semplore: an IR approach to scalable hybrid query of Semantic Web data. In: Proceedings of the 6th International Semantic Web Conference and 2nd Asian Semantic Web Conference. Lecture Notes in Computer Science, vol. 4825, pp. 652–665. Springer, Berlin (2007)

Part II
Reasoning in the Semantic Web

Chapter 7
Reasoning in Semantic Web-based Systems

Florian Fischer and Gulay Unel

Abstract In this chapter, we introduce the basics of formal languages and reasoning in a Web context. Denoting information by means of a logical formalism makes it possible to employ established techniques from the field of automated reasoning. However, reasoning in the context of Web-based systems has a distinct set of requirements in terms of *quality* and *quantity* of the information it has to cope with. In turn, this chapter focuses, in a very foundational way, on reasoning on Semantic Web-oriented data. For this purpose, we briefly identify and describe the basic paradigms forming the background for knowledge representation in Web-based Systems. We then examine how these paradigms are reflected in current standards and trends on the Web and what kinds of reasoning they typically facilitate. Based on this, we proceed to focus on concrete reasoning techniques and their particular properties, including optimizations and various other possibilities, e.g., parallelization and approximation, to meet the scalability requirements in Web-based systems.

7.1 Introduction

Web data grows faster than the capacity of Web-based systems that perform computation on this data. This growth also results in additional requirements for systems to go beyond keyword searches, use of document connectivity and usage patterns. Consider the following question:

Example 7.1 Find the names of the institutions who are involved in Semantic Web research via joint papers in related conferences.

An interpretation of additional data, i.e., metadata, that describes the contents of accessible resources is required to answer questions such as that given in Example 7.1. For this example, the relevant aspects of the natural language content of a document must be described through metadata.

The Semantic Web standardization activity of the World Wide Web Consortium (W3C) aims to design the basic technical standards that allow the representation of

F. Fischer (✉) · G. Unel
STI Innsbruck, University of Innsbruck, Innsbruck, Austria
e-mail: florian.fischer@sti2.at

G. Unel
e-mail: gulay.unel@sti2.at

R. De Virgilio et al. (eds.), *Semantic Web Information Management*,
DOI 10.1007/978-3-642-04329-1_7, © Springer-Verlag Berlin Heidelberg 2010

metadata on the Web, which in turn enables applications to derive answers to questions similar to Example 7.1. These standards can be seen as cornerstones for the development of future large-scale Semantic Web applications that primarily focus on two main aspects: machine readability and machine interpretability [45].

Machine readability requires the definition of a framework for the description of resources on the Web, i.e., the Resource Description Framework(RDF) [22]. RDF can be understood as a semi-structured data model for metadata on the Web. A knowledge-base of Web data typically contains metadata from a collection of information sources, e.g., several Web pages where these information sources are described using the RDF data model.

Machine interpretability is another key aspect for answering questions similar to Example 7.1 on a Web knowledge-base. For instance information, consumers and providers need to agree on the denotation of a common vocabulary, i.e., for Example 7.1, proper nouns such as "Semantic Web", concepts such as "institution" and "conference" as well as the relations such as "involved", must be represented in a structured way to make the evaluation of such queries possible. Web ontology languages allow for the description of this vocabulary by means of logical axioms. Ontology languages, including the RDF vocabulary description language (RDFS) [17], Web Ontology Language (OWL) [26], and the Web Service Modeling Language (WSML) [46], have been standardized for this purpose and are grounded on the assignment of formal semantics to their language constructs. This allows machines to interpret information such that new implicit facts can be derived from asserted facts using a form of symbolic processing, i.e., logical entailment.

In this chapter, we introduce the basics of formal languages and reasoning in a Web context. In Sect. 7.2, we formally introduce the relevant background in particular fundamentals of Logic Programming and Description Logics. Section 7.3 introduces some of the relevant standards for the Semantic Web, namely OWL 2 and WSML. Section 7.4 introduces the most common reasoning techniques that are used for the underlying paradigms introduced in Sect. 7.2. Section 7.5 examines the strategies for scalable reasoning in the context of the Web. Finally, conclusions and future research directions are given in Sect. 7.6.

7.2 Background

This section focuses on the underlying paradigms at a high-level. The content here is not specific to a concrete language.

7.2.1 Logic Programming

This subsection introduces Logic Programming [23] as a knowledge representation paradigm and especially focuses on the different ways to define its semantics.

Efficient query answering, evaluation procedures and relevant reasoning tasks are considered in Sect. 7.4.

The most basic variant of Logic Programming is based on *definite* logic programs and on Horn Logic [18], where logical statements (clauses) in propositional or first order logic are formed as a disjunction of literals with at most one positive literal. Thus, a basic logic program is defined by a finite number of definite Horn clauses such as:

$$\neg B_1 \vee \cdots \vee \neg B_m \vee H$$

A Horn clause with exactly one positive atom is called a definite clause. Horn Clauses are interesting for two reasons:

1. They permit efficient automated reasoning, because the resolution [33] of two Horn Clauses is another Horn Clause.
2. A Horn Clause can be rewritten to be naturally interpreted as a rule of the form: if (something) then (something else).

Such a rule can naturally be written as following:

$$H \leftarrow B_1, \ldots, B_m$$

where $H, B_1, \ldots, B_m$ are positive atoms. H is called the *head* of the rule, while $B_1, \ldots, B_m$ make up the *body*. When a statement has this rule form, it can be seen that to make the statement true when $B_1, \ldots, B_m$ are true, requires that H is also true. In other words, if $B_1, \ldots, B_m$ then H. This allows us to state knowledge (1) as known facts by omitting the body of a rule, and (2) formulate rules that tell us how to derive new knowledge. Furthermore, it is possible to compose queries such as:

$$? \leftarrow B_1, \ldots, B_n$$

where $B_1, \ldots, B_n$ denote positive atoms. Thus, queries are simply Horn clauses with no positive literals.

$$\neg B_1 \vee \cdots \vee \neg B_m$$

Logic Programming environments typically offer several proprietary constructs with built-in semantics, which can be ignored for our purposes. This leads to the presentation offered here, which is a purely declarative one that basically interprets logic programs as a finite set of horn formulae.

Several possibilities to define the semantics of Logic Programs exist, among them model theoretic and fixed-point based approaches. Concrete evaluation methods can be regarded as definitions of the semantics of Logic Programs.

Apart from different methodological differences when defining the semantics of Logic Programs, there also exist specific possibilities regarding the interpretation of specific language constructs, most notably negation. Definite programs give rise to nonmonotonic semantics when extended with negation and/or disjunction.

The motivation to include negation in logic problems is roughly the same as in non-monotonic logics in general, that is to express "default" statements that hold unless special conditions hold, i.e.,

$$H \leftarrow B, \text{ not } C$$

where C denotes some unexpected condition. Thus, definite logic programs are extended to *normal logic programs* by introducing negation:

$$H \leftarrow B_1, \ldots, B_m, \text{ not } C_1, \ldots, \text{ not } C_n$$

This increases the expressive power and convenience of modeling in a specific Logic Programming variant.

A fundamentally more expressive (and more complex) extension of the Logic Programming paradigm is Disjunctive Logic Programming, which also allows disjunctions in the head of a rule. Disjunctive Datalog [41] has applications in Description Logic reasoning [19]. In particular, this approach covers a large subset of OWL DL and shows very favorable performance results in regard to large instance sets, see Sect. 7.4.1.

7.2.2 Description Logics

Description Logics (DLs) are a family of modal logics used in knowledge representation. Research in the area of DLs began under the label *terminological systems*, later the name *concept languages* was used to emphasize the set of concept-forming constructs in the language. In recent years, the term *Description Logics* became popular due to the importance given to the properties of the underlying logical systems. The reason for the success of DLs is that they combine theory and practice to build knowledge representation systems.

The basic notions of DLs are concepts (unary predicates) and roles (binary predicates). Complex concepts and roles are formed from atomic ones using a variety of concept and role constructors (see Table 7.1).[1]

It is useful to think of a DL knowledge-base as consisting of two parts called the *TBox* and the *ABox*. The *TBox* contains a set of terminological axioms, which define subsumption and equivalence relations on concepts and roles. The *ABox* contains a set of assertional axioms that state facts about concrete individuals and the relations of individuals with each other.

The semantics of Description Logics is usually given using a Tarski style model theoretic approach. The interpretations are defined as $\mathfrak{I} = (\Delta^{\mathfrak{I}}, \cdot^{\mathfrak{I}})$ where the non-empty set $\Delta^{\mathfrak{I}}$ is the domain of the interpretation, and $\cdot^{\mathfrak{I}}$ is an interpretation function that assigns a set $A^{\mathfrak{I}} \subseteq \Delta^{\mathfrak{I}}$ to every atomic concept A and a binary relation $R^{\mathfrak{I}} \subseteq \Delta^{\mathfrak{I}} \times \Delta^{\mathfrak{I}}$ to every atomic role R. The interpretation function is extended to concept and role constructors inductively, i.e., as given in the Semantics column

[1] This table captures the DL dialects relevant to this chapter.

Table 7.1 DL concept and role constructors

Syntax	Semantics	Symbol
A	$A^{\mathfrak{I}}$	$\mathcal{AL}(\mathcal{S})$
$\top$	$\Delta^{\mathfrak{I}}$	$\mathcal{AL}(\mathcal{S})$
$\bot$	$\emptyset$	$\mathcal{AL}(\mathcal{S})$
$\neg A$	$\Delta^{\mathfrak{I}} \setminus A^{\mathfrak{I}}$	$\mathcal{AL}(\mathcal{S})$
$C \sqcap D$	$C^{\mathfrak{I}} \cap D^{\mathfrak{I}}$	$\mathcal{AL}(\mathcal{S})$
$\forall R.C$	$\{a \in \Delta^{\mathfrak{I}} \mid \forall b((a,b) \in R^{\mathfrak{I}} \rightarrow b \in C^{\mathfrak{I}})\}$	$\mathcal{AL}(\mathcal{S})$
$\exists R.\top$	$\{a \in \Delta^{\mathfrak{I}} \mid \exists b((a,b) \in R^{\mathfrak{I}})\}$	$\mathcal{AL}(\mathcal{S})$
$\neg C$	$\Delta^{\mathfrak{I}} \setminus C^{\mathfrak{I}}$	$\mathcal{C}(\mathcal{S})$
$C \sqcup D$	$C^{\mathfrak{I}} \cup D^{\mathfrak{I}}$	$\mathcal{U}(\mathcal{S})$
$\exists R.C$	$\{a \in \Delta^{\mathfrak{I}} \mid \exists b((a,b) \in R^{\mathfrak{I}} \wedge b \in C^{\mathfrak{I}})\}$	$\mathcal{E}(\mathcal{S})$
R^+	$\bigcup_{n>1}(R^{\mathfrak{I}})^n$	$\mathcal{R}^+(\mathcal{S})$
$\{i_1,\ldots,i_n\}$	$\{i_1^{\mathfrak{I}},\ldots,i_n^{\mathfrak{I}}\}$	$\mathcal{O}$
R^-	$\{(b,a) \in \Delta^{\mathfrak{I}} \times \Delta^{\mathfrak{I}} \mid (a,b) \in R^{\mathfrak{I}}\}$	$\mathcal{I}$
$\geq [\leq] nR$	$\{a \in \Delta^{\mathfrak{I}} \mid \lvert\{b \in \Delta^{\mathfrak{I}} \mid (a,b) \in R^{\mathfrak{I}}\}\rvert \geq [\leq] n\}$	$\mathcal{N}$

of Table 7.1). The semantics of assertions is given by extending the interpretation function such that it maps each individual a to an element $a \in \Delta^{\mathfrak{I}}$. The semantics of terminological axioms are defined via set relationships.

The basic inference on concept expressions in a DL is *subsumption*, which can be written as $C \sqsubseteq D$. Determining subsumption is the problem of checking whether a concept is more general than another concept. Another inference on concept expressions is concept *satisfiability*, which is the problem of checking whether a concept expression denotes the empty concept or not. Actually, concept satisfiability is a special case of subsumption, where the subsumer is the empty concept.

7.3 Standards on the Semantic Web

In this section, we provide an overview of relevant standards for knowledge representation on the Semantic Web and relate these to relevant knowledge representation paradigms.

7.3.1 OWL 2

OWL 2 [29] extends OWL with several new features that include extra syntactic sugar, property and qualified cardinality constructors, extended data-type support, punning as a simple form of meta-modeling, and a different method for handling annotations (they have no semantic meaning anymore).

OWL 2 DL is an extensions of OWL-DL and corresponds to the Description Logic $\mathcal{SROIQ}$. However, OWL 2 is not given a semantics by mapping to $\mathcal{SROIQ}$ (because punning is not available), but rather directly on the constructs of the functional-style syntax for OWL 2. Similar to OWL, OWL 2 also has several variants (called *profiles*): OWL 2 Full (which is again an extension of the RDFS semantics), OWL 2 DL, OWL 2 EL, OWL 2 QL, and OWL 2 RL, of which we briefly describe the last three and give the motivation to include them.

OWL 2 EL, which is based on $\mathcal{EL}++$ (see [2] and [1]) is a fragment that is tractable in regard to several key inference tasks such as consistency checking, subsumption, instance checking or classification—they can be decided in polynomial time. On the other hand it is still expressive enough to adequately model many real world problems.

OWL 2 QL is based on DL-Lite [7] (which is actually not a single language fragment but rather a family of languages with several slight variations) and tailored for reasoning over large instance sets combined with a relatively inexpressive TBox. More specifically, many important reasoning tasks can be performed in logarithmic space with respect to the size of the ABox. The OWL 2 QL profile picks up from OWL DL-Lite$_R$ and supports property inclusion axioms. A notable feature that goes hand in hand with DL-Lite's complexity results, is that since query answering over knowledge bases has polynomial time data complexity and since it is possible to separate TBox and ABox reasoning for the evaluation of a query, it is therefore possible to delegate the ABox reasoning to a standard SQL database engine, and thus OWL 2 QL also allows for very efficient query answering for large instance sets. As such, OWL 2 QL is optimized for data complexity.

The OWL 2 RL profile is a fragment that is customized to support reasoning with rule-based engines by only considering objects that are explicitly named in the knowledge base. It is a profile that is intended to form a proper extension of RDFS while still being computationally tractable. As such, it realizes a weakened form of the OWL 2 Full semantics and is very similar in spirit to DLP [16] and pD* entailment [39].

7.3.2 WSML

The Web Service Modeling Language WSML [46] is a concrete formal language based on the conceptual model of WSMO [13]. WSML is a formal language for semantically describing various elements of a service-oriented architecture.

The semantic foundation of any description in WSML is the *ontology language* part of WSML, which is used for describing terminology. WSML captures the two knowledge representation paradigms of Description Logics and Logic Programming, introduced in Sect. 7.2. For this purpose WSML comprises several different *variants*, from which the user can choose the most suitable one for the particular domain. These variants are structured as following: WSML-Core is based on DLP [16], at the common intersection of Description Logics and Logic Programming. WSML-Flight and WSML-Rule are the language variants that form an extension in the Logic

Programming direction, with WSML-Flight based on F-Logic [21] and Datalog with inequality and (locally) stratified negation [32]. WSML-Rule extends WSML-Flight with well-founded negation, function symbols and allows unsafe rules. WSML-DL covers the Description Logics paradigm, and is based on the DL $\mathcal{SHIQ}(\mathbf{D})$. Finally, WSML-Full has the semantics of the union of all other language variants.

7.4 Reasoning Techniques

In this section, we introduce the most common reasoning techniques that are used for the underlying paradigms introduced in Sect. 7.2. For this purpose, we rather focus on general and well known approaches instead of very specific optimizations in individual systems.

7.4.1 Description Logic Paradigm

In this section, we describe tableaux methods and translation to rule based systems, which are both common evaluation methods for reasoning with Description Logics.

7.4.1.1 Tableaux Methods

Tableaux methods are one of the most common approaches for implementing both sound and complete reasoning for Description Logics and have been essentially adopted from classical First-Order Logic.

Tableaux algorithms try to prove the satisfiability of a concept D by constructing a model, using an interpretation I in which D^I is not empty. A tableau is a graph that represents such a model, with nodes corresponding to individuals and edges corresponding to relationships between individuals.

A typical algorithm will start with a single individual satisfying D and tries to construct a tableaux, or some structure from which a tableau can be constructed, by inferring the existence of additional individuals or of additional constraints on individuals. The inference mechanism consists of applying a set of expansion rules that correspond to the logical constructs of the language and the algorithm terminates either when the structure is complete (no further inferences are possible) or obvious contradictions have been revealed.

For example, disjunctive concepts give rise to nondeterministic expansions, which are in practice usually dealt with by search, i.e., by trying every possible expansion until (i) a fully expanded and (ii) class free tree is found, or until all possibilities have been shown to arrive at a contradiction. Searching nondeterministic expansions is the main cause of intractability in tableaux subsumption testing algorithms, because they typically make it hard to implement efficient indexing for large data-sets.

Fig. 7.1 Tableaux example

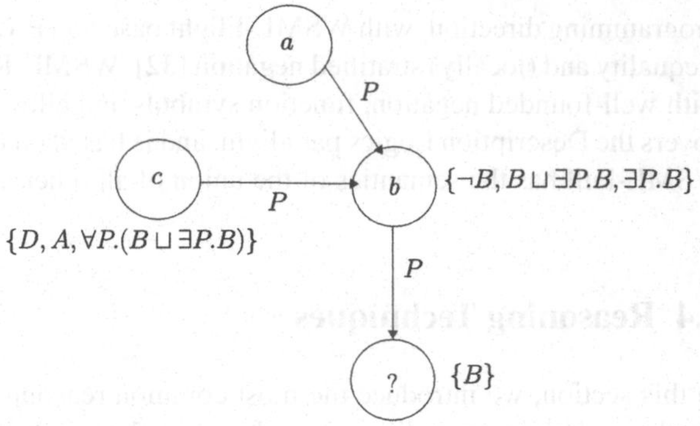

Consequently, naive implementations of tableaux algorithms typically do not result in practically scalable systems. However, a wealth of optimization techniques exist, which accounts for the efficiency of the algorithm in typical cases rather than rare, worst-case scenarios.

Example 7.2 Consider the knowledge base: $\{a\ P\ b,\ c\ P\ b,\ b : \neg B,\ c : D,\ D \equiv A \sqcap \forall P.(B \sqcup \exists P.B)\}$. A tableaux execution trying to construct a concrete example (model) consistent with these KB axioms is shown in Fig. 7.1, which starts from ground facts (ABox axioms) and then explicates the structure implied by complex concepts and TBox axioms.

Pellet Pellet[2] is a reasoner that can be integrated in to semantically-enabled applications for sound and complete reasoning with knowledge represented using OWL-DL.

OWL 2 is a forthcoming revision of the international web standard produced by the W3C for web-friendly ontologies. Pellet currently supports most of the features proposed in OWL 2 including support for OWL 2 profiles such as OWL 2 EL. Pellet can be used as a reasoner for WSML-Core and WSML-DL as it supports the $\mathcal{SHOIQ}$ Description Logic. It also supports XML data types and incorporates various optimization techniques, including novel optimizations for nominals, conjunctive query answering and incremental reasoning.

Pellet is implemented in Java and is available under dual licensing terms (GNU Affero General Public License for open source applications and an alternative license for proprietary applications). Pellet provides various interfaces including a command line interface, an interactive Web form for zero-install use, DIG server implementation and API bindings for RDF/OWL toolkits Jena and Manchester OWL-API.

[2]http://clarkparsia.com/pellet/.

7.4.1.2 Translation to Rule Based Systems

Another approach for reasoning with Description Logics is by applying deductive database techniques along with a translation step that encodes the Description Logic knowledge base into a suitable rule-based formalism. This is motivated by the fact that while optimized tableaux-based systems are very efficient for computing the subsumption hierarchy for a knowledge base, and perform better than their exponential worst-case complexity in most practical cases, efficient reasoning with very large ABoxes is of increasing importance in many applications, including the Semantic Web.

In these applications, one of the main reasoning tasks is query answering over a large set of ground facts. For a tableaux algorithm, this is equivalent to performing a series of consistency checks, since individuals are treated separately. On the other hand, deductive database techniques usually excel at query answering and a wide range of possible optimizations are available.

An example for this approach is [20], which translates $\mathcal{SHIQ}$ knowledge bases to disjunctive Datalog [12]. This reduction does not rely on common features of rule-based formalisms, such as negation-as-failure or minimal model semantics, but rather preserves the original semantics of the $\mathcal{SHIQ}$ knowledge base. However, it still makes use of readily available optimization techniques such as Magic-Sets (see Sect. 7.4.2). Moreover, the fact that a disjunctive database system operates on a set of individuals, rather then considering them one-by-one, makes it possible to employ join-order optimizations according to gathered statistics that estimate the required work.

KAON2 KAON2[3] is a hybrid reasoner that is able to reason with a large subset of OWL DL, corresponding to the Description Logic $\mathcal{SHIQ}(\mathcal{D})$, and Disjunctive Datalog with stratified negation. It has a basic set of built-in predicates and support for integer and string data-types. KAON2 can also be used for reasoning in WSML-Core, WSML-Flight and WSML-DL albeit restricted to the above data-types. The theoretical work underlying KAON2 can be found in [28].

The major advantage of KAON2 is that it is a very efficient reasoner when it comes to reasoning with Description Logics ontologies containing very large ABoxes and small TBoxes.

KAON2 is implemented in Java, owned by the company Ontoprise and is available 'free for use' in noncommercial settings.

7.4.2 Rule Paradigm

A knowledge base consists of ground statements and rules, otherwise known as the extensional database (EDB) and intensional database (IDB), respectively. A statement is entailed by the knowledge base if it exists in the EDB or can be derived

[3] http://kaon2.semanticweb.org/.

from the EDB using the IDB. Reasoning with a knowledge base essentially involves query answering using a logical expression containing between 0 and n variables.

A straightforward reasoning technique involves computing all of the inferences up front before processing any queries. The most naive approach is to apply all of the rules to the ground statements to infer new ground statements and to repeat this process until no new statements are inferred. Such a process is called forward chaining or 'bottom-up'.

A more sophisticated approach is to start with the query and work backwards, finding rules and statements that might be involved in inferring statements that satisfy the query. Such a process is called backward chaining or 'top-down' to reflect the fact that the reasoning process starts with what is required and works backwards (or downwards). This can be a complex process since rules can be singularly (or mutually) recursive and special care must be taken to avoid entering an infinite loop.

7.4.2.1 Bottom-up Techniques

In a model theoretic view, the EDB and IDB define possible models where each model assigns a truth or false value to every possible statement. In logic programming, it is usual to define this model by its set of true statements. To be a model of a set of rules and interpretation must make the rules true for every possible assignment of values from the domain to the variables in each rule [42]. A minimal model of a knowledge-base is that model where not a single true statement can be removed without making the model inconsistent with the rules. Except for certain situations where negation is involved, all rule-sets have a unique minimal model.

One common technique for reasoning with knowledge-bases is based on the computation of the minimal model. This approach can use a variety of methods for executing rules to infer new true statements and adding these statements to the model. When no more new statements can be inferred, then the process has reached a fixed-point and the algorithm terminates. For example, given the knowledge-base:

$$t(X) \leftarrow p(X)$$

$$p(X) \leftarrow q(X)$$

$$q(2)$$

$$p(3)$$

Applying the rules to the set of true statements will initially infer the new statements:

$$t(3)$$
$$p(2)$$

A subsequent application of the rules infers:

$$t(2)$$

And further application of the rules does not infer any new statement that was not previously known, so the algorithm terminates with the minimal model:

$$q(2), p(2), p(3), t(2), t(3)$$

7.4.2.2 Magic-sets Evaluation

While the naive fixed-point computation can be implemented directly, efficient query evaluation engines use more involved techniques such as semi-naive [42] evaluation, goal/join ordering, etc. In addition, whenever the query is known as part of the input, techniques that allow constructing only the relevant parts of the minimal model have been developed. Among these the most prominent is the magic sets [4, 30] rule-rewriting optimization followed by subsequent fixed-point evaluation.

The idea here is that constants in the query can be used to limit the generated minimal model to only those statements that can be used to answer the query.

Example 7.3 Consider the following rules and query [43]:

$$sg(X, X) \leftarrow person(X)$$

$$sg(X, Y) \leftarrow par(X, X_p), sg(X_p, Y_p), par(Y, Y_p)$$
$$? \leftarrow sg(a, W)$$

The Magic-Sets algorithm can re-write these rules to:

$$m\_sg(a)$$

$$m\_sg(X_p) \leftarrow sup(X, X_p)$$
$$sup(X, X_p) \leftarrow m\_sg(X), par(X, X_p)$$

$$sg(X, X) \leftarrow m\_sg(X), person(X)$$
$$sg(X, Y) \leftarrow sup(X, X_p), sg(X_p, Y_p), par(Y, Y_p)$$

The presence of the magic 'seed' $m\_sg(a)$ has the effect of limiting the amount of statements considered for each rule evaluation and so reduces the minimal model down to those statements that can be used to answer the query $sg(a, W)$.

IRIS IRIS[4] (Integrated Rule Inference System) is an extensible rule-based reasoning engine that supports safe or un-safe Datalog (locally) stratified or well-founded 'negation as failure', function symbols, has a comprehensive and extensible set of built-in predicates, and support for all the primitive XML schema data

[4]http://www.iris-reasoner.org/.

types. Reasoning algorithms include bottom-up strategies based on semi-naive rule-evaluation and magic sets, as well as top-down strategies such as SLD, SLDNF and OLDT.

With a suitable translation layer, IRIS can be used for reasoning with OWL 2 profiles RL and EL, as well as WSML-Core, WSML-Flight and WSML-Rule.

IRIS is implemented in Java and is available under the GNU Lesser-GPL license.

7.4.2.3 Top-down (SLD) Resolution with Memoing: SLG

Top-down approaches naturally focus attention on relevant facts. Hence, they avoid, to the maximum extent possible, the production of states that do not need to be searched. The basic top-down evaluation procedure is SLD resolution (Linear resolution with Selection function for Definite programs) [44], which views a program clause as a procedure declaration, and each literal in the body of the clause as a procedure call. The most serious drawback of this approach is that it is not guaranteed to terminate for logic-programming oriented recursive languages. In addition to this, SLD has a tendency to re-derive the same fact. An alternative way is a top-down evaluation with a memoing strategy called SLG resolution (Linear resolution with Selection function for General logic programs) [8, 9, 34], which extends SLD resolution by adding tabling to make evaluations finite and nonredundant, and by adding a scheduling strategy to treat negation efficiently. The idea behind memoing is to maintain a table of procedure calls and the values to return during execution. If the same call is made later in the execution, use the saved answer to update the current state. There are efficient scheduling strategies implemented for tabled logic programs:

- Batched Scheduling: provides space and time reduction over the naive strategy that is called single stack scheduling.
- Local Scheduling: provides speedups for programs that require answer subsumption.

The procedural control in SLD resolution handles parameter passing by matching an atom with the head of a rule and applying the match to every atom in the entire stack. There are several other extensions of SLD resolution. OLD[5] is an incremental version that handles the passing of parameters into and out of procedures explicitly—called refutation. The reason for this representation is to make the procedure calls and returns explicit, so that they can be used for memoing. The OLDT strategy adds memoing to OLD refutation.

It can be shown that the bottom-up technique using magic sets and the top-down approach of SLD Resolution with Memoing (SLG) simulate each other where the magic predicates match the memoing data structures (modulo open terms). For a detailed description of the above techniques, see [4, 30] and [8, 9, 34].

[5] The letters of the name come from *Ordered selection strategy with Linear resolution for Definite clauses*.

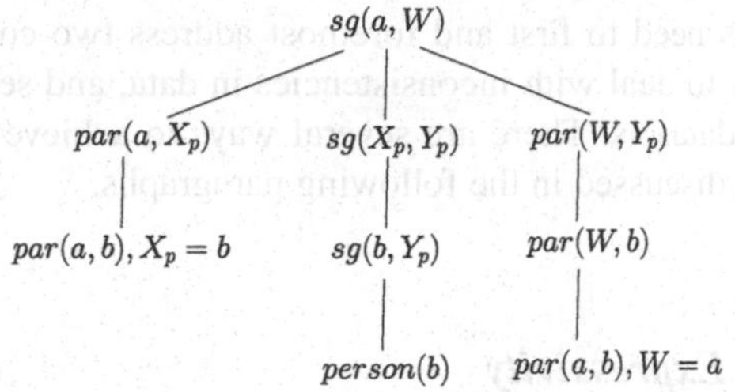

Fig. 7.2 A top-down derivation tree for $sg(a, W)$

Example 7.4 Consider the program and the query given in Example 7.3 and the following fact base:

$$person(a)$$

$$person(b)$$

$$par(a, b)$$

A top-down derivation tree for the query is given in Fig. 7.2.

XSB XSB[6] is a Logic Programming and Deductive Database system with support for different kinds of negation such as stratified negation and negation under the well-founded semantics. The developers of XSB regard it as beyond Prolog because of the availability of SLG resolution and the introduction of HiLog terms.

As a rule-based reasoner XSB can be used for OWL 2 RL reasoning. In terms of the Web service modeling languages, XSB is a suitable reasoner for WSML-Core, WSML-Flight and WSML-Rule.

XSB is available for UNIX and Windows systems, and it is openly distributed under a GNU Lesser-GPL license. XSB also offers interfaces for several programming languages, such as C, Java, Perl, ODBC, SModels and Oracle. These interfaces allow for easy integration of custom built-in predicates.

7.5 Reasoning on the Web

Traditional reasoning operates on well engineered knowledge bases, which are typically confined to one specific domain. These knowledge bases can be assumed to be consistent (often this is even a design goal), of moderate size, and use a well defined vocabulary of a certain expressivity that is required to adequately model the domain under consideration.

In the context of the Web, many of these assumptions do not hold anymore. Datasets are huge and of widely varying quality. Inconsistent and incomplete information can be expected. In order to meet these special requirements, reasoning

[6]http://xsb.sourceforge.org/.

systems need to first and foremost address two concerns: They need to be robust enough to deal with inconsistencies in data, and secondly they need to be scalable to big datasets. There are several ways to achieve this required scalability, which will be discussed in the following paragraphs.

7.5.1 Expressivity

Much research is geared to advancing very expressive formalisms that add increasingly complex modelling constructs. However, this increase in language expressivity is often intrinsically linked to higher computational cost and often leads to formalisms that have high theoretical complexity and that are difficult to implement efficiently. However, the initial sets of standards for knowledge representation on the Web, e.g., OWL [27], are very expressive, and therefore have very high worst-case complexity results for key inference problems (usually ExpTime or higher).

This trade-off between complexity of reasoning and language expressivity has already been outlined in [5]. This jump from a tractable to an effectively intractable language, often called the "computational cliff" usually happens in very distinct steps caused by specific combinations of modelling primitives.

A reduced level of expressivity is often sufficient for many practical scenarios and crucially, absolutely necessary when reasoning with such massive datasets. These requirements have been acknowledged by active research towards more lightweight formalisms and also by industrial implementations that often implement only tractable subsets of existing standards, i.e., they perform total materialization based a subset of OWL. Examples for this are OWLIM,[7] Oracle 11g[8] or AllegroGraph RDFStore.[9]

The theoretical background of a reduced OWL fragment is outlined in [40] and forms the foundation of work on a reduced knowledge representation language called $L2$ within the European project LarKC.[10] $L2$ is defined in terms of entailment rules (essentially Horn rules), which operate directly on RDF triples, similar to [40], but restricts language expressivity even further. The restrictions placed on the language allow for checking the decidability of ground entailment in polynomial time, while still retaining useful expressivity. There have been several approaches aimed at achieving the same result, both in theory and in implementations.

In particular, [38] elaborates on the possible time and space tradeoffs in RDF schema. The authors essentially discuss the implications of materialization of parts of the deductive closure of an RDF graph, which reduces the complexity of query answering, but increases the space requirements as well as maintenance overhead,

---

7 http://www.ontotext.com/owlim/index.html.

8 http://www.oracle.com/technology/tech/semantic_technologies/index.html.

9 http://agraph.franz.com/allegrograph/.

10 http://www.larkc.eu.

e.g., in the case of updates. The paper describes experiments that identify certain modelling primitives that are the major source of this increase and in turn presents a technique that, based on the findings in the evaluation, computes only special parts of the deductive closure in order to avoid exactly these primitives. The purpose of this is to balance query time versus the space requirements of inference.

These results are directly applicable for reasoner implementations of $L2$ and are directly reflected in the design of the language by the fact that a lot of type related inferences are already suppressed due to the exclusion of axiomatic triples. Moreover, [31] presents an in-depth theoretical discussion of the issues presented above, with the main focus on the complexity of entailment in various fragments of RDFS. In particular, a lightweight version of RDFS is presented with favorable complexity properties as well, and further underlines the theoretical feasibility of such an approach.

As already discussed, reducing expressivity to improve scalability is an ongoing research activity leading to more lightweight knowledge representation methods. One such application area is the area of Semantic Web Services, where WSML [6] is used as a modeling language, in order to automate tasks such as location and composition. WSML is actually a family of language variants, based on different logical formalisms. This is because Description Logics alone are not sufficient to describe Web services in many scenarios and the additional expressivity of rules (in the Logic Programming sense) is often needed in order to adequately model services.

Motivated by work on $L2$ and in other standardization bodies, a revised version of WSML (version 2.0) has been produced with the main goal of improving scalability and tractability of the complete language stack, and for improving compatibility with emerging standards. Furthermore, this work has made it possible for all the language variants to be implemented on rule engines (thus, allowing the reuse of deductive database optimizations).

WSML 2.0 consists of several different language variants. These language variants reflect specific application areas and in turn also have different properties concerning scalability, which is one of the main focus points of WSML 2.0. This allows users of the language to decide on (i) the level of expressivity and thus also on (ii) the associated complexity, as well as (iii) the style of modelling.

Figure 7.3 depicts the different variants of WSML 2.0 and their relationships. The variants differ in (i) their expressiveness as well as (ii) in their underlying paradigm. The motivation is to allow an informed choice for a specific application, based on the trade-off between modeling power and scalability.

As can be seen, WSML-Quark and WSML-Core 2.0 form a common, lightweight, yet increasingly expressive foundation for extensions towards the paradigms of both Description Logics (in the form of WSML-DL 2.0) and Logic Programming (in the form of WSML-Flight 2.0 and WSML-Rule 2.0). Consequently, WSML-DL 2.0 and WSML-Flight/Rule 2.0 are both layered on WSML-Core 2.0, which defines a common subset. WSML-Core 2.0 is in turn layered upon WSML-Quark, which is the least expressive variant of all allowing the definition of concept hierarchies suitable for simple classification systems.

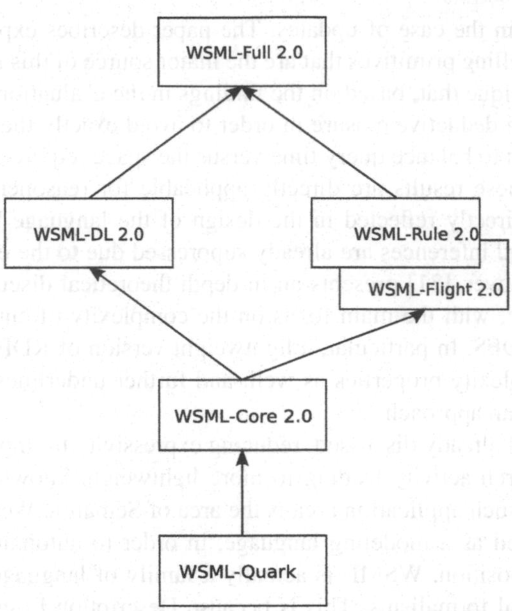

Fig. 7.3 WSML language layering

7.5.2 Approximate Reasoning

In this section, we aim to give a brief overview of various techniques for approximate reasoning *in general*. A more extensive survey can be found in [15] and this is based on a classification of techniques originally given in [14].

There are several possibilities where approximation can be introduced into the inference process. In general, it is possible to approximate:

- The reasoning method itself
- A request (a query)
- The knowledge base used

In [14], this separation is used for classifying the approximation method. These basic possibilities can be broken down as follows.

Approximation of the Reasoning Method In [35], Schaerf and Cadoli define two approximations of classical propositional entailment, named $\vdash_1$ and $\vdash_3$ which are either unsound and complete ($\vdash_1$) or sound and incomplete ($\vdash_3$). Both of these approximations are parameterised over a set of predicate letters S (written $\vdash_1^S$ and $\vdash_3^S$). This set S determines the accuracy of the approximate entailment relations. The idea is that predicate letters in S are given classical truth assignments, while for letters outside S all literals are false. These nonstandard truth-assignments result in nonstandard entailment relations. With increasing S, these are closer approximations of the classical entailment.

In [10] and [11], Dalal and Yang define the family of approximate deduction relations BCP_k, which are variants of Boolean Constraint Propagation (BCP). BCP [25] is a limited form of deduction that is a variant of unit resolution, which performs limited deduction in linear time, at the price of incompleteness. Given a theory T, BCP monotonically expands T by adding literals as follows: in each step, if any single clause in T and all the literals in T taken together entail any other literal (or true), then this literal (or false) is added to the theory T. Allowing BCP to chain on arbitrary clauses would make it sound and complete and would therefore render it uninteresting as an approximate deduction method. This is the motivation for defining BCP_k [10], where chaining is allowed, but only on formulae of limited length: when k increases, BCP_k is allowed to chain on ever more formulae, and will become ever more complete (notice that for $k = 1$, BCP_k reduces to BCP).

Approximation of the Request The most obvious example of approximating the request is query-relaxation. In [37], Stuckenschmidt proposes a query-relaxation method based on the assumption that less complex queries can be answered in shorter time. Following this idea, they propose to compute a sequence of queries $Q_1, \ldots, Q_n$ starting with very simple ones and gradually increasing their complexity. In order to use these simpler queries as approximations for the original query, the quality of the results of the sequence of queries must be nondecreasing.

An alternative approach is formed by so-called "top-k query algorithms" (e.g., [3]). Such algorithms do not change the query, but rather limit the number of answers returned on the original query to k answers, with k increasing in size over time. In other words, the original query Q is changed to a series of queries $Q(k)$, where k limits the size of the answer set. The assumption in this case is that a smaller answer set is cheaper to compute than a larger one.

Approximation of the Knowledge Base Knowledge compilation is the area that deals with translating the knowledge base such that the computational complexity of reasoning decreases. The underlying idea of knowledge compilation is that a knowledge base does not change much over time. The goal of knowledge compilation is to translate the knowledge into (or approximate it by) another knowledge base with better computational properties. This "compiled" knowledge base can be reused to solve many problem instances, thereby saving time and computational resources when compared to solving the problem instances with the original knowledge base. Two classical approaches have been developed for addressing the computational hardness of reasoning problems, which are language restriction and theory approximation. Both can be classified as approximating the knowledge base.

We may restrict the language used to represent knowledge, so that knowledge is compiled into the restricted language. An example of language restriction is the method developed in [36], where a knowledge base is approximated by a set of Horn formulae in order to bound a set of models of the original theory. Another example is the already presented approach in [19], where expressive Description Logic theories are reduced to less expressive but efficiently executable Disjunctive Datalog Programs.

Using theory approximation, one can compile the theory into another "easier" theory (although still expressed in the same language). During the compilation, one can give up the soundness or the completeness in the answer to the original reasoning problem. An example of theory approximation is using an exact knowledge compilation method that can be turned into an approximate method by stopping it before it is completed, because the compilation method is an anytime algorithm. Examples are methods for computing prime implicants and prime implicates like [24]. Another example is the approach of Instance Store, where a retrieval engine is proposed that is sound and complete for role-free A-boxes in Description Logics. In other words: the theory is approximated by removing all roles from the A-box.

7.6 Conclusion

In this chapter, we outlined the different paradigms forming the basis for knowledge representation and reasoning in Web-based Systems. For this purpose, we introduced the logical foundations of Logic Programming and Description Logics, which form a basis for the Semantic Web standards for knowledge representation such as RDF(S), OWL and WSML. In the last section, we focused on the reasoning techniques applicable to the Semantic Web that are based on Logic Programming and Description Logics. Semantic Web standards and reasoning techniques are still evolving and will provide further representations and reasoning techniques in the future.

References

1. Baader, F., Brandt, S., Lutz, C.: Pushing the EL envelope. In: International Joint Conference on Artificial Intelligence, vol. 19, p. 364 (2005)
2. Baader, F., Brandt, S., Lutz, C.: Pushing the EL envelope further. In: Proceedings of the OWLED Workshop (2008)
3. Balke, W.T., Nejdl, W., Siberski, W., Thaden, U.: Progressive distributed top-k retrieval in peer-to-peer networks. In: 21st International Conference on Data Engineering (ICDE'05), pp. 174–185. IEEE Computer Society, Los Alamitos (2005)
4. Beeri, C., Ramakrishnan, R.: On the power of magic. J. Log. Program. **10**(1/2/3&4), 255–299 (1991)
5. Brachman, R., Levesque, H.: The tractability of subsumption in frame-based description languages. In: Proc. of the 4th Nat. Conf. on Artificial Intelligence (AAAI-84), pp. 34–37 (1984)
6. Bruijn, J.D., Heymans, S.: A semantic framework for language layering in WSML. In: Proceedings of the First International Conference on Web Reasoning and Rule Systems (RR2007), Innsbruck, Austria, pp. 103–117. Springer, Berlin (2007)
7. Calvanese, D., De Giacomo, G., Lembo, D., Lenzerini, M., Rosati, R.: DL-Lite: tractable description logics for ontologies. In: Proceedings of the National Conference on Artificial Intelligence, vol. 20(2), p. 602 (2005)
8. Chen, W., Warren, D.: Query evaluation under the well-founded semantics. In: PODS, pp. 168–179 (1993)
9. Chen, W., Swift, T., Warren, D.S.: Efficient implementation of general logical queries. Technical Report, SUNY at Stony Brook (1993)
10. Dalal, M.: Semantics of an anytime family of reasoners. In: Wahlster, W. (ed.) Proceedings of ECAI-96, Budapest, Hungary, pp. 360–364. Wiley, New York (1996)

11. Dalal, M., Yang, L.: Tractable reasoning in knowledge representation systems (1997)
12. Eiter, T., Gottlob, G., Mannila, H.: Disjunctive datalog. ACM Trans. Database Syst. (TODS) **22**(3), 364–418 (1997)
13. Fensel, D., Lausen, H., Polleres, A., Bruijn, J.D., Stollberg, M., Roman, D., Domingue, J.: Enabling Semantic Web Services—The Web Service Modeling Ontology. Springer, Berlin (2006)
14. Groot, P.: A theoretical and empirical analysis of approximation in symbolic problem solving. Ph.D. Thesis, SIKS, Vrije Universiteit, Amsterdam (2003)
15. Groot, P., Hitzler, P., Horrocks, I., Motik, B., Pan, J.Z., Stuckenschmidt, H., Turi, D.: HolgerWache: Methods for approximate reasoning. Technical Report D2.1.2 (2004)
16. Grosof, B., Horrocks, I., Volz, R., Decker, S.: Description Logic Programs: Combining Logic Programs with Description Logic (2003)
17. Hayes, P., McBride, B.: RDF semantics. In: W3C Recommendation, vol. 10 (2004)
18. Horn, A.: On sentences which are true of direct unions of algebras. J. Symb. Log. **16**, 14–21 (1951)
19. Hustadt, U., Motik, B., Sattler, U.: Reducing shiq-description logic to disjunctive datalog programs. In: Proc. KR, pp. 152–162 (2004)
20. Hustadt, U., Motik, B., Sattler, U.: Reducing SHIQ-description logic to disjunctive datalog programs. In: Proc. KR, pp. 152–162 (2004)
21. Kifer, M., Lausen, G., Wu, J.: Logical foundations of object-oriented and frame-based languages. JACM **42**(4), 741–843 (1995)
22. Lassila, O., Swick, R.: Resource description framework (rdf) model and syntax specification. w3c working draft. Internet: http://www.w3.org/tr/rec-rdf-syntax/ (1999)
23. Lloyd, J.: Foundations of Logic Programming. Springer, New York (1987)
24. Marquis, P.: Knowledge compilation using theory prime implicates. In: IJCAI, pp. 837–845 (1995)
25. McAllester, D.A.: Truth maintenance. In: AAAI, pp. 1109–1116 (1990)
26. McGuinness, D.L., van Harmelen, F.: Owl web ontology language overview. technical report,world wide web consortium (w3c). Internet: http://www.w3.org/tr/owl-features/ (2003)
27. McGuinness, D., van Harmelen, F., et al.: OWL web ontology language overview. In: W3C Recommendation, vol. 10, pp. 2004–03 (2004)
28. Motik, B.: Reasoning in description logics using resolution and deductive databases. Ph.D. Thesis, Universitt Karlsruhe (TH), Karlsruhe, Germany (2006)
29. Motik, B., Horrocks, I.: OWL 2 Web Ontology Language. W3C Working Draft, W3C (2008)
30. Mumick, I.S.: Query optimization in deductive and relational databases. Ph.D. Thesis, Department of Computer Science, Stanford University (1991)
31. Munoz, S., Perez, J., Gutierrez, C.: Minimal deductive systems for RDF. Lect. Notes Comput. Sci. **4519**, 53 (2007)
32. Przymusinski, T.C.: On the declarative and procedural semantics of logic programs. J. Autom. Reason. **5**(2), 167–205 (1989)
33. Robinson, J.A.: A machine-oriented logic based on the resolution principle. J. ACM **12**(1), 23–41 (1965)
34. Sagonas, K.F., Swift, T., Warren, D.S.: XSB as an efficient deductive database engine. In: SIGMOD Conference, pp. 442–453 (1994)
35. Schaerf, M., Cadoli, M.: Tractable reasoning via approximation. Artif. Intell. **74**(2), 249–310 (1995)
36. Selman, B., Kautz, H.: Knowledge compilation using horn approximations. In: Proceedings of AAAI-91, pp. 904–909. MIT Press, Cambridge (1991)
37. Stuckenschmidt, H.: Toward multi-viewpoint reasoning with owl ontologies. In: York-Sure, O., Domingue, J. (eds.) Proceedings of the European Semantic Web Conference (ESWC). LNCS, vol. 4011, pp. 259–272. Springer, Berlin (2006)
38. Stuckenschmidt, H., Broekstra, J.: Time-space trade-offs in scaling up rdf schema reasoning. Lect. Notes Comput. Sci. **3807**, 172 (2005)
39. ter Horst, H.J.: Completeness, decidability and complexity of entailment for rdf schema and a semantic extension involving the owl vocabulary. J. Web Semant. **3**(2–3), 79–115 (2005)

40. ter Horst, H.J.: Combining rdf and part of owl with rules: Semantics, decidability, complexity. In: International Semantic Web Conference, pp. 668–684 (2005)
41. Ullman, J.: Principles of Database Systems. Freeman, New York (1983)
42. Ullman, J.: Principles of Database and Knowledge-base Systems, vol. 1. Freeman, New York (1988)
43. Ullman, J.: Principles of Database and Knowledge-base Systems, vol. 2. Freeman, New York (1989)
44. van Emden, M.H., Kowalski, R.: The semantics of predicate logic as programming language. J. ACM 23(4), 733–743 (1976)
45. Volz, R.: Web ontology reasoning with logic databases. Ph.D. Thesis, Institut für Angewandte Informatik und Formale Beschreibungsverfahren (AIFB) (2004)
46. WSML Working Group: WSML language reference. Working Draft D16.1 v0.3, WSML (2008)

Chapter 8
Modular Knowledge Representation and Reasoning in the Semantic Web

Luciano Serafini and Martin Homola

Abstract Construction of *modular ontologies* by combining different modules is becoming a necessity in ontology engineering in order to cope with the increasing complexity of the ontologies and the domains they represent. The modular ontology approach takes inspiration from software engineering, where modularization is a widely acknowledged feature. *Distributed reasoning* is the other side of the coin of modular ontologies: given an ontology comprising of a set of modules, it is desired to perform reasoning by combination of multiple reasoning processes performed locally on each of the modules. In the last ten years, a number of approaches for combining logics has been developed in order to formalize modular ontologies. In this chapter, we survey and compare the main formalisms for modular ontologies and distributed reasoning in the Semantic Web. We select four formalisms build on formal logical grounds of Description Logics: Distributed Description Logics, $\mathcal{E}$-connections, Package-based Description Logics and Integrated Distributed Description Logics. We concentrate on expressivity and distinctive modeling features of each framework. We also discuss reasoning capabilities of each framework.

8.1 Introduction

One of the opportunities opened by the Semantic Web is the possibility of accessing and reusing knowledge bases available via the Internet in the form of RDF/OWL ontologies. In many cases, it is not necessary to build a new ontology from scratch, instead one is able to reuse and compose already existing ontologies, which describe some aspect of the world, by including them or selected parts of them in the newly build knowledge base.[1] This phenomenon is quite similar to modular software development known from software engineering, where software packages that

[1] As this chapter concentrates on ontologies as formally defined knowledge bases with logical semantics, we use the terms knowledge base and ontology interchangeably.

L. Serafini (✉) · M. Homola
Fondazione Bruno Kessler, Via Sommarive 18, 38123 Trento, Italy
e-mail: serafini@fbk.eu

M. Homola (✉)
Fac. of Mathematics, Physics and Informatics, Comenius University, 84248 Bratislava, Slovakia
e-mail: homola@fmph.uniba.sk

R. De Virgilio et al. (eds.), *Semantic Web Information Management*,
DOI 10.1007/978-3-642-04329-1_8,

implement certain algorithms are possibly included and reused in newly developed programs. However, differently from software, there is not a substantial agreement on what does it mean to integrate a set of ontology modules.

The past ten years have seen several proposals of logics which have the explicit goal to define a formal semantics of the integration of modular ontologies. Some of them are based on first order logic or modal logics, other combine dynamic with epistemic logics, etc. The most influential formalisms of modular ontologies for the Semantic Web where the one based on Description Logics (DL) [1]. We study four such formalisms in this chapter.

Distributed Description logics (DDL). A framework for combining DL ontologies by means of directed semantic mapping, which was originally introduced by Borgida and Serafini [9].

$\mathcal{E}$-connections. A framework for combining nonoverlapping ontologies encoded in DL but possibly also other logics by special inter-ontology roles, originally introduced by Kutz et al. [29].

Package-based Description Logics (P-DL). A framework for distributed ontologies that enables import of ontology entities between the modules. P-DL was originally introduced by Bao and Honavar [7].

Integrated Distributed Description Logics (IDDL). A framework for aligning DL ontologies by means of bidirectional semantic mapping, originally introduced by Zimmerman [41].

The idea of modular ontologies opens a number of different issues, each of which deserves for a specific investigation. Even if reductions between the formalisms are known [4, 14, 28] and all of them are reducible into a regular monolithic DL ontology [8, 10, 14, 42], it has to be remarked that each of the formalisms is focused on different modeling scenarios and is suited for different operations that have been enabled by the introduction of modular ontologies. In this respect, we identify the following four important operations associated with modular ontologies.

Ontology combination. Ontology combination is motivated by the combination of ontologies each of which describes a separated portion of the domain. The simple case is when two ontologies O_1 and O_2 describe two distinct dimensions of a complex domain (e.g., one is a geographic ontology and another is an ontology about organization). In order to construct an ontology on a complex domain which encompasses both of these dimensions (e.g., territorial organization), it is necessary to define complex cross domain concepts that combine concepts of O_1 and O_2. The $\mathcal{E}$-connections framework supports this perspective.

Ontology mapping. Ontology mapping is motivated by the resolution of *semantic heterogeneity* between ontologies. A simple case is when two ontologies O_1 and O_2 represent in a heterogeneous way knowledge about the same domain or about partially overlapping domains. To combine the knowledge contained in O_1 and O_2, it is necessary to represent the *semantic mappings* between them (i.e., to indicate the relation between entities from O_1 and O_2). DDL and IDDL are formalisms that support this perspective.

Ontology import. Ontology import is motivated as a flexible mechanism for *partial ontology reuse*. For instance, in order to build an ontology O_2 it is possible to re-use some of the entities (namely concepts, relations and individuals) defined in an already developed ontology O_1. This is done by *importing* entities from one ontology into another, in a similar fashion as when some functionalities of a software package are imported in some other software package. P-DL is a formalism that supports this perspective.

Ontology partitioning. Ontology partitioning is motivated by the problem of dealing with large and very complex ontologies by decomposing them into modules. An example is when a large ontology O is partitioned in a set of ontologies $O_1,\ldots,O_n$ such that the combination of $O_1,\ldots,O_n$ is equivalent to the initial ontology O. Ontology partitioning has been investigated in connection with $\mathcal{E}$-connections [18]. This approach is different from the previous three in that it is more concerned with identifying parts of ontologies which are sufficiently unrelated, in contrast from the previous three focussing on describing the relation between the components.

In addition to the approaches that we compare in this chapter, which all craft distributed and modular ontology frameworks by introducing new constructs to the language and extending the standard DL semantics in order to combine the modules with these constructs, there is also another approach which addresses the problem of ontology modularity by identifying the requirements under which the modules are soundly combined simply by union. One such a requirement is *locality of knowledge* [12, 13]. Another one is the notion of *conservative extension* [22, 30]. In this chapter, however, we concentrate on distributed and modular ontology frameworks of the first kind. A reader interested in comparison of both kinds will find some discussion on this issue in the work of Cuenca Grau and Kutz [14].

We start by introducing the DL $\mathcal{SHOIQ}_\mathrm{b}$ whose sub-languages will serve as local languages of the modular ontology frameworks under comparison. In Sect. 8.3, we discuss on the abstract level the basic unified features shared by all of the logic-based modular ontology frameworks. We then continue by reviewing DDL, $\mathcal{E}$-connections, P-DL and IDDL in Sects. 8.4–8.7. We conclude in the final section.

8.2 Ontologies and Description Logics

Among the languages that are currently used to represent ontologies for the Semantic Web, the most important is OWL Web Ontology Language [31, 32]. The semantics of OWL is derived from DL,[2] thus providing a well founded logical grounding for this language, tractable reasoning algorithms and practical implementations of reasoning engines. For this reason, most modular ontology frameworks supports

[2] OWL actually provides a whole family of languages. Of these, most derive the semantics directly from some specific DL. One exception to this is the OWL Full language which is part of the OWL 1 standard [31]. This language relies on RDF semantics instead.

integration of ontologies expressed in different DL languages. In this section, we briefly introduce syntax and semantics of the DL called $\mathcal{SHOIQ}_b$ [25, 38] whose sublanguages will serve as the underlying logic for the modular ontology frameworks that will be described and compared later on.

8.2.1 Description Logic $\mathcal{SHOIQ}_b$

Definition 8.1 (Syntax of DL $\mathcal{SHOIQ}_b$) Let N_I, N_R and N_C be pairwise disjoint sets of individual names, atomic role names and atomic concept names in the respective order. $\mathcal{SHOIQ}_b$-roles are defined inductively as the smallest set such that:

- each $R \in N_C$ (atomic role) is a role;
- given an atomic role $R \in N_R$, the expression R^- (inverse role) also is a role;
- given two roles R and S each of the expressions $\neg R$ (role complement), $R \sqcap S$ (role intersection) and $R \sqcup C$ (role union) is also a role if it is safe.[3]

An RBox $\mathcal{R}$ is a collection of axioms, each of one of the two forms:

$$R \sqsubseteq S, \qquad \mathrm{Trans}(R)$$

where R and S are roles. First form is called a role inclusion axiom (RIA) and second is called a transitivity assertion. Let $\mathrel{\underline{\circledast}}$ be a transitive-reflexive closure of $\sqsubseteq$. Given an RBox $\mathcal{R}$, a role R is transitive if $\mathrm{Trans}(R) \in \mathcal{R}$; a role S is called simple if there is no transitive role R such that $R \mathrel{\underline{\circledast}} S$. If $R \mathrel{\underline{\circledast}} S$ then R is called a subrole of S. $\mathcal{SHOIQ}_b$-concepts are defined inductively as the smallest set such that:

- each $A \in N_C$ (atomic concept) is a concept;
- given two concepts C, D and a role R the expressions $\neg C$ (complement), $C \sqcap D$ (intersection), $C \sqcup D$ (union), $\exists R.C$ (existential restriction) and $\forall R.C$ (value restriction) are also concepts;
- given a concept C, a simple role S and a natural number $n \geq 0$, the expressions $\geqslant n\, S.C$ and $\leqslant n\, S.C$ (qualified number restrictions) are also concepts,
- given some $o \in N_I$, the expression $\{o\}$ (nominal) is also a concept.

A TBox $\mathcal{T}$ is a set of axioms called General Concept Inclusions (GCI), each of the form:

$$C \sqsubseteq D$$

where C and D are concepts. An ABox $\mathcal{A}$ is a set of axioms of the two possible forms, a concept assertion (on the left) and a role assertion (on the right):

$$C(a), \qquad R(a, b)$$

[3] A $\mathcal{SHOIQ}_b$ role expression is safe if its disjunctive normal form contains at least one non-negated conjunct in every disjunct, please refer work of Tobies [38].

Table 8.1 Semantic constraints on complex $\mathcal{SHOIQ}_b$ concepts and roles

Construct	Condition	
$\neg C$	$(\neg C)^\mathcal{I} = \Delta^\mathcal{I} \setminus C^\mathcal{I}$	
$C \sqcap D$	$(C \sqcap D)^\mathcal{I} = C^\mathcal{I} \cap D^\mathcal{I}$	$\mathcal{A}$
$C \sqcup D$	$(C \sqcup D)^\mathcal{I} = C^\mathcal{I} \cup D^\mathcal{I}$	$\mathcal{L}$
$\forall R.C$	$(\forall R.C)^\mathcal{I} = \{x \in \Delta^\mathcal{I} \mid (\forall y \in \Delta^\mathcal{I})\ (x, y) \in R^\mathcal{I} \Rightarrow y \in C^\mathcal{I}\}$	$\mathcal{C}$
$\exists R.C$	$(\exists R.C)^\mathcal{I} = \{x \in \Delta^\mathcal{I} \mid (\exists y \in \Delta^\mathcal{I})\ (x, y) \in R^\mathcal{I} \wedge y \in C^\mathcal{I}\}$	
$\{o\}$	$\{o\}^\mathcal{I} = \{o^\mathcal{I}\}$	$\mathcal{O}$
$\geqslant n\, S.C$	$(\geqslant n\, S.C)^\mathcal{I} = \{x \in \Delta^\mathcal{I} \mid \sharp\{y \in \Delta^\mathcal{I} \mid (x, y) \in S^\mathcal{I} \wedge y \in C^\mathcal{I}\} \geq n\}$	$\mathcal{Q}$
$\leqslant n\, S.C$	$(\leqslant n\, S.C)^\mathcal{I} = \{x \in \Delta^\mathcal{I} \mid \sharp\{y \in \Delta^\mathcal{I} \mid (x, y) \in S^\mathcal{I} \wedge y \in C^\mathcal{I}\} \leq n\}$	
R^-	$(x, y) \in R^{-\mathcal{I}} \leftrightarrow (y, x) \in R^\mathcal{I}$	$\mathcal{I}$
$\neg R$	$(\neg R)^\mathcal{I} = (\Delta^\mathcal{I} \times \Delta^\mathcal{I}) \setminus R^\mathcal{I}$	
$R \sqcap S$	$(R \sqcap S)^\mathcal{I} = R^\mathcal{I} \cap S^\mathcal{I}$	b
$R \sqcup S$	$(R \sqcup S)^\mathcal{I} = R^\mathcal{I} \cup S^\mathcal{I}$	

where $a, b \in N_\mathrm{I}$ are individuals, C is a concept and R is a role. A $\mathcal{SHOIQ}_b$ knowledge base is a triple $\mathcal{K} = \langle \mathcal{T}, \mathcal{R}, \mathcal{A} \rangle$ formed by a TBox, an RBox and an ABox.

Definition 8.2 (Semantics of $\mathcal{SHOIQ}_b$) An interpretation of a $\mathcal{SHOIQ}_b$ knowledge base $\mathcal{K} = \langle \mathcal{T}, \mathcal{R}, \mathcal{A} \rangle$ is a pair $\mathcal{I} = \langle \Delta^\mathcal{I}, \cdot^\mathcal{I} \rangle$ consisting of a non-empty set $\Delta^\mathcal{I}$ called the interpretation domain of $\mathcal{I}$ and of and interpretation function $\cdot^\mathcal{I}$ which assigns:

- $a^\mathcal{I} \in \Delta^\mathcal{I}$, an element if the domain, to each individual $a \in N_\mathrm{I}$;
- $C^\mathcal{I} \subseteq \Delta^\mathcal{I}$, a subset of the domain, to each concept C that appears in $\mathcal{K}$;
- $R^\mathcal{I} \subseteq \Delta^\mathcal{I} \times \Delta^\mathcal{I}$, a subset of the cross-product of the domain, to each role R that appears in $\mathcal{K}$.

In addition, for complex concepts and roles, the interpretation satisfies the constraints presented in Table 8.1.

Given an RBox $\mathcal{R}$, an interpretation $\mathcal{I}$ satisfies the role hierarchy of $\mathcal{R}$, if for each two roles R and S such that $R \boxtimes S$ we have $R^\mathcal{I} \subseteq S^\mathcal{I}$. $\mathcal{I}$ satisfies a transitivity axiom $\mathrm{Trans}(R) \in \mathcal{R}$ if $R^\mathcal{I}$ is a transitive relation (i.e., for each $x, y, z \in \Delta^\mathcal{I}$, if $\langle x, y \rangle \in R^\mathcal{I}$ and $\langle y, z \rangle \in R^\mathcal{I}$ then also $\langle x, z \rangle \in R^\mathcal{I}$). $\mathcal{I}$ satisfies $\mathcal{R}$ (denoted $\mathcal{I} \models \mathcal{R}$) if it satisfies the role hierarchy of $\mathcal{R}$ and each transitivity axiom of $\mathcal{R}$. Interpretation $\mathcal{I}$ satisfies a GCI axiom $C \sqsubseteq D \in \mathcal{T}$ if $C^\mathcal{I} \subseteq D^\mathcal{I}$. $\mathcal{I}$ satisfies a TBox $\mathcal{T}$ (denoted $\mathcal{I} \models \mathcal{T}$) if it satisfies each GCI axiom of $\mathcal{T}$. $\mathcal{I}$ satisfies a concept assertion $C(a) \in \mathcal{A}$ if $a^\mathcal{I} \in C^\mathcal{I}$. $\mathcal{I}$ satisfies a role assertion $R(a, b) \in \mathcal{A}$ if $\langle a^\mathcal{I}, b^\mathcal{I} \rangle \in R^\mathcal{I}$. $\mathcal{I}$ satisfies an ABox $\mathcal{A}$ (denoted $\mathcal{I} \models \mathcal{A}$) if it satisfies each ABox assertion of $\mathcal{A}$. Interpretation I is a model of $\mathcal{SHOIQ}_b$-knowledge base $\mathcal{K} = \langle \mathcal{T}, \mathcal{R}, \mathcal{A} \rangle$ if $\mathcal{I} \models \mathcal{T}$, $\mathcal{I} \models \mathcal{R}$ and $\mathcal{I} \models \mathcal{A}$.

Basic reasoning tasks for Description Logics include concept satisfiability checking and subsumption entailment checking. These are formally defined as follows.

Definition 8.3 (Reasoning tasks in $\mathcal{SHOIQ}_\mathrm{b}$) Given a $\mathcal{SHOIQ}_\mathrm{b}$-knowledge base $\mathcal{K} = \langle \mathcal{T}, \mathcal{R}, \mathcal{A} \rangle$ we say that:

- a concept, say C, is satisfiable with respect to $\mathcal{K}$, if there exists a model $\mathcal{I}$ of $\mathcal{K}$ such that the set $C^\mathcal{I}$ is nonempty;
- a subsumption formula, say $\phi = C \sqsubseteq D$, is entailed by $\mathcal{K}$ (denoted $\mathcal{K} \models \phi$), if for each model $\mathcal{I}$ of $\mathcal{K}$ we have $C^\mathcal{I} \subseteq D^\mathcal{I}$.

Thanks to the well known reduction [1] in praxis we only need to deal with concept satisfiability checking.

Theorem 8.1 *Given a $\mathcal{SHOIQ}_\mathrm{b}$-knowledge base $\mathcal{K} = \langle \mathcal{T}, \mathcal{R}, \mathcal{A} \rangle$ and a subsumption formula $\phi = C \sqsubseteq D$, ϕ is entailed by $\mathcal{K}$ if and only if $C \sqcap \neg D$ is unsatisfiable with respect to $\mathcal{K}$.*

8.2.2 Sublanguages of $\mathcal{SHOIQ}_\mathrm{b}$

We have introduced such a powerful language like $\mathcal{SHOIQ}_\mathrm{b}$ since we aim at comparing distributed ontology frameworks which all use some sublanguage of $\mathcal{SHOIQ}_\mathrm{b}$ as the underlying logic. Let us briefly introduce selected sublanguages of $\mathcal{SHOIQ}_\mathrm{b}$ that are of particular interest for these in distributed ontology frameworks (see also 3rd column of Table 8.1 for naming conventions):

$\mathcal{ALC}$. A sublanguage of $\mathcal{SHOIQ}_\mathrm{b}$ that only allows for atomic roles (i.e., each $R \in N_\mathrm{R}$), it does not allow RBoxes at all, and from the concept constructors it only allows complement ($\neg$), intersection ($\sqcap$), union ($\sqcup$), existential restriction ($\exists$) and value restriction ($\forall$) in complex concepts. $\mathcal{ALC}$ is one of the most basic DL languages and it is supported by all of the modular ontology frameworks that we will review.

$\mathcal{SHIQ}$. Also known as $\mathcal{ALCQHI}_{\mathrm{R}+}$. It enriches $\mathcal{ALC}$ concept constructors with qualified number restrictions ($\leqslant$ and $\geqslant$), it adds inverse roles, role hierarchies and transitive roles. The basic variant of DDL is built on top of $\mathcal{SHIQ}$.

$\mathcal{SHOIQ}$. Enriches $\mathcal{SHIQ}$ with nominals. Its three sublanguages $\mathcal{SHIQ}$, $\mathcal{SHOQ}$ and $\mathcal{SHIO}$ are of particular interest for $\mathcal{E}$-connections.

$\mathcal{ALCQHI}_\mathrm{b}$. Enriches $\mathcal{ALC}$ with qualified number restrictions, role hierarchies and inverses, and in addition by complex roles derived by role complement ($\neg$), intersection ($\sqcap$) and union ($\sqcup$) constructors. DDL enriched with role mappings is build on top $\mathcal{ALCQHI}_\mathrm{b}$.

The only framework that covers full $\mathcal{SHOIQ}_\mathrm{b}$ (and even goes beyond) is IDDL. However, since such a logic is intractable, reasoning must always happen in some sublanguage here.

8.3 Reference Distributed Ontology Framework

While different ontology frameworks have many distinctive features that make each of them suitable for different applications, in general a unifying view on these frameworks is possible. In this section, we describe the features that are common to all the formalisms of our interest in this chapter. These basic logical components, defined by all the formalisms, are as follows.

Set of modules. Sometimes called local ontologies or knowledge sources, they constitute the modules that have to be integrated. This set is represented by a family of ontologies $\{O_i\}_{i \in I}$ indexed by a set of indexes I. The set of components is finite, and it is fixed and constant (i.e., once specified, there are no means to add, remove or merge components by means of logic). Each index uniquely identifies an ontology O_i which is to be integrated. One important parameter of such a component is the language in which each O_i is expressed, so called local language. For the comparison in this chapter, we assume that the local language is always some language from the family of Description Logics, however also approaches that allow integration of DL with other local logics are known [28].

Connection between the modules. This component represents the connection between the local modules within the framework. Each logic introduces different constructs to represents such a component. This is indeed the core aspect that differentiates the approaches. We distinguish two basic approaches: a *distributed* approach where the connections are expressed between pairs of local ontologies, and an *integrated* approach in which the mappings between local ontologies are represented in a centralized theory. Another important parameter, that should be taken into account in this respect, concerns the type of objects that are connected. Some approaches allow to link only concepts, while other approaches allow to link also relations and individuals.

Semantics. Each of the approaches provides a formal semantics of the logic as an extension (or restriction) of the DL semantics. We distinguish two different philosophies: *centralized semantics*, there is a unique domain of interpretation in which each ontology component is interpreted; *distributed semantics* local ontologies are interpreted in a "private" domain, and the integration is reached by imposing some compatibility constraints on the possible combinations of local semantics.

Axiomatization and reasoning support. All of the approaches provide a sound and complete reasoning algorithm which computes the consequences of the integration. These algorithms are usually based on an extension of the tableaux based reasoning techniques that are available for DL. For some of the approaches, an axiomatization is known. Also here we have two philosophies: some approaches are limited and only consider the consequences of integration within the modules, while others are interested also in reasoning on the mapping component.

In the reminder of the chapter, we review the four formalisms for representing modular ontologies cited in the introduction. For each of them, we will describe the syntax with the associated expressive power, the semantics and, if it is available, the axiomatization. Since our main interest lies in representational aspects, we focus mostly on modeling features of these frameworks which we demonstrate on examples.

8.4 Distributed Description Logics

The Distributed Description Logics framework was originally introduced by Borgida and Serafini [10] and subsequently developed by Serafini et al. [35, 36]. The basic DDL supports local ontologies expressed in $\mathcal{SHIQ}$ and mapping between concepts. This mapping allows for propagations of the concept subsumption hierarchy across the component ontology modules. Successively, Serafini and Tamilin [37] extended DDL with individual correspondences, which encode mapping between individuals of the component ABoxes. With this type of mapping is was possible to propagate not only TBox knowledge (i.e., concept subsumption) but also assertional knowledge stored in the ABoxes of the component modules. In a similar fashion, Ghidini et al. [21] propose an axiomatization of mapping between roles that supports also the propagation of role-hierarchy between the modules. Homola [23] proposed a modification of the DDL semantics in order to improve the propagation of subsumption on complex concepts composed from concepts that are mapped between directly, and successively DDL formalism was modified by Homola and Serafini [24] in order to support the composition of mappings across a chain of ontologies. We limit our review in this chapter to the above listed contributions. However, it is worthwhile to notice that recently the formalism was further extended by Ghidini et al. [20] in order to allow so called heterogeneous mappings, which associate items of different syntactic type, for instance concepts with relations.

8.4.1 Formalization

DDL was build on top of local logics as expressive as $\mathcal{SHIQ}$ and $\mathcal{ALCQHI}_\mathrm{b}$. In this section we build DDL on top of the latter, in order to demonstrate also mapping between roles and modeling with complex roles.

Definition 8.4 (DDLs over $\mathcal{ALCQHI}_\mathrm{b}$) Assume a nonempty index set I, a family of sets of concept names $N_\mathrm{C} = \{N_{\mathrm{C}i}\}_{i\in I}$ a family of sets of role names $N_\mathrm{R} = \{N_{\mathrm{R}i}\}_{i\in I}$ and a family of sets of individual names $\mathcal{ALCQHI}_\mathrm{b}$-role build over $N_{\mathrm{I}i}$.

1. A Distributed TBox is a family of T-Boxes $\mathfrak{T} = \{\mathcal{T}_i\}_{i\in I}$ such that $\mathcal{T}_i$ is a TBox in the language $\mathcal{ALCQHI}_\mathrm{b}$ build over $N_{\mathrm{C}i}$ and $N_{\mathrm{R}i}$.
2. A distributed R-Box $\mathfrak{R} = \{\mathcal{R}_i\}_{i\in I}$ where each $\mathcal{R}_i$, is an RBox in the language $\mathcal{ALCQHI}_\mathrm{b}$ build over $N_{\mathrm{C}i}$ and $N_{\mathrm{R}i}$.
3. To state that a certain axiom ϕ belongs to $\mathcal{T}_i$, $\mathcal{R}_i$ or $\mathcal{A}_i$ we write $i : \phi$.
4. A distributed A-Box $\mathfrak{A} = \{\mathcal{A}_i\}_{i\in I}$ is a family of ABoxes, where each $\mathcal{A}_i$ is an ABox on the language $\mathcal{ALCQHI}_\mathrm{b}$ build over $N_{\mathrm{C}i}$, $N_{\mathrm{R}i}$, and $N_{\mathrm{I}i}$.

5. A bridge rule from i to j is an expression of the form

$$i : X \xrightarrow{\sqsubseteq} j : Y, \qquad i : X \xrightarrow{\sqsupseteq} j : Y, \qquad i : a \longmapsto j : b$$

where X and Y are either two atomic concepts or two atomic roles, and a, b are two individuals, in the respective language. We also define the bridge rule $i : X \xrightarrow{\equiv} j : Y$ as a syntactic shorthand for the pair of bridge rules $i : X \xrightarrow{\sqsubseteq} j : Y$ and $i : X \xrightarrow{\sqsupseteq} j : Y$. A set of bridge rules $\mathfrak{B} = \{\mathfrak{B}_{ij}\}_{i \neq j \in I}$ is a family of sets of bridge rules $\mathfrak{B}_{ij}$ form i to j.
6. A DDL knowledge base over I is a quadruple $\langle \mathfrak{T}, \mathfrak{R}, \mathfrak{A}, \mathfrak{B} \rangle$ with all four components ranging over I.

Bridge rules do not represent semantic relations stated from an external *objective* point of view. As opposed to IDDL (see Sect. 8.7), there is no such global view in the DDL formalism. Instead, bridge rules from i to j express relations between the modules i and j viewed from the *subjective* point of view of the j-th ontology.

Intuitively, the into-bridge rule $i : X \xrightarrow{\sqsubseteq} j : Y$ states that, from the point of view of the module j, that the concept (respectively, the role) X in the module i is less general than its local concept (respectively, local role) Y. Similarly, the onto-bridge rule $i : X \xrightarrow{\sqsupseteq} j : Y$ expresses the fact that, from the viewpoint of the module j, X from the module i is more general than Y from the module j. Bridge rules from i to j provide the possibility of propagating into the local ontology j (under some approximation) the concepts of the foreign ontology i. Note, that since bridge rules reflect a subjective point of view, bridge rules from j to i are not necessarily the inverse of the rules from i to j, and in fact there may be no rules in one or both of these directions.

Definition 8.5 (Semantics of DDL) A distributed interpretation of a distributed knowledge base over an index set I, is a pair $\mathfrak{I} = \langle \{\mathcal{I}_i\}_{i \in I}, \{r_{ij}\}_{i \neq j \in I} \rangle$ consisting of a set of local interpretations $\{\mathcal{I}_i\}_{i \in I}$ and various domain mappings. For each $i \in I$, the local interpretation $\mathcal{I}_i = \langle \Delta^{\mathcal{I}_i}, \cdot^{\mathcal{I}_i} \rangle$ consists of a domain $\Delta^{\mathcal{I}_i}$ and an interpretation function $\cdot^{\mathcal{I}_i}$. The domain is either nonempty, but also possibly empty (in such a case we call $\mathcal{I}_i$ a hole and denote it by $\mathcal{I}_i = \mathcal{I}^{\varepsilon}$).

Given $I, i, j \in I$, a distributed interpretation $\mathfrak{I}$ over I satisfies elements of a distributed knowledge base $\mathfrak{K}$ (denoted by $\mathfrak{I} \models_{\varepsilon} \cdot$) according to the following clauses:

1. $\mathfrak{I} \models_{\varepsilon} i : C \sqsubseteq D$ if $C^{\mathcal{I}_i} \subseteq D^{\mathcal{I}_i}$.
2. $\mathfrak{I} \models_{\varepsilon} \mathcal{T}_i$ if $\mathfrak{I} \models_{\varepsilon} i : C \sqsubseteq D$ for each $i : C \sqsubseteq D \in \mathcal{T}_i$.
3. $\mathfrak{I} \models_{\varepsilon} \mathfrak{T}$ if $\mathfrak{I} \models_{\varepsilon} \mathcal{T}_i$ for each $i \in I$.
4. $\mathfrak{I} \models_{\varepsilon} i : R \sqsubseteq S$ if $R^{\mathcal{I}_i} \subseteq S^{\mathcal{I}_i}$.
5. $\mathfrak{I} \models_{\varepsilon} \mathcal{R}_i$ if $\mathfrak{I} \models_{\varepsilon} i : R \sqsubseteq S$ for each $i : R \sqsubseteq S \in \mathcal{R}_i$.
6. $\mathfrak{I} \models_{\varepsilon} \mathfrak{R}$ if $\mathfrak{I} \models_{\varepsilon} \mathcal{R}_i$ for each $i \in I$.
7. $\mathfrak{I} \models_{\varepsilon} i : C(a)$ if $a^{\mathcal{I}_i} \in C^{\mathcal{I}_i}$.
8. $\mathfrak{I} \models_{\varepsilon} i : R(a, b)$ if $\langle a^{\mathcal{I}_i}, b^{\mathcal{I}_i} \rangle \in R^{\mathcal{I}_i}$.
9. $\mathfrak{I} \models_{\varepsilon} \mathcal{A}_i$ if $\mathfrak{I} \models_{\varepsilon} \phi$ for each $\phi \in \mathcal{A}_i$.
10. $\mathfrak{I} \models_{\varepsilon} \mathfrak{A}$ if $\mathfrak{I} \models_{\varepsilon} \mathcal{A}_i$ for each $i \in I$.

11. $\mathfrak{I} \models_\varepsilon i : X \xrightarrow{\sqsubseteq} j : Y$ if $r_{ij}(X^{\mathcal{I}_i}) \subseteq Y^{\mathcal{I}_j}$.[4]
12. $\mathfrak{I} \models_\varepsilon i : X \xrightarrow{\sqsupseteq} j : Y$ if $r_{ij}(X^{\mathcal{I}_i}) \supseteq Y^{\mathcal{I}_j}$.
13. $\mathfrak{I} \models_\varepsilon i : a \longmapsto j : b$ if $b \in r_{ij}(a)$.
14. $\mathfrak{I} \models_\varepsilon \mathfrak{B}$ if $\mathfrak{I} \models_\varepsilon \phi$ for all axioms $\phi \in \mathfrak{B}$.

The distributed interpretation $\mathfrak{I}$ is a (distributed) model of $\mathfrak{K}$ (denoted by $\mathfrak{I} \models_\varepsilon \mathfrak{K}$) if $\mathfrak{I} \models_\varepsilon \mathfrak{T}$, $\mathfrak{I} \models_\varepsilon \mathfrak{R}$, $\mathfrak{I} \models_\varepsilon \mathfrak{A}$ and $\mathfrak{I} \models_\varepsilon \mathfrak{B}$.

8.4.2 Reasoning in DDL

The two standard decision problems in DL, satisfiability of concepts and entailment of subsumption, play prominent rôle also in context of DDL. Formally, the decision problems are defined as follows.

Definition 8.6 Given a distributed knowledge base $\mathfrak{K}$, an i-local concept C is satisfiable with respect to $\mathfrak{K}$ if there exists a distributed model $\mathfrak{I}$ of $\mathfrak{K}$ such that $C^{\mathcal{I}_i} \neq \emptyset$.

Definition 8.7 Given a distributed knowledge base $\mathfrak{K}$ and two i-local concepts C and D, it is said that C is subsumed by D with respect to $\mathfrak{K}$ if $C^{\mathcal{I}_i} \subseteq D^{\mathcal{I}_i}$ in every distributed model $\mathfrak{I}$ of $\mathfrak{K}$. We also sometimes say that the subsumption formula $i : C \sqsubseteq D$ is entailed by $\mathfrak{K}$ and denote this by $\mathfrak{K} \models_\varepsilon i : C \sqsubseteq D$.

In addition, we also define entailment of ABox expressions.

Definition 8.8 Given a distributed knowledge base $\mathfrak{K}$, a concept expression $i : C(a)$ is entailed by $\mathfrak{K}$ (denoted by $\mathfrak{K} \models_\varepsilon i : C(a)$) if $a^{\mathcal{I}_i} \in C^{\mathcal{I}_i}$ in every distributed model $\mathfrak{I}$ of $\mathfrak{K}$. A role expression $i : R(a, b)$ is entailed by $\mathfrak{K}$ (denoted by $\mathfrak{K} \models_\varepsilon i : R(a, b)$) if $\langle a^{\mathcal{I}_i}, b^{\mathcal{I}_i}\rangle \in R^{\mathcal{I}_i}$ in every distributed model $\mathfrak{I}$ of $\mathfrak{K}$.

DDL mappings may be thought of as inter-module axioms that constrain the interpretations of the ontologies they connect, or analogously, that allow to derive new knowledge via logical consequence. The axiomatization of DDL [21] is provided in terms of *propagation rules* that allows to propagate subsumption statements across different ontology modules. We express propagations rules in the following form:

$$\frac{\begin{array}{l}\text{subsumptions in } i\\ \text{bridge rules from } i \text{ to } j\end{array}}{\text{subsumption in } j}$$

The above rule should be interpreted as: if the subsumptions specified in the premise are proved in the module i and $\mathfrak{B}_{ij}$ contains the bridge rules specified in the premise,

[4]The notation $r_{ij}(d)$ is used for the set $\{d' \mid \langle d, d'\rangle \in r_{ij}\}$ and $r_{ij}(D)$ denotes the set $\bigcup_{d \in D} r_{ij}(d)$.

then the subsumption specified in the conclusion is entailed in the module j. The following propagation rules completely axiomatize the logical consequence in distributed knowledge bases in case of DDL with homogeneous bridge rules between concepts and roles (i.e., disregarding individual correspondences):

$$\frac{\begin{array}{l} i : X \sqsubseteq \bigsqcup_{k=1}^{n} Z_k \\ i : X \xrightarrow{\sqsupseteq} j : Y \\ i : Z_k \xrightarrow{\sqsubseteq} j : W_k \quad \text{for } 1 \leq k \leq n \end{array}}{j : Y \sqsubseteq \bigsqcup_{k=1}^{n} W_k} \qquad \frac{\begin{array}{l} i : \exists P.(\neg \bigsqcup_{k=1}^{p} A_k) \sqsubseteq (\bigsqcup_{k=1}^{m} B_k) \\ i : P \xrightarrow{\sqsupseteq} j : R \\ i : A_k \xrightarrow{\sqsubseteq} j : C_k \quad \text{for } 1 \leq k \leq p \\ i : D_k \xrightarrow{\sqsubseteq} B_k : \quad \text{for } 1 \leq k \leq m \end{array}}{j : \exists R.(\neg \bigsqcup_{k=1}^{p} C_k) \sqsubseteq (\bigsqcup_{k=1}^{m} D_k)} \quad (8.1)$$

In the first rule, X, Y, Z_k, W_k are either all concepts or all roles. In the second rule, A_h, B_h, C_k and D_k are concepts, and P and R are roles or inverse roles, and $p \geq 0$. Furthermore, when $p = 0$, $\bigsqcup_{k=1}^{p} \phi_k$ is defined to be $\bot$. Note that the first rule allows to propagate the concept/role subsumption hierarchy while the second rule allow to propagate the domain and range restriction on atomic and complex roles.

A practical reasoner for Distributed Description Logics has been developed in the system called DRAGO.[5]

8.4.3 Modeling with DDL

The most basic modeling feature of DDL are bridge rules that allow concepts across ontologies to be associated (i.e., they are used to express semantic mapping between concepts).

Example 8.1 Let us build a small ontology that will track all kinds of professions in some IT Company and relations between this professions. In the TBox $\mathcal{T}_1$, we have among others the following axioms:

$$\begin{array}{rr} \mathsf{ITStaff} \sqsubseteq \mathsf{Employee} & \mathsf{SupportStaff} \sqsubseteq \mathsf{Employee} \\ \mathsf{CateringStaff} \sqsubseteq \mathsf{SupportStaff} & \mathsf{AdministrativeStaff} \sqsubseteq \mathsf{SupportStaff} \\ \mathsf{Cook} \sqsubseteq \mathsf{CateringStaff} & \mathsf{Chef} \sqsubseteq \mathsf{Cook} \end{array}$$

Let us also have an individual johnSmith who serves as a chef in the catering division. We assert this in the ABox $\mathcal{A}_1$:

$$\mathsf{Chef(johnSmith)}$$

[5]DRAGO is distributed reasoner specifically developed for DDL. It is based on the Pellet reasoner. It is available via its homepage http://drago.itc.it/.

This simple modeling allows us to derive some entailed knowledge (for instance, Cook(johnSmith), CateringStaff(johnSmith), Cook $\sqsubseteq$ Employee, etc.). Suppose that one day we run into a readily available ontology $\mathcal{T}_2$ based upon the Escoffier's brigade de cuisine system. The excerpt of the ontology $\mathcal{T}_2$ is as follows:

$$\mathsf{KitchenChef} \sqsubseteq \mathsf{Cook} \qquad \mathsf{Saucemaker} \sqsubseteq \mathsf{Cook}$$
$$\mathsf{PastryCook} \sqsubseteq \mathsf{Cook} \qquad \mathsf{Baker} \sqsubseteq \mathsf{PastryCook}$$

Suppose that we decide to reuse the knowledge of $\mathcal{T}_2$ within our organization. We will keep the ontology $\mathcal{T}_1$ cleaner and reuse knowledge of $\mathcal{T}_2$ whenever possible. First, we remove the two axioms Cook $\sqsubseteq$ CateringStaff and Chef $\sqsubseteq$ Cook from $\mathcal{T}_1$ because they are redundant in light of $\mathcal{T}_2$. We do keep however the concepts Cook and Cheff in $\mathcal{T}_1$ as these are positions that some people occupy in our company (e.g., johnSmith). In order to integrate the ontologies, we add the following bridge rules:

$$2:\mathsf{Cook} \xrightarrow{\sqsubseteq} 1:\mathsf{CateringStaff} \qquad 2:\mathsf{Cook} \xrightarrow{\equiv} 1:\mathsf{Cook}$$
$$2:\mathsf{KitchenChef} \xrightarrow{\sqsupseteq} 1:\mathsf{Chef}$$

Thanks to the mapping expressed by the bridge rules, the two subsumptions that we have previously removed from the TBox $\mathcal{T}_1$ are now entailed (i.e., $\mathfrak{K} \models_\varepsilon 1:$ Chef $\sqsubseteq$ Cook and $\mathfrak{K} \models_\varepsilon 1:\mathsf{Cook} \sqsubseteq \mathsf{CateringStaff}$). We are also equally able to derive $\mathfrak{K} \models_\varepsilon 1:\mathsf{Cook(johnSmith)}$, $\mathfrak{K} \models_\varepsilon 1:\mathsf{CateringStaff(johnSmith)}$ and $\mathfrak{K} \models_\varepsilon 1:\mathsf{Cook} \sqsubseteq$ Employee, etc.

With individual correspondence axioms we are able to encode mapping between individuals. We illustrate this by an example.

Example 8.2 Let us extend the distributed ontology from Example 8.1. Suppose that the accounting department decides to create their own ontology where they model things in the company in way that is more practical for the accountants. In the local TBox $\mathcal{T}_3$, we have:

$$\mathsf{Accountant} \sqsubseteq \mathsf{Employee} \qquad \mathsf{Director} \sqsubseteq \mathsf{Employee}$$
$$\mathsf{SeniorExecutive} \sqsubseteq \mathsf{Employee} \qquad \mathsf{JuniorExecutive} \sqsubseteq \mathsf{Employee}$$
$$\mathsf{BasicStaff} \sqsubseteq \mathsf{Employee} \qquad \mathsf{SupportStaff} \sqsubseteq \mathsf{Employee}$$

This ontology then makes reuse of the knowledge already existing within the distributed knowledge base, employing the bridge rules: follows:

$$1:\mathsf{CateringStaff} \xrightarrow{\sqsubseteq} 3:\mathsf{SupportStaff}$$
$$1:\mathsf{ITStaff} \xrightarrow{\sqsubseteq} 3:\mathsf{BasicStaff}$$

In addition, the accounting department keeps its own evidence of all employees in $\mathcal{A}_3$, using individuals with special nomenclature relying on employee numbers (i.e., individuals such as e006B3F, eF9DB15, eE23A28, etc.). Using individual correspondence axioms, these individuals are matched with other representations of the same employee in the knowledge base, for instance:

$$1 : \mathsf{johnSmith} \longmapsto 3 : \mathsf{e006B3F}$$

Now, even without incorporating into $\mathcal{T}_3$ concepts such as Cook and Chef which are of little interest to company accountants and without explicit recording of all information about the precise working position of e006B3F in $\mathcal{T}_3$ and $\mathcal{A}_3$ we are able to derive $\mathfrak{T} \models_{\varepsilon} 3 : \mathsf{SupportStaff}(\mathsf{e006B3F})$.

In DDL, it is also possible to bridge between roles. A practical modeling scenario that makes use of such bridge rules is showed below, by extending our running example.

Example 8.3 In order to improve work efficiency, the accounting department has planned a reorganization of offices. Under the assumption that people do more work when they feel fine in the office, the accounting department asked the employees to create a simple friend or a foe ontology $\mathcal{A}_4$. See, an excerpt from this ontology:

$$\mathsf{friendOf}(\mathsf{johnSmith}, \mathsf{robertKay}) \qquad \mathsf{friendOf}(\mathsf{robertKay}, \mathsf{johnSmith})$$

$$\mathsf{foeOf}(\mathsf{robertKay}, \mathsf{stanCoda}) \qquad \mathsf{foeOf}(\mathsf{stanCoda}, \mathsf{markHoffer})$$

The following bridge rules are used to transfer knowledge that is relevant into the ontology of the accounting department:

$$4 : \mathsf{friendOf} \xrightarrow{\sqsubseteq} 3 : \mathsf{goodOfficeMateOf} \qquad 4 : \mathsf{foeOf} \xrightarrow{\sqsubseteq} 3 : \mathsf{dislikes}$$

$$1 : \mathsf{officeMateOf} \xrightarrow{\sqsubseteq} 3 : \mathsf{currentOfficeMateOf}$$

We are especially interested in employees which do not feel comfortable sharing the office with their current office mates, hence we define a new role that will be called unhappyOfficeMateOf by an axiom in the RBox $\mathcal{R}_3$:

$$\mathsf{currentOfficeMateOf} \sqcap \mathsf{dislikes} \sqsubseteq \mathsf{unhappyOfficeMateOf}$$

Now, by using individual correspondence axioms, the relation between the individuals representing the same employee in different modules is encoded:

$$1 : \mathsf{johnSmith} \longmapsto 3 : \mathsf{e006B3F} \qquad 4 : \mathsf{johnSmith} \longmapsto 3 : \mathsf{e006B3F}$$

and so on for the other individuals. Making use of all this knowledge, we are finally able to derive in $\mathcal{T}_3$ who of the employees is located in the same office with an unfriendly co-worker and also we are able to determine which office mates would be mode suitable for such employees.

The distributed ontology representation framework of DDL allows to combine several ontologies by means of ontology mapping represented by bridge rules. Such an approach allows ontology engineers to reuse existing ontologies when building a new one. DDL also allows ontologies to be modeled in a modular way, keeping each module relatively small and maintainable, as part of the knowledge is imported from remote modules. Apart from other distributed ontology frameworks, $\mathcal{E}$-connections in particular, DDL is able to cope with heterogeneous environments such as for instance the envisioned Semantic Web, not requiring strict separation of modeling domains and being able to deal with inconsistency that may appear locally in such systems.

8.5 $\mathcal{E}$-connections

The motivation behind $\mathcal{E}$-connections, a framework originally introduced by Kutz et al. [26, 28], is the possibility of combining different logics each of which represents one aspect of a complex system. $\mathcal{E}$-connections were defined over so called Abstract Description Systems, a common generalization of Description Logics, modal logics, logics of time and space and some other logical formalisms, as introduced by Baader et al. [2]. Properties of $\mathcal{E}$-connections over Description Logics were studied by Kutz et al. [27] and Cuenca Grau et al. [15, 16]. $\mathcal{E}$-connections of OWL ontologies were also introduced by Cuenca Grau et al. [17].

A distinctive feature of $\mathcal{E}$-connections, different from other modular ontology frameworks presented in this chapter, is that each local ontology is supposed to model a portion of the domain that is complementary and nonoverlapping with respect to the other local ontologies (e.g., the two domains of people and vehicles are non-overlapping). Hence, in $\mathcal{E}$-connections it is not possible to have a concept in some ontology module that has subconcepts or instances in some other ontology module. For further illustration of nonoverlapping modeling domains, see Example 8.4 below.

In $\mathcal{E}$-connections, the ontology modules are combined using so called *link properties*, in short also called *links*. Links are effectively inter-ontology roles, they are allowed in restrictions and thus they allow the local ontologies to be connected. In contrast with DDL and some other distributed ontology frameworks, links are not intended to represent semantic mappings between ontologies.

8.5.1 Formalization

The two most commonly explored flavours of $\mathcal{E}$-connections of Description Logics are $\mathcal{C}^{\mathcal{E}}_{\mathcal{HQ}}(\mathcal{SHIQ},\mathcal{SHOQ},\mathcal{SHIO})$ and $\mathcal{C}^{\mathcal{E}}_{\mathcal{HI}}(\mathcal{SHIQ},\mathcal{SHOQ},\mathcal{SHIO})$ [15–17]. These allow $\mathcal{SHIQ}$, $\mathcal{SHOQ}$, and $\mathcal{SHIO}$ local ontologies to be connected with links, the former allowing link hierarchies and qualified number restrictions on links, the latter link hierarchies and inverse links. It has been noted that more general frameworks such as $\mathcal{C}^{\mathcal{E}}_{\mathcal{HIQ}}(\mathcal{SHOIQ})$ and even $\mathcal{C}^{\mathcal{E}}_{\mathcal{HIQ}}(\mathcal{SHIQ},\mathcal{SHOQ},\mathcal{SHIO})$ lead to undesired behaviour such as projection of nominals from one local model to another [17, 28].

In addition, two extended frameworks named $\mathcal{C}^{\mathcal{E}}_{\mathcal{HQ}+}(\mathcal{SHIQ},\mathcal{SHOQ},\mathcal{SHIO})$ and $\mathcal{C}^{\mathcal{E}}_{\mathcal{HI}+}(\mathcal{SHIQ},\mathcal{SHOQ},\mathcal{SHIO})$ [15, 34] were also studied. These extend the framework with several tweaks useful from the modeling perspective: same property name is freely reusable as a role name (within a module) and as well as a link name (between the modules), transitive links are allowed and transitivity of roles and links is now controlled by so called general transitivity axiom which enables switching the transitivity on and off based on the context of modules within/between which the role/link is used. For sake of simplicity, we introduce a slightly more general $\mathcal{C}^{\mathcal{E}}_{\mathcal{HIQ}+}(\mathcal{SHIQ},\mathcal{SHOQ},\mathcal{SHIO})$, of which $\mathcal{C}^{\mathcal{E}}_{\mathcal{HQ}+}(\mathcal{SHIQ},\mathcal{SHOQ},\mathcal{SHIO})$ is the sub-language that does not allow inverse links and $\mathcal{C}^{\mathcal{E}}_{\mathcal{HI}+}(\mathcal{SHIQ},\mathcal{SHOQ},\mathcal{SHIO})$ is the sub-language that does not allow links in number restrictions.

Definition 8.9 (Syntax of $\mathcal{C}^{\mathcal{E}}_{\mathcal{HIQ}+}(\mathcal{SHIQ},\mathcal{SHOQ},\mathcal{SHIO})$) Given a finite index set I, for $i \in I$, let m_i be a constant either equal to $\mathcal{SHIQ}$, $\mathcal{SHOQ}$ or $\mathcal{SHIO}$ that serves to identify the local language of a component knowledge base. For $i \in I$, let $N_{C_i}^{m_i}$ and $N_{I_i}^{m_i}$ be pairwise disjoint sets of concepts names and individual names, respectively. For $i, j \in I$, i and j not necessarily distinct, let $\varepsilon_{ij}^{m_i}$ be sets of properties, not necessarily mutually disjoint, but disjoint w.r.t. $N_{C_k}^{m_k}$ and $N_{I_k}^{m_k}$ for any $k \in I$ and let ρ_{ij} be sets of ij-properties defined as follows:

- if $i = j$ and $m_i = \mathcal{SHOQ}$ then $\rho_{ij} = \varepsilon_{ij}^{m_i}$;
- otherwise $\rho_{ij} = \varepsilon_{ij}^{m_i} \cup \{P^- \mid P \in \varepsilon_{ji}^{m_j}\}$.

For $P_1, P_2 \in \rho_{ij}$ an ij-property axiom is an assertion of the form $P_1 \sqsubseteq P_2$. A general transitivity axiom is of the form $\mathrm{Trans}(P; (i_1,i_2), (i_2,i_3), \ldots, (i_{n-1},i_n))$ provided that for each $k \in \{1,\ldots,p\}$ we have $P \in \varepsilon_{i_k j_k}^{m_{i_k}}$. An ij-property box $\mathcal{R}_{ij}$ is a finite set of ij-property axioms. The combined property box $\mathcal{R}$ contains all the property boxes for each $i, j \in I$ (not necessarily distinct) and also all transitivity axioms. Let us denote by $\boxtimes$ the transitive-reflexive closure on $\sqsubseteq$. A property P is said to be transitive in (i, j), if $\mathrm{Trans}(P; (i_1,i_2), \ldots, (i_{n-1},i_n)) \in \mathcal{R}$ such that $i_k = i$ and $i_{k+1} = j$, for some $1 \le k < n$. An ij-property P is called simple if there is no S that is transitive in (i, j) and $S \boxtimes P$.

Given some $i \in I$ the set of i-concepts is defined inductively, as the smallest set such that:

- each atomic concept $A \in N_{C_i}^{m_i}$ and two special symbols $\top_i$ and $\bot_i$ are i-concepts;
- given i-concepts C, D a j-concept Z and $P \in \rho_{ij}$, also $\neg C$, $C \sqcap D$, $C \sqcup D$, $\exists P^{(j)}.Z$, and $\forall P^{(j)}.Z$ are i-concepts;

- if $m_i \in \{\mathcal{SHOQ}, \mathcal{SHIO}\}$ and $o \in N_{\mathrm{I}i}$ then $\{o\}$ is an i-concept;
- given a j-concept Z, a natural number n and a simple property $S \in \rho_{ij}$ such that if $i = j$ then $m_i \in \{\mathcal{SHIQ}, \mathcal{SHOQ}\}$, also $\geqslant n\, S^{(j)}.Z$ and $\leqslant n\, S^{(j)}.Z$ are i-concepts.[6]

Given two individuals $a, b \in N_{\mathrm{I}i}$, an i-concept C and some role $R \in \rho_{ii}$, the expression $C(a)$ is called an i-local concept assertion and the expression $R(a, b)$ is called an i-local role assertion. In addition, given two individuals $a \in N_{\mathrm{I}i}$ and $b \in N_{\mathrm{I}j}$ such that $i \neq j$, and some link property $E \in \rho_{ij}$, an object assertion is an axiom of the form:

$$a \cdot E \cdot b$$

A combined TBox is a tuple $\mathcal{K} = \{\mathcal{K}_i\}_{i \in I}$ where each $\mathcal{K}_i$ is a set of i-local GCI each of the form $C \sqsubseteq D$, where C and D are i-concepts. A combined ABox $\mathcal{A} = \{\mathcal{A}_i\}_{i \in I} \cup \mathcal{A}_{\mathcal{E}}$ is a set containing local ABoxes[7] $\mathcal{A}_i$, each comprising of a finite number of i-local concept and role assertions, and a finite number of object assertions $\phi \in \mathcal{A}_{\mathcal{E}}$. A combined knowledge base $\Sigma = \langle \mathcal{K}, \mathcal{R}, \mathcal{A} \rangle$ is composed of a combined TBox, a combined property box, and a combined ABox, all of them defined over same index set I.

Semantics of $\mathcal{E}$-connections employs so called combined interpretations which are similar to distributed interpretations of DDL. A combined interpretation $\mathcal{I}$ consists of local domains and interpretation functions. Local domains $\Delta^{\mathcal{I}_i}$ are pairwise disjoint and unlike in DDL they are strictly nonempty. There is no distinctive domain relation as in DDL, instead there are special interpretation functions for links which assign to each link $E \in \varepsilon_{ij}$ a subset of $\Delta^{\mathcal{I}_i} \times \Delta^{\mathcal{I}_j}$ thus effectively turning them into a form of inter-ontology properties.

Definition 8.10 (Semantics of $\mathcal{C}^{\mathcal{E}}_{\mathcal{HIQ}+}(\mathcal{SHIQ}, \mathcal{SHOQ}, \mathcal{SHIO})$) Let us assume a combined knowledge base $\Sigma = \langle \mathcal{K}, \mathcal{R}, \mathcal{A} \rangle$ with some index set I. A combined interpretation is a triple $\mathcal{I} = \langle \{\Delta^{\mathcal{I}_i}\}_{i \in I}, \{\cdot^{\mathcal{I}_i}\}_{i \in I}, \{\cdot^{\mathcal{I}_{ij}}\}_{i,j \in I} \rangle$, where for each $i \in I$, $\Delta^{\mathcal{I}_i} \neq \emptyset$ and for each $i, j \in I$ such that $i \neq j$ we have $\Delta^{\mathcal{I}_i} \cap \Delta^{\mathcal{I}_j} = \emptyset$. Interpretation functions $\cdot^{\mathcal{I}_i}$ provide denotation for i-concepts and interpretation functions $\cdot^{\mathcal{I}_{ij}}$ are employed for sake of denotation of ij-properties.

[6]Note that even if the local language of the i-th module is $\mathcal{SHIO}$ (i.e., $m_i = \mathcal{SHIO}$) for some index $i \in I$, number restrictions may still appear in i-concepts as long as they are specified on link properties [15, 34].

[7]While local ABoxes are not included in $\mathcal{C}^{\mathcal{E}}_{\mathcal{HQ}}(\mathcal{SHIQ}, \mathcal{SHOQ}, \mathcal{SHIO})$, $\mathcal{C}^{\mathcal{E}}_{\mathcal{HI}}(\mathcal{SHIQ}, \mathcal{SHOQ}, \mathcal{SHIO})$, $\mathcal{C}^{\mathcal{E}}_{\mathcal{HQ}+}(\mathcal{SHIQ}, \mathcal{SHOQ}, \mathcal{SHIO})$, $\mathcal{C}^{\mathcal{E}}_{\mathcal{HI}+}(\mathcal{SHIQ}, \mathcal{SHOQ}, \mathcal{SHIO})$ $\mathcal{E}$-connections as defined by Cuenca Grau et al. [15–17] nor as given by Parsia and Cenca Grau [34], they are present in the previous work of Kutz et al. [27, 28]. Since they do not constitute any problem semantically, we add them for sake of comparison. Note also that even if the inter-module object assertions are possibly expressed using the same syntax as role assertions, we favor a syntax similar to the one of Cuenca Grau and Kutz [14] in order to make a clear distinction here.

Table 8.2 Semantic constraints on complex i-concepts in $\mathcal{E}$-connections. C, D are i-concepts, Z is a j-concept, P, S are either roles or links, S is simple

Construct	Condition
$\neg C$	$(\neg C)^{\mathcal{I}_i} = \Delta^{\mathcal{I}_i} \setminus C^{\mathcal{I}_i}$
$C \sqcap D$	$(C \sqcap D)^{\mathcal{I}_i} = C^{\mathcal{I}_i} \cap D^{\mathcal{I}_i}$
$C \sqcup D$	$(C \sqcup D)^{\mathcal{I}_i} = C^{\mathcal{I}_i} \cup D^{\mathcal{I}_i}$
$\{o\}$	$\{o\}^{\mathcal{I}_i} = \{o^{\mathcal{I}_i}\}$
$\forall P.Z$	$(\forall P.Z)^{\mathcal{I}_i} = \{x \in \Delta^{\mathcal{I}_i} \mid (\forall y \in \Delta^{\mathcal{I}_j})\, (x, y) \in P^{\mathcal{I}_{ij}} \Rightarrow y \in Z^{\mathcal{I}_j}\}$
$\exists P.Z$	$(\exists P.Z)^{\mathcal{I}_i} = \{x \in \Delta^{\mathcal{I}_i} \mid (\exists y \in \Delta^{\mathcal{I}_j})\, (x, y) \in P^{\mathcal{I}_{ij}} \wedge y \in Z^{\mathcal{I}_j}\}$
$\geqslant n\, S.Z$	$(\geqslant n\, S.Z)^{\mathcal{I}_i} = \{x \in \Delta^{\mathcal{I}_i} \mid \sharp\{y \in \Delta^{\mathcal{I}_j} \mid (x, y) \in S^{\mathcal{I}_{ij}}\} \geq n\}$
$\leqslant n\, S.Z$	$(\leqslant n\, S.Z)^{\mathcal{I}_i} = \{x \in \Delta^{\mathcal{I}_i} \mid \sharp\{y \in \Delta^{\mathcal{I}_j} \mid (x, y) \in S^{\mathcal{I}_{ij}}\} \leq n\}$

Each ij-property $P \in \rho_{ij}$ is interpreted by $P^{\mathcal{I}_{ij}}$ a subset of $\Delta^{\mathcal{I}_i} \times \Delta^{\mathcal{I}_j}$. If $P \in \rho_{ij}$ is an inverse, say $P = Q^-$, $Q \in \rho_{ji}$, then $P^{\mathcal{I}_{ij}} = \{(x, y) \in \Delta^{\mathcal{I}_i} \times \Delta^{\mathcal{I}_j} \mid (y, x) \in Q^{\mathcal{I}_{ji}}\}$. A combined interpretation $\mathcal{I}$ satisfies an ij-property axiom $P_1 \sqsubseteq P_2$ if ${P_1}^{\mathcal{I}_{ij}} \subseteq {P_2}^{\mathcal{I}_{ij}}$. It satisfies a transitivity axiom Trans$(P; (i_1, i_2), \ldots, (i_{n-1}, i_n))$ if both of the following conditions are true:[8]

1. for each $1 \leq k < n$, $P^{\mathcal{I}_{i_k i_{k+1}}}$ is transitive relation;
2. for each $1 \leq k < h < n$, $P^{\mathcal{I}_{i_k i_h}} = P^{\mathcal{I}_{i_k i_{k+1}}} \circ \cdots \circ P^{\mathcal{I}_{i_h i_{h+1}}}$.

A combined interpretation satisfies an ij-property box $\mathcal{R}_{ij}$ if it satisfies all ij-property axioms of $\mathcal{R}_{ij}$ and it satisfies a combined property box $\mathcal{R}$ if it satisfies each ij-property box and each transitivity axiom contained in $\mathcal{R}$.

Each i-concept C is interpreted by some subset $C^{\mathcal{I}_i}$ of $\Delta^{\mathcal{I}_i}$. For special symbols, we have $\top_i = \Delta^{\mathcal{I}_i}$ and $\bot_i = \emptyset$. In addition, denotation of complex i-concepts must satisfy the constraints as given in Table 8.2. Combined interpretation $\mathcal{I}$ satisfies an i-local GCI $C \sqsubseteq D$ (denoted by $\mathcal{I} \models C \sqsubseteq D$) if $C^{\mathcal{I}_i} \subseteq D^{\mathcal{I}_i}$; it satisfies a local TBox $\mathcal{K}_i$ (denoted $\mathcal{I} \models \mathcal{K}_i$) if it satisfies each i-local GCI thereof; and is satisfies a combined TBox $\mathcal{K}$ over I (denoted $\mathcal{I} \models \mathcal{K}$) if it satisfies $\mathcal{K}_i$ for each $i \in I$.

A combined interpretation $\mathcal{I}$ satisfies an i-local concept assertion $C(a)$ (denoted $\mathcal{I} \models C(a)$), if $a^{\mathcal{I}_i} \in C^{\mathcal{I}_i}$; it satisfies an i-local role assertion $R(a, b)$ (denoted $\mathcal{I} \models R(a, b)$), if $\langle a^{\mathcal{I}_i}, b^{\mathcal{I}_i}\rangle \in R^{\mathcal{I}_{ii}}$; $\mathcal{I}$ satisfies an object assertion $a \cdot E \cdot b$ (denoted $\mathcal{I} \models a \cdot E \cdot b$), $a \in N_{\mathrm{I}i}$, $b \in N_{\mathrm{I}j}$, $E \in \rho_{ij}$, if $\langle a^{\mathcal{I}_i}, b^{\mathcal{I}_j}\rangle \in E^{\mathcal{I}_{ij}}$. Putting this together, $\mathcal{I}$ satisfies a combined ABox $\mathcal{A}$ (denoted $\mathcal{I} \models \mathcal{A}$) if it satisfied each ABox assertion of each $\mathcal{A}_i \in \mathcal{A}$ and as well each object assertion contained in $\mathcal{A}$.

[8] This definition of the semantics of general transitivity axioms differs from that originally given by Cuenca Grau et al. [15] and Parsia and Cuenca Grau [34], however, we believe that this new definition actually suits the intuition behind the general transitivity axiom as it is explained in these works.

Finally, a combined interpretation $\mathcal{I}$ over some index set I is a model of a combined knowledge base $\Sigma = \langle \mathcal{K}, \mathcal{R}, \mathcal{A} \rangle$ defined over I (denoted by $\mathcal{I} \models \Sigma$) if $\mathcal{I}$ satisfies all three $\mathcal{K}$, $\mathcal{R}$ and $\mathcal{A}$.

8.5.2 Reasoning in $\mathcal{E}$-connections

A key reasoning task for $\mathcal{E}$-connections is the satisfiability of i-concepts with respect to a combined knowledge base. Other reasoning tasks such as entailment of subsumption between i-concepts are reducible.

Definition 8.11 (Reasoning tasks for $\mathcal{E}$-connections) Given a combined knowledge base Σ over some index set I and $i \in I$, an i-concept C is satisfiable with respect to Σ if there exists a combined interpretation $\mathcal{I}$ of Σ that is a model of Σ such that $C^{\mathcal{I}_i} \neq \emptyset$. Given two i-concepts C and D, it is said that Σ entails the subsumption $C \sqsubseteq D$ (denoted $\mathcal{I} \models C \sqsubseteq D$) if in each model $\mathcal{I}$ of Σ we have $C^{\mathcal{I}_i} \subseteq D^{\mathcal{I}_i}$.

As for regular DL, the entailment of subsumption decision problem is reducible into satisfiability [15, 28].

Theorem 8.2 *Given a combined knowledge base Σ over some index set I, $i \in I$ and two i-concepts C and D, the subsumption formula $C \sqsubseteq D$ is entailed by Σ if and only if the complex i-concept $C \sqcap \neg D$ is unsatisfiable with respect to Σ.*

Other classic decision problem that have been considered for $\mathcal{E}$-connections are the problem of entailment of ABox knowledge [28].

Definition 8.12 (Entailment of ABox formulae) A combined knowledge base Σ entails an i-local expression $C(a)$, if in each model $\mathcal{I}$ of Σ we have $a^{\mathcal{I}_i} \in C^{\mathcal{I}_i}$. Σ entails an i-local expression $R(a, b)$, if in each model $\mathcal{I}$ of Σ we have $\langle a^{\mathcal{I}_i}, b^{\mathcal{I}_i} \rangle \in R^{\mathcal{I}_{ii}}$.

Tableaux reasoning algorithms for the $\mathcal{E}$-connections languages $\mathcal{C}^{\mathcal{E}}_{\mathcal{HQ}}(\mathcal{SHIQ}, \mathcal{SHOQ}, \mathcal{SHIO})$, $\mathcal{C}^{\mathcal{E}}_{\mathcal{HI}}(\mathcal{SHIQ}, \mathcal{SHOQ}, \mathcal{SHIO})$, $\mathcal{C}^{\mathcal{E}}_{\mathcal{HQ}+}(\mathcal{SHIQ}, \mathcal{SHOQ}, \mathcal{SHIO})$, and $\mathcal{C}^{\mathcal{E}}_{\mathcal{HI}+}(\mathcal{SHIQ}, \mathcal{SHOQ}, \mathcal{SHIO})$ were introduced by Cuenca Grau et al. [15] and Parsia and Cuenca Grau [34]. For each of these algorithms, the complexity of deciding the satisfiability of an i-concept C with respect to a combined knowledge base Σ is 2NExpTime in the size of C and Σ in the worst case. The Pellet reasoner[9] supports $\mathcal{C}^{\mathcal{E}}_{\mathcal{HQ}}(\mathcal{SHIQ}, \mathcal{SHOQ}, \mathcal{SHIO})$ and $\mathcal{C}^{\mathcal{E}}_{\mathcal{HI}}(\mathcal{SHIQ}, \mathcal{SHOQ}, \mathcal{SHIO})$ [15, 17]; Pellet's extension towards $\mathcal{C}^{\mathcal{E}}_{\mathcal{HQ}+}(\mathcal{SHIQ}, \mathcal{SHOQ}, \mathcal{SHIO})$ and also $\mathcal{C}^{\mathcal{E}}_{\mathcal{HO}+}(\mathcal{SHIQ}, \mathcal{SHOQ}, \mathcal{SHIO})$ is planned [34].

[9] Pellet OWL DL reasoner is an open-source competitive DL reasoner currently available. Pellet is available though its homepage http://clarkparsia.com/pellet/.

8.5.3 Modeling with $\mathcal{E}$-connections

Since DDL and $\mathcal{E}$-connections take a different modelling perspective, the examples that we present bellow in this section do not intend to remodel precisely the scenario of Sect. 8.4. Instead, they aim to demonstrate the practical modeling features offer to us by $\mathcal{E}$-connections.

Example 8.4 Let us build a combined knowledge base $\mathcal{K}$ about people and their occupation in a modular way. Let us split the modeling domain into three local ontologies:

- People, that contains individuals such as johnSmith, rickDeckard, etc., and concepts such as Man, Woman, Adult, Parent, etc.;
- Organizations, with individuals such as googleInc, operaSA, teatroAllaScala, etc., and concepts such as Enterprise, Theatre, ITCompany, etc.;
- Locations, that contains concepts such as Oslo, Milan, MountainView, Norway, Italy, EU, USA, etc.

We are allowed to model this way, since people clearly are disjoint from institutions, and hence no individual will ever be an instance of some concept from People and some other concept from Organizations. The same holds for Locations.

However, in order to introduce yet another local ontology Professions that will contain concepts such as Researcher, Chef or Pilot, we ought to be cautious. We need to think twice about how do we really want to use these concepts: given an individual that represents a person, say johnSmith that comes from the ontology People, do we want this individual to possibly become an instance of one of the concepts in Professions? This kind of modeling is not possible in $\mathcal{E}$-connections. In fact, as showed below, we will be able to keep professions in a separate local ontology, but under certain restrictions.

Let us continue Example 8.4 as a running example in order to illustrate the usage of links.

Example 8.5 Assume the Organizations module contains the following knowledge:

$$\mathsf{ITCompany(operaSA)}$$

$$\mathsf{ITCompany(googleInc)}$$

$$\mathsf{ITCompany} \sqsubseteq \mathsf{Enterprise}$$

As people and institutions are separated between two distinct modules, we will need the link worksAt to indicate employment. It is important to specify the source and the destination ontology for links; the source module for the worksAt link is People and its destination module is Organizations. We also add another link locatedIn between Organizations and Locations in order to indicate where the institutions are located. We do so by introducing the following object assertions:

johnSmith · worksAt · googleInc googleInc · locatedIn · MountainView
rickDeckard · worksAt · operaSA operaSA · locatedIn · Oslo

In addition, we employ links in restrictions in order to derive new knowledge within People in form of complex concepts, for instance by including the following GCI axiom:

$$\exists \mathsf{worksAt.Enterprise} \sqsubseteq \mathsf{IndustryEmployee}$$

Using the $\mathcal{E}$-connections semantics, one is able to derive that both johnSmith and rickDeckard are in fact industry employees.

As mentioned above, $\mathcal{E}$-connections require strict separation of modeling domains between modules. Hence, if we want to introduce a new local ontology Professions that will contain concepts such as Chef or Pilot this comes at some cost. Particularly, we will not be able to assert in the ABox of People that some its individuals belongs to any of the concepts of Professions. Also, we will not be able to relate directly concepts such as Adult of People with say Policeman of Professions by means of subsumption. In part, these issues are overcome by using links instead of class membership, as we show in the following example. While inter-ontology class membership is ruled by this approach, it possibly yields satisfactory modeling.

Example 8.6 Let us now include a new local ontology Professions containing concepts such as Chef, Pilot, Researcher, Policeman, etc. In order to express that some people belong to certain profession, we use the link hasProfession between People and Professions:

johnSmith · hasProfession · Chef
rickDeckard · hasProfession · Researcher

The two more expressive $\mathcal{E}$-connections frameworks $\mathcal{C}^{\mathcal{E}}_{\mathcal{HQ}+}(\mathcal{SHIQ}, \mathcal{SHIQ}, \mathcal{SHOQ})$ and $\mathcal{C}^{\mathcal{E}}_{\mathcal{HI}+}(\mathcal{SHIQ}, \mathcal{SHIQ}, \mathcal{SHOQ})$ also include the general transitivity axiom [15, 34]. Taking advantage of the fact that names are freely allowed to be reused for role and link properties, this allows very for flexible transitivity control. In order to demonstrate this feature, we borrow an example that originally appears in these works.

Example 8.7 Let us add some more knowledge into our running example. First, we add to Organizations (indexed by 2) further structure for the Google company:

partOf(gCateringDpt, gEmployeeServicesDiv)
partOf(gEmployeeServicesDiv, googleInc)

In addition, for whatever reason we decide to also include knowledge about human body parts in the component ontology. In accordance, we add the following axiom into People (indexed by 1):

$$\mathsf{patOf(finger47, johnSmith)}$$

Finally, we are also free to use the property patOf as a link, and so we add the following object assertion between these two component ontologies:

$$\mathsf{johnSmith} \cdot \mathsf{partOf} \cdot \mathsf{gCateringDpt}$$

With previous flavors of $\mathcal{E}$-connections, we would need to use a separate role name for each component ontology an for each linkbox between each two component modules. In this case, we would be forced to use three names.

However, the real utility of this feature only comes in combination with general transitivity axioms. Before these axioms were introduced, $\mathcal{E}$-connections only included the possibility to declare transitive roles inside each component RBox. This would allow us to derive $\mathcal{K} \models \mathsf{patOf(gCateringDpt, googleInc)}$ in our case, if we have previously declared the role partOf transitive in the Organizations component, but not anything more. General transitivity axioms allow us to assert transitivity on the combined relation resulting from the composition of all partOf properties, whether roles or links, e.g., by the following axiom:

$$\mathrm{Trans}\big(\mathsf{partOf}; (1,1), (1,2), (2,2)\big)$$

By including this axiom in $\mathcal{K}$ we derive that $\mathcal{K} \models \mathsf{johnSmith} \cdot \mathsf{partOf} \cdot \mathsf{googleInc}$ which is intuitively justified, but as well $\mathcal{K} \models \mathsf{finger47} \cdot \mathsf{partOf} \cdot \mathsf{googleInc}$ which may not be justified for each modeling scenario. However, the transitivity axiom is versatile enough, and we easily rule out the second consequence, if undesired, by replacing the above transitivity axiom by:

$$\mathrm{Trans}\big(\mathsf{partOf}; (1,2), (2,2)\big)$$

$\mathcal{E}$-connections allow to connect several ontologies under the assumption that their modeling domains are separated. Knowledge from one local ontology is reused in the other ontologies thanks to use of link properties. Such a framework is of demand and is easily applicable if one is about to build a new an ontology in a modular way, and from the very beginning clearly perceives how to split the modeling domain into modules. Highly developed reasoning algorithms and readily available reasoning engines make $\mathcal{E}$-connections also available for practical use. A tool that allows to automatically partition a monolithic ontology is also available [18]. On the other hand, the separate domains assumption is a serious obstacle if one wishes to combine several already existing ontologies. In such a case, we consider the assumption of separate domains too strict, as with fair probability the modeling domains covered by these existing ontologies overlap to some extent.

8.6 Package-based Description Logics

Package-based Description Logics (P-DL) was originally introduced by Bao and Honavar under the name Package-extended Ontologies [7]. Later the framework was developed by Bao et al. [4–6, 8]. Within this framework, a modular ontology is composed of several packages. Each ontological entity (namely, each individual, concept and role) is assigned its home package – the package it primarily belongs to. Given a package P_i, besides for its home terms, also other terms are free to appear in P_i, even if their home package is different from P_i. These terms are said to be *foreign terms* in P_i, and they are said to be *imported into* P_i.

Similarly to the formalisms presented above, in the semantics of P-DL each packages is interpreted in a local model. The denotation of foreign symbols is related to the denotation of these symbols in their home package. P-DL also includes several other modularisation features inspired by modular software engineering [6]. Package nesting is possible, by virtue of which packages are organized into a hierarchy. The package hierarchy in a P-DL ontology constitutes an organizational structure, in contrast to the semantic structure imposed by ontology axioms and importing. In addition, P-DL includes scope limitation modifiers which allow ontology engineers to limit the visibility of certain terms from the perspective of packages other than their home package. Most typical examples of these are the three predefined modifiers public, protected and private, however P-DL allows users to introduce their own modifiers.

8.6.1 Formalization

We now proceed by introducing the P-DL framework formally. The review in this section is based on the most recent publication of Bao et al. to date [8]. Here, P-DL is built over the local language $\mathcal{SHOIQ}$ resulting into the P-DL language $\mathcal{SHOIQP}$.

Definition 8.13 (Syntax of $\mathcal{SHOIQP}$ PD-L) A package based ontology is any $\mathcal{SHOIQ}$ ontology $\mathcal{P}$, which partitions into a finite set of packages $\{P_i\}_{i\in I}$, where I is some finite index set, and such that for every term (namely, concept, role and individual symbol) t of the alphabet of $\mathcal{P}$, there is a unique package, called the *home package* of t.

Given a package-based ontology $\mathcal{P} = \{P_i\}_{i\in I}$, we will use the following terminology:

- the set of home terms of a package $P_i \in \mathcal{P}$ is denoted by Δ_{S_i};
- the index of the home package of a term t is denoted by home(t);
- term t occurring in P_i is a *local term* in P_i if home$(t) = i$, otherwise it is said to be a *foreign term* in P_i;

- if t is a foreign term in P_j, and home $(t) = i$, then we write $i \xrightarrow{t} j$;
- $i \rightarrow j$ means that $i \xrightarrow{t} j$ for some t;
- $i \xrightarrow{*} j$ if $i = i_1 \rightarrow i_2 \ldots i_{n-1} \rightarrow i_n = j$ for some $i_1, \ldots, i_n \in I$;
- $P_j^* = P_j \cup \{P_i | i \xrightarrow{*} j\}$.

When a package P_j imports another package P_i, it imports also the domain of P_i. In order to denote in P_j the domain of an imported package P_i, the language of P-DL introduces the concept symbol $\top_i$. Within the local model of P_j, the denotation of $\top_i$ represents the domain of P_i (it is an image of this domain). P-DL also introduces so called *contextualized negation* $\neg_i$, which is a concept constructor applicable within the package P_i and the packages that import P_i. When it occurs in P_i, $\neg_i$ stands for normal concept complement. However, if $\neg_i C$ occurs in P_j is the complement with respect to the domain of P_i as imported into P_j (i.e., within P_j we have $\neg_i C \equiv \top_i \sqcap \neg_j C$).

The semantics of P-DL is also called semantics of importing by Bao et al. [4] due to its ability to import concepts from one ontology to another. In this sense, it is similar to the approach of Pan et al. [33] who also investigate semantic imports in distributed ontologies. The P-DL semantics is reminiscent of the DDL semantics in that sense that it also relies on a domain relation which projects interpretation of terms from one package to another. Unlike to the original DDL semantics, strict constraints are placed on the domain relation in P-DL. It is worthwhile to note that some later works on DDL experiment with incorporating some of these restrictions into the DDL framework [24].

Definition 8.14 (Semantics of $\mathcal{SHOIQP}$ P-DL) Given a package-based ontology $\mathcal{P} = \{P_i\}_{i \in I}$, a distributed interpretation of $\mathcal{P}$ is a pair $\mathcal{I} = \langle \{\mathcal{I}_i\}_{i \in I}, \{r_{ij}\}_{i \xrightarrow{*} j} \rangle$ such that each $\mathcal{I}_i = \langle \Delta^{\mathcal{I}_i}, \cdot^{\mathcal{I}_i} \rangle$ is an interpretation of the local package P_i and each $r_{ij} \subseteq \Delta^{\mathcal{I}_i} \times \Delta^{\mathcal{I}_j}$ is a domain relation between $\Delta^{\mathcal{I}_i}$ and $\Delta^{\mathcal{I}_j}$. A distributed interpretation $\mathcal{I}$ is a model of $\{P_i\}_{i \in I}$ if the following conditions hold:

1. there is at least one $i \in I$ such that $\Delta^{\mathcal{I}_i} \neq \emptyset$;
2. $\mathcal{I}_i \models P_i$;
3. r_{ij} is an injective partial function, and r_{ii} is the identity function;
4. If $i \xrightarrow{*} j$ and $j \xrightarrow{*} k$, then $r_{ik} = r_{ij} \circ r_{jk}$;
5. if $i \xrightarrow{t} j$, then $r_{ij}(t^{\mathcal{I}_i}) = t^{\mathcal{I}_j}$;
6. if $i \xrightarrow{R} j$, then if $(x, y) \in R^{\mathcal{I}_i}$ and $r_{ij}(x)$ is defined then, also $r_{ij}(y)$ is defined.

In a nutshell, the P-DL semantics is characterized as follows. If two terms t_1 and t_2 appear within some package P_i, and they are related by means of axioms in P_i, then this relation is propagated into any other package P_j where both these terms also appear, as long as P_j directly or indirectly imports P_i.

8.6.2 Reasoning in P-DL

The three main reasoning tasks for P-DL are consistency of knowledge bases, concept satisfiability and concept subsumption entailment with respect to a knowledge base. In addition, these three decision problems are always defined with respect to a so called witness package P_w of the knowledge base $\mathcal{P}$. When answering the decision problems, we only care about the importing closure P_w^* of the witness package and we neglect the rest of the knowledge base. Given two different packages P_1 and P_2, the answer to these decision problems may be different when witnessed by P_1 as it is when witnessed by P_2.

Definition 8.15 (Reasoning tasks for P-DL) A package-based ontology $\mathcal{P}$ is consistent as witnessed by a package P_w of $\mathcal{P}$, if there exists a model $\mathcal{I}$ of P_w^* such that $\Delta^{\mathcal{I}_w} \neq \emptyset$. A concept C is satisfiable as witnessed by a package P_w of $\mathcal{P}$, if there exists a model $\mathcal{I}$ of P_w^* such that $C^{\mathcal{I}_w} \neq \emptyset$. A subsumption formula $C \sqsubseteq D$ is valid as witnessed by a package P_w of $\mathcal{P}$ (denoted $\mathcal{P} \models C \sqsubseteq_w D$), if for every model $\mathcal{I}$ of P_w^* we have $C^{\mathcal{I}_w} \subseteq D^{\mathcal{I}_w}$.

While not formally introduced in by Bao et al. [8] we analogously define also ABox formulae entailment, as follows.

Definition 8.16 (ABox reasoning for P-DL) A formula $C(a)$ is valid as witnessed by a package P_w of $\mathcal{P}$, if for every model $\mathcal{I}$ of P_w^* we have $a^{\mathcal{I}_w} \in C^{\mathcal{I}_w}$. A formula $R(a,b)$ is valid as witnessed by a package P_w of $\mathcal{P}$, if for every model $\mathcal{I}$ of P_w^* we have $\langle a^{\mathcal{I}_w}, b^{\mathcal{I}_w}\rangle \in R^{\mathcal{I}_w}$.

A distributed reasoning algorithm for the P-DL language $\mathcal{ALCP_C}$, a sublanguage of $\mathcal{SHOIQP}$ which is build on top the local DL $\mathcal{ALC}$ and only allows for importing of concepts, was given by Bao et al. [5]. To our best knowledge, no implementation is known. The decidability and the computational complexity of reasoning for the full expressive P-DL language $\mathcal{SHOIQP}$ are shown via a reduction of a package-based ontology into a standard DL knowledge base. $\mathcal{SHOIQP}$ is decidable and the computational complexity for the decision problems is NExpTime-complete [8].

8.6.3 Modeling with P-DL

The $\mathcal{E}$-connections users will find P-DL familiar. In fact, one is able to model in P-DL in a very similar fashion. In order to illustrate this, we remodel Example 8.4 in P-DL.

Example 8.8 Let us build a package based ontology $\{P_1, P_2, P_3\}$ where P_1 will contain knowledge about people, P_2 about organizations, and P_3 about locations. Let us fix the home terms for these packages as follows: $\Delta_{S_1} = \{$Person, Man, Woman,

Child, Adult, hasChild, IndustryEmployee, worksAt, johnSmith, rickDeckard}, $\Delta_{S_2} =$ {ITCompany, Enterprise, Theatre, googleInc, operaSA, locatedIn}, and we fix $\Delta_{S_3} =$ {Oslo, Milan, MountainView, Norway, Italy, EU, USA}.

It shows that we are able to mimic the conceptual modeling that we have done in case of $\mathcal{E}$-connections. In this respect, we put into P_1 the following axioms:

$$\mathsf{Child} \sqsubseteq \neg\mathsf{Adult}$$

$$\mathsf{Woman} \sqsubseteq \neg\mathsf{Man}$$

$$\mathsf{Parent} \sqsubseteq \exists\mathsf{hasChild.Person}$$

$$\exists\mathsf{worksAt.Enterprise} \sqsubseteq \mathsf{IndustryEmployee}$$

Since worksAt now turns into a regular role with its home package being P_1, role assertions are used to express where our P_1-individuals work. In accordance, we add the following axioms into P_1:

$$\mathsf{worksAt(johnSmith, googleInc)}$$

$$\mathsf{worksAt(rickDeckard, operaSA)}$$

In the TBox of P_2, we put:

$$\mathsf{ITCompany} \sqsubseteq \mathsf{Enterprise}$$

And in the P_2's ABox, we put:

$$\mathsf{ITCompany(operaSA)} \qquad \mathsf{locatedIn(operaSA, Oslo)}$$

$$\mathsf{ITCompany(googleInc)} \qquad \mathsf{locatedIn(googleInc, MountainView)}$$

Altogether we have done the following imports:

$$2 \overset{\mathsf{operaSA}}{\rightarrow} 1 \qquad 3 \overset{\mathsf{Oslo}}{\rightarrow} 2$$

$$2 \overset{\mathsf{googleInc}}{\rightarrow} 1 \qquad 3 \overset{\mathsf{MountainView}}{\rightarrow} 2$$

$$2 \overset{\mathsf{Enterprise}}{\rightarrow} 1$$

Notice that in the last axiom of P_1 we have build the 1-concept ∃worksAt.Enterprise in a very similar fashion as we would do in $\mathcal{E}$-connections. The only foreign term that comes into play here is Enterprise. The fact that worksAt in not a link but a 1-role here is only a minor difference compared to $\mathcal{E}$-connections.

Given the importing relation, under the P-DL semantics we derive that both individuals johnSmith and rickDeckard are instances of the concept IndustryEmployee, as witnessed by the package P_1. This does not follow from P_1 directly, distributed reasoning is required.

P-DL offers more freedom in modeling however. Let us now extend Example 8.8 in order to demonstrate this. We will introduce a new package P_4 that will cover the domain of professions. However, even if we have decided to split the modeling domain into the domain of persons in P_1 and the domain of professions in P_4, we will still be able to relate the concepts Policeman and Adult by a GCI, even if each of them belongs to a different home package. Moreover, we will be allowed to assert membership of individuals of P_1 in concepts imported from P_4. Recall from our conclusion from Sect. 8.5, that such modeling is not possible in $\mathcal{E}$-connections.

Example 8.9 Let us now enrich the P-DL knowledge base from Example 8.8 with new package P_4 that will deal with professions. The home terms of P_4 are $\Delta_{S_4} =$ {Chef, Pilot, Researcher, Policeman}. In addition, let us add into the home terms of P_1 a new individual enderWiggin.

We record conceptual knowledge about professions in P_4, such as, for instance, for some professions only adults are eligible. Hence, in the TBox of P_4, we have:

$$\mathsf{Policeman} \sqsubseteq \mathsf{Adult} \qquad \mathsf{Pilot} \sqsubseteq \mathsf{Adult}$$

And, in the ABox of P_1, we indicate:

$$\mathsf{Pilot(enderWiggin)} \qquad \mathsf{Chef(johnSmith)}$$

$$\mathsf{Child(enderWiggin)}$$

Altogether, the importing relation is enriched by the following imports:

$$4 \overset{\mathsf{Chef}}{\to} 1 \qquad 1 \overset{\mathsf{Adult}}{\to} 4$$

$$4 \overset{\mathsf{Pilot}}{\to} 1$$

Expectedly, in this case, the P-DL semantics renders the knowledge base inconsistent as witnessed by the package P_1. This is because the individual enderWiggin is an instance of both Child and Pilot, the second concept being imported from P_4. The semantics of importing will assure that also in P_1 the imported concept Pilot is a subconcept of Adult; this subsumption relation is imported from P_4. This in turn implies that the individual enderWiggin is also an instance of Adult, a concept disjoint with Child to which enderWiggin must belong because it was explicitly asserted in the P_1's ABox.

As we have seen, the prominent feature of P-DL is term importing which allows us to reuse in any local ontology also terms defined in some other part of the system together with the knowledge associated with these terms. This makes P-DL an attractive formalism for modelling distributed ontologies. The reasoning algorithm is, however, known only for a rather limited case of package-based $\mathcal{ALC}$ with only concept imports allowed. Also no implementation of a P-DL reasoner is available, a serious obstacle towards its practical use.

8.7 Integrated Distributed Description Logics

Integrated Distributed Description Logics (IDDL) was introduced by Zimmerman [41] with the main motivation of overcoming some of the limitations of the already existing formalisms for ontology mapping. IDDL was particularly designed to support reasoning about ontology mappings and mapping composition. The basic intuition of IDDL is to represent mappings in a separate logical language, on which it is possible to define a calculus, that allows to determine logical consequence between mappings. A second motivation for the introduction of IDDL was the fact that DDL, $\mathcal{E}$-connections and P-DL considers ontology mappings as a method linking the items of a source ontology (concepts, roles and individuals) with the items of a target ontology, and they are expressed from the perspective of the target ontology. In the vision of IDDL, mappings are semantic relations between items of different ontologies, stated form an external perspective and so they do not distinguish between a source and a target ontology. This vision is much more similar to peer-to-peer information integration approach introduced by Ullman [39] and further formalized by Calvanese et al. [11], in which mappings are represented as implication formulas of two data sources.

8.7.1 Formalization

Theoretically, IDDL is built on top of an underlying DL that employs basic $\mathcal{ALC}$ features, plus qualified number restrictions, nominals, role complement, union, intersection and composition, inverse roles and the transitive-reflexive closure role constructor [41, 42] (i.e., this language extends $\mathcal{SHOIQ}_b$ introduced in Sect. 8.2 with composition of roles and role transitive-reflexive closure constructors). This language is known to be undecidable [3]. It has been showed, however, that reasoning in IDDL is decidable as long as each local KB uses a sub-language which is decidable [42].

Definition 8.17 (Syntax of IDDL) An IDDL knowledge base, called distributed system (DS), is a pair $\langle \mathbf{O}, \mathbf{A} \rangle$ where $\mathbf{O} = \{O_i\}_{i \in I}$ is a set of DL ontologies and $\mathbf{A} = \{A_{ij}\}_{i,j \in I}$ is a family of alignments, each A_{ij} consisting of correspondence axioms of the following six possible forms:

$$i : C \overset{\sqsubseteq}{\longleftrightarrow} j : D, \qquad i : R \overset{\sqsubseteq}{\longleftrightarrow} j : S$$

$$i : C \overset{\perp}{\longleftrightarrow} j : D, \qquad i : R \overset{\perp}{\longleftrightarrow} j : S$$

$$i : a \overset{\in}{\longleftrightarrow} j : C, \qquad i : a \overset{=}{\longleftrightarrow} j : b$$

where C, D are concepts, R, S, are roles, a, b are individuals, and $k : \phi$ means that the expression ϕ belongs to the local ontology O_i and conforms to its local language. From left to right from top to bottom, the above correspondence axioms are called cross-ontology concept subsumption, cross-ontology role subsumption, cross-ontology concept disjointness, cross-ontology role disjointness, cross-ontology membership and cross-ontology identity.

In order to simplify the notation, we add a syntactic shorthand $i : X \stackrel{\equiv}{\longleftrightarrow} j : Y$, representing the pair of cross-ontology subsumptions $i : X \stackrel{\sqsubseteq}{\longleftrightarrow} j : Y$, $j : Y \stackrel{\sqsubseteq}{\longleftrightarrow} i : X$, where X, Y are either both concepts or both roles.

Definition 8.18 (Semantics of IDDL) Given a distributed system $S = \langle \mathbf{O}, \mathbf{A} \rangle$ over an index set I, a distributed interpretation of S is a pair $\langle \mathbf{I}, \boldsymbol{\varepsilon} \rangle$ where $\mathbf{I} = \{\mathcal{I}_i\}_{i \in I}$ is a family of local interpretations such that each $\mathcal{I}_i = \langle \Delta^{\mathcal{I}_i}, \cdot^{\mathcal{I}} \rangle$ is an interpretation of $\mathcal{O}_i$ in its own language with a non-empty local domain $\Delta^{\mathcal{I}_i}$, and the equalizing function $\boldsymbol{\varepsilon} = \{\varepsilon_i\}_{i \in I}$ is a family of functions $\varepsilon_i : \Delta^{\mathcal{I}_i} \to \Delta_\varepsilon$ that map all elements of each local domain $\Delta^{\mathcal{I}_i}$ into a single global domain Δ_ε[10].

A distributed interpretation $\mathcal{I} = \langle \mathbf{I}, \boldsymbol{\varepsilon} \rangle$ satisfies a local axiom $i : \phi \in O_i$ (denoted by $\mathcal{I} \models_{\mathrm{d}} i : \phi$) if ϕ is satisfied by $\mathcal{I}_i$ in according to its local DL language. A local ontology $\mathcal{O}_i$ is satisfied by $\mathcal{I}$ (denoted $\mathcal{I} \models_{\mathrm{d}} O_i$) if each its axiom $i : \phi \in O_i$ is satisfied by $\mathcal{I}$. A correspondence axiom ψ is satisfied by $\mathcal{I}$ depending on its type as follows:

$$\mathcal{I} \models_{\mathrm{d}} i : C \stackrel{\sqsubseteq}{\longleftrightarrow} j : D \quad \text{if } \varepsilon_i\big(C^{\mathcal{I}_i}\big) \subseteq \varepsilon_j\big(D^{\mathcal{I}_j}\big)$$

$$\mathcal{I} \models_{\mathrm{d}} i : R \stackrel{\sqsubseteq}{\longleftrightarrow} j : S \quad \text{if } \varepsilon_i\big(R^{\mathcal{I}_i}\big) \subseteq \varepsilon_j\big(S^{\mathcal{I}_j}\big)$$

$$\mathcal{I} \models_{\mathrm{d}} i : C \stackrel{\perp}{\longleftrightarrow} j : D \quad \text{if } \varepsilon_i\big(C^{\mathcal{I}_i}\big) \cap \varepsilon_j\big(D^{\mathcal{I}_j}\big) = \emptyset$$

$$\mathcal{I} \models_{\mathrm{d}} i : R \stackrel{\perp}{\longleftrightarrow} j : R \quad \text{if } \varepsilon_i\big(R^{\mathcal{I}_i}\big) \cap \varepsilon_j\big(S^{\mathcal{I}_j}\big) = \emptyset$$

$$\mathcal{I} \models_{\mathrm{d}} i : a \stackrel{\in}{\longleftrightarrow} j : C \quad \text{if } \varepsilon_i\big(a^{\mathcal{I}_i}\big) \in \varepsilon_j\big(D^{\mathcal{I}_j}\big)$$

$$\mathcal{I} \models_{\mathrm{d}} i : a \stackrel{=}{\longleftrightarrow} j : b \quad \text{if } \varepsilon_i\big(a^{\mathcal{I}_i}\big) = \varepsilon_j\big(b^{\mathcal{I}_j}\big)$$

An alignment A_{ij} is satisfied by $\mathcal{I}$ (denoted $\mathcal{I} \models_{\mathrm{d}} A_{ij}$) if for each correspondence axiom $\psi \in A_{ij}$ we have $\mathcal{I} \models_{\mathrm{d}} \psi$.

Given an index set I, a distributed system $S = \langle \mathbf{O}, \mathbf{A} \rangle$ and a distributed interpretation $\mathcal{I} = \langle \mathbf{I}, \boldsymbol{\varepsilon} \rangle$ both over I, we say that $\mathcal{I}$ is a model of S (denoted by $\mathcal{I} \models_{\mathrm{d}} S$) if for each $i \in I$ we have $\mathcal{I} \models_{\mathrm{d}} O_i$ and for each pair $i, j \in I$ we have $\mathcal{I} \models_{\mathrm{d}} A_{ij}$.

---

[10] Each of ε_i is a function, hence it certainly assigns to each element $x \in \Delta^{\mathcal{I}_i}$ some element $y \in \Delta_\varepsilon$. As the local domain $\Delta^{\mathcal{I}_i}$ is required to be nonempty for each $i \in I$, it follows that the global domain Δ_ε is also nonempty.

8.7.2 Reasoning in IDDL

The main reasoning task described for IDDL is consistency checking for distributed systems. Since the definition of a consistent distributed system is not given by Zimmerman and Duc [41, 42], we assume the usual definition, which is as follows.

Definition 8.19 (DS consistency in IDDL) A distributed system S is consistent if there exists a distributed interpretation $\mathcal{I}$ that is a model of S.

The other reasoning tasks for IDDL are local formula entailment and also correspondence formula entailment.

Definition 8.20 (Other reasoning tasks in IDDL) A formula ϕ (either a local formula or an correspondence formula) is entailed by S (denoted $S \models_{\mathrm{d}} \phi$) if for each distributed interpretation $\mathcal{I}$ that is a model of S it holds that $\mathcal{I} \models_{\mathrm{d}} \phi$.

All the other reasoning tasks are reducible into distributed system consistency checking [42]. A sound and complete algorithm for consistency checking of IDDL distributed systems with alignments limited to cross-ontology concept subsumption, disjointness and role subsumption was given by Zimmerman and Duc [42]. This reasoning algorithm is based on a reduction of a distributed system into a set of independent ontologies which are all consistent if and only if the original distributed system is consistent. Worst-case complexity of this procedure is 3ExpTime [42].

An attempt to provide an axiomatization of the effects of the correspondences in terms of propagation rules, similar to the rules presented for DDL, is presented in [41]. The completeness of these rules is still an open problem.

8.7.3 Modeling with IDDL

IDDL is particularly intended for reasoning about ontology mapping. In IDDL the mapping is not primarily viewed as a mean of knowledge transfer between ontologies, instead it is viewed as an integrating element that forms the global semantics of a distributed system on top of the local semantics of each of the components thereof. As such, the mapping is bidirectional—a unique feature among the frameworks part of this review. This poses some implications on the way how one models with IDDL. In order to demonstrate this, we remodel in part of the scenario created in Examples 8.1–8.3.

Example 8.10 In our example company, three ontologies are used. The first one is O_1, the ontology of employees. An excerpt:

$$\mathsf{ITStaff} \sqsubseteq \mathsf{Employee} \qquad \mathsf{SupportStaff} \sqsubseteq \mathsf{Employee}$$

$$\mathsf{CateringStaff} \sqsubseteq \mathsf{SupportStaff} \qquad \mathsf{AdministrativeStaff} \sqsubseteq \mathsf{SupportStaff}$$

$$\mathsf{Cook} \sqsubseteq \mathsf{CateringStaff} \qquad \mathsf{Chef} \sqsubseteq \mathsf{Cook}$$

There is also O_2, the brigade de cuisine ontology of kitchen jobs. An excerpt:

$$\mathsf{KitchenChef} \sqsubseteq \mathsf{Cook} \qquad \mathsf{Saucemaker} \sqsubseteq \mathsf{Cook}$$

$$\mathsf{PastryCook} \sqsubseteq \mathsf{Cook} \qquad \mathsf{Baker} \sqsubseteq \mathsf{PastryCook}$$

And, in addition, the accounting department prefers to model things according to their own taste, so there is O_3, the accounting ontology. An excerpt:

$$\mathsf{Accountant} \sqsubseteq \mathsf{Employee} \qquad \mathsf{Director} \sqsubseteq \mathsf{Employee}$$

$$\mathsf{SeniorExecutive} \sqsubseteq \mathsf{Employee} \qquad \mathsf{JuniorExecutive} \sqsubseteq \mathsf{Employee}$$

$$\mathsf{BasicStaff} \sqsubseteq \mathsf{Employee} \qquad \mathsf{SupportStaff} \sqsubseteq \mathsf{Employee}$$

With IDDL we are able to integrate these three ontologies into a DS $S = \langle \mathbf{O} = \{O_1, O_2, O_3\}, \mathbf{A} \rangle$ using the alignment $\mathbf{A}$ as follows:

$$2:\mathsf{KitchenChef} \overset{\sqsubseteq}{\longleftrightarrow} 1:\mathsf{Chef} \qquad 2:\mathsf{Cook} \overset{\equiv}{\longleftrightarrow} 1:\mathsf{Cook}$$

$$3:\mathsf{Employee} \overset{\equiv}{\longleftrightarrow} 1:\mathsf{Employee} \qquad 3:\mathsf{Accountant} \overset{\sqsubseteq}{\longleftrightarrow} 1:\mathsf{AdministrativeStaff}$$

$$1:\mathsf{ITStaff} \overset{\sqsubseteq}{\longleftrightarrow} 3:\mathsf{BasicStaff} \qquad 1:\mathsf{SupportStaff} \overset{\equiv}{\longleftrightarrow} 3:\mathsf{SupportStaff}$$

In the DS S, we now derive, for instance, $S \models_{\mathrm{d}} 2:\mathsf{Baker} \overset{\sqsubseteq}{\longleftrightarrow} 1:\mathsf{CateringStaff}$ and as well $S \models_{\mathrm{d}} 2:\mathsf{Baker} \overset{\sqsubseteq}{\longleftrightarrow} 3:\mathsf{SupportStaff}$. In fact, the entailed relation $S \models_{\mathrm{d}} i:X \overset{\sqsubseteq}{\longleftrightarrow} j:Y$ provides us with a global view, i.e., ontological organization of all concepts regardless of what ontology they originally belonged to.

Besides for mapping between concepts, IDDL allows to map between roles, in a very analogous fashion. We move on and demonstrate working with individuals in IDDL in the following example.

Example 8.11 After asserting in O_1 the following axiom:

$$\mathsf{Cook(johnSmith)}$$

and asserting the following correspondence:

$$1:\mathsf{johnSmith} \overset{=}{\longleftrightarrow} 3:\mathsf{e006B3F}$$

we are immediately able to derive as a consequence the cross-ontology membership $S \models_{\mathrm{d}} 3:\mathsf{e006B3F} \overset{\in}{\longleftrightarrow} 1:\mathsf{CateringStaff}$. In addition, if we want to further indicate the specialization of this employee (a 1-individual), it is not necessary to copy the desired target concept from O_2 to O_1, instead we use the cross-ontology membership correspondence as an axiom. We add:

$$1:\mathsf{johnSmith} \overset{\in}{\longleftrightarrow} 3:\mathsf{Baker}$$

Sometimes it is handy to indicate the disjointness of concepts (also roles) across ontologies. IDDL provides us with means to do it.

Example 8.12 Since the company does not specialize in catering services but in IT instead, we add the following cross-ontology disjointness:

$$1:\mathsf{CateringStaff} \overset{\perp}{\longleftrightarrow} 3:\mathsf{Director}$$

We are immediately able to derive both $S \models_{\mathrm{d}} 1:\mathsf{johnSmith} \overset{\in}{\longleftrightarrow} 3:\neg\mathsf{Director}$ and $S \models_{\mathrm{d}} 3:\mathsf{e006B3F} \overset{\in}{\longleftrightarrow} 3:\neg\mathsf{Director}$ which are consequences on the global semantics.

It also sometimes happens in IDDL that the global semantics resulting from the mapping influences the local semantics of a particular component ontology. For instance, in our example the entailed consequence $S \models_{\mathrm{d}} 3:\mathsf{e006B3F} \overset{\in}{\longleftrightarrow} 3:\neg\mathsf{Director}$ causes that within $\mathcal{O}_3$ we derive $s \models_{\mathrm{d}} 3:\neg\mathsf{Director}(\mathsf{e006B3F})$.

As we have seen, IDDL is especially suitable for ontology integration, representing mapping and reasoning about mapping. In contrast, the other approaches concentrate on reuse of knowledge, for instance, when building a new ontology one may reuse some ontologies that already exist. DDL, $\mathcal{E}$-connections and P-DL are more suitable for this task than IDDL because of two reasons; first, in IDDL the mapping is bidirectional, and hence if ontology O_1 wishes to reuse ontology O_2 also O_2 is affected by O_1; and second, IDDL creates a global view which is rather centralized and not distributed.

A typical application scenario for IDDL is for instance reasoning about mapping computed by one of the ontology matching algorithms [19]. These algorithms typically produce bidirectional mapping and the main reasoning task here would be determining the consistency of the resulting integrated ontology.

8.8 Conclusion

This chapter gives a comparative presentation of the most important logical representation frameworks for modular ontologies. Above all, we have concentrated on expressivity and modeling with these formalisms: by which practical features the modular ontology development is supported in each of the formalisms and how one is able to use these features in order to model ontologies in a modular fashion. We summarize our observations as follows.

- Distributed Description Logics allow for distributed ontologies in which the component modules are connected by directional semantic mapping. With this mapping, concepts, roles and individuals from distinct components are semantically associated. This allows for reuse of knowledge between the component ontologies. This reuse is directed, that is, if ontology O_1 reuses ontology O_2, the latter is not affected at all. DDL is able to cope with partially overlapping modeling domains and as well with inconsistency that appears locally in one of the component modules.
- $\mathcal{E}$-connections allow to combine several component ontology modules under the assumption that the local modeling domains are strictly disjoint. In $\mathcal{E}$-connections, one connects ontologies with links, practically inter-ontology roles. This framework is especially applicable when building a complex ontology in a modular fashion, and from the beginning it is understood how the local modeling domains should be separated. $\mathcal{E}$-connections also provide an elaborate transitivity control for combinations of local and inter-ontology roles.
- Package-based Description Logic allow to combine several ontology modules by semantic importing of ontology entities, that is, concepts, roles and individuals. Semantically, P-DL overcomes some of the limitations of the other approaches and improves their expressivity.
- Integrated Distributed Description Logics allow for integration of several ontologies with bi-directional semantic mapping, while maintaining both the local view (of each component ontology) and as well the global view (the result of integration). While the previous approaches aim at ontology combination and reuse, IDDL aims more at ontology integration. Typical application for IDDL is reasoning about automatically computed ontology mapping.

All four frameworks feature distributed reasoning algorithms, however, only for DDL and $\mathcal{E}$-connections the reasoning support is available in form of practical implementations (DDL reasoner DRAGO and $\mathcal{E}$-connections support in the reasoner Pellet). To our best knowledge, no practical implementations of reasoners for the other two frameworks is known, which leaves them, for the time being, at the level of theoretical proposals without practical applicability.

This chapter is not the first attempt for comparison of modular ontology representation frameworks. Wang et al. propose a first qualitative comparison of the different approaches [40]. More formal approach to comparison of the expressivity of the frameworks also exits. First formal comparison between expressive power of DDL and $\mathcal{E}$-connections was carried out by Kutz et al. [28]; Cuenca Grau and Kutz [14] compare DDL, $\mathcal{E}$-connections and P-DL, and in addition they compare these three approaches with the approach that combines ontologies by simple union under specific conditions as discussed in Sect. 8.1; and Bao et al. [4] claim that DDL with mapping on concepts and $\mathcal{E}$-connections are strictly less expressive than Package-based Description Logics. Also, all four approaches are reducible into regular Description Logics [8, 10, 14, 42].

References

1. Baader, F., Calvanese, D., McGuinness, D., Nardi, D., Patel-Schneider, P. (eds.): The Description Logic Handbook. Cambridge University Press, Cambridge (2003)
2. Baader, F., Lutz, C., Sturm, H., Wolter, F.: Fusions of description logics and abstract description systems. J. Artif. Intell. Res. (JAIR) **16**, 1–58 (2002)
3. Baader, F., Sattler, U.: Number restrictions on complex roles in description logics. In: Procs. of the Fifth International Conference on Principles of Knowledge Representation and Reasoning (KR'96). Morgan Kaufmann, San Mateo (1996)
4. Bao, J., Caragea, D., Honavar, V.: On the semantics of linking and importing in modular ontologies. In: Procs. of ISWC 2006. LNCS, vol. 4273. Springer, Berlin (2006)
5. Bao, J., Caragea, D., Honavar, V.G.: A tableau-based federated reasoning algorithm for modular ontologies. In: Procs. of IEEE/WIC/ACM International Conference on Web Intelligence (WI'06). IEEE Press, New York (2006)
6. Bao, J., Caragea, D., Honavar, V.G.: Towards collaborative environments for ontology construction and sharing. In: Procs. of the 2006 International Symposium on Collaborative Technologies and Systems, Las Vegas, Nevada, USA (2006)
7. Bao, J., Honavar, V.: Ontology language extensions to support collaborative ontology building. In: 3rd International Semantic Web Conference (ISWC2004) (2004)
8. Bao, J., Voutsadakis, G., Slutzki, G., Honavar, V.: Package-based description logics. In: Modular Ontologies: Concepts, Theories and Techniques for Knowledge Modularization. LNCS, vol. 5445, pp. 349–371. Springer, Berlin (2009)
9. Borgida, A., Serafini, L.: Distributed description logics. In: Horrocks, I., Tessaris, S. (eds.) Proceedings of the 2002 Intl. Workshop on Description Logics (DL2002), CEUR-WS, Toulouse (2002)
10. Borgida, A., Serafini, L.: Distributed description logics: Assimilating information from peer sources. J. Data Semant. **1**, 153–184 (2003)
11. Calvanese, D., Giacomo, G.D., Lenzerini, M., Rosati, R.: Logical foundations of peer-to-peer data integration. In: PODS, pp. 241–251 (2004)
12. Cuenca Grau, B., Horrocks, I., Kazakov, Y., Sattler, U.: A logical framework for modularity of ontologies. In: IJCAI 2007, Proceedings of the 20th Joint Conference on Artificial Intelligence, Hyderabad, India, January 6–12, 2007, pp. 298–303 (2007)
13. Cuenca Grau, B., Horrocks, I., Kutz, O., Sattler, U.: Will my ontologies fit together? In: Procs. of the 2006 International Workshop on Description Logics (DL'06), pp. 175–182 (2006)
14. Cuenca Grau, B., Kutz, O.: Modular ontology languages revisited. In: SWeCKa 2007: Proc. of the IJCAI-2007 Workshop on Semantic Web for Collaborative Knowledge Acquisition, Hyderabad, India, January 7, 2007
15. Cuenca Grau, B., Parsia, B., Sirin, E.: Tableaux algorithms for $\mathcal{E}$-connections of description logics. Tech. Rep., University of Maryland Institute for Advanced Computer Studies (2004)
16. Cuenca Grau, B., Parsia, B., Sirin, E.: Working with multiple ontologies on the Semantic Web. In: Procs. of ISWC2004. LNCS, vol. 3298. Springer, Berlin (2004)
17. Cuenca Grau, B., Parsia, B., Sirin, E.: Combining OWL ontologies using $\mathcal{E}$-connections. J. Web Semant. **4**(1), 40–59 (2006)
18. Cuenca Grau, B., Parsia, B., Sirin, E., Kalyanpur, A.: Modularity of web ontologies. In: Proc. of the 10th International Conference on Principles of Knowledge Representation and Reasoning (KR 2006), pp. 198–209. AAAI Press, Menlo Park (2006)
19. Euzenat, J., Shvaiko, P.: Ontology Matching. Springer, Berlin (2007)
20. Ghidini, C., Serafini, L., Tessaris, S.: On relating heterogeneous elements from different ontologies. In: Procs. of the Sixth International and Interdisciplinary Conference on Modeling and Using Context (CONTEXT'07). LNCS, vol. 4635. Springer, Berlin (2007)
21. Ghidini, C., Serafini, L., Tessaris, S.: Complexity of reasoning with expressive ontology mappings. In: FOIS, pp. 151–163 (2008)

22. Ghilardi, S., Lutz, C., Wolter, F.: Did I damage my ontology? A case for conservative extensions in description logics. In: Procs. of the Tenth International Conference on Principles of Knowledge Representation and Reasoning (KR 2006), pp. 187–197. AAAI Press, Menlo Park (2006)
23. Homola, M.: Distributed description logics revisited. In: Procs. of the 20th International Workshop on Description Logics (DL-2007), CEUR-WS, vol. 250 (2007)
24. Homola, M., Serafini, L.: Towards distributed tableaux reasoning procedure for DDL with increased subsumption propagation between remote ontologies. In: Advances in Ontologies, Procs. of Knowledge Representation Ontology Workshop (KROW 2008). CRPIT, vol. 90. Australian Computer Society, Canberra (2008)
25. Horrocks, I., Sattler, U.: A tableaux decision procedure for $\mathcal{SHOIQ}$. In: Proc. of the 19th International Joint Conference on Artificial Intelligence (IJCAI-05), pp. 448–453 (2005)
26. Kutz, O.: $\mathcal{E}$-connections and logics of distance. Ph.D. Thesis, University of Liverpool, UK (2004)
27. Kutz, O., Lutz, C., Wolter, F., Zakharyaschev, M.: $\mathcal{E}$-connections of description logics. In: Procs. of the 2003 International Workshop on Description Logics (DL2003), CEUR-WS, vol. 81 (2003)
28. Kutz, O., Lutz, C., Wolter, F., Zakharyaschev, M.: $\mathcal{E}$-connections of abstract description systems. Artif. Intell. **156**(1), 1–73 (2004)
29. Kutz, O., Wolter, F., Zakharyaschev, M.: Connecting abstract description systems. In: Proceedings of the 8th Conference on Principles of Knowledge Representation and Reasoning (KR 2002), pp. 215–226. Morgan Kaufmann, San Mateo (2002)
30. Lutz, C., Walther, D., Wolter, F.: Conservative extensions in expressive description logics. In: IJCAI 2007, Proceedings of the 20th International Joint Conference on Artificial Intelligence, Hyderabad, India, January 6–12, 2007, pp. 453–458 (2007)
31. McGuinness, D.L., van Harmelen, F. (eds.): OWL Web Ontology Language Overview. A W3C Recommendation. Available online, at http://www.w3.org/TR/owl-features/
32. Motik, B., Cuenca Grau, B., Horrocks, I., Wu, Z., Fokoue, A., Lutz, C. (eds.): OWL 2 Web Ontology Language Profiles. A W3C Candidate Recommendation. Available online, at http://www.w3.org/TR/owl2-profiles/
33. Pan, J.Z., Serafini, L., Zhao, Y.: Semantic import: An approach for partial ontology reuse. In: Haase, P., Honavar, V., Kutz, O., Sure, Y., Tamilin, A. (eds.) Procs. of the 1st International Workshop on Modular Ontologies (WoMo-06), CEUR-WS, vol. 232, Athens, Georgia, USA (2006)
34. Parsia, B.: Cuenca Grau, B.: Generalized link properties for expressive $\mathcal{E}$-connections of description logics. In: Proc. of the Twentieth National Conference on Artificial Intelligence (AAAI-2005). AAAI Press, Menlo Park (2005)
35. Serafini, L., Borgida, A., Tamilin, A.: Aspects of distributed and modular ontology reasoning. In: Procs. of the Nineteenth International Joint Conference on Artificial Intelligence (IJCAI-05), pp. 570–575 (2005)
36. Serafini, L., Tamilin, A.: Local tableaux for reasoning in distributed description logics. In: Procs. of the 2004 International Workshop on Description Logics (DL2004), CEUR-WS, vol. 104 (2004)
37. Serafini, L., Tamilin, A.: Distributed instance retrieval in heterogeneous ontologies. In: Proc. of the 2nd Italian Semantic Web Workshop Semantic Web Applications and Perspectives (SWAP'05), Trento, Italy (2006)
38. Tobies, S.: Complexity results and practical algorithms for logics in knowledge representation. Ph.D. Thesis, RWTH Aachen, Germany (2001)
39. Ullman, J.D.: Information integration using logical views. In: Afrati, F.N., Kolaitis, P.G. (eds.) Database Theory—ICDT '97, 6th International Conference, Delphi, Greece, January 8–10, 1997, Proceedings. Lecture Notes in Computer Science, vol. 1186, pp. 19–40. Springer, Berlin (1997)
40. Wang, Y., Bao, J., Haase, P., Qi, G.: Evaluating formalisms for modular ontologies in distributed information systems. In: Web Reasoning and Rule Systems, First International Confer-

ence, RR 2007, Proceedings. Lecture Notes in Computer Science, vol. 4524, pp. 178–193. Springer, Berlin (2007)
41. Zimmermann, A.: Integrated distributed description logics. In: Procs. of 20th International Workshop on Description Logics (DL-2007), CEUR-WS, vol. 250 (2007)
42. Zimmermann, A., Le Duc, C.: Reasoning on a network of aligned ontologies. In: Calvanese, D., Lausen, G. (eds.) Web Reasoning and Rule Systems, Second International Conference, RR 2008, Karlsruhe, Germany, October/November 2008, Proceedings. Lecture Notes in Computer Science, vol. 5341, pp. 43–57. Springer, Berlin (2008)

Chapter 9
Semantic Matching with S-Match

Pavel Shvaiko, Fausto Giunchiglia, and Mikalai Yatskevich

Abstract We view *matching* as an operation that takes two graph-like structures (e.g., lightweight ontologies) and produces an alignment between the nodes of these graphs that correspond semantically to each other. *Semantic matching* is based on two ideas: (i) we discover an alignment by computing *semantic relations* (e.g., equivalence, more general); (ii) we determine semantic relations by analyzing the *meaning* (concepts, not labels) which is codified in the entities and the structures of ontologies. In this chapter, we first overview the state of the art in the ontology matching field. Then we present basic and optimized algorithms for semantic matching as well as their implementation within the S-Match system. Finally, we evaluate S-Match against state of the art systems, thereby justifying empirically the strength of the approach.

9.1 Introduction

Matching is an important operation in many applications, such as ontology integration, data warehouses, peer-to-peer data sharing, etc. The matching operation takes two graph-like structures (e.g., lightweight ontologies [14]) and produces an alignment, that is a set of mapping elements (or correspondences), between the nodes of the graphs that correspond semantically to each other.

There exist various solutions of matching, see [7, 37, 40, 41] for recent surveys. In turn, some recent examples of individual matching approaches can be found in [2, 3, 6, 8, 10–12, 23, 27, 32, 38].[1] We concentrate on a schema-based solution, i.e.,

---

[1] See www.OntologyMatching.org for a complete information on the topic.

The first and the third authors performed this work while at the University of Trento.

P. Shvaiko (✉)
TasLab, Informatica Trentina S.p.A., Trento, Italy
e-mail: pavel.shvaiko@infotn.it

F. Giunchiglia
Dipto. Ingegneria e Scienza dell'Informazione, Università di Trento, Via Sommarive 14, 38100 Povo TN, Italy
e-mail: fausto@dit.unitn.it

M. Yatskevich
Faculté de Médecine, Université Rennes 1, Rennes, France
e-mail: mikalai.yatskevich@univ-rennes1.fr

R. De Virgilio et al. (eds.), *Semantic Web Information Management*,
DOI 10.1007/978-3-642-04329-1_9, © Springer-Verlag Berlin Heidelberg 2010

a matching system that exploits only the schema information and does not consider the instance information. We follow an approach called *semantic matching* [15]. This approach is based on two key ideas. The first is that we calculate correspondences between ontology entities by computing *semantic relations* (e.g., equivalence, more general, disjointness), instead of computing coefficients rating match quality in the [0, 1] range, as it is the case in most previous approaches, see, for example, [6, 10, 30, 33]. The second idea is that we determine semantic relations by analyzing the *meaning* (concepts, not labels) which is codified in the entities and the structures of ontologies. In particular, labels at nodes, written in natural language, are automatically translated into propositional formulas which explicitly codify the labels' intended meaning. This allows us to translate the matching problem into a propositional validity problem, which can then be efficiently resolved using (sound and complete) state of the art propositional satisfiability (SAT) deciders, e.g., [28].

A vision for the semantic matching approach and some of its implementation within S-Match were reported in [15–17, 19, 22]. In turn, the works in [18, 21, 23, 43] focused on the following aspects of S-Match: (i) algorithms and implementation, (ii) discovering missing background knowledge in matching tasks, (iii) explanation of matching results and (iv) large-scale evaluation. This chapter builds on top of the above mentioned works and provides a summative account for the semantic matching approach (hence, the key algorithms are identical to those in the above mentioned works).

The rest of the chapter is organized as follows. Section 9.2 overviews the state of the art in the ontology matching field. Section 9.3 presents the semantic matching approach. Section 9.4 introduces the optimizations that allow improving efficiency of the basic version of Sect. 9.3. Section 9.5 outlines the S-Match architecture. The evaluation results are presented in Sect. 9.6. Finally, Sect. 9.7 provides conclusions and discusses future work.

9.2 State of the Art

A good survey and a classification of ontology[2] matching approaches up to 2001 was provided in [40], a semantics driven extension of its schema-based part and a user-centric classification of matching systems was provided in [41], while the work in [9] considered both [40, 41] as well as some other classifications.

In particular, for individual matchers, [41] introduced the following criteria which allow for detailing further the element and structure level of matching: *syntactic* techniques (these interpret their input as a function of their sole structures following some clearly stated algorithms, e.g., iterative fix point computation for

[2] An ontology typically provides a vocabulary that describes a domain of interest and a specification of the meaning of terms used in the vocabulary. Depending on the precision of this specification, the notion of ontology includes various data and conceptual models [9]. The term ontology is used here in a wide sense, and, hence, encompasses, e.g., sets of terms, classifications, database schemas, thesauri, or fully axiomatized theories.

matching graphs), *external* techniques (these exploit external resources of knowledge, e.g., WordNet [35]), and *semantic* techniques (these use formal semantics, e.g., model-theoretic semantics) in order to interpret the input and justify their results.

The distinction between the hybrid and composite matching algorithms of [40] is useful from an architectural perspective. The work in [41] extended this view by taking into account how the systems can be distinguished in the matter of considering the alignments and the matching task, thus representing the end-user perspective. In this respect, the following criteria were used: *alignments as solutions* (these systems consider the matching problem as an optimization problem and the alignment is a solution to it, e.g., [10, 33]); *alignments as theorems* (these systems rely on semantics and require the alignment to satisfy it, e.g., the approach discussed in this chapter); *alignments as likeness clues* (these systems produce only reasonable indications to a user for selecting the alignment, e.g., [5, 30]).

So far there have been developed more than 50 various matching approaches, such as Harmony [36], Falcon [26], RiMOM [29], Sambo [27], to name a few, see [9] for the detailed comparison of the state of the art systems. Here, we only consider the closest to S-Match schema-based systems in light of the above mentioned criteria.

Rondo implements the Similarity Flooding (SF) [33] approach, and utilizes a hybrid matching algorithm based on the ideas of similarity propagation [34]. Schemas are presented as directed labeled graphs. The algorithm exploits only syntactic techniques at the element and structure level. It starts from the string-based comparison, such as common prefixes and suffixes tests, of the nodes' labels to obtain an initial alignment which is further refined within the fix-point computation. Rondo considers the alignments as a solution to a clearly stated optimization problem.

Cupid implements a hybrid matching algorithm comprising syntactic techniques at the element (e.g., common prefixes test) and structure (e.g., tree matching weighted by leaves) levels [30]. It also exploits external resources, such as a precompiled thesaurus. Cupid falls into the alignments as likeness clues category.

COMA implements a composite matching approach which exploits syntactic and external techniques [5, 6]. It provides a library of matching algorithms; a framework for combining obtained results, and a platform for the evaluation of the effectiveness of the different matchers. The matching library is extensible and contains six elementary matchers, five hybrid matchers and one reuse-oriented matcher. Most of them implement string-based techniques, such as n-gram and edit distance; others share techniques with Cupid, such as tree matching weighted by leaves; reuse-oriented matcher tries to reuse previously obtained results for entire new ontologies or for their fragments. Specialties of COMA with respect to Cupid include a more flexible architecture and a possibility of performing iterations in the matching process. COMA falls into the alignments as likeness clues category.

Semantic heterogeneity is typically reduced in two steps. We have focused so far only on the first step, i.e., establishing an alignment between semantically related entities of ontologies. The second step includes interpreting an alignment according to application needs, such as data translation or query answering. Here, alignments are taken as input and are analyzed in order to generate, e.g., query expressions, that automatically translate/exchange data instances between the information sources. Notice that taking as input semantic relations, instead of coefficients in the [0, 1] range, enables, e.g., data translation systems, to produce better results, since, e.g., in such systems as Clio [25], the first step is to interpret the correspondences by giving them a clear semantics.

9.3 Semantic Matching

We assume that all the data and conceptual models (e.g., lightweight ontologies [14]) can be generally represented as graphs (see [15] for a detailed discussion). This allows for the statement and solution of a *generic (semantic) matching problem* independently of specific conceptual or data models, very much along the lines of what is done in Cupid [30] and COMA [5]. We focus on tree-like structures or such types of ontologies as classifications and XML schemas. Real-world schemas are seldom trees, however, there are (optimized) techniques, transforming a graph representation of a schema into a tree representation, e.g., the graph-to-tree operator of Protoplasm [1]. From now on, we assume that a graph-to-tree transformation can be done by using existing systems, and therefore, we focus on other issues instead.

The semantic matching approach is based on two key notions, namely:

- *Concept of a label*, which denotes the set of documents (data instances) that one would classify under a *label* it encodes;
- *Concept at a node*, which denotes the set of documents (data instances) that one would classify under a node, given that it has a certain *label* and that it is in a certain *position* in a tree.

Our approach can discover the following semantic relations between the *concepts at nodes* of two ontologies: *equivalence* ($=$); *more general* ($\sqsupseteq$); *less general* ($\sqsubseteq$); *disjointness* ($\perp$). When none of the relations holds, the special *idk* (i do not know) relation is returned.[3] The relations are ordered according to decreasing binding strength, i.e., from the strongest ($=$) to the weakest (*idk*), with more general and less general relations having equal binding power. Notice that the strongest semantic relation always exists since, when holding together, more general and less general relations are equivalent to equivalence. These relations have the obvious set-theoretic semantics.

A *mapping element* is a 4-tuple $\langle ID_{ij}, a_i, b_j, R\rangle$, $i = 1, \ldots, N_A$; $j = 1, \ldots, N_B$; ID_{ij} is a unique identifier of the given mapping element; a_i is the i-th node of the first tree, N_A is the number of nodes in the first tree; b_j is the j-th node of the second

[3] Notice *idk* is an explicit statement that the system is unable to compute any of the declared (four) relations. This should be interpreted as either there is not enough background knowledge, and therefore, the system cannot explicitly compute any of the declared relations or, indeed, none of those relations hold according to an application.

tree, N_B is the number of nodes in the second tree; and R specifies a semantic relation which may hold between the concepts at nodes a_i and b_j. *Semantic matching* can then be defined as the following problem: given two trees T_A and T_B, compute the $N_A \times N_B$ mapping elements $\langle ID_{ij}, a_i, b_j, R' \rangle$, with $a_i \in T_A$, $i = 1, \ldots, N_A$; $b_j \in T_B$, $j = 1, \ldots, N_B$; and R' is the strongest semantic relation holding between the concepts at nodes a_i and b_j. Since we look for the $N_A \times N_B$ correspondences, the cardinality of mapping elements we are able to determine is $1 : N$. Also, these, if necessary, can be decomposed straightforwardly into mapping elements with the $1 : 1$ cardinality.

9.3.1 The Tree Matching Algorithm

We discuss the semantic matching algorithm with the help of an example, see Fig. 9.1. Here, numbers are the unique identifiers of nodes. We use "C" for concepts of labels and concepts at nodes. For instance, in the tree A, $C_{History}$ and C_4 are, respectively, the concept of the label *History* and the concept at node 4. To simplify the presentation, whenever it is clear from the context we assume that the concept of a label can be represented by the label itself. In this case, for example, $C_{History}$ becomes denoted as *History*. Finally, we sometimes use subscripts to dis-

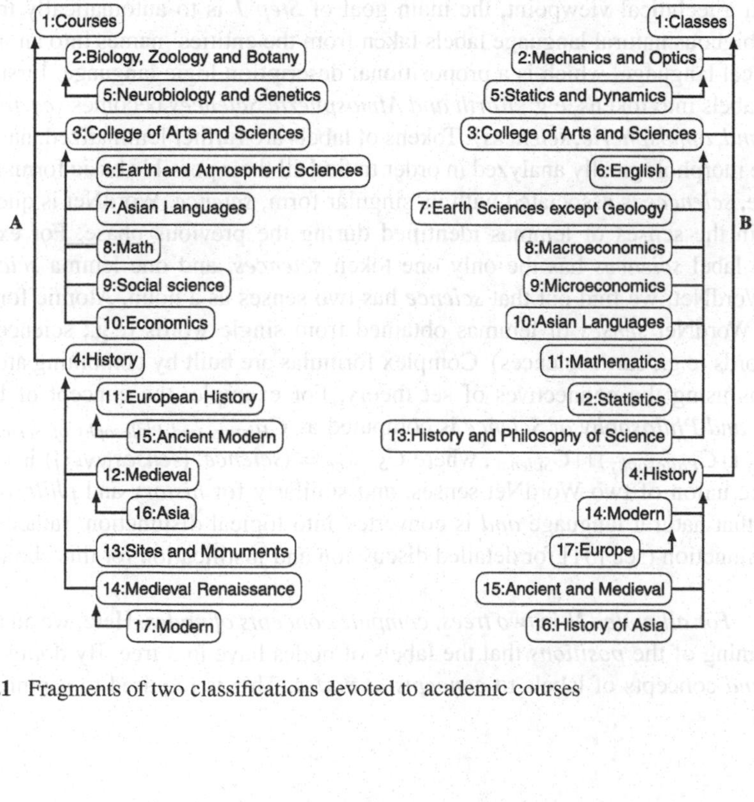

Fig. 9.1 Fragments of two classifications devoted to academic courses

tinguish between trees in which the given concept of a label occurs. For instance, $History_A$, means that the concept of the label *History* belongs to the tree A.

The algorithm discussed below was first published in [16] and later updated in [17, 23]. It takes as input two ontologies and computes as output a set of mapping elements in four macro steps:

- *Step 1*: for all labels L in two trees, compute concepts of labels, C_L.
- *Step 2*: for all nodes N in two trees, compute concepts at nodes, C_N.
- *Step 3*: for all pairs of labels in two trees, compute relations among C_L's.
- *Step 4*: for all pairs of nodes in two trees, compute relations among C_N's.

The first two steps represent the preprocessing phase, while the third and the fourth steps are the element level and structure level matching, respectively. It is important to notice that *Step 1* and *Step 2* can be done once, independently of the specific matching problem. *Step 3* and *Step 4* can only be done at run time, once two trees which must be matched have been chosen.

Step 1. *For all labels L in two trees, compute concepts of labels.* We view labels of nodes as concise descriptions of the data that is stored under the nodes. Here, we compute the meaning of a label at a node (in isolation) by taking as input a *label*, by analyzing its real-world semantics (e.g., using WordNet [35]), and by returning as output a *concept of the label*. For example, by writing $C_{History}$ we move from the natural language label *History* to the concept $C_{History}$, which codifies explicitly its intended meaning, namely the data (documents) which are about history.

From a technical viewpoint, the main goal of *Step 1* is to automatically translate ambiguous natural language labels taken from the entities' names into an internal logical language, which is a propositional description logic language. First, we chunk labels into tokens, e.g., *Earth and Atmospheric Sciences* becomes ⟨*earth sciences, and, atmospheric, sciences*⟩. Tokens of labels are further lemmatized, namely they are morphologically analyzed in order to find all their possible basic forms. For instance, *sciences* is associated with its singular form, *science*. WordNet is queried to obtain the senses of lemmas identified during the previous phase. For example, the label *sciences* has the only one token *sciences*, and one lemma *science*. From WordNet, we find out that *science* has two senses as a noun. Atomic formulas are WordNet *senses* of lemmas obtained from single words (e.g., science) or multiwords (e.g., earth sciences). Complex formulas are built by combining atomic formulas using the connectives of set theory. For example, the concept of label *History and Philosophy of Science* is computed as $C_{History\ and\ Philosophy\ of\ Science} = (C_{History} \sqcup C_{Philosophy}) \sqcap C_{Science}$, where $C_{Science} = \langle science, \{senses_{WN\#2}\}\rangle$ is taken to be the union of two WordNet senses, and similarly for *history* and *philosophy*. Notice that natural language *and* is converted into logical disjunction, rather than into conjunction (see [31] for detailed discussion and justification for this choice).

Step 2. *For all nodes N in two trees, compute concepts of nodes.* Here, we analyze the meaning of the *positions* that the labels of nodes have in a tree. By doing this, we *extend* concepts of labels to *concepts at nodes*. This is required to capture the knowledge residing in the structure of a tree, namely the *context* in which the given concept of label occurs [13]. For example, in the tree A, when we write C_4 we mean the concept describing all the documents of the (academic) courses, which are about history.

From a technical viewpoint, concepts of nodes are written in the same propositional logical language as concepts of labels. Classifications and XML schemas are hierarchical structures where the path from the root to a node uniquely identifies that node and also its meaning. Thus, following an access criterion semantics [24], the logical formula for a concept at node is defined as a conjunction of concepts of labels located in the path from the given node to the root. For example, in the tree A, the concept at node four is computed as follows: $C_4 = C_{Courses} \sqcap C_{History}$.

Step 3. *For all pairs of labels in two trees, compute relations among concepts of labels* (*label matching*). Relations between concepts of labels are computed with the help of a library of element level semantic matchers [20]. These matchers take as input two concepts of labels and produce as output a semantic relation (e.g., equivalence, more/less general) between them. Some of them are reimplementations of the well-known matchers used in Cupid [30] and COMA [5]. The most important difference is that our matchers ultimately return a semantic relation, rather than an affinity level in the [0, 1] range, although sometimes using customizable thresholds.

The label matchers are briefly summarized in Table 9.1. The first column contains the names of the matchers. The second column lists the order in which they are executed. The third column introduces the matchers' approximation level. The relations produced by a matcher with the first approximation level are always correct. For example, *name* $\sqsupseteq$ *brand* as returned by the *WordNet* matcher. In fact, according

Table 9.1 Element level semantic matchers [17, 23]

Matcher name	Execution order	Approximation level	Matcher type	Schema info
Prefix	2	2	String-based	Labels
Suffix	3	2	String-based	Labels
Edit distance	4	2	String-based	Labels
Ngram	5	2	String-based	Labels
Text corpus	13	3	String-based	Labels + corpus
WordNet	1	1	Sense-based	WordNet senses
Hierarchy distance	6	3	Sense-based	WordNet senses
WordNet gloss	7	3	Gloss-based	WordNet senses
Extended WordNet gloss	8	3	Gloss-based	WordNet senses
Gloss comparison	9	3	Gloss-based	WordNet senses
Extended gloss comparison	10	3	Gloss-based	WordNet senses
Semantic gloss comparison	11	3	Gloss-based	WordNet senses
Extended semantic gloss comparison	12	3	Gloss-based	WordNet senses

to WordNet *name* is a hypernym (superordinate word) of *brand*. Notice that *name* has 15 senses and *brand* has 9 senses in WordNet. We use some sense filtering techniques to discard the irrelevant senses [23]. The relations produced by a matcher with the second approximation level are likely to be correct (e.g., *net* ≡ *network*, but *hot* ≡ *hotel* by *Prefix*). The relations produced by a matcher with the third approximation level depend heavily on the context of the matching task (e.g., *cat* ≡ *dog* by *Extended gloss comparison* in the sense that they are both pets). Notice that by default matchers are executed following the order of increasing approximation level. The fourth column reports the matchers' type. The fifth column describes the matchers' input.

We have three main categories of matchers. *String-based* matchers have two labels as input (with exception of *Text corpus* which takes in input also a text corpus). These compute only equivalence relations (e.g., equivalence holds if the weighted *distance* between the input strings is lower than an empirically established threshold). *Sense-based* matchers have two WordNet senses in input. The *WordNet* matcher computes equivalence, more/less general, and disjointness relations; while *Hierarchy distance* computes only the equivalence relation. *Gloss-based* matchers also have two WordNet senses as input, however they exploit techniques based on comparison of textual definitions (*glosses*) of the words whose senses are taken in input. These compute, depending on a particular matcher, the equivalence, more/less general relations, see for details [18, 20].

The result of *Step 3* is a matrix of relations holding between atomic concepts of labels; Table 9.2 shows a part of it for the example of Fig. 9.1.

Step 4. *For all pairs of nodes in two trees, compute relations among concepts of nodes* (*node matching*). Here, we initially reformulate the tree matching problem into a set of node matching problems (one problem for each pair of nodes). Then we translate each node matching problem into a propositional validity problem.

The tree matching algorithm is concerned with the decomposition of the tree matching task into a set of node matching tasks. It takes as input two preprocessed trees obtained as a result of *Step 1*, *Step 2* and a matrix of semantic relations holding between the atomic concepts of labels in both trees obtained as a result of *Step 3*. It produces as output the matrix of semantic relations holding between concepts at nodes in both trees. The pseudo code in Algorithm 9.1 illustrates the tree matching algorithm.

Table 9.2 Matrix of semantic relations holding between concepts of labels (*ClabsMatrix*)

A	B			
	Classes	*History*	*Modern*	*Europe*
Courses	=	*idk*	*idk*	*idk*
History	*idk*	=	*idk*	*idk*
Medieval	*idk*	*idk*	⊥	*idk*
Asia	*idk*	*idk*	*idk*	⊥

Algorithm 9.1 The pseudo code of the tree matching algorithm [23]

```
900.  String[ ][ ] treeMatch(Tree of Nodes source, target, String[ ][ ] cLabsMatrix)
910.    Node sourceNode, targetNode;
920.    String[ ][ ] cNodesMatrix, relMatrix;
930.    String axioms, context_A, context_B;
940.    int i, j;
960.    for each sourceNode ∈ source
970.      i = getNodeId(sourceNode);
980.      context_A = getCnodeFormula(sourceNode);
990.      for each targetNode ∈ target
1000.       j = getNodeId(targetNode);
1010.       context_B = getCnodeFormula(targetNode);
1020.       relMatrix = extractRelMatrix(cLabsMatrix, sourceNode, targetNode);
1030.       axioms = mkAxioms(relMatrix);
1040.       cNodesMatrix[i][j] = nodeMatch(axioms, context_A, context_B);
1050. return cNodesMatrix;
```

Table 9.3 Matrix of relations among the concepts at nodes (*cNodesMatrix*)

A	B: C_1	C_4	C_{14}	C_{17}
C_1	$=$	$\sqsupseteq$	$\sqsupseteq$	$\sqsupseteq$
C_4	$\sqsubseteq$	$=$	$\sqsupseteq$	$\sqsupseteq$
C_{12}	$\sqsubseteq$	$\sqsubseteq$	$\bot$	$\bot$
C_{16}	$\sqsubseteq$	$\sqsubseteq$	$\bot$	$\bot$

In particular, treeMatch takes two trees of Nodes (source and target) and the matrix of relations holding between atomic concepts of labels (cLabsMatrix) as input. It starts from two loops over all the nodes of source and target trees in lines 960–1040 and 990–1040. The node matching problems are constructed within these loops. For each node matching problem, we take a pair of propositional formulas encoding concepts at nodes and relevant relations holding between the atomic concepts of labels using the getCnodeFormula and extractRelMatrix functions, respectively. The former are memorized as context_A and context_B in lines 980 and 1010. The latter are memorized in relMatrix in line 1020. In order to reason about relations between concepts at nodes, we build the premises (axioms) in line 1030. These are a conjunction of the concepts of labels which are related in relMatrix. For example, the semantic relations in Table 9.2, which are considered when we match C_4 in the tree A and C_4 in the tree B are $Classes_B \equiv Courses_A$ and $History_B \equiv History_A$. In this case, axioms is $(Classes_B \equiv Courses_A) \sqcap (History_B \equiv History_A)$. Finally, in line 1040, the semantic relations holding between the concepts at nodes are calculated by nodeMatch and are reported as a bidimensional array (cNodesMatrix); Table 9.3 shows a part of it for the example of Fig. 9.1.

Table 9.4 The relationship between semantic relations and propositional formulas [17, 23]

rel(*a*, *b*)	Translation of *rel*(*a*, *b*) into propositional logic	Translation of (9.2) into Conjunctive Normal Form
$a \equiv b$	$a \leftrightarrow b$	N/A
$a \sqsubseteq b$	$a \rightarrow b$	$axioms \wedge context_A \wedge \neg context_B$
$a \sqsupseteq b$	$b \rightarrow a$	$axioms \wedge context_B \wedge \neg context_A$
$a \perp b$	$\neg(a \wedge b)$	$axioms \wedge context_A \wedge context_B$

9.3.2 Node Matching Algorithm

Each node matching problem is converted into a propositional validity problem. Semantic relations are translated into propositional connectives using the rules described in Table 9.4 (second column).

The criterion for determining whether a relation holds between concepts of nodes is the fact that it is entailed by the premises. Thus, we have to prove that the following formula:

$$axioms \rightarrow rel(context_A, context_B) \tag{9.1}$$

is valid, namely that it is true for all the truth assignments of all the propositional variables occurring in it. *axioms*, $context_A$ and $context_B$ are the same as they were defined in the tree matching algorithm. *rel* is the semantic relation that we want to prove holding between $context_A$ and $context_B$. The algorithm checks the validity of (9.1) by proving that its negation, i.e., (9.2), is unsatisfiable.

$$axioms \wedge \neg rel(context_A, context_B) \tag{9.2}$$

Table 9.4 (third column) describes how (9.2) is translated before testing each semantic relation. Notice that (9.2) is in Conjunctive Normal Form (CNF), namely it is a conjunction of disjunctions of atomic formulas. The check for equivalence is omitted in Table 9.4, since $A \equiv B$ holds if and only if $A \sqsubseteq B$ and $A \sqsupseteq B$ hold, i.e., both $axioms \wedge context_A \wedge \neg context_B$ and $axioms \wedge context_B \wedge \neg context_A$ are unsatisfiable formulas.

Let us consider the pseudo code of a basic node matching algorithm, see Algorithm 9.2. In line 1110, nodeMatch constructs the formula for testing disjointness. In line 1120, it converts the formula into CNF, while in line 1130, it checks the CNF formula for unsatisfiability. If the formula is unsatisfiable, the disjointness relation is returned. Then the process is repeated for the less and more general relations. If both relations hold, then the equivalence relation is returned (line 1220). If all the tests fail, the *idk* relation is returned (line 1280). In order to check the unsatisfiability of a propositional formula in a basic version of our NodeMatch algorithm, we use the standard DPLL-based SAT solver [28].

Algorithm 9.2 The pseudo code of the node matching algorithm [23]

```
String nodeMatch(String axioms, context_A, context_B)
    formula = And(axioms, context_A, context_B);
    formulaInCNF = convertToCNF(formula);
    boolean isOpposite = isUnsatisfiable(formulaInCNF);
    if (isOpposite)
        return "⊥";
    String formula = And(axioms, context_A, Not(context_B));
    String formulaInCNF = convertToCNF(formula);
    boolean isLG = isUnsatisfiable(formulaInCNF)
    formula = And(axioms, Not(context_A), context_B);
    formulaInCNF = convertToCNF(formula);
    boolean isMG = isUnsatisfiable(formulaInCNF);
    if (isMG && isLG)
        return "=";
    if (isLG)
        return "⊑";
    if (isMG)
        return "⊒";
    return "idk";
```

From the example in Fig. 9.1, trying to prove that C_4 in the tree B is less general than C_4 in the tree A, requires constructing the following formula:

$$\big((Classes_B \leftrightarrow Courses_A) \wedge (History_B \leftrightarrow History_A)\big)$$
$$\wedge\, (Classes_B \wedge History_B) \wedge \neg(Courses_A \wedge History_A)$$

The above formula turns out to be unsatisfiable, and therefore, the less general relation holds. Notice, if we test for the more general relation between the same pair of concepts at nodes, the corresponding formula would be also unsatisfiable. Thus, the final relation returned by the NodeMatch algorithm for the given pair of concepts at nodes is the equivalence.

9.4 Efficient Semantic Matching

The node matching problem in semantic matching is a CO-NP hard problem, since it is reduced to the validity problem for the propositional calculus. In this section, we present a set of optimizations for the node matching algorithm. In particular, we show that when dealing with conjunctive concepts at nodes, i.e., the concept at node is a conjunction (e.g., C_7 in the tree A in Fig. 9.1 is defined as $Asian_A \wedge Languages_A$), the node matching tasks can be solved in linear time. When we have disjunctive concepts at nodes, i.e., the concept at node contains both conjunctions and disjunctions in any order (e.g., C_3 in the tree B in Fig. 9.1 is defined as $College_B \wedge (Arts_B \vee Sciences_B)$), we use techniques allowing us to avoid the exponential space explosion which arises due to the conversion of disjunctive formulas into CNF. This modification is required since all state of the art SAT deciders take CNF formulas in input.

9.4.1 Conjunctive Concepts at Nodes

Let us make some observations with respect to Table 9.4. The first observation is that the *axioms* part remains the same for all the tests, and it contains only clauses with two variables. In the worst case, it contains $2 \times n_A \times n_B$ clauses, where n_A and n_B are the number of atomic concepts of labels occurred in $context_A$ and $context_B$, respectively. The second observation is that the formulas for testing less and more general relations are very similar and they differ only in the negated context formula (e.g., in the test for less general relation $context_B$ is negated). This means that (9.2) contains one clause with n_B variables plus n_A clauses with one variable. In the case of disjointness, test $context_A$ and $context_B$ are not negated. Therefore, (9.2) contains $n_A + n_B$ clauses with one variable. Let us consider tests for more/less general relations, see [22, 23] for details on the other tests.

Tests for Less and More General Relations Using the above observations concerning Table 9.4, (9.2), with respect to the tests for less/more general relations, can be represented as follows:

$$\overbrace{\bigwedge_{q=0}^{n*m}(\neg A_s \vee B_t) \wedge \bigwedge_{w=0}^{n*m}(A_k \vee \neg B_l) \wedge \bigwedge_{v=0}^{n*m}(\neg A_p \vee \neg B_r)}^{Axioms} \wedge \overbrace{\bigwedge_{i=1}^{n} A_i}^{Context_A} \wedge \overbrace{\bigvee_{j=1}^{m} \neg B_j}^{\neg Context_B} \quad (9.3)$$

where n is the number of variables in $context_A$, m is the number of variables in $context_B$. The A_i's belong to $context_A$, and the B_j's belong to $context_B$. s, k, p are in the $[0..n]$ range, while t, l, r are in the $[0..m]$ range. q, w and v define the number of particular clauses. *Axioms* can be empty. Equation (9.3) is composed of clauses with one or two variables plus one clause with possibly more variables (the clause corresponding to the negated context). The key observation is that the formula in (9.3) is Horn, i.e., each clause contains at most one positive literal. Therefore, its satisfiability can be decided in linear time by the *unit resolution rule* [4]. Notice, that DPLL-based SAT solvers require quadratic time in this case.

In order to understand how the linear time algorithm works, let us prove the unsatisfiability of (9.3) in the case of matching C_{16} in the tree A and C_{17} in the tree B in Fig. 9.1. In this case, (9.3) is as follows:

$$\begin{aligned}
&(\neg \boldsymbol{course}_A \vee class_B) \wedge (\boldsymbol{course}_A \vee \neg class_B) \wedge (\neg \boldsymbol{history}_A \vee history_B) \\
&\wedge (\boldsymbol{history}_A \vee \neg history_B) \wedge (\neg \boldsymbol{medieval}_A \vee modern_B) \wedge (\neg \boldsymbol{asia}_A \vee \neg europe_B) \\
&\wedge \boldsymbol{course}_A \wedge \boldsymbol{history}_A \wedge \boldsymbol{medieval}_A \wedge \boldsymbol{asia}_A \\
&\wedge (\neg class_B \vee \neg history_B \vee \neg modern_B \vee \neg europe_B) \qquad (9.4)
\end{aligned}$$

In (9.4), the variables from $context_A$ are written in bold face. First, we assign *true* to all unit clauses occurring in (9.4) positively. Notice these are all and only the clauses in $context_A$. This allows us to discard the clauses where $context_A$ variables occur positively (in this case: $\boldsymbol{course}_A \vee \neg class_B, \boldsymbol{history}_A \vee \neg history_B$). The resulting formula is as follows:

$$class_B \wedge history_B \wedge \neg modern_B \wedge \neg europe_B \\ \wedge (\neg class_B \vee \neg history_B \vee \neg modern_B \vee \neg europe_B) \tag{9.5}$$

Equation (9.5) does not contain any variable derived from $context_A$. Notice that, by assigning *true* to $class_B$, $history_B$ and *false* to $modern_B$, $europe_B$ we do not derive a contradiction. Therefore, (9.5) is satisfiable. In fact, a (Horn) formula is unsatisfiable if and only if the empty clause is derived (and it is satisfiable otherwise).

Let us consider again (9.5). For this formula to be unsatisfiable, all the variables occurring in the negation of $context_B$ ($class_B \vee \neg history_B \vee \neg modern_B \vee \neg europe_B$ in our example) should occur positively in the unit clauses obtained after resolving *axioms* with the unit clauses in $context_A$ ($class_B$ and $history_B$ in our example). For this to happen, for any B_j in $context_B$ there must be a clause of form $\neg A_i \vee B_j$ in *axioms*, where A_i is a formula of $context_A$. Formulas of form $\neg A_i \vee B_j$ occur in (9.3) if and only if we have the axioms of form $A_i \equiv B_j$ and $A_i \sqsubseteq B_j$. These considerations suggest the following macro steps for testing satisfiability (see [23] for details):

- *Step 1.* Create an array of size m. Each entry in the array stands for one B_j in (9.3).
- *Step 2.* For each axiom of type, $A_i \equiv B_j$ and $A_i \sqsubseteq B_j$ mark the corresponding B_j.
- *Step 3.* If all the B_j's are marked, then the formula is unsatisfiable.

9.4.2 Disjunctive Concepts at Nodes

Now, we allow for the concepts of nodes to contain conjunctions and disjunctions in any order. As from Table 9.4, *axioms* is the same for all the tests. However, $context_A$ and $context_B$ may contain any number of disjunctions. Some of them are coming from the concepts of labels, while others may appear from the negated $context_A$ or $context_B$ (e.g., see less/more generality tests). With disjunctive concepts at nodes, (9.1) is a full propositional formula, and hence, no hypothesis can be made on its structure. Thus, its satisfiability must be tested by using a standard SAT decider.

In order to avoid the exponential space explosion, which may arise when converting (9.1) into CNF, we apply a set of structure preserving transformations [39]. The main idea is to replace disjunctions occurring in the original formula with newly introduced variables and to explicitly state that these variables imply the subformulas they substitute. Therefore, the size of the propositional formula in CNF grows linearly with respect to the number of disjunctions in the original formula. Thus, nodeMatch (see Algorithm 9.2) should be optimized by replacing all the calls to convertToCNF with calls to optimizedConvertToCNF.

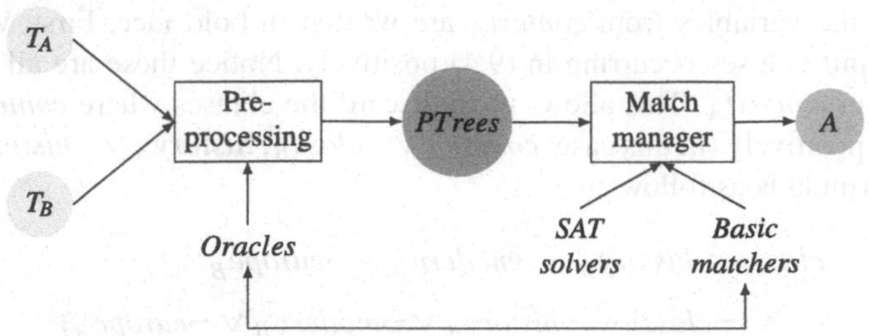

Fig. 9.2 The S-Match architecture (adapted from [9])

9.5 The S-Match Architecture

S-Match was designed and developed (in Java) as a platform for semantic matching, i.e., a modular system with the core of computing semantic relations where single components can be plugged, unplugged or suitably customized, see Fig. 9.2. It is a sequential system with a parallel composition at the element level.

The input tree-like structures (T_A and T_B) are codified in a standard internal XML format. The module taking input ontologies performs *preprocessing* (*Steps 1, 2*) with the help of *oracles*, such as WordNet. The output of the module is an enriched tree. These enriched trees are stored in an internal database (*PTrees*) where they can be browsed, edited and manipulated. The *Match manager* coordinates the matching process. S-Match libraries contain *basic element level matchers* of Table 9.1 (*Step 3*) and structure level matchers that include *SAT solvers* [28] and ad hoc reasoning methods [22] (*Step 4*). Finally, the Match manager outputs the computed alignment A.

9.6 Evaluation

Let us discuss the performance and quality evaluation of S-Match. In particular, we evaluate basic and optimized versions of our system, called (S-Match$_B$) and (S-Match), respectively, against three state of the art systems, such as Cupid [30], COMA [5] and SF [33] as implemented in Rondo [34]. All the systems under consideration are fairly comparable because they are all schema-based. They differ in the specific matching techniques they use and in the way they compute alignments (see Sect. 9.2).

9.6.1 Evaluation Set Up

The evaluation was performed on six matching tasks from different application domains, see Table 9.5.[4]

[4]Source files and description of the ontologies tested can be found at the Knowdive project website: http://www.dit.unitn.it/~knowdive/description_SMatch_experiments.php.

Table 9.5 Some indicators of the complexity of the test cases [23]

#	Matching task	Max depth	# nodes	#Labels per tree	Concepts of nodes
(a)	Cornell vs. Washington	3/3	34/39	62/64	Conjunctive Disjunctive
(b)	CIDX vs. Excel	3/3	34/39	56/58	Conjunctive Disjunctive
(c)	Looksmart vs. Yahoo	10/8	140/74	222/101	Conjunctive Disjunctive
(d)	Yahoo vs. Standard	3/3	333/115	965/242	Conjunctive Disjunctive
(e)	Google vs. Yahoo	11/11	561/665	722/945	Conjunctive Disjunctive
(f)	Google vs. Looksmart	11/16	706/1081	1048/1715	Conjunctive Disjunctive

There is one matching task from the academy domain: (a). It describes in a minimal way courses taught at the Cornell University and at the University of Washington. There are two tasks from the business domain: (b) and (d), e.g., BizTalk,[5] purchase order schemas CIDX and Excel. Finally, there are three matching tasks on general topics: (c), (e), (f) as represented by the well-known web directories, such as Google,[6] Yahoo[7] and Looksmart.[8]

The reference alignments for the tasks (a) and (b) were established manually. Then the results computed by the systems have been compared with the reference alignments. In this evaluation study, we focus mostly on the performance characteristics of S-Match, involving large matching tasks, namely ontologies with hundreds and thousands of nodes. Quality characteristics of the S-Match results which are presented here address only medium size ontologies; see [18, 21] for a large-scale quality evaluation.

There are three further observations that ensure a fair (qualitative) comparative study. The first observation is that Cupid, COMA and Rondo can discover only the correspondences which express similarity between entities. Instead, S-Match, among others, discovers the disjointness relation which can be interpreted as strong dissimilarity in terms of other systems under consideration. Therefore, we did not take into account the disjointness relations when specifying the reference alignments. The second observation is that, since S-Match returns a matrix of relations,

[5] http://www.microsoft.com/biztalk.

[6] http://www.google.com/Top/.

[7] http://dir.yahoo.com/.

[8] http://www.looksmart.com/.

while all other systems return a list of the best correspondences, we used some filtering rules. More precisely we have the following two rules: (i) discard all the correspondences where the relation is *idk*; (ii) return always the *core* relations, and discard relations whose existence is implied by the core relations. Finally, whether S-Match returns the equivalence or subsumption relations does not affect the quality indicators. What only matters is the presence of the correspondences standing for those relations.

As match quality measures, we have used the following indicators: *precision*, which is a correctness measure, *recall*, which is a completeness measure, *overall*, which is an estimate of the post match efforts needed for adding false negatives and removing false positives, and *F-measure*, computed as the harmonic mean of precision and recall, see for details [9]. As a performance measure, we have used *time*. It estimates how fast systems are when producing alignments fully automatically. Time is important, since it shows the ability of matching systems to scale up.

In our experiments, each test has two degrees of freedom: *directionality* and *use of oracles*. By directionality, we mean here the direction in which correspondences have been computed: from the first ontology to the second one (forward direction), or vice versa (backward direction). We report the best results obtained with respect to directionality, and use of oracles allowed. We were not able to plug a thesaurus in Rondo, since the version we have is standalone, and it does not support the use of external thesauri. Thesauri of S-Match, Cupid and COMA were expanded with terms necessary for a fair competition (e.g., expanding *uom* into *unitOfMeasure*, a complete list is available at the URL in Footnote 3).

All the tests have been performed on a P4-1700, with 512 MB of RAM, with the Windows XP operating system, and with no applications running but a single matching system. The systems were limited to allocate no more than 512 MB of memory. All the tuning parameters (e.g., thresholds, combination strategies) of the systems were taken by default (e.g., for COMA we used *NamePath* and *Leaves* matchers combined in the *Average* strategy) for all the tests. S-Match was also used in default configuration, e.g., threshold for string-based matchers was 0.6.

9.6.2 Evaluation Results

We present the time performance results for all the tasks of Table 9.5, while quality results, as from the previous discussion are presented for the tasks (a) and (b).

The evaluation results were first published in [23] and are shown in Fig. 9.3. For example, on task (a), since all the labels at nodes in the given test case were correctly encoded into propositional formulas, all the quality measures of S-Match reach their highest values. In fact, as discussed before, the propositional SAT solver is correct and complete. This means that once the element level matchers have found all and only the correspondences, S-Match will return all of them and only the correct ones. In turn, on task (b), S-Match performs as good as COMA and outperforms other systems in terms of quality indicators. Also, the optimized version of S-Match works

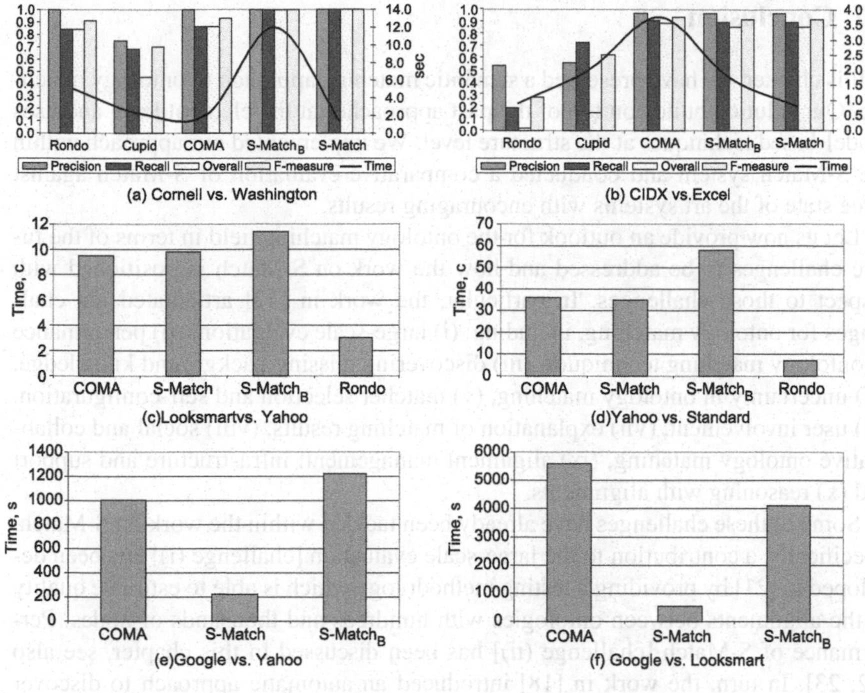

Fig. 9.3 The evaluation results

more than 4 times faster than COMA, more than 2 times faster than Cupid, and as fast as Rondo.

For what concerns the other tasks, whenever a tested system (e.g., Cupid) went out of memory, its results were not reported. On the task (d), S-Match works about 40% faster than S-Match$_B$. It performs 1% faster than COMA and about 5 times slower than Rondo. The relatively small improvement in this case can be explained by noticing that the maximum depth in both trees is 3 and that the average number of labels at nodes is about 2. Hence, here the optimizations cannot significantly influence the system performance.

In the case of task (e), S-Match is more than 6 times faster than S-Match$_B$. COMA performs about 5 times slower than S-Match. Finally, in the case of the biggest matching task, i.e., (f), S-Match performs about 9 times faster than COMA, and about 7 times faster than S-Match$_B$.

Having considered matching tasks of Table 9.5, we conclude that our system performs (in terms of execution time) slightly slower than COMA and Rondo on the ontologies with one up to three hundred of nodes. At the same time, it is considerably faster on the ontologies with more than five hundreds nodes, thereby indicating for system scalability.

9.7 Conclusion

In this chapter, we have presented a semantic matching approach to ontology matching. Our solution builds on top of the past approaches at the element level and uses model-based techniques at the structure level. We implemented our approach within the S-Match system and conducted a comparative evaluation of S-Match against three state of the art systems with encouraging results.

Let us now provide an outlook for the ontology matching field in terms of the future challenges to be addressed and how the work on S-Match is positioned with respect to those challenges. In particular, the work in [42] articulated ten challenges for ontology matching, including: (i) large-scale evaluation, (ii) performance of ontology matching techniques, (iii) discovering missing background knowledge, (iv) uncertainty in ontology matching, (v) matcher selection and self-configuration, (vi) user involvement, (vii) explanation of matching results, (viii) social and collaborative ontology matching, (ix) alignment management: infrastructure and support and (x) reasoning with alignments.

Some of these challenges have already been tackled within the work on S-Match. Specifically, a contribution to the large-scale evaluation [challenge (i)] has been developed in [21] by providing a testing methodology which is able to estimate quality of the alignments between ontologies with hundreds and thousands of nodes. Performance of S-Match [challenge (ii)] has been discussed in this chapter, see also [22, 23]. In turn, the work in [18] introduced an automatic approach to discover the missing background knowledge [challenge (iii)] in matching tasks by using semantic matching iteratively. Finally, explanations [challenge (vii)] of the S-Match results has been tackled in [43].

Future work includes user involvement [challenge (vi)], e.g., through the development of an interactive semantic matching system. It will improve the quality of the alignments by focusing user's attention on the critical points where his/her input is maximally useful. Moreover, users have to be provided with the system that is configurable and customizable, such that they themselves can improve it, thereby arriving to the exact solution that fits best their needs and preferences.

References

1. Bernstein, P., Melnik, S., Petropoulos, M., Quix, C.: Industrial-strength schema matching. ACM SIGMOD Rec. (2004)
2. Bouquet, P., Serafini, L., Zanobini, S.: Semantic coordination: a new approach and an application. In: Proceedings of ISWC (2003)
3. Chai, X., Sayyadian, M., Doan, A., Rosenthal, A., Seligman, L.: Analyzing and revising mediated schemas to improve their matchability. In: Proceedings of VLDB (2008)
4. Davis, M., Putnam, H.: A computing procedure for quantification theory. J. ACM (1960)
5. Do, H., Rahm, E.: COMA—a system for flexible combination of schema matching approaches. In: Proceedings of VLDB (2002)
6. Do, H., Rahm, E.: Matching large schemas: approaches and evaluation. Inf. Syst. (2007)
7. Doan, A., Halevy, A.: Semantic integration research in the database community: a brief survey. AI Mag. (2005). Special issue on Semantic integration

8. Ehrig, M., Staab, S., Sure, Y.: Bootstrapping ontology alignment methods with APFEL. In: Proceedings of ISWC (2005)
9. Euzenat, J., Shvaiko, P.: Ontology Matching. Springer, Berlin (2007)
10. Euzenat, J., Valtchev, P.: Similarity-based ontology alignment in OWL-lite. In: Proceedings of ECAI (2004)
11. Falconer, S., Storey, M.: A cognitive support framework for ontology mapping. In: Proceedings of ISWC/ASWC (2007)
12. Gal, A., Anaby-Tavor, A., Trombetta, A., Montesi, D.: A framework for modeling and evaluating automatic semantic reconciliation. VLDB J. (2005)
13. Giunchiglia, F.: Contextual reasoning. Epistemologia (1993)
14. Giunchiglia, F., Marchese, M., Zaihrayeu, I.: Encoding classifications into lightweight ontologies. J. Data Semant. (2007)
15. Giunchiglia, F., Shvaiko, P.: Semantic matching. Knowl. Eng. Rev. (2003)
16. Giunchiglia, F., Shvaiko, P., Yatskevich, M.: S-Match: an algorithm and an implementation of semantic matching. In: Proceedings of ESWS (2004)
17. Giunchiglia, F., Shvaiko, P., Yatskevich, M.: Semantic schema matching. In: Proceedings of CoopIS (2005)
18. Giunchiglia, F., Shvaiko, P., Yatskevich, M.: Discovering missing background knowledge in ontology matching. In: Proceedings of ECAI (2006)
19. Giunchiglia, F., Shvaiko, P., Yatskevich, M.: Semantic matching. In: Encyclopedia of Database Systems (2009)
20. Giunchiglia, F., Yatskevich, M.: Element level semantic matching. In: Proceedings of the workshop on Meaning Coordination and Negotiation at ISWC (2004)
21. Giunchiglia, F., Yatskevich, M., Avesani, P., Shvaiko, P.: A large scale dataset for the evaluation of ontology matching systems. Knowl. Eng. Rev. (2009)
22. Giunchiglia, F., Yatskevich, M., Giunchiglia, E.: Efficient semantic matching. In: Proceedings of ESWC (2005)
23. Giunchiglia, F., Yatskevich, M., Shvaiko, P.: Semantic matching: algorithms and implementation. J. Data Semant. (2007)
24. Guarino, N.: The role of ontologies for the Semantic Web (and beyond). Tech. Rep., Laboratory for Applied Ontology, Institute for Cognitive Sciences and Technology (ISTC-CNR) (2004)
25. Haas, L., Hernández, M., Ho, H., Popa, L., Roth, M.: Clio grows up: from research prototype to industrial tool. In: Proceedings of SIGMOD (2005)
26. Hu, W., Qu, Y., Cheng, G.: Matching large ontologies: a divide-and-conquer approach. Data Knowl. Eng. (2008)
27. Lambrix, P., Tan, H.: SAMBO—a system for aligning and merging biomedical ontologies. J. Web Semant. (2006)
28. Le Berre, D.: Sat4j: A satisfiability library for Java (2004). http://www.sat4j.org/
29. Li, J., Tang, J., Li, Y., Luo, Q.: RiMOM: a dynamic multi-strategy ontology alignment framework. Trans. Knowl. Data Eng. (2008)
30. Madhavan, J., Bernstein, P., Rahm, E.: Generic schema matching with Cupid. In: Proceedings of VLDB (2001)
31. Magnini, B., Serafini, L., Speranza, M.: Making explicit the semantics hidden in schema models. In: Proceedings of the Workshop on Human Language Technology for the Semantic Web and Web Services at ISWC (2003)
32. McCann, R., Shen, W., Doan, A.: Matching schemas in online communities: a web 2.0 approach. In: Proceedings of ICDE (2008)
33. Melnik, S., Garcia-Molina, H., Rahm, E.: Similarity flooding: a versatile graph matching algorithm. In: Proceedings of ICDE (2002)
34. Melnik, S., Rahm, E., Bernstein, P.: Developing metadata-intensive applications with Rondo. J. Web Semant. (2003)
35. Miller, G.: WordNet: a lexical database for English. Commun. ACM (1995)
36. Mork, P., Seligman, L., Rosenthal, A., Korb, J., Wolf, C.: The harmony integration workbench. J. Data Semant. (2008)

37. Noy, N.: Semantic integration: a survey of ontology-based approaches. ACM SIGMOD Rec. (2004)
38. Noy, N., Musen, M.: The PROMPT suite: interactive tools for ontology merging and mapping. Int. J. Hum.-Comput. Stud. (2003)
39. Plaisted, D., Greenbaum, S.: A structure-preserving clause form translation. J. Symb. Comput. (1986)
40. Rahm, E., Bernstein, P.: A survey of approaches to automatic schema matching. VLDB J. (2001)
41. Shvaiko, P., Euzenat, J.: A survey of schema-based matching approaches. J. Data Semant. (2005)
42. Shvaiko, P., Euzenat, J.: Ten challenges for ontology matching. In: Proceedings of ODBASE (2008)
43. Shvaiko, P., Giunchiglia, F., Pinheiro da Silva, P., McGuinness, D.: Web explanations for semantic heterogeneity discovery. In: Proceedings of ESWC (2005)

Chapter 10
Preserving Semantics in Automatically Created Ontology Alignments

Giorgio Orsi and Letizia Tanca

Abstract In an open world such as the Internet, one of the most challenging tasks is ontology alignment, which is the process of finding relationships among their elements. Performing this work in an automated fashion is, however, subject to errors, because of the different semantics carried by the same concept in different application domains or because of different ontology design styles which often produce incompatible ontology structures. In this chapter, we relate the most important approaches to ontology mapping revision, proposing a revision technique which aims at preserving the semantics of the original ontologies.

10.1 Introduction

Nowadays, ontologies are extensively used to negotiate common vocabularies in semantic Web applications in particular in biomedical knowledge bases [3], and to achieve interoperability among networked enterprise information systems (EIS) [1]. Ontologies are suitable because they are explicit models of conceptualizations with a well-defined semantics. In an "open world", such as the Internet, one of the most challenging tasks is their alignment (also called matching or mapping) which is the process of finding relationships among their elements (e.g., concepts, roles and individuals).

Relating and integrating ontologies is a hard task because of the difficulty of finding high quality correspondences between different ontologies, and because possible mismatches can arise during the alignment process. Mismatches may emerge because of the different semantics carried by the same concept in different application domains or because of different ontology design styles which often produce incompatible ontology structures. Sometimes, their languages have different expressive powers and something that can be expressed in one language cannot be expressed in the other one, even if they are the same concept. In ontology matching/integration,

G. Orsi (✉)
Politecnico di Milano, Via Ponzio 34/5, Milan, Italy
e-mail: orsi@elet.polimi.it

L. Tanca
Dipto. Elettronica e Informazione (DEI), Politecnico di Milano, Via Ponzio 34/5, 20133 Milan, Italy
e-mail: tanca@elet.polimi.it

R. De Virgilio et al. (eds.), *Semantic Web Information Management*,
DOI 10.1007/978-3-642-04329-1_10,

more than in ontology evolution and learning, it is necessary to achieve inter-ontology consistency in such a way that as little information as possible is lost during the process, especially because in some cases only the correspondences can be accessed for modification while the input ontologies cannot be modified.

As also seen in Chap. 9, the automatic discovery of correspondences among ontologies is a quite challenging task. The fundamental problem is the strict connection between ontology matching (and schema matching in general) with meaning comprehension, which makes this problem inherently unsolvable by machines. Finding alignments between two ontologies, as well as other problems related or derived from meaning comprehension such as Natural Language Processing (NLP [28]) and Computer Vision [15], are usually known as AI-complete problems [33]. The belonging of a problem to this class of problems usually implies that its solution is in some way equivalent to the solution of the central problem of artificial intelligence i.e., making an artificial system as intelligent as humans (i.e., *strong AI*).

Despite the numerous solutions proposed for the ontology matching problem (see [11] for an up-to-date review of the problem and approaches), ontology matching tools produced, up to now, results with a significant amount of wrong alignments (lack of precision) and they are unable to retrieve all the correct ones (lack of recall). One of the reasons is the presence of numerous heuristics encoded within the matching algorithms that try to cope with the intrinsic complexity of the problem. In most situations, automatically-created ontology alignments need to be *revised* by a human expert and, since this process is extremely time-consuming, many research efforts have been put in the definition of automated support for their analysis and repairing.

Current approaches to mapping revision are mainly based on another set of heuristics which, in turn, are affected by the same problems which affect the heuristics used to "find" the correspondences. Sometimes, these techniques produce a loss of the original structure of the conceptualization during the process but they are very useful when associated to an explanation phase to make the resolution of mismatches easier. A remarkable exception is the work of Meilicke et al. [29] which debugs a set of alignments using logical reasoning in order to produce an alignment which is logically sound. However, in many situations, even after a process of logical revision of the alignments, which produces a logically consistent result, the produced mapping remains faulty because it is *semantically incoherent* w.r.t. the application domain or the intended semantics of the original ontologies.

In this chapter, we overview the most interesting approaches to ontology mapping revision as follows: Sect. 10.3 recalls some basic definitions about ontologies, DLs and alignments. In Sect. 10.4, we report on the major line of research in ontology mapping revision, while Sect. 10.2 is devoted to the related research fields. Finally, Sect. 10.5 draws some conclusions.

10.2 Related Research Fields

Mapping revision is strongly connected to several other research fields. Perhaps, the most related one is that of ontology debugging; Haase and Qi [21] survey various approaches for resolving inconsistencies in DL Ontologies and the most relevant approaches are those coming from the field of belief revision [37] in particular those that adapt the AGM (Alchourrón, Gärdenfors and Makinson) theory [14] to the case of description logics. These approaches address logical theory revision and debugging in general, however none of them deal specifically with the revision of correspondences between ontologies.

Schlobach et al. [32] and Parsia et al. [25] discuss approaches to ontology diagnosis and debugging. In particular, we can distinguish between glass-box techniques, that analyze the tableaux proof to find causes of inconsistencies [5], and black-box techniques that use the reasoning algorithm as a black box and try to detect inconsistencies by the iterative application of reasoning tasks.

Another notable research field is that of alignment systems, which uses propositional logical reasoning to compute the correspondences in such a way that no inconsistent correspondences are generated in the first place [18] or the correspondences adhere to a given property (e.g., minimality) as in [17]. These systems however trade precision for recall, because the use of logical reasoning for proving semantic relations is often too restrictive and may miss many reasonable matches.

Finally, the problem of modeling uncertainty is becoming interesting in ontology modeling and description logic research. Early approaches to uncertainty management under probabilistic settings started with the probabilistic extension of interpretation function at the TBox and ABox level [10, 23, 24, 26]. More recent work aims at integrating several approaches to uncertainty representation into a single and coherent framework [20] like that of rule-based languages [27].

10.3 Preliminaries

In this section, we recall some basic terminology used in this paper such as ontologies, alignments, faults and diagnoses. The reader already familiar with such concepts can skip this section and proceed with Sect. 10.4.

10.3.1 Ontologies

An *ontology* is a shared and formal description of a conceptualization of a domain of interest [19] encoded in a certain language. Formally, it can be seen as a 5-tuple $\mathcal{O} = \langle N_C, N_R, N_U, N_I, A \rangle$, where N_C is a set of concept names, N_R is a set of role names, N_U is a set of attribute names, N_I is a set of individual names (i.e., constants) and A is a set of axioms that are valid in the conceptualization and define its logical structure. An ontology is conveniently seen as a *Knowledge Base* i.e., a triple $\mathcal{KB} = \langle \mathcal{T}, \mathcal{R}, \mathcal{A} \rangle$, respectively called TBox, RBox and ABox, where $\mathcal{T}$ contains the definitions and axioms about concepts (terminological knowledge), $\mathcal{R}$ contains the axioms related to roles and $\mathcal{A}$ contains assertions about individuals (factual knowledge). In this work we focus on DL-ontologies i.e., ontologies described using a decidable Description Logic [2], whose semantics is given in terms of standard first-order interpretations.

Given a domain of individuals Δ and an interpretation function $I(\cdot)$, an individual o is interpreted as $o^I \in \Delta$, a concept C is interpreted as $C^I \subset \Delta$, a role R is interpreted as $R^I \subseteq \Delta \times \Delta$ and an attribute U is interpreted as $U^I \subset \Delta \times D$ where D is a concrete datatype (e.g., integers).

Terminological knowledge is constructed by means of the subsumption relationships between concepts ($C \sqsubseteq D$) or roles ($R \sqsubseteq S$) and is interpreted as a containment between their interpretations ($C^I \subseteq D^I$ and $R^I \subseteq S^I$ respectively). An equivalence relationship between two concepts or roles is simply a double subsumption (e.g., $C \equiv D \Leftrightarrow C \sqsubseteq D$ and $C \sqsupseteq D$ for two concepts C and D) and is interpreted accordingly. Moreover, the negated formula $\neg C$ is interpreted as $\Delta \setminus C^I$. We refer to [2] for the additional constructors and their interpretations.

Given a knowledge base $\mathcal{KB} = \langle \mathcal{T}, \mathcal{R}, \mathcal{A} \rangle$, an interpretation $\mathcal{I}$ is a *model* for $\mathcal{KB}$ if and only if, for each axiom of the form $C_i \sqsubseteq D_i$ in $\mathcal{T}$, we have that $C_i^I \subseteq D_i^I$. By consistency check we mean the process of testing if the global TBox is consistent and coherent, w.r.t. the following definitions proposed in [13]. A concept C, defined in a TBox $\mathcal{T}$, is *unsatisfiable* if and only if, for every model of $\mathcal{T}$, $C^I = \emptyset$ (i.e., it is unsatisfiable in every interpretation); a TBox $\mathcal{T}$ where all concepts are satisfiable is called *coherent* and a $\mathcal{KB}$ with a coherent TBox is also coherent. There exist situations in which the TBox is coherent, but the facts contained into the ABox are such that it is impossible to find an interpretation satisfying both the TBox and the ABox; in these situations, the $\mathcal{KB}$ is *inconsistent*. Note that also an incoherent TBox may have a model, thus the presence of unsatisfiable concepts is a *symptom* of inconsistency, but does not imply it.

10.3.2 Correspondences and Mappings

As described in [11], an *alignment* between two ontologies $\mathcal{O}_i$ and $\mathcal{O}_j$ is defined as a set of *correspondences* among the elements of the input ontologies defined as follows:

Definition 10.1 (Correspondence) [11] Given two ontologies $\mathcal{O}_i, \mathcal{O}_j$ and a function Q, defining the sets of matchable elements for a given ontology, a correspondence is a 5-tuple $\langle id, i{:}e, j{:}e', r, n\rangle$ such that *id* is a unique identifier for the correspondence, $i{:}e \in Q(\mathcal{O}_i)$, $j{:}e' \in Q(\mathcal{O}_j)$, r is an alignment relation, and n is a confidence value from a suitable structure $\langle D, \preceq\rangle$, where D is the support set and $\preceq$ is a partial order for the values in D.

In order to relate terms from two ontologies, we consider only the following set of alignment relationships $r = \{\sqsubseteq, \sqsupseteq, \equiv, \perp\}$ because they have the same semantics in every DL.[1] Moreover, we assume $D = [0, 1]$ and $\preceq$ to be interpreted as $\leqslant$.

In the following, we use the term *matching* to indicate a set of correspondences which carry a confidence value n, and the term *mapping* to refer to a set of correspondences wherefrom the confidence value has been removed because they have been *validated* through user intervention or an automated revision process. We want to stress this terminology in order to distinguish between the output of an ontology matching tool and the outcome of a revision procedure which validates and applies the correspondences. After the revision process, the mapping can be considered as a piece of the logical theory which comprehends the input ontologies and the mapping itself.

Alignments are called *simple* when directly relating ontology elements one to one e.g.,

$$\langle 1, i\text{:JournalPaper}, j\text{:ScientificArticle}, \sqsubseteq, 1.0\rangle$$

When the alignment involves a complex expression, in at least one side of the alignment, it is referred to as *complex* alignments [16], e.g.,

$$\langle 2, i\text{:Mother}, j\text{:Person} \sqcap \exists j\text{:hasGender}.\{\text{Female}\} \sqcap \exists j\text{:hasChild}.j\text{:Person}), \sqsubseteq, 1.0\rangle$$

Another classification distinguishes *homogeneous* correspondences i.e., when elements are mapped with elements of the same kind as in the above examples e.g., concepts with concepts, roles with roles and individuals with individuals. By contrast, a *heterogeneous* correspondence relates elements of different nature e.g.,

$$\langle 3, i\text{:Parent}, j\text{:fatherOf}, \equiv, 0.85\rangle$$

where the class Parent is put into correspondence with the role fatherOf. Such correspondences may be extremely useful to annotate ontology fragments.

10.3.3 Distributed Ontologies

Despite the fact that we focus our attention on the restricted setting of DL-ontologies, we must take into account the fact that ontologies are distributed across the semantic-web and possibly described using different description logics. This heterogeneity in the language expressivity necessarily influences the mapping revision process and calls for an appropriate theoretical setting to reason in such distributed environments.

In Chap. 8, we have seen an overview of suitable formalisms for distributed reasoning and, in order to illustrate the techniques for mapping revisions, we rely here on the Distributed Description Logics [4] (DDL) formalism due to its intuitiveness.

[1]In the most general case, an alignment might be expressed by making use of more general alignment relationships that carry their own semantics.

We remark that DDL is used here only as a means to describe the revision approaches. The actual feasibility of the techniques is contingent to those families of description logics which are decidable when used in a DDL setting.

We recall that, assumed a non empty index set $\mathcal{I}$, a distributed knowledge base can be seen as a 4-tuple $\mathfrak{KB} = \langle \mathfrak{T}, \mathfrak{R}, \mathfrak{A}, \mathfrak{B} \rangle$ where:

1. $\mathfrak{T} = \bigcup_{i \in \mathcal{I}} \mathcal{T}_i$ is a distributed TBox and each $\mathcal{T}_i$ is a TBox in a given language L_i.
2. $\mathfrak{R} = \bigcup_{i \in \mathcal{I}} \mathcal{R}_i$ is a distributed RBox and each $\mathcal{R}_i$ is a RBox.
3. $\mathfrak{A} = \bigcup_{i \in \mathcal{I}} \mathcal{A}_i$ is a distributed ABox where each $\mathcal{A}_i$ represents the ABox of a particular ontology.
4. In order to state that a certain axiom ϕ belongs to an ontology $\mathcal{O}_i$, the syntax $i{:}\phi$ is used.
5. $\mathfrak{B} = \bigcup_{i \neq j \in \mathcal{I}} \mathcal{B}_{i,j}$ is a set of *bridge rules* from $\mathcal{O}_i$ to $\mathcal{O}_j$ which are expressions of the form:

$$i{:}X \xrightarrow{\sqsubseteq} j{:}Y, \qquad i{:}X \xrightarrow{\sqsupseteq} j{:}Y, \qquad i{:}X \xrightarrow{\perp} j{:}Y, \qquad i{:}a \mapsto j{:}b$$

   where X and Y are either two atomic concepts or two atomic roles, and a, b are two individuals, in the respective language.

It is immediate to see that bridge rules can be used to straightforwardly encode correspondences.

A distributed knowledge base $\mathfrak{KB}$ is interpreted in terms of distributed interpretations which extend standard first-order interpretations to the distributed setting. A distributed interpretation $\mathfrak{I}$ is a (distributed) model for $\mathfrak{KB}$ (denoted by $\mathfrak{I} \models_\varepsilon \mathfrak{KB}$) if $\mathfrak{I} \models_\varepsilon \mathfrak{T}$, $\mathfrak{I} \models_\varepsilon \mathfrak{R}$, $\mathfrak{I} \models_\varepsilon \mathfrak{A}$ and $\mathfrak{I} \models_\varepsilon \mathfrak{B}$.

DDL formalizes also two distributed reasoning tasks which are prominent for mapping revision: distributed concept satisfiability and distributed subsumption check. A i-local concept $i{:}C$ is satisfiable with respect to $\mathfrak{KB}$ if there exists a distributed model $\mathfrak{I}$ for $\mathfrak{KB}$ such that $C^{\mathcal{I}_i} \neq \emptyset$. A i-local subsumption $i{:}C \sqsubseteq D$ holds in $\mathfrak{KB}$ iff $C^{\mathcal{I}_i} \subseteq D^{\mathcal{I}_i}$ in every distributed model $\mathfrak{I}$.

10.3.4 Faults and Diagnoses

In 1987, Raymond Reiter proposed a general theory based on first-order logic for the identification and the diagnosis of faults in a system [31]. Reiter formalized a *system* as a triple $S = \langle SD, COMP, OBS \rangle$ where SD is the system description given in terms of first-order formulae, $COMP$ is a set of constants describing the system's components and OBS is a set of observations of the input, status and output of the system, also given in terms of first-order formulae. In such a framework, if a system behaves correctly the set of formulae $\Gamma = SD \cup OBS$ is logically consistent; a *fault* occurs when an external entity observes a misbehavior i.e., Γ becomes inconsistent. In Reiter's theory, a *diagnosis task* is then the process that leads to the identification of a minimal set of components that misbehave w.r.t. the behavior determined by the system description and a given set of inputs and status variables. We use the predicate $AB(c)$ to indicate that the component c has an abnormal behavior.

A *diagnosis* is then a conjecture that some minimal set of components is faulty. This is defined in Reiter's theory as a set $\Delta \subseteq COMP$ such that:

$$\Gamma = SD \cup OBS \cup \{\neg AB(c) \mid c \in COMP - \Delta\}$$

is a consistent set of formulae.

The computation of a diagnosis is done by first identifying a set $\{c_1, c_2, \ldots, c_k\} \subset COMP$ of components that are faulty. Such a set is called a *conflict set* and it is *minimal* whenever none of its proper subsets is a *conflict set*. Once all the minimal conflict sets have been identified, there exists a procedure based on Hitting Sets which can compute all the repairs to restore the consistency of the system.

By leveraging on the property of minimality of conflict sets, it is easy to see that a *repair* for a system is obtained by removing (or substituting) a single component from each conflict set until no conflict set can be computed anymore. It is also easy to see that this framework is particularly suited to represent the mapping revision problem and to compare the various approaches.

10.4 Mapping Revision

In order to proceed to the analysis of mapping revision techniques, we first introduce the problem, then proceed to a classification of the *faults* in automatically-generated correspondences and finally recall a method to evaluate the effectiveness of a revision procedure.

In general, a mapping revision process starts from a set of automatically-created, and potentially flawed, correspondences C between two ontologies $\mathcal{O}_i, \mathcal{O}_j$ and produces another set of correspondences C' which enjoys a set of properties $\mathcal{P}$.

Wang et al. [36] propose a classification of the most common types of flaws in automatically generated correspondences between two ontologies. They classify the flaws in four categories:

- *Inconsistent correspondences.* This is the most dangerous class of flaws since they destroy the satisfiability of the distributed ontology and make the ontologies useless unless we introduce approximate reasoning [22].
- *Redundant correspondences.* A correspondence is redundant if it can be inferred from other correspondences already present in the solution. Anyway, the presence of redundant correspondences is not always useless; sometimes they can be stored in order to avoid the burden of their recomputation when an inference mechanism is not available or is too expensive for the considered application.
- *Imprecise correspondences.* Due to the limitation of some mapping algorithms (e.g., most of them compute only simple correspondences), imprecise correspondences may occur, which means that the algorithm has not found the best answer but an approximate one.

- *Abnormal correspondences.* Some suspicious correspondences do not belong to the above three categories and constitute symptoms of possible problems in the theory. Unfortunately, the term *suspicious* highly depends on a subjective consideration of what is considered abnormal for an application or by a designer. A common example of abnormal behavior discussed in [36] occurs when a set of correspondences connects entities which are *close* to one another in $\mathcal{O}_i$ but whose counterparts are *distant* from each other in $\mathcal{O}_j$.

Notice that the above categories are not mutually exclusive.

In order to evaluate a debugging process, we resort to the following formalization, due to [29], which defines how to evaluate the quality of a set of correspondences and of the revision process. A set of correspondences can be defined as $C = C^+ \cup C^-$ where $C^+ = C \cap \mathfrak{C}$ and $C^- = C - \mathfrak{C}$ and $\mathfrak{C}$ is a given set of "reference correspondences", i.e., correspondences that are considered as correct by a domain expert. The quality of a set of correspondences C is usually evaluated in terms of recall ($Rec = \frac{C^+}{\mathfrak{C}}$) and precision ($Prec = \frac{C^+}{C}$) w.r.t. the reference correspondences $\mathfrak{C}$. On the other hand, the effectiveness of a mapping revision process is defined in terms of recall and precision of the repair process. Given the set Δ of correspondences removed by the revision process (i.e., the repair), the precision of the repair is defined as $Rep_{prec} = \frac{\Delta \cap C^-}{\Delta}$ while the recall is defined as $Rep_{rec} = \frac{\Delta \cap C^-}{C^-}$. We now proceed to the description of the current research results on ontology mapping revision.

10.4.1 Model-based Mapping Revision

As a matter of fact, since aligned ontologies are ontologies themselves, early approaches to mapping revision applied the known debugging mechanisms such as axiom pinpointing [32] (white-box) and inconsistency debugging [25] (black-box). These techniques mainly rely on the model-theoretic semantics associated to ontologies and thus share the advantages (soundness and completeness) and disadvantages (high computational complexity) associated to logical reasoning.

10.4.1.1 Consistency-Preserving Revision

In 2007, Meilicke et al. [29] published a seminal work on mapping revision which proceeds from a first systematization [35]. Given a set C of correspondences between $\mathcal{O}_i$ and $\mathcal{O}_j$, their revision process ensures that the final set C' of correspondences does not cause inconsistencies in any of the input ontologies.

The revision framework is based on distributed description logics; input ontologies are considered as members of a distributed ontology while correspondences are encoded as bridge rules. As an example, the correspondence:

$$\langle id, i{:}e, j{:}e, \sqsubseteq, n\rangle$$

is encoded as two bridge rules:

$$\{i{:}e \overset{\sqsubseteq}{\rightarrow} j{:}e,\ j{:}e \overset{\sqsupseteq}{\rightarrow} i{:}e\}$$

Since in the DDL framework the direction of mapping matters, the correspondences are expressed w.r.t. both ontologies.

The main idea is that, if one of the bridge rules is responsible for an inconsistency in the distributed ontology, then the correspondence that originated that bridge rule must be revised. Diagnoses are formulated within an adaptation of Reiter's theory to mapping revision. The distributed ontology is used as the system description *SD*, bridge rules represents the system's components *COMP* and the observations *OBS* are the (possibly infinite) subsumptions that could be inferred within the distributed ontology. A component (i.e., a bridge rule) is considered to misbehave if it causes an inconsistency in the distributed ontology and a diagnosis is then a set Δ of correspondences such that $C - \Delta$ produces a set of bridge rules which preserves consistency when applied to the distributed ontology.

The computation of a diagnosis is done by resorting to the computation of minimal conflict sets using Reiter's theory as seen in Sect. 10.3. In this scenario, the repair is obtained by removing a single bridge rule from the corresponding conflict set. Differently from Reiter's approach, where the repair was computed by means of the Hitting-Set algorithm, the framework of Meilicke et al. [29] resorts to the confidence value associated to correspondences and removes from the conflict sets the bridge rule with lower confidence in order to restore consistency. In addition, they show how the Hitting-Set method may lead to the removal of the wrong bridge rules since it uses no prior knowledge about the problem such as the confidence value. Moreover, since a matching algorithm might not associate a confidence value to the produced correspondences, they resort to a linguistic distance measure based on WordNet to compute the missing confidence value for the elements involved in a correspondence.

10.4.1.2 Coherence-Preserving Revision

By *semantic coherence check*, we mean the process of *verifying whether the inferences enabled by the alignment process change the semantics of some terms as defined in the original ontologies*. As a consequence, in [8], we propose to restore the original semantics while preserving as much as possible information coming from the correspondences. This fact implies that, if a contradiction arises after an alignment process, the problem is solved by looking at the sets of computed correspondences and by removing or weakening some of them. This approach faces the problem of guaranteeing the *semantic coherence*.

Semantic coherence is harder to guarantee than consistency because it partially depends on the semantics of the application domain and therefore the faults are not easily identifiable as it is for logical consistency.

In the X-SOM mapper [9], the technique used to identify the faults is based on the notion of i-local subsumption [4] whose definition is recalled here.

Definition 10.2 (i-local subsumption) A subsumption $i{:}C \sqsubseteq D$ is said to be *i-local* to a TBox $\mathcal{T}_i$ of a distributed $\mathcal{KB}$ if $C^{\mathcal{I}_i} \subseteq D^{\mathcal{I}_i}$ in every distributed model $\mathfrak{I}$.

Based on the previous definition, we can say that there is a change in a representation when a i-local subsumption is added or removed. A semantic incoherence arises when, after an alignment process, the set of i-local subsumptions of the TBox of a $\mathcal{KB}$ has been modified (e.g., a subsumption becomes an equivalence and two concepts collapse into each other). Since, in general, the possible i-local subsumptions to be checked are infinite, we restrict the analysis to the subsumptions between named concepts and roles on the classified global ontology i.e., the set of subsumptions that results from the execution of the classification task.

Given two TBoxes $\mathcal{T}_i$ and $\mathcal{T}_j$, and a set of correspondences C_{ij} between them, $\mathfrak{T} = \mathcal{T}_i \sqcup \mathcal{T}_j \sqcup C_{ij}$ is the *aligned Tbox*. Let Δ be a set of i-local subsumptions and $\mathcal{T}_i$ a TBox; the function $\mathcal{L} : (\Delta, i) \mapsto \mathcal{L}(\Delta, i) \in \wp(\Delta)$ computes the subset of Δ which contains the subsumptions that are local to the given TBox $\mathcal{T}_i$. Then we have the following definitions.

Definition 10.3 (Semantics-preserving correspondences) C_{ij} is a set of semantics-preserving correspondences (SP-Correspondences) between two Tboxes $\mathcal{T}_i$ and $\mathcal{T}_j$ if and only if $\mathcal{L}(\mathcal{T}_i, i) = \mathcal{L}(\bar{\mathcal{T}}, i)$ and $\mathcal{L}(\mathcal{T}_j, j) = \mathcal{L}(\bar{\mathcal{T}}, j)$.

According to the above definition, a mapping derived from a set of SP-correspondences does not change the relationship between any two resources belonging to the same $\mathcal{KB}$. The distributed TBox is then called *semantically coherent*:

Definition 10.4 (Semantically coherent Distributed TBox) Let $\mathcal{T}_i$ and $\mathcal{T}_j$ be two coherent Tboxes. The distributed Tbox $\mathfrak{T} = \langle \mathcal{T}_i, \mathcal{T}_j, C_{ij} \rangle$ is *semantically coherent* iff C_{ij} is a set of SP-Correspondences.

Thus, to achieve semantic coherence, this technique will analyze the computed correspondences and only keep those that, when applied, become semantics-preserving correspondences. If the TBoxes $\mathcal{T}_i$ and $\mathcal{T}_j$ are coherent before the alignment process, and this process does not add or remove any local subsumption, then the distributed TBox $\mathfrak{T}$ is also coherent, since an unsatisfiable concept can be introduced only by enabling at least a new subsumption in $\mathcal{T}_i$ or $\mathcal{T}_j$. As a consequence, if an aligned TBox is semantically coherent, then it is also coherent.

Note that, since this approach preserves the semantics of the application domains represented by the input ontologies, nothing can be done if a set of correspondences enables anomalous inferences without modifying any subsumption into the original representations. Indeed, this kind of incoherence can be only detected either when the application interacts with its application domain or by a human designer.

The identification of the correspondences enabling a given suspicious local subsumption is done by means of the same procedure used in [29] to find the source of logical inconsistencies. The identification of all the new i-local subsumptions produced by the alignment process can be achieved by classifying the distributed

TBox and retrieving all the i-local subsumptions from the local TBoxes. This set of axioms is compared with the set of i-local subsumption which are true in the local ontologies without the bridge rules. The difference between the computed sets represents all the new i-local subsumptions we want to remove. We call this set $N_{\sqsubseteq}$ and define it as:

$$N_{\sqsubseteq} = \frac{\mathcal{L}(\mathfrak{T},i)}{(\mathcal{L}(\mathcal{T}_i,i) \cup \mathcal{L}(\mathcal{T}_j,j))}$$

Once $N_{\sqsubseteq}$ has been computed, we use the model-based approaches described in Sect. 10.4.1 to compute the diagnoses for the adjunctive i-local subsumptions, and then remove one bridge rule from each conflict set starting from those that appear in multiple conflict sets, since they have the highest probability to be the true responsible for the new i-local subsumption.

This approach, however, is very conservative, and thus may cause an undesirable loss of information. It is possible to relax it by removing only the local subsumptions that deeply change the semantics of an ontology, for instance, correspondences which cause two concepts to collapse or enforce a restriction as suggested in Wang et al.; to this end, heuristics that ensure semantic coherence can be used, presented in the next section.

10.4.2 Heuristic Mapping Revision

Model-based techniques for mapping revision are in general too expensive from a computational point of view when dealing with large-scale ontologies. In order to address this problem, a possible solution is to resort to heuristics which trade the soundness and the completeness of model-theoretic approaches for improvements in performance when these issues are not essential for the final application.

10.4.2.1 Static Heuristic Revision

One of the first attempts made in order to formalize the problem of mapping revision was done in 2007 by Wang et al. The work resulted in a set of heuristics used to identify and repair suspicious correspondences which are statistically present in automatically-aligned ontologies. Differently from Stuckenschmidt et al. [29], these heuristics address a broader class of faults than mapping consistency.

- *Redundant correspondences.* Every redundant correspondence (i.e., one already implied by a set of correspondences which are already part of the solution), is added to a *warning list* which is then handed to the user for manual evaluation or used by other heuristics to solve other suspicious situations.
- *Imprecise correspondences.* An imprecise correspondence c maps a concept $i{:}C$ to multiple concepts $j{:}D_k$ with $D_i \sqsubseteq \neg D_j \ \forall i \neq j$. If the alignment relation is $\stackrel{\sqsubseteq}{\rightarrow}$, then the original correspondence is replaced with $i{:}C \stackrel{\sqsubseteq}{\rightarrow} j{:}\bigwedge_k D_k$. When the

alignment relation is $\stackrel{\sqsupseteq}{\rightarrow}$, then the correspondence $i{:}C \stackrel{\sqsupseteq}{\rightarrow} j{:}\bigvee_k D_k$ is substituted. When the correspondence is an equivalence relation, more knowledge is needed in order to decide which is the more precise correspondence.

- *IS-A circles.* Given an ontology graph, an IS-A circle is a chain of subsumption relations which starts and ends on the same concept. This anomaly collapses the involved concepts into one and, since this must be caused by (at least) two correspondences, it is a symptom of badly-aligned ontologies. Also in this case, the proposed solution is to hand the probably flawed correspondences over to the user for manual evaluation.
- *Inconsistent correspondences.* Given a set of equivalent concepts $\{i{:}A_k\}$ and a set of correspondences $\{c_k\}$, which map $\{A_k\}$ to a set of concepts $\{j{:}B_t\}$, if any B_t is not equivalent with the others in $\{B_t\}$ then some correspondence must be faulty. As usual the user support is needed in order to solve the problem.
- *Abnormal correspondences.* As said in the beginning of this section, a set of abnormal correspondences connects concepts which are close in one ontology, to concepts which are distant in the other. Wang et al. defined a measure called *behavior* in order to quantify this anomaly. Given a set of correspondences $\{c_k = \langle id, i{:}a_k, j{:}b_k, r, n_k\rangle\}$, the behavior is defined as a relative measure:

$$Bh(c_k \mid c_1, \ldots, c_n) = \frac{1}{n}\sum_{t=1}^{n} \frac{d(i{:}a_k, i{:}a_t)}{d(j{:}b_k, j{:}b_t)} \quad (t \neq k)$$

  where $d(\cdot,\cdot)$ is a suitable distance measure between ontology terms. The closer the behavior is to value 1, the more normal the correspondence is considered. If the behavior goes lower than a predefined threshold, it is handed to the user for manual evaluation.

The main problem of the above heuristic approach is the absence of a theoretical framework which justifies the heuristics and helps evaluating their effectiveness.

10.4.2.2 Heuristics for Coherence Preservation

Logic-based approaches to consistency and coherence of ontology mapping are quite expensive from a computational point of view. Since an inconsistent aligned model is of little use, it is generally not convenient to trade the soundness of a consistency checking process for increased performance. Anyway, since this is not true for the coherence check, we single out a number of specific anomalies and, for each one, propose a heuristic technique to restore the coherence of the mapping, similar but more general than those of [36]:

Bowtie Rule (B-Rule) The bowtie problem is a particular situation that may arise when mapping two hierarchies. The kernel of this pattern is represented by the following set of axioms: $i{:}A_h \stackrel{\sqsubseteq^*}{\rightarrow} i{:}A_k$, $j{:}B_h \stackrel{\sqsubseteq^*}{\rightarrow} j{:}B_k$, $i{:}A_h \stackrel{\equiv}{\rightarrow} j{:}B_k$, $i{:}A_k \stackrel{\equiv}{\rightarrow} j{:}B_h$,

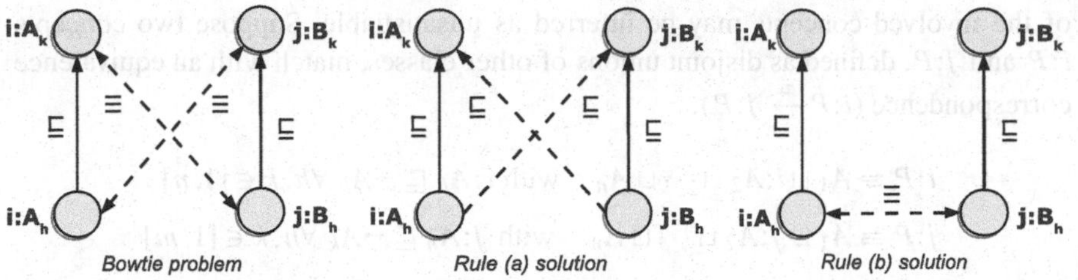

Fig. 10.1 The bowtie problem

where $\sqsubseteq *$ represents the transitive closure of $\sqsubseteq$. From these axioms, we can derive the following set of correspondences that leads to semantic incoherence:

$$M_{ij} = \left\{\begin{matrix} i{:}A_h \xrightarrow{\sqsubseteq} j{:}B_k \ (1) \\ i{:}A_h \xrightarrow{\sqsubseteq} j{:}B_k \ (2) \\ i{:}A_k \xrightarrow{\sqsubseteq} j{:}B_h \ (3) \\ i{:}A_k \xrightarrow{\sqsubseteq} j{:}B_h \ (4) \end{matrix}\right\} \cup \left\{\begin{matrix} i{:}A_h \sqsubseteq A_k \\ j{:}B_h \sqsubseteq B_k \end{matrix}\right\} \models_{\varepsilon} \left\{\begin{matrix} i{:}A_h \equiv A_k \\ j{:}B_h \equiv B_k \\ i{:}A_k \xrightarrow{\equiv} j{:}B_h \end{matrix}\right\}$$

The problem here is that correspondences (2) and (3) create a cycle which causes the bowtie to collapse. The collapse changes the semantics of the original ontologies: in fact, concepts that before were considered to be in a subclass relationship now are equivalent. We have to engineer a solution to avoid this behavior, preserving the original semantics. Our heuristic solution applies rule (a), weakening the correspondences, to obtain the situation described in the middle of Fig. 10.1, where we keep only correspondences (1) and (4). Note that in the figures the correspondences are denoted by dashed lines.

$$\text{(a)} \quad \frac{i{:}A_h \sqsubseteq A_k,\ j{:}B_h \sqsubseteq B_k,\ i{:}A_k \xrightarrow{\equiv} j{:}B_k,\ i{:}A_k \xrightarrow{\equiv} j{:}B_h}{i{:}A_h \sqsubseteq A_k,\ j{:}B_h \sqsubseteq B_k, i{:}A_h \xrightarrow{\equiv} j{:}B_k, i{:}A_k \xrightarrow{\equiv} j{:}B_h}$$

Weakening the axioms removes the incoherence but, under certain circumstances, we can capture the semantics of correspondences better. An alternative solution can be proposed, by noticing that the leaves of the bowtie ($i{:}A$ and $j{:}B$) are concepts that have the same characteristics but inherit them from their hierarchies in a different order. If the inherited properties are the same for the two hierarchies, the leaves of a bowtie can be considered as equivalent classes, and the solution to the bowtie problem is:

$$\text{(b)} \quad \frac{i{:}A_h \sqsubseteq A_k,\ j{:}B_h \sqsubseteq B_k,\ i{:}A_k \xrightarrow{\equiv} j{:}B_k,\ i{:}A_k \xrightarrow{\equiv} j{:}B_h}{i{:}A_h \sqsubseteq A_k,\ j{:}B_h \sqsubseteq B_k,\ i{:}A_h \xrightarrow{\equiv} j{:}B_h}$$

Partition Rule (P-Rule) A very common problem is the matching of partitions: if two similar partitions (each in one of the input ontologies) partially overlap, some of the involved concepts may be inferred as unsatisfiable. Suppose two concepts $i{:}P$ and $j{:}P$, defined as disjoint unions of other classes, match with an equivalence correspondence ($i{:}P \xrightarrow{\equiv} j{:}P$).

$$i{:}P \equiv A_1 \sqcup i{:}A_2 \sqcup \cdots \sqcup A_n \quad \text{with } i{:}A_h \sqsubseteq \neg A_k \ \forall h, k \in [1, n]$$

$$j{:}P \equiv A_1 \sqcup j{:}A_2 \sqcup \cdots \sqcup A_n \quad \text{with } j{:}A_h \sqsubseteq \neg A_k \ \forall h, k \in [1, m]$$

and a number of correspondences $i{:}A_h \xrightarrow{\equiv} j{:}A_k$ for some $h \in [1, n]$ and for some $k \in [1, m]$. The P-Rule creates a third concept $m : P$ defined as a disjoint union:

$$m{:}P = i{:}A_1 \sqcup \cdots \sqcup A_r \sqcup j{:}A_1 \sqcup \cdots \sqcup A_s$$

by merging the original partitions in such a way that the common concepts are taken only once. The original correspondence $i{:}P \xrightarrow{\equiv} j{:}P$ is substituted by two correspondences $i{:}P \xrightarrow{\sqsubseteq} m{:}P$ and $j{:}P \xrightarrow{\equiv} m{:}P$.

Cycle Rule (CYC-Rule) This rule removes cycles of subsumptions. A cycle of subsumptions causes the involved concepts to collapse into a unique concept; this means that the expressed subsumptions are modified to equivalence relationships, thus modifying the semantics of the original ontologies. One problem is the role of reflexivity; to avoid that an equivalence correspondence be interpreted as a cycle, we check for cycles of subsumptions involving $n > 2$ concepts.

$$\text{(c)} \quad \frac{i{:}A_h \sqsubseteq A_k,\ i{:}A_h \xrightarrow{\sqsupseteq} j{:}H,\ i{:}A_k \xrightarrow{\sqsubseteq} j{:}H}{i{:}A_h \sqsubseteq A_k\ (i{:}A_h \xrightarrow{\sqsupseteq} j{:}H \mid i{:}A_k \xrightarrow{\sqsubseteq} j{:}H \mid \emptyset)}$$

The presence of both correspondences changes an axiom in T_i. The cycle must be broken in some way. The notation $(m_1 \mid m_2)$ means that the algorithm randomly choses one of the options to solve the mismatch.

Blind Multiple Correspondences Special attention is deserved by the most difficult situations, in which the system must choose among multiple correspondences with no prior knowledge available about the concepts involved, or the knowledge is not enough to take a decision. To deal with this kind of mismatches, along with multiple correspondences whose solution is based on the similarity value, the algorithm isolates *clusters of concepts* involved in multiple correspondences and, for each of them, computes the subset that maximizes the sum of the similarity values of the correspondences and do not modify the semantics of the original ontologies. However, there exist situations in which a multiple correspondence represents a knowledge refinement to be preserved. In order to distinguish such situations, we give the following definitions: Let C_{ij} be a set of correspondences between two ontologies O_i and O_j, let $m = \langle C_h, C_k, s\rangle$ be a correspondence in C_{ij} between a concept $i{:}C_h$ and a concept $j{:}C_k$.

Definition 10.5 (Cluster of concepts) C_{ij} is a cluster of concepts if and only if the graph which has as nodes the concepts in C_{ij} and as edges the correspondences in C_{ij} is connected.

After all clusters have been identified, the algorithm looks for a semantically coherent set of correspondences defined as follows:

Given a set of correspondences C_{ij} identified as a cluster, and the related TBoxes $\mathcal{T}_i$ and $\mathcal{T}_j$ we can state the following definitions.

Definition 10.6 (Semantics-preserving cluster) C_{ij} is a semantics-preserving cluster (SPC) if and only if it is a cluster and the contained correspondences are semantics-preserving.

Since we can have many SPC's for a given cluster, we want to select the one that maximizes the sum of the similarity degrees:

$$\psi(SPC) = \sum_{m \in SPC} s \tag{10.1}$$

Definition 10.7 (Optimal semantics-preserving cluster) We define an *optimal semantics-preserving cluster* (OSPC) as a SPC such that:

$$OSPC = \text{argmax}^2(\psi(SPC)) \tag{10.2}$$

We recall that a cluster includes all the correspondences that can be solved only relying on the similarity value. Information among nodes belonging to the same ontology can be ignored because it is useless for the resolution of the conflict. Thus, the cluster can be seen as a bipartite graph as shown in Fig. 10.2. Since correspondences belonging to the cluster have the property that everything that can be inferred changes or adds at least one axiom in one of the original ontologies, the problem of finding the OSPC is equivalent to the problem of finding a subgraph of maximum cost in which there exist not paths with length greater than one. A path of length $n = 2$ exists if and only if there exist one of the following configurations:

- $i{:}A_h \overset{\sqsubseteq}{\rightarrow} j{:}B \overset{\sqsubseteq}{\rightarrow} i{:}A_k$ with $h \neq k$
- $i{:}A_h \overset{\perp}{\rightarrow} j{:}B \overset{\perp}{\rightarrow} i{:}A_k$ with $h \neq k$
- $i{:}A_h \overset{\sqsubseteq}{\rightarrow} j{:}B \overset{\perp}{\rightarrow} i{:}A_k$ with $h \neq k$

In the same way, the reverse situations also generate paths. Given a cluster of correspondences, the OSPC can be computed by Algorithm 10.8. It is easy to show that the OSPC has two properties: all cycles have been removed and it is semantic-incoherence-free. Both properties come from the fact that the algorithm that computes the OSPC removes the paths with cardinality greater than two, forbidding every possible inference between nodes belonging to the same ontology.

[2] In mathematics, argmax stands for the argument of the maximum, i.e., the set of points of the given argument for which the value of the given expression attains its maximum value.

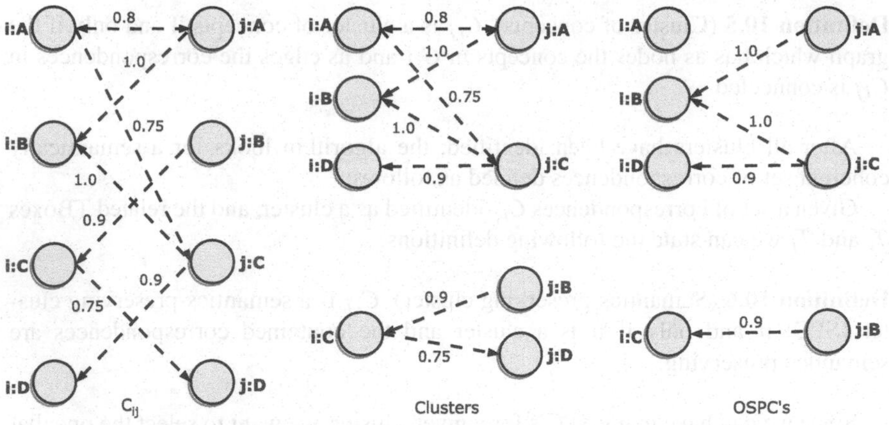

Fig. 10.2 Clusters and SPCs

Algorithm 10.8 The OSPC Algorithm

```
Input: C_ij
Output: OSPC
OSPC = ∅;
while C_ij has correspondences do
    pick the m = ⟨t_i, t_j, s⟩ from C_ij with maximum weight;
    if m = ⟨t_i, t_j, s⟩ does not generate a path of length 2 then OSPC ← OSPC ∪ m = ⟨t_i, t_j, s⟩
    else remove m = ⟨t_i, t_j, s⟩
end while
M_ij ← OSPC;
```

The approaches presented so far implicitly assume that, given a set of bugged correspondences, there exists a repair able to resolve inconsistency and/or incoherence of the mapping between two ontologies. However, in many practical cases the problem has not a clear solution but there exist more than one sub-optimal sets of correspondences which "minimizes" in some way the faults in the mapping. It is not difficult to foresee that, in an open scenario such as that of the Semantic-Web, with the spreading of independent and overlapping ontologies, the presence of inconsistency and incoherence is somewhat unavoidable. For this reason, in the next section, we briefly discuss debugging techniques able to deal with uncertainty in the correspondences in order to tolerate inconsistent or incoherent solutions.

10.4.3 Uncertainty-Aware Mapping Revision

Since 2007, a great amount of work has been done in order to support uncertainty in ontologies [10, 27]. In these frameworks, inconsistency and incoherence are tolerated and the intrinsic uncertainty of certain axioms is modeled within well-defined theoretical frameworks. This idea was considered interesting also within the ontology mapping community and it has been applied to existing revision techniques [6]. In the following, we report two interesting approaches to mapping revision with uncertainty.

10.4.3.1 Probabilistic Mapping Revision

In 2008 Castano et al. [7] proposed a mapping revision technique based on probabilistic reasoning. Given a set of automatically-generated correspondences, these are first represented as *conditional constraints*. A conditional constraint is an expression of the form:

$$(C \mid D)[l, u]$$

and represents a lower bound l and an upper bound u for the conditional probability for two concepts C, D. C is called the *evidence* and D the *hypothesis*. In such a framework, each ontological axiom of the input ontologies along with the correspondences produce one or more conditional constraints; in particular, a correspondence $\langle id, C, D, \sqsubseteq, n\rangle$ is then interpreted as a conditional constraint of the form $(D \mid C)[n, n]$. Since the set of conditional constraints can be interpreted as a set of linear equations, consistency holds whenever the system of equations associated to the theory has a solution.

In such a setting, the fault is not only a logical contradiction as in the classical sense, but also the unsolvability of the system of equations associated to the theory. Thus, a correspondence can produce contradictions in two ways: (i) the constraint is logically contradictory in the classical way; (ii) the constraint is consistent with the theory, but the associated probability does not satisfy the lower and upper bounds (*incoherence*). An incoherence, in turn, might be caused by (i) incompatibility of the correspondence with the ontology axioms or (ii) incompatibility of the correspondence is incompatible with other correspondences.

The repairing procedure takes as input a set of correspondences along with the input ontologies. In the first place, a descending order over the correspondences is produced (i.e., from the most probable to the less probable). Then the correspondences are applied to the model one by one starting from the most probable; if an incoherence is detected, the conditional constraint is removed from the model and the correspondence is discarded. The order itself privileges the most probable correspondences but, in order to refine the process, when a correspondence is incoherent w.r.t. an ontological axiom, the latter is preferred and the correspondence is discarded in order to preserve the semantics of the original ontologies.

10.4.3.2 Fuzzy Mapping Revision

An advancement w.r.t. to the previous approach to mapping revision is that of Ferrara et al. [12]. Differently from [7], where a probabilistic setting has been used, here the theoretical framework is that of ontologies with fuzzy description logics [34]. Roughly speaking, the main difference between classical and fuzzy description logic resides in the interpretation function which is actually a fuzzy membership function in the sense of fuzzy logic [38]. The interpretations of concepts and relations are intuitively extended by replacing the standard set operators with their fuzzy counterparts i.e., t-norms and t-conorms. The notion of consistency is then relaxed to tolerate inconsistencies if the axioms of the theory at least w.r.t. the constraints imposed by the fuzzy membership functions. See [34] for the details.

A fuzzy correspondence is defined in the same way as a standard correspondence, i.e., as a 5-tuple $\langle id, i{:}e, j{:}e, r, n\rangle$. Differently from the standard setting, the value n is the empirical evidence of the semantics relation r between the involved entities. This particular meaning given to the confidence value leads to the following interpretations for correspondences, where $\mu_C(a)$ is the membership degree of the individual a to the concept C:

$$\mathcal{I} \models i{:}e \xrightarrow{\equiv} j{:}e : n \iff \forall a\ a \in i{:}e^{\mathcal{I}} \rightarrow \mu_{j:e}(a) = n$$

$$\mathcal{I} \models i{:}e \xrightarrow{\sqsubseteq} j{:}e : n \iff \forall a \text{ such that } a \in i{:}e^{\mathcal{I}} \rightarrow \mu_{j:e}(a) \geq n$$

$$\mathcal{I} \models i{:}e \xrightarrow{\sqsupseteq} j{:}e : n \iff \forall a \text{ such that } a \in i{:}e^{\mathcal{I}} \rightarrow \mu_{j:e}(a) \leq n$$

$$\mathcal{I} \models i{:}e \xrightarrow{\perp} j{:}e : n \iff \forall a \text{ such that } a \in i{:}e^{\mathcal{I}} \rightarrow \mu_{j:e}(a) = 0$$

The above interpretation implicitly defines a way to build a set of fuzzy membership assertions from a set of correspondences and enable a revision procedure based on the membership degrees.

In such a setting, the faults are the inconsistencies detected in the fuzzy theory as a whole. As an example, if the fuzzy assertions state at the same time that for a certain individual a both $\mu_C(a) \leq 0.5$ and a $\mu_C(a) \geq 0.6$ hold, we are in the presence of an inconsistency in the fuzzy theory. Inconsistencies i.e., faults are detected by means of a fuzzy reasoning engine which traces the deductions in order to debug the theory when needed.

Differently from [7], the repairing is not obtained by simply discarding the problematic correspondences on the basis of their confidence value. Since the above formalization of correspondences leaves room for certain adjustments of the membership degrees, the repair mechanism first tries to adjust the membership degrees associated to fuzzy correspondences in order to restore consistency. When this first attempt fails, the problematic correspondences are removed on the basis of how many times they are identified as responsible of an inconsistency. This is done on the basis of a complete analysis of the conflict sets as in [32], adapted to the fuzzy setting.

10.5 Conclusion

Despite its importance for the Semantic Web vision, the mapping revision problem is still not completely solved. Indeed, it suffers from the inherent problem of the automatization of semantics understanding, that is, none of the adopted heuristics is completely able to take into account the initial intentions of the ontology designers. Moreover, these techniques may produce a change of the original structure of the ontologies, which may cause a loss of semantics.

In this work, we have presented the most recent and significant approaches to the mapping revision problem, trying to give a short and comprehensive view of the different techniques, along with their main strengths and weaknesses.

A fundamental distinction is between exact and approximate techniques. The main aim of the former is to preserve the correctness of the theory, with the consequence that more correspondences than necessary might be pruned. The latter approaches, on the other hand, introduce approximation to accept a larger number of correspondences, which ultimately may correspond to alternative, but possibly incompatible, views of the domain. This means that the different input semantics are accommodated, but no choice is made among them.

In our approach, we privilege the first attitude, trying not only to keep the logical consistency but also to capture the intentions of the ontology designers as much as possible. We believe that this crisp approach lends itself to be "related" in different ways than by adopting approximate techniques, and we are investigating a context-based method [30] for tolerating anomalies.

References

1. Antoniou, G., Van Harmelen, F.: A Semantic Web Primer. MIT Press, Cambridge (2004)
2. Baader, F., Calvanese, D., McGuinness, D.L., Nardi, D., Patel-Schneider, P.F.: The Description Logic Handbook: Theory, Implementation, and Applications. Cambridge University Press, Cambridge (2007)
3. Bodenreider, O.: The Unified Medical Language System (UMLS): integrating biomedical terminology. Nucleic Acids Res. J. **32**, 267–270 (2004)
4. Borgida, A., Serafini, L.: Distributed description logics: assimilating information from peer sources. J. Data Semant. **1**, 153–184 (2003)
5. Borgida, A., Franconi, E., Horrocks, I., McGuinness, D.L., Patel-Schneider, P.F.: Explaining ALC subsumption. In: Lambrix, P., Borgida, A., Lenzerini, M., Müller, R., Patel-Schneider, P. (eds.) Description Logics, CEUR-WS, Linköping (1999)
6. Calí, A., Lukasiewicz, T., Predoiu, L., Stuckenschmidt, H.: A framework for representing ontology mappings under probabilities and inconsistency. In: Bobillo, F., da Costa, P.G., d'Amato, C., Fanizzi, N., Fung, F., Lukasiewicz, T., Martin, T., Nickles, M., Peng, Y., Pool, M., Smrz, P., Vojtás, P. (eds.) Proceedings of the 3rd ISWC Workshop on Uncertainty Reasoning for the Semantic Web Busan, Korea (2008)
7. Castano, S., Ferrara, A., Lorusso, D.: Mapping validation by probabilistic reasoning. In: Bechhofer, S., Hauswirth, M., Hoffmann, J., Koubarakis, M. (eds.) Proceedings of the 5th European Semantic Web Conference, Tenerife, Greece (2008)
8. Curino, C.A., Orsi, G., Tanca, L.: X-SOM: Ontology mapping and inconsistency resolution. In: European Semantic Web Conference 2007—Poster Session. http://www.polibear.net/blog/wp-content/uploads/2008/01/final.pdf
9. Curino, C.A., Orsi, G., Tanca, L.: X-SOM: A flexible ontology mapper. In: Proceedings of 1st Intl Workshop on Semantic Web Architectures for Enterprises, Regensburg, Germany, pp. 424–428 (2007)

10. Ding, Z., Peng, Y., Pan, R.: BayesOWL: Uncertainty modeling in semantic web ontologies. Stud. Fuzziness Soft Comput. (2006)
11. Euzenat, J., Shvaiko, P.: Ontology Matching. Springer, Berlin (2007)
12. Ferrara, A., Lorusso, D., Stamou, G., Stoilos, G., Tzouvaras, V., Venetis, T.: Resolution of conflicts among ontology mappings: a fuzzy approach. In: Sheth, A., Staab, S., Dean, M., Paolucci, M., Maynard, D., Finin, T., Thirunarayan, K. (eds.) Proceedings of the 7th International Semantic-Web Conferencem Karlsruhe, Germany (2008)
13. Flouris, G., Huang, Z., Pan, J.Z., Plexousakis, D., Wache, H.: Inconsistencies, negations and changes in ontologies. In: Gil, Y., Mooney, R.J. (eds.) Proceedings of the 21st AAAI Conference on Artificial Intelligence, Boston, Massachusetts, USA (2006)
14. Flouris, G., Plexousakis, D., Antoniou, G.: On applying the AGM theory to DLS and OWL. In: Gil, Y., Motta, E., Benjamins, R., Musen, M. (eds.) Proceedings of the 4th International Semantic Web Conference, pp. 216–231 (2005)
15. Forsyth, D.A., Ponce, J.: Computer Vision: A Modern Approach. Prentice Hall, Englewood Cliffs (2002)
16. Ghidini, C., Serafini, L.: Reconciling concepts and relations in heterogeneous ontologies. In: Sure, Y., Domingue, J. (eds.) Proceedings of the 3rd European Semantic Web Conference, pp. 50–64, Budva, Montenegro (2006)
17. Giunchiglia, F., Maltese, V., Autayeu, A.: Computing minimal mappings. In: DISI Technical Report. http://eprints.biblio.unitn.it/archive/00001525/01/078.pdf
18. Giunchiglia, F., Yatskevich, Y., Shvaiko, P.: Semantic matching: Algorithms and implementation. J. Data Semant. **9**, 1–38 (2007)
19. Gruber, T.: Toward principles for the design of ontologies used for knowledge sharing. In: Guarino, N., Poli, R. (eds.) International Workshop on Formal Ontology, Padova, Italy (1993)
20. Haarslev, V., Pai, H.I., Shiri, N.: A generic framework for description logics with uncertainty. In: Cesar, P., da Costa, G., Laskey, K.B., Laskey, K.J., Pool, M. (eds.) Proceedings of the ISWC Workshop on Uncertainty Reasoning for the Semantic Web, Galway, Ireland (2005)
21. Haase, P., Qi, G.: An analysis of approaches to resolving inconsistencies in dl-based ontologies. In: Proceedings of ESWC Workshop on Ontology Dynamics (2007)
22. Halpern, J.Y.: Reasoning about Uncertainty. MIT Press, Cambridge (2003)
23. Heinsohn, J.: Probabilistic description logics. In: López de Mántaras, R., Poole, D. (eds.) Proceedings of the 10th Conference on Uncertainty in Artificial Intelligence, Seattle, Washington, USA, pp. 311–318 (1994)
24. Jaeger, M.: Probabilistic reasoning in terminological logics. In: Doyle, J., Sandewall, E., Torasso, P. (eds.) Proceedings of the 4th International Conference on Knowledge Representation and Reasoning, Bonn, Germany, pp. 305–316 (1994)
25. Kalyanpur, A., Parsia, B., Sirin, E., Hendler, J.: Debugging unsatisfiable classes in OWL ontologies. J. Web Semant. **3** (2006)
26. Koller, D., Levy, A.Y., Pfeffer, A.: P-classic: A tractable probabilistic description logic. In: Proceedings of the 14th AAAI Conference on Artificial Intelligence, Providence, Rhode Island, USA (1997)
27. Lukasiewicz, T.: Expressive probabilistic description logics. Artif. Intell. (2007)
28. Manning, C.D., Schutze, H.: Foundations of Statistical Natural Language Processing. MIT Press, Cambridge (1999)
29. Meilicke, C., Stuckenschmidt, H., Tamilin, A.: Repairing Ontology Mappings. In: Holte, R.C., Howe, A. (eds.) Proceedings of the 22nd AAAI Conference on Artificial Intelligence, Vancouver, Canada, pp. 1408–1413 (2007)
30. Orsi, G., Tanca, L.: Ontology driven, context-aware query distribution for on-the-fly dataintegration. Technical Report
31. Reiter, R.: A theory of diagnosis from first principles. Artif. Intell. **32**, 57–95 (1987)
32. Schlobach, S., Cornet, R.: Non-standard reasoning services for the debugging of description logic terminologies. In: Gottlob, G., Walsh, T. (eds.) Proceedings of the 18th International Joint Conference on Artificial Intelligence, Acapulco, Mexico (2003)

33. Shahaf, D., Amir, E.: Towards a theory of AI completeness. In: Proceedings of the 8th International Symposium on Logical Formalizations of Commonsense Reasoning, Stanford, California, USA (2006)
34. Stamou, G., Stoilos, G., Pan, J.: Handling imprecise knowledge with fuzzy description logics. In: Parsia, B., Sattler, U., Toman, D. (eds.) Proceedings of the International Workshop on Description Logics, Windermere, Lake District, UK (2006)
35. Stuckenschmidt, H., Serafini, L., Wache, H.: Reasoning about ontology mappings. In: Proceedings of the 2nd Intl Workshop on Contextual Representation and Reasoning (2006)
36. Wang, P., Xu, B.: Debugging ontology mappings: a static approach. Comput. Inform. **22**, 1001–1015 (2007)
37. Wassermann, R.: An algorithm for belief revision. In: Giunchiglia, F., Selman, B. (eds.) Proceedings of the 7th International Conference on Principles of Knowledge Representation and Reasoning, Breckenridge, Colorado, USA (2000)
38. Zadeh, L.A.: Fuzzy Sets. World Scientific, Singapore (1996)

Chapter 11
tOWL: Integrating Time in OWL

**Flavius Frasincar, Viorel Milea,
and Uzay Kaymak**

Abstract The Web Ontology Language (OWL) is the most expressive standard language for modeling ontologies on the Semantic Web. In this chapter, we present the temporal OWL (tOWL) language: a temporal extension of the OWL DL language. tOWL is based on three layers added on top of OWL DL. The first layer is the Concrete Domains layer, which allows the representation of restrictions using concrete domain binary predicates. The second layer is the Time Representation layer, which adds time points, intervals, and Allen's 13 interval relations. The third layer is the Change Representation layer which supports a perdurantist view on the world, and allows the representation of complex temporal axioms, such as state transitions. A Leveraged Buyout process is used to exemplify the different tOWL constructs and show the tOWL applicability in a business context.

11.1 Introduction

In its role as reference system, time is, beyond any doubt, one of the most encountered dimensions in a variety of domains. Naturally, dealing with time has been, and continues to be, one of the major concerns in different fields, including knowledge representation.

When including time in a knowledge representation language, one can choose to model linear time or branching time. Linear time uses a single line of time (one future), while branching time employs many time lines (possible futures). Based on the inclusion of time representations in the language, we distinguish between explicit and implicit approaches. In an explicit approach, time is part of the language, and in an implicit approach, time is inherent in the ordering of states. For an explicit temporal representation, we differentiate between time points and time intervals. Also, the explicit representations can further be defined using an internal

F. Frasincar (✉) · V. Milea · U. Kaymak
Erasmus University Rotterdam, Burgemeester Oudlaan 50, 3062 PA Rotterdam,
The Netherlands
e-mail: frasincar@ese.eur.nl

V. Milea
e-mail: milea@ese.eur.nl

U. Kaymak
e-mail: kaymak@ese.eur.nl

R. De Virgilio et al. (eds.), *Semantic Web Information Management*,
DOI 10.1007/978-3-642-04329-1_11, © Springer-Verlag Berlin Heidelberg 2010

or an external view on time. In an external view, an individual has different states at different moments in time, and in the internal view, an individual is seen as collection of different parts, each one holding at a certain moment in time. In other words, the external view uses an endurantist view on the world, and the internal view uses a perdurantist view on the world.

For modeling time one has at least two options to consider: valid time and transaction time. Valid time denotes the time during which the data is true in the modeled world. Transaction time represents the time at which the data was stored. Another differentiation pertains to whether we model relative time as "next week" or absolute time as "24 May 2009 15:00 CEST".

The considerable and ever-increasing volume of data present on the Web today motivates a need to move from free-text representations of data to semantically rich representations of information. Endeavors in this direction are being undertaken under a common denominator: the Semantic Web [4]. The state-of-the-art tools and languages provided under this umbrella, such as RDF(S) [5, 11] and OWL [3], go beyond the Web and provide the means for data sharing and reuse outside this platform, i.e., in the form of semantic applications. Despite the omnipresence of time in any Web knowledge representation, the current RDF(S) and OWL standards do not support at language level temporal representations, failing thus to provide a uniform way of specifying and accessing temporal information.

Previous attempts [6] to represent time and change relate to RDF extensions that are able to cope only to a limited extent with the semantics of temporal representations. Also, these languages are difficult to use in practice as they do not have an RDF/XML serialization. Other solutions are based on proposing ontologies [9, 17] for modeling time and/or change. These approaches also present shortcomings when modeling temporal semantics as they are bound to the OWL expressivity power.

In this chapter, we present a temporal ontology language, i.e., tOWL, addressing the current limitations on representing temporality on the Semantic Web. We model valid time using an absolute time representation. By employing a similar approach, one can model also transaction time, and by determining the context of temporal expressions it is also possible to use relative time by converting it internally to an absolute representation. Our language is able to represent *linear time* using an *explicit time* specification. It supports both *time points* and *time intervals*, and adopts an *internal* (*predurantist*) *view* on the world. The proposed language builds upon OWL, the most expressive Semantic Web standard in knowledge representation. The current contribution is focused around employing the tOWL language for the representation of business processes, the Leveraged Buyout process.

Section 11.2 presents the concrete domains and fluents notions needed in order to understand the tOWL language. In Sect. 11.3 we describe the tOWL language by providing its layered architecture, and the OWL schema representation in RDF/XML of its vocabulary. After that, in Sect. 11.4, we present the TBox and ABox of the tOWL ontology for a Leveraged Buyout example. Section 11.5 compares the related work with the tOWL approach. Last, in Sect. 11.6, we present our concluding remarks and identify possible future work.

11.2 Preliminaries

The language proposed in this paper builds on previous work on concrete domains in description logics, and fluents representation in Semantic Web languages. In Sect. 11.2.1, we present a scheme for integrating concrete domains and their predicates in description logics. After that, in Sect. 11.2.2, we present the 4D Fluents approach for modeling change in OWL DL.

11.2.1 Concrete Domains

Current DL-based languages as OWL DL are well-equipped for representing abstract concepts, but experience limitations when modeling concrete features as price, weight, age, etc. For this purpose, in [2], an approach is proposed for including concrete domains in the description logic $\mathcal{ALC}$. A concrete domain $\mathcal{D}$ is defined as a set $\Delta_{\mathcal{D}}$, the domain of $\mathcal{D}$, and a set *pred*($\mathcal{D}$), the predicate names of $\mathcal{D}$. Each predicate name is associated with a predicate of arity n, $P^{\mathcal{D}} \subseteq \Delta^n_{\mathcal{D}}$.

In order to maintain the decidability of the extended language, the concrete domains need to be admissible. A concrete domain is considered admissible if it satisfies three conditions: (i) the set of predicate names is closed under negation, (ii) the set of predicate names contains a name for $\Delta_{\mathcal{D}}$, and (iii) the satisfiability of conjunctions of the form:

$$\bigwedge_{i=1}^{k} P_i(\underline{x}^{(i)})$$

where $P_1, \ldots, P_k$ are predicate names in *pred*($\mathcal{D}$) of arity $n_1, \ldots, n_k$, respectively, and $\underline{x}^{(i)}$ represents an n_i-tuple $(x_1^{(i)}, \ldots, x_{n_i}^{(i)})$ of variables, is decidable.

From a tOWL perspective, we identify one concrete domain that has been proven in the literature [12] to be admissible, the set of rational numbers with the comparison operators $<, \leq, =, \neq, \geq$, and $>$. The set of time intervals with the 13 Allen operators *equal*, *before*, *after*, *meets*, *met-by*, *overlaps*, *overlapped-by*, *during*, *contains*, *starts*, *started-by*, *finishes* and *finished-by* can be translated to operations on the previously identified concrete domain. The intervals concrete domain is not admissible based on the previous definition, but it is a well-behaved concrete domain that has been proven to maintain the decidability of the extended language [12].

In [2], the authors propose $\mathcal{ALC}(\mathcal{D})$, $\mathcal{ALC}$ extended with an admissible concrete domain $\mathcal{D}$. The extension is based on the following concrete domain constructor:

$$\exists u_1 \ldots u_n.P$$

where u_i are concrete feature chains, i.e., compositions of the form $f_1 \ldots f_m g$ where $f_1, \ldots, f_m$ are abstract features, and g is a concrete feature. The semantics of the concrete domain constructor is defined as follows:

$$(\exists u_1 \ldots u_n.P)^{\mathcal{I}} = \{a \in \Delta_{\mathcal{I}} \mid \exists x_1, \ldots, x_n \in \Delta_{\mathcal{D}} : \\ u_i^{\mathcal{I}}(a) = f_1^{\mathcal{I}} \ldots f_{m_i}^{\mathcal{I}} g^{\mathcal{I}}(a) = x_i, 1 \le i \le n, (x_1, \ldots, x_n) \in P^{\mathcal{D}}\}$$

where $\Delta_{\mathcal{I}}$ is the abstract domain of the interpretation.

In the same paper, the authors prove that $\mathcal{ALC}(\mathcal{D})$ is decidable. In addition, it is proven that the union of two admissible domains yields an admissible domain, i.e., admissibility is closed under union. The previous concrete domain constructor has been generalized to roles in [7] as follows:

$$\exists u_1 \ldots u_n.P$$

$$\forall u_1 \ldots u_n.P$$

where u_i are concrete role chains, i.e., compositions of the form $r_1 \ldots r_m g$ where $r_1, \ldots, r_m$ are abstract roles, and g is a concrete feature.

The semantics of the generalized concrete domain constructor is defined as:

$$(\exists u_1 \ldots u_n.P)^{\mathcal{I}} = \{a \in \Delta_{\mathcal{I}} \mid \exists x_1, \ldots, x_n \in \Delta_{\mathcal{D}} : \\ u_i^{\mathcal{I}}(a) = r_1^{\mathcal{I}} \ldots r_{m_i}^{\mathcal{I}} g^{\mathcal{I}}(a) = x_i, 1 \le i \le n, (x_1, \ldots, x_n) \in P^{\mathcal{D}}\}$$

$$(\forall u_1 \ldots u_n.P)^{\mathcal{I}} = \{a \in \Delta_{\mathcal{I}} \mid \forall x_1, \ldots, x_n \in \Delta_{\mathcal{D}} : \\ u_i^{\mathcal{I}}(a) = r_1^{\mathcal{I}} \ldots r_{m_i}^{\mathcal{I}} g^{\mathcal{I}}(a) = x_i, 1 \le i \le n, (x_1, \ldots, x_n) \in P^{\mathcal{D}}\}$$

The earlier decidability results have been generalized in [13] to the more powerful description logic $\mathcal{SHIQ}(\mathcal{D})$. As tOWL aims at extending OWL with temporal information based on the previously identified concrete domains, the decidable subset of tOWL is given by $\mathcal{SHIN}(\mathcal{D})$, i.e., OWL DL with two well-behaved concrete domains but without nominals.

11.2.2 4D Fluents

Most of the existing knowledge representation formalisms on the Semantic Web deal with the representation of static domains, failing to capture the semantics of dynamic domains. A notable exception is the 4D Fluents approach from [17], which is based on an OWL DL ontology for modeling a perdurantist view on the world. The abstract syntax of the proposed ontology is defined as follows:

```
Ontology(4dFluents
  Class(TimeSlice)
  DisjointClasses(TimeSlice TimeInterval)
  Property(fluentProperty
    domain(TimeSlice)
    range(TimeSlice))
  Property(tsTimeSliceOf Functional
    domain(TimeSlice)
    range(complementOf(TimeInterval))
  Property(tsTimeInterval Functional
    domain(TimeSlice)
    range(TimeInterval)))
```

The cornerstone of the ontology is given by fluents, i.e., object properties that change through time. The authors investigate several solutions for the fluents representation in OWL. The first solution is provided by adding an extra temporal dimension to RDF triples that leads to ternary predicates which are not supported by the OWL language unless reification is used. Unfortunately, reification has no clear semantics so this solution is discarded. A second solution is provided by adding a meta-logical predicate *holds* which makes triples valid at certain moments in time. This solution is also rejected as OWL DL does not support second order logic.

The authors propose to represent fluents as properties that have as domain and range timeslices. Timeslices stand for entities that are stretched through the temporal dimension (temporal worms). For timeslice representation, two properties are used: *tsTimeSliceOf* to refer to the corresponding entity, and *tsTimeInterval* to point to the associated interval. For representing intervals, the 4D Fluents ontology imports the OWL-Time ontology [9]. The definition of *TimeInterval* in OWL-Time is given as follows:

```
Ontology(OWL-Time
  Class(TimeInterval)
  Class(InstantThing)
  Property(begins Functional
    domain(TimeInterval)
    range(InstantThing)
  Property(ends Functional
    domain(TimeInterval)
    range(InstantThing))
  Property(inCalendarClockDataType
    domain(InstantThing)
    range(xsd:dateTime))
  ...)
```

TimeInterval is defined as a class with two properties *begins* and *ends* that refer to *InstantThings*. *InstantThing* has the property *inCalendarClockDataType* to refer to one time instant given using XML Schema *xsd:dateTime*. When using fluents to link two different timeslices (possibly belonging to two different entities), one needs to make sure that these two timeslices correspond to the same time interval. This constraint goes outside the OWL DL expressivity as it accesses information from two possibly different entities and needs to be enforced before further processing the ontology.

Fig. 11.1 tOWL layer cake

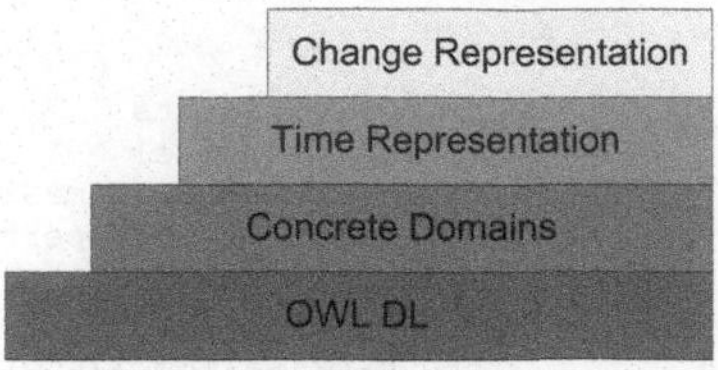

11.3 tOWL

This section presents the temporal OWL (tOWL) language [15], focusing on its abstract syntax and semantics. First, Sect. 11.3.1 gives an overview of the tOWL language and its layer-based architecture. Then, Sect. 11.3.2 introduces the tOWL OWL Schema in RDF/XML.

11.3.1 tOWL Overview

As given in Fig. 11.1, the tOWL language is composed of 4 layers, the bottom layer being the OWL DL layer.

The first layer introduced by tOWL concerns the expressiveness of the language in a general, rather than in a strictly temporal sense. The *Concrete Domains* layer enables the representation of restrictions on property chains based on concrete domain predicates.

Partly enabled by the *Concrete Domains* layer, the *Temporal Representation* layer adds a temporal reference system to the language, in the form of concrete time and concrete temporal relations. For this purpose, we use two concrete domains: the set of time instants given by XML Schema *xsd:dateTime* (which is equivalent to the set of rational numbers) with the comparison predicates, and the set of time intervals with the Allen predicates. The *Interval* is defined using the time instant concrete domain as follows:

$$Interval \equiv \exists\ start\ end. <$$

Upon enabling temporal reference in the language, the representation of change and state transitions is provided through the *Change Representation* layer. This extension enables the modeling of temporal parts of individuals that may have different property values at various moments in time. For this purpose, we employ the fluents approach of the 4D Fluents ontology.

11.3.2 OWL Schema of tOWL

In this section, we present an OWL schema of the tOWL language constructs. This is done in the same fashion as for OWL in the form of an "RDF Schema of OWL" [3].

The main purpose of this section is to provide a clear overview of the tOWL vocabulary.

The presentation of the OWL schema of tOWL starts off with the usual preliminaries in the form of namespace declarations as for any OWL ontology:

```
<?xml version="1.0"?>
<!DOCTYPE rdf:RDF [
     <!ENTITY rdf  "http://www.w3.org/1999/02/22-rdf-syntax-ns#">
     <!ENTITY rdfs "http://www.w3.org/2000/01/rdf-schema#">
     <!ENTITY xsd  "http://www.w3.org/2001/XMLSchema#">
     <!ENTITY owl  "http://www.w3.org/2002/07/owl#">
     <!ENTITY towl "http://www.towl.org/towl#">
     <!ENTITY towl_ "http://www.towl.org/towl">
   ]>
<rdf:RDF xmlns:rdf  = "&rdf;"
         xmlns:rdfs = "&rdfs;"
         xmlns:xsd  = "&xsd;"
         xmlns:owl  = "&owl;"
         xmlns      = "&towl;"
         xml:base   = "&towl_;">
```

The class *TimeSlice* is the superclass of all timeslices. This concept is introduced in the language by the *Change Representation* layer as follows:

```
<owl:Class rdf:ID="TimeSlice">
  <rdfs:label>TimeSlice</rdfs:label>
  <rdfs:subClassOf rdf:resource="&owl;Class"/>
</owl:Class>
```

Individuals of type *TimeSlice*, as presented in the previous paragraph, describe a regular individual over some period of time. Indicating which individual is described by an instance of type *TimeSlice* is achieved through the *timeSliceOf* functional property:

```
<owl:FunctionalProperty rdf:ID="timeSliceOf">
  <rdfs:label>timeSliceOf</rdfs:label>
  <rdf:type rdf:resource="&owl;ObjectProperty"/>
  <rdfs:domain rdf:resource="#TimeSlice"/>
  <rdfs:range>
    <owl:Class>
      <owl:complementOf>
        <owl:Class>
          <owl:unionOf rdf:parseType="Collection">
            <owl:Class rdf:about="#TimeSlice"/>
            <owl:Class rdf:about="#Interval"/>
            <owl:Class rdf:about="&rdfs;Literal"/>
          <owl:unionOf/>
        </owl:Class>
      </owl:complementOf>
    </owl:Class>
  </rdfs:range>
</owl:FunctionalProperty>
```

Another property describing individuals of type *TimeSlice* indicates the period of time for which these individuals hold. This is specified through the *time* functional property, that points to individuals of type *Interval*. This property, as well as the *Interval* class, are specified as follows:

```
<owl:FunctionalProperty rdf:ID="time">
  <rdfs:label>time</rdfs:label>
  <rdf:type rdf:resource="&owl;ObjectProperty"/>
  <rdfs:domain rdf:resource="#TimeSlice"/>
  <rdfs:range rdf:resource="#Interval"/>
</owl:FunctionalProperty>

<owl:Class rdf:ID="Interval">
  <rdfs:label>Interval</rdfs:label>
  <rdfs:subClassOf rdf:resource="&owl;Class"/>
</owl:Class>
```

Intervals are characterized by a starting point and an ending point, respectively. These bounds of an interval are represented as XML Schema *xsd:dateTime* datatypes, and connected to the respective interval through the *start* and *end* properties, respectively:

```
<owl:FunctionalProperty rdf:ID="start">
  <rdf:type rdf:resource="&owl;DatatypeProperty"/>
  <rdfs:domain rdf:resource="#Interval"/>
  <rdfs:range rdf:resource="&xsd;dateTime"/>
</owl:FunctionalProperty>

<owl:FunctionalProperty rdf:ID="end">
  <rdf:type rdf:resource="&owl;DatatypeProperty"/>
  <rdfs:domain rdf:resource="#Interval"/>
  <rdfs:range rdf:resource="&xsd;dateTime"/>
</owl:FunctionalProperty>
```

Indicating change for timeslices is achieved in the tOWL language through the use of fluents. A *FluentProperty* may come in one of two flavors, namely *FluentObjectProperty* or *FluentDatatypeProperty*. The first type links a timeslice to another timeslice, while the second type is used to indicate changing concrete values and thus links a timeslice to an XML Schema datatype. The fluent property types are defined as follows:

```
<owl:Class rdf:ID="FluentProperty">
  <rdfs:label>FluentProperty</rdfs:label>
  <rdfs:subClassOf rdf:resource="&rdf;Property"/>
</owl:Class>

<owl:Class rdf:ID="FluentObjectProperty">
  <rdfs:label>FluentObjectProperty</rdfs:label>
  <rdfs:subClassOf rdf:resource="#FluentProperty"/>
</owl:Class>

<owl:Class rdf:ID="FluentDatatypeProperty">
  <rdfs:label>FluentDatatypeProperty</rdfs:label>
  <rdfs:subClassOf rdf:resource="#FluentProperty"/>
</owl:Class>
```

The 13 Allen relations [1] that describe any possible relation that may exist between 2 intervals are introduced in the language through the *TimeIntervalPredicate* class, limited to 13 individuals corresponding to the Allen predicates in a one-to-one fashion:

```
<owl:Class rdf:ID="TimeIntervalPredicate">
  <rdfs:label>TimeIntervalPredicate</rdfs:label>
  <owl:equivalentClass>
    <owl:Class>
      <owl:oneOf rdf:parseType="Collection">
        <owl:Thing rdf:ID="equal"/>
        <owl:Thing rdf:ID="met-by"/>
        <owl:Thing rdf:ID="meets"/>
        ...
      </owl:oneOf>
    </owl:Class>
  </owl:equivalentClass>
</owl:Class>
```

In the same fashion, we describe $<$, $\leq$, $=$, $\neq$, $\geq$, and $>$ relations that may hold between concrete *xsd:dateTime* values that represent the end points of intervals:

```
<owl:Class rdf:ID="DateTimePredicate">
  <rdfs:label>DateTimePredicate</rdfs:label>
  <owl:equivalentClass>
    <owl:Class>
      <owl:oneOf rdf:parseType="Collection">
        <owl:Thing rdf:ID="dateTime-less-than"/>
        <owl:Thing rdf:ID="dateTime-greater-than"/>
        <owl:Thing rdf:ID="dateTime-equal"/>
        ...
      </owl:oneOf>
    </owl:Class>
  </owl:equivalentClass>
</owl:Class>
```

Concrete features, i.e., functional properties over the concrete domain, are introduced in tOWL through the *ConcreteFeature* class:

```
<owl:Class rdf:ID="ConcreteFeature">
  <rdfs:label>ConcreteFeature</rdfs:label>
  <rdfs:subClassOf rdf:resource="&owl;FunctionalProperty"/>
  <rdfs:subClassOf rdf:resource="&owl;DatatypeProperty"/>
</owl:Class>
```

One of the novelties of the tOWL language consists of the introduction of chains of roles ending in a concrete feature. This is present in the language through the *ConcreteRoleChain* construct:

```
<owl:Class rdf:ID="ConcreteRoleChain">
  <rdfs:label>ConcreteRoleChain</rdfs:label>
  <rdfs:subClassOf rdf:resource="&rdf;List"/>
</owl:Class>
```

Introducing such chains has impact on the type of restrictions allowed in the language. For this purpose, the OWL construct *owl:onProperty* is extended with the *onPropertyChains* construct, thus allowing restrictions on tOWL chains:

```
<owl:ObjectProperty rdf:ID="onPropertyChains">
  <rdfs:label>onPropertyChains</rdfs:label>
  <rdfs:domain rdf:resource="&owl;Restriction"/>
  <rdfs:range rdf:resource="&tow;ConcreteRoleChains">
</owl:ObjectProperty>

<owl:Class rdf:ID="ConcreteRoleChains">
  <rdfs:label>ConcreteRoleChains</rdfs:label>
  <rdfs:subClassOf rdf:resource="&rdf;List"/>
</owl:Class>
```

In the same fashion, the OWL restrictions *allValuesFrom* and *someValuesFrom* are extended to include the *TimeIntervalPredicate* and *DateTimePredicate* classes:

```
<owl:ObjectProperty rdf:ID="dataAllValuesFrom">
  <rdfs:label>allValuesFrom</rdfs:label>
  <rdfs:domain rdf:resource="&owl;Restriction"/>
  <rdfs:range>
    <owl:Class>
      <owl:unionOf rdf:parseType="Collection">
        <owl:Class rdf:about="#TimeIntervalPredicate"/>
        <owl:Class rdf:about="#DateTimePredicate"/>
      </owl:unionOf>
    </owl:Class>
  </rdfs:range>
</owl:ObjectProperty>

<owl:ObjectProperty rdf:ID="dataSomeValuesFrom">
  <rdfs:label>someValuesFrom</rdfs:label>
  <rdfs:domain rdf:resource="&owl;Restriction"/>
  <rdfs:range>
    <owl:Class>
      <owl:unionOf rdf:parseType="Collection">
        <owl:Class rdf:about="#TimeIntervalPredicate"/>
        <owl:Class rdf:about="#DateTimePredicate"/>
      </owl:unionOf>
    </owl:Class>
  </rdfs:range>
</owl:ObjectProperty>
```

11.4 A tOWL Ontology for the Leveraged Buyouts

In order to show the usefulness of the proposed language, in this section, we illustrate how one can model a business process for which the temporal aspects are essential. For this purpose, we decided to focus on Leveraged Buyouts (LBO), one of the most complex processes encountered in business acquisitions. First, in Sect. 11.4.1, we introduce the LBO example. Then, in Sect. 11.4.2, we present the TBox of the LBO example. After that, in Sect. 11.4.3, we give the ABox of the LBO example.

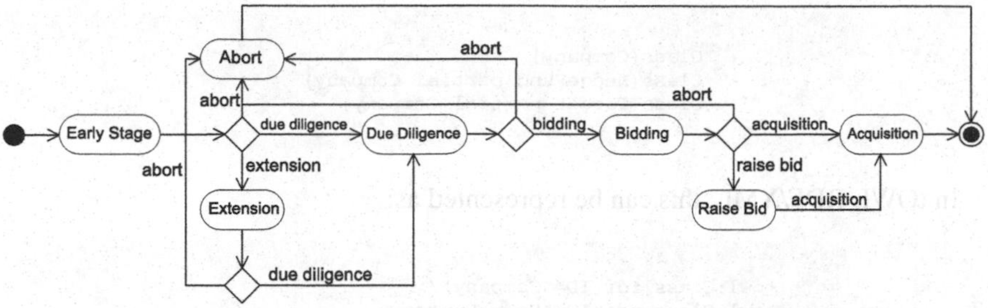

Fig. 11.2 The Leverged Buyout process

Last, in Sect. 11.4.4, we show some use cases for the tOWL in the context of the LBO example.

The focus of this section is to illustrate how the information regarding an LBO process can be represented in the tOWL language. For this purpose, we provide a representation of this example in tOWL abstract syntax and RDF/XML syntax. This is done for both TBox and ABox level representations.

11.4.1 Leveraged Buyouts

A Leveraged Buyout is a special type of an acquisition in which a company buys another company by using loans guaranteed with assets of the bought company. Figure 11.2 shows the activity diagram of an LBO process associated to one of the buyer/buyee companies. After each stage, but the last one, the system can go in the *Abort* stage, which ends the process without acquisition. The first state is the *Early Stage*. From this stage, a transition can be made to the *Due Diligence* stage or the current state might be extended. After *Due Diligence* stage follows the *Bidding* stage, from which the process can optionally go to *Raise Bid* stage. Last, the process ends with *Acquisition*.

The running example in this paper is based on the largest LBO acquisition in Europe. In 2007, two hedge funds did compete for the acquisition of a target company. From the two hedge funds, Kohlberg Kravis Roberts & Co and Terra Firma, the first won the bidding and acquired the target company Alliance Boots.

11.4.2 TBox

At TBox level, we represent conceptual information that is known about LBO processes in general. In this context, two types of companies that take part in an LBO are known: *HedgeFund* and *Target*, which we define as subclasses of the *Company* class. In tOWL abstract syntax, this translates to the following:

```
Class(Company)
Class(HedgeFund partial Company)
Class(Target partial Company)
```

In tOWL RDF/XML, this can be represented as:

```
<owl:Class rdf:ID="Company"/>
<owl:Class rdf:ID="HedgeFund">
  <rdfs:subClassOf rdf:resource="#Company"/>
</owl:Class>
<owl:Class rdf:ID="Target>
  <rdfs:subClassOf rdf:resource="#Company"/>
</owl:Class>
```

The different stages of an LBO process are represented as subclasses of the *Stage* class, such as for example in the case of the *Bidding* stage. In tOWL abstract syntax, this is represented as:

```
Class(Bidding partial Stage)
```

The tOWL RDF/XML representation of the above expression takes the form:

```
<owl:Class rdf:ID="Stage"/>
<owl:Class rdf:ID="Bidding">
  <rdfs:subClassOf rdf:resource="#Stage"/>
</owl:Class>
```

All stages are pairwise disjoint, which can be represented in tOWL abstract syntax as follows:

```
DisjointClasses(EarlyStage, DueDiligence, ..., Extension)
```

In tOWL RDF/XML, for each unique pair of stages their disjunction is expressed like:

```
<owl:Class rdf:ID="RaiseBid">
  <rdfs:subClassOf rdf:resource="#Stage"/>
  <owl:disjointWith rdf:resource="#Acquisition"/>
</owl:Class>
```

We define the class of all timeslices of an LBO process as follows, in tOWL abstract syntax:

```
Class(LBOProcess_TS complete
  restriction(timeSliceOf(someValuesFrom LBOProcess)))
```

The same representation takes the following form in tOWL RDF/XML:

```
<owl:Class rdf:ID="LBOProcess_TS">
  <owl:quivalentClass>
    <owl:Restriction>
       <owl:onProperty rdf:resource="&towl;timeSliceOf"/>
       <owl:someValuesFrom rdf:resource="#LBOProcess"/>
    </owl:Restriction>
  </owl:equivalentClass>
</owl:Class>
```

In similar fashion, we define, for each stage, the class of all timeslices of that stage. For the *EarlyStage* this achieved as follows, in tOWL abstract syntax:

```
Class (EarlyStage_TS complete
   restriction(timeSliceOf(someValuesFrom EarlyStage)))
```

The tOWL RDF/XML serialization of this fact takes the form:

```
<owl:Class rdf:ID="EarlyStage_TS">
  <owl:equivalentClass>
    <owl:Restriction>
       <owl:onProperty rdf:resource="&towl;timeSliceOf"/>
       <owl:someValuesFrom rdf:resource="#EarlyStage"/>
    </owl:Restriction>
  </owl:equivalentClass>
</owl:Class>
```

For each stage, we define a functional property that links a particular LBO process timeslice to the timeslice of the stage belonging to it. Please note that this property is not a fluent as it links timeslices corresponding to different temporal intervals and it does not change in time. In tOWL abstract syntax, this is represented as:

```
ObjectProperty(earlyStage
  domain(LBOProcess_TS)
  range(EarlyStage_TS)
  Functional)
```

Representing the same fact in tOWL RDF/XML resumes to the following expression:

```
<towl:ObjectProperty rdf:ID="earlyStage">
  <rdf:type rdf:resource="&owl;FunctionalProperty"/>
  <rdfs:domain rdf:resource="#LBOProcess_TS"/>
  <rdfs:range rdf:resource="#EarlyStage_TS"/>
</towl:ObjectProperty>
```

Next, we move on to define the *inStage* fluent, that for each timeslice of a company points to the stage in which the company finds itself. In tOWL abstract syntax, it is represented as:

```
FluentObjectProperty(inStage
  domain(
    restriction(timeSliceOf(someValuesFrom Company)))
  range(
    restriction(timeSliceOf(someValuesFrom Stage)))
```

In tOWL RDF/XML serialization the previously fluent is described as:

```
<towl:FluentObjectProperty rdf:ID="inStage">
  <rdfs:domain>
    <owl:Restriction>
      <owl:onProperty rdf:resource="&towl;timeSliceOf"/>
        <owl:someValuesFrom rdf:resource="#Company"/>
      </owl:Restriction>
  </rdfs:domain>
  <rdfs:range>
    <owl:Restriction>
      <owl:onProperty rdf:resource="&towl;timeSliceOf"/>
      <owl:someValuesFrom rdf:resource="#Stage"/>
    </owl:Restriction>
  </rdfs:range>
</towl:FluentObjectProperty>
```

Timeslices of an LBO process are defined by the sequence of stages that a company may follow in this process. Representing such sequences relies on concrete role chains, and reduces to assessing the order of the intervals associated with the different stages.

For example, representing that the *EarlyStage* always starts an LBO process can be represented in tOWL abstract syntax as follows:

```
Class(LBOProcess_TS complete
  intersectionOf(
    restriction(
      dataSomeValuesFrom((earlyStage time) time starts))
    ...))
```

For the RDF/XML serialization of the above type of restriction, we need two types of lists: lists for representing each concrete role chain, and a list that stores the property chains on which the binary concrete domain predicate is applied. Please note that for concrete features that stand for concrete feature chains used in restrictions, the list construct is not needed.

Serializing the previous axiom in tOWL RDF/XML results in the following:

```
<towl:ConcreteRoleChain rdf:ID="iEarlyStageChain">
  <rdf:first rdf:resource="#earlyStage"/>
  <rdf:rest>
    <towl:ConcreteRoleChain>
      <rdf:first rdf:resource="#time"/>
      <rdf:rest rdf:resource="&rdf;nil"/>
    </towl:ConcreteRoleChain>
  </rdf:rest>
</towl:ConcreteRoleChain>

<owl:Class rdf:ID="LBOProcess_TS">
  <owl:equivalentClass>
    <owl:intersectionOf parseType="Collection">
      <owl:Restriction>
        <towl:onPropertyChains>
          <towl:ConcreteRoleChains>
            <rdf:first rdf:resource="#iEarlyStageChain"/>
            <rdf:rest>
              <towl:ConcreteRoleChains>
                <rdf:first rdf:resource="#time"/>
                <rdf:rest rdf:resource="&rdf;nil"/>
              </towl:ConcreteRoleChains>
            <rdf:rest>
          </towl:ConcreteRoleChains>
        </towl:onPropertyChains>
        <towl:dataSomeValuesFrom rdf:resource="#starts"/>
      </owl:Restriction>
      ...
    </owl:intersectionOf>
  </owl:equivalentClass>
</owl:Class>
```

Similarly, *meets* is used between the other stages of the LBO process, while the last stage, i.e., *Acquisition finishes* the LBO process.

11.4.3 ABox

At ABox level, we represent particular information that is known about the specific LBO process presented in this section. We start off by instantiating the relevant individuals that are known to play a role in the LBO process.

First, we represent the participating companies. In tOWL abstract syntax, this is represented as follows:

```
Individual(iAllianceBoots Target)
Individual(iKKR HedgeFund)
Individual(iTerraFirma HedgeFund)
```

Similarly, we represent the same in tOWL RDF/XML:

```
<Target rdf:ID="iAllianceBoots"/>
<HedgeFund rdf:ID="iTerraFirma"/>
<HedgeFund rdf:ID="iKKR"/>
```

For each of the hedgefunds involved, we instantiate a process and define its stages, such as in the case of the TerraFirma. In tOWL abstract syntax, we define the following:

```
Individual(iLBOProcess1 type(LBOProcess)
  value(earlyStage iEarlyStage1)
  value(dueDiligence iDueDiligence1)
  value(bidding iBidding1)
  value(abort iAbort1))

Individual(iLBOProcess_TS1 type(LBOProcess_TS)
  value(timeSliceOf iLBOProcess1))}
```

The tOWL RDF/XML representation of the above two individuals takes the following form:

```
<LBOProcess rdf:ID="iLBOProcess1">
  <earlyStage rdf:ID="iEarlyStage1"/>
  <dueDiligence rdf:ID="iDueDiligence1"/>
  <bidding rdf:ID="iBidding1"/>
  <abort rdf:ID="iAbort1"/>
</LBOProcess>

<LBOProcess_TS rdf:ID="iLBOProcess_TS1">
  <towl:timesliceOf rdf:ID="iLBOProcess1"/>
</LBOProcess_TS>
```

Next, we represent the information contained by the individual news messages associated with the LBO process. We illustrate this by employing the first news message that describes the hedgefund *TerraFirma* entering the *EarlyStage* phase. This is described in the following news message:

Buyout firm Terra Firma mulls Boots bid
Sun Mar 25, 2007 8:42 am EDT

This news message signals the beginning of the LBO, mentioning that Terra Firma is considering a bid for Alliance Boots (*EarlyStage*).

For representing the information contained in the news message, we create a timeslice for the hedgefund and the target, respectively, a time interval associated to the stage, and employ the *inStage* fluent to associate the companies to the stage. In tOWL abstract syntax, this resumes to the following:

```
Individual(t1 type(Interval))
Individual(iEarlyStage1 type(EarlyStage))
Individual(iEarlyStage1_TS1 type(TimeSlice)
  value(timeSliceOf iEarlyStage1)
  value(time t1))
Individual(iAllianceBoots_TS1 type(TimeSlice)
  value(timeSliceOf iAllianceBoots)
  value(time t1)
  value(inStage iEarlyStage1_TS1))
Individual(iTerraFirma_TS1 type(TimeSlice)
  value(timeSliceOf iTerraFirma)
  value(time t1)
  value(inStage iEarlyStage1_TS1))
```

The tOWL RDF/XML representation of this news message is formulated as follows:

```
<towl:Interval rdf:ID="t1"/>
<EarlyStage rdf:ID="iEarlyStage1"/>
<towl:TimeSlice rdf:ID="iEarlyStage1_TS1">
  <towl:timeSliceOf rdf:ID="iEarlyStage1"/>
  <towl:time rdf:ID="t1"/>
</towl:TimeSlice>
<towl:TimeSlice rdf:ID="iAllianceBoots_TS1">
  <towl:timeSliceOf rdf:ID="iAllianceBoots"/>
  <towl:time rdf:ID="t1"/>
  <inStage rdf:ID="iEarlyStage1_TS1"/>
</towl:TimeSlice>
<towl:TimeSlice rdf:ID="iTerraFirma_TS1">
  <towl:timeSliceOf rdf:ID="iTerraFirma"/>
  <towl:time rdf:ID="t1"/>
  <inStage rdf:ID="iEarlyStage1_TS1"/>
</towl:TimeSlice>
```

Finally, it should be remarked that although the representation proposed here is not an exhaustive one with regard to an arbitary LBO process, i.e., it does not cover the whole process, it is sufficient for illustrating the fulfillment of the two objectives it set out to achieve: (i) illustrating the power and use of the tOWL language constructs in a temporal context, and (ii) how an LBO process can be modeled by employing the tOWL language.

11.4.4 Use Cases

The usefulness of the tOWL representation of the LBO process is explained by means of three use cases depicted in Fig. 11.3: (a) historical analysis, (b) stock prediction, and (c) regulatory conformance.

In the historical analysis use case, it can be determined in which stage the LBO process is, given a certain time instant. In this way, the LBO process evolution can be analyzed at every moment in time. In the example from Fig. 11.3, the LBO process is in *Early* stage at time t_1 and in *Due Diligence* at time t_2.

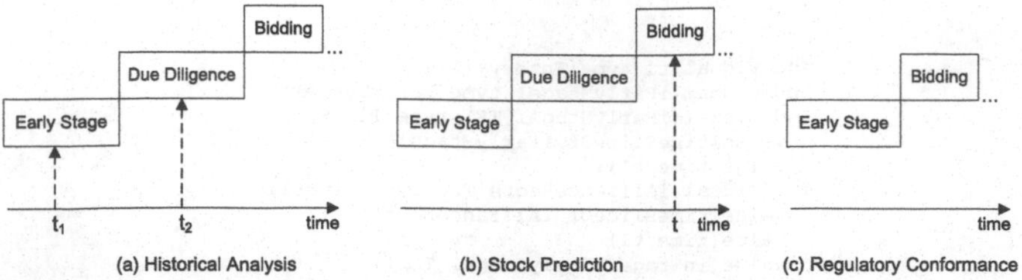

Fig. 11.3 Three use cases for the tOWL representation of the LBO process

In the stock prediction use case it can be estimated what is the impact on the stock price of a certain company given its stage in the LBO process. For instance, knowing that the LBO process is in an advanced stage has a positive effect on the price of the target company stocks. In the example from Fig. 11.3, the LBO process is in *Bidding* stage at time t, which means that the *Alliance Boots*' stock price will possibly increase.

In the regulatory conformance use case, it can be checked if a given LBO process (ABox) obeys its temporal obligations from the regulatory specification (TBox). In the example from Fig. 11.3, the *Bidding* stage comes immediately after the *Early Stage* which conflicts with the LBO process regulation that says that after *Early Stage* should follow the *Due Diligence* stage.

11.5 Related Work

In this section, we compare our approach with related work for representing time and change on the Semantic Web. In Sect. 11.5.1, we analyse Temporal RDF, an RDF extension to represent both time and change. Then, in Sect. 11.5.2, we discuss OWL-Time, an OWL ontology able to represent time. Last, in Sect. 11.5.3, we relate to the 4D Fluents ontology able to represent time and change.

11.5.1 Temporal RDF

Temporal RDF [6] extends RDF with temporal information. The approach is based on temporal graphs which are sets of triples with time intervals or instants (temporal labels) associated to them. The time intervals represent the time in which a triple holds true, and have *intial* and *final* properties defined. The authors focus on valid time, while stating that transaction time can be defined in a similar way. The proposed approach extends the RDF semantics with a temporal semantics and defines temporal entailment of RDF graphs.

An interesting feature of temporal RDF is that it supports anonymous time which represents a time variable instead of a constant. One such temporal variable introduced in the language is *NOW* which stands for the current time. This variable is a place holder for the time at which the corresponding triple is evaluated. Temporal RDF has a temporal query language, and it is proven that the temporal labeling of triples does not introduce any complexity overhead in query answering.

Despite using reification for associating time intervals to triples, the lack of semantics of reification is overcame by defining temporal rules that provide for equivalent representations. Nevertheless, from a practical perspective, the authors do not show how reification can be avoided from the serialization of RDF graphs. In addition, as XML is the lingua franca on the Semantic Web, temporal RDF doesn't have an RDF/XML serialization which makes this approach difficult to use in practice.

Temporal RDF and tOWL are able to specify both temporal instants and intervals. In tOWL, the reification problem is avoided by employing a perdurantist view on the world, extending objects in a temporal dimension. In addition, we target OWL instead of RDF, which allows a more precise definition (e.g., functional properties, restrictions, etc.) of the provided vocabulary. We also make use of concrete domains which allows a more accurate definition of intervals (the start time point of an interval has to be before the end time point of the same interval) as well as employing the Allen calculus for defining temporal relationships between object states. Differently than temporal RDF, tOWL makes use of existing standards, when possible, for representing temporal information (e.g., *xsd:dateTime* for representing time points).

11.5.2 OWL-Time

One of the first OWL ontologies seeking to represent time is OWL-Time [9]. The initial purpose of OWL-Time was to describe the temporal content of Web pages and services. It later grew to a reference time ontology able to represent time, duration, clock, calendar, and temporal aggregates in may domains. Some of the applications of OWL-Time are information retrieval and question answering. OWL-Time is currently a W3C working draft [10].

The root node of OWL-Time ontology is the *TemporalEntity* which is refined in two types: *Instant* and *Interval*. Any *TemporalEntity* has a *begins* and *ends* property which refer to *InstantThing*s. In addition, the ontology defines *CalendarClockDescription*, *DurationDescription* and *TemporalUnit*. OWL-Time provides two alternative ways to represent time points *CalendarClockDescription* and *xsd:dateTime*. The advantage of the first representation is that it allows one to express more information (e.g., the first day of a week, i.e., Sunday), while the second one is based on a standard which has a wider acceptance and usage.

OWL-Time defines the *inside* relation between instants and intervals, and the Allen temporal relations between intervals. The Allen relations can be specified based the transitive *before* relation between begin and end points. Unfortunately, this translation scheme goes beyond the OWL expressivity and thus needs to be encoded separately from the OWL inference rules. From the 13 Allen relations, six have inverses (*equal* doesn't have an inverse) which can be easily expressed based on OWL semantics.

For time representations that are not based on *xsd:dateTime*, OWL-Time defines a time zone ontology that allows to define time zones (e.g., +1 hour from Greenwich Mean Time) and link them to geographical locations (e.g., the Netherlands). Additionally, OWL-Time allows the representation of temporal aggregates [16]. For this purpose, it builds upon the inherent ordering of temporal entities. For example, in OWL-Time, one is able to specify "every other Friday in 2009" which takes in consideration the days ordering in a specific context, i.e., "2009".

The semantics of the introduced concepts is given in first order logic and to some extent also in second order logic (quantifying over predicates for the definition of temporal aggregates) and thus goes beyond the expressivity power of OWL DL. It is not clear which set of the proposed vocabulary provides for a decidable language. Also, some of the introduced primitives as *xsd:duration* have ambiguous semantics (e.g., a duration of 1 month can represent 28 days, 29 days, 30 days, and 31 days) and for this reason they have been left out from the XML Schema datatypes included in RDF and OWL [8].

For tOWL, we have identified that the decidable language subset is $\mathcal{SHIN}(\mathcal{D})$. Also, tOWL is able to better capture the semantics of intervals (e.g., impose an ordering between the start and end time points of an interval), and make use of Allen calculus for defining temporal relations at TBox level by employing the functionality offered by concrete domains (OWL-Time is able to do this only at ABox level). tOWL does not make use of durations avoiding thus their ambiguous semantics. Differently than OWL-Time, tOWL is able to represent the objects' dynamics by specifying object properties that change in time.

11.5.3 4D Fluents

As identified in Sect. 11.2, the 4D Fluents ontology [17] allows to represent both time and change. Unfortunately, as it makes use of OWL-Time ontology for the time representation, it suffers from the shortcomings previously identified for this approach. While 4D Fluents defines timeslices and fluents as an ontology, tOWL brings these primitives as first class citizens of the new language enabling anyone devising a tOWL ontology to make use of these constructs in modeling the domain dynamics. In addition, this approach allows a tOWL reasoner to translate the Allen relations between intervals as temporal relations between their end points, and enforce that two timeslices connected by the same fluent correspond to the same interval.

The 4D Fluents solution for representing a dynamic world suffers from the proliferation of objects. One fluent requires two timeslices, each timeslice referring to one entity and one temporal interval, in total 7 triples (including the triple in which the fluent is employed) need to be created in the dynamic domain for 1 triple in the static domain. In order to alleviate this problem, tOWL differentiates between two types of fluents, FluentObjectProperty and FluentDatatypeProperty. FluentDatatypeProperty has as range datatypes which means that one timeslice and its two required relationships are not needed. This yields a reduction from 7 triples to 4 triples in the case of FluentDatatypeProperty.

Differently than 4D Fluents, tOWL allows the use of the Allen calculus at TBox level as for expressing temporal relations between the different concept states. Also, by extending the OWL language with concrete domains, one can add to the language other concrete domains than the temporal concrete domains as for example the Region Connection Calculus (RCC8) for specifying spatial relationships, or the price concrete domain for representing price changes.

11.6 Conclusion

The tOWL language is an extension of OWL DL that enables the representation of time and change in dynamic domains. It comes to meet shortcomings of previous approaches, such as [6, 9, 17] that only address these representations to a limited extent. For this purpose, tOWL makes use of concrete domains and a perdurantist view on the world based on fluents. The expressivity power of the language is demonstrated by means of one of the most complex use cases known from business process modeling, i.e., a real world Leveraged Buyout (LBO) process. The knowledge regarding this LBO is modeled at TBox level by means of axioms describing the possible paths through such a process. At ABox level we are able to describe the actual process through the representation of the information contained in real news messages associated with this particular LBO.

Currently, we are working towards providing a tOWL Protege plugin that would foster the tOWL usage by allowing users to build tOWL ontologies using a simple user interface. For this purpose, we plan to keep the new interface compatible with the Protege OWL interface so that the transition to the new language is made as smooth as possible for existing Protege users. As far as the reasoner is concerned, we would like to implement the $\mathcal{SHIQ}(\mathcal{D})$ reasoning algorithm from [13], or use a hybrid reasoner in which one of the existing DL reasoners (e.g., Pellet) is extended with a concrete domain reasoning box.

In order to further reduce the proliferation of objects in tOWL, we would like to investigate the merging of timeslices by coalescing their corresponding intervals. Also, we would like to investigate the decidability of tOWL (in this paper it is shown that tOWL without nominals is decidable) by considering what is the influence of nominals on $\mathcal{SHIQ}(\mathcal{D})$ decidability results. We also plan also to examine how to extend the tOWL language with a spatial dimension by including the RCC8 calculus. As Allen calculus, RCC8 has the jointly exhaustive and pairwise disjoint property that ensures the decidability of the extended DL language [14].

Acknowledgements The authors are supported by the EU funded IST-STREP Project FP6-26896: *Time-determined ontology-based information system for realtime stock market analysis* (TOWL). More information is available on the official website[1] of the TOWL project.

[1] http://www.semlab.nl/towl.

References

1. Allen, J.F.: Maintaining knowledge about temporal intervals. Commun. ACM **26**(11), 832–843 (1983)
2. Baader, F., Hanschke, P.: A scheme for integrating concrete domains into concept languages. In: 12th International Joint Conference on Artificial Intelligence (IJCAI 1991), pp. 452–457. Morgan Kaufmann, San Mateo (1991)
3. Bechhofer, S., van Harmelen, F., Hendler, J., Horrocks, I., McGuinness, D.L., Patel-Schneider, P.F., Stein, L.A.: OWL Web Ontology Language reference. W3C Recommendation 10 February 2004 (2004). http://www.w3.org/TR/owl-ref/
4. Berners-Lee, T., Hendler, J., Lassila, O.: The Semantic Web. Sci. Am. **284**(5), 34–43 (2001)
5. Brickley, D., Guha, R.: RDF Vocabulary Description Language 1.0: RDF Schema. W3C Recommendation 10 February 2004 (2004). http://www.w3.org/TR/rdf-schema/
6. Gutierrez, C., Hurtado, C.A., Vaisman, A.A.: Introducing time into RDF. IEEE Trans. Knowl. Data Eng. **19**(2), 207–218 (2007)
7. Hanschke, P.: Specifying role interaction in concept languages. In: Third International Conference on Principles of Knowledge Representation and Reasoning (KR 2002), pp. 318–329. Morgan Kaufmann, San Mateo (1992)
8. Hayes, P.: RDF semantics. W3C Recommendation 10 February 2004 (2004). http://www.w3.org/TR/rdf-mt
9. Hobbs, J.R., Pan, F.: An ontology of time for the Semantic Web. ACM Trans. Asian Lang. Inf. Process. **3**(1), 66–85 (2004)
10. Hobbs, J.R., Pan, F.: Time ontology in OWL. W3C Working Draft 27 September 2006 (2006). http://www.w3.org/TR/2006/WD-owl-time-20060927/
11. Klyne, G., Carroll, J.J.: Resource Description Framework (RDF): Concepts and abstract syntax. W3C Recommendation 10 February 2004 (2004). http://www.w3.org/TR/rdf-concepts/
12. Lutz, C.: Interval-based temporal reasoning with general tboxes. In: Seventeenth International Joint Conference on Artificial Intelligence (IJCAI 2001), pp. 89–96. Morgan Kaufmann, San Mateo (2001)
13. Lutz, C.: Adding numbers to the SHIQ description logic: first results. In: Eighth International Conference on Principles of Knowledge Representation and Reasoning (KR 2002), pp. 191–202 (2002)
14. Lutz, C., Milicic, M.: A tableau algorithm for description logics with concrete domains and general TBoxes. J. Autom. Reason. **38**(1–3), 227–259 (2007)
15. Milea, V., Frasincar, F., Kaymak, U.: Knowledge engineering in a temporal Semantic Web context. In: Eighth International Conference on Web Engineering (ICWE 2008), pp. 65–74. IEEE Computer Society, Los Alamitos (2008)
16. Pan, F., Hobbs, J.R.: Temporal aggregates in OWL-Time. In: 18th International Florida Artificial Intelligence Research Society Conference (FLAIRS 2005), pp. 560–565. AAAI Press, Menlo Park (2005)
17. Welty, C.A., Fikes, R.: A reusable ontology for fluents in OWL. In: Fourth International Conference on Formal Ontology in Information Systems (FOIS 2006). Frontiers in Artificial Intelligence and Applications, vol. 150, pp. 226–336. IOS Press, Amsterdam (2006)

Part III
Semantic Web Data Querying

Chapter 12
Datalog Extensions for Tractable Query Answering over Ontologies

Andrea Calì, Georg Gottlob, and Thomas Lukasiewicz

Abstract We survey a recently introduced family of expressive extensions of Datalog, called Datalog$^{\pm}$, which is a new framework for representing ontologies in the form of integrity constraints, and for query answering under such constraints. Datalog$^{\pm}$ is derived from Datalog by allowing existentially quantified variables in rule heads, and by enforcing suitable properties in rule bodies, to ensure decidable and efficient query answering. We first present different languages in the Datalog$^{\pm}$ family, providing tight complexity bounds for nearly all cases. We then show that such languages are general enough to capture the most common tractable ontology languages. In particular, Datalog$^{\pm}$ can express the *DL-Lite* family of description logics and F-Logic Lite. Datalog$^{\pm}$ is a natural and very general framework that can be employed in different contexts such as data integration and exchange.

12.1 Introduction

In this paper, we give an overview on the results of two recent works [9, 10] on a family of expressive extensions of Datalog, called Datalog$^{\pm}$, towards query answering over ontologies. Rules in Datalog$^{\pm}$ are rules in Datalog that additionally admit existentially quantified variables in the head, but on which restrictions are enforced on the body to ensure desirable decidability and tractability properties.

A. Calì (✉)
Oxford-Man Institute of Quantitative Finance, University of Oxford, Eagle House, Walton Well Road, Oxford OX2 6ED, UK
e-mail: andrea.cali@oxford-man.ox.ac.uk

A. Calì · G. Gottlob · T. Lukasiewicz
Computing Laboratory, University of Oxford, Wolfson Building, Parks Road, Oxford OX1 3QD, UK

G. Gottlob
Oxford-Man Institute of Quantitative Finance, University of Oxford, Blue Boar Court, 9 Alfred Street, Oxford OX1 4EH, UK
e-mail: georg.gottlob@comlab.ox.ac.uk

T. Lukasiewicz
Institut für Informationssysteme, Technische Universität Wien, Favoritenstraße 9-11, 1040 Wien, Austria
e-mail: thomas.lukasiewicz@comlab.ox.ac.uk

R. De Virgilio et al. (eds.), *Semantic Web Information Management*,
DOI 10.1007/978-3-642-04329-1_12, © Springer-Verlag Berlin Heidelberg 2010

Ontologies are fundamental to the development of the Semantic Web [6]; they are also gaining importance in databases, since they provide the necessary expressive power for tasks such as data modeling and data integration [30]. Among formalisms for representing ontologies, *description logics* (DLs) have played a crucial role in the last decade, especially in the Semantic Web. Currently, much research on DLs is directed towards scalable and efficient query answering over ontologies. In particular, the DLs of the *DL-Lite* family [13, 34] are the most common DLs in the Semantic Web and databases that allow for tractable query answering.

Example 12.1 A DL knowledge base consists of an ABox and a TBox. For example, the knowledge that John is a manager can be expressed by the axiom *Manager(john)* in the ABox, while the knowledge that (i) every manager is an employee, (ii) every manager supervises someone, (iii) employees are not employers and (iv) every employee is supervised by at most one manager, can be expressed by the axioms $Manager \sqsubseteq Employee$, $Manager \sqsubseteq \exists Supervises$, $Employee \sqsubseteq \neg Employer$, and $(\mathsf{funct}\, Supervises^{-})$ in the TBox, respectively. A Boolean conjunctive query (BCQ) asking whether John supervises someone is $\exists X Supervises(john, X)$.

The ABox and the TBox of DL knowledge bases are closely related to extensional databases and intensional sets of rules in Datalog [15, 36]. Datalog is a language with simple syntax and natural semantics, which make it easily understandable and usable. It has also been successfully used in many applications such as Web data extraction [24]. Moreover, there are several optimization techniques for Datalog, which improve its applicability. But not all ontological statements can be expressed in plain Datalog, as discussed in [33] and illustrated below.

Example 12.2 The knowledge that every manager is an employee can be expressed in Datalog by the rule $manager(X) \rightarrow employee(X)$. However, we cannot express in Datalog that every manager supervises someone, which requires a rule with an existential quantification in its head: $manager(X) \rightarrow \exists Y\, supervises(X, Y)$. Such assertions are special *tuple-generating dependencies* (*TGDs*), which generalize *inclusion dependencies* (*IDs*). We also cannot express in plain Datalog that employees are not employers, which requires a rule of the form $employee(X), employer(X) \rightarrow \bot$. Similarly, we cannot express that every employee is supervised by at most one manager, which requires a rule of the form $supervises(X, Y), supervises(X', Y) \rightarrow X = X'$. Such assertions are special *equality-generating dependencies* (*EGDs*), which generalize *functional dependencies* (*FDs*).

As the above example shows, an extension of Datalog by TGDs, negative constraints, and EGDs allows to express forms of ontological knowledge beyond plain Datalog. However, the interaction among TGDs and EGDs leads to undecidability of query answering [12, 16, 18, 28, 32] in general. Interesting subclasses of TGDs and EGDs have been studied in the literature, e.g., in the fundamental work [28]. All these works make use of a technique called *chase* [5, 16, 28], which amounts to "repairing" violations of TGDs and EGDs starting from a database, until a fixpoint is reached. The chase can be seen as a tableaux technique. One of the main difficulties behind all these approaches is the fact that such a fixpoint may be infinite. Several works in the literature consider classes of TGDs for which the chase terminates and therefore generates a finite instance; for example, the *weakly acyclic TGDs*, first introduced in [21] and extensively studied in [22].

The Datalog$^{\pm}$ family is an expressive extension of Datalog by integrity constraints as illustrated in Example 12.2 towards query answering over ontologies. Datalog$^{\pm}$ deals with certain TGDs as rules (as well as negative constraints and EGDs) for which the chase does not terminate, but for which query answering is nonetheless decidable in general and tractable in many cases in the data complexity. Datalog$^{\pm}$ is divided into the sublanguages of *guarded, linear*, and *weakly guarded* Datalog$^{\pm}$, having *guarded, linear* and *weakly guarded* TGDs as rules, respectively:

- Guarded TGDs are characterized by the presence of a *guard*, i.e., an atom in the body that contains all the (universally quantified) variables in the rule body.
- Weakly guarded TGDs have instead a *weak guard*, i.e., an atom in the body that contains all the (universally quantified) variables in the body that appear in the so-called *affected positions*, which are informally the only arguments of atoms where newly invented values can appear during the chase process.
- Linear TGDs have exactly one atom in the body and one in the head; they are the class which is closest to inclusion dependencies among the three, and they correspond to inclusion dependencies with repetition of columns.

We characterize the complexity of query answering for all three sublanguages of Datalog$^{\pm}$ for variable and fixed sets of TGDs. The results are compactly summarized in Tables 12.1 and 12.2. In detail, query answering is complete for PSPACE and 2EXPTIME in the linear and the guarded/weakly guarded case, respectively, for variable sets of TGDs. It is complete for NP and EXPTIME in the linear/guarded and the weakly guarded case, respectively, for fixed sets of TGDs. Finally, query answering is in AC_0 (which is the complexity of evaluating fixed first-order formulas over a database or finite structure), PTIME-complete, and EXPTIME-complete when

Table 12.1 Summary of complexity results: variable set of TGDs

BCQ type	Linear TGDs	Guarded TGDs	Weakly Guarded TGDs
general	PSPACE-complete	2EXPTIME-complete	2EXPTIME-complete
bounded width, fixed, and atomic	PSPACE-complete	EXPTIME-complete	2EXPTIME-complete

Table 12.2 Summary of complexity results: fixed set of TGDs

BCQ type	Linear TGDs	Guarded TGDs	Weakly Guarded TGDs
general	NP-complete	NP-complete	EXPTIME-complete
bounded width, fixed, and atomic	in AC_0	PTIME-complete	EXPTIME-complete

the query is of bounded width, fixed, or atomic in the linear, the guarded, and the weakly guarded case, respectively, for fixed sets of TGDs.

We then further enrich Datalog$^\pm$ with additional features, which serve to represent ontology languages. In particular, we add negative constraints, which are Horn clauses with a (not necessarily guarded) conjunction of atoms in their body and the truth constant *false*, denoted $\perp$, in the head. Negative constraints are easy to handle, and we actually show that their introduction does not increase the complexity of query answering in Datalog$^\pm$. As a second extension, we add *non-conflicting keys*, which are special EGDs that do not interact with TGDs, and thus also do not increase the complexity of query answering in Datalog$^\pm$. We deal only with *keys*, since this suffices to capture the most common tractable ontology languages in the literature. The class of *non-conflicting keys* is a generalization of the one in [12].

We finally show that the Datalog$^\pm$ family is able to express the most common tractable ontology languages. More concretely, linear Datalog$^\pm$ with negative constraints and non-conflicting keys, called *Datalog*$_0^\pm$, can be used for query answering in *DL-Lite*$_\mathcal{A}$ in a natural and unified way. Here, Datalog$_0^\pm$ is strictly more expressive than *DL-Lite*$_\mathcal{A}$. Furthermore, weakly guarded Datalog$^\pm$ with a single non-conflicting key can be used for query answering in F-Logic Lite ontologies. Other DLs of the *DL-Lite* family [13] (such as *DL-Lite*$_\mathcal{F}$ and *DL-Lite*$_\mathcal{R}$) can be similarly translated to Datalog$_0^\pm$. Since *DL-Lite*$_\mathcal{R}$ is able to fully capture (the DL fragment of) RDF Schema [7], Datalog$_0^\pm$ is also able to fully capture (the DL fragment of) RDF Schema. Furthermore, note that the F-Logic formalism [29] is able to offer the *meta-querying* facility, i.e., the possibility of querying the schema as well as the data, in a homogeneous fashion. This is considered important for service discovery and in information integration in the Semantic Web, for example; however, the facilities for meta-querying have been usually awkward to the user, for example, the SQL system catalog, or the Java Reflection API. In F-Logic Lite [11], rules are indeed TGDs, and our goal is to generalize the F-Logic Lite framework, and to have the results of [11] as a special case of Datalog$^\pm$.

Note that in [10], we also show how stratified negation can be added to Datalog$^\pm$ while keeping ontology querying tractable in the data complexity. More specifically, we provide a canonical model and a perfect model semantics, and we show that they coincide. We thus provide a natural stratified negation for query answering over ontologies, which has been an open problem to date, since it is in general based on several strata of infinite models. By the results of Sect. 12.7, this also provides a natural stratified negation for the *DL-Lite* family of description logics.

12.2 Preliminaries

In this section, we briefly recall some basics on databases, queries, (tuple- and equality-generating) dependencies, and the chase. We also provide some notions about the treewidth of a graph and of a database instance.

Databases and Queries We assume (i) an infinite universe of *data constants* Δ (which constitute the "normal" domain of a database), (ii) an infinite set of (*labeled*) *nulls* Δ_N (used as "fresh" Skolem terms, which are placeholders for unknown values, and can thus be seen as variables), and (iii) an infinite set of variables $\mathcal{X}$ (used in dependencies and queries). Different constants represent different values (*unique name assumption*), while different nulls may represent the same value. We assume a lexicographic order on $\Delta \cup \Delta_N$, with every symbol in Δ_N following all symbols in Δ. We denote by $\mathbf{X}$ sequences of variables $X_1, \ldots, X_k$ with $k \geqslant 0$.

A *relational schema* $\mathcal{R}$ is a finite set of *relation names* (or *predicates*). A *position* $p[i]$ identifies the i-th argument of a predicate p. A *term* t is a constant, null, or variable. An *atomic formula* (or *atom*) $\mathbf{a}$ has the form $p(t_1, \ldots, t_n)$, where p is an n-ary predicate, and $t_1, \ldots, t_n$ are terms. We denote by $dom(\mathbf{a})$, $pred(\mathbf{a})$, and $vars(\mathbf{a})$ the set of all arguments, the predicate symbol, and the set of all variables of an atom $\mathbf{a}$, respectively. This notation naturally extends to sets of atoms. Conjunctions of atoms are often identified with the sets of their atoms.

A *database* (*instance*) D for $\mathcal{R}$ is a (possibly infinite) set of atoms with predicates from $\mathcal{R}$ and arguments from $\Delta \cup \Delta_N$. Such D is *ground* iff all arguments of its atoms are from Δ. A *conjunctive query* (*CQ*) over $\mathcal{R}$ has the form $q(\mathbf{X}) = \exists \mathbf{Y} \Phi(\mathbf{X}, \mathbf{Y})$, where $\Phi(\mathbf{X}, \mathbf{Y})$ is a conjunction of atoms having as arguments variables $\mathbf{X}$ and $\mathbf{Y}$ and constants (but no nulls). A *Boolean CQ* (*BCQ*) over $\mathcal{R}$ is a CQ having head predicate q of arity 0 (i.e., no variables in $\mathbf{X}$). BCQs are often identified with the sets of their atoms. Answers to CQs and BCQs are defined via *homomorphisms*, which are mappings $\mu \colon \Delta \cup \Delta_N \cup \mathcal{X} \to \Delta \cup \Delta_N \cup \mathcal{X}$ such that (i) $c \in \Delta$ implies $\mu(c) = c$, (ii) $c \in \Delta_N$ implies $\mu(c) \in \Delta \cup \Delta_N$, and (iii) μ is naturally extended to atoms, sets of atoms, and conjunctions of atoms. The set of all *answers* to a CQ $Q(\mathbf{X}) = \exists \mathbf{Y} \Phi(\mathbf{X}, \mathbf{Y})$ over a database D, denoted $Q(D)$, is the set of all tuples $\mathbf{t}$ over Δ for which there exists a homomorphism $\mu \colon \mathbf{X} \cup \mathbf{Y} \to \Delta \cup \Delta_N$ such that $\mu(\Phi(\mathbf{X}, \mathbf{Y})) \subseteq D$ and $\mu(\mathbf{X}) = \mathbf{t}$. The *answer* to a BCQ Q over D is *Yes*, denoted $D \models Q$, iff $Q(D) \neq \emptyset$.

Dependencies Given a relational schema $\mathcal{R}$, a *tuple-generating dependency* (or *TGD*) σ is a first-order formula $\forall \mathbf{X} \forall \mathbf{Y}\, \Phi(\mathbf{X}, \mathbf{Y}) \to \exists \mathbf{Z}\, \Psi(\mathbf{X}, \mathbf{Z})$, where $\Phi(\mathbf{X}, \mathbf{Y})$ and $\Psi(\mathbf{X}, \mathbf{Z})$ are conjunctions of atoms over $\mathcal{R}$, called the *body* and the *head* of σ, respectively. Such σ is satisfied in a database D for $\mathcal{R}$ if every homomorphism h with $h(\Phi(\mathbf{X}, \mathbf{Y})) \subseteq D$ can be extended to a homomorphism h' with $h'(\Psi(\mathbf{X}, \mathbf{Y})) \subseteq D$.

Example 12.3 The following formula σ is a tuple-generating dependency (note that we use the comma as logical conjunction symbol):

$$\forall X \forall Y r_1(X, Y), r_2(Y, X) \to \exists Z r_3(X, Z), r_3(Y, Z)$$

The database $D_1 = \{r_1(a, b), r_2(b, a), r_3(a, c), r_3(b, c)\}$ satisfies σ. In fact, every homomorphism h mapping the body to D_1 is such that $h(X) = a$ and $h(Y) = b$, and we can extend it to h' by choosing $h'(Z) = c$. It is immediately seen that, instead, the database $D_2 = \{r_1(a, b), r_2(b, a), r_3(a, c), r_3(b, d)\}$ does not satisfy σ: h maps the body of σ to D_2, but no extension h' of h exists that maps the head of σ to D_2.

The notion of *query answering* under TGDs is defined as follows. For a set of TGDs Σ on $\mathcal{R}$, and a database D for $\mathcal{R}$, the set of *models* of D given Σ, denoted $mods(\Sigma, D)$, is the set of all databases B such that $B \models D \cup \Sigma$. The set of *answers* to a CQ Q on D given Σ, denoted $ans(Q, \Sigma, D)$, is the set of all tuples $\mathbf{a}$ such that $\mathbf{a} \in Q(B)$ for all $B \in mods(\Sigma, D)$. The *answer* to a BCQ Q over D given Σ is *Yes*, denoted $D \cup \Sigma \models Q$, iff $ans(Q, \Sigma, D) \neq \emptyset$.

We recall that the two problems of CQ and BCQ evaluation under TGDs are LOGSPACE-equivalent [17, 20, 22, 28]. Moreover, it is easy to see that the query output tuple (QOT) problem (as a decision version of CQ evaluation) and BCQ evaluation are AC_0-reducible to each other. Henceforth, we thus focus only on BCQ evaluation. All complexity results carry over to the other problems. We also recall that query answering under TGDs is equivalent to query answering under TGDs with only singleton atoms in their heads [9]. This is shown by means of a transformation from general TGDs to TGDs with single-atom heads [9]. Moreover, the transformation preserves the properties of the classes of TGDs that we are going to consider in the rest of the paper (*weakly-guarded*, *guarded*, and *linear* TGDs). Therefore, all our results carry over to TGDs with multiple atoms in the head. In the sequel, we thus assume w.l.o.g. that every TGD has a singleton atom in its head.

An *equality-generating dependency* (or *EGD*) σ is a first-order formula of the form $\forall \mathbf{X}\, \Phi(\mathbf{X}) \rightarrow X_i = X_j$, where $\Phi(\mathbf{X})$, called the *body* of σ, is a conjunction of atoms, and X_i and X_j are variables from $\mathbf{X}$. We call $X_i = X_j$ the *head* of σ. Such σ is satisfied in a database D for $\mathcal{R}$ if, whenever there exists a homomorphism h such that $h(\Phi(\mathbf{X}, \mathbf{Y})) \subseteq D$, it holds that $h(X_i) = h(X_j)$.

Example 12.4 The following formula σ is an equality-generating dependency:

$$\forall X \forall Y \forall Z r_1(X, Y), r_2(Y, Z) \rightarrow Y = Z$$

The database $D_1 = \{r_1(a, b), r_2(b, b)\}$ satisfies σ, because every homomorphism h mapping the body of σ to D_1 is such that $h(Y) = h(Z)$. On the contrary, the database $D_1 = \{r_1(a, b), r_2(b, c)\}$ does not satisfy σ. It is important to notice that EGDs generalize *functional dependencies* and, in particular, *key dependencies* [1]. For example, to express that the first attribute of a ternary predicate r is a key, thus asserting a key dependency, we can use the following pair of EGDs:

$$r(X, Y_1, Z_1), r(X, Y_2, Z_2) \rightarrow Y_1 = Y_2$$
$$r(X, Y_1, Z_1), r(X, Y_2, Z_2) \rightarrow Z_1 = Z_2$$

The body (resp., head) of a TGD or EGD σ is denoted by *body*(σ) (resp., *head*(σ)). We usually omit the universal quantifiers in TGDs and EGDs, and all sets of TGDs and EGDs are finite here.

The Chase The *chase* was introduced to enable checking implication of dependencies [31], and later also for checking query containment [28]. It is a procedure for repairing a database relative to a set of dependencies, so that the result of the chase satisfies the dependencies. By "chase", we refer both to the chase procedure and to its output. The chase works on a database through so-called TGD and EGD *chase rules*. The TGD chase rule comes in two flavors: *oblivious* and *restricted*, where the restricted one repairs TGDs only when they are not satisfied. We focus on the oblivious one, since it makes proofs technically simpler. The *(oblivious) TGD chase rule* defined below is the building block of the chase.

TGD CHASE RULE. Consider a database D for a relational schema $\mathcal{R}$, and a TGD σ on $\mathcal{R}$ of the form $\Phi(\mathbf{X}, \mathbf{Y}) \rightarrow \exists \mathbf{Z}\, \Psi(\mathbf{X}, \mathbf{Z})$. Then, σ is *applicable* to D if there exists a homomorphism h such that $h(\Phi(\mathbf{X}, \mathbf{Y})) \subseteq D$. Let σ be applicable, and h_1 be a homomorphism that extends h as follows: for each $X_i \in \mathbf{X}$, $h_1(X_i) = h(X_i)$; for each $Z_j \in \mathbf{Z}$, $h_1(Z_j) = z_j$, where z_j is a "fresh" null, i.e., $z_j \in \Delta_N$, z_j does not occur in D, and z_j lexicographically follows all other nulls already introduced. The application of σ adds to D the atom $h_1(\Psi(\mathbf{X}, \mathbf{Z}))$ if not already in D.

The notion of the *(derivation) level* of an atom in a TGD chase is defined as follows. Let D be the *initial* database from which the chase is constructed. Then: (1) The atoms in D have level 0. (2) Let a TGD $\Phi(\mathbf{X}, \mathbf{Y}) \rightarrow \exists \mathbf{Z}\, \Psi(\mathbf{X}, \mathbf{Z})$ be applied at some point in the construction of the chase, and let h and h_1 be as in the TGD chase rule. If the atom with highest level among those in $h_1(\Phi(\mathbf{X}, \mathbf{Y}))$ has level k, then the added atom $h_1(\Psi(\mathbf{X}, \mathbf{Z}))$ has level $k+1$.

Given a set of TGDs Σ and a database D, the chase algorithm for Σ and D consists of an exhaustive application of the TGD chase rule in a breadth-first (level-saturating) fashion, which leads as result to a (possibly infinite) chase for Σ and D. Formally, the *chase* of D relative to Σ, denoted *chase*(Σ, D), is the database built by an iterative application of the TGD chase rule as follows: let $I_1, \ldots, I_k$ be all possible images of bodies of TGDs in Σ relative to some homomorphism, and $\mathbf{a}_i$ be the atom with highest level in I_i; let M be such that $\text{level}(\mathbf{a}_M) = \min_{1 \leqslant i \leqslant k}\{\text{level}(\mathbf{a}_i)\}$: among the possible applications of TGDs, choose the lexicographically first among those that utilize a homomorphism from the body of a TGD to I_M. For brevity, the application of the chase rule with a TGD σ on a database D is called application of σ on D. The *chase of level up to* $k \geqslant 0$ for Σ and D, denoted *chase*$^k(\Sigma, D)$, is the set of all atoms in *chase*(Σ, D) of level at most k.

Example 12.5 Consider the two TGDs

$$\sigma_1 \colon r(X, Y), r(Z, X) \rightarrow \exists W\, s(W, Z, X)$$
$$\sigma_2 \colon r(X, Y), s(Z, X, Y) \rightarrow \exists W\, r(W, X)$$

and the database D consisting of the two atoms $r(a, b)$ and $s(c, a, b)$. Then, in the construction of *chase*$(\{\sigma_1, \sigma_2\}, D)$, we apply first the TGD σ_2 on $r(a, b)$ and $s(c, a, b)$, adding $r(z_1, a)$ (where z_1 is a new null), and we apply then σ_1 on $r(a, b)$ and $r(z_1, a)$, adding $s(z_2, z_1, a)$ (where z_2 is a new null). The two added facts have the derivation depths 1 and 2, respectively.

The (possibly infinite) chase for Σ and D is a *universal model*, i.e., for every $B \in \mathit{mods}(\Sigma, D)$, there exists a homomorphism that maps *chase*(Σ, D) onto B [9, 20].

EGD CHASE RULE. Consider a database D for a relational schema $\mathcal{R}$, and an EGD σ on $\mathcal{R}$ of the form $\Phi(\mathbf{X}) \to X_i = X_j$. Such an EGD σ is *applicable* to D if there exists a homomorphism η: $\Phi(\mathbf{X}) \to D$ such that $\eta(X_i)$ and $\eta(X_j)$ are different and not both constants. If $\eta(X_i)$ and $\eta(X_j)$ are different constants, then there is a *hard violation* of σ, and the chase *fails*. Otherwise, the result of the application of σ to D is the database $h(D)$ obtained from D by replacing every occurrence of a nonconstant element $e \in \{\eta(X_i), \eta(X_j)\}$ in D by the other element e' (if e and e' are both nulls, then e precedes e' in the lexicographic order).

Example 12.6 Consider the following set $\Sigma = \{\sigma_1, \sigma_2, \sigma_3\}$ of TGDs and EGDs:

$$\sigma_1 : \forall X \forall Y \, r(X, Y) \to \exists Z \, s(X, Y, Z)$$
$$\sigma_2 : \forall X \forall Y \forall Z \, s(X, Y, Z) \to Y = Z$$
$$\sigma_3 : \forall X \forall Y \forall Z \, r(X, Y), s(Z, Y, Y) \to X = Y$$

Let D be the instance $\{r(a, b)\}$. In the computation of $chase(\Sigma, D)$, we first apply σ_1 and add the fact $s(a, b, z_1)$, where z_1 is a labeled null. Then, the application of σ_2 on $s(a, b, z_1)$ yields $z_1 = b$, thus turning $s(a, b, z_1)$ into $s(a, b, b)$. Now, we apply σ_3 on $r(a, b)$ and $s(a, b, b)$, and by equating $a = b$, the chase fails; this is a hard violation, since both a and b are constants in Δ.

The *chase* of a database D, in the presence of two sets Σ_T and Σ_E of TGDs and EGDs, respectively, denoted $chase(\Sigma_T \cup \Sigma_E, D)$, is computed by iteratively applying (1) a single TGD once, according to the order specified above, and (2) the EGDs, as long as they are applicable (i.e., until a fixpoint is reached).

Treewidth We finally recall the notions of treewidth, tree decomposition and bounded-treewidth model property (see, e.g., [23]).

A *tree decomposition* of a graph $G = (V, E)$ consists of a tree $T = (N, A)$ and a labeling function $\lambda : N \to 2^V$ such that (i) for every $v \in V$, there exists $n \in N$ with $v \in \lambda(n)$, (ii) for every $(v_1, v_2) \in E$, there exists $n \in N$ such that $\{v_1, v_2\} \subseteq \lambda(n)$ and (iii) for every $v \in V$, the set $\{n \in N \mid v \in \lambda(n)\}$ induces a (connected) subtree in T.

The *Gaifman graph* of a database D (or of any set of atoms) is a nondirected graph defined as follows: (i) the nodes are the symbols in $dom(D)$ (in general, constants in Δ and nulls in Δ_N), and (ii) there exists an arc (c_1, c_2) between c_1 and c_2 if there exist some atom in D that has both c_1 and c_2 as arguments.

The *width* of a tree decomposition (T, λ), with $T = (N, A)$, of a graph $G = (V, E)$ is the integer $\max_{n \in N} |\lambda(n)|$. The *treewidth* of a graph $G = (V, E)$, denoted $tw(G)$, is the minimum width among all tree decompositions. Given a relational instance D (or any set of atoms), its treewidth $tw(D)$ is the treewidth of its Gaifman graph.

A class $\mathcal{C}$ of formulas has the *bounded treewidth model property* if for every $\phi \in \mathcal{C}$, whenever ϕ is satisfiable, then it is possible to compute a number $f(\phi)$ such that ϕ has a model of treewidth at most $f(\phi)$.

12.3 Guarded Datalog$^{\pm}$

Query answering under general TGDs is undecidable [4], even when the schema and the TGDs are fixed [9]. In this section, we discuss *guarded* TGDs, also called *guarded* Datalog$^{\pm}$, as a special class of TGDs relative to which query answering is decidable in the general case and even tractable in the data complexity. Queries relative to such TGDs can be evaluated on a finite part of the chase, which is of constant size when the query and the TGDs are fixed.

A TGD σ is *guarded* if it contains an atom in its body that contains all universally quantified variables of σ. The leftmost such atom is the *guard atom* (or *guard*) of σ. The nonguard atoms in the body of σ are the *side atoms* of σ.

Example 12.7 The TGD $r(X,Y), s(Y,X,Z) \to \exists W s(Z,X,W)$ is guarded (via the guard $s(Y,X,Z)$), while the TGD $r(X,Y), s(Y,Z) \to t(X,Z)$ is not guarded, since no body atom contains all the (universally quantified) variables in the body.

Sets of guarded TGDs (with single-atom heads) are theories in the guarded fragment of first-order logic [2]. Guardedness is a truly fundamental class ensuring decidability. As the following theorem shows, adding a single unguarded Datalog rule to a guarded Datalog$^{\pm}$ program may destroy decidability.

Theorem 12.1 [9] *There is a fixed set of TGDs Σ_u where all but one are guarded, such that for instances D for a schema $\mathcal{R}$ and atomic queries Q, determining whether $D \cup \Sigma_u \models Q$, or, equivalently, whether $Q \in chase(\Sigma_u, D)$, is undecidable.*

Combined Complexity The next theorem establishes combined complexity results for conjunctive query evaluation under guarded Datalog$^{\pm}$.

Theorem 12.2 [9] *Let Σ be a guarded Datalog$^{\pm}$ program (i.e., a set of guarded TGDs) over a schema $\mathcal{R}$, and let D be an instance for $\mathcal{R}$. Let, moreover, w denote the maximum arity of any predicate appearing in $\mathcal{R}$, and let $|\mathcal{R}|$ denote the total number of predicate symbols. Then:*

1. *If Q is an atomic query, then checking whether $D \cup \Sigma \models Q$ is* PTIME*-complete in case both w and $|\mathcal{R}|$ are bounded, and remains* PTIME*-complete even in case Σ is fixed.*[1] *This problem is* EXPTIME*-complete if w is bounded and* 2EXPTIME*-complete in general. It remains* 2EXPTIME*-complete even when $|\mathcal{R}|$ is bounded.*
2. *If Q is a general conjunctive query, checking whether $D \cup \Sigma \models Q$ is* NP*-complete in case both w and $|\mathcal{R}|$ are bounded, and thus also in case of a fixed set Σ. Checking whether $D \cup \Sigma \models Q$ is* EXPTIME*-complete if w is bounded and* 2EXPTIME*-complete in general (and even when $|\mathcal{R}|$ is bounded).*
3. *Query containment under guarded TGDs is* NP*-complete if both w and $|\mathcal{R}|$ are bounded, and even in case the set of guarded TGDs Σ is fixed.*

[1] This is just a mild extension of the data complexity case in Sect. 12.3, where also Q is fixed.

4. *Query containment under guarded TGDs is* EXPTIME*-complete if w is bounded and* 2EXPTIME*-complete in general (and even when $|\mathcal{R}|$ is bounded).*

For unguarded Datalog$^{\pm}$, and, in particular, for plain Datalog, even when we fix both, the width w and the number of predicates $|\mathcal{R}|$ that are allowed to occur in a program, we can still formulate an infinity of mutually non-equivalent programs. In contrast to this, it is not hard to see that in case both w and $|\mathcal{R}|$ are bounded, there are—up to isomorphism—only constantly many guarded Datalog$^{\pm}$ programs. It is thus not very astonishing that conjunctive query answering on the basis of such drastically limited programs is not harder than the standard task of evaluating a query over an extensional database. The EXPTIME and 2EXPTIME upper bounds of Theorem 12.2 can be established via alternating computations in a similar way as those for the more general *weakly guarded* Datalog$^{\pm}$ programs, which will be dealt with in Sect. 12.5. The EXPTIME-hardness results of the above theorem are achieved via simulations of an alternating PSPACE Turing machine, and an alternating EXPSPACE Turing machine, respectively. Simulating an alternating PSPACE Turing machine is not difficult. The (polynomially many) rules that simulate such a machine can contain explicit symbols for each of the polynomially many worktape cell positions. Simulating an EXPSPACE Turing machine via guarded rules is much harder. Here, the problem is that to this aim we can no longer explicitly address each worktape cell i, or each pair of cells i, j, given that there is now an *exponential* number of worktape cells. The idea is thus to encode tape cell indexes as *vectors* of variables $(V_1, \ldots, V_k)$ where the value of each V_i ranges over 0 and 1. We can then define a successor relation $succ(V_1, \ldots, V_k, W_1, \ldots, W_k)$ with a polynomial number of Datalog rules. However, there is a further difficulty. We now have two different types of variables, the V_i, W_j variables representing the bits in the above-described bit vectors, and other variables say, X, Y, Z, for denoting configurations. A major difficulty is to ensure that we do not violate guardedness, when using both types of variables in a rule body. In our proof in the full version of [10], we employ some sophisticated technical tricks in order to achieve this.

The next result, which tightens parts of Theorem 12.2, shows that the above EXPTIME and 2EXPTIME-completeness results hold even for a fixed input database.

Theorem 12.3 [9] *Let Σ be a guarded Datalog$^{\pm}$ program over a schema $\mathcal{R}$. Let w denote the maximum arity of any predicate appearing in $\mathcal{R}$, and let $|\mathcal{R}|$ denote the total number of predicate symbols. Then, for fixed databases D and for both fixed atomic and variable queries Q, checking whether $chase(\Sigma, D) \models Q$ is* EXPTIME*-complete if w is bounded, and* 2EXPTIME*-complete in general. This problem remains* 2EXPTIME*-complete even when $|\mathcal{R}|$ is bounded.*

From the above 2EXPTIME-completeness result, it follows that the satisfiability problem for very simple guarded theories is already at the same complexity level as decidability for the entire guarded fragment GFO of first-order logic, for which Grädel [26] has shown 2EXPTIME-completeness. In fact, atomic queries and their (universally quantified) negation are guarded. If Σ is a guarded Datalog$^{\pm}$ program, i.e., a set of guarded TGDs with single right-hand sides, and Q an (existentially quantified) atomic Boolean conjunctive query, then $D \wedge \Sigma \wedge \neg Q$ is a guarded FO theory of a particularly simple form. It is clear that $chase(\Sigma, D) \models Q$ iff $D \cup \Sigma \models Q$ iff $D \wedge \Sigma \wedge \neg Q$ is satisfiable. It is quite astonishing that the satisfiability of theories in such simple disjunction-free subfragments of GFO is as hard to decide as deciding whether an arbitrary GFO theory is satisfiable. On the other hand, it is less surprising that deciding the satisfiability of guarded Π_2-theories, i.e., guarded universal-existential first-order theories, is 2EXPTIME hard. In fact, Grädel [26] has shown a Π_2 normal form for satisfiability in the guarded fragment. Note, however, that this normal form is not disjunction-free.

Data Complexity We next focus on the data complexity of evaluating BCQs relative to guarded TGDs, which turns out to be polynomial in general and linear for atomic queries. In the sequel, let $\mathcal{R}$ be a relational schema, D be a database for $\mathcal{R}$, and Σ be a set of guarded TGDs on $\mathcal{R}$. We first give some preliminary definitions.

The *chase graph* for Σ and D is the directed graph consisting of $chase(\Sigma, D)$ as the set of nodes and having an arrow from $\mathbf{a}$ to $\mathbf{b}$ iff $\mathbf{b}$ is obtained from $\mathbf{a}$ and possibly other atoms by a one-step application of a TGD $\sigma \in \Sigma$. Here, we mark $\mathbf{a}$ as *guard* iff $\mathbf{a}$ is the image of the guard of σ w.r.t. the homomorphism h associated with the application of σ, as in the definition of the TGD chase rule. The *guarded chase forest* for Σ and D is the restriction of the chase graph for Σ and D to all atoms marked as guards and their children. The *subtree* of an atom $\mathbf{a}$ in this forest, denoted *subtree*($\mathbf{a}$), is the restriction of the forest to all successors of $\mathbf{a}$. The *type* of an atom $\mathbf{a}$, denoted *type*($\mathbf{a}$), is the set of all atoms $\mathbf{b}$ in $chase(\Sigma, D)$ that have only constants from $\mathbf{a}$ and nulls from $\mathbf{a}$ as arguments. Informally, the type of $\mathbf{a}$ is the set of all atoms that determine the subtree of $\mathbf{a}$ in the guarded chase forest.

Example 12.8 Consider the two TGDs

$$\sigma_1 : r_1(X, Y), r_2(Y) \rightarrow \exists Z\, r_1(Z, X)$$

$$\sigma_2 : r_1(X, Y) \rightarrow r_2(X)$$

applied on a database $D = \{r_1(a, b), r_2(b)\}$. The first part of the (infinite) chase graph for $\{\sigma_1, \sigma_2\}$ and D is shown in Fig. 12.1, where every arrow is labeled with the corresponding TGD. The figure also shows the corresponding guarded chase forest, depicting its arrows with continuous lines and the others with dashed lines. The numbers in small circles indicate the derivation levels of every atom.

Given a finite set $S \subseteq \Delta \cup \Delta_N$, two sets of atoms A_1 and A_2 are *S-isomorphic* (or *isomorphic* if $S = \emptyset$) iff there exists a bijection $\beta : A_1 \cup dom(A_1) \rightarrow A_2 \cup dom(A_2)$ such that (i) β and β^{-1} are homomorphisms, and (ii) $\beta(c) = c = \beta^{-1}(c)$ for all $c \in S$. Two atoms $\mathbf{a}_1$ and $\mathbf{a}_2$ are *S-isomorphic* (or *isomorphic* if $S = \emptyset$) iff $\{\mathbf{a}_1\}$ and $\{\mathbf{a}_2\}$ are S-isomorphic. The notion of S-isomorphism (or isomorphism if $S = \emptyset$) is naturally extended to more complex structures, such as pairs of two subtrees (V_1, E_1) and (V_2, E_2) of the guarded chase forest, and two pairs $(\mathbf{b}_1, S_1)$ and $(\mathbf{b}_2, S_2)$, where $\mathbf{b}_1$ and $\mathbf{b}_2$ are atoms, and S_1 and S_2 are sets of atoms.

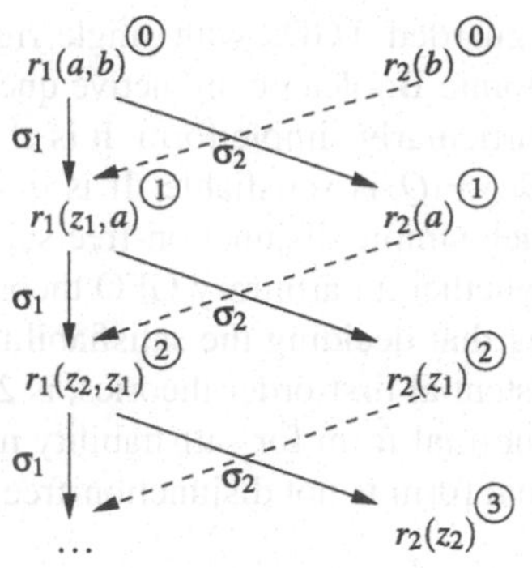

Fig. 12.1 Chase graph and guarded chase forest for Example 12.8

Example 12.9 Let $\mathbf{a} = r(a, b, z_1)$, where $a, b \in \Delta$ and $z_1 \in \Delta_N$. Then, $s(b, z_3)$ and $s(b, z_4)$ are $dom(\mathbf{a})$-isomorphic, while $s(b, z_3)$ and $s(b, z_1)$ are not (with $z_3, z_4 \in \Delta_N$).

The following key lemma shows that for each set of guarded TGDs Σ, there exists a constant k such that for every database D and every atom $\mathbf{a}$ generated at some depth level d while chasing D with Σ, such that whenever the same chase generates an atom $\mathbf{b}$ whose arguments are among those of $\mathbf{a}$, then $\mathbf{b}$ must be generated at depth at most $d + k$. Here, the *(guarded) depth* of an atom $\mathbf{a}$ in the guarded chase forest for Σ and D, denoted $depth(\mathbf{a})$, is the length of the path from some atom in D to $\mathbf{a}$ in the forest. The main idea behind the proof is that the subtree of an atom $\mathbf{a}$ depends only on $\mathbf{a}$ and the type of $\mathbf{a}$, and the number of non-$dom(\mathbf{a})$-isomorphic pairs consisting of an atom and its type is bounded by a constant, depending only on $\mathcal{R}$.

Lemma 12.1 [10] *Let $\mathcal{R}$ be a relational schema, D be a database for $\mathcal{R}$, and Σ be a set of guarded TGDs on $\mathcal{R}$. Let $\mathbf{a}$ be a guard in the chase graph for Σ and D, and $\mathbf{b} \in type(\mathbf{a})$. Then, $depth(\mathbf{b}) \leqslant depth(\mathbf{a}) + k$, where k depends only on $\mathcal{R}$.*

Note that the guarded depth of an atom in the guarded chase forest is generally different from the derivation level in the chase, as the following example shows.

Example 12.10 Consider the following set of guarded TGDs:

$$\sigma_1: r_3(X, Y) \to r_2(X)$$
$$\sigma_2: r_1(X, Y) \to \exists Z\, r_3(Y, Z)$$
$$\sigma_3: r_1(X, Y), r_2(Y) \to r_1(Y, X)$$

Let D be the database $\{r_1(a, b)\}$. Then, the chase graph of $chase(\Sigma, D)$ is depicted in Fig. 12.2, with the usual notation. Observe that the derivation level of $r_1(b, a)$ is 3, while the guarded depth of $r_1(b, a)$ is 1.

The next lemma shows that query evaluation can be done on only a finite, initial portion of the forest, whose size is determined by the query Q and $\mathcal{R}$ only. Here,

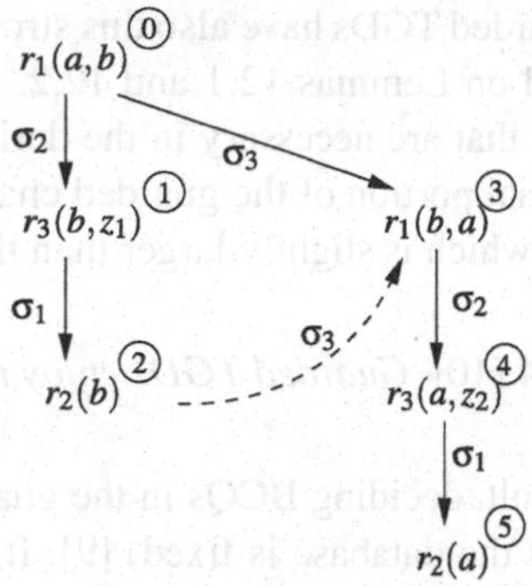

Fig. 12.2 Chase graph and guarded chase forest for Example 12.10

the *guarded chase* of level up to $k \geqslant 0$ for Σ and D, denoted $g\text{-}chase^k(\Sigma, D)$, is the set of all atoms in the forest of depth at most k. The result is proved similarly to Lemma 12.1, showing that every path from D to (the image of) a query atom in the guarded chase forest, whose length exceeds a certain value (depending on Q and $\mathcal{R}$), has two atoms with $dom(\mathbf{a})$-isomorphic subtrees (since two atoms and their types are $dom(\mathbf{a})$-isomorphic), and thus Q can also be evaluated "closer" to D.

Lemma 12.2 [10] *Let $\mathcal{R}$ be a relational schema, D be a database for $\mathcal{R}$, Σ be a set of guarded TGDs on $\mathcal{R}$, and Q be a BCQ over $\mathcal{R}$. If there is a homomorphism μ that maps Q into chase(Σ, D), then there is a homomorphism λ that maps Q into $g\text{-}chase^k(\Sigma, D)$, where k depends only on Q and $\mathcal{R}$.*

Example 12.11 Intuitively, the chase under guarded TGDs has a "periodicity" of atoms and their types. In Example 12.8, every level of the guarded chase forest is given by two atoms $r_1(z_k, z_{k-1})$ and $r_2(z_{k-1})$, where the type of the former is given by the atoms $r_1(z_k, z_{k-1})$, $r_2(z_{k-1})$, and $r_2(z_k)$. This "pattern" repeats indefinitely in the chase, as it is easily seen. For example, a query $Q = \{r_1(X,Y), r_1(Z,X), r_1(W,Z)\}$ will necessarily map onto three atoms that form a path in the guarded chase forest: however deep these atoms are in the chase, Q can anyway also be mapped onto the first levels, e.g., onto $\{r_1(z_2, z_1), r_1(z_3, z_2), r_1(z_4, z_3)\}$.

The above lemma says that (homomorphic images of) the query atoms are contained in a finite, initial portion of the guarded chase forest, whose size is determined only by the query and $\mathcal{R}$. But it does not yet ensure that also the whole derivation of the query atoms are contained in such a portion of the guarded chase forest. This slightly stronger property is captured by the following definition.

Definition 12.1 (Bounded guard-depth property) We say that Σ has the *bounded guard-depth property* (*BGDP*) iff, for each database D for $\mathcal{R}$ and for each BCQ Q, whenever there is a homomorphism μ that maps Q into *chase*(Σ, D), then there is a homomorphism λ of this kind such that all ancestors of $\lambda(Q)$ in the chase graph for Σ and D are contained in $g\text{-}chase^{\gamma_g}(\Sigma, D)$, where γ_g depends only on Q and $\mathcal{R}$.

In fact, guarded TGDs have also this stronger bounded guard-depth property. The proof is based on Lemmas 12.1 and 12.2, where the former now also assures that all side atoms that are necessary in the derivation of the query atoms are contained in a finite, initial portion of the guarded chase forest, whose size is determined only by Q and $\mathcal{R}$ (which is slightly larger than the one for the query atoms only).

Theorem 12.4 [10] *Guarded TGDs enjoy the BGDP.*

By this result, deciding BCQs in the guarded case is in P in the data complexity (where all but the database is fixed) [9]. It is also hard for P, as can be proved by reduction from propositional logic programming [10].

Theorem 12.5 [9, 10] *Let $\mathcal{R}$ be a relational schema, D be a database for $\mathcal{R}$, Σ be a set of guarded TGDs on $\mathcal{R}$, and Q be a BCQ over $\mathcal{R}$. Then, deciding $D \cup \Sigma \models Q$ is* P*-complete in the data complexity.*

Deciding atomic BCQs in the guarded case is even possible in linear time in the data complexity, as can be proved by reduction to propositional logic programming.

Theorem 12.6 [10] *Let $\mathcal{R}$ be a relational schema, D be a database for $\mathcal{R}$, Σ be a finite set of guarded TGDs on $\mathcal{R}$, and Q be a Boolean atomic query over $\mathcal{R}$. Then, deciding $D \cup \Sigma \models Q$ can be done in linear time in the data complexity.*

12.4 Linear Datalog$^{\pm}$

Linear Datalog$^{\pm}$ is a variant of guarded Datalog$^{\pm}$, where query answering is even FO-rewritable in the data complexity. Nonetheless, linear Datalog$^{\pm}$ is still expressive enough for representing ontologies, as we will show in Sect. 12.7. A TGD is *linear* iff it contains only a singleton body atom. Note that linear Datalog$^{\pm}$ generalizes the well-known class of *inclusion dependencies*. Note also that linear TGDs are more expressive than inclusion dependencies. For example, the linear TGD $\mathit{supervises}(X, X) \rightarrow \mathit{manager}(X)$, which asserts that all people supervising themselves are managers, is not expressible with inclusion dependencies.

Combined Complexity Query answering with linear Datalog$^{\pm}$ is PSPACE-com plete when the program is not fixed, which holds by results in [14, 25, 28, 37].

Theorem 12.7 [14, 25, 28, 37] *Let $\mathcal{R}$ be a relational schema, Σ be a set of linear TGDs over $\mathcal{R}$, D be a database for $\mathcal{R}$, and Q be a BCQ over $\mathcal{R}$. Then, deciding $D \cup \Sigma \models Q$ is* PSPACE*-complete. It remains* PSPACE*-complete when Q is fixed.*

Data Complexity A class $\mathcal{C}$ of TGDs is *first-order rewritable* (or *FO-rewritable*) iff for every set of TGDs Σ in $\mathcal{C}$ and for every BCQ Q, there exists a first-order query Q_Σ such that, for every database instance D, it holds that $D \cup \Sigma \models Q$ iff $D \models Q_\Sigma$. Since answering first-order queries is in AC_0 in the data complexity [38], also BCQ answering under FO-rewritable TGDs is in AC_0 in the data complexity.

We next define the bounded derivation-depth property, which is strictly stronger than the bounded guard-depth property. Informally, this property says that (homomorphic images of) the query atoms along with their derivations are contained in a finite, initial portion of the chase graph (rather than the guarded chase forest), whose size is determined only by the query and $\mathcal{R}$.

Definition 12.2 (Bounded derivation-depth property) A set of TGDs Σ has the *bounded derivation-depth property* (*BDDP*) iff, for every database D for $\mathcal{R}$ and for every BCQ Q over $\mathcal{R}$, whenever $D \cup \Sigma \models Q$, then $\mathit{chase}^{\gamma_d}(\Sigma, D) \models Q$, where γ_d depends only on Q and $\mathcal{R}$.

Clearly, in the case of linear TGDs, for every $\mathbf{a} \in \mathit{chase}(\Sigma, D)$, the subtree of $\mathbf{a}$ is now determined only by $\mathbf{a}$ itself, while in the case of guarded TGDs it depends on $\mathit{type}(\mathbf{a})$. Therefore, for a single atom, its depth coincides with the number of applications of the TGD chase rule that are necessary to generate it. That is, the guarded chase forest coincides with the chase graph. Thus, by Theorem 12.4, we immediately obtain that linear TGDs have the bounded derivation-depth property.

Corollary 12.1 [10] *Linear TGDs enjoy the BDDP.*

The next result shows that BCQs Q relative to TGDs Σ with the bounded derivation-depth property are FO-rewritable. The main ideas behind its proof are informally summarized as follows. Since the derivation depth and the number of body atoms in TGDs in Σ is bounded, the number of all database ancestors of query atoms is also bounded. Thus, the number of all non-isomorphic sets of potential database ancestors with variables as arguments is also bounded. Take the existentially quantified conjunction of every such ancestor set where the query Q is answered positively. Then, the FO-rewriting of Q is the disjunction of all these formulas.

Theorem 12.8 [10] *Let $\mathcal{R}$ be a relational schema, Σ be a set of TGDs over $\mathcal{R}$, D be a database for $\mathcal{R}$, and Q be a BCQ over $\mathcal{R}$. If Σ enjoys the BDDP, then Q is FO-rewritable.*

As an immediate consequence of Corollary 12.1 and Theorem 12.8, BCQs are FO-rewritable in the linear case.

Corollary 12.2 [10] *Let $\mathcal{R}$ be a relational schema, Σ be a set of linear TGDs over $\mathcal{R}$, D be a database for $\mathcal{R}$, and Q be a BCQ over $\mathcal{R}$. Then, Q is FO-rewritable.*

12.5 Weakly Guarded Datalog$^{\pm}$

In this section, we introduce *weakly-guarded Datalog*$^{\pm}$, or *weakly guarded TGDs* (*WGTGDs*), which is a generalization of guarded Datalog$^{\pm}$.

We first define the notion of *affected* position of a relational schema, given a set of TGDs Σ. (a) If an existentially quantified variable appears in π in some TGD in Σ, then π is affected relative to Σ. (b) If, for some $\sigma \in \Sigma$, the same universally quantified variable appears both in π in $head(\sigma)$, and *only* in affected positions in $body(\sigma)$, then π is affected relative to Σ. It is not difficult to see that affected positions are the only ones where a null can appear, during the chase construction.

Example 12.12 Consider the following set of TGDs:

$$\sigma_1 : p_1(X,Y), p_2(X,Y) \rightarrow \exists Z\, p_2(Y,Z)$$

$$\sigma_2 : p_2(X,Y), p_2(W,X) \rightarrow p_1(Y,X)$$

Notice that $p_2[2]$ is affected since Z in σ_1 is existentially quantified in σ_1. Considering again σ_1, the variable Y appears in $p_2[2]$ but also in $p_1[2]$, therefore it does not make $p_2[1]$ affected. In σ_2, X appears in the affected position $p_2[2]$ but also in $p_2[1]$, which is not affected; therefore, it does not make $p_1[2]$ affected. On the contrary, in σ_2, Y appears in $p_2[2]$ and nowhere else, thus causing $p_1[1]$ to be affected.

A TGD is *weakly-guarded* relative to a set Σ of TGDs if there is an atom in its body that contains all the universally quantified variables that appear *only* in positions that are affected relative to Σ.

Example 12.13 Consider the two TGDs in Example 12.12. In σ_1, both atoms are guards (and obviously weak guards), since they contain all universally quantified variables in the TGD. In σ_2, the only variable that appears only in affected positions is Y; therefore, the first atom is a weak guard.

We now give some preliminary definitions, which serve for the subsequent complexity analysis. Let D be a possibly infinite relational instance for a schema $\mathcal{R}$, and let S be a set of symbols. An S-join forest of D is an undirected labeled forest $T = (V, E, \lambda)$, with labeling function $\lambda : V \rightarrow D$ such that: (i) $D \subseteq \lambda(V)$, and (ii) T is S-connected, i.e., for each $c \in dom(D) - S$, the set $\{v \in V \mid c \text{ occurs in } \lambda(v)\}$ induces a connected subtree in T. We say that D is S-acyclic iff D has an S-join forest. This generalizes the classical notion of hypergraph acyclicity [3] of an instance (or, equivalently, of a query). In fact, an instance or a query (seen as an instance) is hypergraph-acyclic iff it is $\emptyset$-acyclic. From the definitions of S-acyclicity, we straightforwardly get that, if an instance D for a schema $\mathcal{R}$ is S-acyclic, then $tw(D) \leqslant |S| + w$, where w is the maximum arity of any predicate symbol in $\mathcal{R}$.

Note that $chase(\Sigma, D)$ can be partitioned into two sets: $chase^{\perp}(\Sigma, D)$, the set of the atoms in $chase(\Sigma, D)$ that have *only* values in $dom(D)$ as arguments, and $chase^{+}(\Sigma, D)$, the rest of the atoms. Note also that $chase^{+}(\Sigma, D)$ is $dom(D)$-acyclic.

The proof of the following lemma is easily derived from the above results.

Lemma 12.3 [9] *If Σ is a set of WGTGDs and D an instance of a schema $\mathcal{R}$, then $tw(chase(\Sigma, D)) \leqslant |D| + w$, where w is the maximum arity of a predicate in $\mathcal{R}$.*

We now come to the decidability of query answering under WGTGDs. From [19] (see also [23, 26]) we have that if a set of first-order formulas has the bounded-treewidth model property, then checking satisfiability for such formulas is decidable. Observing that both $chase(\Sigma, D) \wedge Q$ and $chase(\Sigma, D) \wedge \neg Q$ have a (possibly infinite) model of bounded treewidth, when they are satisfiable, we get the following result.

Theorem 12.9 [9] *Query answering under WGTGDs is decidable.*

This theorem establishes decidability of query answering under WGTGDs, but nothing about the complexity. This will be the subject of the following sections.

Combined Complexity We now tackle the complexity of query answering under WGTGDs. We start from determining the lower bound.

Theorem 12.10 [9] *Query answering under WGTGDs is* 2EXPTIME*-hard. The same problem is* EXPTIME*-hard in case the arity of predicates in the schema is fixed. The same complexity bound holds in the case of atomic queries and even fixed queries.*

Note that this result was already shown for the more restricted class of guarded TGDs (see Theorems 12.2 and 12.3).

Now, we come to the upper bound for query answering under WGTGDs. We start by defining notion of *squid decomposition*, and prove a lemma called "Squid Lemma" which will be a useful tool for proving the upper complexity bound of the query answering problem.

We first define the notion of $\mathcal{R}$-cover. Given a BCQ Q on a schema $\mathcal{R}$ having n body atoms, an *$\mathcal{R}$-cover* of Q is a Boolean conjunctive query Q^+ on $\mathcal{R}$ that contains in its body all atoms of Q and that may, in addition, contain at most n further $\mathcal{R}$-atoms whose variables can be either from $vars(Q)$ or new.

For example, consider the schema $\mathcal{R} = \{r/2, s/3, t/3\}$, and let Q be the Boolean conjunctive query $r(X,Y), r(Y,Z), t(Z,X,X)$. The following query Q^+ is an $\mathcal{R}$-cover of Q: $Q^+ = \{r(X,Y), r(Y,Z), t(Z,X,X), t(Y,Z,Z), s(Z,U,U)\}$.

It is possible to show, given an instance (finite or infinite) D for a schema $\mathcal{R}$ and a BCQ Q, that $D \models Q$ iff there exists an $\mathcal{R}$-cover Q^+ of Q such that $D \models Q^+$. We refer the reader to [9] for the proof of this result.

The following definition amends and replaces the one in [9], which was correct for relational schemas with binary predicates only; the present definition and the subsequent results are general and can deal with predicates of arbitrary arity.

Definition 12.3 (Squid decomposition) Let Q be a BCQ over a schema $\mathcal{R}$. A *squid decomposition* $\delta = (Q^+, h, H, T)$ of Q consists of an $\mathcal{R}$-cover Q^+ of Q, a mapping $h : vars(Q^+) \to vars(Q^+)$, and a decomposition of $h(Q^+)$ into two sets H and T, with $T = h(Q^+) - H$, such that (i) there exists $V_\delta \subseteq vars(Q^+)$ with $H = \{\mathbf{a} \in h(Q^+) \mid vars(\mathbf{a}) \subseteq V_\delta\}$, and (ii) T is V_δ-acyclic. We refer to H as the *head* of δ, and to T as the *tentacles* of δ. The set of all squid decompositions of Q is referred to as $squidd(Q)$.

One may imagine the set H in a squid decomposition as the head of a squid, and the set T as a forest of tentacles attached to that head. Note that a squid decomposition $\delta = (Q^+, h, H, T)$ of Q does not necessarily define a query folding [17, 35] of Q^+, because h does not need to be an endomorphism of Q^+: in other terms, we do not require that $h(Q^+) \subseteq Q^+$. Of course, h is a homomorphism.

Example 12.14 Consider the following BCQ (the schema is omitted for brevity):

$$\begin{aligned} Q = \{ & r(X,Y), r(X,Z), r(Y,Z), \\ & r(Z,V_1), r(V_1,V_2), r(V_2,V_3), r(V_3,V_4), r(V_4,V_5), \\ & r(V_1,V_6), r(V_6,V_5), r(V_5,V_7), r(Z,U_1), s(U_1,U_2,U_3), \\ & r(U_3,U_4), r(U_3,U_5), r(U_4,U_5)\} \end{aligned}$$

Let Q^+ be the Boolean query where we add the atom $s(U_3, U_4, U_5)$ to the body. A possible squid decomposition (Q^+, h, H, T) can be based on the homomorphism h, where $h(V_6) = V_2$, $h(V_4) = h(V_5) = h(V_7) = V_3$, and where $h(\xi) = \xi$ for each other variable ξ. The result of the decomposition with $V_\delta = \{X, Y, Z\}$ is the query shown in Fig. 12.3, where its join graph is depicted, in order to better distinguish the (cyclic) head from the (acyclic) tentacles. Note that if we eliminated the additional atom $s(U_3, U_4, U_5)$, the original atoms $r(U_3, U_4), r(U_3, U_5), r(U_4, U_5)$ would form an uncovered cycle, and could therefore not simultaneously be part of the tentacles, as T would then no longer be V_δ-acyclic.

The following lemma (Squid Lemma) serves as a main tool in the complexity analysis of the problem of query answering under WGTGDs.

Lemma 12.4 *Let Σ be a set of WGTGDs on a schema $\mathcal{R}$, let D be a ground database instance for $\mathcal{R}$, and let Q be a conjunctive query. Then, $chase(\Sigma, D) \models Q$ iff there is a squid decomposition $\delta = (Q^+, h, H, T) \in squidd(Q)$, and a homomorphism $\theta : dom(h(Q^+)) \to dom(chase(\Sigma, D))$ such that:* (i) $\theta(H) \subseteq chase^\perp(\Sigma, D)$, *and* (ii) $\theta(T) \subseteq chase^+(\Sigma, D)$.

We now come to our main result.

Theorem 12.11 [9] *Query answering under WGTGDs is decidable in* 2EXPTIME. *The same problem is decidable in* EXPTIME *in case the arity of the predicates in the schema is bounded.*

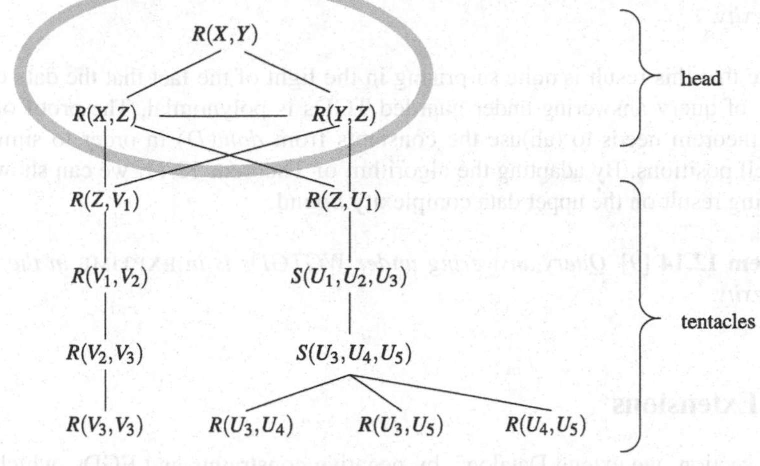

Fig. 12.3 Squid decomposition for Example 12.14

The above result is proved by exhibiting an alternating algorithm that decides the query answering problem. We preliminarily define the notion of *cloud* of an atom in the chase: $cloud(\Sigma, D, \mathbf{a})$ is the set of atoms in $chase(\Sigma, D)$ that have as arguments symbols from $dom(\mathbf{a}) \cup dom(D)$. Notice that the notion of cloud is similar to the one of type, with the difference that $cloud(\Sigma, D, \mathbf{a})$ can have as arguments symbols in $dom(D)$ that do not occur in $\mathbf{a}$. First of all, given a BCQ Q, the algorithm can guess a path in the guarded chase forest from some atom in D to an atom $\mathbf{b}$ which is a homomorphic image of some atom in Q. For each atom $\mathbf{a}$ in such a path, a subset S of $cloud(\Sigma, D, \mathbf{a})$ and a configuration are generated, where the configuration is basically an ordering on the atoms of S; by guessing that the atoms in S until the i-th are derived, and the others are yet to be derived in the chase, the algorithm checks whether the set S is actually in the chase. Now, given a query Q, the alternating algorithm guesses a squid decomposition of it such that the head maps onto $chase^{\perp}(\Sigma, D)$ via a homomorphism θ_0. Then, the algorithm tries to find an extension θ of θ_0 that maps the tentacles of the squid decomposition to $chase^{+}(\Sigma, D)$. By using a technique similar to the one described above, that checks whether the image of some atom is in the chase, the algorithm is then able, based on Lemma 12.4, to check whether θ exists.

By combining Theorems 12.10 and 12.11 we get the following complexity characterization for reasoning under WGTGDs.

Theorem 12.12 [9] *Query answering under WGTGDs is* 2-EXPTIME *complete. It is* EXPTIME *complete in case of bounded predicate arities, and even in case the WGTGDs are fixed.*

Data Complexity With a reduction from a PSPACE alternating Turing Machine, we can show the following result on the lower data complexity bound.

Theorem 12.13 [9] *Query answering under WGTGDs is* EXPTIME-*hard in the data complexity.*

Note that this result is quite surprising in the light of the fact that the data complexity of query answering under guarded TGDs is polynomial. The proof of the above theorem needs to (ab)use the constants from *dom*(*D*) in order to simulate tape cell positions. By adapting the algorithm of Theorem 12.11, we can show the following result on the upper data complexity bound.

Theorem 12.14 [9] *Query answering under WGTGDs is in* EXPTIME *in the data complexity.*

12.6 Extensions

In this section, we extend Datalog$^{\pm}$ by negative constraints and EGDs, which are both important when representing ontologies.

Example 12.15 If the unary predicates c and c' represent two classes, we may use the constraint $c(X), c'(X) \rightarrow \bot$ to assert that the two classes have no common instances. Similarly, if additionally the binary predicate r represents a relationship, we may use $c(X), r(X, Y) \rightarrow \bot$ to enforce that no member of the class c participates to r. Similarly, we may use the EGD $r(X, Y), r(X, Y') \rightarrow Y = Y'$ to express that the second argument of the binary predicate r functionally depends on the first argument of r.

However, while adding negative constraints is effortless from a computational perspective, adding EGDs is more problematic: The interaction of TGDs and EGDs leads to undecidability of query answering even in simple cases, such that of functional and inclusion dependencies [18], or keys and inclusion dependencies (see, e.g., [12], where the proof of undecidability is done in the style of Vardi as in [28]). It can even be seen that a *fixed* set of EGDs and guarded TGDs can simulate a universal Turing machine, and thus query answering and even propositional ground atom inference is undecidable with such fixed sets of dependencies.

For this reason, after dealing with negative constraints, we consider a restricted class of EGDs, namely, *non-conflicting key dependencies* (or *NC keys*), which show a controlled interaction with TGDs (and negative constraints), such that they do not increase the complexity of answering BCQs. Nonetheless, this class is sufficient for modeling ontologies.

12.6.1 Negative Constraints

A *negative constraint* (or *constraint*) is a first-order formula $\forall \mathbf{X} \Phi(\mathbf{X}) \rightarrow \bot$, where $\Phi(\mathbf{X})$ is a (not necessarily guarded or weakly guarded) conjunction of atoms. It is often also written as $\forall \mathbf{X} \Phi'(\mathbf{X}) \rightarrow \neg p(\mathbf{X})$, where $\Phi'(\mathbf{X})$ is obtained from $\Phi(\mathbf{X})$ by removing the atom $p(\mathbf{X})$. We usually omit the universal quantifiers.

Query answering on a database D under TGDs Σ_T and constraints Σ_C can be done effortless by additionally checking that every constraint $\sigma = \Phi(\mathbf{X}) \rightarrow \bot \in \Sigma_C$ is satisfied in D given Σ_T, each of which can be done by checking that the BCQ $Q_\sigma = \Phi(\mathbf{X})$ evaluates to false in D given Σ_T. We write $D \cup \Sigma_T \models \Sigma_C$ iff every $\sigma \in \Sigma_C$ is false in D given Σ_T. We thus obtain immediately the following result. Here, a BCQ Q is *true* in D given Σ_T and Σ_C, denoted $D \cup \Sigma_T \cup \Sigma_C \models Q$, iff (i) $D \cup \Sigma_T \models Q$ or (ii) $D \cup \Sigma_T \not\models \Sigma_C$ (as usual in DLs).

Theorem 12.15 [10] *Let $\mathcal{R}$ be a relational schema, Σ_T and Σ_C be sets of TGDs and constraints on $\mathcal{R}$, respectively, D be a database for $\mathcal{R}$, and Q be a BCQ on $\mathcal{R}$. Then, $D \cup \Sigma_T \cup \Sigma_C \models Q$ iff* (i) *$D \cup \Sigma_T \models Q$ or* (ii) *$D \cup \Sigma_T \models Q_\sigma$ for some $\sigma \in \Sigma_C$.*

The next theorem shows that constraints do not increase the data and combined complexity of answering BCQs in the guarded, linear, and weakly guarded case. It follows from Theorem 12.15. For the data complexity in the guarded and linear case, the result is known from [10].

Theorem 12.16 [10] *Let $\mathcal{R}$ be a relational schema, Σ_T and Σ_C be sets of TGDs and constraints on $\mathcal{R}$, respectively, D be a database for $\mathcal{R}$, and Q be a BCQ. Then, deciding $D \cup \Sigma_T \cup \Sigma_C \models Q$ in the guarded (resp., linear, weakly guarded) case has the same data complexity and also the same combined complexity as deciding $D \cup \Sigma_T \models Q$ in the guarded (resp., linear, weakly guarded) case.*

12.6.2 Non-conflicting Keys

We now first concentrate on the semantic notion of separability for EGDs, which formulates a controlled interaction between EGDs and TGDs (and negative constraints), such that the EGDs do not increase the complexity of answering BCQs. We then provide a sufficient syntactic condition for the separability of EGDs, where we transfer a result by [12] about *non-key-conflicting* inclusion dependencies to the more general setting of Datalog$^{\pm}$. In the context of description logics, general EGDs cannot be formulated, but only keys. Therefore, we mainly focus on keys here.

Definition 12.4 (Separability) Let $\mathcal{R}$ be a relational schema, and Σ_T and Σ_E be sets of TGDs and EGDs on $\mathcal{R}$, respectively. Then, Σ_E is *separable* from Σ_T iff for every database D for $\mathcal{R}$, the following two conditions are both satisfied:

1. If there is a hard violation of an EGD in *chase*$(\Sigma_T \cup \Sigma_E, D)$, then there is also a hard violation of some EGD of Σ_E, when this EGD is directly applied to D.
2. If there is no chase failure, then for every BCQ Q, *chase*$(\Sigma_T \cup \Sigma_E, D) \models Q$ iff *chase*$(\Sigma_T, D) \models Q$.

The following result shows that adding separable EGDs to TGDs and constraints does not increase the data and combined complexity of answering BCQs in the guarded, linear, and weakly guarded case. It follows immediately from the fact that the separability implies that chase failure can be directly evaluated on D. For the data complexity in the guarded and linear case, the result is known from [10].

Theorem 12.17 [10] *Let $\mathcal{R}$ be a relational schema, Σ_T and Σ_C be sets of TGDs and constraints on $\mathcal{R}$, respectively, and D be a database for $\mathcal{R}$. Let Σ_E be a set of EGDs that is separable from Σ_T, and Q be a BCQ. Then, deciding $D \cup \Sigma_T \cup \Sigma_C \cup \Sigma_E \models Q$ in the guarded (resp., linear, weakly guarded) case has the same data complexity and also the same combined complexity as deciding $D \cup \Sigma_T \models Q$ in the guarded (resp., linear, weakly guarded) case.*

We next provide a sufficient syntactic condition for the separability of EGDs. We assume that the reader is familiar with the notions of *functional dependency* (*FD*) and *key* [1]. Clearly, FDs are special types of EGDs. A key κ of a relation r can be written as a set of FDs that specify that κ determines each other attribute of r. Thus, keys can be identified with sets of EGDs. It will be clear from the context when we regard a key as a set of attribute positions, and when as a set of EGDs. The following definition generalizes the notion of "non-key-conflicting" dependency relative to a set of keys, introduced in [12], to the context of arbitrary TGDs.

Definition 12.5 (Non-conflicting property) Let κ be a key, and σ be a TGD of the form $\Phi(\mathbf{X}, \mathbf{Y}) \rightarrow \exists \mathbf{Z}\, r(\mathbf{X}, \mathbf{Z})$. Then, κ is *non-conflicting* (*NC*) with σ iff either (i) the relational predicate on which κ is defined is different from r, or (ii) the positions of κ in r are not a proper subset of the $\mathbf{X}$-positions in r in the head of σ, and every variable in $\mathbf{Z}$ appears only once in the head of σ. We say κ is *non-conflicting* (*NC*) with a set of TGDs Σ_T iff κ is NC with every $\sigma \in \Sigma_T$. We say a set of keys Σ_K is *non-conflicting* (*NC*) with Σ_T iff every $\kappa \in \Sigma_K$ is NC with Σ_T.

Example 12.16 Consider the four keys κ_1, κ_2, κ_3, and κ_4 defined by the key attribute sets $\mathbf{K}_1 = \{r[1], r[2]\}$, $\mathbf{K}_2 = \{r[1], r[3]\}$, $\mathbf{K}_3 = \{r[3]\}$, and $\mathbf{K}_4 = \{r[1]\}$, respectively, and the TGD $\sigma = p(X, Y) \rightarrow \exists Z\, r(X, Y, Z)$. Then, the head predicate of σ is r, and the set of positions in r with universally quantified variables is $\mathbf{H} = \{r[1], r[2]\}$. Observe that all keys but κ_4 are NC with σ, since only $\mathbf{K}_4 \subset \mathbf{H}$. Roughly, every atom added in a chase by applying σ would have a fresh null in some position in $\mathbf{K}_1$, $\mathbf{K}_2$, and $\mathbf{K}_3$, thus never firing κ_1, κ_2, and κ_3, respectively.

The following theorem shows that the property of being NC between keys and TGDs implies their separability. This generalizes a useful result of [12] on inclusion dependencies to the much larger class of all TGDs.

Theorem 12.18 [10] *Let $\mathcal{R}$ be a relational schema, Σ_T and Σ_K be sets of TGDs and keys, respectively, such that Σ_K is NC with Σ_T. Then, Σ_K is separable from Σ_T.*

We conclude this section by stating that in the NC case, keys do not increase the data and the combined complexity of answering BCQs under guarded (resp., linear, weakly guarded) TGDs and constraints. This result follows immediately from Theorems 12.18 and 12.17. For the data complexity in the guarded and linear case, this result is known from [10].

Corollary 12.3 [10] *Let $\mathcal{R}$ be a relational schema, Σ_T and Σ_C be sets of TGDs and constraints on $\mathcal{R}$, respectively, and D be a database for $\mathcal{R}$. Let Σ_E be a set of EGDs that is NC with Σ_T, and Q be a BCQ. Then, deciding $D \cup \Sigma_T \cup \Sigma_C \cup \Sigma_E \models Q$ in the guarded (resp., linear, weakly guarded) case has the same data complexity and also the same combined complexity as deciding $D \cup \Sigma_T \models Q$ in the guarded (resp., linear, weakly guarded) case.*

12.7 Ontology Querying

In this section, we show how Datalog$^\pm$ can be used for query answering in *DL-Lite*$_\mathcal{A}$ and F-Logic Lite ontologies.

12.7.1 DL-Lite$_\mathcal{A}$

We now describe how the DL *DL-Lite*$_\mathcal{A}$ [34] can be translated to linear Datalog$^\pm$ with (negative) constraints and NC keys, called *Datalog*$_0^\pm$, and that the former is strictly less expressive than the latter. We first recall *DL-Lite*$_\mathcal{A}$. We then define the translation and provide the expressivity result.

Note that other DLs of the *DL-Lite* family [13] can be similarly translated to Datalog$_0^\pm$. In particular, the translation for *DL-Lite*$_\mathcal{F}$ and *DL-Lite*$_\mathcal{R}$ is given in [10]. Note also that *DL-Lite*$_\mathcal{R}$ is able to fully capture (the DL fragment of) RDF Schema [7], the vocabulary description language for RDF; see [8]. Consequently, Datalog$_0^\pm$ is also able to fully capture (the DL fragment of) RDF Schema.

Intuitively, DLs model a domain of interest in terms of concepts and roles, which represent classes of individuals and binary relations on such classes, respectively. A DL knowledge base (or ontology) encodes in particular subset relationships between concepts, subset relationships between roles, the membership of individuals to concepts, the membership of pairs of individuals to roles, and functional dependencies on roles. Important additional ingredients of *DL-Lite*$_\mathcal{A}$ are datatypes and attributes, which are collections of data values and binary relations between individuals and data values, respectively, along with the possibility to encode subset relationships between datatypes and between attributes, the membership of individual-value pairs to attributes, and functional dependencies on attributes.

We first describe the elementary ingredients of *DL-Lite*$_\mathcal{A}$. We assume a finite set $\mathbf{D}$ of *atomic datatypes* d, which are associated with pairwise disjoint sets of *data values* $\mathbf{V}_d$. We also assume pairwise disjoint sets $\mathbf{A}$, $\mathbf{R}_A$, $\mathbf{R}_D$, and $\mathbf{I}$ of *atomic concepts*, *atomic roles*, *atomic attributes*, and *individuals*, respectively. We denote by $\mathbf{V}$ the union of all $\mathbf{V}_d$ with $d \in \mathbf{D}$.

These elementary ingredients are used to construct roles, concepts, attributes, and datatypes, which are defined as follows:

- A *basic role* Q is either an atomic role $P \in \mathbf{R}_A$ or its inverse P^-. A (*general*) *role* R is either a basic role Q or the negation of a basic role $\neg Q$.
- A *basic concept* B is either an atomic concept $A \in \mathbf{A}$, or an existential restriction on a basic role Q, denoted $\exists Q$, or the domain of an atomic attribute U, denoted $\delta(U)$. A (*general*) *concept* C is either the *universal concept* $\top_C$, or a basic concept B, or the negation of a basic concept $\neg B$, or an existential restriction on a basic role Q of the form $\exists Q.C$, where C is a concept.
- A (*general*) *attribute* V is either an atomic attribute U or the negation of an atomic attribute $\neg U$.
- A *basic datatype* E is the range of an atomic attribute U, denoted $\rho(U)$. A (*general*) *datatype* F is either the *universal datatype* $\top_D$ or an atomic datatype.

Statements about roles, concepts, attributes, and datatypes are expressed via *axioms*, which have the following forms: (1) $B \sqsubseteq C$ (*concept inclusion axiom*), where B is a basic concept, and C is a concept; (2) $Q \sqsubseteq R$ (*role inclusion axiom*), where Q is a basic role, and R is a role; (3) $U \sqsubseteq V$ (*attribute inclusion axiom*), where U is an atomic attribute, and V is an attribute; (4) $E \sqsubseteq F$ (*datatype inclusion axiom*), where E is a basic datatype, and F is a datatype; (5) (funct Q) (*role functionality axiom*), where Q is a basic role; (6) (funct U) (*attribute functionality axiom*), where U is an atomic attribute; (7) $A(a)$ (*concept membership axiom*), where A is an atomic concept and $a \in \mathbf{I}$, (8) $P(a,b)$ (*role membership axiom*), where P is an atomic role and $a, b \in \mathbf{I}$; (9) $U(a, v)$ (*attribute membership axiom*), where U is an atomic attribute, $a \in \mathbf{I}$, and $v \in \mathbf{V}$.

We next define knowledge bases, which consist of a restricted finite set of inclusion and functionality axioms, called TBox, and a finite set of membership axioms, called ABox. We also describe CQs and BCQs to such knowledge bases.

We first define the restriction on inclusion and functionality axioms. A basic role Q (resp., atomic attribute U) is an *identifying property* in a set of axioms $\mathcal{S}$ iff $\mathcal{S}$ contains a functionality axiom (funct Q) (resp., (funct U)). Given an inclusion axiom α of the form $X \sqsubseteq Y$ (resp., $X \sqsubseteq \neg Y$), a basic role (resp., atomic attribute) Y appears *positively* (resp., *negatively*) in the right-hand side of α. A basic role (resp., atomic attribute) is *primitive* in $\mathcal{S}$ iff it does not appear positively in the right-hand side of an inclusion axiom in $\mathcal{S}$ and it does not appear in an expression $\exists Q.C$ in $\mathcal{S}$.

We can now define knowledge bases. A *TBox* is a finite set $\mathcal{T}$ of inclusion and functionality axioms such that every identifying property in $\mathcal{T}$ is primitive. Intuitively, identifying properties cannot be specialized in $\mathcal{T}$, i.e., they cannot appear positively in the right-hand side of inclusion axioms in $\mathcal{T}$. An *ABox* $\mathcal{A}$ is a finite set of membership axioms. A *knowledge base* $KB = (\mathcal{T}, \mathcal{A})$ consists of a TBox $\mathcal{T}$ and an ABox $\mathcal{A}$. *Conjunctive queries* (*CQs*) and *Boolean CQs* (*BCQs*) are defined as usual, where concept, role, and attribute membership axioms (over variables, individuals, and values as arguments) are used as atoms.

The semantics of *DL-Lite*$_{\mathcal{A}}$ is defined in terms of standard first-order interpretations as usual. In particular, the *satisfiability* of knowledge bases *KB* and the *answers* for *CQs* and *BCQs* to such *KB* are defined as usual in first-order logic.

Example 12.17 We use a knowledge base $KB = (\mathcal{T}, \mathcal{A})$ in *DL-Lite*$_{\mathcal{A}}$ to specify some simple information about scientists and their publications. Consider the following sets of atomic concepts, atomic roles, atomic attributes, individuals, and data values:

$$\mathbf{A} = \{\mathit{Scientist}, \mathit{Article}, \mathit{ConfPaper}, \mathit{JournPaper}\}$$
$$\mathbf{R}_A = \{\mathit{hasAuthor}, \mathit{isAuthorOf}, \mathit{hasFirstAuthor}\}$$
$$\mathbf{R}_D = \{\mathit{name}, \mathit{title}, \mathit{yearOfPub}\}$$
$$\mathbf{I} = \{i_1, i_2\}, \qquad \mathbf{V} = \{\text{“}\mathit{mary}\text{”}, \text{“}\mathit{Semantic\ Web\ search}\text{”}, 2008\}$$

The TBox $\mathcal{T}$ contains the subsequent axioms, which informally express that (i) conference and journal papers are articles, (ii) conference papers are not journal papers, (iii) every scientist has at least one publication, (iv) *isAuthorOf* relates scientists and articles, (v) *isAuthorOf* is the inverse of *hasAuthor*, and (vi) *hasFirstAuthor* is a functional binary relationship:

$$\begin{array}{l} \mathit{ConfPaper} \sqsubseteq \mathit{Article},\ \mathit{JournPaper} \sqsubseteq \mathit{Article},\ \mathit{ConfPaper} \sqsubseteq \neg \mathit{JournPaper} \\ \mathit{Scientist} \sqsubseteq \exists \mathit{isAuthorOf},\ \exists \mathit{isAuthorOf} \sqsubseteq \mathit{Scientist},\ \exists \mathit{isAuthorOf}^- \sqsubseteq \mathit{Article} \\ \mathit{isAuthorOf}^- \sqsubseteq \mathit{hasAuthor},\ \mathit{hasAuthor}^- \sqsubseteq \mathit{isAuthorOf},\ (\mathrm{funct}\ \mathit{hasFirstAuthor}) \end{array}$$

The ABox $\mathcal{A}$ contains the following axioms, which express that the individual i_1 is a scientist whose name is "*mary*" and who is the author of article i_2, which is entitled "*Semantic Web search*" and has been published in the year 2008:

$$\begin{array}{l} \mathit{Scientist}(i_1),\ \mathit{name}(i_1, \text{“}\mathit{mary}\text{”}),\ \mathit{isAuthorOf}(i_1, i_2),\ \mathit{Article}(i_2) \\ \mathit{title}(i_2, \text{“}\mathit{Semantic\ Web\ search}\text{”}),\ \mathit{yearOfPub}(i_2, 2008) \end{array}$$

Querying for all scientists who published an article in 2008 yields the following CQ:

$$Q(x) = \exists y \big(\mathit{Scientist}(x) \wedge \mathit{isAuthorOf}(x, y) \wedge \mathit{Article}(y) \wedge \mathit{yearOfPub}(y, 2008)\big)$$

It is not difficult to verify that $KB = (\mathcal{T}, \mathcal{A})$ is satisfiable, and that the answer to $Q(x)$ contains the tuple (i_1). Informally, *mary* published an article in 2008.

The translation τ from the elementary ingredients and axioms of *DL-Lite*$_{\mathcal{A}}$ into *Datalog*$_0^{\pm}$ is defined as follows:

1. Every data value v has a constant $\tau(v) = c_v \in \Delta$ such that the $\tau(\mathbf{V}_d)$'s for all datatypes $d \in \mathbf{D}$ are pairwise disjoint. Every datatype $d \in \mathbf{D}$ has under τ a predicate $\tau(d) = p_d$ along with the constraint $p_d(X) \wedge p_{d'}(X) \rightarrow \bot$ for all pairwise distinct $d, d' \in \mathbf{D}$. Every atomic concept $A \in \mathbf{A}$ has a unary predicate $\tau(A) =$

$p_A \in \mathcal{R}$, every abstract role $P \in \mathbf{R}_A$ has a binary predicate $\tau(P) = p_P \in \mathcal{R}$, every attribute $U \in \mathbf{R}_D$ has a binary predicate $\tau(U) = p_U \in \mathcal{R}$, and every individual $i \in \mathbf{I}$ has a constant $\tau(i) = c_i \in \Delta - \bigcup_{d \in \mathbf{D}} \tau(\mathbf{V}_d)$.

2. Every concept inclusion axiom $B \sqsubseteq C$ is translated to the TGD or constraint $\tau(B \sqsubseteq C) = \tau'(B) \to \tau''(C)$, where
   a. $\tau'(B)$ is defined as $p_A(X), p_P(X, Y), p_P(Y, X)$, and $p_U(X, Y)$, if B is of the form $A, \exists P, \exists P^-$, and $\delta(U)$, respectively, and
   b. $\tau''(C)$ is defined as $p_A(X)$, $\exists Z p_P(X, Z)$, $\exists Z p_P(Z, X)$, $\exists Z p_U(X, Z)$, $\neg p_A(X)$, $\neg p_P(X, Y)$, $\neg p_P(Y, X)$, $\neg p_U(X,Y)$, $\exists Z p_P(X, Z) \wedge p_A(Z)$, and $\exists Z p_P(Z, X) \wedge p_A(Z)$, if C is of form $A, \exists P, \exists P^-, \delta(U), \neg A, \neg\exists P, \neg\exists P^-, \neg\delta(U), \exists P.A$, and $\exists P^-.A$, respectively.

   Note that concept inclusion axioms $B \sqsubseteq \top_C$ can be safely ignored, and concept inclusion axioms $B \sqsubseteq \exists Q.C$ can be expressed by the two concept inclusion axioms $B \sqsubseteq \exists Q.A$ and $A \sqsubseteq C$, where A is a fresh atomic concept. Note also that the TGDs with two atoms in their heads abbreviate their equivalent sets of TGDs with singleton atoms in the heads.
3. The functionality axioms (funct P) and (funct P^-) are under τ translated to the EGDs $p_P(X, Y) \wedge p_P(X, Y') \to Y = Y'$ and $p_P(X, Y) \wedge p_P(X', Y) \to X = X'$, respectively. The functionality axiom (funct U) is under τ translated to the EGD $p_U(X, Y) \wedge p_U(X, Y') \to Y = Y'$.
4. Every concept membership axiom $A(a)$ is under τ translated to the database atom $p_A(c_a)$. Every role membership axiom $P(a, b)$ is under τ translated to the database atom $p_P(c_a, c_b)$. Every attribute membership axiom $U(a, v)$ is under τ translated to the database atom $p_U(c_a, c_v)$.
5. Every role inclusion axiom $Q \sqsubseteq R$ is translated to the TGD or constraint $\tau(Q \sqsubseteq R) = \tau'(Q) \to \tau''(R)$, where
   a. $\tau'(Q)$ is defined as $p_P(X, Y)$ and $p_P(Y, X)$, if Q is of the form P and P^-, respectively, and
   b. $\tau''(R)$ is defined as $p_P(X, Y)$, $p_P(Y, X)$, $\neg p_P(X, Y)$, and $\neg p_P(Y, X)$, if R is of the form P, P^-, $\neg P$, and $\neg P^-$, respectively.
6. Attribute inclusion axioms $U \sqsubseteq U'$ and $U \sqsubseteq \neg U'$ are under τ translated to the TGD $p_U(X, Y) \to p_{U'}(X, Y)$ and the constraint $p_U(X, Y) \to \neg p_{U'}(X, Y)$, respectively.
7. Every datatype inclusion axiom $\rho(U) \sqsubseteq d$ is under τ translated to the TGD $p_U(Y, X) \to p_d(X)$. Note that datatype inclusion axioms $\rho(U) \sqsubseteq \top_D$ can be safely ignored.

Example 12.18 The concept inclusion axioms of Example 12.17 are translated to the following TGDs and constraints (where we identify atomic concepts and roles with their predicates):

$$\mathit{ConfPaper}(X) \to \mathit{Article}(X),\ \mathit{JournPaper}(X) \to \mathit{Article}(X)$$

$$\mathit{ConfPaper}(X) \to \neg \mathit{JournPaper}(X),\ \mathit{Scientist}(X) \to \exists Z\ \mathit{isAuthorOf}(X, Z)$$

The role inclusion and functionality axioms of Example 12.17 are translated to the following TGDs and EGDs:

$$isAuthorOf(X,Y) \rightarrow Scientist(X),\ isAuthorOf(Y,X) \rightarrow Article(X)$$

$$isAuthorOf(Y,X) \rightarrow hasAuthor(X,Y),\ hasAuthor(Y,X) \rightarrow isAuthorOf(X,Y)$$

$$hasFirstAuthor(X,Y), hasFirstAuthor(X,Y') \rightarrow Y = Y'$$

The membership axioms of Example 12.17 are translated to the following database atoms (where we also identify individuals and values with their constants):

$$Scientist(i_1),\ name(i_1, \text{"mary"}),\ isAuthorOf(i_1, i_2),\ Article(i_2)$$

$$title(i_2, \text{"Semantic Web search"}),\ yearOfPub(i_2, 2008)$$

Every knowledge base *KB* in *DL-Lite*$_{\mathcal{A}}$ is then translated into a database D_{KB}, set of TGDs Σ_{KB}, and set of queries $\mathcal{Q}_{KB}$ as follows: (i) D_{KB} is the set of all $\tau(\phi)$ such that ϕ is a membership axiom in *KB* along with "type declarations" $p_d(v)$ for all their data values; (ii) Σ_{KB} is the set of all TGDs resulting from $\tau(\phi)$ such that ϕ is an inclusion axiom in *KB*; and (iii) $\mathcal{Q}_{KB}$ is the set of all queries resulting from datatype constraints and from constraints and EGDs $\tau(\phi)$ such that ϕ is an inclusion or functionality axiom in *KB*. The TGDs and EGDs that are generated via τ from a *DL-Lite*$_{\mathcal{A}}$ knowledge base are in fact linear TGDs and NC keys, respectively.

The following result shows that BCQs to knowledge bases in *DL-Lite*$_{\mathcal{A}}$ can be reduced to BCQs in Datalog$_0^{\pm}$. This result follows immediately from the above lemma and Theorem 12.18. As an immediate consequence, the satisfiability of knowledge bases in *DL-Lite*$_{\mathcal{A}}$ can then also be reduced to BCQs in Datalog$_0^{\pm}$.

Theorem 12.19 [10] *Let KB be a knowledge base in DL-Lite*$_{\mathcal{A}}$*, and Q be a BCQ for KB. Then,* $KB \models Q$ *iff* (i) $D_{KB} \cup \Sigma_{KB} \models Q$*, or* (ii) $D_{KB} \cup \Sigma_{KB} \models Q_c$ *for some* $Q_c \in \mathcal{Q}_{KB}$.

The next result shows that Datalog$_0^{\pm}$ is strictly more expressive than *DL-Lite*$_{\mathcal{A}}$.

Theorem 12.20 [10] *Datalog*$_0^{\pm}$ *is strictly more expressive than DL-Lite*$_{\mathcal{A}}$.

12.7.2 F-Logic Lite

In this section, we briefly present a formalism for object-oriented schemas called F-Logic Lite, and we then show that it is a special case of weakly-guarded Datalog$^{\pm}$. We will also show, with a different proof, the same result appearing in [11], i.e., that query answering under F-Logic Lite rules is NP-complete.

F-Logic Lite is a smaller but still expressive version of F-logic [29], a well-known formalism introduced for object-oriented deductive databases. We refer the reader to [11] for details about F-Logic Lite. Roughly speaking, with respect to F-Logic, F-Logic Lite excludes negation and default inheritance, and allows only for a limited form of cardinality constraints.

We now show that F-Logic Lite can be expressed by using weakly-guarded Datalog$^\pm$ rules and a single EGD. We denote the Datalog$^\pm$ that we obtain in this translation with Σ_{FLL}, with $\Sigma_{FLL} = \{\rho_i\}_{1 \leqslant i \leqslant 12}$. The rules are shown below.

1. $type(O, A, T), data(O, A, V) \rightarrow member(V, T)$.
2. $sub(C_1, C_3), sub(C_3, C_2) \rightarrow sub(C_1, C_2)$.
3. $member(O, C), sub(C, C_1) \rightarrow member(O, C_1)$.
4. $data(O, A, V), data(O, A, W), funct(A, O) \rightarrow V = W$.
   Note that this is the only EGD in this axiomatization.
5. $mandatory(A, O) \rightarrow \exists V\, data(O, A, V)$.
   Note that this is a TGD with an existential variable in the head (variable V).
6. $member(O, C), type(C, A, T) \rightarrow type(O, A, T)$.
7. $sub(C, C_1), type(C_1, A, T) \rightarrow type(C, A, T)$.
8. $type(C, A, T_1), sub(T_1, T) \rightarrow type(C, A, T)$.
9. $sub(C, C_1), mandatory(A, C_1) \rightarrow mandatory(A, C)$.
10. $member(O, C), mandatory(A, C) \rightarrow mandatory(A, O)$.
11. $sub(C, C_1), funct(A, C_1) \rightarrow funct(A, C)$.
12. $member(O, C), funct(A, C) \rightarrow funct(A, O)$.

Now, we present a set Σ'_{FLL} of TGDs and EGDs that is equivalent to Σ_{FLL}, but enjoys the desirable property that the single EGD in it is a key dependency. The set of rules Σ'_{FLL} is obtained from Σ_{FLL} by: (1) adding to $\mathcal{R}$ the ternary predicate $data'$, thus obtaining $\mathcal{R}'$, (2) replacing ρ_4 with the rule $data'(O, A, V), data'(O, A, W) \rightarrow V = W$, denoted ρ'_4, and (3) adding the rule $mandatory(A, O), funct(A, O) \rightarrow \exists V\, data'(O, A, V)$, denoted ρ_{13}. It can be straightforwardly shown that: (1) all TGDs in Σ'_{FLL} are weakly-guarded, (2) the single EGD ρ'_4 in Σ'_{FLL} is a key dependency, and (3) ρ'_4 is non-conflicting with all the other TGDs in Σ'_{FLL}. Moreover, it is not difficult to prove that, for every query Q expressed on $\mathcal{R}'$ but without the predicate $data'$ (i.e., with predicates in $\mathcal{R}$ only), and for every instance D, we have that $D \cup \Sigma_{FLL} \models Q$ iff $D \cup \Sigma'_{FLL} \models Q$. By the above considerations, and by Theorem 12.18, we can restrict our attention solely on the TGDs in Σ_{FLL}.

By a polynomial reduction from the 3-COLORABILITY problem, we can show the following complexity result.

Theorem 12.21 [9, 11] *Query answering under F-Logic Lite rules is* NP*-hard.*

F-Logic Lite rules have also some interesting properties, which are formalized as *Polynomial Clouds Criterion* in [9]. First, for every instance D, the number of clouds in $chase(\Sigma_{FLL}, D)$ that are pairwise non-D-isomorphic is polynomial in the size $|D|$ of D. Second, for every atom $\mathbf{a}$, the set $cloud(\Sigma_{FLL}, D, \mathbf{a})$ can be computed in time polynomial in $|D|$ from $\mathbf{a}$ and $cloud(\Sigma, D, \mathbf{b})$ (whenever $\mathbf{b}$ exists), where

b is the predecessor of **a** in the chase forest. Starting from the above considerations, it is possible to get the following result, which then immediately implies that answering CQs under F-Logic Lite rules is NP-complete.

Theorem 12.22 [9, 11] *Answering CQs under F-Logic Lite rules is in* NP.

12.8 Conclusion

In this paper, we have surveyed recent results about Datalog$^\pm$, a family of expressive extensions of Datalog that allow for a general and natural formalization of ontologies. We have presented the different languages in the Datalog$^\pm$ family along with tight complexity bounds for all cases. We have then shown that the Datalog$^\pm$ family is capable of expressing the most common tractable ontology languages that are currently adopted in the Semantic Web and databases, namely, the *DL-Lite* family of DLs and F-Logic Lite. In [10], we have shown how stratified negation can be added to Datalog$^\pm$ while keeping ontology querying tractable in the data complexity.

Datalog$^\pm$ is a natural and very general framework that closes the gap between query answering in databases, on the one hand, and ontology querying in DLs and the Semantic Web, on the other hand. It is an exciting family of languages for ontology querying, which are important in their own right and well worth being studied more deeply. Datalog$^\pm$ allows to naturally satisfy the emerging need of incorporating ontologies in the database area. Furthermore, it paves the way for applying standard database technology in the areas of DLs and the Semantic Web, as it has been shown in this paper for stratified negation, but which is also highly interesting for areas such as data integration and exchange [22]. In particular, such a transfer of database technology may help to satisfy the current need of DLs and the Semantic Web for scalable and efficient techniques.

In future research, we aim especially at making Datalog$^\pm$ even more powerful, without destroying its nice computational properties, so to also allow for embedding further, more expressive ontology languages, especially further tractable ontology languages, such as e.g. Horn-$\mathcal{SHIQ}$ [27], but also those involving disjunctive knowledge. Furthermore, we work on generalizations of the class of non-conflicting keys, which does not interact with TGDs. We also intend to find a syntactic criterion to restrict the class of weakly guarded TGDs and to lower its complexity. A semantic criterion is found in [9], which ensures that there are polynomially many clouds relative to the size of the database. Finally, we plan to investigate relevant first-order fragments, and get for them precise time bounds for Courcelle's theorem.

Acknowledgements The work of Andrea Calì and Georg Gottlob was supported by the EPSRC grant Number EP/E010865/1 "Schema Mappings and Automated Services for Data Integration". Georg Gottlob, whose work was partially carried out at the Oxford-Man Institute of Quantitative Finance, gratefully acknowledges support from the Royal Society as the holder of a Royal Society-Wolfson Research Merit Award. Thomas Lukasiewicz's work was supported by the German Research Foundation (DFG) under the Heisenberg Programme.

References

1. Abiteboul, S., Hull, R., Vianu, V.: Foundations of Databases. Addison-Wesley, Reading (1995)
2. Andréka, H., Németi, I., van Benthem, J.: Modal languages and bounded fragments of predicate logic. J. Philos. Logic **27**(3), 217–274 (1998)
3. Beeri, C., Fagin, R., Maier, D., Mendelzon, A.O., Ullman, J.D., Yannakakis, M.: Properties of acyclic database schemes. In: Proc. STOC 1981, pp. 355–362. ACM, New York (1981)
4. Beeri, C., Vardi, M.Y.: The implication problem for data dependencies. In: Proc. ICALP 1981. LNCS, vol. 115, pp. 73–85. Springer, Berlin (1981)
5. Beeri, C., Vardi, M.Y.: A proof procedure for data dependencies. J. ACM **31**(4), 718–741 (1984)
6. Berners-Lee, T., Hendler, J., Lassila, O.: The Semantic Web. Sci. Am. **284**(5), 34–43 (2001)
7. Brickley, D., Guha, R.V.: RDF vocabulary description language 1.0: RDF Schema (2004). W3C Recommendation
8. de Bruijn, J., Heymans, S.: Logical foundations of (e)RDF(S): Complexity and reasoning. In: Proc. ISWC 2007. LNCS, vol. 4825, pp. 86–99. Springer, Berlin (2007)
9. Calì, A., Gottlob, G., Kifer, M.: Taming the infinite chase: Query answering under expressive relational constraints (2008). Unpublished Technical Report. Available at http://benner.dbai.tuwien.ac.at/staff/gottlob/CGK.pdf. This is the full and revised version of a preliminary short version in Proc. KR 2008, pp. 70–80. AAAI Press (2008)
10. Calì, A., Gottlob, G., Lukasiewicz, T.: A general Datalog-based framework for tractable query answering over ontologies. In: Proc. PODS 2009, pp. 77–86. ACM, New York (2009)
11. Calì, A., Kifer, M.: Containment of conjunctive object meta-queries. In: Proc. VLDB 2006, pp. 942–952. ACM, New York (2006)
12. Calì, A., Lembo, D., Rosati, R.: On the decidability and complexity of query answering over inconsistent and incomplete databases. In: Proc. PODS 2003, pp. 260–271. ACM, New York (2003)
13. Calvanese, D., De Giacomo, G., Lembo, D., Lenzerini, M., Rosati, R.: Tractable reasoning and efficient query answering in description logics: The *DL-Lite* family. J. Autom. Reason. **39**(3), 385–429 (2007)
14. Casanova, M.A., Fagin, R., Papadimitriou, C.H.: Inclusion dependencies and their interaction with functional dependencies. J. Comput. Syst. Sci. **28**(1), 29–59 (1984)
15. Ceri, S., Gottlob, G., Tanca, L.: Logic Programming and Databases. Springer, Berlin (1990)
16. Chandra, A.K., Lewis, H.R., Makowsky, J.A.: Embedded implicational dependencies and their inference problem. In: Proc. STOC 1981, pp. 342–354. ACM, New York (1981)
17. Chandra, A.K., Merlin, P.M.: Optimal implementation of conjunctive queries in relational data bases. In: Proc. STOC 1977, pp. 77–90. ACM, New York (1977)
18. Chandra, A.K., Vardi, M.Y.: The implication problem for functional and inclusion dependencies is undecidable. SIAM J. Comput. **14**(3), 671–677 (1985)
19. Courcelle, B.: The monadic second-order logic of graphs. I. Recognizable sets of finite graphs. Inf. Comput. **85**(1), 12–75 (1990)
20. Deutsch, A., Nash, A., Remmel, J.B.: The chase revisited. In: Proc. PODS 2008, pp. 149–158. ACM, New York (2008)
21. Deutsch, A., Tannen, V.: Reformulation of XML queries and constraints. In: Proc. ICDT 2003. LNCS, vol. 2572, pp. 225–241. Springer, Berlin (2003)
22. Fagin, R., Kolaitis, P.G., Miller, R.J., Popa, L.: Data exchange: Semantics and query answering. Theor. Comput. Sci. **336**(1), 89–124 (2005)
23. Goncalves, M.E., Grädel, E.: Decidability issues for action guarded logics. In: Proc. DL 2000, pp. 123–132 (2000). CEUR-WS.org
24. Gottlob, G., Koch, C., Baumgartner, R., Herzog, M., Flesca, S.: The Lixto data extraction project—Back and forth between theory and practice. In: Proc. PODS 2004, pp. 1–12. ACM, New York (2004)
25. Gottlob, G., Papadimitriou, C.H.: On the complexity of single-rule Datalog queries. Inf. Comput. **183**(1), 104–122 (2003)

26. Grädel, E.: On the restraining power of guards. J. Symb. Log. **64**(4), 1719–1742 (1999)
27. Hustadt, U., Motik, B., Sattler, U.: Data complexity of reasoning in very expressive description logics. In: Proc. IJCAI 2005, pp. 466–471 (2005)
28. Johnson, D.S., Klug, A.C.: Testing containment of conjunctive queries under functional and inclusion dependencies. J. Comput. Syst. Sci. **28**(1), 167–189 (1984)
29. Kifer, M., Lausen, G., Wu, J.: Logical foundations of object-oriented and frame-based languages. J. ACM **42**(4), 741–843 (1995)
30. Lenzerini, M.: Data integration: A theoretical perspective. In: Proc. PODS 2002, pp. 233–246. ACM, New York (2002)
31. Maier, D., Mendelzon, A.O., Sagiv, Y.: Testing implications of data dependencies. ACM Trans. Database Syst. **4**(4), 455–469 (1979)
32. Mitchell, J.C.: The implication problem for functional and inclusion dependencies. Inform. Control **56**(1/2), 154–173 (1983)
33. Patel-Schneider, P.F., Horrocks, I.: Position paper: A comparison of two modelling paradigms in the Semantic Web. In: Proc. WWW 2006, pp. 3–12. ACM, New York (2006)
34. Poggi, A., Lembo, D., Calvanese, D., De Giacomo, G., Lenzerini, M., Rosati, R.: Linking data to ontologies. J. Data Semant. **10**, 133–173 (2008)
35. Qian, X.: Query folding. In: Proc. ICDE 1996, pp. 48–55. IEEE Computer Society, Los Alamitos (1996)
36. Ullman, J.D.: Principles of Database and Knowledge-Base Systems. Computer Science Press, New York (1989)
37. Vardi, M.Y.: (1984). Personal communication reported in [28]
38. Vardi, M.Y.: On the complexity of bounded-variable queries. In: Proc. PODS 1995, pp. 266–176. ACM, New York (1995)

Chapter 13
On the Semantics of SPARQL

Marcelo Arenas, Claudio Gutierrez, and Jorge Pérez

Abstract The Resource Description Framework (RDF) is the standard data model for representing information about World Wide Web resources. In January 2008, it was released the recommendation of the W3C for querying RDF data, a query language called SPARQL. In this chapter, we give a detailed description of the semantics of this language. We start by focusing on the definition of a formal semantics for the core part of SPARQL, and then move to the definition for the entire language, including all the features in the specification of SPARQL by the W3C such as blank nodes in graph patterns and bag semantics for solutions.

13.1 Introduction

The Resource Description Framework (RDF) is a data model for representing information about World Wide Web resources. Jointly with its release in 1998 as recommendation of the W3C, the natural problem of querying RDF data was raised. Since then, several designs and implementations of RDF query languages have been proposed. In 2004, the RDF Data Access Working Group, part of the W3C Semantic Web Activity, released a first public working draft of a query language for RDF, called SPARQL [15].[1] Since then, SPARQL has been rapidly adopted as the standard for querying Semantic Web data. In January 2008, SPARQL became a W3C recommendation.

RDF is a directed labeled graph data format and, thus, SPARQL is essentially a graph-matching query language. SPARQL queries are composed by three parts.

[1]The name SPARQL is a recursive acronym that stands for *SPARQL Protocol and RDF Query Language*.

M. Arenas (✉) · J. Pérez
Department of Computer Science, Pontificia Universidad Católica de Chile,
Vicuña Mackenna 4860, 7820436 Macul, Santiago, Chile
e-mail: marenas@ing.puc.cl

J. Pérez
e-mail: jperez@ing.puc.cl

C. Gutierrez
Department of Computer Science, Universidad de Chile, Blanco Encalada 2120,
8370459 Santiago, Santiago, Chile
e-mail: cgutierr@dcc.uchile.cl

R. De Virgilio et al. (eds.), *Semantic Web Information Management*,
DOI 10.1007/978-3-642-04329-1_13, © Springer-Verlag Berlin Heidelberg 2010

The *pattern matching part*, which includes several interesting features of pattern matching of graphs, like optional parts, union of patterns, nesting, filtering values of possible matchings, and the possibility of choosing the data source to be matched by a pattern. The *solution modifiers*, which once the output of the pattern has been computed (in the form of a table of values of variables), allow to modify these values applying classical operators like projection, distinct, order and limit. Finally, the *output* of a SPARQL query can be of different types: yes/no queries, selections of values of the variables which match the patterns, construction of new RDF data from these values and descriptions of resources.

The definition of a formal semantics for SPARQL has played a key role in the standardization process of this query language. Although taken one by one the features of SPARQL are intuitive and simple to describe and understand, it turns out that the combination of them makes SPARQL into a complex language. Reaching a consensus in the W3C standardization process about a formal semantics for SPARQL was not an easy task. The initial efforts to define SPARQL were driven by use cases, mostly by specifying the expected output for particular example queries. In fact, the interpretations of examples and the exact outcomes of cases not covered in the initial drafts of the SPARQL specification, were a matter of long discussions in the W3C mailing lists. In [11], the authors presented one of the first formalizations of a semantics for a fragment of the language. Currently, the official specification of SPARQL [15], endorsed by the W3C, formalizes a semantics based on [11].

A formalization of a semantics for SPARQL is beneficial for several reasons, including to serve as a tool to identify and derive relations among the constructors that stay hidden in the use cases, to identify redundant and contradicting notions, to drive and help the implementation of query engines and to study the complexity, expressiveness and further natural database questions like rewriting and optimization. In this chapter, we present a streamlined version of the core fragment of SPARQL with precise algebraic syntax and a formal compositional semantics based on [11–13].

One of the delicate issues in the definition of a semantics for SPARQL is the treatment of *optional matching* and incomplete answers. The idea behind optional matching is to allow information to be added if the information is available in the data source, instead of just failing to give an answer whenever some part of the pattern does not match. This feature of optional matching is crucial in Semantic Web applications, and more specifically in RDF data management, where it is assumed that every application have only partial knowledge about the resources being managed. The semantics of SPARQL is formalized by using *partial mappings* between variables in the patterns and actual values in the RDF graph being queried. This formalization allows one to deal with partial answers in a clean way, and is based on the extension of some classical relational algebra operators to work over sets of partial mappings.

The rest of the chapter is organized as follows. In Sect. 13.2, we describe the official syntax of SPARQL proposed by the W3C. In Sect. 13.3, we introduce an algebraic syntax for the language and compare it with the official syntax. In Sect. 13.4, we formalize the semantics of SPARQL. We begin formalizing a set semantics for the language without considering blank nodes in patterns. We then extend the semantics to consider blank nodes and we provide a bag semantics for SPARQL. In

Sect. 13.5, we review some of the results in the literature about the complexity of evaluating SPARQL graph patterns. Section 13.6 describes some related work about the formalization of a semantics for SPARQL. Concluding remarks are in Sect. 13.7.

13.2 The W3C Syntax of SPARQL

The RDF query language SPARQL was adopted as a W3C recommendation on January 15, 2008. Its syntax and semantics are specified in [15]. SPARQL is a language designed to query data in the form of sets of triples, namely RDF graphs (see Sect. 13.3 for a formal definition of the notion of RDF graph). The basic engine of the language is a pattern matching facility, which uses some graph pattern matching functionalities (sets of triples can be viewed also as graphs). The overall structure of the language—from a syntactic point of view—resembles SQL with its three main blocks (as shown in Fig. 13.1):

- A WHERE clause, which is composed of a graph pattern. Informally speaking, this clause is given by a pattern that corresponds to an RDF graph where some resources have been replaced by variables. But not only that, more complex expressions (patterns) are also allowed, which are formed by using some algebraic operators. This pattern is used as a filter of the values of the dataset to be returned.
- A FROM clause, which specifies the sources or datasets to be queried.
- A SELECT clause, which specifies the final form in which the results are returned to the user. SPARQL, in contrast to SQL, allows several forms of returning the data: a table using SELECT, a graph using DESCRIBE or CONSTRUCT, or a TRUE/FALSE answer using ASK.

In what follows, we explain in more detail each component of the language. Of course, for ultimate details the reader should consult [15].

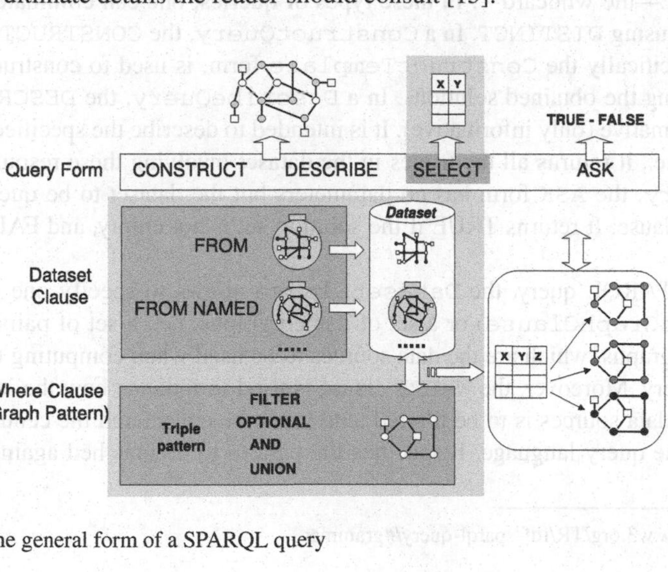

Fig. 13.1 The general form of a SPARQL query

13.2.1 Basic Definitions

There are several basic concepts used in the definition of the syntax of SPARQL, many of which are taken from the RDF specification with some minor modifications. For the sake of completeness, we review them here.

An *IRI* (Internationalized Resource Identifier [5]) is an identifier of resources, which essentially extends the syntax of URIs to a much wider repertoire of characters for internationalization purposes. For denoting resources, SPARQL uses IRIs instead of the URIs of RDF. A *literal* is used to identify values such as numbers and dates by means of a lexical representation. Anything represented by a literal could also be represented by a IRI, but it is often more convenient or intuitive to use literals. All literals have a lexical form that is a Unicode string. There are two types of literals: plain and typed. A *plain literal* is a string combined with an optional language tag. This may be used for plain text in a natural language. A *typed literal* is a string combined with a datatype IRI.

13.2.2 Basic Structures

In order to present the language, we follow the grammar given in Fig. 13.2 that specifies the basic structure of the SPARQL Query Grammar [15].[2]

As shown in Fig. 13.2, a SPARQL `Query` is given by a `Prologue` followed by any of the four types of SPARQL queries: `SelectQuery`, `ConstructQuery`, `DescribeQuery` or `AskQuery`. The `Prologue` contains the declaration of variables, namespaces and abbreviations to be used in the query. The `SELECT` clause in a `SelectQuery` selects a group of variables, or all of them using—as in SQL—the wildcard `*`. In these types of queries, one can eliminate duplicate solutions using `DISTINCT`. In a `ConstructQuery`, the `CONSTRUCT` form, and more specifically the `ConstructTemplate` form, is used to construct an RDF graph using the obtained solutions. In a `DescribeQuery`, the `DESCRIBE` form is not normative (only informative). It is intended to describe the specified variables or IRIs, i.e., it returns all the triples in the dataset involving these resources. In an `AskQuery`, the `ASK` form has no parameters but the dataset to be queried and a `WHERE` clause. It returns TRUE if the solution set is not empty, and FALSE otherwise.

In a SPARQL query, the `DatasetClause` allows to specify one graph (the `DefaultGraphClause`) or a set of named graphs, i.e., a set of pairs of identifiers and graphs, which are the data sources to be used when computing the answer to the query. Moreover, the `WHERE` clause is used to indicate how the information from the data sources is to be filtered, and it can be considered the central component of the query language. It specifies the pattern to be matched against the data

---

[2] http://www.w3.org/TR/rdf-sparql-query/#grammar.

```
Query          ::=  Prologue ( SelectQuery | ConstructQuery |
                                DescribeQuery | AskQuery )

SelectQuery ::=  "SELECT" ( "DISTINCT" | "REDUCED" )?
                           ( Var+ | "*" )
                 DatasetClause* WhereClause SolutionModifier

ConstructQuery ::= "CONSTRUCT" ConstructTemplate
                   DatasetClause* WhereClause
                   SolutionModifier

DescribeQuery  ::=  "DESCRIBE" ( VarOrIRIref+ | "*" )
                    DatasetClause* WhereClause?
                    SolutionModifier

AskQuery       ::=  "ASK" DatasetClause* WhereClause

DatasetClause  ::=  "FROM" ( DefaultGraphClause |
                             NamedGraphClause )

WhereClause    ::=  "WHERE"? GroupGP

GroupGP        ::= "{" TB? ((GPNotTr | Filter) "."? TB?)* "}"
GPNotTr        ::= OptionalGP | GroupOrUnionGP | GraphGP
OptionalGP     ::= "OPTIONAL" GroupGP
GraphGP        ::= "GRAPH" VarOrIRIref GroupGP
GroupOrUnionGP ::= GroupGP ( "UNION" GroupGP )*
Filter         ::= "FILTER" Constraint

SolutionModifier  ::=  OrderClause? LimitOffsetClauses?
```

Fig. 13.2 A fragment of the SPARQL Query Grammar [15]

sources. In particular, it includes sets of triples with some of the IRIs or blank elements replaced by variables, called "triple blocks" (`TB` in the grammar), an operator for collecting triples and blocks (denoted by `{A . B}`, and with no fixed arity), an operator `UNION` for specifying alternatives, an operator `OPTIONAL` to provide optional matchings, and an operator `FILTER` that allows filtering results of patterns under certain basic constraints.

Example 13.1 Consider the following query: "Give the name and the mailbox of each person who has a mailbox with domain .cl". This query can be expressed in SPARQL as follows:

```
PREFIX foaf:   <http://xmlns.com/foaf/0.1/>
PREFIX ex:     <http://example.com/ns#>

SELECT ?name ?mbox
FROM   <myDataSource.rdf>
WHERE  {
         ?x  foaf:name  ?name .
```

```
        ?x   foaf:mbox   ?mbox .
        ?mbox  ex:domain   ".cl"
      }
```

The first two lines in this example form the `Prologue` of the query, which specifies the namespaces to be used. In this case, one is the well-known FOAF ontology, and the other one is an example namespace. The keywords `foaf` and `ex` are abbreviations for the namespaces, which are used in the body of the query.

The `SELECT` keyword indicates that the query returns a table with two columns, corresponding to the values obtained from the matching of the variables `?name` and `?mbox` against the graph pointed to in the `FROM` clause (`myDataSource.rdf`), and according to the pattern described in the `WHERE` clause. It should be noticed that a string starting with the symbol `?` denotes a variables in SPARQL.

In the above query, the `WHERE` clause is composed by a pattern with three triples: `?x foaf:name ?name`, `?x foaf:mbox ?mbox` and `?mbox ex:domain ".cl"`, where `.cl` is a literal. This pattern indicates that one is looking for the elements `?x`, `?name` and `?mbox` in the RDF graph `myDataSource.rdf` such that the `foaf:name` of `?x` is `?name`, the `foaf:mbox` of `?x` is `?mbox` and the `ex:domain` of `?mbox` is `.cl`. Thus, an expression of the form `{A . B}` in SPARQL denotes the conjunction of `A` and `B`, as this expression holds if both `A` and `B` holds.

13.2.3 More Complex Queries

SPARQL allows to write more complex queries than the ones presented in the previous section. The syntax of these queries becomes slightly involved and, in particular, two important issues are the use of the `OPTIONAL` and of the `FILTER` operator. We discuss these issues in this section.

Example 13.2 (Querying optional values) Consider the following query: "Give the name and the mailbox, if it is provided, of each person in the FOAF file of Bob". This query can be expressed in SPARQL as follows:

```
PREFIX foaf: <http://xmlns.com/foaf/0.1/>

SELECT ?name ?mbox
FROM  <http://example.org/foaf/bobFoaf>
WHERE  {
         ?x  foaf:name ?name .
         OPTIONAL { ?x  foaf:mbox  ?mbox }
       }
```

In this case, the `WHERE` clause is composed by the conjunction of two patterns, the triple pattern `?x foaf:name ?name` and the optional pattern:

```
OPTIONAL { ?x  foaf:mbox  ?mbox },
```

which in turn includes the triple pattern `?x foaf:mbox ?mbox`. The `WHERE` clause indicates that one is looking for the elements `?name` and `?mbox` in the RDF graph `http://example.org/foaf/bobFoaf` such that the `foaf:name` of `?x` is `?name` and the `foaf:mbox` of `?x` is `?mbox`, provided that `?x` has a `foaf:mbox`. In the case where `?x` does not have a mailbox, the variable `?mbox` is not instantiated and, thus, the corresponding tuple in the answer table only has a value in the attribute `?name`.

As shown in the previous example, the keyword `OPTIONAL` in the W3C SPARQL syntax works as a unary operator. In the following example, we show a query where this operator has to be used in conjunction with the notion of named graph.

Example 13.3 (Querying different data sources) Consider the following query: "For every person known by Alice and Bob, give the nicknames by which are known by Alice and Bob." We note that in this case the query must be posed against two different data sets, the FOAF data of Bob and of Alice. Moreover, it could be the case that Bob and Alice know different nicknames for a person, or that Bob knows a nickname for a person which is not known by Alice, or vice versa. Hence, to express the query in SPARQL, we need to use named graphs and the `OPTIONAL` operator:

```
PREFIX foaf: <http://xmlns.com/foaf/0.1/>
PREFIX data: <http://example.org/foaf/>

SELECT ?nickA ?nickB
FROM NAMED <http://example.org/foaf/aliceFoaf>
FROM NAMED <http://example.org/foaf/bobFoaf>
WHERE
  {
    GRAPH data:bobFoaf { ?x foaf:knows ?comm
                OPTIONAL { ?comm foaf:nick ?nickB } } .
    GRAPH data:aliceFoaf { ?y foaf:knows ?comm .
                OPTIONAL { ?comm foaf:nick ?nickA } }
  }
```

Notice that in the `WHERE` clause, the operator `GRAPH` is used to specify over which dataset the pattern enclosed in braces should be matched. Also, notice the use of the `OPTIONAL` operator to avoid losing information for people that only has a registered nickname in the FOAF data of either Alice or Bob.

It is important to notice that nesting of optional patterns is allowed in the official specification of SPARQL [15]. Unfortunately, the rules that define this nesting are rather involved (see rules 20–23 in [15]).

As mentioned above, the operator `FILTER` is another interesting and complex feature of SPARQL. More specifically, SPARQL filters restrict the solutions of a graph pattern match according to a given expression, which includes several functions and operators that are defined over the elements of the RDF graphs and the variables of SPARQL queries. A subset of these functions and operators are taken from XQuery and XPath (see [15] for further details). Among them, one of the most useful is the unary operator `bound(?x)`, which checks if the variable `?x` is bounded in the answer (this turns out to be really useful in combination with the `OPTIONAL` operator [1]). The functions `isIRI`, `isBlank` and `isLiteral` play similar roles. As expected, the Boolean connectives OR, AND and NOT (denoted by `logical-or`, `logical-and` and `!`, respectively) have also been included, as well as some functionalities for checking equality and order. The following example shows one of these features.

Example 13.4 (Filtering values) Consider the following query: "Give the list of people for whom Alice knows at least two nicknames." This query can be expressed by the following SPARQL query:

```
PREFIX foaf: <http://xmlns.com/foaf/0.1/>

SELECT ?y
FROM <http://example.org/foaf/aliceFoaf>
WHERE
  {
     ?x foaf:knows ?y .
     ?y foaf:nick ?nick1 .
     ?y foaf:nick ?nick2 .
       FILTER (?nick1 != ?nick2) }
  }
```

The filter expression `FILTER (?nick1 != ?nick2)` is used to check that the nicknames `?nick1` and `?nick2` of `?y` are distinct. Thus, this expression is used to ensure that Alice knows at least two distinct nicknames for `?y`.

We conclude our discussion by pointing out that one important aspect of SPARQL is the scope of the `FILTER` operator, which is a source of difficulties in the current specification of SPARQL (see [1] for more details).

13.2.4 Final Remarks

We conclude this section by providing a list of some important syntactic features of SPARQL, which are widely used in practice (for a complete list see the official specification of SPARQL [15]).

- A literal in SPARQL is a string (enclosed in either double quotes or single quotes), with either an optional language tag (introduced by `@`) or an optional datatype IRI or prefixed name (introduced by `^^`).
- Variables are prefixed by either "`?`" or "`$`", and these two symbols are not considered to be part of the variable name. Furthermore, variables in SPARQL queries have global scope; the use of a given variable name anywhere in a query identifies the same variable.

- There is syntactic sugar for expressing namespaces. As we pointed out, in general it is more convenient to declare them in the `Prologue` of the query, but this is not mandatory. For example, these three expressions represent the same query:

```
PREFIX  dc: <http://purl.org/dc/elements/1.1/>
SELECT  ?title
WHERE   { <http://example.org/book/book1> dc:title ?title }

PREFIX  dc: <http://purl.org/dc/elements/1.1/>
PREFIX  : <http://example.org/book/>
SELECT  $title
WHERE   { :book1  dc:title  $title }

BASE    <http://example.org/book/>
PREFIX  dc: <http://purl.org/dc/elements/1.1/>
SELECT  $title
WHERE   { <book1>  dc:title  ?title }
```

  The clause `BASE` is used to indicate the base IRI for a query. In the last example, this base IRI is `http://example.org/book/` and, thus, the element `book1` in the query refers to this namespace.
- SPARQL allows a simplified notation for sets of triple patterns with a common subject; the symbol '`;`' can be used to express that a set of pairs is associated with a particular subject, thus writing the subject only once. For example, the following sequence of triples:

```
?x  foaf:name  ?name .
?x  foaf:mbox  ?mbox .
```

  is the same in SPARQL as:

```
?x  foaf:name  ?name ;
    foaf:mbox  ?mbox .
```

13.3 An Algebraic Syntax for SPARQL

In this section, we present the algebraic formalization of the core fragment of SPARQL proposed in [11–13], and show that it is equivalent in expressive power to the core fragment of SPARQL defined in [15]. Thus, this formalization is used in this chapter to give a formal semantics to SPARQL, as well as to study some fundamental properties of this language.

We start by introducing the necessary notions about RDF (for details on the formalization of RDF see [7]). Assume that there are pairwise disjoint infinite sets I, B and L (IRIs [5], Blank nodes, and Literals, respectively). A triple $(s, p, o) \in (I \cup B) \times I \times (I \cup B \cup L)$ is called an *RDF triple*. In this tuple, s is the *subject*, p the *predicate* and o the *object*. We denote the union $I \cup B \cup L$ by T (RDF Terms). Assume additionally the existence of an infinite set V of variables disjoint from the above sets.

Definition 13.1 (RDF Graph) An *RDF graph* [10] is a set of RDF triples. If G is an RDF graph, then $\text{term}(G)$ is the set of elements of T appearing in the triples of G, and $\text{blank}(G)$ is the set of blank nodes appearing in G ($\text{blank}(G) = \text{term}(G) \cap B$).

SPARQL queries are evaluated against an *RDF dataset* [15], that is, a set of RDF graphs in which every graph is identified by an IRI, except for a distinguished graph in the set called the *default* graph. Formally, an RDF dataset is a set:

$$\mathcal{D} = \{G_0, \langle u_1, G_1 \rangle, \dots, \langle u_n, G_n \rangle\}$$

where $G_0, \dots, G_n$ are RDF graphs, $u_1, \dots, u_n$ are distinct IRIs, and $n \geq 0$. In the dataset, G_0 is the *default graph*, and the pairs $\langle u_i, G_i \rangle$ are *named graphs*, with u_i being the name of G_i. We assume that every dataset $\mathcal{D}$ is equipped with a function $d_{\mathcal{D}}$ such that $d_{\mathcal{D}}(u) = G$ if $\langle u, G \rangle \in \mathcal{D}$ and $d_{\mathcal{D}}(u) = \emptyset$, otherwise. Additionally, $\text{name}(\mathcal{D})$ stands for the set of IRIs that are names of graphs in $\mathcal{D}$, and $\text{term}(\mathcal{D})$ and $\text{blank}(\mathcal{D})$ stand for the set of terms and blank nodes appearing in the graphs of $\mathcal{D}$, respectively. For the sake of simplicity, and without loss of generality, we assume that the graphs in a dataset have disjoint sets of blank nodes, i.e., for $i \neq j$, $\text{blank}(G_i) \cap \text{blank}(G_j) = \emptyset$.

As we have seen in the previous section, the official syntax of SPARQL [15] considers operators `GRAPH`, `OPTIONAL`, `UNION`, `FILTER` and *conjunction* via a point symbol (`.`). The syntax also considers `{ }` to group patterns, and some implicit rules of precedence and association. For example, the point symbol (`.`) has precedence over `OPTIONAL`, and `OPTIONAL` is left associative. In order to avoid ambiguities in the parsing, in this section, we present the syntax of SPARQL graph patterns in a more traditional algebraic formalism, using binary operators AND (`.`), UNION (`UNION`), OPT (`OPTIONAL`), FILTER (`FILTER`) and GRAPH (`GRAPH`). We fully parenthesize expressions making explicit the precedence and association of operators.

To define the algebraic syntax of SPARQL, we need to introduce the notions of *triple pattern* and *basic graph pattern*. A triple pattern is a tuple $t \in (I \cup L \cup V) \times (I \cup V) \times (I \cup L \cup V)$, and a basic graph pattern is a finite set of triple patterns. Notice that a triple pattern is essentially an RDF triple with some positions replaced by variables. Also notice that in our definitions of triple and basic graph pattern, we are not considering blank nodes. We make this simplification here to focus on the pattern matching part of the language. In Sect. 13.4.1, we discuss how these definitions should be extended to deal with blank nodes in basic graph patterns.

We use basic graph patterns as the base case for the syntax of SPARQL graph pattern expressions. A SPARQL graph pattern expression is defined recursively as follows:

1. A basic graph pattern is a graph pattern.
2. If P_1 and P_2 are graph patterns, then expressions (P_1 AND P_2), (P_1 OPT P_2) and (P_1 UNION P_2) are graph patterns (*conjunction graph pattern*, *optional graph pattern*, and *union graph pattern*, respectively).
3. If P is a graph pattern and $X \in I \cup V$, then (X GRAPH P) is a graph pattern.

4. If P is a graph pattern and R is a SPARQL *built-in* condition, then the expression (P FILTER R) is a graph pattern (a *filter graph pattern*).

A SPARQL *built-in* condition is constructed using elements of the set $I \cup L \cup V$ and constants, logical connectives ($\neg$, $\wedge$, $\vee$), ordering symbols ($<$, $\leq$, $\geq$, $>$), the equality symbol ($=$), unary predicates like bound, isBlank, and isIRI, plus other features (see [15] for a complete list). In this chapter, we restrict to the fragment of SPARQL where a built-in condition is a Boolean combination of terms constructed by using $=$ and bound, that is:

1. If $?X, ?Y \in V$ and $c \in I \cup L$, then bound($?X$), $?X = c$ and $?X = ?Y$ are (atomic) built-in conditions.
2. If R_1 and R_2 are built-in conditions, then $(\neg R_1)$, $(R_1 \vee R_2)$ and $(R_1 \wedge R_2)$ are built-in conditions.

Let P be a SPARQL graph pattern. In the rest of this chapter, we use var(P) to denote the set of variables occurring in P. In particular, if P is a basic graph pattern, then var(P) denotes the set of variables occurring in the triple patterns that form P. Similarly, for a built-in condition R, we use var(R) to denote the set of variables occurring in R.

We conclude the definition of the algebraic framework by describing the formal syntax of the SELECT query result form. A SELECT SPARQL query is simply a tuple (W, P), where P is a SPARQL graph pattern expression and W is a set of variables such that $W \subseteq \text{var}(P)$.

13.3.1 *Translating* SPARQL *into the Algebraic Formalism*

In this section, we show that every SPARQL query can be translated into the algebraic terminology introduced above. But before providing the procedure that performs this translation, we show how the examples of Sect. 13.2 can be written in the algebraic formalism.

Example 13.5 First, consider the query "Give the name and the mailbox of each person who has a mailbox with domain .cl" from Example 13.1. The following algebraic expression represents this query (when evaluated over the RDF graph `myDataSource.rdf`):

```
({?name, ?mbox},
  ((?x, http://xmlns.com/foaf/0.1/name, ?name) AND
   (?x, http://xmlns.com/foaf/0.1/mbox, ?mbox) AND
   (?mbox, http://example.com/ns#domain, ".cl")))
```

Second, consider the query "Give the name and the mailbox, if it is provided, of each person in the FOAF file of Bob", which was considered in Example 13.2. The following algebraic expression represents this query (when evaluated over the graph `http://example.org/foaf/bobFoaf`):

```
({?name, ?mbox},
   ((?x, http://xmlns.com/foaf/0.1/name, ?name) OPT
    (?x, http://xmlns.com/foaf/0.1/mbox, ?mbox)))
```

Third, consider the query: "For every person known by Alice and Bob, give the nicknames by which are known by Alice and Bob" from Example 13.3. This query can be expressed as follows in the algebraic formalism:

```
({?nickA, ?nickB},
   ((http://example.org/foaf/bobFoaf GRAPH
        ((?x, http://xmlns.com/foaf/0.1/knows, ?comm) OPT
          (?comm, http://xmlns.com/foaf/0.1/nick, ?nickB))) AND
     (http://example.org/foaf/aliceFoaf GRAPH
        ((?y, http://xmlns.com/foaf/0.1/knows, ?comm) OPT
          (?comm, http://xmlns.com/foaf/0.1/nick, ?nickA)))))
```

Finally, consider the query: "Give the list of people for whom Alice knows at least two nicknames" from Example 13.4. The following expression represents this query (when evaluated over the graph `http://example.org/foaf/aliceFoaf`):

```
({?y},
   (((?x, http://xmlns.com/foaf/0.1/knows, ?y) AND
     (?y, http://xmlns.com/foaf/0.1/nick, ?nick1) AND
     (?y, http://xmlns.com/foaf/0.1/nick, ?nick2))
                             FILTER (?nick1 != ?nick2)))
```

In Algorithm 13.1, we show a transformation function $\mathcal{T}$ of patterns in the SPARQL syntax into the algebraic formalism presented in this section. For the sake of readability, we assume that the translation of Triple Blocks (`TB`) is given (this translation is straightforward, but tedious due to the multiple representations of triples allowed in the SPARQL syntax).

Algorithm 13.1 Transformation $\mathcal{T}$ of SPARQL pattern syntax into algebraic syntax

// Input: a SPARQL graph pattern `GroupGP`
// Output: an algebraic expression $E = \mathcal{T}(\texttt{GroupGP})$
$E \leftarrow \emptyset$; $FS \leftarrow \emptyset$
for each syntactic form f in `GroupGP` **do**
  if f is `TB` **then** $E \leftarrow (E$ AND $\mathcal{T}(\texttt{TB}))$
  if f is `OPTIONAL GroupGP`$_1$ **then** $E \leftarrow (E$ OPT $\mathcal{T}(\texttt{GroupGP}_1))$
  if f is `GroupGP`$_1$ `UNION` $\cdots$ `UNION GroupGP`$_n$ **then**
    if $n > 1$ **then** $E' \leftarrow (\mathcal{T}(\texttt{GroupGP}_1)$ UNION $\cdots$ UNION $\mathcal{T}(\texttt{GroupGP}_n))$
    else $E' \leftarrow \mathcal{T}(\texttt{GroupGP}_1)$
    $E \leftarrow (E$ AND $E')$
  if f is `GRAPH VarOrIRIref GroupGP`$_1$ **then**
    $E \leftarrow (E$ AND (`VarOrIRIref` GRAPH $\mathcal{T}(\texttt{GroupGP}_1)))$
  if f is `FILTER constraint` **then** $FS \leftarrow (FS \wedge \texttt{constraint})$
end for
if $FS \neq \emptyset$ **then** $E \leftarrow (E$ FILTER $FS)$

For example, consider the following pattern written according to the official syntax of SPARQL:

```
{
    ?x :age ?y
    FILTER (?y > 30)
    ?x :knows ?z .
    ?z :home_country ?c
    FILTER (?c = "Chile")
    OPTIONAL { ?z :phone ?p }
}
```

Following the grammar of SPARQL given in Fig. 13.2, the above pattern is parsed as a single `GroupGP` that contains the syntactic forms `TB`, `Filter`, `TB`, `Filter` and `OptionalGP` (in that order), with the `OptionalGP` syntactic form containing a `GroupGP` composed by a single `TB` syntactic form.

The translation function in Algorithm 13.1 starts with $E = \{\}$ and $FS = \{\}$. Then it considers all the syntactic forms in the pattern obtaining that:

$$E = (((\{\} \text{ AND } \mathcal{T}(\texttt{TB}_1)) \text{ AND } \mathcal{T}(\texttt{TB}_2)) \text{ OPT } \mathcal{T}(\texttt{GroupGP}_1))$$
$$FS = (?Y > 30 \wedge ?C = \text{Chile})$$

where $\texttt{TB}_1$ is `?x :age ?y`, $\texttt{TB}_2$ is `?x :knows ?z . ?z :home_country ?c`, and $\texttt{GroupGP}_1$ is `{ ?z :phone ?p }`. The translations $\mathcal{T}(\texttt{TB}_1)$ and $\mathcal{T}(\texttt{TB}_2)$ are simply $\{(?X, \text{:age}, ?Y)\}$ and $\{(?X, \text{:knows}, ?Z), (?Z, \text{:home\_country}, ?C)\}$, respectively. To compute $\mathcal{T}(\texttt{GroupGP}_1)$, the algorithm proceeds recursively and gives as output the pattern:

$$E' = (\{\} \text{ AND } \{(?Z, \text{:phone}, ?P)\})$$

Thus, the final output of the algorithm is:

$$\begin{aligned}[((((\{\} \text{ AND } \{(?X, \text{:age}, ?Y)\}) \\ \text{AND } \{(?X, \text{:knows}, ?Z), (?Z, \text{:home\_country}, ?C)\}) \\ \text{OPT } (\{\} \text{ AND } \{(?Z, \text{:phone}, ?P)\})) \\ \text{FILTER } (?Y > 30 \wedge ?C = \text{Chile})]\end{aligned}$$

13.4 Semantics of SPARQL

To define the semantics of SPARQL graph pattern expressions, we use the algebraic representation of SPARQL introduced in the previous section.

We start by introducing some terminology. A *mapping* μ from V to T is a partial function $\mu : V \to T$. The domain of μ, denoted by $\text{dom}(\mu)$, is the subset of V where μ is defined. The empty mapping $\mu_\emptyset$ is a mapping such that $\text{dom}(\mu_\emptyset) = \emptyset$ (i.e. $\mu_\emptyset = \emptyset$). Given a triple pattern t and a mapping μ such that $\text{var}(t) \subseteq \text{dom}(\mu)$,

$\mu(t)$ is the triple obtained by replacing the variables in t according to μ. Similarly, given a basic graph pattern P and a mapping μ such that $\mathrm{var}(P) \subseteq \mathrm{dom}(\mu)$, we have that $\mu(P) = \bigcup_{t \in P}\{\mu(t)\}$, i.e., $\mu(P)$ is the set of triples obtained by replacing the variables in the triples of P according to μ.

We can now define the semantics for basic graph patterns as a function $[\![\cdot]\!]_G$ that given a basic graph pattern P returns a set of mappings.

Definition 13.2 Let G be an RDF graph, and P a basic graph pattern. The *evaluation* of P over G, denoted by $[\![P]\!]_G$, is defined as the set of mappings

$$[\![P]\!]_G = \{\mu : V \to T \mid \mathrm{dom}(\mu) = \mathrm{var}(P) \text{ and } \mu(P) \subseteq G\}$$

Notice that for every RDF graph G, it holds that $[\![\{\}]\!]_G = \{\mu_\emptyset\}$, i.e. the evaluation of an empty basic graph pattern against any graph results in the set containing only the empty mapping. For every basic graph pattern $P \neq \{\}$, we have that $[\![P]\!]_\emptyset = \emptyset$.

To define the semantics of more complex patterns, we need to introduce some more notions. Two mappings μ_1 and μ_2 are *compatible* when for all $x \in \mathrm{dom}(\mu_1) \cap \mathrm{dom}(\mu_2)$, it is the case that $\mu_1(x) = \mu_2(x)$, i.e., when $\mu_1 \cup \mu_2$ is also a mapping. Intuitively, μ_1 and μ_2 are compatible if μ_1 *can be extended* with μ_2 to obtain a new mapping, and vice versa. Note that two mappings with disjoint domains are always compatible and that the empty mapping $\mu_\emptyset$ is compatible with every other mapping.

Let Ω_1 and Ω_2 be sets of mappings. We define the join of, the union of and the difference between Ω_1 and Ω_2 as:

$$\Omega_1 \bowtie \Omega_2 = \{\mu_1 \cup \mu_2 \mid \mu_1 \in \Omega_1, \mu_2 \in \Omega_2 \text{ and } \mu_1, \mu_2 \text{ are compatible mappings}\}$$

$$\Omega_1 \cup \Omega_2 = \{\mu \mid \mu \in \Omega_1 \text{ or } \mu \in \Omega_2\}$$

$$\Omega_1 \smallsetminus \Omega_2 = \{\mu \in \Omega_1 \mid \text{ for all } \mu' \in \Omega_2,\ \mu \text{ and } \mu' \text{ are not compatible}\}$$

Based on the previous operators, we define the left outer-join as:

$$\Omega_1 ⟕ \Omega_2 = (\Omega_1 \bowtie \Omega_2) \cup (\Omega_1 \smallsetminus \Omega_2)$$

Intuitively, $\Omega_1 \bowtie \Omega_2$ is the set of mappings that result from extending mappings in Ω_1 with their compatible mappings in Ω_2, and $\Omega_1 \smallsetminus \Omega_2$ is the set of mappings in Ω_1 that cannot be extended with any mapping in Ω_2. The operation $\Omega_1 \cup \Omega_2$ is the usual set theoretical union. A mapping μ is in $\Omega_1 ⟕ \Omega_2$ if it is the extension of a mapping of Ω_1 with a compatible mapping of Ω_2, or if it belongs to Ω_1 and cannot be extended with any mapping of Ω_2. These operations resemble the relational algebra operations but over sets of mappings (partial functions).

We are ready to define the semantics of SPARQL graph pattern expressions as a function $[\![\cdot]\!]_G^{\mathcal{D}}$ which given a dataset $\mathcal{D}$ and a (target) graph G in $\mathcal{D}$, takes a pattern expression and returns a set of mappings. For the sake of readability, the semantics of filter expressions is presented in a separate definition.

Definition 13.3 Let $\mathcal{D}$ be an RDF dataset and G an RDF graph in $\mathcal{D}$. The *evaluation* of a graph pattern P over G in the dataset $\mathcal{D}$, denoted by $[\![\cdot]\!]_G^{\mathcal{D}}$, is defined recursively as follows:

1. if P is a basic graph pattern, then $[\![P]\!]_G^{\mathcal{D}} = [\![P]\!]_G$.
2. if P is $(P_1 \text{ AND } P_2)$, then $[\![P]\!]_G^{\mathcal{D}} = [\![P_1]\!]_G^{\mathcal{D}} \bowtie [\![P_2]\!]_G^{\mathcal{D}}$.
3. if P is $(P_1 \text{ OPT } P_2)$, then $[\![P]\!]_G^{\mathcal{D}} = [\![P_1]\!]_G^{\mathcal{D}} ⟕ [\![P_2]\!]_G^{\mathcal{D}}$.
4. if P is $(P_1 \text{ UNION } P_2)$, then $[\![P]\!]_G^{\mathcal{D}} = [\![P_1]\!]_G^{\mathcal{D}} \cup [\![P_2]\!]_G^{\mathcal{D}}$.
5. if P is $(X \text{ GRAPH } P_1)$, then:
   - if $X \in I$, then $[\![P]\!]_G^{\mathcal{D}} = [\![P_1]\!]_{d_{\mathcal{D}}(X)}^{\mathcal{D}}$,
   - if $X \in V$, then

$$[\![P]\!]_G^{\mathcal{D}} = \bigcup_{v \in \text{name}(\mathcal{D})} \left([\![P_1]\!]_{d_{\mathcal{D}}(v)}^{\mathcal{D}} \bowtie \{\mu_{X \to v}\}\right)$$

   where $\mu_{X \to v}$ is a mapping such that $\text{dom}(\mu) = \{X\}$ and $\mu(X) = v$.

Given a dataset $\mathcal{D}$ with default graph G_0, and a SPARQL pattern P, we say that the evaluation of P over dataset $\mathcal{D}$, denoted by $[\![P]\!]^{\mathcal{D}}$, is simply $[\![P]\!]_{G_0}^{\mathcal{D}}$.

The idea behind the OPT operator is to allow for *optional matching* of patterns. Consider pattern expression $(P_1 \text{ OPT } P_2)$ and let μ_1 be a mapping in $[\![P_1]\!]_G^{\mathcal{D}}$. If there exists a mapping $\mu_2 \in [\![P_2]\!]_G^{\mathcal{D}}$ such that μ_1 and μ_2 are compatible, then $\mu_1 \cup \mu_2$ belongs to $[\![(P_1 \text{ OPT } P_2)]\!]_G^{\mathcal{D}}$. But if no such a mapping μ_2 exists, then μ_1 belongs to $[\![(P_1 \text{ OPT } P_2)]\!]_G^{\mathcal{D}}$. Thus, operator OPT allows information to be added to a mapping μ if the information is available, instead of just rejecting μ whenever some part of the pattern does not match. This feature of *optional matching* is crucial in Semantic Web applications, and more specifically in RDF data management, where it is assumed that every application has only partial knowledge about the resources being managed.

The operator GRAPH is used to change the *target* RDF graph over which a pattern is being evaluated. An expression of the form $(X \text{ GRAPH } P)$, with X an IRI and P a graph pattern, is used to change the target RDF graph to the one whose name is X, and then to continue evaluating P over that RDF graph. The expression $(X \text{ GRAPH } P)$, with X a variable, is used to evaluate the pattern P over all the named RDF graphs in a dataset $\mathcal{D}$, and its result is the union of all these evaluations. Notice that before taking the union, for every $v \in \text{name}(\mathcal{D})$, the set of mappings obtained by evaluating pattern P over $d_{\mathcal{D}}(v)$ is joined with a mapping that assigns to variable X the value v. It should also be noticed that GRAPH is the only operator that can change the target RDF graph. Thus, if a pattern P does not contain any GRAPH expression, then the entire pattern is evaluated over a single RDF graph (the default graph of the RDF dataset). Therefore, if P is a SPARQL graph pattern expression that does not contain any GRAPH sub-expression, we simply write $[\![P]\!]_G$ to denote the set $[\![P]\!]_G^{\mathcal{D}}$. We use this notation in the following section when studying the complexity of evaluating graph pattern expressions.

The semantics of filter expressions goes as follows. Given a mapping μ and a built-in condition R, we define a notion of satisfaction of R by μ, denoted by $\mu \models R$, in a three valued logic (with values `true`, `false` and `error`). For an atomic built-in condition of the form $?X = c$, if $?X \notin \mathrm{dom}(\mu)$ the evaluation results in `error`; else, the evaluation results in `true` if $\mu(?X) = c$ and results in `false` otherwise. Similarly, for an atomic built-in condition of the form $?X = ?Y$, if $?X \notin \mathrm{dom}(\mu)$ or $?Y \notin \mathrm{dom}(\mu)$ the evaluation results in `error`; else, the evaluation results in `true` if $\mu(?X) = \mu(?Y)$ and results in `false` otherwise. For the case of bound(?X), the evaluation results in `true` if $?X \in \mathrm{dom}(\mu)$, and in `false` otherwise. For non-atomic constraints, the evaluation is defined as usual in a three valued logic:

R_1	R_2	$R_1 \wedge R_2$	$R_1 \vee R_2$
true	true	true	true
true	error	error	true
true	false	false	true
error	true	error	true
error	error	error	error
error	false	false	error
false	true	false	true
false	error	false	error
false	false	false	false

R_1	$\neg R_1$
true	false
error	error
false	true

Then $\mu \models R$ if and only if the evaluation of R against μ results in `true`.

Definition 13.4 Given an RDF dataset $\mathcal{D}$, an RDF graph G in $\mathcal{D}$, and a filter expression (P FILTER R), we have that $[\![(P \text{ FILTER } R)]\!]_G^{\mathcal{D}} = \{\mu \in [\![P]\!]_G^{\mathcal{D}} \mid \mu \models R\}$.

Several algebraic properties of graph patterns are proved in [11]. A simple property is that AND and UNION are associative and commutative. This permits us to avoid parentheses when writing sequences of AND operators or UNION operators. This is consistent with the definitions of Group Graph Pattern and Union Graph Pattern in [15]. To simplify the notation, when considering basic graph patterns composed by a single triple pattern $\{t\}$, we do not write the braces enclosing t. For example, for the pattern $((\{t_1\} \text{ UNION } \{t_2\}) \text{ OPT } \{t_3\})$, we simply write $((t_1 \text{ UNION } t_2) \text{ OPT } t_3)$. The following lemma shows that the base case for the syntax and semantics of SPARQL can also be defined in terms of triple patterns (instead of sets of triple patterns), as the semantics of basic graph patterns can be obtained by using the AND operator between triple patterns.

Lemma 13.1 *Let $\{t_1, t_2, \ldots, t_n\}$ be a basic graph pattern, where $n \geq 1$. Then for every dataset $\mathcal{D}$, it holds that:*

$$[\![\{t_1, t_2, \ldots, t_n\}]\!]^{\mathcal{D}} = [\![(t_1 \text{ AND } t_2 \text{ AND } \cdots \text{ AND } t_n)]\!]^{\mathcal{D}}$$

To formally define the semantics of SELECT SPARQL queries, we need the following notion. Given a mapping $\mu : V \to T$ and a set of variables $W \subseteq V$, the *restriction* of μ to W, denoted by $\mu_{|W}$, is a mapping such that $\text{dom}(\mu_{|W}) = \text{dom}(\mu) \cap W$ and $\mu_{|W}(?X) = \mu(?X)$ for every $?X \in \text{dom}(\mu) \cap W$.

Definition 13.5 Given a SELECT query (W, P), the evaluation of (W, P) in a dataset $\mathcal{D}$ is the set of mappings $[\![(W, P)]\!]^{\mathcal{D}} = \{\mu_{|W} \mid \mu \in [\![P]\!]^{\mathcal{D}}\}$.

In the rest of this chapter, we usually represent sets of mappings as tables where each row represents a mapping in the set. We label every row with the name of a mapping, and every column with the name of a variable. If a mapping is not defined for some variable, then we simply leave empty the corresponding position. For instance, the table:

	?X	?Y	?Z	?V	?W
μ_1 :	a	b			
μ_2 :		c			d
μ_3 :			e		

represents the set of mappings $\Omega = \{\mu_1, \mu_2, \mu_3\}$, where:

$$\text{dom}(\mu_1) = \{?X, ?Y\}, \quad \mu_1(?X) = a, \quad \text{and} \quad \mu_1(?Y) = b$$
$$\text{dom}(\mu_2) = \{?Y, ?W\}, \quad \mu_2(?Y) = c, \quad \text{and} \quad \mu_2(?W) = d$$
$$\text{dom}(\mu_3) = \{?Z\}, \quad \text{and} \quad \mu_3(?Z) = e$$

We sometimes write $\{\{?X \to a, ?Y \to b\}, \{?Y \to c, ?W \to d\}, \{?Z \to e\}\}$ for a set of mappings as the one above.

Example 13.6 Consider an RDF graph G storing information about professors in a university:

$$G = \big\{(B_1, \text{name}, \text{paul}), (B_1, \text{phone}, 777\text{-}3426), (B_2, \text{name}, \text{john}), (B_2, \text{email}, \text{john@acd.edu}), (B_3, \text{name}, \text{george}), (B_3, \text{webPage}, \text{www.george.edu}), (B_4, \text{name}, \text{ringo}), (B_4, \text{email}, \text{ringo@acd.edu}), (B_4, \text{webPage}, \text{www.starr.edu}), (B_4, \text{phone}, 888\text{-}4537)\big\}$$

Let $\mathcal{D}$ be an RDF dataset with G as its default graph and with no named graphs. The following are graph pattern expressions and their evaluations over $\mathcal{D}$. Since the graph patterns do not use the GRAPH operator, we denote their evaluation by $[\![\cdot]\!]_G$.

- $P_1 = ((?A, \text{email}, ?E) \text{ OPT } (?A, \text{webPage}, ?W))$. Then

$[\![P_1]\!]_G =$

	?A	?E	?W
μ_1 :	B_2	john@acd.edu	
μ_2 :	B_4	ringo@acd.edu	www.starr.edu

– $P_2 = (((?A, \text{name}, ?N) \text{ OPT } (?A, \text{email}, ?E)) \text{ OPT } (?A, \text{webPage}, ?W))$. Then

$[\![P_2]\!]_G =$

	?A	?N	?E	?W
μ_1:	B_1	paul		
μ_2:	B_2	john	john@acd.edu	
μ_3:	B_3	george		www.george.edu
μ_4:	B_4	ringo	ringo@acd.edu	www.starr.edu

– $P_3 = ((?A, \text{name}, ?N) \text{ OPT } ((?A, \text{email}, ?E) \text{ OPT } (?A, \text{webPage}, ?W)))$. Then

$[\![P_3]\!]_G =$

	?A	?N	?E	?W
μ_1:	B_1	paul		
μ_2:	B_2	john	john@acd.edu	
μ_3:	B_3	george		
μ_4:	B_4	ringo	ringo@acd.edu	www.starr.edu

Notice the difference between $[\![P_2]\!]_G$ and $[\![P_3]\!]_G$. These two examples show that $[\![((A \text{ OPT } B) \text{ OPT } C)]\!]_G \neq [\![(A \text{ OPT } (B \text{ OPT } C))]\!]_G$ in general.

– $P_4 = ((?A, \text{name}, ?N) \text{ AND } ((?A, \text{email}, ?E) \text{ UNION } (?A, \text{webPage}, ?W)))$. Then

$[\![P_4]\!]_G =$

	?A	?N	?E	?W
μ_1:	B_2	john	john@acd.edu	
μ_2:	B_3	george		www.george.edu
μ_3:	B_4	ringo	ringo@acd.edu	
μ_4:	B_4	ringo		www.starr.edu

– $P_5 = (((?A, \text{name}, ?N) \text{ OPT } (?A, \text{phone}, ?P)) \text{ FILTER } (?N = \text{paul}))$. Then

$[\![P_5]\!]_G =$

	?A	?N	?P
μ_1:	B_1	paul	777-3426

– $P_6 = (((?A, \text{name}, ?N) \text{ OPT } (?A, \text{phone}, ?P)) \text{ FILTER } (\neg \text{bound}(?P)))$. Then

$[\![P_6]\!]_G =$

	?A	?N	?P
μ_1:	B_2	john	
μ_2:	B_3	george	

The following example shows the evaluation of patterns that use operator GRAPH.

Example 13.7 Let G be the graph in Example 13.6 and consider the following RDF graph H:

$$H = \{(R_1, \text{name}, \text{mick}), (R_1, \text{email}, \text{mj@acd.edu}), (R_2, \text{name}, \text{keith}), (R_2, \text{email}, \text{keith@acd.edu})\}$$

Let $\mathcal{D} = \{\emptyset, \langle \text{tb}, G\rangle, \langle \text{trs}, H\rangle\}$ be an RDF dataset with empty default graph. The following are graph pattern expressions and their evaluations over $\mathcal{D}$.

– P_7 = (trs GRAPH (?A, name, ?N)). Then

$\llbracket P_7 \rrbracket^{\mathcal{D}} =$

	?A	?N
μ_1 :	R_1	mick
μ_2 :	R_2	keith

– P_8 = (?G GRAPH {(?A, name, ?N), (?A, email, ?E)}). Then

$\llbracket P_8 \rrbracket^{\mathcal{D}} =$

	?G	?A	?N	?E
μ_1 :	tb	B_2	john	john@acd.edu
μ_2 :	tb	B_4	ringo	ringo@acd.edu
μ_3 :	trs	R_1	mick	mj@acd.edu
μ_4 :	trs	R_2	keith	keith@acd.edu

Finally, the following example shows the evaluation of a SELECT pattern.

Example 13.8 Let $\mathcal{D}$ be the dataset in Example 13.7 and consider the pattern P_8 in that example. Then the evaluation of the SELECT query ({?G, ?N, ?E}, P_8) over $\mathcal{D}$ is the following set of mappings:

$\llbracket(\{?G, ?N, ?E\}, P_8)\rrbracket =$

	?G	?N	?E
μ_1 :	tb	john	john@acd.edu
μ_2 :	tb	ringo	ringo@acd.edu
μ_3 :	trs	mick	mj@acd.edu
μ_4 :	trs	keith	keith@acd.edu

13.4.1 Blank Nodes in Graph Patterns

The official specification of SPARQL [15] allows basic graph patterns to have blank nodes in their triple patterns. Blank nodes in graph patterns are essentially defined as variables whose values cannot be retrieved by a query. In what follows, we extend the definitions of the previous sections to consider graph patterns with blank nodes.

We extend the definition of triple patterns to be tuples in the set $(T \cup V) \times (I \cup V) \times (T \cup V)$, that is, triple patterns are now allowed to have blank nodes as components. Similarly, we extend the definition of basic graph patterns. Also for a triple pattern t and a basic graph pattern P, we define blank(t) and blank(P) as the sets of blank nodes appearing in t and P, respectively.

Definition 13.6 Let G be an RDF graph and P a basic graph pattern with blank nodes. Then the evaluation of P over G, denoted by $\llbracket P \rrbracket_G$, is defined as the set of all mappings μ such that:

- dom(μ) = var(P),
- and there exists a substitution θ : blank(P) $\to$ term(G) such that $\mu(\theta(P)) \subseteq G$,

where $\theta(P)$ is the basic graph pattern that results from replacing the blank nodes of P according to θ.

This definition extends the definition of the semantics of a basic graph pattern P not mentioning blanks nodes, as by using the substitution $\theta : \emptyset \rightarrow \text{term}(G)$, we obtain the same set of mappings as in Definition 13.2 for pattern P (since $\theta(P) = P$).

Now, given a dataset $\mathcal{D}$ and a general graph pattern P constructed from basic graph patterns possibly with blank nodes, the evaluation of P over $\mathcal{D}$ is defined as in the previous section but with Definition 13.6 as the base case.

Example 13.9 Let G be the RDF graph in Example 13.6, and consider the basic graph pattern $P = \{(X, \text{name}, ?N), (X, \text{email}, ?E)\}$, where X is a blank node. Notice that, if we use a substitution $\theta : \text{blank}(P) \rightarrow \text{term}(G)$ such that $\theta(X) = B_2$, and a mapping $\mu = \{?N \rightarrow \text{john}, ?E \rightarrow \text{john@acd.edu}\}$, then we have that $\mu(\theta(P)) \subseteq G$. Thus, μ is in the evaluation of P over G. In fact, the evaluation of P over G is the set of mappings:

$[\![P]\!]_G =$

	?N	?E
μ_1:	john	john@acd.edu
μ_2:	ringo	ringo@acd.edu

13.4.2 Bag Semantics of SPARQL

A *bag* Ω of mappings is a set of mappings in which every mapping is *annotated* with a positive integer that represents its *cardinality* in Ω. We denote the cardinality of the mapping μ in the bag Ω by $\text{card}_\Omega(\mu)$ (or simply $\text{card}(\mu)$ when Ω is understood from the context). If $\mu \notin \Omega$, then $\text{card}_\Omega(\mu) = 0$.

In Sect. 13.4, we consider operations between sets of mappings. Those operations can be extended to bags by, roughly speaking, making the operations not to discard duplicates. Formally, if Ω_1, Ω_2 are bags of mappings, then:

$$\text{for } \mu \in \Omega_1 \bowtie \Omega_2, \quad \text{card}_{\Omega_1 \bowtie \Omega_2}(\mu) = \sum_{\mu = \mu_1 \cup \mu_2} \text{card}_{\Omega_1}(\mu_1) \cdot \text{card}_{\Omega_2}(\mu_2)$$

$$\text{for } \mu \in \Omega_1 \cup \Omega_2, \quad \text{card}_{\Omega_1 \cup \Omega_2}(\mu) = \text{card}_{\Omega_1}(\mu) + \text{card}_{\Omega_2}(\mu)$$

$$\text{for } \mu \in \Omega_1 \smallsetminus \Omega_2, \quad \text{card}_{\Omega_1 \smallsetminus \Omega_2}(\mu) = \text{card}_{\Omega_1}(\mu)$$

The bag semantics of basic graph patterns that contain blank nodes is formalized in the following definition. This formalization is used as the base case for the bag semantics of SPARQL graph patterns.

Definition 13.7 Consider a basic graph pattern P (possibly with blank nodes) and an RDF graph G. The cardinality of the mapping $\mu \in [\![P]\!]_G$ is defined as the number of distinct substitutions $\theta : \text{blank}(P) \rightarrow \text{term}(G)$ such that $\mu(\theta(P)) \subseteq G$, i.e.,

$$\text{card}_{[\![P]\!]_G}(\mu) = \left|\{\theta : \text{blank}(P) \rightarrow \text{term}(G) \mid \mu(\theta(P)) \subseteq G\}\right|$$

For a basic graph pattern P, without blank nodes, every solution $\mu \in [\![P]\!]_G$ has cardinality 1, as in this case the only possible substitution is $\theta : \emptyset \rightarrow \text{term}(G)$.

Given a dataset $\mathcal{D}$ and a general graph pattern P constructed from basic graph patterns possibly with blank nodes, we define the bag semantics of P over $\mathcal{D}$ simply as in Definition 13.3, but applying bag operators and considering the semantics of basic graph patterns as in Definition 13.7.

We define now the bag semantics of SPARQL SELECT queries. Informally, when considering bag semantics, to evaluate a SELECT query $q = (W, P)$, we simply take the projection of the evaluation of P over W but without discarding duplicates. Formally, given a SPARQL SELECT query (W, P) and a mapping μ in the evaluation of (W, P) over a dataset $\mathcal{D}$, we define the cardinality of μ in $[\![P]\!]^{\mathcal{D}}$ as:

$$\text{card}_{[\![(W,P)]\!]^{\mathcal{D}}}(\mu) = \sum_{\nu \in [\![P]\!]^{\mathcal{D}} \,:\, \nu_{|W} = \mu} \text{card}_{[\![P]\!]^{\mathcal{D}}}(\nu).$$

Example 13.10 Consider the RDF graph:

$$G = \{(\text{Alice}, \text{knows}, \text{Bob}), (\text{Alice}, \text{knows}, \text{Peter}), (\text{Bob}, \text{knows}, \text{Peter})\}$$

and the basic graph pattern $P = \{(?X, \text{knows}, B)\}$ with B a blank node. Now consider the mapping $\mu_1 = \{?X \rightarrow \text{Alice}\}$, and the substitutions θ_1 and θ_2 from blank(P) to term(G) such that $\theta_1(B) = \text{Bob}$ and $\theta_2(B) = \text{Peter}$. Then it holds that $\mu_1(\theta_1(P)) \subseteq G$ and that $\mu_1(\theta_2(P)) \subseteq G$. Thus, we have that μ_1 is in $[\![P]\!]_G$ and that the cardinality of μ_1 is 2. If we consider the mapping $\mu_2 = \{?X \rightarrow \text{Bob}\}$, then we have that μ_2 is also in $[\![P]\!]_G$ and that the cardinality of μ_2 is 1.

Example 13.11 As an example of the evaluation of a SELECT query under bag semantics, consider the dataset $\mathcal{D}$ and the pattern P_8 of Example 13.7, and the SELECT query $(\{?G\}, P_8)$. Then the evaluation of $(\{?G\}, P_8)$ over $\mathcal{D}$ is composed by the mappings $\mu_1 = \{?G \rightarrow \text{tb}\}$ and $\mu_2 = \{?G \rightarrow \text{trs}\}$, both with cardinality 2.

13.5 On the Complexity of the Evaluation Problem

A fundamental issue in every query language is the complexity of query evaluation and, in particular, what is the influence of each component of the language in this complexity.

In this section, we study the complexity of the evaluation of SPARQL graph patterns, reviewing some of the results in the literature regarding this problem. The first study about the complexity of SPARQL was published in [11], and some refinements of the complexity results of [11] were presented in [13, 17]. We present here a study of the complexity that follows [11], considering fragments of SPARQL graph patterns built incrementally, and presenting complexity results for each such fragment.

In this section, we focus on the core fragment of SPARQL and, thus, we impose the following restrictions to graph patterns and to the evaluation process. First, we will be mainly focused on the evaluation of SPARQL patterns, that is, we do not consider SELECT queries, and we restrict to the evaluation over a single RDF graph, that is, we do not consider the GRAPH operator. Second, we assume that graph patterns do not contain blank nodes. And third, we focus on the set semantics of graph patterns, that is, we do not consider the cardinality of mappings when evaluating SPARQL patterns. It would be interesting to investigate whether the complexity results that we present in this section can be extended to the bag-semantics case. We left this study for future work.

As is customary when studying the complexity of the evaluation problem for a query language [18], we consider its associated decision problem. We denote this problem by EVALUATION and we define it as follows:

INPUT	: An RDF graph G, a graph pattern P, and a mapping μ.
QUESTION	: Is $\mu \in [\![P]\!]_G$?

It is important to recall that we are assuming that P in the above definition does not contain blank nodes, and that $[\![P]\!]_G$ is the set-based evaluation of P over the RDF graph G. Also notice that the evaluation problem that we study considers the mapping as part of the input. That is, we study the complexity by measuring how difficult it is to verify whether a given mapping is a solution for a pattern evaluated over an RDF graph. This is the standard *decision* problem considered when studying the complexity of a query language [18], as opposed to the *computation* problem of actually listing the set of solutions (finding all the mappings). To focus on the associated decision problem allows us to obtain a fine grained analysis of the complexity of the evaluation problem, classifying the complexity for different fragments of SPARQL in terms of standard complexity classes. Also notice that the pattern P and the graph G are both inputs in the definition of EVALUATION. Thus, we study the *combined complexity* of the query language [18].

We start this study by considering the fragment consisting of graph pattern expressions constructed by using only AND and FILTER operators. This simple fragment is interesting as it does not use the two most complicated operators in SPARQL, namely UNION and OPT. Given an RDF graph G, a graph pattern P in this fragment and a mapping μ, it is possible to efficiently check whether $\mu \in [\![P]\!]_G$ by using the following simple algorithm [11]. First, for each triple t in P, verify whether $\mu(t) \in G$. If this is not the case, then return *false*. Otherwise, by using a bottom-up approach, verify whether the expression generated by instantiating the variables in P according to μ satisfies the FILTER conditions in P. If this is the case, then return *true*, else return *false*.

Theorem 13.1 [11] EVALUATION *can be solved in time* $O(|P| \cdot |G|)$ *for graph pattern expressions constructed by using only* AND *and* FILTER *operators.*

We continue this study by adding the UNION operator to the AND-FILTER fragment. It is important to notice that the inclusion of UNION in SPARQL is one of the most controversial issues in the definition of this language. The following theorem proved in [11], shows that the inclusion of the UNION operator makes the evaluation problem for SPARQL considerably harder.

Theorem 13.2 [11] EVALUATION *is NP-complete for graph pattern expressions constructed by using only* AND, FILTER *and* UNION *operators.*

It is straightforward to prove that EVALUATION is in NP for the case of graph pattern expressions constructed by using only AND, UNION and FILTER operators. The NP-hardness proof presented in [11] relies on a reduction from the satisfiability problem for propositional formulas in CNF (SAT-CNF). An instance of SAT-CNF is a propositional formula φ of the form $C_1 \wedge \cdots \wedge C_n$, where each C_i ($i \in [1, n]$) is a clause, that is, a disjunction of propositional variables and negations of propositional variables. Then the problem is to verify whether there exists a truth assignment satisfying φ. It is well known that SAT-CNF is NP-complete [6]. In the encoding presented in [11], the authors use a fixed RDF graph D and a fixed mapping μ. Then they show how to encode a SAT-CNF formula by using SPARQL variables to encode literals (propositional variables and negations of propositional variables), AND and UNION to encode $\wedge$ and $\vee$, respectively, and FILTER restrictions to ensure that if a truth assignment assigns value true to a literal ℓ, then it must assign value false to the negation of ℓ (and vice versa).

We now consider the OPT operator, which is the most involved operator in graph pattern expressions and, definitively, the most difficult to define. The following theorem proved in [11] shows that when considering all the operators in SPARQL graph patterns, the evaluation problem becomes considerably harder.

Theorem 13.3 [11] EVALUATION *is PSPACE-complete.*

The membership in PSPACE is given by Algorithm 13.2. Given a mapping μ, a pattern P, and an RDF graph G, the algorithm verifies whether $\mu \in [\![P]\!]_G$. In the procedure, we use $\text{pos}(P, G)$ to denote the set of mappings ν such that $\text{dom}(\nu) \subseteq \text{var}(P)$ and for every variable $?X \in \text{dom}(\nu)$, it holds that $\nu(?X)$ is a value in $\text{term}(G)$.

It is easy to see that the procedure is correct (it is essentially applying the definition of the set-semantics of the SPARQL operators). Given that the size needed to store the name of a variable in $\text{var}(P)$ is $O(\log|P|)$ and the size needed to store an element of G is $O(\log|G|)$, we obtain that the size of a mapping in $\text{pos}(P, G)$ is $O(|P| \cdot (\log|P| + \log|G|))$. Thus, given that the depth of the tree of recursive calls to **Eval** is $O(|P|)$, we have that procedure **Eval** can be implemented by using a polynomial amount of space.

To prove the PSPACE-hardness of EVALUATION, the authors show in [11] how to reduce in polynomial time the quantified boolean formula problem (QBF) to

Algorithm 13.2 Eval(μ: mapping, P: graph pattern, G: RDF graph)

```
case:
P is a triple pattern t:
  if dom(μ) = var(t) and μ(t) ∈ G then return true
  return false
P is a pattern of the form (P1 FILTER R):
  if Eval(μ, P1, G) = true and μ ⊨ R then return true
  return false
P is a pattern of the form (P1 UNION P2):
  if Eval(μ, P1, G) = true or Eval(μ, P2, G) = true then return true
  return false
P is a pattern of the form (P1 AND P2):
  for each pair of mappings μ1 ∈ pos(P1, G) and μ2 ∈ pos(P2, G)
   if Eval(μ1, P1, G) = true and Eval(μ2, P2, G) = true and μ = μ1 ∪ μ2 then return
    true
  return false
P is a pattern of the form (P1 OPT P2):
  if Eval(μ, (P1 AND P2), G) = true then return true
  if Eval(μ, P1, G) = true then
    for each mapping μ' ∈ pos(P2, G)
      if Eval(μ', P2, G) = true and μ is compatible with μ' then return false
    return true
  return false
```

EVALUATION. An instance of QBF is a quantified propositional formula φ of the form:

$$\forall x_1 \exists y_1 \forall x_2 \exists y_2 \cdots \forall x_m \exists y_m \, \psi,$$

where ψ is a quantifier-free formula of the form $C_1 \wedge \cdots \wedge C_n$, with each C_i ($i \in \{1, \ldots, n\}$) being a clause, that is, a disjunction of propositional variables and negations of propositional variables. Then the problem is to verify whether φ is valid. It is known that QBF is PSPACE-complete [6]. In the encoding presented in [11], the authors use a fixed RDF graph G and a fixed mapping μ. Then they encode formula φ with a pattern P_φ that uses nested OPT operators to encode the *quantifier alternation* of φ, and a graph pattern not mentioning the optional operator to encode the satisfiability of formula ψ.

When verifying whether $\mu \in [\![P]\!]_G$, it is natural to assume that the size of P is considerably smaller than the size of G. This assumption is very common when studying the complexity of a query language. In fact, it is named *data complexity* in the database literature [18], and it is defined as the complexity of the evaluation problem for a fixed query. More precisely, for the case of SPARQL, given a graph pattern expression P, the evaluation problem for P, denoted by EVALUATION(P), has as input an RDF graph G and a mapping μ, and the problem is to verify whether $\mu \in [\![P]\!]_G$. The following result shows that the data-complexity of the evaluation problem for SPARQL patterns is in LOGSPACE.

Theorem 13.4 EVALUATION(P) *is in LOGSPACE for every graph pattern expression P.*

To see why the above theorem holds, consider Algorithm 13.2. The space needed to store a mapping in $\text{pos}(P, G)$ is $O(|P| \cdot (\log|P| + \log|G|))$, and this bound becomes $O(\log|G|)$ when P is considered to be fixed. Thus, given that the depth of the tree of recursive calls to **Eval** is a fixed constant if P is considered to be fixed, we obtain that **Eval** can be implemented by using logarithmic space in this case.

13.6 Related Work

Most of the material presented in this chapter comes from [11]. At the time when [11] was published, there were two main proposals for the semantics of SPARQL graph pattern expressions. The first was an operational semantics, consisting essentially in the execution of a depth-first traversal of parse trees of graph pattern expressions, and the use of intermediate results to avoid some computations. At that time, this approach was followed by ARQ [2] (a language developed by HPLabs), and by the W3C when evaluating graph pattern expressions containing nested optionals [16]. For instance, the computation of the mappings satisfying (A OPT (B OPT C)) was done by first computing the mappings that match A, then checking which of these mappings match B and for those that match B checking whether they also match C [16]. The second approach, compositional in spirit and the one advocated in [11], extended classical conjunctive query evaluation [7] and was based on a bottom up evaluation of parse trees of graph pattern expressions, borrowing notions of relational algebra evaluation [4, 8] plus some additional features. Currently, the official specification of SPARQL [15], endorsed by the W3C, formalizes a semantics based on [11], that we also follow in this chapter.

Since the beginning of the SPARQL standardization process by the W3C there have been efforts to formalize the semantics of the language. In [4], Cyganiak presents a relational model of SPARQL. The author uses modified versions of the standard relational algebra operators (join, left outer join, projection, selection, etc.) to model SPARQL `SELECT` clauses. The central idea in [4] is to make a correspondence between SPARQL queries and relational algebra queries over a single relation *Triple*(*subject*, *predicate*, *object*), that stores RDF graphs in the form of triples. In [4], the author discusses some drawbacks of using classical relational algebra operators to define the semantics of SPARQL, and identifies cases in which his formalization does not match the SPARQL official specification. Additionally, a translation system between SPARQL and SQL is outlined in [4]. The system extensively uses `COALESCE` and `IS NULL`/`IS NOT NULL` operators to accurately resemble some SPARQL features. With different motivations, but similar philosophy, Harris et al. present in [8] an implementation of a simple fragment of SPARQL in a relational database engine (they use relational algebra operators similar to the ones used in [4]).

As noted in [4], the treatment of null values is the major problem encountered when trying to specify the semantics of SPARQL by means of standard relational algebra. Since mappings must be modeled as relational tuples, null values need to be used to model unbounded variables. Zaniolo introduces in [19] an algebra to deal with null values in relational databases. The author interprets null values as standing for "no information", as opposed with the more complex "unknown" and "nonexistent" interpretations [9]. In [19], a *relation with null values* is defined as a set of tuples of not necessarily the same arity, which possibly contain null values in some of their components. The author then defines operators over those relations with nulls that generalize the standard relational algebra operators. The treatment of null values in [19] matches the treatment of unbounded variables in SPARQL. Thus, the operators over sets of mappings introduced in Sect. 13.3 can be easily modeled within the framework of [19]. Although the formalization in [19] can be used to define the semantics of SPARQL, we follow a simplified approach formalizing only what is strictly necessary in the SPARQL context, and thus simplifying the subsequent study of the language.

DeBruin et al. [3] study the semantics of the conjunctive fragment of SPARQL (graph patterns using only the AND operator, plus the `SELECT` clause) from a logical point of view. This semantics slightly differs from the definition in [15] on the issue of blank nodes. In their approach, blanks play the role of "non-distinguished" variables, that is, variables that are not presented in the answer.

In [14], Polleres studies the problem of translating SPARQL queries into Datalog queries. Based on [11], the author proposes three different semantics: (1) bravely-joining, (2) cautiously-joining and (3) strictly-joining semantics. These semantics are obtained by strengthening the notion of compatible mappings, and thus, strengthening the conditions under which unbound variables are joined. Strictly-joining semantics essentially resembles the inner-join condition of SQL, allowing a simple translation into Datalog. Bravely-joining semantics coincides with the semantics presented in Sect. 13.4. To translate the bravely-joining semantics into Datalog, a special predicate *BOUND*(·) is needed to test whether a variable is bounded to a non-null value. As a result, the translation generates a program with disjunctions in the bodies of the rules that extensively uses ¬*BOUND*(·). The program is then transformed into Datalog by using standard techniques [14].

13.7 Conclusion

The query language SPARQL has been in the process of standardization since 2004. In this process, the semantics of the language has played a key role. A formalization of a semantics is beneficial on several grounds: help in identifying relationships among the constructors that stay hidden in the use cases, identify redundant and contradicting notions, study the expressiveness and complexity of the language, help in optimizing the evaluation of queries, etc. In this chapter, we have provided such a formal semantics for SPARQL, and we have reviewed some results concerning the complexity of evaluating SPARQL graph patterns.

Acknowledgements We would like to thank Alejandro Mallea for many useful comments. The authors were supported by: Arenas—Fondecyt grant 1090565; Gutierrez—Fondecyt grant 1070348; Pérez—Conicyt Ph.D. Scholarship. We would like to thank Alejandro Mallea for many useful comments.

References

1. Angles, R., Gutierrez, C.: The expressive power of SPARQL. In: Proceedings of the Seventh International Semantic Web Conference, pp. 114–129 (2008)
2. ARQ. A SPARQL processor for Jena, version 1.3 March 2006, Hewlett-Packard Development Company. http://jena.sourceforge.net/ARQ
3. de Bruijn, J., Franconi, E., Tessaris, S.: Logical reconstruction of normative rdf. In: OWLED
4. Cyganiak, R.: A relational algebra for SPARQL. Tech. Rep. HPL-2005-170, HP-Labs. http://www.hpl.hp.com/techreports/2005/HPL-2005-170.html
5. Durst, M., Suignard, M.: RFC 3987, Internationalized Resource Identifiers (IRIs). http://www.ietf.org/rfc/rfc3987.txt
6. Garey, M.R., Johnson, D.S.: Computers and Intractability: A Guide to the Theory of NP-Completeness. Freeman, New York (1979)
7. Gutierrez, C., Hurtado, C., Mendelzon, A.: Foundations of Semantic Web databases. In: Proceedings of the Twenty-Third ACM Symposium on Principles of Database Systems (PODS), pp. 95–106 (2004)
8. Harris, S., Shadbolt, N.: SPARQL query processing with conventional relational database systems. In: WISE Workshops, pp. 235–244
9. Imielinski, T., Lipski, W.: Incomplete information in relational databases. J. ACM **31**(4), 761–791 (1984)
10. Klyne, G., Carroll, J.J., McBride, B.: Resource Description Framework (RDF): Concepts and Abstract Syntax. W3C Recommendation 10 February 2004. http://www.w3.org/TR/rdf-concepts/
11. Pérez, J., Arenas, M., Gutierrez, C.: Semantics and complexity of SPARQL. In: Proceedings of the Fifth International Semantic Web Conference (ISWC), pp. 30–43 (2006)
12. Pérez, J., Arenas, M., Gutierrez, C.: Semantics of SPARQL. Technical Report, Universidad de Chile TR/DCC-2006-17, October 2006
13. Pérez, J., Arenas, M., Gutierrez, C.: Semantics and complexity of SPARQL. ACM Trans. Database Syst. **34**(3) (2009)
14. Polleres, A.: From SPARQL to rules (and back). In: WWW, pp. 787–796
15. Prud'hommeaux, E., Seaborne, A.: SPARQL Query Language for RDF. W3C Recommendation 15 January 2008. http://www.w3.org/TR/2008/REC-rdf-sparql-query-20080115/
16. Seaborne, A.: Personal communication (2006)
17. Schmidt, M., Meier, M., Lausen, G.: Foundations of SPARQL Query Optimization. arXiv.org paper arXiv:0812.3788v1, December 19, 2008
18. Vardi, M.Y.: The complexity of relational query languages (extended abstract). In: STOC 1982, pp. 137–146
19. Zaniolo, C.: Database relations with null values. J. Comput. Syst. Sci. **28**(1), 142–166 (1984)

Chapter 14
Labeling RDF Graphs for Linear Time and Space Querying

Tim Furche, Antonius Weinzierl, and François Bry

Abstract Indices and data structures for web querying have mostly considered tree shaped data, reflecting the view of XML documents as tree-shaped. However, for RDF (and when querying ID/IDREF constraints in XML) data is indisputably graph-shaped. In this chapter, we first study existing indexing and labeling schemes for RDF and other graph datawith focus on support for efficient adjacency and reachability queries. For XML, labeling schemes are an important part of the wide-spread adoption of XML, in particular for mapping XML to existing (relational) database technology. However, the existing indexing and labeling schemes for RDF (and graph data in general) sacrifice one of the most attractive properties of XML labeling schemes, the constant time (and per-node space) test for adjacency (child) and reachability (descendant). In the second part, we introduce the first labeling scheme for RDF data that retains this property and thus achieves linear time and space processing of acyclic RDF queries on a significantly larger class of graphs than previous approaches (which are mostly limited to tree-shaped data). Finally, we show how this labeling scheme can be applied to (acyclic) SPARQL queries to obtain an evaluation algorithm with time and space complexity *linear in the number of resources* in the queried RDF graph.

T. Furche (✉) · F. Bry
Institute for Informatics, University of Munich, Oettingenstraße 67, 80538 Munich, Germany
e-mail: tim@furche.net
url: http://www.pms.ifi.lmu.de/

F. Bry
e-mail: bry@lmu.de

A. Weinzierl
Knowledge-based Systems Group, Technische Universität Wien, Favoritenstraße 9-11, 1040 Wien, Austria
e-mail: aweinz@kr.tuwien.ac.at
url: http://www.kr.tuwien.ac.at/staff/aweinz/

R. De Virgilio et al. (eds.), *Semantic Web Information Management*,
DOI 10.1007/978-3-642-04329-1_14, © Springer-Verlag Berlin Heidelberg 2010

14.1 Introduction

"Interesting data is *relationships*" (Tim Berners-Lee).[1] To support this view of data, initiatives such as RDF (resource description framework) and Linked Data have been launched and are increasingly adopted beyond just an enthusiast and academic community (cf. RDFa's use by Google).

What relationships exist between entities (resources) on the web can not be regulated in advance. From a data management perspective, this renders storage and access schemes that rely on fixed, pre-established schemata mostly void in the web context. Rather than storing and accessing relations of a particular schema, web data management solutions have to deal with data in widely varying, constantly changing schemata.

Storage and access schemes specifically tailored to these properties of relationships on the web are therefore needed. For XML (extensible markup language), where data is mostly considered tree shaped, such schemes have been developed and implemented with great success, in particular in the form of labeling schemes.

Labeling schemes assign labels to nodes in a tree or graph in such a way that various relations between nodes can be decided given just the labels of two nodes. They have proved to be one of the most pertinent techniques for time and space efficient XML processing and are nowadays employed in most XML databases [6, 35]. Labeling schemes are particularly interesting if queries are mostly concerned with the relationships between entities in a query, e.g., the existence of a certain relation, the reachability between two entities, etc.

For RDF, however, previously proposed storage and access schemes have, with few exceptions, been adjacency- (storing triples directly and using standard joins for reconstructing the graph structure) or schema-based (exploiting regularities in the shape of RDF sub-graphs, e.g., that most resources of a given type have certain properties). The reason for this lack is that graph data poses a greater challenge for labeling schemes than tree data. Though labeling schemes for RDF and similar graph data have been developed [1, 10, 43, 44], these labeling schemes have failed to preserve, for all or at least a significant number of RDF graphs, those essential properties that have made tree labeling schemes a success.

In this chapter, we describe the first labeling scheme for RDF that retains most of the following characteristics of tree labeling schemes:

1. *Constant* time *adjacency* test. In other words, the ability to test, in constant time, whether a given triple holds in the queried RDF graph.
2. *Enumeration* of all adjacent resources for a given resource in time *linear* in the number of adjacent resources (but independent of the number of overall resources in the graph). In other words, the ability to enumerate all properties of a given resource in time linear in the number of these properties.
3. *Constant* time *reachability* test. In other words, the ability to test, in constant time, whether there is a path between two resources in the RDF graph. Just

[1]Talk on "The Next Web and Linked Data", at TED 2009, http://www.ted.com/index.php/talks/lang/eng/tim_berners_lee_on_the_next_web.html.

like for adjacency, enumeration of reachable resources is linear in the number of reachable resources, rather than the overall graph.
4. *Constant* size labels[2] and thus a *linear overall size* of the labeling (index) in the number of resources in the graph.
5. *Polynomial* labeling algorithm that computes the labeling for a given graph.

All these characteristics hold for tree data, e.g., for the pre-/post-encoding used in [6]. However, none of the previously proposed labeling scheme for graph (or specifically RDF data) retains these properties. Though on arbitrary graphs, our approach degenerates to quadratic space complexity (as previous approaches), we present the first characterisation of a class of graphs for which these properties are retained yet that is a nontrivial proper super-class of all structures (like XML trees) for which such a guarantee has been shown previously.

14.1.1 Contributions

To summarize, we present a labeling scheme for RDF data that:

- Generalizes interval based tree labeling schemes, such as the pre-/post-encoding [6] or the labeling schemes used in SPEX [31, 33] and CAA [30], to arbitrary graphs. It combines a fast adjacency test (at worst logarithmic in the number of nodes) with often significantly lower storage than adjacency-based schemes (including adjacency lists), see Sect. 14.5.
- Retains the most important properties of tree labeling schemes (see Sect. 14.4.1) to a significantly larger class of graphs, so-called CIGs, than any previous labeling scheme (see Sect. 14.4.2 on previous graph labeling schemes):

  1. constant-time adjacency (and reachability) test,
  2. constant label size, thus linear overall size of the labeling,
  3. linear time enumeration of adjacent (and reachable) nodes,
  4. polynomial time labeling algorithm.

  The formal definition of CIGs and their properties are given in Sect. 14.6.
- Performs on tree data as good as the best known tree labeling schemes and thus is ideally suited when both tree, CIG, and general graph data is to be processed, see Sect. 14.7.
- Allows the linear time and space evaluation of acyclic SPARQL queries and provides an efficient basis for full SPARQL implementation, see Sect. 14.7.

Table 14.1 summarizes the complexity results for evaluating three subsets of SPARQL based on the CIG-labeling: for single, ground triple patterns (i.e., testing

[2]In this chapter, we adopt the common convention to disregard that the bit size of labels scales logarithmically with the size of the data. This is reasonable as such labels are usually stored in attributes of a fixed numerical type (such as SQL's `INT` or `BIGINT` type). If label bit size is of concern, a logarithmic, multiplicative factor in the size of the graph is to be added to all complexities.

Table 14.1 Complexity of query evaluation with the CIG-labeling (time and space complexity are the same in all cases except for single, ground triple patterns, where the space complexity is given after the time complexity); q query size, n data size, q_g: number of "graph" variables, i.e., variables with multiple incoming query edges)

Data	Single, ground triple pattern	Acyclic basic graph pattern	Full graph pattern
tree	$\mathcal{O}(\log n), \mathcal{O}(1)$	$\mathcal{O}(q \cdot n)$	$\mathcal{O}(n^{q_g} + q \cdot n)$
CIG	$\mathcal{O}(\log n), \mathcal{O}(1)$	$\mathcal{O}(q \cdot n)$	$\mathcal{O}(n^{q_g} + q \cdot n)$
graph	$\mathcal{O}(\log n), \mathcal{O}(n^2)$	$\mathcal{O}(q \cdot n^2)$	$\mathcal{O}(n^{q_g} + q \cdot n^2)$

whether a graph contains a given triple of only named resources), which corresponds to testing adjacency between the two resources in the triple; for acyclic (as in [21]) SPARQL graph patterns with variables and filters; for full SPARQL graph patterns. Note, that there is no penalty at all to going from tree data to CIG data, but arbitrary graph data does incur a logarithmic penalty in time (and a linear penalty in space).

The rest of this chapter is organized as follows: First, we briefly introduce or revisit a few notions on RDF and SPARQL needed in the rest of the paper (Sect. 14.3). Then we investigate existing labeling schemes for RDF and graph data in general, with a brief perspective also on XML labeling schemes (Sect. 14.4), as these form the basis for many RDF labeling schemes. Section 14.5 finally introduces the general CIG-labeling scheme and its properties on arbitrary graphs. For trees and the novel class of CIGs, it is shown in Sect. 14.6 that a CIG-labeling with constant label size can be found in polynomial time. In Sect. 14.7, we briefly discuss how the CIG-labeling is used to evaluate acyclic and full SPARQL queries and even some nSPARQL [38] path expressions.

14.2 Motivating Example

The principle idea of the proposed labeling builds on a property from XML query engines such as SPEX [33] and CAA [30]: to order the nodes of the XML tree in such a way, that we can describe adjacency between nodes through intervals over that order, rather than through explicit storage of the pairs of adjacent nodes.

Our labeling scheme, called CIG-labeling, generalizes this property to general graphs: In a CIG-labeling, each node n is labeled with a pair (l_n, I_n) such that:

1. l_n is the position of n in some order over the nodes of the graph and
2. I_n is a set of non-overlapping intervals that covers all adjacent nodes of n.

Figure 14.1 shows an RDF graph about roman emperors, their relations, and the provinces they ruled.[3] We only show provinces that changed ownership in the

[3]For clarity of presentation, we omit technical details of RDF not relevant for this discussion. For instance, which URLs (if any) are chosen to identify the emperors and provinces is of no concern here. We also depict `rdf:label` by adjacent labels, `rdf:type` triples through different node shapes, `ex:father-of` edges black, and `ex:ruled` edges dotted blue.

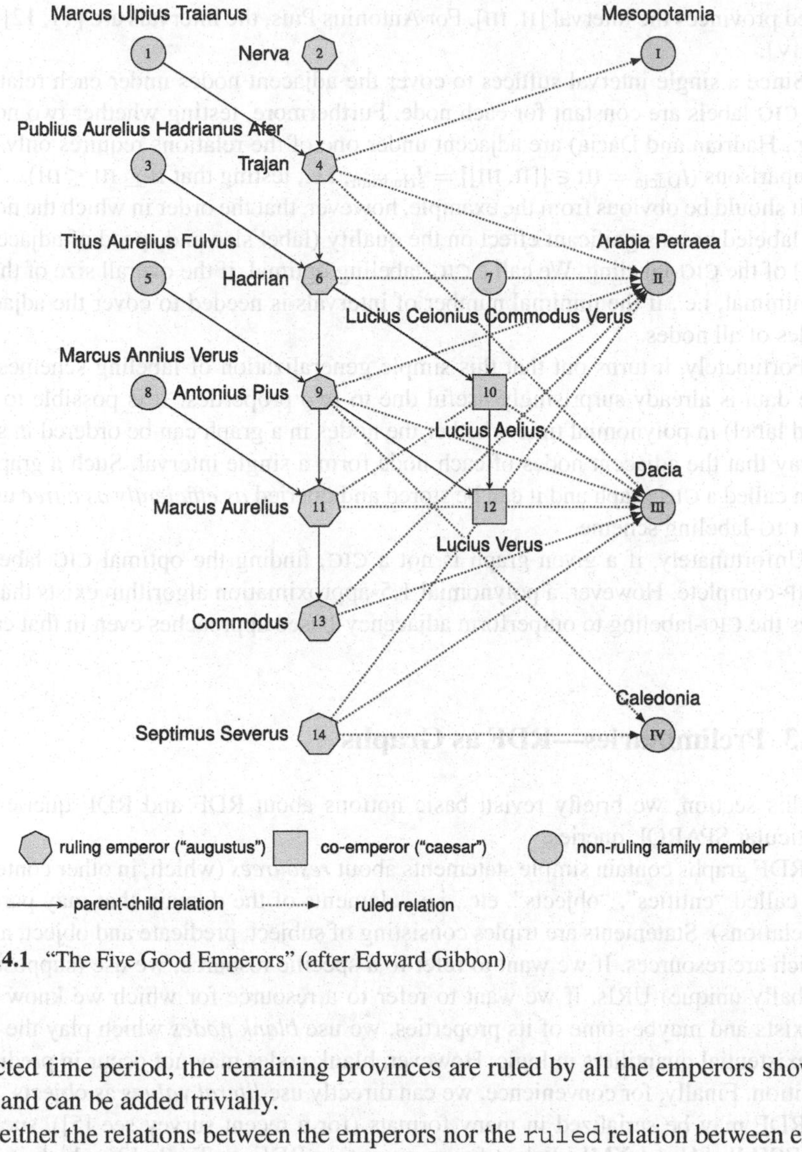

Fig. 14.1 "The Five Good Emperors" (after Edward Gibbon)

depicted time period, the remaining provinces are ruled by all the emperors shown here and can be added trivially.

Neither the relations between the emperors nor the `ruled` relation between emperors and provinces is tree shaped. In fact, some provinces are ruled by nearly all of the depicted emperors (e.g., Dacia) while others where only in roman hands for a short period of time (e.g., Mesopotamia). The relation between emperors is not tree shaped as the emperors of this time used legal adoption (rather than blood relation) to choose their heir and the depicted parent-child relation mixed legal and biological relations.

Despite the considerable complexity of the relations involved in this example, the adjacent nodes of each emperor can be represented as a single interval for each of the two relations. For instance, the sons of Hadrian form the interval [9, 10], his ruled provinces the interval [II, III]. For Antonius Pius, the intervals are [11, 12] and [II, IV].

Since a single interval suffices to cover the adjacent nodes under each relation, the CIG labels are constant for each node. Furthermore, testing whether two nodes (e.g., Hadrian and Dacia) are adjacent under one of the relations requires only two comparisons ($l_{\text{Dacia}} = \text{III} \in \{[\text{II}, \text{III}]\} = I_{\text{Hadrian}}$, i.e., testing that $\text{II} \leq \text{III} \leq \text{III}$).

It should be obvious from the example, however, that the order in which the nodes are labeled has a significant effect on the quality (label size and speed of adjacency test) of the CIG-labeling. We call a CIG-labeling optimal, if the overall size of the I_n is minimal, i.e., if the minimal number of intervals is needed to cover the adjacent nodes of all nodes.

Fortunately, it turns out that this simple generalization of labeling schemes for tree data is already surprisingly useful due to two properties: It is possible to test (and label) in polynomial time whether the nodes in a graph can be ordered in such a way that the adjacent nodes of each node form a single interval. Such a graph is then called a CIG graph and it can be stored and queried *as efficiently as a tree* using the CIG-labeling scheme.

Unfortunately, if a given graph is not a CIG, finding the optimal CIG labeling is NP-complete. However, a polynomial 1.5-approximation algorithm exists that allows the CIG-labeling to outperform adjacency-based approaches even in that case.

14.3 Preliminaries—RDF as Graphs

In this section, we briefly revisit basic notions about RDF and RDF queries, in particular SPARQL queries.

RDF graphs contain simple statements about *resources* (which, in other contexts, are called "entities", "objects", etc., i.e., elements of the domain that may partake in relations). Statements are triples consisting of subject, predicate and object, all of which are resources. If we want to refer to a specific resource, we use (supposedly globally unique) URIs, if we want to refer to a resource for which we know that it exists and maybe some of its properties, we use *blank nodes* which play the role of existential quantifiers in logic. However, blank nodes may not occur in predicate position. Finally, for convenience, we can directly use *literal values* as objects.

RDF may be serialized in many formats (for a recent survey see [5]), such as RDF/XML [4], an XML dialect for representing RDF, or Turtle [3] which is also used in SPARQL. The following Turtle data, e.g., describes a number of (fictitious) articles, their titles, creators and relations to conferences.

```
@prefix dc: <http://purl.org/dc/elements/1.1/> .
@prefix dct: <http://purl.org/dc/terms/> .
@prefix vcard: <http://www.w3.org/2001/vcard-rdf/3.0#> .
@prefix bib: <http://www.edutella.org/bibtex#> .
@prefix ulp: <http://example.org/roman/libraries/ulpia#> .
ulp:cicero-46-wt a bib:Article ; dc:title "Wax Tablets" ;
```

```
7       dc:creator [ a rdf:Seq ;
            rdf:_1 ulp:cicero ; rdf:_2 ulp:tiro ] ;
9       ulp:cites ulp:hirtius-47-bc ;
        dct:isPartOf ulp:conf-46-mutina .
11 ulp:cicero a bib:Person ; vcard:FN "M. T. Cicero" .
   ulp:tiro a bib:Person ; vcard:FN "M. T. Tiro" .
13 ulp:hirtius-47-bc a bib:Article ;
        ulp:cites ulp:cicero-46-wt ;
15      dct:isPartOf ulp:conf-46-mutina .
   ulp:conf-46-mutina a bib:InProceedings ;
17      rdfs:label "Storage Media" .
```

Following the definition of namespace prefixes used in the remainder of the Turtle document (omitting common RDF namespaces), each line contains one or more statements separated by colon or semi-colon. If separated by semi-colon, the subject of the previous statement is carried over. E.g., line 6 reads as ulp:cicero-46-wt is a bib:Article and has dc:title "Wax Tablets". Lines 7–9 show a blank node: the creator of the article is neither Cicero nor Tiro, but some unnamed resource that is a sequence of those two authors.

For the rest of this chapter, we consider RDF as plain data without much consideration for concepts of interpretations, models, entailment, etc. However, as holds for SPARQL, the discussed labeling could as well be applied on an entailment graph containing inferred (rather than explicitly stated) triples.

It is also worth pointing out that all graphs we consider in this chapter are directed and we use "adjacent" and "reachable" accordingly. That is, a node m' is adjacent to m if there is an edge from m to m' (the other direction does not matter), m' is reachable from m if there is a directed path from m to m'.

This RDF data is mapped to a graph as shown in Fig. 14.2. There is a single node in the graph for each named resource that occurs in the RDF data. The same literal may occur multiple times. Each blank node is depicted as a rectangular node. As in Turtle [3] and SPARQL, blank nodes are labeled with local identifiers prefixed by `_:`. There is one node for each blank node in the RDF data, though the graph does not need to be lean.

14.3.1 Queries on RDF Graphs

We consider three types of queries on RDF graphs, all sub-languages of SPARQL. The first and simplest type, called **1-SPARQL queries**, corresponds to single, ground SPARQL triple patterns. For instance, the triple pattern

```
ulp:cicero vcard:FN 'M. T. Cicero'
```

matches a given graph if the given triple occurs in the graph, i.e., if there is a `vcard:FN` labeled edge from `ulp:cicero` to a literal node with label "M. T. Cicero".

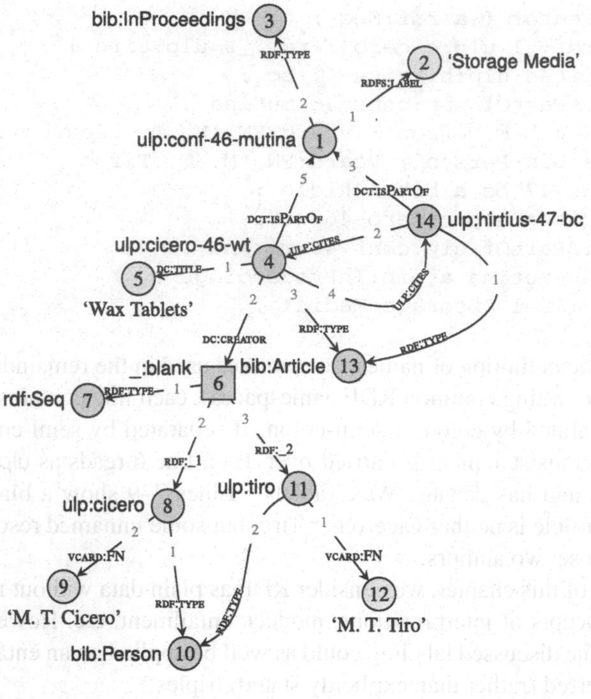

Fig. 14.2 Exemplary RDF Graph: RDF Conference Data

The second type of queries, called **A-SPARQL queries**, are essentially acyclic conjunctive queries on RDF and correspond to acyclic SPARQL basic graph patterns. For instance, the basic graph pattern[4]

```
?a rdf:type bib:Article
  AND ?a dc:creator ?p
  AND ?p vcard:FN 'M. T. Cicero'
```

selects from a given graph all articles created by someone with the full-name "M. T. Cicero" and binds the article to `?a` and the creator to `?p`. We only allow acyclic basic graph patterns:

Definition 14.1 (Acyclic Basic Graph Pattern) Let P be a basic SPARQL graph pattern. Then P is acyclic, if it contains no variable in predicate position and no variable in P depends directly or indirectly on itself.

We say a variable `?x` depends (directly) on a variable `?y` (a resource R) if there is a triple pattern `?x` P `?y` (`?x` P R) for some property P. We say a variable `?x`

[4]We use the variant syntax for SPARQL from [37] and in Chap. 8 of this volume to ease the presentation.

depends indirectly on a variable `?y` if there are variables or resources $z_1, \ldots, z_l$ such `?x` depends on z_1, z_1 on $\ldots$, and z_l depends on `?y`.

The most common case of acyclic graph patterns are tree patterns, where the variables of the query form a proper hierarchy.

The third type of queries are full SPARQL graph patterns. They may be cyclic and include **UNION**, **MINUS**, **OPTIONAL**, **FILTER**. We use the variant syntax for SPARQL discussed in [37] to ease the definition of syntax and semantics of the language. We omit named graphs and assume that all queries are on the single input graph. An extension of the discussion to named graphs is easy (and partially demonstrated in [39]) but only distracts from the salient points of the discussion.

The full grammar of SPARQL graph patterns considered here is as follows:

⟨*pattern*⟩ ::= ⟨*triple*⟩ | '{' ⟨*pattern*⟩ '}'
  | ⟨*pattern*⟩ 'FILTER' '(' ⟨*condition*⟩ ')' |
  | ⟨*pattern*⟩ 'AND' ⟨*pattern*⟩ | ⟨*pattern*⟩ 'UNION' ⟨*pattern*⟩
  | ⟨*pattern*⟩ 'MINUS' ⟨*pattern*⟩ | ⟨*pattern*⟩ 'OPT' ⟨*pattern*⟩
⟨*triple*⟩ ::= ⟨*resource*⟩ ',' ⟨*predicate*⟩ ',' ⟨*resource*⟩
⟨*resource*⟩ ::= ⟨*iri*⟩ | ⟨*variable*⟩ | ⟨*literal*⟩ | ⟨*blank*⟩
⟨*predicate*⟩ ::= ⟨*iri*⟩ | ⟨*variable*⟩
⟨*variable*⟩ ::= '?' ⟨*identifier*⟩
⟨*condition*⟩ ::= ⟨*variable*⟩ '=' ⟨*variable*⟩ | ⟨*variable*⟩ '=' (⟨*literal*⟩ | ⟨*iri*⟩)
  | 'BOUND(' ⟨*variable*⟩ ')' | 'isBLANK(' ⟨*variable*⟩ ')'
  | 'isLITERAL(' ⟨*variable*⟩ ')' | 'isIRI(' ⟨*variable*⟩ ')'
  | ⟨*negation*⟩ | ⟨*conjunction*⟩ | ⟨*disjunction*⟩
⟨*negation*⟩ ::= '¬' ⟨*condition*⟩
⟨*conjunction*⟩ ::= ⟨*condition*⟩ '∧' ⟨*condition*⟩
⟨*disjunction*⟩ ::= ⟨*condition*⟩ '∨' ⟨*condition*⟩

We pose some additional syntactic restrictions: SPARQL graph patterns must be *error-free* SPARQL expressions, i.e., for each **FILTER** expression all variables occurring in the (right-hand) condition must also occur in the (left-hand) pattern. This can easily be ensured a-priori and queries violating this condition rewritten to the canonical false **FILTER** expression (as **FILTER** expressions with unbound variables raise errors which, in turn, are treated as a false filter, see "effective boolean value" in [40]).

Following [39], we define the semantics of SPARQL graph patterns based on *substitutions*. A substitution $\theta = \langle v_1, n_1, \ldots, v_k : n_k \rangle$ with $v_i \in \mathsf{Vars}(Q) \wedge n_i \in$ *nodes*(D) for a query Q over an RDF graph D maps some variables from Q to nodes in D. For a substitution θ, we denote with $dom(\theta)$ the variables mapped by θ. Given a triple pattern $t = (s, p, o)$, we denote with $t\theta$ the application of θ to t replacing all occurrences of variables mapped in θ by their mapping in t. For a triple (s, p, o) containing no variables, we say $(s, p, o) \in D$ if there is a p labeled edge between s and o labeled nodes in D.

On sets of substitutions the usual relational operations $\bowtie$, $\cup$, and $\setminus$ apply. We define the (left) semi-join as $(R \bowtie S) \cup (R \setminus S)$.

Table 14.2 Semantics for SPARQL graph patterns

$[\![(s,p,o)]\!]^D_{\mathsf{Subst}}$	$= \{\theta : dom(\theta) = \mathsf{Vars}((s,p,o)) \wedge t\theta \in D\}$
$[\![pattern_1 \text{ AND } pattern_2]\!]^D_{\mathsf{Subst}}$	$= [\![pattern_1]\!]^D_{\mathsf{Subst}} \bowtie [\![pattern_2]\!]^D_{\mathsf{Subst}}$
$[\![pattern_1 \text{ UNION } pattern_2]\!]^D_{\mathsf{Subst}}$	$= [\![pattern_1]\!]^D_{\mathsf{Subst}} \cup [\![pattern_2]\!]^D_{\mathsf{Subst}}$
$[\![pattern_1 \text{ MINUS } pattern_2]\!]^D_{\mathsf{Subst}}$	$= [\![pattern_1]\!]^D_{\mathsf{Subst}} \setminus [\![pattern_2]\!]^D_{\mathsf{Subst}}$
$[\![pattern_1 \text{ OPT } pattern_2]\!]^D_{\mathsf{Subst}}$	$= [\![pattern_1]\!]^D_{\mathsf{Subst}} \ltimes [\![pattern_2]\!]^D_{\mathsf{Subst}}$
$[\![pattern \text{ FILTER } condition]\!]^D_{\mathsf{Subst}}$	$= \{\theta \in [\![pattern]\!]^D_{\mathsf{Subst}} : \mathsf{Vars}(condition) \subset dom(\theta)$ $\wedge [\![condition]\!]^D_{\mathsf{Bool}}(\theta)\}$
$[\![condition_1 \wedge condition_2]\!]^D_{\mathsf{Bool}}(\theta)$	$= [\![condition_1]\!]^D_{\mathsf{Bool}}(\theta) \wedge [\![condition_2]\!]^D_{\mathsf{Bool}}(\theta)$
$[\![condition_1 \vee condition_2]\!]^D_{\mathsf{Bool}}(\theta)$	$= [\![condition_1]\!]^D_{\mathsf{Bool}}(\theta) \vee [\![condition_2]\!]^D_{\mathsf{Bool}}(\theta)$
$[\![\neg condition]\!]^D_{\mathsf{Bool}}(\theta)$	$= \neg [\![condition]\!]^D_{\mathsf{Bool}}(\theta)$
$[\![\text{BOUND}(?v)]\!]^D_{\mathsf{Bool}}(\theta)$	$= v\theta \neq \textbf{nil}$
$[\![\text{isLITERAL}(?v)]\!]^D_{\mathsf{Bool}}(\theta)$	$= v\theta \in L$
$[\![\text{isIRI}(?v)]\!]^D_{\mathsf{Bool}}(\theta)$	$= v\theta \in I$
$[\![\text{isBLANK}(?v)]\!]^D_{\mathsf{Bool}}(\theta)$	$= v\theta \in B$
$[\![?v = literal]\!]^D_{\mathsf{Bool}}(\theta)$	$= v\theta = literal$
$[\![?u = ?v]\!]^D_{\mathsf{Bool}}(\theta)$	$= u\theta = v\theta \wedge u\theta \neq \textbf{nil}$

Using these definitions, Table 14.2 gives the semantics of SPARQL graph patterns. It produces a set of substitutions (or bindings) for variables in P. Triple patterns t (Case 1) are evaluated to the set of substitutions θ such that the $t\theta$ contains no more variables and falls in D. Pattern compositions **AND**, **UNION**, **MINUS**, and **OPT** are reduced to the appropriate operations on sets of substitutions (Cases 2–4). **FILTER** expressions (Case 5) are again evaluated straightforwardly, as restrictions on the substitutions returned by the (left-hand) pattern with the boolean formula that is provided the second semantic function for the condition of the filter expression. $\mathsf{Vars}(condition) \subset dom(\theta)$ is not strictly necessary as it merely restates that we only consider error-free SPARQL queries.

The semantics of A-SPARQL and 1-SPARQL patterns are the obvious specializations of the semantics for full SPARQL patterns. For 1-SPARQL patterns, this yields a boolean semantics, with {} as false and $\{\emptyset\}$ as true (the empty substitution is a solution, if $t\emptyset = t \in D$).

14.3.2 Triple Patterns and Adjacency

Triple patterns as in 1-SPARQL are a form of adjacency test between the two named resources (or the named resource and the literal) in the given triple pattern. In this chapter, we often prefer to speak of adjacency test to emphasize the general nature of CIG-labelings. In particular, whether the edges are labeled or not has no impact on the labeling: If the number of edge labels is fixed and small, we can choose different CIG-labelings for each of the induced sub-graphs. Otherwise, we can, e.g., choose to represent edges as special nodes (connected to its source and sink) with a label property for storing the edge label. We can also choose a mixture of both approaches, e.g., to use separate CIG-labelings for each of the k most used edge labels and the second approach for all remaining edge labels.

It is worth noting that this holds, more or less, for most labeling schemes and thus allows us to consider also labeling schemes intended for un-labeled graph data for RDF, see Sect. 14.4.2.

Though not part of SPARQL, reachability is also a property that is often useful in graph queries. There are already proposals for extending SPARQL with reachability or even full path expressions [9, 38]. Here, we only mention in passing that CIG-labelings can handle reachability testing just as well as adjacency testing. For more details, see Sect. 14.7.4.

14.4 Labeling Schemes for RDF Graphs

Though RDF and, in particular, SPARQL are fairly new technologies, there is significant relevant related work on labeling schemes for graph data in general. Though little of that has been specifically considered for RDF, most is easily adapted to RDF.

Before turning to graph labeling schemes, we briefly revisit labeling schemes for *tree data*, as most graph labeling schemes are extensions of one of the tree labeling schemes. Moreover, tree labeling schemes have seen significant attention from academia and implementation in most XML-enabled relational databases.

14.4.1 Foundation: Tree Labeling

Labeling schemes of XML data fall into one of three categories: interval-based, prefix-based and arithmetic. *Interval-based labeling* schemes order the nodes of the tree in one or more orders and describe the structural relations (such as child, descendant, etc.) as windows over the assigned orders. For instance, the pre-/post-encoding (first proposed in [15] and adapted for use in XML querying in [6, 22]) assigns each node its positions in pre- and in post-order traversal. The descendants of a node are then all nodes with higher pre- and lower post-order number. With an additional label for the nesting level, all XPath axes can be expressed analogously. *Prefix-based labeling* schemes such as the Dewey ID-based ORDPATH [35] (used in Microsoft SQL server for XML storage) assign each node a label, such that the label of a parent is the prefix of the labels of all its children. For instance, if the parent is labeled 1.7.2, its children are labeled 1.7.2.x for some (positive or negative integer x). Notable is that ORDPATH leaves gaps in the assignment of the child portions of a label to allow updates without relabeling the entire tree. However, prefix-based labeling schemes are, in general, best suited for rather regular, flat trees. If the tree becomes too deep or fan-outs vary significantly, the label sizes quickly degenerate (up to $\mathcal{O}(n)$ where n is the number of nodes in the tree). Finally, *arithmetic labeling* schemes (such as BIRD [45]) use some kind of arithmetic relation between labels to express child-parent, ancestor-descendant relationships. For example, prime numbers are assigned to the leaf nodes in the tree and labels of parent nodes become the product of the labels of their child nodes. Thus, testing whether a node is an ancestor subsumes to testing whether the label of the node is a multiple of the label of the original node. Here, we focus primarily on interval-based labeling schemes, as these have been extended to graph data and are particularly well suited for large data sets (where prefix-based labeling schemes often fail due to the large label size and arithmetic labeling schemes often fail due to the high computational cost for computing a labeling). For a more detailed comparison of labeling schemes for XML, see [42].

Aside of labeling schemes as separate indices (often for relational storage and access of XML), it is also worth to briefly consider different approaches for XML query evaluation as these often exploit properties of tree data similar to those exploited by interval-based labelings.

There are five approaches to XML query evaluation that are particularly relevant for a comparison with interval-based labeling schemes. The time and space complexity for evaluating various classes of queries (path, tree, and graph queries) on various classes of data (tree, DAG, graph) are given in Table 14.3. Note, that in all cases, we consider pointers of constant size (as in most related work [8, 31] and

Table 14.3 Comparison of Related Approaches. n: number of nodes in the data, d: depth, resp. diameter of data; e: number of edges; q: size of query, q_a: number of result or answer variables; q_g: number of "graph" variables, i.e., variables with multiple incoming query edges

Approach	Query	Data	Time	Space
Structural Joins [2, 6]	path	tree	$\mathcal{O}(n^{q_a} + q \cdot n \cdot \log n)$	$\mathcal{O}(n^{q_a} + q \cdot n^2)$
	tree	tree/DAG	$\mathcal{O}(n^{q_a} + q \cdot n \cdot \log n)$	$\mathcal{O}(n^{q_a} + q \cdot n^2)$
	graph	tree	$\mathcal{O}(n^q)$	$\mathcal{O}(n^q)$
	graph	graph	$\mathcal{O}(n^q)$	$\mathcal{O}(n^q)$
Twig or Stack Joins [8]	tree (c/d)	tree	$\mathcal{O}(q \cdot n)$	$\mathcal{O}(q \cdot n + n \cdot d)$
	tree (c/d)	DAG	$\mathcal{O}(q \cdot n^2 + e)$	$\mathcal{O}(q \cdot n + e)$
SPEX (streaming) [31, 32]	tree	tree	$\mathcal{O}(q \cdot n^2)$	$\mathcal{O}(q \cdot n \cdot d)$
CAA [30]	tree	tree	$\mathcal{O}(q \cdot n \cdot \log n \cdot d)$	$\mathcal{O}(q \cdot n)$
CIG-labeling & Interval Join	tree (c/d)	tree	$\mathcal{O}(q \cdot n)$	$\mathcal{O}(q \cdot d)$
	tree	tree, CIG	$\mathcal{O}(q \cdot n)$	$\mathcal{O}(q \cdot n)$
	tree	graph	$\mathcal{O}(q \cdot n^2)$	$\mathcal{O}(q \cdot n^2)$
	graph	tree, CIG	$\mathcal{O}(n^{q_g} + q \cdot n)$	$\mathcal{O}(n^{q_g} + q \cdot n)$
	graph	graph	$\mathcal{O}(n^{q_g} + q \cdot n^2)$	$\mathcal{O}(n^{q_g} + q \cdot n^2)$

[30]). In fact, all approaches need an additional $\log n$ multiplicative factor if pointer size is taken into consideration. The assumption of constant pointer (or label) size is reasonable in practice, as these are usually stored in attributes of a reasonably sized, constant length numerical type such as SQL's `INT` or `BIGINT`.

The first approach, dubbed *structural joins* [2], is predominantly used in relational storage of XML. It uses some form of labeling scheme, here pre-/post-encoding as in [6], to find nodes that fulfill each of the structural conditions of the query and joins the result (either using standard relational joins or using a tree-aware join such as the staircase join [23]). This results in a very flexible evaluation technique (it can, e.g., deal with all 13 XPath axes), but is not quite as space efficient as more specialized approaches. Though structural join approaches can be easily extended to graph data, they do not perform well on graph data. CIG-labelings can be easily integrated into structural join approaches, but as we illustrate in Sect. 14.7.2 a specialized interval join yields even better results (linear time and *space* processing).

In contrast to structural join approaches, twig (or stack) join approaches [8, 11, 12, 28] use a single ("holistic") operator for matching tree patterns. They are limited to tree and DAG data and only consider child and descendant relations. The basic idea of twig join approaches is the use of one stack per query variable (or XPath step) containing nodes that may be matches for that variable. Relations between such potential matches are established in form of explicit parent pointers. However, since queries may only contain child and descendant relations, at most d such parent pointers may exist per node. The essential observation from twig joins is, that we need to limit the space (and management overhead) to describe the relations between potential matches of different variables. In twig joins, the combination of tree data and tree queries with only child and descendant relations together with an efficient stack management ensures this property. Similarly, the evaluation of A-SPARQL using a specialized interval join as discussed in Sect. 14.7.2 uses CIG-labelings to represent relations and ensures that, if the data is a tree or CIG, the relations between potential matches can always be represented by a linear space CIG labeling. Thus, on tree and CIG data CIG-labelings with the interval join are actually more space efficient and as fast as twig joins on tree data, yet are not limited to only child and descendant relations.

Twig joins can be considered a hybrid of in-memory and streaming evaluation approach. Specialized streaming engines for XML query evaluation, such as SPEX [33], also often use stacks for collecting potential matches. In contrast to twig joins, SPEX buffers nodes centrally and manages only annotations (or conditions) that represent relations among potential matches in the stacks of its transducers (roughly, one for each query variable). SPEX compacts these annotations into intervals where possible, but (partially due to its streaming nature) can not always achieve this compaction as the CIG-labeling scheme can on tree and CIG data. SPEX can process all forward [34] XPath axes, but is limited to tree data.

The approach closest in spirit to ours are the complete answer aggregates (CAA) [30]. Like twig joins and other polynomial approaches to XPath tree query processing (e.g., [20]), the (potential) answers for each query variable are stored separately. Unlike the other approaches (and like CIG-labelings), the relations between these potential answers may be described using intervals (rather than lists of pointers or keys). CAAs are unique among the discussed approaches in that they always store answers for all query variables (therefore *complete* answer aggregates), which is helpful in the context of query refinement and exploration of the database, but otherwise often undesirable.

14.4.2 Reachability in Graphs

When we turn from tree data to graph data, the use of labeling schemes becomes less predominant. However, there have been a number of approaches for exploiting labeling schemes to provide an efficient test for *reachability* in graph data. For RDF, as discussed in [13] and [43], this is particularly relevant as these approaches allow efficient querying of the RDFs subsumption hierarchy. Though SPARQL does not provide specific means for reachability queries, several extensions for SPARQL, most notably nSPARQL [38], have been proposed that include such support. Furthermore, SPARQL can be used to query also, e.g., the RDFS entailment (rather than the raw) graph where the subsumption is expanded. For either case, labeling schemes can be exploited. In the latter case, we can use the CIG-labeling scheme as for adjacency testing (on the expanded relation). However, it is often preferable not to expand the reachability relation a-priori. We call this case *ad-hoc reachability test*.

Considerable research on indexing arbitrary graph data for ad-hoc reachability testing has basically fallen into two classes. Table 14.4 summarizes the most relevant approaches for comparison with the CIG-labeling. As baselines, we also include the naive storage of the full reachability matrix as well as the online (shortest path)

Table 14.4 Cost of Reachability Test in Graph Data. n, e: number of nodes, edges in the data, e_g: number of non-tree edges, c_{opt} the number of intervals needed to cover the children of a single node in an optimal CIG-labeling and i_{opt} the total sum of these intervals

Approach	Reachability test time	Index time	Index size
No index [36]	$\mathcal{O}(n+e)$	$O(n+e)$	$O(n+e)$
Full Reachability Matrix	$\mathcal{O}(1)$	$\mathcal{O}(n^3)$	$\mathcal{O}(n^2)$
2-Hop [14]	$\mathcal{O}(\sqrt{e}) \le \mathcal{O}(n)$	$\mathcal{O}(n^4)$	$\mathcal{O}(n \cdot \sqrt{e})$
HOPI [41]	$\mathcal{O}(\sqrt{e}) \le \mathcal{O}(n)$	$\mathcal{O}(n^3)$	$\mathcal{O}(n \cdot \sqrt{e})$
Graph labeling [1]	$\mathcal{O}(n)$	$\mathcal{O}(n^3)$	$\mathcal{O}(n^2)$
SSPI [10]	$\mathcal{O}(e-n)$	$\mathcal{O}(n+e)$	$\mathcal{O}(n+e)$
Dual labeling [44]	$\mathcal{O}(1)$	$\mathcal{O}(n+e+e_g^3)$	$\mathcal{O}(n+e_g^2)$
GRIPP [43]	$\mathcal{O}(e-n)$	$\mathcal{O}(n+e)$	$\mathcal{O}(n+e)$
CIG labeling on trees, CIGs	$\mathcal{O}(1)$	$\mathcal{O}(e)$	$\mathcal{O}(n)$
—on arbitrary graphs	$\mathcal{O}(\log(1.5 \cdot c_{\text{opt}})) < \mathcal{O}(\log n)$	$\mathcal{O}(n^3)$	$\mathcal{O}(1.5 \cdot i_{\text{opt}}) < \mathcal{O}(n^2)$

computation with no index at all. For large graphs, neither of these baseline approaches is feasible. Therefore, two classes of approaches have been developed that allow with significantly lower space to obtain sub-linear time for membership test.

The first class is based on the idea of a *2-hop cover* [14]: Instead of storing a full reachability matrix, we allow that reachable nodes are reached via at most one other node (i.e., in two "hops"). More precisely, each node n is labeled with two connection sets, $in(n)$ and $out(n)$. $in(n)$ contains a set of nodes that can reach n, $out(n)$ a set of nodes that are reachable from n. Both sets are assigned in such a way, that a node m is reachable from n iff $out(n) \cap in(m) \neq \emptyset$. Unfortunately, computing the optimal 2-hop cover is NP-hard. Approximation algorithms [41] that can provide very good guarantees have been developed, but still require rather significant time for index computation.

A different approach [1, 10, 43, 44] is to use *interval encoding* for labeling a spanning tree of the graph and treating the remaining non-tree edges separately. This allows for sublinear or even constant membership test, though constant membership test incurs lower but still considerable indexing cost, e.g., in Dual Labeling [44] where a full transitive closure over the non-tree edges is built. GRIPP [43] and SSPI [10] use a different trade-off by attaching additional interval labels to non-tree edges. This leads to linear index size and time at the cost of increased query time.

In comparison, the CIG-labeling combines many of the best characteristics of these approaches: It is even better suited to sparse, tree-like graphs than pre-/post-based interval encoding approaches (as it provides guaranteed constant reachability test not only for trees but also for CIGs). At the same time, we can give very strong guarantees for maximum time (and space) for reachability testing on general graphs (see Sect. 14.5.3). These guarantees come with an increased indexing time ($O(n^3)$), yet we can also choose to spend less time indexing and choose a rougher heuristics.

14.5 CIG-labeling Scheme

The CIG-labeling scheme is designed around a generalization of interval labels, called here CIG-labeling. CIG-labelings provide flexible, yet simple description of arbitrary relations with attractive properties: In essence, we map each node to a single (integer) label and describe the children of each node as a set of intervals over the above mapping.

Definition 14.2 (CIG-Labeling) Let $G = (N, E)$ be an (arbitrary) graph. Then a CIG-labeling $\mathcal{L}$ of G, is a pair $(l, \mathcal{I})$ such that

1. $l : N \to \mathbb{N}_{|N|}$ is a bijective labeling function that assigns to each node in G an (integer) label from $\{1, \dots, |N|\} = \mathbb{N}_{|N|}$.
2. $\mathcal{I} : N \to 2^{\mathbb{N}_{|N|} \times \mathbb{N}_{|N|}}$ is a mapping from nodes in G to sets of closed, non-empty, non-overlapping, non-adjacent intervals over $\mathbb{N}_{|N|}$.
3. $\mathcal{I}(n)$ covers all adjacent nodes of n for each $n \in N$, i.e.,

$$\{n' \in N : (n, n') \in E\} = \{n' \in N : \exists [s, e] \in \mathcal{I}(n) : s \leq l(n') \leq e\}$$

For an interval $[a, b]$, we say that $[a, b]$ "covers" the nodes with $a \leq l(n) \leq b$. Recall, that an interval $[a, b]$ is closed, if their start and end point is part of the nodes covered by the interval, and nonempty, if $a \leq b$ and thus at least one node is covered by the interval. A pair of intervals $[a, b]$ and $[c, d]$ are called nonoverlapping, if no node is covered by both intervals, and nonadjacent if neither $b = c$ nor $d = a$. Thus, in a set of closed, nonempty, nonoverlapping and nonadjacent intervals each index occurs in no more than one interval (there is no start- or endpoint that is start- or endpoint of another interval).

Compared to other interval labelings, it is worth pointing out that a CIG-labeling uses only a single integer label per node, but at the cost of requiring explicit descriptions of the children intervals. The often used pre-/post-encoding [22] for trees, e.g., uses three such labels (the pre- and the post-numer as well as the level of the node), but does not need to explicitly store the interval boundaries (they follow from the labels) and can cover multiple relations with these three labels.

However, the main difference is that most labeling schemes assign labels in a predetermined way (e.g., by means of a pre- and post-order traversal of the tree). The CIG-labeling, on the other hand, allows us to choose rather flexibly among possible orderings (and thus labels) of the node. Thus, the CIG-labeling scheme consists in the CIG-labeling together with an algorithm for generating that labeling. We will suggest such algorithms for general graphs (Sect. 14.5.3), as well as trees and CIGs (Sect. 14.6).

To emphasize this flexibility, it is worth explicitly stating that each graph can be labeled by some CIG-labeling:

Theorem 14.1 *For any graph G there exists a* CIG*-labeling.*

Proof Let $G = (N, E)$. Then we assign labels from $\mathbb{N}_{|N|}$ to the nodes in N arbitrarily. Given the resulting labeling function l, we set $\mathcal{L}(n)$ to the set of all intervals $[l(n'), l(n')]$ where $(n, n') \in E$. The resulting intervals are trivially closed, nonoverlapping and nonempty. As long as there are still adjacent intervals in any of the interval sets, we merge those adjacent intervals into a single interval. This procedure terminates after at most n merge steps per node resulting in interval sets that are also nonadjacent. □

The challenge is finding an optimal labeling for our purpose. For querying a single relation, we call a CIG-labeling *optimal*, if the total size of the interval labels is minimal, i.e., the sum of the sizes of the interval labels over all nodes in the graph.

Definition 14.3 (Optimal CIG-Labeling) Let $G = (N, E)$ be a graph and $\mathcal{L}$ a CIG-labeling for G. We call $\sum_{n \in N} |\mathcal{I}(n)|$ the size of $\mathcal{L}$, denoted $|\mathcal{L}|$. $\mathcal{L}$ is optimal for G iff there is no other CIG-labeling $\mathcal{L}'$ for G with $|\mathcal{L}'| < |\mathcal{L}|$.

It turns out that for trees we can define several labeling strategies that yield a CIG-labeling with similar properties as a pre-/post-encoding, most notably with linear size for the entire labeling (and constant per node size). With a slight extension, it is also possible to define a CIG-labeling that can cover all forward XPath axes in one labeling.

In contrast to tree labelings such as pre-/post-encoding, the CIG-labeling is, however, flexible enough to be used also for many non-tree graphs. It can even provide constant reachability test for a significantly larger class of graphs than trees (at linear size), see Sect. 14.6. Even on arbitrary graphs, we can still profit from a CIG-labeling compared to, e.g., a full (quadratic) reachability matrix or previous graph labeling schemes (see Sect. 14.4.2 for an overview). Though finding the optimal CIG-labeling is NP-complete for general graphs, a polynomial 1.5 approximation exists that gives very compact representations in most practical cases.

Before we turn to the question *how* to compute an optimal CIG-labeling, we first summarize the main properties of a given CIG-labeling (whether optimal or not), namely its label size (Sect. 14.5.1) and the complexity of its adjacency test (Sect. 14.5.2).

14.5.1 Label Size

The first property to be investigated is the size of a CIG-labeling. It is easy to give an upper bound for arbitrary graphs:

Theorem 14.2 *For any given graph G with n nodes and e edges, a* CIG*-labeling uses exactly n integer labels and $\mathcal{O}(e)$ intervals.*

Proof From the definition, it follows directly that each node is associated with an integer label. Furthermore, in the worst case each child of every node is covered by a single interval (i.e., no two children are adjacent in the order of the nodes). Thus, $\mathcal{O}(e)$ total intervals are used. This is indeed the worst-case as intervals are closed nonempty, nonoverlapping and nonadjacent. □

We can also characterize the space complexity in terms of space used per node.

Proposition 14.1 *For any given graph G with n nodes and e edges, each node m requires a single integer label and an interval set label containing at most* $\max(\mathsf{out\text{-}degree}(m), \frac{1}{2}n)$ *intervals.*

Proof Again for the integer label, this follows directly from the definition. For the interval set label, observe that m has $\mathsf{out\text{-}degree}(m)$ children that need to be covered by an interval. Since all intervals are empty and nonoverlapping, each does cover a node that is not covered by any of the others, and thus we can cover all $\mathsf{out\text{-}degree}(m)$ children with at most $\mathsf{out\text{-}degree}(m)$ intervals. Furthermore, $\frac{1}{2}n$ is an upper bound for the number of intervals per node, as $\mathsf{out\text{-}degree}(m) - \frac{1}{2}n$ of the children of m must have an integer label consecutive with one or more of the other children in any order over the nodes, if $\mathsf{out\text{-}degree}(m) > \frac{1}{2}n$. Thus, no additional intervals are needed for these nodes. □

The above are the label sizes for the adjacency relation on a given graph G. If we consider the reachability relation on G the same considerations apply, but w.r.t. the reachability graph G' of G. Thus, the number of nodes remains the same, but the number of edges increases to the number of pairs of reachable nodes which is, even for sparse graphs, often close to $\mathcal{O}(n^2)$.

Fortunately, this is in practice partially offset by the observation (see Sect. 14.6.1) that both graphs with sparse and almost complete graphs are more likely CIGs than graphs that are neither.

14.5.2 Adjacency & Reachability Test

Given a CIG-labeling (for the original graph or for the reachability graph), we can test adjacency and reachability fairly efficiently.

Theorem 14.3 *Let G be a graph with n nodes. Given any* CIG*-labeling for G and two nodes m, m' we can test whether there is an edge from m to m' in $\mathcal{O}(\log i_m)$ where i_m is the number of intervals in the interval set label of m ($i_m \leq \max(\text{out-degree}(m), \frac{1}{2}n)$ by Proposition* 14.1).

Proof When constructing a CIG-labeling, we can easily assure that the intervals in each interval set are stored ordered by start position (and thus by end position since they are non-overlapping), e.g., by sorting them. Then testing whether m' is a child of m subsumes to looking up $l(m')$ in constant time, looking up $\mathcal{I}(m)$, performing a binary search on the sorted intervals in $\mathcal{I}(m)$, see Fig. 14.3. Obviously, the latter runs in $\log i_m$. □

Again, the same applies for reachability testing but on the reachability graph G' for G. Note, that the out-degree of a node is affected by the step from G to G', but not the number of nodes. Thus, in both cases $\log \frac{n}{2}$ is an upper bound.

In addition to testing adjacency and reachability, the iteration over the adjacent or reachable nodes of a given node is an important operation for evaluating SPARQL. In the optimal case, this iteration depends only on the number of these nodes and not on the (size or shape of) the remaining graph. With a CIG-labeling we obtain this optimal case, simply by iterating over the ordered intervals in the interval set of each node:

```
input : nodes m, m', CIG-labeling (l, I)
output: true if (m, m') ∈ E, false otherwise
first ← 1; last ← |I(m)| ;
while first ≤ last do
    mid ← (first+last)/2; [s,e] ← I(m)[mid] ;
    if l(m') < s then last ← mid − 1 ;
    else if l(m') > e then first ← mid + 1 ;
    else return true;
return false;
```

Fig. 14.3 Binary search in interval set

Corollary 14.1 *Let G be a graph with n nodes. Given any* CIG*-labeling for G and a node m we can iterate over the c_m adjacent (reachable nodes) of m in $\mathcal{O}(c_m)$.*

14.5.3 Optimal CIG*-labeling*

So far we have only investigated the properties of CIG-labelings in general, without considering how to compute a "good" or even optimal CIG-labeling. For an arbitrary graph, it turns out that computing an optimal CIG-labeling is hard.

Theorem 14.4 *Let G be an arbitrary graph. Then computing an* optimal CIG-*labeling for G is* NP*-complete.*

Proof In particular, it is NP-complete to determine whether there is a CIG-labeling $\mathcal{L}$ for G with $|\mathcal{L}| \leq k$.

Obviously, we can find such a CIG-labeling by guessing a suitable order and verifying that $\mathcal{L} \leq k$ in linear time.

NP-hardness is established by reduction from the consecutive block minimization (or CBM) problem for binary matrices, first introduced in [29]. Following [18], the consecutive block minimization problem is the problem of computing a permutation of the columns of a binary matrix such that results in a matrix B with at most k consecutive blocks of 1's. In other words, B must not have more than k entries b_{ij} such that $b_{ij} = 1$ and either $b_{ij} = 0$ or $j = n$. The problem remains NP-hard for quadratic matrices as well as for sparse matrices.

A block of 1's in row i in CBM corresponds to an interval in the interval set of node $l^{-1}(i)$ in a CIG-labeling: Each of the nodes covered by the interval is a child of $l^{-1}(i)$ and thus the corresponding entry in the adjacency matrix of G is 1. As in CBM, we aim to find a permutation of the nodes that minimize the number of such intervals where the next node in the permutation is not a child of $l^{-1}(i)$, i.e., the corresponding entry in the adjacency matrix is 0.

Thus, the reduction is very easy: We just take the quadratic matrix (for which the problem is still NP-hard) and consider it as adjacency matrix of the graph for which to find an optimal CIG-labeling. Given that labeling, we can compute the matrix B as the adjacency matrix of the graph where the columns are ordered by l. □

Though finding an *optimal* CIG-labeling is thus infeasible even for small graphs, [25] proposes an 1.5 approximation algorithm for CBM based on a (fairly straightforward) transformation to the traveling salesmen problem.

Corollary 14.2 *Let G be an arbitrary graph. Then we can compute, in polynomial time, a* CIG*-labeling with a size that does not differ more than* 50% *from the optimal one (i.e., its size is* $1.5 i_{\text{opt}}$ *where* i_{opt} *is the optimal number of intervals for any* CIG*-labeling).*

More precisely, the computation is in $\mathcal{O}(n^3)$ (it is dominated by the time for finding a maximum matching in a graph).

14.6 CIG-labeling on Trees and CIGs

We have established that CIG-labelings on arbitrary graphs can give us logarithmic adjacency test and linear adjacency iteration, yet with optimal or near optimal CIG-labelings we can have significantly smaller size than full adjacency lists or matrices.

However, CIG-labelings have another desirable property: On certain graphs, including all trees and forest, but extending significantly beyond, we can test adjacency in constant time and require only constant labels (thus, linear total space).

In this section, we first characterize and illustrate the class of graphs where this property holds and then show how to compute a CIG-labeling with constant labels for this class.

14.6.1 CIGs: Sharing-Limited Graphs

In a sense, a graph with a CIG-labeling with constant labels (called a CIG) exhibits a certain regularity: It limits the way child nodes may be shared among parents such that two parents may share a node, but only if there is still a way to order the nodes such that the shared nodes of both parents are adjacent to its non-shared nodes. This can be seen as a generalization of similar restrictions on trees and the reachability graphs of trees: In trees, each child has at most one parent and thus there is no sharing of child nodes. In reachability graphs for trees (i.e., the graph for the transitive closure of the edges of a tree), if two nodes share a child, then one is a descendant of the other and thus all its children are shared with the other node. These differences are mirrored in the way intervals for covering the children of nodes in these three structures behave: Fig. 14.4 illustrates how in a tree these intervals can be made not to overlap at all. In the reachability graph for a tree they may be contained in each other, but no other form of overlapping is allowed. In a CIG, these intervals may overlap arbitrarily, but they still must be single, continuous intervals. In an arbitrary graph, the latter restriction is also lifted, as seen above.

More formally, CIGs are a proper superset of trees defined as follows.

Definition 14.4 (CIG) Let G be a graph. Then G is called a *continuous-image graph* (or CIG) if there is a CIG-labeling for G where all the interval set labels contain a single interval only.

Thus, a graph $G = (N, E)$ is a CIG if there is

1. a bijective labeling function $l : N \to \mathbb{N}_{|N|}$ that assigns to each node in G an (integer) label from $\{1, \dots, |N|\} = \mathbb{N}_{|N|}$,
2. a partial mapping from nodes in G to closed, non-empty intervals $\mathcal{I} : N \to \mathbb{N}_{|N|} \times \mathbb{N}_{|N|}$ and

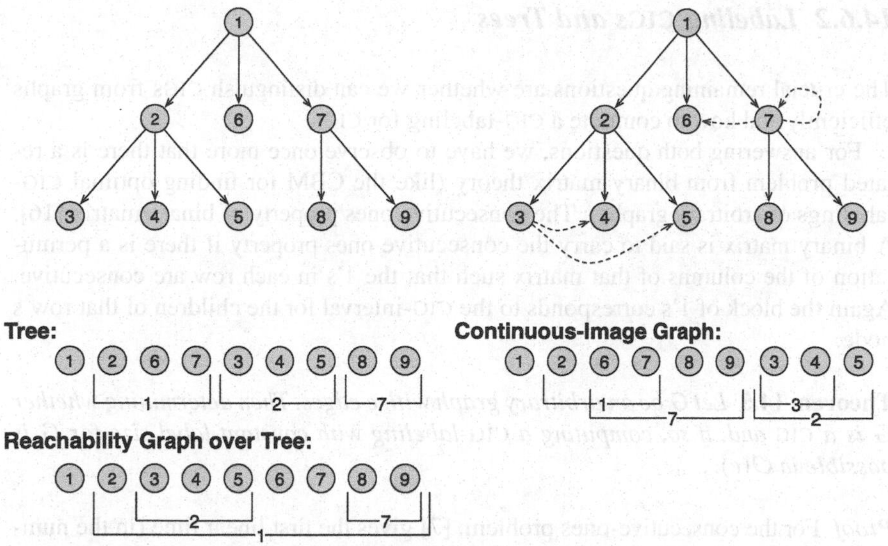

Fig. 14.4 Sharing of children in trees, reachability graphs over trees, and CIGs

3. $\mathcal{I}(n)$ covers all adjacent nodes of n for each $n \in N$, i.e.,

$$\{n' \in N : (n,n') \in E\} = \{n' \in N : \exists [s,e] = \mathcal{I}(n) : s \leq l(n') \leq e\}$$

Essentially, this is a slight simplification of the conditions for a CIG-labeling where each node is assigned a single interval (or none).

In practice, we belief that CIGs are fairly common, in particular where hierarchical or mostly hierarchical ontologies as well as time-related (e.g., event) data is considered. If relations, e.g., between England and its rulers, are time-related, it is quite likely that there will be some overlapping, e.g., for periods where two persons were claiming the rulership of England at the same time. Similarly, hierarchical data often has some limited anomalies that make a modelling as strict tree data impossible. Both points are illustrated in Fig. 14.1 where we show the relationships (both by law and by blood) between emperors of the "Five Good Emperors" (Edward Gibbon) period (roughly 2nd century A.D.) as well which provinces they ruled (provinces not shown have been ruled by all of these emperors).[5] Despite the rather complicated shape of the relations (they are obviously not tree-shaped and there is considerable overlapping, in particular w.r.t. province rulership), the whole graph is a CIG and can be stored with constant size labels and its adjacency can be queried in constant time.

[5]The name and status of the province between the wall of Hadrian and the wall of Antonius Pius in northern Britain is controversial. For simplicity, we refer to it as "Caledonia", though that actually denotes all land north of Hadrian's wall.

14.6.2 Labeling CIGs and Trees

The crucial remaining questions are whether we can distinguish CIGs from graphs efficiently and how to compute a CIG-labeling for CIGs.

For answering both questions, we have to observe once more that there is a related problem from binary matrix theory (like the CBM for finding optimal CIG-labelings of arbitrary graphs): The consecutive ones property of binary matrix [16]. A binary matrix is said to carry the consecutive ones property if there is a permutation of the columns of that matrix such that the 1's in each row are consecutive. Again the block of 1's corresponds to the CIG-interval for the children of that row's node.

Theorem 14.5 *Let G be an arbitrary graph with e edges. Then determining whether G is a* CIG *and, if so, computing a* CIG*-labeling with constant label size for G is possible in $\mathcal{O}(e)$.*

Proof For the consecutive-ones problem, [7] gives the first linear time (in the number of nodes) algorithm based on so called PQ-trees, a compact representation for permutations of rows in a matrix. More recent refinements in [24] and [27] show that simpler algorithms, based on the PC-tree [26], can be achieved. To decide whether a given graph is a CIG we use the PC-tree algorithm on that graph's adjacency matrix which runs in $\mathcal{O}(e)$. If the matrix carries the consecutive ones property, the graph is a CIG and any of the consecutive ones order in the PC-tree can be used to label the nodes of the graph. The intervals are then computed accordingly and we obtain a single interval per node (thus the node label is constant, one integer label and one interval). Both is possible in $\mathcal{O}(e)$. □

14.6.3 Properties of CIG-labelings on CIGs and Trees

The previous section establishes that CIGs can be characterized and labeled in linear time. However, we have yet to note the precise time and space complexities for adjacency/reachability testing with a CIG-labeling. The same complexities as for CIGs hold also for trees (which are, after all, a special case of CIGs) and are as good as those of the best known complexities for tree-only labeling schemes such as the pre-/post-encoding.

Theorem 14.6 *Let G be a* CIG *(or tree, forest, reachability graph over a tree) with n nodes and $\mathcal{L}$ a* CIG*-labeling computed as in Theorem* 14.5*. Then the size of each node label is constant and thus the overall space complexity of the* CIG*-labeling $\mathcal{O}(n)$. Furthermore, testing the adjacency of two nodes in G is possible in constant time.*

Proof The labels are constant by the construction in Theorem 14.5: A single interval is needed to represent all children, as all children are consecutive in the computed order. For testing the adjacency of two nodes m, m' in G it suffices to test if $\{[s, e]\} = \mathcal{I}(m) \wedge s \leq l(m) \leq e$. □

14.6.4 Limitations and Extensions

Though CIGs already cover many practical graphs, it is still worth considering the limits of this class. There are even (fairly) simple graphs that are no CIGs, see Fig. 14.5. The figure shows two graphs that are *no* CIGs. Incidentally, both graphs are acyclic and, if we take away any one edge in either graph, the resulting graph becomes a CIG. The first illustrates an easy to grasp sufficient but not necessary condition for being a non-CIG: if a node has at least three parents and each of the parents has at least one (other) child not shared by the others then the graph can not be a CIG.

To overcome these limitations, CIG-labelings can be extended in at least three aspects while retaining the constant label size and constant adjacency test (for more details see [46]):

1. We can allow more than one, but still a constant number of k intervals per node. It turns out, however, that already for $k = 2$ even determining whether there is such a labeling is NP-hard [19].
2. Another promising extension is to allow multiple integer labels per node, i.e., to consider intervals over multiple orders. In some sense, this extension generalizes intervals over one dimension to those over multiple dimensions. However, it has been shown in [46] recently (by reduction from k-colorability) that finding an optimal labeling for this extension also becomes NP-hard quickly (in fact, already determining whether there is a labeling with 2 orders is NP-complete).
3. Localizing maximum CIG subgraphs also turns out to be an intractable problem (cf. consecutive ones submatrix [18]).

Though these extensions cover additional graphs, we would, once more, have to rely on heuristics or approximations for finding optimal labelings. This strongly indicates that CIGs are very much a "sweet spot" w.r.t. size of the class and complexity of the labeling algorithm.

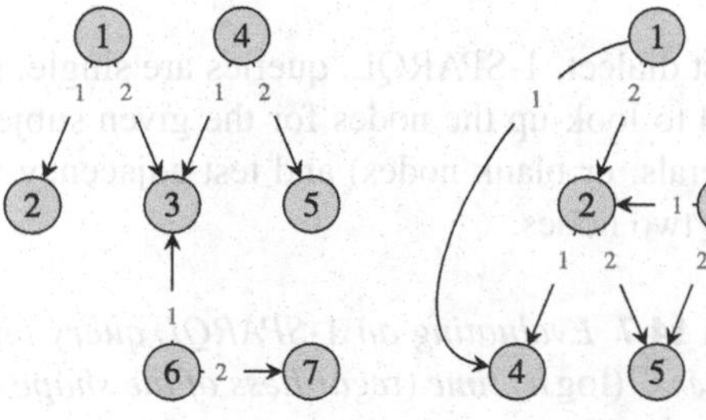

Fig. 14.5 Limits of continuous-image graphs

14.7 Processing SPARQL with CIG-labelings

The previous sections introduce the CIG-labeling, its properties on arbitrary graphs, on CIGs, the novel class of graphs with constant time adjacency test, and on trees. In this section, we use these results to sketch how to evaluate queries in the three SPARQL dialects introduced in Sect. 14.3 efficiently.

For all three dialects, the first issue to address is how to label an RDF graph. Node labels and typed nodes (the distinction between literals, URIs, and blank nodes) are easily represented in a CIG-labeling. However, we have to consider what to do with edge labels which are not present in the plain directed graphs used so far for defining the CIG-labeling. There are two possibilities to dealing with edge labels:

1. The RDF graph can be transformed by introducing a new node of type edge-node n_l for each node n and edge label l if n has outgoing edges labeled with l. We also add edges (n, n_l) and one outgoing edge to each n' with (n, l, n') in the original graph. Finally, we delete the edge (n, l, n'). The resulting graph has only unlabeled edges and we can rewrite each query (s, p, o) to (s, p), (p, o), and edge-node(p). This representation is obviously linear in the number of triples in the graph.
2. The graph induced by the edges of each edge label can be considered separately and queries adapted to query the appropriate graph.

The first approach has advantages if the number of edge labels (i.e., properties) in the RDF graph is very large and most properties occur infrequently. The second approach requires slightly more space (at least one integer label per node and edge label), but allows the use of different node orders for different edge labels. Thus, graphs that are, if we consider edges with any label, no CIG, may turn out to be CIGs if we consider each edge label separately, which provides a significant advantage.

It is tempting to consider an extension of the CIG-labeling scheme where we aim to find compatible orders for multiple relations (edge sets) on the same nodes. Such an extension allows us to combine the advantages of both approaches: Where necessary separate CIG-labelings are created, but where possible the integer labels are shared. Determining an optimal compatible order is an open question.

14.7.1 Processing 1-SPARQL

In the first dialect, 1-SPARQL, queries are single, ground triple patterns. Thus, we only need to look-up the nodes for the given subject and object (whether they are URIs, literals, or blank nodes) and test adjacency wrt. the given property URI between the two nodes.

Theorem 14.7 *Evaluating an* 1*-SPARQL query on a* CIG*-labeled graph G with n nodes takes $\mathcal{O}(\log n)$ time (regardless of the shape of G).*

Proof Finding the nodes and their labels for the given subject and object is in $\log|\Sigma|$ (e.g., if data URIs are held in an appropriate dictionary) where Σ is the set of unique URIs and literals that occur in the data. Obviously, $|\Sigma| \leq n$. In both of the above representations, the adjacency test given the node labels is constant, if the RDF graph can be represented as a CIG. Otherwise, the test is in $\log n$. The overall complexity is in both cases $\mathcal{O}(\log n)$ □

14.7.2 Processing A-SPARQL

For processing A-SPARQL a basic algorithm can be expressed as follows: Evaluate each triple pattern separately and then join the resulting substitutions. The challenge lies in representing the result of the join compactly. Intuitively the idea is as follows: Rather than storing all (possibly exponential) combinations of bindings for answer variables, we store candidates for each variable separately. Relations between the candidates are stored, as in a CIG labeling, as intervals over these candidates. It turns out that for acyclic queries, we can ensure that a single such interval suffices for each candidate and sub-variable. There are two issues we have to solve to ensure this: We have to extend normal join algorithms to deal with these interval and we have to avoid that invalidating candidates for variable requires updating candidates for all other variables. The first, we achieve by a new interval join, the second by only marking invalidated candidates and propagating this information only once at the end of the evaluation:

- For each variable v, store candidate nodes in form of their integer label and interval sets for each dependent variable. Order these candidate nodes in the order of the relation between v and its parent in the query (if there are multiple parents clone v, but not its dependent variables). Initialize these candidate stores with all nodes and the interval sets $\{[1, |N|]\}$. This can be done in $\mathcal{O}(n)$ as the nodes are stored in order in the CIG-labeling.
- For each triple pattern (v, p, v') involving two variables v and v', we look at each of the candidates for v and intersect its current interval set over v' with the one retrieved from the CIG-labeling for p. The intersection of ordered interval sets can be performed in time linear in the total number of intervals over v' in candidates for v. The details of the algorithm are shown in Fig. 14.6: It is performed once for each dependent variable and computes in $\mathcal{O}(i_1 + i_2)$, where $i_1, i_2 \leq n$ are the sizes of the two interval sets, a minimal set of nonoverlapping, nonempty, nonadjacent, closed intervals that covers all nodes covered by both input interval sets.
- For each conditions (such as URI labels, type restrictions) on a variable, we mark all candidates for that variable that do not match that condition.
- Finally, we compute the actual answers by iterating (bottom-up) over each candidate store and computing for each index in the store its new index, the index of the next and the previous actual answer: For leave variables that is the first variable that is not marked (including itself). For inner variables this is the first

```
input : Sets Intervals_1, Intervals_2 of intervals
output: Minimal set of intervals covering all nodes covered by both Intervals_1 and
        Intervals_2
1  NewIntervals ← ∅ ; start ← ⊥ ;
2  [s_1, e_1] ← interval in Intervals_1 with minimal start index s_1;
3  [s_2, e_2] ← interval in Intervals_2 with minimal start index s_2;
4  while true do
5      while e_2 < s_1 do
           // Current [s_2, e_2] do not overlap, get the next
6          Intervals_2 ← Intervals_2 \ {[s_2, e_2]};
7          if Intervals_2 = ∅ then break 2 (line 5);
8          [s_2, e_2] ← interval in Intervals_2 with minimal start index s_2;
       // There is some overlapping
9      if s_2 ≤ e_1 then
10         NewIntervals ← NewIntervals ∪ {[max(s_1, s_2), min(e_1, e_2)]};
11     if e_1 ≤ e_2 or s_2 > e_1 then
           // Current [s_1, e_1] do not overlap (any further), get the next
12         Intervals_1 ← Intervals_1 \ {[s_1, e_1]};
13         if Intervals_1 = ∅ then break (line 5);
14         [s_1, e_1] ← interval in Intervals_1 with minimal start index s_1;
15 return NewIntervals ;
```

Fig. 14.6 Intersect interval sets

variable that is (a) not marked and for which (b) the interval sets for each dependent variable are nonempty. Analog for the previous actual answer. Whenever we have computed the actual answers of a variable v we adjust the indices of the parent variable(s) p as follows: The start index of each interval in the interval set of a candidate for p is advanced to the index of the next actual answer for p, the end index is reduced to the index of the previous actual answer. If the interval is now empty, it is dropped.

This algorithm runs in time linear to the total number of candidates and intervals in candidates of any variable. The details of the algorithm are shown in Fig. 14.7. It uses a log of 3-tuples that contains, for each index, a $\hookrightarrow$ (a $\hookleftarrow$) triple that associates the index with the index of the next (previous) *actual answer* and, for all indices of candidates that are also actual answers, a $\downarrow$ triple that associates the original index with the index of the actual answer. Such a log is computed (in linear time and space) while adapting the answers of each dependent variable. With the log, the algorithm in Fig. 14.7 adapts the interval sets for each dependent variable.

Theorem 14.8 *Evaluating an A-SPARQL query of size q on a* CIG*-labeled graph G with n nodes takes*:

1. $\mathcal{O}(q \cdot n)$ *time and space if G is a tree or* CIG.
2. $\mathcal{O}(q \cdot n^2)$ *time and space otherwise*.

Proof In both cases, step 1 is performed $\mathcal{O}(q)$ times, thus takes in total $\mathcal{O}(q \cdot n)$ time.

```
input : Non-overlapping set of intervals Ints and set of "log" entries
output: Set of intervals modified according to Log
NewInts ← ∅ ;
lastStart ← ∞; lastEnd ← ∞;
foreach [s,e] ∈ Ints in order of start index do
    if (↪,s,next) ∈ Log then s ← next;
    if (↩,e,prev) ∈ Log then e ← prev;
    if s > e then continue;
    // Now there must be ↓ entries for s and e, as ↪ and ↩ entries always reference
       "good" entries or ∞ or 0 which are excluded above
    (↓,s,s_new), (↓,e,e_new) ∈ Log ;
    // If we cannot extend the last interval, add it ...
    if lastEnd ≠ s_new + 1 then
        NewInts ← NewInts ∪ {[lastStart, lastEnd]};
        lastStart = s_new ;
    // ... otherwise lastStart remains unchanged
    lastEnd ← e_new ;
// Collect remaining interval
if lastStart ≠ ∞ then NewInts ← NewInts ∪ {[lastStart, lastEnd]};
return NewInts
```

Fig. 14.7 Log-based adaption of interval sets

For steps 2 and 3, we distinguish between CIGs and arbitrary graphs:

If G is a tree or CIG then there is a single interval per node and relation. Step 2 is performed once for triple pattern and at most n intervals are intersected (as each of the at most n candidates for v only contains one interval over v'). Thus, it takes in total at most $\mathcal{O}(q \cdot n)$ time. Step 3 is performed once and takes at most $\mathcal{O}(q \cdot n)$ time as that is the upper bound for the total number of intervals in all candidate answers.

If G is an arbitrary graph, there are up to $\frac{1}{2}n$ intervals per node and relation. Step 2 thus intersects at most n^2 intervals and takes $\mathcal{O}(q \cdot n^2)$ time. Step 3 is performed once and takes at most $\mathcal{O}(q \cdot n^2)$ time as that is the upper bound for the total number of intervals in all candidate answers. □

For the actual implementation, we adapt a number of aspects of the algorithm, in particular the handling of marked nodes and the initialization that improve space usage in most cases, but do not affect the complexity and are therefore omitted here.

14.7.3 Towards Full SPARQL

For a given SPARQL query, we essentially compute an A-SPARQL core of the query, evaluate that core and then compute the rest of the query as in the relational algebra, accessing the results of the A-SPARQL core when needed.

It is worth pointing out that we can add many of SPARQL's features also to the A-SPARQL core (without sacrificing the linear time evaluation). E.g., many forms of `UNION`, most `FILTER` expressions, and some cases of `OPTIONAL`. Though `UNION` and `OPTIONAL` somewhat complicate the evaluation algorithm sketched above, it is well-worth in practice. None of these changes, however, changes the overall complexity significantly and they are omitted here. For more details, see [17].

Corollary 14.3 *Evaluating a SPARQL query of size q with q_g triples not covered by a chosen A-SPARQL core of the query on a* CIG*-labeled graph G with n nodes takes $\mathcal{O}(n^{q_g} + q \cdot n)$ time and space on* CIGs *and $\mathcal{O}(n^{q_g} + q \cdot n^2)$ time and space on other graphs.*

14.7.4 Towards Path Expressions

As discussed in Sect. 14.4.2, the CIG-labeling is particularly well suited for reachability graphs. Though SPARQL does not explicitly support reachability queries, it may be evaluated, e.g., against the RDFS-entailment graph of a given RDF graph which includes reachability semantics for, e.g., rdfs:subClassOf. Furthermore, CIG-labelings can be used to support efficient iteration and constant time reachability test for extensions of SPARQL with reachability queries. For instance, nSPARQL [38] proposes such and more powerful operators (full path expressions). The latter, unfortunately, can no longer be iterated in time linear to the matches (rather than to the entire graph) or tested in constant time, not even with CIG-labelings.

14.8 Conclusion

In this chapter, we introduce the CIG-labeling, a novel, easy and efficiently implementable, yet surprisingly powerful labeling scheme for trees and graphs. We show that CIG-labelings allow for constant time, constant per-node space adjacency (and reachability) testing not only on trees, but also on many graphs. We precisely characterize the class of graphs with this property.

CIG-labelings can be easily applied to RDF and give us linear time evaluation for large classes of SPARQL queries on many RDF graphs. They also have the potential to significantly speed-up the processing of general SPARQL queries, however, current indexing algorithms may prove to be too expensive for very large RDF graphs.

The development of more efficient heuristics and approximations for very large RDF graphs is therefore clearly called for. On the other hand, it is also worth investigating how to increase the class of graphs which can still be queried in constant time, even if we increase the indexing time (this is relevant, e.g., when indexing is done infrequently and en-bloc as in search engines). In Sect. 14.6.4, we discussed several such extensions, though optimal labeling algorithms turn out to be NP-complete even for small extensions.

Another candidate is the exploitation of results on the zero-partitionable property of adjacency matrix. This is, in some sense, a generalization of the consecutive ones property that CIGs are based on: Intuitively in a zero-partitionable matrix we can push all 0s either to the right or to the bottom: A binary matrix is zero-partitionable if every 0 can be labeled either by R, in which case every position to its right must be an R labeled 0; or by C, in which case every position below must be a C labeled 0. On a graph with a zero-partitionable adjacency matrix, we can still provide constant time and constant per-node space adjacency testing though the class is a proper superclass of CIGs. The best known labeling algorithm is polynomial but with a very large constant in the exponent. It is an open question whether the labeling is effective for realistic RDF graphs.

Acknowledgements We are very deeply indebted to Simon Brodt and Norbert Eisinger for many revealing and stimulating discussions on CIG-labelings and related issues. The research leading to these results has received funding from the European Community's Seventh Framework Programme (FP7/2007–2013) under grant agreement n° 211932 (cf. http://www.kiwi-project.eu/).

References

1. Agrawal, R., Borgida, A., Jagadish, H.V.: Efficient management of transitive relationships in large data and knowledge bases. In: Proc. ACM Symp. on Management of Data (SIGMOD), pp. 253–262. ACM, New York (1989)
2. Al-Khalifa, S., Jagadish, H.V., Koudas, N., Patel, J.M., Srivastava, D., Wu, Y.: Structural joins: a primitive for efficient XML query pattern matching. In: Proc. Int. Conf. on Data Engineering, p. 141. IEEE Computer Society, Los Alamitos (2002)
3. Backett, D.: Turtle—Terse RDF Triple Language. Technical Report, Institute for Learning and Research Technology, University of Bristol (2007)
4. Beckett, D., McBride, B.: RDF/XML Syntax Specification (Revised). Recommendation, W3C (2004)
5. Bolzer, O.: Towards Data-Integration on the Semantic Web: Querying RDF with Xcerpt. Diplomarbeit/diploma Thesis, University of Munich (2005)
6. Boncz, P., Grust, T., van Keulen, M., Manegold, S., Rittinger, J., Teubner, J.: MonetDB/X-Query: a fast XQuery processor powered by a relational engine. In: Proc. ACM Symp. on Management of Data (SIGMOD), pp. 479–490. ACM, New York (2006)
7. Booth, K.S., Lueker, G.S.: Linear algorithms to recognize interval graphs and test for the consecutive ones property. In: Proc. of ACM Symposium on Theory of Computing, pp. 255–265. ACM, New York (1975)
8. Bruno, N., Koudas, N., Srivastava, D.: Holistic twig joins: optimal XML pattern matching. In: Proc. ACM SIGMOD Int. Conf. on Management of Data, pp. 310–321. ACM, New York (2002)
9. Bry, F., Furche, T., Linse, B., Pohl, A.: Xcerpt^{RDF}: A pattern-based answer to the versatile web challenge. In: Proc. Workshop on (Constraint) Logic Programming (WLP) (2008)
10. Chen, L., Gupta, A., Kurul, M.E.: Stack-based algorithms for pattern matching on dags. In: Proc. Int'l. Conf. on Very Large Data Bases (VLDB), pp. 493–504. VLDB Endowment (2005)
11. Chen, T., Lu, J., Ling, T.W.: On boosting holism in XML twig pattern matching using structural indexing techniques. In: Proc. ACM SIGMOD Int. Conf. on Management of Data, pp. 455–466. ACM, New York (2005)
12. Chen, Z., Gehrke, J., Korn, F., Koudas, N., Shanmugasundaram, J., Srivastava, D.: Index structures for matching XML twigs using relational query processors. Data Knowl. Eng. (DKE) **60**(2), 283–302 (2007)
13. Christophides, V., Plexousakis, D., Scholl, M., Tourtounis, S.: On labeling schemes for the semantic web. In: Proc. Int'l. World Wide Web Conf. (WWW), pp. 544–555. ACM, New York (2003)

14. Cohen, E., Halperin, E., Kaplan, H., Zwick, U.: Reachability and distance queries via 2-hop labels. In: Proc. ACM Symposium on Discrete Algorithms, pp. 937–946. Society for Industrial and Applied Mathematics, Philadelphia (2002)
15. Dietz, P.F.: Maintaining order in a linked list. In: Proc. ACM Symp. on Theory of Computing (STOC), pp. 122–127. ACM, New York (1982)
16. Fulkerson, D.R., Gross, O.A.: Incidence matrices and interval graphs. Pac. J. Math. **15**(3), 835–855 (1965)
17. Furche, T.: Implementation of web query language reconsidered: beyond tree and single-language algebras at (almost) no cost. Dissertation/doctoral Thesis, Ludwig-Maxmilians University Munich (2008)
18. Garey, M.R., Johnson, D.S.: Computers and Intractability: A Guide to the Theory of NP-Completeness. Freeman, New York (1979)
19. Goldberg, P.W., Golumbic, M.C., Kaplan, H., Shamir, R.: Four strikes against physical mapping of DNA. J. Comput. Biol. **2**(1), 139–152 (1995)
20. Gottlob, G., Koch, C., Pichler, R.: Efficient algorithms for processing XPath queries. ACM Trans. Database Syst. (2005)
21. Gottlob, G., Leone, N., Scarcello, F.: The complexity of acyclic conjunctive queries. J. ACM **48**(3), 431–498 (2001)
22. Grust, T.: Accelerating XPath location steps. In: Proc. ACM Symp. on Management of Data (SIGMOD) (2002)
23. Grust, T., van Keulen, M., Teubner, J.: Staircase join: teach a relational DBMS to watch its (axis) steps. In: Proc. Int. Conf. on Very Large Databases (2003)
24. Habib, M., McConnell, R., Paul, C., Viennot, L.: Lex-BFS and partition refinement, with applications to transitive orientation, interval graph recognition and consecutive ones testing. Theor. Comput. Sci. **234**(1–2), 59–84 (2000)
25. Haddadi, S., Layouni, Z.: Consecutive block minimization is 1.5-approximable. Inf. Process. Lett. **108**(3), 132–135 (2008)
26. Hsu, W.L.: PC-trees vs. PQ-trees. In: Proc. Int'l. Conf. on Computing and Combinatorics. LNCS, vol. 2108. Springer, Berlin (2001)
27. Hsu, W.L.: A simple test for the consecutive ones property. J. Algorithms **43**(1), 1–16 (2002)
28. Jiang, H., Wang, W., Lu, H., Yu, J.X.: Holistic twig joins on indexed XML documents. In: Proc. Int'l. Conf. on Very Large Data Bases (VLDB), pp. 273–284. VLDB Endowment (2003)
29. Kou, L.T.: Polynomial complete consecutive information retrieval problems. SIAM J. Comput. **6**(1), 67–75 (1977)
30. Meuss, H., Schulz, K.U.: Complete answer aggregates for treelike databases: a novel approach to combine querying and navigation. ACM Trans. Inf. Syst. **19**(2), 161–215 (2001)
31. Olteanu, D.: SPEX: streamed and progressive evaluation of XPath. IEEE Trans. Knowl. Data Eng. (2007)
32. Olteanu, D., Furche, T., Bry, F.: Evaluating complex queries against XML streams with polynomial combined complexity. In: Proc. British National Conf. on Databases (BNCOD), pp. 31–44 (2003)
33. Olteanu, D., Furche, T., Bry, F.: An efficient single-pass query evaluator for XML data streams. In: Data Streams Track, Proc. ACM Symp. on Applied Computing (SAC) pp. 627–631 (2004)
34. Olteanu, D., Meuss, H., Furche, T., Bry, F.: XPath: looking forward. In: Proc. EDBT Workshop on XML-Based Data Management. Lecture Notes in Computer Science, vol. 2490. Springer, Berlin (2002)
35. O'Neil, P., O'Neil, E., Pal, S., Cseri, I., Schaller, G., Westbury, N.: ORDPATHs: insert-friendly XML node labels. In: Proc. ACM Symp. on Management of Data (SIGMOD), pp. 903–908. ACM, New York (2004)
36. Paige, R., Tarjan, R.E.: Three partition refinement algorithms. SIAM J. Comput. **16**(6), 973–989 (1987)
37. Perez, J., Arenas, M., Gutierrez, C.: Semantics and complexity of SPARQL. In: Proc. Int'l. Semantic Web Conf. (ISWC) (2006)

38. Pérez, J., Arenas, M., Gutierrez, C.: nSPARQL: A navigational language for rdf. In: Proc. Int'l. Semantic Web Conf. (ISWC), pp. 66–81 (2008)
39. Polleres, A.: From SPARQL to rules (and back). In: Proc. Int'l. World Wide Web Conf. (WWW), pp. 787–796. ACM, New York (2007)
40. Prud'hommeaux, E., Seaborne, A.: SPARQL Query Language for RDF. Proposed Recommendation, W3C (2007)
41. Schenkel, R., Theobald, A., Weikum, G.: HOPI: an efficient connection index for complex XML document collections. In: Proc. Extending Database Technology (2004)
42. Su-Cheng, H., Chien-Sing, L.: Node labeling schemes in XML query optimization: A survey and trends. IETE Tech. Rev. **26**(2), 88–100 (2009)
43. Trißl, S., Leser, U.: Fast and practical indexing and querying of very large graphs. In: Proc. ACM Symp. on Management of Data (SIGMOD), pp. 845–856. ACM, New York (2007)
44. Wang, H., He, H., Yang, J., Yu, P.S., Yu, J.X.: Dual labeling: Answering graph reachability queries in constant time. In: Proc. Int'l. Conf. on Data Engineering (ICDE), p. 75. IEEE Computer Society, Los Alamitos (2006)
45. Weigel, F., Schulz, K.U., Meuss, H.: The BIRD numbering scheme for XML and tree databases—deciding and reconstructing tree relations using efficient arithmetic operations. In: Proc. Int'l. XML Database Symposium (XSym). LNCS, vol. 3671, pp. 49–67. Springer, Berlin (2005)
46. Weinzierl, A.: Interval-based graph representations for efficient web querying. Diplomarbeit/diploma Thesis, Ludwig-Maxmilians University Munich (2009)

Chapter 15
SPARQLog: SPARQL with Rules and Quantification

François Bry, Tim Furche, Bruno Marnette, Clemens Ley, Benedikt Linse, and Olga Poppe

Abstract SPARQL has become the gold-standard for RDF query languages. Nevertheless, we believe there is further room for improving RDF query languages. In this chapter, we investigate the addition of rules and quantifier alternation to SPARQL. That extension, called SPARQLog, extends previous RDF query languages by arbitrary quantifier alternation: blank nodes may occur in the scope of all, some, or none of the universal variables of a rule. In addition, SPARQLog is aware of important RDF features such as the distinction between blank nodes, literals and IRIs or the RDFS vocabulary. The semantics of SPARQLog is closed (every answer is an RDF graph), but lifts RDF's restrictions on literal and blank node occurrences for intermediary data. We show how to define a sound and complete operational semantics that can be implemented using existing logic programming techniques. While SPARQLog is Turing complete, we identify a decidable (in fact, polynomial time) fragment SwARQLog ensuring polynomial data-complexity inspired from the notion of super-weak acyclicity in data exchange. Furthermore, we prove that SPARQLog with no universal quantifiers in the scope of existential ones (∀∃ fragment) is

F. Bry (✉) · T. Furche · B. Linse · O. Poppe
Institute for Informatics, University of Munich, Oettingenstraße 67, 80538 Munich, Germany
e-mail: bry@lmu.de
url: http://www.pms.ifi.lmu.de/

T. Furche
e-mail: tim@furche.net

B. Linse
e-mail: Benedikt.Linse@ifi.lmu.de

O. Poppe
e-mail: olga.poppe@pms.ifi.lmu.de

B. Marnette · C. Ley
Computing Laboratory, Oxford University, Wolfson Building, Parks Road, Oxford OX1 3QD, UK

B. Marnette
e-mail: Bruno.Marnette@comlab.ox.ac.uk

C. Ley
e-mail: Clemens.Ley@comlab.ox.ac.uk
url: http://web.comlab.ox.ac.uk/oucl/people/clemens.ley.html

R. De Virgilio et al. (eds.), *Semantic Web Information Management*,
DOI 10.1007/978-3-642-04329-1_15, © Springer-Verlag Berlin Heidelberg 2010

equivalent to full SPARQLog in presence of graph projection. Thus, the convenience of arbitrary quantifier alternation comes, in fact, for free. These results, though here presented in the context of RDF querying, apply similarly also in the more general setting of data exchange.

15.1 Introduction

Access to data in a machine-processable, domain-independent manner plays a central role in the future growth of the Internet. Information on legislative proceedings, census data, scientific experiments and databases, as well as the data gathered by social network applications is now accessible in form of RDF data. The Resource Description Framework (RDF) is a data format for the Web with a formal semantics that is achieving considerable popularity. Compared to relational databases, RDF is mostly distinguished by (1) a specialization to ternary statements or "triples" relating a subject, via a predicate, to an object, (2) the presence of blank nodes that allow statements where subject or object are unknown and (3) specific semantics for a small, predefined vocabulary (RDF Schema, or RDFS) reminiscent of an object-oriented type system.

With the staggering amount of data available in RDF form on the Web, the second indispensable ingredient becomes the easy selection and processing of RDF data. For that purpose, a large number of RDF query languages (see [9] for a recent survey) has been proposed, with SPARQL [19] the most prominent representative. In this paper, we build on SPARQL to remedy two of the most significant weaknesses of SPARQL from our perspective: SPARQLog extends SPARQL to support the distinguishing features of RDF such as blank nodes and the logical core [15] of the RDFS vocabulary. More technically speaking, we extend SPARQLog with rules and quantifier alternation. In SPARQLog, Blank nodes can be constructed by existentially quantified variables in rule heads. It allows *full alternation* between existential and universal quantifiers in a rule. This sharply contrasts with previous approaches to rule-based query languages that either do not support blank nodes (in rule heads) at all [18, 23], or only a limited form of quantifier alternation [10, 21, 25].

To illustrate the benefits of full quantifier alternation, imagine an information system about university courses. We distinguish three types of rules with existential quantifiers (and thus blank nodes) based on the alternation of universal and existential quantifiers:

(1) "Someone knows each professor" can be represented in SPARQLog as:

```
PREFIX uni: <http://example.org/uni>
FROM    <http://lmu.de/staff/>

EX ?pers ALL ?prof
CONSTRUCT { ?pers foaf:knows ?prof }
WHERE     { ?prof rdf:type uni:professor }
```

We call such rules ∃∀ rules (i.e., rules in the Bernays–Schönfinkel class). Some approaches such as [25] are limited to rules of this form. We show that a recursive rule language that is limited to these kind of rules is strictly less expressive than a language that allows rules also of the form discussed under (2) and (3). The gain is that languages with only ∃∀ rules are still decidable. However, as shown in Sect. 15.5.1.1, there are larger fragments of SPARQLog that are still decidable.

(2) Imagine, that we would like to state that each lecture must be "practiced" by another course (such as a tutorial or practice lab) without knowing more about that course. This statement can not be expressed by ∃∀ rules. In SPARQLog, it can be represented as:

```
PREFIX uni: <http://example.org/uni>
FROM   <http://lmu.de/staff/>

ALL ?lec EX ?crs
CONSTRUCT { ?crs uni:practices ?lec }
WHERE     { ?lec rdf:type uni:lecture }
```

Such rules are referred to as ∀∃ rules (sometimes also denoted as ∀*∃* rules). Recent proposals for rule extensions to SPARQL are limited to this form, if they consider blank nodes in rule heads at all. The reason is that in SPARQL CONSTRUCT patterns a fresh blank node is constructed for every binding of the universal variables (see Sect. 10.2.1 in [19]). For a more detailed comparison of SPARQL and SPARQLog, see Sects. 15.4 and 15.3.

(3) To the best of our knowledge, SPARQLog is the first RDF query language that supports the third kind of rules, where quantifiers are allowed to alternate freely: This allows to express statements such as, for each lecture there is a course that "practices" that lecture and is attended by all students attending the lecture. This is represented in SPARQLog as:

```
PREFIX uni: <http://example.org/uni>
FROM   <http://lmu.de/staff/>

ALL ?lec EX ?crs ALL ?stu
CONSTRUCT { ?crs uni:practices ?lec . ?stu uni:attends ?crs }
WHERE     { ?lec rdf:type uni:lecture . ?stu uni:attends ?lec }
```

In Sect. 15.5.2, we show (for the first time) that rules with full quantifier alternation can be normalized to ∀∃ form if we allow triple projection (more precisely, if we consider only the default graph in the RDF dataset as semantic of a SPARQLog program). Thus, full quantifier alternation does not add to the expressiveness of SPARQLog under default-graph semantics. Rather, for all languages with ∀∃ rules and triple projection the rewriting in Sect. 15.5.2 allows arbitrary quantifier alternation to be added for free.

In addition to flexible support for existential information through full quantifier alternation, SPARQLog captures the essentials of RDF through two further characteristics: First, SPARQLog is a closed RDF query language, i.e., the answer to an SPARQLog program is again an RDF dataset. Second, SPARQLog can express the logical core of the RDFS semantics (ρdf from [15]).

In particular, we follow RDF in allowing blank nodes not in predicate position for answers (as well as literals only in object position). We show that these limitations make the traditional approach of defining a closed semantics for a rule based query language as initial models unpractical. Nonetheless, we show how a closed semantics of a rule based query language for RDF can be defined that captures the consequences of the program under RDF entailment. A consequence of that semantics is that intermediary data, but only intermediary data, may violate the limitations posed by RDF (see also [24]).

With this semantics, SPARQLog is unsurprisingly Turing complete. Therefore, we also consider fragments of SPARQLog that are decidable in polynomial time. We (slightly) extend results from [13] to also cover quantifier alternation and identify a tractable fragment, called SwARQLog. It is based on the notion of super-weak acyclicity from [13] (which is itself inspired from, though strictly more general than, the notion of *weak-acyclicity* in data-exchange [6]). SwARQLog also remains strictly more expressive than restrictions of SPARQLog to ∃∀ rules as in [25].

Contributions The paper is organized along the following contributions:

1. An extension of SPARQL with *rules and free quantifier alternation*, called SPARQLog is introduced in Sect. 15.4.
2. The semantics of SPARQLog is defined in terms of entailment in Sect. 15.4.2. We show how this semantics can be implemented by a *reduction to the evaluation of a standard logic program* without existential quantifiers in Sect. 15.4.3.
3. SPARQLog is shown to be Turing-complete, but a significant *decidable fragment* is identified in Sect. 15.5.1.1.
4. A rewriting for SPARQLog programs to reduce quantifier alternation to ∀∃ form, i.e., rules where no universal quantifier occurs in the scope of an existential one, is given in Sect. 15.5.2 and shown to be equivalent under default-graph semantics. It is worth emphasizing that this rewriting is not possible in general first-order logic, unless we allow an extension of the vocabulary with helper constants that are not part of the semantics of the program. The latter is provided by the default-graph semantics of SPARQLog.
5. The experimental evaluation of a basic prototype shows that the reduction to standard logic programming easily competes with existing SPARQL engines even when considering only the restricted fragment of SPARQLog equivalent to SPARQL, see Sect. 15.5.3.

The results in this chapter are partially based on previous results on RDFLog, a Datalog extension with quantifier alternation, see [2, 3].

15.2 Preliminaries

In this paper, we adopt the notions of RDF vocabulary, RDF graph, (simple) RDF interpretation and (simple) RDF entailment from [11].

Definition 15.1 (RDF Graph [11]) An *RDF vocabulary* V consists of two disjoint sets called *IRIs* U and *literals* L. The *blank nodes* B is a set disjoint from U and L. An *RDF graph* is a set of RDF triples where an *RDF triple* is an element of $(\mathsf{U} \cup \mathsf{B}) \times \mathsf{U} \times (\mathsf{U} \cup \mathsf{L} \cup \mathsf{B})$. If $t = (\mathsf{s}, \mathsf{p}, \mathsf{o})$ is an RDF triple then s is the *subject*, p is the *predicate*, and o is the *object* of t.

The set L of literals consists of three subsets, *plain literals*, *typed literals* and *literals with language tags*. In this work, we consider only plain literals (and thus drop IL, the interpretation function for typed literals, see Sect. 1.3 in [11], in the following definitions).

Definition 15.2 (RDF Interpretation [11]) An *interpretation* I of an RDF vocabulary $\mathsf{V} = (\mathsf{U}, \mathsf{L})$ is a tuple $(\mathsf{IR}, \mathsf{LV}, \mathsf{IP}, \mathsf{IEXT}, \mathsf{IS})$ where IR is a nonempty set of *resources* such that $\mathsf{L} \subseteq \mathsf{LV} \subseteq \mathsf{IR}$, IP is a set of *properties* and $\mathsf{IEXT} : \mathsf{IP} \rightarrow 2^{\mathsf{IR} \times \mathsf{IR}}$, and $\mathsf{IS} : \mathsf{U} \rightarrow \mathsf{IR} \cup \mathsf{IP}$ are mappings.

RDF assigns a special meaning to a predefined vocabulary, called RDFS (RDF Schema) vocabulary. For example, it is required that IEXT(IP(rdfs:subPropertyOf)) is transitive and reflexive. The formulation of theses constraints on RDF interpretation makes use of a notion of a *class*. We have omitted this notion in the definition above for simplicity. The logical core of RDFS has been identified in [15], denoted as ρdf. An RDF interpretation I is a ρdf *interpretation* if I satisfied the constraints specified in Definition 3 in [15]. ρdf entailment is the same as RDF entailment, but assigns specific semantics to the RDFS vocabulary (e.g., transitivity of rdf:subClassOf).

Definition 15.3 (Interpretation of an RDF Graph [11]) Let I be the RDF (ρdf) interpretation $(\mathsf{IR}, \mathsf{LV}, \mathsf{IP}, \mathsf{IEXT}, \mathsf{IS})$ and $\mathsf{A} : \mathsf{B} \rightarrow \mathsf{IR}$ a mapping. Then $[\mathsf{I} + \mathsf{A}](\mathsf{e}) = \mathsf{a}$ if e is the literal a, $[\mathsf{I} + \mathsf{A}](\mathsf{e}) = \mathsf{IS}(\mathsf{e})$ if e is a IRI, $[\mathsf{I} + \mathsf{A}](\mathsf{e}) = \mathsf{A}(\mathsf{e})$ if e is a blank node, and $[\mathsf{I} + \mathsf{A}](\mathsf{e}) = \text{true}$ if $\mathsf{e} = (\mathsf{s}, \mathsf{p}, \mathsf{o})$ is an RDF triple over V, $\mathsf{I}(\mathsf{p}) \in \mathsf{IP}$ and $(\mathsf{I}(\mathsf{s}), \mathsf{I}(\mathsf{o})) \in \mathsf{IEXT}(\mathsf{I}(\mathsf{p}))$. Finally, $\mathsf{I}(\mathsf{g}) = \text{true}$ if there is a mapping $\mathsf{A} : \mathsf{B} \rightarrow \mathsf{IR}$ such that $[\mathsf{I} + \mathsf{A}](t) = \text{true}$ for all RDF triples $\mathsf{t} \in \mathsf{g}$.

The semantics of RDF is completed by the notion of entailment: An RDF graph g *RDF-entails* (ρdf*-entails*) an RDF graph h if for all RDF (ρdf) interpretations I, $\mathsf{I}(\mathsf{h}) = \text{true}$ if $\mathsf{I}(\mathsf{g}) = \text{true}$ [11]. This is equivalent to saying that there is a homomorphism from g to h.

We extend the notion of RDF graph to an RDF dataset as in SPARQL. In [19], an RDF dataset is defined as a set of RDF graphs each associated with an identifying IRI of which one is marked as the default graph. Here, we choose a formalization of RDF dataset close to an RDF graph that simplifies latter notation, but captures the same intuition.

Definition 15.4 (RDF Dataset) An RDF dataset D is a set of quadruples from $(\mathsf{U} \cup \mathsf{B}) \times \mathsf{U} \times (\mathsf{U} \cup \mathsf{L} \cup \mathsf{B}) \times (\mathsf{U} \cup \{\diamond\})$ such that for all (s, p, o, g), (s', p', o', g') it holds that if $\{s, o\} \cap \{s', o'\} = b \neq \emptyset$ and $b \in \mathsf{B}$ then $g = g'$.

Thus, an RDF dataset is a set of triples each extended with an IRI or $\diamond$ that indicates the provenance of the triple from one RDF graphs. Triples from two distinct RDF graphs in a same RDF dataset may not share any blank node. In other words, a RDF dataset is a set of extended RDF triples, where extended means that each triple is assigned a provenance in the form of the name of an RDF graph. A RDF dataset requires that if the same blank node occur in two extended triples of the dataset, then these triples have the same provenance. $\diamond$ indicates that the triple occurs in the default graph, otherwise the IRI identifies the named graph the triple originates from.

For an RDF dataset D, we denote with $\mathsf{D}[g] = \{(s, p, o) : \exists (s, p, o, g) \in \mathsf{D}\}$ the triples (without the graph identifier) in D that belong to the RDF graph with IRI $g \in \mathsf{U} \cup \{\diamond\}$.

We can lift the notion of RDF-entailment to RDF datasets as follows: An RDF dataset D *RDF-entails* (*ρdf-entails*) an RDF dataset E iff for all $g \in \mathit{IRI} \cup \{\diamond\}$ $\mathsf{D}[g]$ RDF-entails $\mathsf{E}[g]$.

For the semantics of SPARQLog, we make use of the following mapping from RDF graphs and datasets to first-order formulas.

Definition 15.5 (Canonical Formula) For an RDF graph, $\mathsf{g} = \{(s_1, p_1, o_1), \ldots, (s_n, p_n, o_n)\}$ and we define the canonical formula

$$\phi(\mathsf{g}) = \exists b_1 \ldots \exists b_m \big(R(s_1, p_1, o_1) \wedge \cdots \wedge R(s_n, p_n, o_n)\big)$$

where $b_1, \ldots, b_m$ are the blank nodes occurring in g and R is a fixed ternary relation symbol.

For an RDF dataset D containing the graph identifiers $u_1, \ldots, u_n$, we define the canonical formula

$$\phi(\mathsf{D}) = \bigwedge_{1 \le i \le n} \exists b_1^{u_i} \ldots \exists b_{m_{u_i}}^{u_i} \Bigg(\bigwedge_{(s,p,o,u_i) \in \mathsf{D}} R(s, p, o, u_i) \Bigg)$$

where $b_1^{u_i}, \ldots, b_{m_{u_i}}^{u_i}$ are the blank nodes occurring in the graph with identifier u_i and R is a fixed relation symbol with arity 4.

It is worth noting (and easy to prove) that the notion of RDF entailment coincides with first-order entailment on the canonical formulas of RDF graphs, resp. RDF datasets.

Lemma 15.1 *Let* g, h *be RDF graphs* (*datasets*). *Then* g *RDF-entails* h *iff* $\phi(\mathsf{g})$ *FO-entails* $\phi(\mathsf{h})$.

15.3 SPARQL Rule Languages

15.3.1 SPARQL and Rule Extensions of SPARQL

As briefly outlined above, SPARQLog is distinguished from previous RDF query languages by the support for arbitrary quantifier alternation. SPARQL [19], which is quickly becoming the yardstick for RDF query languages, supports only ∀∃ quantification in what corresponds to rule heads: Each blank node in a CONSTRUCT clause is instantiated once for each binding tuple of the (universal) variables in that clause. Otherwise, SPARQLog and SPARQL queries are roughly equivalent with the exception of negation and typed literals that are not supported in SPARQLog. Furthermore, SPARQL only considers what amounts to a single (nonrecursive) rule.

There have been several proposals [18, 21] for extending SPARQL with multiple rules. Typically these either explicitly do not deal with blank nodes in CONSTRUCT clauses as [18] or consider only ∀∃ quantification as in basic SPARQL [21]. Their semantics also differs considerably from SPARQLog as they support negation with answer-set or well-founded semantics. It is worth noting that the characterization of the decidable class of super-weakly acyclic programs as well as the ∀∃ rewriting carry over to SPARQLog with negation fairly immediately.

As SPARQLog [21] consider querying not a single RDF graph but a set of named RDF graphs with may contain dynamically computed views. The authors extend named RDF graphs to so called *networked graphs* allowing:

1. "reuse of RDF graphs enabling the dynamic copying of contents from one graph to the other,
2. viewing RDF graphs in a way that is defined by another RDF graph and
3. dynamic networking of RDF graphs. RDF graphs constitute databases and the meaning they describe comes from their dynamic networking" [21].

In a sense, networked graphs are a mixture of SPARQL datasets and SPARQLog programs.

Definition 15.6 (Networked Graph, adopted from [21]) A *networked graph* $G_N = (N, G, [G_1, \ldots, G_n], v)$ is encoded in a named RDF graph with name N where G is an RDF graph containing the explicit triples to be included in G_N. $[G_1, \ldots, G_n]$ is a list of networked graphs and v a mapping from that list of networked graphs to an RDF graph called the view definition of G_N. The *view definition* is included in G_N by statements of the form:

```
N g:definedBy "query".
```

where the prefix g is appropriately bound and "query" a literal containing a CONSTRUCT rule. We call the literal a *sub-query* of the networked graph definition. The view definition is the union of the sub-queries.

The following example from [21] illustrates the notion of networked graph. We assume that the named RDF graph ISWebGraph contains information about researchers working at the Information Systems and Semantic Web lab of the Institute of computer science (IFI) and the named RDF graph IFIAdminGraph information about the administrative staff at IFI. Then the named graph u : IFIGraph shown below is a networked graph: (u:IFIGraph,{ u:ISWeb u:workingGroupOf u:IFI . u:IFI u:belongsTo u:CSDepartment }, [ISWebGraph, IFIAdminGraph], v). v maps the RDF named graph IFIAdminGraph to itself and the RDF named graph ISWebGraph to an RDF graph about persons that work at `u:IFI` if they are known to work at u:ISWeb.

```
u:IFIGraph {
  u:ISWeb u:workingGroupOf u:IFI . u:IFI u:belongsTo u:CSDepartment .
  u:IFIGraph g:definedBy "CONSTRUCT { ?s ?p ?o }
                          FROM NAMED u:IFIAdminGraph
                          WHERE { GRAPH u:IFIAdminGraph { ?s ?p ?o } }"
  u:IFIGraph g:definedBy "CONSTRUCT { ?person u:worksAt u:IFI }
                          FROM NAMED u:ISWebGraph
                          WHERE { GRAPH u:ISWebGraph {
                                      ?person u:worksAt u:ISWeb. }" }
```

The advantage of this approach is the ability to encode the view definitions directly into RDF graphs where their definitions can also be processed by RDF tools that are not networked aware.

In SPARQLog, we can provide the same definition (using `u:IFIGraph` as default graph). However, SPARQLog also allows multiple different named graphs as targets for the same construction. More importantly, SPARQLog provides full quantifier alternation and has a far simpler semantics (admittedly partly due to the absence of negation):

```
FROM NAMED u:IFIAdminGraph
FROM NAMED u:ISWebGraph

CONSTRUCT { u:ISWeb u:workingGroupOf u:IFI.
            u:IFI u:belongsTo u:CSDepartment }

ALL ?s ?p ?o
CONSTRUCT { ?s ?p ?o }
WHERE     GRAPH u:IFIAdminGraph { ?s ?p ?o }

ALL ?person
CONSTRUCT { ?person u:worksAt u:IFI }
WHERE     GRAPH u:ISWebGraph { ?person u:worksAt u:ISWeb. }
```

15.3.2 Other Rule-based RDF Query Languages

The other class of recursive, rule-based query languages for RDF are adaptations of F-Logic for RDF: As in the case of extending SPARQL, these often do not consider blank nodes in rule heads at all [23]. To the best of our knowledge, the only *decidable* rule-based RDF query language with *blank nodes in rule heads* has been proposed in [25]. Decidability is obtained by restricting rules to $\exists\forall$ form. In this paper, we show that a much less restrictive (and strict super-) class of SPARQLog programs is still decidable, viz. super-weakly acyclic SPARQLog.

Most other RDF query languages such as RQL [10, 12], or SeRQL [1] are limited to what amounts to single SPARQLog rules and do not treat issues such as rule chaining, query closure (i.e., that an answer to a query is again an RDF graph or dataset), and arbitrary quantifier alternation.

SPARQLog shares some similarity with rule extensions for description logics. [20] gives an overview over the limits and possibilities of combining description logics and datalog with and without negation, thereby pointing out minimal undecidable combinations of the two methodologies. Due to the possibility of deriving concepts from base concepts, concept and role inclusion axioms, which are not present in SPARQLog, this problem is fundamentally different and harder to tackle. In particular, the undecidability results from [20] do not carry over to SPARQLog. Moreover, such approaches either disallow existential quantifiers in *rule heads* (but allow them in facts or TBox-Axioms), or use full logic programming with function symbols and negation as in dlvhex.

15.3.3 Quantifier Alternation in Data Exchange

As discussed in more detail in Chap. 14, existential quantification and its expressiveness have been extensively studied in data exchange [6]. A data exchange setting consists of two database schemata, a source schema S and the target schema T, and a set of constraints Σ. The data exchange problem is to find, given a source database I over schema S, a target database J over schema T such that (I, J) satisfies Σ. In this case, J is called a solution for the data exchange problem for I and Σ. A solution J is universal, if there is a homomorphism from J to any other solution J' of the setting. In RDF terms, such a homomorphisms is the identity function on IRIs and literals, but allows blank nodes to be mapped either to other blank nodes or to IRIs or literals.

Different classes of constraints have been considered. An important class are tupel generating dependencies (TGD). These are roughly SPARQLog rules where the quantifier alternation is restricted to one alternation of the form $\forall\exists$. Therefore, a data exchange problem for TGDs resembles the problem of computing the semantics for a given SPARQLog program P with dataset D. Hence, the set of universal solutions could be considered a suitable semantics for P. Universal solutions have a drawback though: they are not closed under homomorphism: Given a universal solution J for a set of constraints Σ, there may be databases J' such that there is a homomorphism from J to J', yet J' is not even a solution (let alone a universal solution) for Σ. For instance, let $\Sigma = \{r(a,b), \forall x, y \exists z : r(x,y) \rightarrow s(x,z), \forall x : s(x,x) \rightarrow q(x)\}$. Then $J = \{r(a,b), \exists x : s(a,x)\}$ is a universal solution for Σ and there is a homomorphism from J to $K = \{r(a,b), s(a,a)\}$ (the identity function up to x which is mapped to a). However, K is not a solution of Σ (and thus also no universal solution) as $s(a,a)$ requires also $q(a)$ to hold in a solution for Σ due to the third constraint. Still it is easy to see that the set of universal solutions of P is a subset of the denotational semantics $[\![P]\!]$ defined in Sect. 15.4.2. In addition, we show that the operational semantics $[P]$ is a universal solution (Lemma 15.2). This is not surprising since our operational semantics is closely related to the chase procedure which can be used to compute universal solutions [4]. Nonetheless, one could state that we have extended the chase procedure to a wider class of constraints (by allowing arbitrary quantifier alternation) and to a more general data model where the input database can contain blank nodes.

It has been observed in [8] that TGDs are not closed under composition. That is there are two finite sets of TGDs Σ_1 and Σ_2 such that there is no finite set of TGDs that defines the same database to database mapping as $\Sigma_1 \circ \Sigma_2$. Nonetheless, [8] shows that there is a finite set Σ of non-TGDs constraints that is equivalent to $\Sigma_1 \circ \Sigma_2$. It turns out that this set Σ is in fact a set constraints with $\forall\exists\forall$ quantifier alternation that can be expressed in SPARQLog. This shows that if projection is not allowed (as in the standard data exchange setting or when all rules in a SPARQLog program are required to construct into the default graph), then the extra quantifier alternation does indeed add expressive power.

15.4 SPARQLog: SPARQL with Rules and Quantification

SPARQL has quickly become *the* standard for querying RDF data. Part of its success is certainly that it is a fairly compact language. Here we want to investigate how SPARQL can be extended with two features, rules and arbitrary quantification, without sacrificing most of its simplicity and the basic flavor of the language.

Rules are an acknowledged part of the Semantic Web vision. The `CONSTRUCT` query form of SPARQL can be seen as a form of non-recursive single-rule program and offer an obvious start point for a full rule language. With full rules SPARQL becomes by itself capable of computing such important concepts as the subsumption hierarchy in RDFS data or a person's social network in FOAF (*friend of a friend*) data.

The following SPARQLog program illustrates how we extend SPARQL's syntax to accommodate rules: Rather than a single `CONSTRUCT-WHERE` clause, in the following called *rule*, we allow any number of these to occur in the document. The bodies of SPARQLog rules are mostly standard SPARQL `WHERE` clauses. The heads are `CONSTRUCT` clauses that may be adorned with `GRAPH` patterns that specify the target graph of the rule. If no such pattern is present, the result of the rule is added to the default graph of the dataset. If such a pattern is present, it is added to the graph named in the `GRAPH` pattern. This allows, e.g., for hiding intermediary results. Note, that the dataset clauses `FROM` and `FROM NAMED` occur only once for all rules. Thus all rules query the same dataset.

```
PREFIX   :     <http://example.org/#ns>.
PREFIX   foaf: <http://xmlns.com/foaf/0.1/>.
PREFIX   wine: <http://www.w3.org/TR/2003/PR-owl-guide-20031209/wine#>
FROM       <http://example.org>
```

```
5  FROM NAMED <http://example.org/bavarians>

7  ALL ?x ?y
   CONSTRUCT { ?x rdf:type :bavarian-look-alike }                            R3
9  WHERE { { { ?x :likes      ?y .         ?y rdf:type      wine:Wine .
               ?y wine:locatedIn wine:ItalianRegion } UNION
11             { ?x :likes      ?y .         ?y rdf:type      wine:Wine .
               ?y wine:locatedIn wine:FrenchRegion } } .
13           GRAPH <http://example.org/bavarians>
               { ?x rdf:type    :bavarian }
15
   ALL ?x
17 CONSTRUCT GRAPH <http://example.org/bavarians>                             R2
             { ?x rdf:type    :bavarian }
19 WHERE     { ?x rdf:type    :european.    ?x foaf:knows    "Edmund" }

21 ALL ?x
   CONSTRUCT { ?x rdf:type    :european }                                    R1
23 WHERE     { ?x foaf:knows "Angela" .     ?x foaf:knows    "Nicolas" .
               ?x foaf:knows "Elisabeth" }
```

In the example above, R_1 queries the default dataset (there is no GRAPH pattern in the body) to find people who know the German chancellor, the French president, and the British queen. Triples classifying these people as European are added to the default graph. In R_2 that default graph is queried for such people that also know the former Bavarian prime minister. Triples classifying such people as Bavarian are added to the named graph `http://example.org/bavarians` that is also included in the dataset in the dataset clause of line 5. R_3 queries that named graph (containing the results of R_2 as well as any statements contained in the graph from the beginning) for Bavarians. If the default graph contains the information that such a person also likes Italian or French wine, then we that person can not be a real Bavarian, but must be a look-alike posing as a Bavarian.

Note that all rules carry explicit quantification clauses, e.g., ALL ?x. These clauses are added to support SPARQLog's second major addition over SPARQL.

SPARQL's CONSTRUCT rules allow the construction of RDF graphs. Unfortunately, the construction of one of RDF's most significant innovations, the provision of existential information in form of *blank nodes*, is poorly supported: Blank nodes can be constructed, but they are always scoped over all (universal) variables of the query. This makes most grouping tasks involving blank nodes (e.g., the construction of a container for all authors for each paper) impossible. In absence of rules, this is a significant limitation. We suggest the use of an explicit quantifier clause to overcome this limitation: Rather than assuming that all blank nodes to be constructed are in the scope of all universal variables, we allow arbitrary quantifier quantification as in first-order logic.

To illustrate the issue of quantifier alternation and what kind of queries can be expressed, consider three examples. We choose to use explicit existential variables rather than blank nodes as their use in SPARQL is somewhat confusing (in bodies they play the role of normal variables, but in heads they are treated as existential).

The first, B_1, asserts that there is a Presenter for each TalkEvent who also attends that same event.

B_1

```
PREFIX eswc: <http://www.eswc2006.org/technologies/ontology#>

ALL ?x EX ?y
CONSTRUCT { ?y eswc:attendeeAt ?x . ?y rdf:type eswc:Presenter }
WHERE     { ?x rdf:type           eswc:TalkEvent }
```

The second, B_2, asserts that there is a MeetingRoomPlace that is the location of all talks.

B_2

```
EX ?x ALL ?y
CONSTRUCT { ?y eswc:hasLocation ?x . ?x rdf:type eswc:MeetingRoomPlace }
WHERE     { ?y rdf:type            eswc:TalkEvent }
```

The third, B_3, asserts that there for each TalkEvent there is someone that holds that talk and therefore is known by all attendees of the talk.

B_3

```
ALL ?x EX ?y ALL ?z
CONSTRUCT { ?x eswc:heldBy ?y .                ?z foaf:knows ?y }
WHERE     { ?x rdf:type      eswc:TalkEvent. ?z eswc:attendeeAt ?x }
```

The difference between the three cases is, of course, the scope of the existential variable (or blank node): In the first case, which is the only one unmodified SPARQL supports, one *fresh* blank node is created for each binding of the universal variable. In the second case, a single blank node is created that is the object in all hasLocation triples. In the third case, one *fresh* blank node is created for each binding of `?x` (each talk), but that same blank node is object in all knows triples for attendees of that talk.

It is worth noting that the latter two cases are essential for constructing many group or set like structures in RDF. For instance for RDF containers, RDF representations of *n*-ary relations [16], and RDF reification it is best and common practice to use blank nodes for the container, relation, or statement object. Unfortunately, SPARQL does not support either of these cases.

In presence of rules (and thus not in SPARQL) and graph projection, we show in Sect. 15.5.2 that quantifier alternation, though convenient, actually does not increase the expressiveness. In other words, if rules and graph projection is present cases 2 and 3 can be expressed using only rules as in case 1. Nevertheless, even in these cases quantifier alternation is far more convenient (see rewriting in Sect. 15.5.2).

15.4.1 SPARQLog Syntax

As illustrated above, SPARQLog mostly adds rules and quantifier alternation to SPARQL. There are a few other restrictions and simplifications:

1. We do not consider `OPTIONAL` and `FILTER` expressions in this chapter. As negation in SPARQL is expressed via `OPTIONAL` and `isBound`, SPARQLog as presented here is based on positive SPARQL.
2. As stated above, we do not allow blank nodes to occur in bodies or heads of SPARQLog rules. In bodies blank nodes can be replaced by fresh universal variables, in heads with fresh existential ones.

```
⟨program⟩              ::= ⟨prefix-clause⟩* ⟨dataset-clause⟩ ⟨rule⟩+
⟨dataset-clause⟩       ::= 'FROM' ⟨iri⟩ ('FROM' 'NAMED' ⟨iri⟩)*
⟨prefix-clause⟩        ::= 'PREFIX' ⟨identifier⟩? ':' ⟨iri⟩
⟨rule⟩                 ::= ⟨quantifier-clause⟩* ⟨construct-clause⟩ ⟨where-clause⟩?
⟨quantifier-clause⟩    ::= 'ALL' ⟨variable⟩+ | 'EX' ⟨variable⟩+
⟨construct-clause⟩     ::= 'CONSTRUCT' '{' ⟨triple-pattern⟩ '}'?
                           ⟨construct-template⟩*
⟨construct-template⟩   ::= 'GRAPH' (⟨iri⟩ | ⟨variable⟩) '{' ⟨triple-pattern⟩ '}'
⟨where-clause⟩         ::= 'WHERE' '{' ⟨graph-pattern⟩ '}'
⟨graph-pattern⟩        ::= ('GRAPH' (⟨iri⟩ | ⟨variable⟩))? '{' ⟨graph-pattern⟩ '}'
                         | '{' ⟨graph-pattern⟩ '}' 'UNION' '{' ⟨graph-pattern⟩ '}'
                         | ⟨graph-pattern⟩ ('.' ⟨graph-pattern⟩)?
⟨basic-graph-pattern⟩  ::= ⟨triple-pattern⟩ ('.' ⟨basic-graph-pattern⟩)?
⟨triple-pattern⟩       ::= ⟨resource⟩ ⟨predicate⟩ ⟨resource⟩
⟨resource⟩             ::= ⟨iri⟩ | ⟨variable⟩ | ⟨literal⟩
⟨predicate⟩            ::= ⟨iri⟩ | ⟨variable⟩
⟨variable⟩             ::= '?' ⟨identifier⟩
```

Fig. 15.1 Syntax of SPARQLog

3. We allow only IRIs or universal variables, but no existential variables, for the graph identifier (directly after `GRAPH`) in rule heads.
4. In contrast to SPARQL, we do require that all SPARQLog rules are range-restricted: If x is an universal variable in the head of a rule R, then x must occur in the body of R. If there is an existential variable y in the head of R that is in the scope of an universal variable x, then x must occur in the body of R.
5. For simplicity, we only consider basic triple patterns and none of the abbreviation syntaxes from SPARQL (no predicate-object or object lists, no syntactic sugar for collections or `rdf:type`).

Literals and IRIs are as in RDF graphs (see Sect. 15.2), variables are from an infinite set disjoint with IRIs, literals, and blank nodes.

With the above restrictions, Fig. 15.1 gives the syntax of SPARQLog. For simplicity, we ignore namespace prefixes and all associated issues in the following. Prefix resolution can be added easily, but only distracts from the salient points of this chapter. We allow `WHERE` clauses to be omitted entirely. In this case, the rule head is always true (a fact).

15.4.2 Denotational Semantics for SPARQLog

SPARQL's semantic is defined with a rather ad-hoc algebra in [19]. A more complete algebraic semantics of SPARQL is given in Chap. 12 of this volume. For SPARQLog, a semantics based on (simple) RDF entailment seems the most natural, in particular since RDF entailment coincides with FO entailment of the canonical formulas of RDF datasets.

To this end, we first define a canonical formula also for SPARQLog programs. This can be seen as a translation of SPARQLog to first-order logic.

Definition 15.7 (Canonical Formula for SPARQLog Program) Let P be a SPARQLog program and $u_1, \dots, u_n$ the identifiers for RDF graphs $G_1, \dots, G_n$. Then the canonical formula $\phi(P)$ of P is defined as follows:

$\phi(\texttt{FROM}\ u_i\ Q)$	$= \bigwedge_{(s,p,o)\in G_i} (s, p, o, \diamond) \wedge \phi(Q)$
$\phi(\texttt{FROM NAMED}\ u_i\ Q)$	$= \bigwedge_{(s,p,o)\in G_i} (s, p, o, u_i) \wedge \phi(Q)$
$\phi(\mathit{ALL\ vars}\ Q)$	$= \forall\, \mathit{vars} : \phi(Q)$
$\phi(\mathit{EX\ vars}\ Q)$	$= \exists\, \mathit{vars} : \phi(Q)$
$\phi(\texttt{CONSTRUCT}\ \mathit{template}\ Q)$	$= \phi_g(\mathit{template}, \diamond)\ \phi(Q)$
$\phi(\texttt{WHERE}\ \mathit{pattern})$	$= \leftarrow \phi_g(\mathit{pattern}, \diamond)$
$\phi_g(\mathit{pattern}\ \texttt{UNION}\ Q, c)$	$= \phi_g(\mathit{pattern}, c) \vee \phi_g(Q, c)$
$\phi_g(\texttt{GRAPH}\ \mathit{var}\ Q, c)$	$= \phi_g(Q, \mathit{var})$
$\phi_g(\texttt{GRAPH}\ \mathit{iri}\ Q, c)$	$= \phi_g(Q, \mathit{iri})$
$\phi_g(\mathit{pattern}\ \texttt{.}\ Q, c)$	$= \phi_g(\mathit{pattern}, c) \wedge \phi_g(Q, c)$
$\phi_g(\texttt{\{}\ \mathit{pattern}\ \texttt{\}}, c)$	$= \phi_g((\mathit{pattern}), c)$
$\phi_g(\mathit{sub\ pred\ obj}, c)$	$= R(\phi(\mathit{sub}), \phi(\mathit{pred}), \phi(\mathit{obj}), c)$

The canonical formula is pretty straightforward: the head of a SPARQLog rule, i.e., the `CONSTRUCT` clause, is translated into a conjunction that forms the consequence of an implication. The `WHERE` clause is translated into the condition of the implication. It may contain both disjunctions and conjunctions. Noteworthy is the propagation of the identifier of the current query graph in the dataset by means of the second parameter of ϕ_g.

For instance, rule B_3 from Sect. 15.4 has the following canonical formula (brackets are normalized):

$$\forall x \exists y \forall z : R(x, \text{eswc:heldBy}, y, \diamond) \wedge R(z, \text{foaf:knows}, y, \diamond)$$
$$\leftarrow R(x, \text{rdf:type}, \text{eswc:TalkEvent}, \diamond) \wedge R(z, \mathit{eswc{:}attendeeAt}, x, \diamond)$$

Here all triples occur in the default graph. In contrast, the canonical formula for rule R_2 highlights that the default graph is queried, but that the consequences are triples in a named graph:

$$\forall x : R(x, \text{rdf:type}, \text{:bavarian}, \texttt{<http://example.org/bavarians>})$$
$$\leftarrow R(x, \text{rdf:type}, \text{:european}, \diamond) \wedge R(z, \text{foaf:knows}, \text{"Edmund"}, \diamond)$$

It is not generally agreed upon what the semantics of a rule based RDF query language should be if existential variables are allowed in the head. In contrast, it is agreed that the semantics of a logic program with only universally quantified variables is its minimal Herbrand model.

We deal with this problem by defining the semantics of SPARQLog in terms of entailment. More precisely, we define the semantics of an SPARQLog program P to be the set of all RDF datasets D whose canonical formulas entail the same RDF datasets as the canonical formula of P.

Definition 15.8 (Denotational Semantics of SPARQLog) Let P be an SPARQLog program. The *denotational semantics* $[\![P]\!]$ of P is the set of all RDF datasets D, such that for all RDF datasets E it holds that $\phi(\mathsf{D})$ entails $\phi(\mathsf{E})$ if and only if $\phi(P)$ entails $\phi(\mathsf{E})$.

Observe that the semantics of an SPARQLog program is an infinite set of possibly infinite RDF datasets. However, we choose the above semantics (and not, e.g., the set of all datasets whose canonical formulas follow logically from $\phi(P)$) to ensure that $[\![P]\!]$ forms an equivalence class under (RDF) entailment. Therefore, any element (in particular, any finite element if such exists) of $[\![P]\!]$ characterizes the entire set. We consider an implementation of SPARQLog *sound* and *complete* if it returns any element of $[\![P]\!]$ for a given SPARQLog program P.

This semantics is not RDFS aware. However, as stated above [15] gives a set of first-order formulas that characterize the logical core of RDFS (there called ρfs). These formulas can be expressed by SPARQLog rules and added to a program, if an RDFS aware semantics is desired.

15.4.3 Relational Operational Semantics for SPARLog

The goal of this section is to give an evaluation of an SPARQLog program P by first translating P into a logic program $s(P)$, using the well-studied notion of Skolemisation [5], and then evaluating this program $s(P)$ using standard logic programming or relational technology. Two post processing steps (Unskolemization and RDF normalization) make sure that the result is an RDF graph in the denotational semantics of P.

We use the well studied notion of Skolemisation [5] to translate an SPARQLog program into a logic program.

Definition 15.9 (Skolemisation [5]) Let Σ and Γ be disjoint alphabets, $\varphi = \forall \bar{x} \exists y (\psi)$ a formula over $\Sigma \cup \Gamma$ and $f \in \Gamma$. A *Γ-Skolemisation step* s_f maps φ to $s_f(\varphi) := \forall \bar{x} \psi\{y \leftarrow f(\bar{x})\}$. (We denote with $\phi\{t \leftarrow t'\}$ the formula ϕ where all occurrences of the term t are replaced by the term t'.) A *Γ-Skolemisation* s is a composition $s_{f_1} \circ \cdots \circ s_{f_n}$ of Γ-Skolemisation steps such that f_i does not occur in $s_{f_{i+1}} \circ \cdots \circ s_{f_n}(\varphi)$ and $s(\varphi)$ contains no existential variables. The definition of a Skolemisation is extended to sets in the usual way.

The Skolemisation of (the canonical formula of) an SPARQLog program P is equivalent to a range restricted logic program, which we denote by $s(\phi(P))$. If necessary, disjunction in rule bodies and conjunction in rule heads is expanded into multiple rules as usual. Any logic programming engine can compute the minimal Herbrand model $M_{s(\phi(P))}$ of $s(\phi(P))$.

For instance, the following logic program is the Skolemisation $s(\phi(P))$ of the SPARQLog rule B_3 from Sect. 15.4 where s replaces the existential variable y in P by the term $s_y(x)$:

$$\{\forall xz : R(x, \text{eswc:heldBy}, s_y(x), \diamond)$$
$$\leftarrow R(x, \text{rdf:type}, \text{eswc:TalkEvent}, \diamond) \wedge R(z, \textit{eswc:attendeeAt}, x, \diamond)$$
$$\forall xz : R(z, \text{foaf:knows}, s_y(x), \diamond)$$
$$\leftarrow R(x, \text{rdf:type}, \text{eswc:TalkEvent}, \diamond) \wedge R(z, \textit{eswc:attendeeAt}, x, \diamond)\}$$

We define $\phi(M_{s(\phi(P))})$ to be the conjunction of all ground atoms that are true in $M_{s(\phi(P))}$. However, $\phi(M_{S(P)})$ might not be the canonical formula of an element of $[\![P]\!]$ for two reasons. First, the example shows that $\phi(M_{S(P)})$ might contain atoms with skolem terms, which are not entailed by $\phi(P)$. Second, $\phi(M_{S(P)})$ can contain atoms with literals in subject or predicate position or blank nodes in predicate position. Such atoms are not allowed in an RDF graph, and therefore never part of an element of $[\![P]\!]$.

We can avoid the first problem by "undoing" the Skolemization: replacing each Skolem term in $\phi(M_{S(P)})$ by a fresh, distinct blank node. We formalize this operation as the inverse of a Skolemization called *Unskolemization*.

Definition 15.10 (Unskolemization) Let Σ and Γ be disjoint alphabets and φ a ground, possibly infinite, and quantifier free formula over $\Sigma \cup \Gamma$. Let $\bar{t}$ be the sequence of all ground terms $f(\bar{u})$ where f is in Γ and $\bar{u}$ is a sequence of terms over $\Sigma \cup \Gamma$. Then the *Γ-Unskolemization u* maps φ to $u(\varphi) := \exists\bar{x}(\varphi\{\bar{t} \leftarrow \bar{x}\})$, where $\bar{x}$ is a sequence of fresh variables.

To address the second issue, we remove all atoms with literals or blank nodes in predicate position (no RDF graph may contain such a triple or any triple entailed by it). In addition we remove each triple t in graph u that contains a literal l in subject position and add two triples t_1 and t_2 to u where t_1 is obtained from t by replacing an occurrence of a literal l in subject position by a fresh blank node b_l and t_2 is obtained from t by replacing all occurrences of l by b_l. Dropping these atoms does not affect the soundness or completeness (see below) as these atoms can by definition not be part of an RDF dataset. Nevertheless, allowing them during the evaluation is useful and even necessary for certain programs (for details see [15]).

Definition 15.11 (Normalization Operator) Let φ be a formula of the form $\exists\bar{x}(a_1(\bar{x}) \wedge \cdots \wedge a_n(\bar{x}))$ where each $a_i(\bar{x}) = T(t_1, t_2, t_3)$ for some $t_1, t_2, t_3 \in (\mathsf{U} \cup \mathsf{B} \cup \mathsf{L})$. Let $\mathsf{L}' \subseteq \mathsf{L}$ be the set of literals that occur in the first argument of an atom in φ. We define $\mu : \mathsf{U} \cup \mathsf{B} \cup \mathsf{L} \rightarrow \mathsf{U} \cup \mathsf{B} \cup \mathsf{L}$ to be the injection such that

$\mu(t) = b$ for some fresh blank node b (not in φ) if $t \in \mathsf{L}'$ and $\mu(t) = t$ otherwise. Then $\Pi(\varphi) = \{\Pi(a_1(\bar{x})), \ldots, \Pi(a_n(\bar{x}))\}$ and

$$\Pi\big(T(t_1,t_2,t_3)\big) = \begin{cases} \top & \text{if } t_2 \in \mathsf{B} \cup \mathsf{L} \\ (\mu(t_1), t_2, t_3) \wedge (\mu(t_1), t_2, \mu(t_3)) & \text{otherwise} \end{cases}$$

The normalization operator ensures that, though intermediary atoms may contain blank nodes in predicate position (see [24] for examples where this is useful), the final answer of an SPARQLog program never contains such atoms.

Armed with these notions of Skolemization, Unskolemization and Normalization, we finally define the operational semantics of SPARQLog as follows.

Definition 15.12 (Operational Semantics of SPARQLog) Let P be an SPARQLog program over Σ, s a Γ-Skolemization for P, and u an Γ-Unskolemization. Then the *operational semantics* $[P]$ of P is $[P] := \Pi(u(\phi(M_{s(\phi(P))})))$ where $\phi(M_{s(\phi(P))})$ is as defined above: the conjunction of all ground atoms that are true in the minimal Herbrand model of $s(\phi(P))$.

15.4.3.1 Soundness and Completeness

Even though we do not require that elements of the denotational semantics $[\![P]\!]$ of an SPARQLog program P are models of P it holds that $u(\phi(M_{s(\phi(P))}))$ has a canonical structure that is not only a model of P but even a universal model (or universal solution in the sense of [7]). Thus, if we allow literals in subject position and blank nodes in subject or predicate position, we can omit Π from the operational semantics and compute a model of P.

To formulate this more precisely, we define an *extended Herbrand structure A* over alphabet Σ and variables *Var* as a structure (D, Rel, Fun) where D is the set of (possibly nonground) terms over Σ and *Var*, and every function f^A is defined by $f^A(t_1,\ldots,t_n) = f(t_1,\ldots,t_n)$. We extend the definition of Unskolemization from formulas to extended Herbrand structures: if u is an Unskolemization that replaces $\bar{t}$ by $\bar{x}$ then $u(M)$ is the extended Herbrand structure obtained from M by renaming the domain elements $\bar{t}$ by $\bar{x}$.

Lemma 15.2 *Let P be an SPARQLog program. Then* $A_P = u(M_{s(\phi(P))}) \models^s \phi(P)$ *and* $\phi(P) \models^e u(\phi(M_{s(\phi(P))})) = \psi_P$.

Intuitively, $A_P \models^s \phi(P)$ means that ψ_P captures all the information in P and $\phi(P) \models^e \psi_P$ means that it does not assert anything that is not asserted by P. From these two key observations, we can prove that the operational semantics of SPARQLog is both sound and complete with respect to the denotational semantics.

Theorem 15.1 *Let P be an SPARQLog program. Then* $[P] \in [\![P]\!]$.

15.4.3.2 Proof of Lemma 15.2 and Theorem 15.1

In the proof of Lemma 15.2, we often make use of the Substitution lemma, which we state here without proof.

Lemma 15.3 (Substitution Lemma) *Let φ be a sentence and M an interpretation. Then*

$$M \models^s \varphi \quad \text{iff} \quad M, d \models^s \psi(x)$$

if $\psi = \varphi\{t \leftarrow x\}$ and M interprets t as d.

We now recall some well-known results about Skolemization. Symmetric proofs show the following properties of Unskolemization.

Lemma 15.4 (Skolemization Lemma) *Let Σ, Γ and Π be disjoint alphabets and φ a finite formula over $\Sigma \cup \Gamma$. Let s be a Π-Skolemization for φ, u an Γ-Unskolemization for φ. Then*

- $\varphi \models^e u(\varphi)$.
- $s(\varphi) \models^e \varphi$.
- *$u(\varphi)$ is satisfiable iff φ is satisfiable.*
- *φ is satisfiable iff $s(\varphi)$ is satisfiable.*

Corollary 15.1 (of the Skolemization Lemma) *Let φ be a finite formula over $\Sigma \cup \Gamma$ and u an Γ-Unskolemization for φ. If S is a model of $u(\varphi)$ over Σ then there exists an extension T of S on Γ which is a model of φ.*

Before we can turn to the actual proofs of the soundness and completeness of the operational semantics, we have to establish some further properties of Unskolemization. These are the central observations to show that every RDF dataset which is entailed by the operational semantics of an SPARQLog program P is entailed by $\phi(P)$.

Lemma 15.5 *Let φ and ψ be formulas over $\Sigma \cup \Gamma$ where φ is finite and ψ is possibly infinite and ground. Let u be an Γ-Unskolemization for φ. Then*

$$\varphi \models^e \psi \quad \text{implies that} \quad u(\varphi) \models^e u(\psi)$$

Proof Let S be a model over Σ of $u(\varphi)$. As φ is finite, by Corollary 15.1 there is an extension T of S on Γ which is a model of φ. By the assumption, T is also a model of ψ. Then it follows from Lemma 15.4 that T is a model of $u(\psi)$. As $u(\psi)$ contains no symbol from Γ and T is an extension of S on Γ, S is a model of $u(\psi)$. □

Lemma 15.6 *Let φ be a formula over Σ, M an extended Herbrand structure over Σ and Var, and u an Γ-Unskolemization for φ. Then*

$$M \models^s \varphi \quad \text{implies that} \quad u(M) \models^s u(\varphi)$$

Proof Assume that $M \models^s \varphi$. Let $\forall \bar{x}(\psi) = \varphi$. Then for all sequences of terms $\bar{t}$ it holds that $M \models^s \psi(\bar{t})$. As M is an extended Herbrand structure, it interprets every constant c by c. Therefore, it follows from the substitution Lemma that $M \models^s (\psi\{\bar{c} \leftarrow \bar{y}\})(\bar{t}, \bar{c})$. Observe that $u(M)$ be the extended Herbrand structure obtained from M by renaming the domain elements $\bar{c}$ by $\bar{y}$. Thus $u(M) \models^s (\psi\{\bar{c} \leftarrow \bar{y}\})(\bar{t})$. Finally, by the definition of entailment and Unskolemization it holds that $u(M) \models^s u(\varphi)$. □

Proof of Lemma 15.2 Let P be an SPARQLog program over alphabet Σ. We need to show that $A_P = u(M_{s(\phi(P))}) \models^s \phi(P)$ and $\phi(P) \models^e u(\phi(M_{s(\phi(P))})) = \psi_P$.

To show that $A_P \models^s \phi(P)$, observe that by definition $M_{s(\phi(P))}$ is a model of $s(\phi(P))$. It therefore follows from Lemma 15.6 that $u(M_{s(\phi(P))})$ is a model of P.

For the second part, observe that as $s(\phi(P))$ is a logic program it follows that $s(\phi(P))$ entails each atom that is true in $M_{s(\phi(P))}$. Thus, $s(\phi(P))$ also entails the canonical formula $\phi(M_{s(\phi(P))})$ of $M_{s(\phi(P))}$. Let u be the inverse of s. As $s(\phi(P))$ is a finite set of finite formulas and ψ_P is a ground formula it follows from Lemma 15.5 that $u \circ s(\phi(P)) = \phi(P)$ entails $u(\phi(M_{s(\phi(P))}))$. □

Proof of Theorem 15.1 The aim is to show that every RDF dataset that is entailed by an SPARQLog program is also entailed by the operational semantics. First, we need to establish a few more properties of canonical formulas of SPARQLog programs. □

Lemma 15.7 *Let P be a logic program over alphabet Σ and M_P its minimal Herbrand model. Let* g *be an RDF dataset and $\phi(\mathsf{g}) = \exists \bar{x}(\bigwedge \psi)$ its canonical formula. Then the following statements are equivalent*

(a) $P \models^e \bigwedge \psi\{\bar{x} \leftarrow \bar{t}\}$ *for some sequence of variables $\bar{x}$ and ground terms $\bar{t}$.*
(b) $P \models^e \phi(\mathsf{g})$.
(c) $M_P \models^s \phi(\mathsf{g})$.

Proof It is trivial that (a) implies (b). To see that (b) implies (c) observe that M_P is a model of P. To show that (c) implies (a) assume that (c) is true. As M_P is a Herbrand model there is a sequence of terms $\bar{t}$ such that $M_P, \bar{t}$ is a model of $\bigwedge \Phi(\bar{x})$. In addition, M_P interprets all terms by themselves. Thus, it follows from the substitution lemma that M_P is a model of $\bigwedge \Phi\{\bar{x} \leftarrow \bar{t}\}$. Therefore, M_P is a model of $a\{\bar{x} \leftarrow \bar{t}\}$ for every $a \in \Phi$. As $a\{\bar{x} \leftarrow \bar{t}\}$ is a ground atom it follows that $P \models^e a\{\bar{x} \leftarrow \bar{t}\}$. As this is true for every $a \in \Phi$ it holds that $P \models^e \bigwedge \Phi\{\bar{x} \leftarrow \bar{t}\}$ for some sequence of terms $\bar{t}$. □

With these properties, we can now show the Theorem 15.1: Let P be an SPARQLog program and $\psi_P = u(\phi(M_{s(\phi(P))}))$. We first show that for any RDF graph g

$$\phi(P) \models^e \phi(\mathsf{g}) \quad \text{iff} \quad \psi_P \models^e \phi(\mathsf{g})$$

The direction from right to left follows from the second part of Theorem 15.2. For the direction from left to right, let $\phi(\mathsf{g}) = \exists \bar{x}(\bigwedge \xi)$ where ξ is a set of atom. Assume that $\phi(P) \models^e \phi(\mathsf{g})$. By Lemma 15.4, $s(\phi(P)) \models^e \phi(\mathsf{g})$ for any Skolemization s of $\phi(P)$. As $s(\phi(P))$ is a logic program it follows from Lemma 15.7 that there is a sequence $\bar{t}$ of terms such that $s(\phi(P)) \models^e \bigwedge \xi\{\bar{x} \leftarrow \bar{t}\}$. Thus, for all atoms $a \in \xi\{\bar{x} \leftarrow \bar{t}\}$ it holds that $s(\phi(P)) \models^e a$. As $M_{s(\phi(P))}$ is a model of $s(\phi(P))$ it follows that $M_{s(\phi(P))}$ is a model of a. Let $\bigwedge M_{s(\phi(P))}$ be the conjunction of all ground atoms which are true in $M_{s(\phi(P))}$. Then a is a conjunct in $M_{s(\phi(P))}$ and thus $\bigwedge M_{s(\phi(P))} \models^e a$. As this is true for any $a \in \xi\{\bar{x} \leftarrow \bar{t}\}$ it holds that $\bigwedge M_{s(\phi(P))} \models^e \xi\{\bar{x} \leftarrow \bar{t}\}$.

Thus, $\bigwedge M_{s(\phi(P))} \models^e \phi(\mathsf{g})$ and there is a homomorphism μ from $M_{s(\phi(P))}$ to g. Observe that there is a mapping ν from $D^{M_{s(\phi(P))}}$ to $D^{u(M_{s(\phi(P))})}$ such that (i) $\nu(c^{M_{s(\phi(P))}}) = c^{u(M_{s(\phi(P))})}$ if c is a IRI or literal, (ii) if f is a skolem symbol then $\nu(f(\bar{t})) = x_{f(\bar{t})}$ where $x_{f(\bar{t})}$ is a nonconstant domain element in $D^{u(M_{s(\phi(P))})}$, and (iii) $R^{M_{s(\phi(P))}}(\bar{d})$ iff $R^{u(M_{s(\phi(P))})}(\nu(\bar{t}))$ for every relation symbol R. Observe that $\mu \circ \nu$ is a homomorphism from G to $u(M_{s(\phi(P))})$. Thus, the operational semantics $u(M_{s(\phi(P))})$ of P entails φ^{g}.

It remains to show that $\theta \models^e \phi(\mathsf{g})$ iff $\Pi(\theta) \models^e \phi(\mathsf{g})$ where θ is a formula as in the definition of the normalization operator Π. The direction from right to left is immediate since $\Pi(\theta) \models^e \theta$. The other direction follows from the definition of Π and the structure of RDF triples.

15.5 Properties of SPARQLog

15.5.1 Designing Tractable Fragments of SPARQLog

Since the full SPARQLog captures some classes of expressive formulas (such as the $\forall\exists$-rules) it is easy to adapt some standard proofs of Turing completeness (see, e.g., [4]) to show the following.

Proposition 15.1 *SPARQLog is Turing complete.*

This section focuses on the description of fragments of SPARQLog, recognizable in PTIME, that ensure polynomial complexity when given a fixed (or fairly small) program P and a potentially very large RDF dataset (playing the role of a *database*). We can formalize the desired notion of tractability as follows.

Definition 15.13 (Tractability) We say that an SPARQLog program P containing the RDF graph identifiers $u_1, \ldots, u_n$ in its dataset clause is tractable iff the following holds: For all RDF graphs, $G_1, \ldots, G_n$ associated with $u_1, \ldots, u_n$ of total size n, the RDF dataset $[P]$ is finite and can be computed in time $O(n^k)$ for some k depending only on P.

It follows from Theorem 2 in [13] that the finiteness of $[P]$ (for all $G_1, \ldots, G_n$) is actually a sufficient condition for polynomial data-complexity. By using a standard encoding of general relational constraints into RDF constraints, we can adapt the proof of Theorem 4 in [13] to show that the finiteness of $[P]$ is undecidable.

Proposition 15.2 *The following problem is undecidable: given an SPARQLog program P, is P tractable?*

Note that the union $P_1 \cup P_2$ of two tractable SPARQLog programs P_1 and P_2 is not necessarily tractable. Consider for instance the two following rules, where `:a` and `:b` denotes two distinct IRIs:

```
R1 = ALL ?x ?y EX ?z
    CONSTRUCT { ?y <b> ?z } FROM { ?x <a> ?y }
R1 = ALL ?x ?y EX ?z
    CONSTRUCT { ?y <a> ?z } FROM { ?x <b> ?y }
```

Even though $P_1 = \{R_1\}$ and $P_2 = \{R_2\}$ are tractable, we can check that the SPARQLog program $P_{12} = \{R_1, R_2\}$ is *not* tractable. In particular, in the case of an RDF graph G containing a triple (<c>, <a>, <d>) we can observe that $[P]$ is infinite as it must contain an infinite path of the form

{(<c>, <a>, <d>); (<d>, <b>, _:1); (_:1, <a>, _:2); (_:2, <b>, _:3); ...}

where _:i is a blank node.

As also illustrated by this example, there is very little hope of identifying an interesting *local* criterion (testing each rule independently) ensuring the right notion of tractability. In particular, the notion of *guarded Datalog*$^{\pm}$ from Chap. 14 of this volume, designed to ensure (only) the tractability of query answering, does not ensure the tractably of the data-exchange problem (i.e., the materialization of $[P]$). We can indeed observe that P_{12} is not tractable in the sense of Definition 15.13 even though it is *guarded* (each rule contains an atom in its body that contains all universally quantified variables of that rule).

A more relevant approach would consist in relying on the notion of *weak-acylicity* (WA), introduced in [6], and based on the study of two different processes: the creation of new terms in some positions and the migration of newly-created terms from initial positions to new positions. A criteria of acyclicity then ensures that there is no infinite loop in this process of creation and migration of new terms, and that the evaluation of $[P]$ terminates in polynomial time.

Even though WA is a fairly simple way of ensuring tractability, we argue in this section that the more technical notion of *Super-weak Acyclicity* (SwA) introduced in [13] turns out to be a very significant and useful generalization of WA in the context of RDF.

First, SwA allows to take in account the numerous constants that usually occur in a SPARQLog program while relying on efficient unification technics to distinguish distinct constants. This contrasts with WA which was only defined for constraints without constants.

Second, SwA relies on a richer notion of *positions* (called *places*). A standard approach in the context of relational databases is indeed to define a *position* as a pair

(R, A) where R is a relational symbol, and A is a single attribute (or column) of R. In the context of RDF, since we have only a single predicate symbol of small arity we would only consider a fixed and very small number (typically 3) of positions and large programs are almost never acyclic in the sense of WA. In contrast, the SwA relies on *places* of the form (a, i) where a is an atom of the logic program $s(\phi(P))$ and $i \in \{1, 2, 3\}$. SwA distinguishes therefore a polynomial number $O(\|P\|^3)$ of *places* instead of distinguishing only 3 positions.

Third, SwA enjoys some natural closure properties (missing in WA) which make the design of SwA programs easier (see Theorem 5 in [13]). In particular, adding more atoms in the body of some rule in P never hurts: if P is SwA then the resulting set of rules is also SwA.

Note that other generalizations of WA (incomparable with SwA) have been proposed in the literature, in particular, the notion of *Stratification* [4], the notion of *Safe Restriction* [22], and the notion of *Inductive Restriction* [14]. However, none of these notions solves the problems of WA discussed above. In particular, the tractable program

```
ALL ?x ?y EX ?z
CONSTRUCT { ?y <b> ?z } FROM { ?x <a> ?y }
```

belongs to none of these classes because none of them take into account the fact that the two IRIs (constants) a and b are distinct. Moreover, these three classes only ensure the termination of the so-called *restricted chase*, and—unlike SwA—they do not ensure the termination of the logic program $s(\phi(P))$ (i.e., $[P]$ could be infinite).

15.5.1.1 SwARQLog

We define in this section a tractable fragment called SwARQLog (for super-weakly acyclic SPARQLog) relying on the notion of *super-weak acyclicity* (SwA) introduced in [13] in the context of data-exchange with ∀∃-rules only, and adapted here to the case of rules with quantifier alternation.

Given an SPARQLog program P we let P^* be the logic program $P^* = s(\phi(P))$ and define a *place* as a pair (a, i) where a is a atom of P^* and $i \leq 3$. We write $(a, i) \sim (a, i')$ when $i = i'$ and the atoms a and a' are unifiable. Given two sets of places Q and Q', we write $Q \sqsubseteq Q'$ iff for all $p \in Q$ there exists $p' \in Q'$ such that $p \sim p'$. Given a rule $r : B_r \rightarrow H_r$ and a variable x, we let $\rho(x, B_r)$ and $\rho(x, H_r)$ be the set of places $(R(t_1, t_2, t_3, u), i)$ in the body B_r and the head H_r such that $t_i = x$. Given a function symbol f, we let $\rho(f, H_r)$ be the set of places $(R(t_1, t_2, t_3, u), i)$ in the head H_r such that t_i is of the form $f(\ldots)$. Given a set of places Q, we define $\mathsf{Fix}^*(Q)$ as the smallest set of places Q' such that $Q \subseteq Q'$ and for all rules $r : B_r \rightarrow H_r$ and all variables x we have $(\rho(x, B_r) \sqsubseteq Q') \Rightarrow (\rho(x, H_r) \subseteq Q')$. Let F^* be the set of function symbols occurring in P^*, then we can observe that each $f \in F^*$ occurs in exactly one rule denoted $r_f : B_f \rightarrow H_f$ and that each occurrence of f in this rule uses the same vector of arguments denoted $\mathsf{arg}(f)$. Given two function symbols $f \in F^*$ and $g \in F^*$, we say that f *feeds* g iff there exists some

$$\phi(P) = \begin{cases} \forall lec \exists crs \forall stu (R(lec, \text{rdf:type}, \text{uni:lecture}, \diamond) \wedge R(stu, \text{uni:attends}, lec, \diamond) \\ \quad \rightarrow R(crs, \text{uni:practices}, lec, \diamond) \wedge R(stu, \text{uni:attends}, crs, \diamond)) \\ \forall x \exists prf \forall stu (R(stu, \text{uni:attends}, x) \\ \quad \rightarrow R(x, \text{uni:taught-by}, prf, \diamond) \wedge R(prf, \text{people:knows}, stu, \diamond)) \end{cases}$$

$$s(\phi(P)) = \begin{cases} R(\underset{1}{\underline{lec}}, \text{rdf:type}, \text{uni:lecture}, \diamond) \wedge R(\underset{2}{\underline{stu}}, \text{uni:attends}, \underset{3}{\underline{lec}}, \diamond) \\ \quad \rightarrow R(\underset{4}{\underline{f(lec)}}, \text{uni:practices}, \underset{5}{\underline{lec}}, \diamond) \wedge R(\underset{6}{\underline{stu}}, \text{uni:attends}, \underset{7}{\underline{f(lec)}}, \diamond) \\ R(\underset{8}{\underline{stu}}, \text{uni:attends}, \underset{9}{\underline{x}}, \diamond) \\ \quad \rightarrow R(\underset{10}{\underline{x}}, \text{uni:taught-by}, \underset{11}{\underline{g(x)}}, \diamond) \wedge R(\underset{12}{\underline{g(x)}}, \text{people:knows}, \underset{13}{\underline{stu}}, \diamond) \end{cases}$$

Fig. 15.2 Super-weakly acyclic program P

$x \in \mathsf{arg}(g)$ such that $\rho(x, B_g) \sqsubseteq \mathsf{Fix}^*(\rho(f, H_f))$ and we define the feeding graph $\mathcal{G}(P)$ of P as the graph $(F^*, \rightsquigarrow)$ containing an edge $(f \rightsquigarrow g)$ iff f feeds g.

Definition 15.14 (SwARQLog) An SPARQLog program P is super-weakly acyclic (SwA) and is called an SwARQLog program iff the feeding graph $\mathcal{G}(P)$ is acyclic.

Consider, for instance, the following SwARQLog program P:

```
PREFIX uni:  <http://example.org/uni>
FROM     <http://example.org/oxford>

ALL ?lec EX ?crs ALL ?stu
CONSTRUCT { ?crs uni:practices ?lec    . ?stu uni:attends ?crs }
WHERE     { ?lec rdf:type uni:lecture . ?stu uni:attends ?lec }

ALL ?lec EX ?prf ALL ?stu
CONSTRUCT { ?lec uni:taught-by ?prf  . ?prf foaf:knows  ?stu }
WHERE     { ?stu uni:attends ?lec }
```

Figure 15.2 illustrates the places in P: $p_1 = (R(lec, \text{rdf:type}, \text{uni:lecture}, \diamond), 1)$; $p_2 = (R(stu, \text{uni:attends}, lec, \diamond), 1)$; $p_3 = (R(stu, \text{uni:attends}, lec, \diamond), 3)$; $\ldots$; $p_{13} = (R(prf, \text{people:knows}, stu, \diamond), 3)$. Note that there are more places, but we show only the useful ones. With letting f and g the skolem functions used in $s(\phi(P))$ we can check that P is indeed super-weakly acyclic:

- f feeds g: We have indeed $\rho(f, H_f) = \{p_4, p_7\}$ and $\mathsf{Fix}^*(\{p_4, p_7\}) = \{p_4, p_7, p_{10}\}$ while $\mathsf{arg}(g) = \{x\}$ and $\rho(x, B_g) = \{p_9\}$. Since p_9 unifies with p_{11} we have therefore $\rho(x, B_g) \sqsubseteq \mathsf{Fix}^*(\rho(f, H_f))$.
- f does not feed f: We have indeed$\rho(f, H_f) = \{p_4, p_7\}$ and $\mathsf{Fix}^*(\{p_4, p_7\}) = \{p_4, p_7, p_{10}\}$ while $\mathsf{arg}(f) = \{lec\}$ and $\rho(lec, B_f) = \{p_1, p_3\}$. Since none of the places in $\{p_4, p_7, p_{10}\}$ unifies with p_1 we have $\rho(lec, B_f) \not\sqsubseteq \mathsf{Fix}^*(\rho(f, H_f))$.

- We can check similarly that g does not feed f and g does not feed g.

The definition above coincides precisely with the definition of SwA given in [13] for the case of ∀∃-rules and we can easily adapt the proofs given in [13] to also cover quantifier alternation and thus show the following.

Theorem 15.2 (Tractability of SwARQLog)

(1) *We can decide whether an SPARQLog program is SwA in* PTIME.
(2) *Every SwARQLog program is tractable.*

15.5.2 Expressiveness of Quantifier Alternation in SPARQLog

SPARQLog allows existential variables in any position of the quantifier of a rule. This contrasts to other RDF query languages that are either limited to rules in ∀∃ or to ∃∀ form: In ∀∃ approaches, such as [21], existential quantifiers occur in the scope of *all* universal variables of a rule. In ∃∀ approaches, such as [25], existential variables occur in the scope of *no* universal variables.

In this section, we show that an SPARQLog program P can be translated into an SPARQLog program $F_{\forall\exists}(P)$ such that the two programs are default-graph equivalent and $F_{\forall\exists}(P)$ contains only rules in ∀∃ form. Such an equivalence does not hold for the ∃∀ form.

Default-graph equivalence captures the notion that they both construct the same default graph, but may differ on the named graphs they query and construct in intermediary rules.

Definition 15.15 (Default-graph Equivalence) Let P and P' be two SPARQLog programs. Then P is *default-graph equivalent* to P' if for all datasets $\mathsf{D} \in [\![P]\!]$, $\mathsf{D}' \in [\![P']\!]$ it holds that $\mathsf{D}[\diamond] \models\!\!\!\!\mid \mathsf{D}'[\diamond]$.

Thus, two SPARQLog programs that are default-graph equivalent can be considered equivalent up to results in intermediary named graphs.

First, we define $F_{\forall\exists}$. For convenience, we abbreviate for any IRI H and sequence of variables $\bar{x} = x_1, \ldots, x_n$, the conjunction of triple patterns

```
(H rdf:_1 ?x1) . \ldots . (H rdf:_n xn)
```

by $H(\bar{x})$ and, for any graph IRI I,

$$\tilde{H}(\bar{x}, I) = R(H, \mathtt{rdf:\_1}, x_1, I) \wedge \cdots \wedge R(H, \mathtt{rdf:\_n}, x_n, I)$$

Definition 15.16 (∀∃ Rewriting) Let P be an SPARQLog program and

```
1 ALL x̄ EX ȳ Qz̄
  CONSTRUCT { ξ(x̄, ȳ, z̄) } WHERE { ψ(x̄, ȳ, z̄) }
```

a rule R in P with $Q\bar{z}$ some sequence of quantifier clauses over the variables $\bar{z}$, $\xi(\bar{x}, \bar{y}, \bar{z})$ a construct template over the given variables and $\psi(\bar{x}, \bar{y}, \bar{z})$ a graph pattern over the given variables.

Then we define the *∀∃-rewriting* $F_{\forall\exists}(\phi)$ as

$$F_{\forall\exists}(\phi) = \begin{cases} R & \text{if } R \text{ is in } \forall\exists \text{ form} \\ R_1 R_2 R_3 & \text{otherwise} \end{cases}$$

where

```
R_1 = ALL x̄ ALL ȳ ALL z̄
  CONSTRUCT GRAPH <I> { Proj_R(x̄) } WHERE { ψ(x̄, ȳ, z̄) }

R_2 = ALL x̄ EX ȳ
  CONSTRUCT GRAPH <I> { Gen_R(x̄, ȳ) } WHERE GRAPH <I> { Proj_R(x̄) }

R_3 = F_∀∃(ALL x̄ ALL ȳ Qz̄
  CONSTRUCT { ξ(x̄, ȳ, z̄) } WHERE { ψ(x̄, ȳ, z̄) . GRAPH <I> { Gen_R(x̄, ȳ) } } )
```

and Gen_R, Proj_R, I are new IRIs that do not occur in P. The definition is analog for rules with graph specification in the head.

The idea of the rewriting is to extract all existential variables $\bar{y}$ that depend only on the universal variables $\bar{x}$ from ϕ. A specific *generator rule* R_{gen} states their existential dependence on $\bar{x}$ separately. To allow R_{gen} in ∀∃ form, we first project all variables in ψ on only the relevant variables $\bar{x}$ in R_{proj}, the *projection rule*. Finally, we query both the original body and the generator rule in R_{join}. Since Gen is a new IRI (and thus there can be no further rules with Gen in the head) it suffices together with $\bar{x}$ to identify the corresponding $\bar{y}$.

Even though a classical logic formula with arbitrary quantifier alternation has, in general, no logical equivalent in the prefix class ∀∃, this does no longer hold if we allow the extension of the vocabulary with "helper constants" that are ignored when considering equivalence. Here this is provided by the notion of default-graph equivalence introduced above. The above rewriting extends the vocabulary of the SPARQLog program in two ways:

1. It introduces, for each rewritten rule, a new graph identifier constant (I in Definition 15.16). All intermediary tuples introduced by the rewriting of that rule are constructed to belong to I (only $\xi(\bar{x}, \bar{y}, \bar{z})$ remains in the original graph).
2. It introduces, for each rewritten rule, two new RDF resource IRIs Gen_R, Proj_R. It would actually suffice to use introduce two such new IRIs overall, as the rewriting of different rules can reuse these constants without clash (due to the separate graph identifiers). But for clarity we use also in this case distinct new constants. In fact, the rewriting remains applicable even if no concept such as graph identifiers exists in the rule language. But in this case, we need a form of equivalence up to certain constants or predicate symbols (see, e.g., the notion of relativised equivalence in [17]).

To illustrate the rewriting consider again rule B_3 from Sect. 15.4:

```
ALL ?x EX ?y ALL ?z                                                  B3
CONSTRUCT { ?x eswc:heldBy ?y .            ?z foaf:knows ?y }
WHERE     { ?x rdf:type    eswc:TalkEvent. ?z eswc:attendeeAt ?x }
```

For this rule, we obtain the following rewriting $F_{\forall\exists}(B_3)$ using `http../I` as IRI for the intermediary graph, `http../Gen1` as IRI for R_1 and `http../Proj1` as IRI for R_2:

```
ALL ?x ALL ?y ALL ?z
CONSTRUCT { ?x eswc:heldBy ?y . ?z foaf:knows ?y }
WHERE GRAPH <http../I> { ?x rdf:type eswc:TalkEvent. ?z eswc:attendeeAt ?x.
                  <http../Gen1> rdf:_1 ?x . <http../Gen1> rdf:_2 ?y }

ALL ?x EX ?y
CONSTRUCT GRAPH <http../I> {<http../Gen1> rdf:_1 ?x. <http../Gen1> rdf:_2
     ?y}
WHERE GRAPH <http../I> { <http../Proj1> rdf:_1 ?x }

ALL ?x, ?y, ?z
CONSTRUCT GRAPH <http../I> { (<http../Proj1> rdf:_1 ?x }
WHERE      { ?x rdf:type eswc:TalkEvent. ?z eswc:attendeeAt ?x }
```

Observe that the rewriting essential splits the prefix of the original rule at any $\forall$ after an $\exists$ and distributes the prefix parts over several rules. The triples with fresh IRIs allow us to link the bindings for parts of the prefix between different rules.

The $\forall\exists$ rewriting of an SPARQLog program is, if restricted to the default graph, equivalent to the original program.

Theorem 15.3 *Let P be an SPARQLog program. Then $F_{\forall\exists}(P)$ is default-graph equivalent to P.*

In other words, SPARQLog restricted to $\forall\exists$ rules is as expressive as full SPARQLog if we consider default-graph semantics.

Proof Let R be an SPARQLog rule as in the definition of $F_{\forall\exists}$. We show that (1) $\phi(F_{\forall\exists}(R))$ FO-entails $\phi(R)$ and (2) if $A = (D, \mathrm{Rel}, \mathrm{Fun})$ is a first-order model of R then there is an extension B of A with only triples from the auxiliary relations in the auxiliary graph I that is a model of $\phi(F_{\forall\exists}(R))$. We omit sub- and superscripts if they are clear from the context. Finally, let $R_3 = F_{\forall\exists}(R_3')$.

We first show that $\phi(F_{\forall\exists}(R))$ FO-entails $\phi(R)$. The proof is by induction on the number of quantifier alternations in R. The base case is trivial. For the induction step, let $A = (D, \mathrm{Rel}, \mathrm{Fun})$ be a FO-model of $\phi(F_{\forall\exists}(R))$. To show that $A \models^s \phi(R)$, let $\bar{d} \in D^*$ be a sequence of domain elements with the same length as $\bar{x}$. If for all $e \in D$ and $\bar{f} \in D^*$ with $|\bar{f}| = |\bar{z}|$, it holds that $A \not\models^s \psi(\bar{d}, e, \bar{f})$ then we are done. Otherwise, there are $e \in D$ and $\bar{f} \in D^*$ such that $A \models^s \psi(\bar{d}, e, \bar{f})$. As by hypothesis $A \models^s \phi(R_1)$ if follows that $A \models^s \tilde{\mathsf{Proj}}_R(\bar{d}, I)$. Therefore, as $A \models^s \phi(R_2)$ there is an $e' \in D$, such that $A \models^s \tilde{\mathsf{Gen}}_R(\bar{d}, e', I)$. Finally, as $A \models^s \phi(R_3)$ if follows from the induction hypothesis that $A \models^s \phi(R_3')$, and thus $A \models^s \phi(R)$.

We now show that if $A = (D, \mathrm{Rel}, \mathrm{Fun})$ is a model of $\phi(R)$ then there are triples $T_1 = \{\tilde{\mathsf{Proj}}(\bar{x}, I) \ldots \tilde{\mathsf{Proj}}(\bar{x}, y, \bar{z}, I)\}$ and $T_2 = \{\tilde{Gen}(\bar{x}, I) \ldots \tilde{Gen}(\bar{x}, y, \bar{z}, I)\}$ such that the extension $B = (D, \mathrm{Rel} \cup T_1 \cup T_2, \mathrm{Fun})$ of A is a model for $\phi(F_{\forall\exists}(R))$.

The proof is by induction on the number of quantifier alternations in R. Again the base case is trivial. For the induction step, let A be a model of $\phi(R)$. We define

$$T_1 = \{\tilde{\mathsf{Proj}}(\bar{x}, I) : \exists y, \bar{z} : \phi(\psi(\bar{x}, y, \bar{z}))\}$$

$$T_2 = \{\tilde{\mathsf{Gen}}(\bar{x}, y, I) : \phi(Qz : \texttt{CONSTRUCT}\ \xi(\bar{x}, y, \bar{z})\ \texttt{WHERE}\ \psi(\bar{x}, y, \bar{z}))\}$$

and $C = (D, \mathrm{Rel} \cup T_1 \cup T_2, \mathrm{Fun})$. With this definition, it is a tautology that $C \models^s \phi(R_1)$. To show that $C \models^s R_2$ let $\bar{d} \in D^*$. As $A \models^s \phi(R)$ it holds that there is an $e \in D$ such that $A \models^s \phi(Qz : \texttt{CONSTRUCT}\ \xi(\bar{x}, y, \bar{z})\ \texttt{WHERE}\ \psi(\bar{x}, y, \bar{z}))$. Thus, $C \models^s \phi(R_2)$. Finally, we observe that $\phi(R) \models^s \phi(\theta)$ where

```
θ = ALL x̄ ALL ȳ Qz̄
CONSTRUCT { ξ(x̄, ȳ, z̄) } WHERE { ψ(x̄, ȳ, z̄) . GRAPH <I> { Gen_R(x̄, ȳ) } }
```

As C is a model of $\phi(R)$ it is also a model of $\phi(\theta)$. By the induction hypothesis, there is an extension B of C that is model of $R_3 = F_{\forall\exists}(\theta)$. □

15.5.3 Experimental Comparison with SPARQL Engines

The reduction of SPARQLog to standard logic programs (Sect. 15.4.3) allows for a direct implementation of SPARQLog on top of any logic programming or database engine that supports value invention and recursion. In the following, we compare experimentally the performance of a very simple prototype based on that principle with two of the more common SPARQL implementations. Our implementation of SPARQLog uses a combination of Perl pre- and post-filters for Skolemization, Unskolemization, and normalization of SPARQLog programs and XSB Prolog to evaluate the Skolemized programs.

We compare our implementation with the ARQ SPARQL processor of Jena (Version 2.1) and the SPARQL engine provided by the Sesame RDF Framework. For Sesame, we choose the main-memory store as it is "by far the fastest type of repository that can be used" according to Sesame's authors. With this store, Sesame becomes a main-memory, ad-hoc query engine just like SPARQLog and ARQ. As common for ad-hoc queries, we measure overall execution time including both loading of the RDF data and execution of the SPARQL or SPARQLog query. For the comparison, we only consider rules without existential quantification (rule 1 below) or with ∀∃ quantification (rule 2 below, expressible by blank nodes in the `CONSTRUCT` graph pattern in SPARQL). Rules with arbitrary quantifier alternation are not considered as they are not expressible in SPARQL (the rewriting from Sect. 15.5.2 does not apply as SPARQL is single-rule and provides no projection).

In the experiments, we evaluate three different queries against an RDF graph consisting of Wikipedia data. The experiments have been carried out on a Intel Pentium M Dual-Core with 1.86 GHz, 1 MB cache and 2 GB main memory. For each setting, the running time is averaged over 25 runs. We compare the following rules (with appropriate prefix definitions and dataset clauses).

```
Rule 1: ALL ?x ALL ?y
  CONSTRUCT { ?x test:connected ?y } WHERE {?x wiki:internalLink ?y }
Rule 2: ALL ?x ALL ?z EX ?z
  CONSTRUCT { ?x test:connected ?z } WHERE {?x wiki:internalLink ?y }
Rule 3: EX ?z ALL ?x ALL ?y
  CONSTRUCT { ?x test:connected ?z } WHERE {?x wiki:internalLink ?y }
```

Figure 15.3 shows the performance of SPARQLog for each of the rules. Note that the running time increases from rule 1 to rule 3 and from rule 3 to rule 2. The difference between rule 1 and rule 3 might be due to overhead of Skolemization, Unskolemization and normalization. The running time difference between rule 3 and rule 2 may be attributed to the lower amount of blank nodes generated in rule 3, as the existential quantifier is outside of the scope of all universal quantifiers.

Figure 15.4 compares the performance of SPARQLog with that of ARQ and Sesame for rule 1 and rule 2 (we omit rule 3 as it is not expressible in SPARQL). Despite its light-weight, ad-hoc implementation, SPARQLog outperforms ARQ and Sesame in this setting. The figures show moreover that also for ARQ and Sesame, blank node construction does not bear any significant additional computational effort.

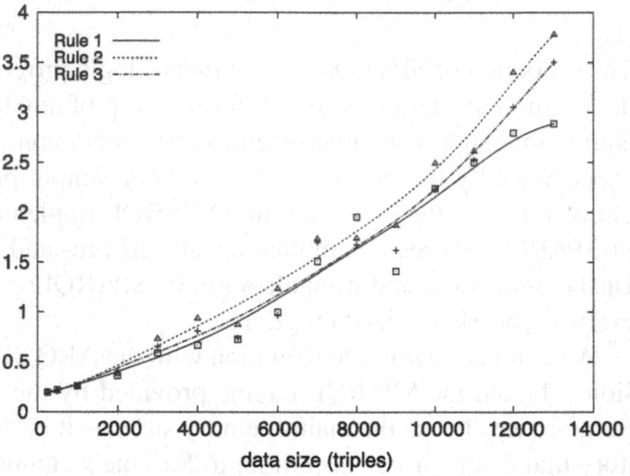

Fig. 15.3 Performance of SPARQLog on rules 1, 2 and 3

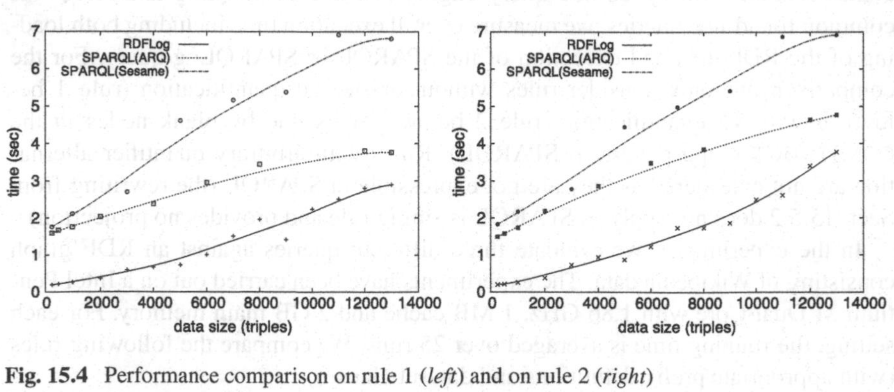

Fig. 15.4 Performance comparison on rule 1 (*left*) and on rule 2 (*right*)

15.6 Conclusion

Blank nodes are one of RDF's distinguishing features. Yet they have been entirely neglected or treated only in a limit fashion in previous approaches to RDF querying. With SPARQLog, we advance the knowledge about the combination of blank nodes and rules (and thus RDF and rules) in three directions: (1) We show that restrictions of RDF wrt. blank nodes occurrence can be treated in a semantics based purely on entailment. (2) Though unrestricted combinations of recursive rules and blank nodes in rule heads lead, unsurprisingly, to a undecidable, Turing-complete language, we identify a large fragment of such rules that is still decidable. This fragment is strictly larger than previous decidable languages with recursive rules and blank nodes in the head. (3) Finally, we show that quantifier alternation does not add to the expressiveness or complexity of a language with $\forall\exists$ rules and projection. The latter form of rules is commonly found in data exchange or SPARQL rule extensions. In other words, quantifier alternation comes for free for such languages.

Though we present the results here in the context of RDF querying, they apply to a wide range of logic languages with horn rules extended by existential quantification. In particular, in data exchange such languages are common but mostly limited to $\forall\exists$ rules.

References

1. Broekstra, J., Kampman, A.: An rdf query and transformation language. In: Semantic Web and Peer-to-Peer, pp. 23–39. Springer, Berlin (2006)
2. Bry, F., Furche, T., Ley, C., Linse, B., Marnette, B.: Rdflog: It's like datalog for rdf. In: Proc. Workshop on (Constraint) Logic Programming (WLP) (2008)
3. Bry, F., Furche, T., Ley, C., Linse, B., Marnette, B.: Taming existence in rdf querying. In: Proc. Int'l. Conf. on Web Reasoning and Rule Systems (RR) (2008)
4. Deutsch, A., Nash, A., Remmel, J.: The chase revisited. In: Proc. ACM Symp. on Principles of Database Systems (PODS), pp. 149–158. ACM, New York (2008)
5. Ebbinghaus, H.D., Flum, J., Thomas, W.: Mathematical Logic. Springer, Berlin (1994)
6. Fagin, R., Kolaitis, P.G., Miller, R.J., Popa, L.: Data exchange: Semantics and query answering. In: Proc. Int'l. Conf. on Database Theory (ICDT), pp. 207–224 (2003)
7. Fagin, R., Kolaitis, P.G., Popa, L.: Data exchange: Getting to the core. ACM Trans. Database Syst. **30**(1), 174–210 (2005)
8. Fagin, R., Kolaitis, P.G., Popa, L., Tan, W.C.: Composing schema mappings: Second-order dependencies to the rescue. ACM Trans. Database Syst. **30**(4), 994–1055 (2005)
9. Furche, T., Linse, B., Bry, F., Plexousakis, D., Gottlob, G.: RDF querying: language constructs and evaluation methods compared. In: Tutorial Lectures Int'l. Summer School 'Reasoning Web'. Lecture Notes in Computer Science, vol. 4126, pp. 1–52. Springer, Berlin (2006). 19 citations [Google Scholar]
10. Gutierrez, C., Hurtado, C., Mendelzon, A.O.: Foundations of Semantic Web databases. In: Proc. ACM Symp. on Principles of Database Systems (PODS), pp. 95–106. ACM, New York (2004)
11. Hayes, P., McBride, B.: Rdf semantics. Recommendation, W3C (2004)
12. Karvounarakis, G., Alexaki, S., Christophides, V., Plexousakis, D., Scholl, M.: Rql: a declarative query language for rdf. In: Proc. Int'l. World Wide Web Conf. (WWW), pp. 592–603. ACM, New York (2002)

13. Marnette, B.: Generalized schema-mappings: From termination to tractability. In: Proc. ACM Symp. on Management of Data (SIGMOD). ACM, New York (2009)
14. Meier, M., Schmidt, M., Lausen, G.: Stop the chase. CoRR (2009). arXiv:0901.3984
15. Muñoz, S., Pérez, J., Gutierrez, C.: Minimal deductive systems for rdf. In: Proc. European Semantic Web Conf. (ESWC). Lecture Notes in Computer Science, vol. 4519, pp. 53–67. Springer, Berlin (2007)
16. Noy, N., Rector, A., Hayes, P., Welty, C.: Defining n-ary relations on the Semantic Web. Working group note, W3C (2006)
17. Oetsch, J., Tompits, H., Woltran, S.: Facts do not cease to exist because they are ignored: Relativised uniform equivalence with answer-set projection. In: Proc. Nat'l. Conf. on Artificial Intelligence (AAAI), pp. 458–464 (2007)
18. Polleres, A.: From sparql to rules (and back). In: Proc. Int'l. World Wide Web Conf. (WWW), pp. 787–796. ACM, New York (2007)
19. Prud'hommeaux, E., Seaborne, A.: SPARQL Query Language for RDF. Proposed Recommendation, W3C (2007)
20. Rosati, R.: The limits and possibilities of combining description logics and datalog. In: Proc. Int. Conf. on Rule Markup Languages (RuleML), pp. 3–4 (2006)
21. Schenk, S., Staab, S.: Networked graphs: a declarative mechanism for sparql rules, sparql views and rdf data integration on the web. In: Proc. Int'l. World Wide Web Conf. (WWW), pp. 585–594. ACM, New York (2008)
22. Schmidt, M., Meier, M., Lausen, G.: Foundations of sparql query optimization. CoRR (2008). arXiv:0812.3788
23. Sintek, M., Decker, S.: Triple—a query, inference, and transformation language for the Semantic Web. In: Proc. Int'l. Semantic Web Conf. (ISWC) (2002)
24. ter Horst, H.J.: Completeness, decidability and complexity of entailment for rdf schema and a semantic extension involving the owl vocabulary. In: Web Semantics: Science, Services and Agents on the World Wide Web3 (2005)
25. Yang, G., Kifer, M.: Reasoning about anonymous resources and meta statements on the Semantic Web. J. Data Semant. **1**, 69–97 (2003)

Chapter 16
SP^{2}Bench: A SPARQL Performance Benchmark

Michael Schmidt, Thomas Hornung, Michael Meier, Christoph Pinkel, and Georg Lausen

Abstract A meaningful analysis and comparison of both existing storage schemes for RDF data and evaluation approaches for SPARQL queries necessitates a comprehensive and universal benchmark platform. We present SP^{2}Bench, a publicly available, language-specific performance benchmark for the SPARQL query language. SP^{2}Bench is settled in the DBLP scenario and comprises a data generator for creating arbitrarily large DBLP-like documents and a set of carefully designed benchmark queries. The generated documents mirror vital key characteristics and social-world distributions encountered in the original DBLP data set, while the queries implement meaningful requests on top of this data, covering a variety of SPARQL operator constellations and RDF access patterns. In this chapter, we discuss requirements and desiderata for SPARQL benchmarks and present the SP^{2}Bench framework, including its data generator, benchmark queries and performance metrics.

16.1 Introduction

In the recent years, many proposals for the efficient evaluation of SPARQL [35] have been made. These approaches comprise a wide range of optimization techniques, including normal forms [23], graph pattern reordering based on selectivity estimations [22, 30] (similar to relational join reordering), syntactic rewriting of SPARQL queries [17, 27], RISC-style query processing [22] and Semantic Query

M. Schmidt (✉) · T. Hornung · M. Meier · G. Lausen
Albert-Ludwigs-Universität Freiburg, Georges-Köhler-Allee, Geb. 51, 79110 Freiburg, Germany
e-mail: mschmidt@informatik.uni-freiburg.de

T. Hornung
e-mail: hornungt@informatik.uni-freiburg.de

M. Meier
e-mail: meierm@informatik.uni-freiburg.de

G. Lausen
e-mail: lausen@informatik.uni-freiburg.de

C. Pinkel
MTC Infomedia OHG, Kaiserstr. 26, 66121 Saarbrücken, Germany
e-mail: c.pinkel@mtc-infomedia.de

R. De Virgilio et al. (eds.), *Semantic Web Information Management*,
DOI 10.1007/978-3-642-04329-1_16, © Springer-Verlag Berlin Heidelberg 2010

Optimization [18]. In addition, there has been a corpus of research on specialized indices [13, 16] and storage schemes [1, 4, 7, 15, 31, 36] for RDF data [34], with the aim to provide efficient data access paths. Another notable line of research is the translation of SPARQL queries into established data models like SQL [9, 10] or Datalog [3, 24], thus facilitating SPARQL evaluation with traditional engines and allowing to exploit optimization techniques implemented in existing systems.

A meaningful analysis and comparison of all these optimization approaches necessitates a comprehensive and universal benchmark platform. Systematic benchmarking has been an important topic in database research from the beginning [12] and, over time, a variety of benchmarks have been proposed, covering both different aspects of data processing and different data models. Examples include the prominent TPC[1] benchmark suite for Relational data, the OO7 [8] benchmark for Object-oriented databases, and the XMark [25] benchmark for the XML data model. Coming along with the proliferation of the Semantic Web, benchmarking has become an increasingly important topic in the context of Semantic Web data formats like RDF(S) [34] and OWL [33]. As a response, also in this context several benchmark platforms have been developed. These platforms address structural aspects of the data (e.g., [21]) as well as the issue of efficient data processing (e.g., [2, 6, 14]).

One well-known benchmark that falls into the latter category is the Lehigh University Benchmark (LUBM) [14]. It comes with a data generator, which allows to generate synthetic OWL documents, a set of 14 benchmark queries, implementing different reasoning tasks with varying complexity over the generated data, and several performance metrics, allowing to evaluate and compare benchmark results. The LUBM benchmark suite has a strong focus on testing the inference and reasoning capabilities of Semantic Web repositories and—although there exist SPARQL versions of the benchmark queries—is not primarily a SPARQL benchmark.

The Barton Library benchmark [2] is a more traditional database benchmark in the sense that it shifts the focus from inference and reasoning to query answering. It uses the real-world RDF Barton online catalog as underlying data. The benchmark queries implement tasks that are derived from a typical browsing session through the catalog data, so Barton is highly use-case driven. The queries are encoded in SQL and it is assumed that RDF data is stored in a Relational database (as proposed in [1]). Given the current SPARQL specification [35], not all of the Barton benchmark queries can be expressed in SPARQL, due to missing support for aggregation.

The application-oriented Berlin SPARQL Benchmark [6] (BSBM) is SPARQL-specific and tests the performance of SPARQL engines in a prototypical e-commerce scenario. Also BSBM is use-case driven and provides a set of benchmark queries that are intended to be run in a work load fashion over generated data sets of different size. This setting is particularly interesting to compare the overall performance of engines that expose SPARQL endpoints via the SPARQL protocol.

In this chapter, we present the SP^{2}Bench **SP**ARQL **P**erformance **Bench**mark [26, 28], which comprises a data generator and a set of queries, implementing meaningful requests on top of the generated data. SP^{2}Bench is freely available online in a

[1] See http://www.tpc.org.

ready-to-use format.[2] The focus and design goals of SP^{2}Bench vary from the benchmark projects discussed before. In particular, SP^{2}Bench differs in that is neither application-oriented nor use-case driven, but falls into the class of *language-specific* benchmarks. This means that, compared to the other benchmarks, the document and query design in SP^{2}Bench is not driven by a specific use-case, but instead specifically laid out to test common SPARQL constructs, operator constellations, and a variety of RDF data access patterns. In this line, SP^{2}Bench covers a broad range of challenges that SPARQL engines might face in different contexts and constitutes a benchmark that allows for comprehensive performance evaluation, rather than performance assessment in a specific, application-driven scenario. The SP^{2}Bench queries, which differ in their characteristics and complexity, are not intended to be evaluated in a work load setting, but rather on a one by one basis, where each query poses different challenges to the tested SPARQL engine and might help to identify deficiencies in the underlying evaluation strategy. With these design goals, SP^{2}Bench allows to assess the generality of optimization approaches and to compare evaluation strategies in a universal, application-independent setting.

The first component of SP^{2}Bench is the data generator, which supports the creation of DBLP-like[3] models in RDF format. The generated documents mirror vital key characteristics and distributions found in the original DBLP database [19], making it possible to create arbitrarily large documents with realistic data that exhibits many real-world characteristics. The data mimics natural correlations between entities, such as power law distributions and limited growth curves. Complementary to the generator, SP^{2}Bench comprises 17 meaningful queries specified over the generated documents. These queries cover important SPARQL constructs, operator constellations, and vary in their characteristics, such as complexity and result size. The detailed knowledge of data characteristics, which is established by an elaborate analysis of the original DBLP database, makes it possible to predict the challenges that the queries impose on SPARQL engines. This, in turn, contributes to the understanding of the benchmark and facilitates the interpretation of benchmark results.

Structure We start with a discussion of general and SPARQL-specific desiderata for benchmarks in Sect. 16.2, including a summary of design decisions made in the SP^{2}Bench framework. Subsequently, in Sect. 16.3 we turn towards a study of the SP^{2}Bench data generator. This discussion includes an analysis of key characteristics of the DBLP data set, which forms the basis for the implementation of the data generator. The profound knowledge of the DBLP main characteristics then helps to understand the key challenges of the SP^{2}Bench queries, which are presented in Sect. 16.4. The chapter ends with a discussion of possible performance metrics for the SP^{2}Bench suite (Sect. 16.5) and a short conclusion (Sect. 16.6).

---

[2] See http://dbis.informatik.uni-freiburg.de/index.php?project=SP2B.

[3] DBLP [19] is a well-known bibliographic library that contains publications made in the area of databases and, more generally, Computer Science.

16.2 Benchmark Design Decisions

A central aspect in the design of a benchmark is the choice of an appropriate domain. Clearly, the domain of a language-specific benchmark should not only constitute a representative scenario that captures the philosophy behind the data format, but also leave room for challenging benchmark queries. With the choice of the DBLP [19] library, a bibliographic database that contains a large collection of publications in the area of Computer Science, SP^2Bench satisfies both desiderata. First, the RDF data format has been particularly designed to encode metadata (cf. [34]), which makes DBLP an excellent candidate for an RDF scenario. Further, as shown in [11], DBLP reflects interesting social-world distributions. One might expect that such distributions are frequently encountered in the Semantic Web, which integrates a great many of individual databases into one global database and therefore can be seen as a large social network. As an example, it has been shown in [32] that power-law distributions are naturally contained in large RDF Schema specifications. These observations justify the choice of DBLP as the underlying scenario.

Rather than using an RDF version of the existing DBLP data set (such as [5]), SP^2Bench comes with a generator that supports the creation of arbitrarily large DBLP-like documents in RDF format, hence overcoming an upper limit on the size of benchmark documents. The generator itself relies on an in-depth study of characteristics and relationships between entities found in the original DBLP database, comprising the analysis of data entities (such as articles and authors), their properties, frequency and also their interaction. Consequently, the generated documents mimic a broad range of natural, social-world distributions such as power laws (found in the citation system or the distribution of publications among authors) and limited growth curves (e.g., the increasing number of venues and publications over time).

Requirements for Domain-specific Benchmarks In the Benchmark Handbook [12], four key requirements for domain specific benchmarks are postulated. First, a domain-specific benchmark should be (1) *relevant*, thus testing typical operations within the specific domain. Second, the benchmark should be (2) *portable*, i.e., should be executable on different platforms. Third, such a benchmark should be (3) *scalable*, which particularly this means that it should be possible to run the benchmark on both small and very large data sets. Last but not least, a benchmark must be (4) *understandable*, since otherwise it will not be adopted in practice.

For a language-specific benchmark, the relevance requirement (1) suggests that queries implement realistic requests on top of the data. Further, the queries should not focus on verifying the correctness of the tested engine, but on common operator constellations that impose particular challenges. To give a concrete example for the manifestation of these ideas in SP^2Bench, two benchmark queries (i.e., $Q6$ and $Q7$) test negation, which (under closed-world assumption) can be expressed in SPARQL through a combination of operators OPTIONAL, FILTER, and BOUND (cf. [3]).

Requirements (2) portability and (3) scalability mainly bring along technical challenges concerning the implementation of the data generator. Addressing those, the SP^2Bench data generator is deterministic, platform independent and accurate w.r.t. the desired size of generated documents. Furthermore, the C++ implementation is both efficient and effective, i.e., it gets by with a constant amount of main memory, making it possible to generate arbitrarily large RDF documents.

Finally, from the viewpoint of an engine developer, a benchmark should give hints on deficiencies in the design and implementation of the respective engine. This is where the (4) understandability requirement comes into play, i.e., it is important to keep queries simple and understandable. At the same time, they should still be challenging and leave room for diverse optimizations. In this regard, the SP^{2}Bench queries are carefully designed in such a way that they are amenable to a wide range of optimization strategies. Ultimately, also the fact that these queries operate on top of data with realistic, natural distributions contributes to the understanding of the benchmark queries and permits to predict the challenges that the queries impose to SPARQL engines, allowing to better interpret the benchmark results.

16.3 The SP^{2}Bench Data Generator

Having discussed general aspects of benchmarking and the SP^{2}Bench design decisions, we now turn towards a study of the DBLP database [19], which lays the foundations for the implementation of the SP^{2}Bench data generator. We analyze properties, relations and distributions of bibliographic entities and persons in the DBLP data. The study of correlations in scientific production is not new and has first been performed in [20]. A previous study of characteristics of DBLP has been presented in [11], showing that DBLP—restricted to publications and authors in the database area—reflects many distributions typically encountered in social networks and, with this regard, it forms a "small world" on its own. While the latter analysis forms valuable groundwork for the study in this section, our approach here is more pragmatic: we pursue the goal to approximate distributions by concrete functions that can be used to implement the SP^{2}Bench data generator. With this goal in mind, we approximate distributions found in the original database by function families that naturally reflect the characteristics of interest, such as logistics curves for limited growth scenarios or power equations for power law distributions.

16.3.1 Characteristics of DBLP Data

In the following, we sketch different aspects of the DBLP analysis that were considered in the design of the SP^{2}Bench data generator. We leave out technical details, referring the interested reader to [28] for a deeper, more technical discussion.

16.3.1.1 Structure of Document Classes

The starting point for our study is the XML version of the DBLP database [19]. Abstracting from the details, this database contains nine different types of bibliographic entities, namely ARTICLE, INPROCEEDINGS, JOURNAL, PROCEEDINGS,

Table 16.1 Probability distribution for selected attributes and document classes

	Article	Inproc.	Proc.	Book	WWW	PhDTh.	MastTh.	Incoll
author	0.9895	0.9970	0.0001	0.8937	0.9973	1.0000	1.0000	0.8459
cite	0.0048	0.0104	0.0001	0.0079	0.0000	0.0000	0.0000	0.0047
editor	0.0000	0.0000	0.7992	0.1040	0.0004	0.0000	0.0000	0.0000
isbn	0.0000	0.0000	0.8592	0.9294	0.0000	0.0222	0.0000	0.0073
journal	0.9994	0.0000	0.0004	0.0000	0.0000	0.0000	0.0000	0.0000
month	0.0065	0.0000	0.0001	0.0008	0.0000	0.0333	0.0000	0.0000
pages	0.9261	0.9489	0.0000	0.0000	0.0000	0.0000	0.0000	0.6849
title	1.0000	1.0000	1.0000	1.0000	1.0000	1.0000	1.0000	1.0000

BOOK, INCOLLECTION, PHDTHESIS, MASTERSTHESIS and WWW documents. We call these entities *document classes* and instances thereof *documents*.

Each document in the DBLP XML database is described by a set of *attributes*, such as `author`, `cite`, `editor`, `title` or `pages`. As one might expect, the document classes differ in their structure; even instances of the same document class do not necessarily have the same set of describing attributes. For instance, attribute `pages` is never associated with WWW documents, but typically (though not necessarily) used in combination with INPROCEEDINGS documents.

A first and very basic step in the analysis of the DBLP data therefore is an investigation of the structure of document classes. We illustrate our analysis in Table 16.1, which—for selected attribute/document class pairs—shows the probability that the attribute describes a document of the respective class. To give an example, about 92.61% of all ARTICLE documents are described by attribute `pages`, but none of them has an `editor` associated. In contrast, about 79.92% of all PROCEEDINGS documents are described by one or more `editor` attributes. This probability distribution forms the basis for generating document class instances of any type.

We note that the latter distribution does not yet consider the issue of attributes that are repeatedly used to describe a single document, e.g., article documents are typically described by several `author` attributes (i.e., one `author` attribute for each article author). Tackling this issue, we next turn towards an investigation of repeated attributes. We will exemplarily discuss our analysis for attribute `cite`, which is used to model outgoing citations of bibliographic entities.

Figure 16.1(a) shows, for each document that is described by at least one `cite` attribute, the probability (y-axis) that the document has exactly n `cite` attributes (x-axis). We observe that, given a publication with at least one outgoing citation, the average number of outgoing citations is about fifteen. Recalling the goal to approximate the distributions encountered in DBLP by natural function families, we decided to use bell-shaped Gaussian curves for approximating the distribution of repeated `cite` attributes, i.e., functions of the form

$$p_{\text{gauss}}^{(\mu,\sigma)}(x) = \frac{1}{\sigma\sqrt{2\pi}} e^{-0.5(\frac{x-\mu}{\sigma})^2} \quad (16.1)$$

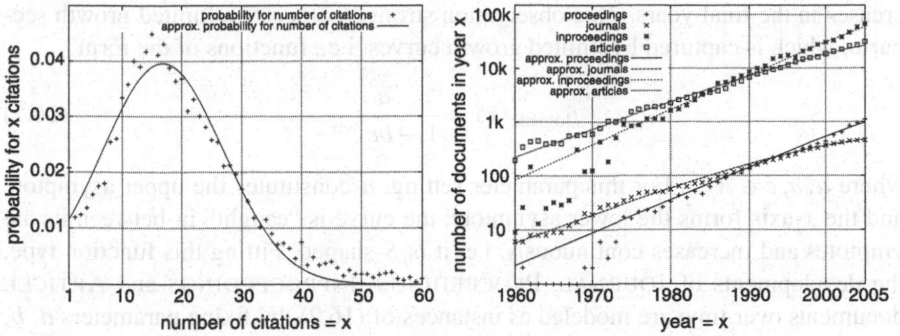

Fig. 16.1 (**a**) Distribution of citations for documents having at least one outgoing citation and (**b**) Development of document class instances over time

where parameter $\mu \in \mathbb{R}$ fixes the x-position of the peak and $\sigma \in \mathbb{R}_{>0}$ specifies the statistical spread. Such functions are typically used to model normal distributions.[4] The approximation function for the distribution of outgoing citations that is implemented in our data generator hence is an instance of the Gaussian curve equation above, obtained by choosing appropriate values for parameters μ and σ.

The analysis for other repeated attributes in DBLP, such as `editor` and `author`, is very similar and therefore we omit the details. A notable observation in the context of the `author` attribute was that the average number of authors per publication has steadily increased over time. Similar observations were made in [11] and explained by the increasing pressure to publish and the proliferation of new communication platforms, like the Internet, which facilitates the collaboration among authors. Due to the prominent role of authors in DBLP, this increase in the average number of authors is also implemented in the SP²Bench data generator.

16.3.1.2 Development of Document Classes over Time

Another important subject of our DBLP study is the development of document class instances over time. Figure 16.1(b) exemplarily plots the number of PROCEEDINGS, JOURNAL, INPROCEEDINGS and ARTICLE documents as a function of time. Note that the y-axis is in log scale. It can be seen that inproceedings and articles are closely coupled to the proceedings and journals, respectively. For instance, there are always about 50–60 times more inproceedings than proceedings. This indicates that the average number of inproceedings per proceeding is stable over time. Similar observations hold with respect to the articles and the journals they appeared in.

Figure 16.1(b) clearly indicates exponential growth for all four document classes and we observe that the growth rate of JOURNAL and ARTICLE documents de-

[4]Note that, strictly speaking, our data is not normally distributed, due to the left limit at position $x = 1$. Still, the Gaussian curve shown in Fig. 16.1(a) nicely fits the data.

creases in the final years. This observation strongly suggests a limited growth scenario, which is captured by limited growth curves, i.e., functions of the form

$$f_{\text{logistic}}(x) = \frac{a}{1 + be^{-cx}} \tag{16.2}$$

where $a, b, c \in \mathbb{R}_{>0}$. For this parameter setting, a constitutes the upper asymptote and the x-axis forms the lower asymptote; the curve is "caught" in-between its asymptotes and increases continuously, i.e. it is S-shaped. Fitting this function type, the developments of JOURNAL, PROCEEDINGS, INPROCEEDINGS and ARTICLE documents over time are modeled as instances of (16.2), by fixing parameters a, b, and c, appropriately. The resulting approximations are plotted in Fig. 16.1(b).

A similar analysis leads to approximation functions for the document classes BOOK, and INCOLLECTION. As for PHDTHESIS, MASTERSTHESIS, and WWW documents we found that they were distributed unsteadily; they are implemented in SP²Bench as random functions that reflect their distribution in the original data set.

16.3.1.3 Other Characteristics

In the following, we shortly sketch selected other characteristics that were considered in the SP²Bench data generator design. A complete discussion can be found in [28].

- *Authors*: special care in the analysis of DBLP was spent in the analysis of authors. The study includes the total number of authors per year (i.e., the sum of `author` attributes), the number of distinct authors per year (obtained from the total authors by eliminating duplicates), as well as the number of new authors in each year. Among others, this analysis shows that the total number of authors has increased steadily over time [accounting for the increasing number of publications over time sketched in Fig. 16.1(b)] and that the number of distinct authors relative to the number of total authors decreases over time, which reflects an increasing productivity of authors, as discussed before in Sect. 16.3.1.1.
- *Editors*: as one might expect, an analysis of connections between authors and editors in DBLP reveals that editors are typically persons that have published before, i.e., persons that are well known in the community.
- *Publications*: the distribution of publications among authors follows a prototypical power law distribution: there are only few authors with many publications, whereas many authors have few publications. Power law distributions are natural distributions that can be modeled as power equations (cf. [28]).
- *Incoming Citations*: in addition to the study of outgoing citations discussed in Sect. 16.3.1.1 [Fig. 16.1(a)], we consider the number of incoming citations for publications. Like for the distribution of publications among authors, we observe a power law distributions, i.e., few publications have many incoming citations, but many of them have few citations. Consequently, we use power equations to implement this distribution in the SP²Bench data generator.

- *Completeness of the Citation System*: it is worth mentioning that, according to Table 16.1, only 0.5% of all article and only about 1% of inproceedings have outgoing citations. Arguably, this value should be close to 100% in a complete scenario, i.e., DBLP contains only a fraction of all existing citations. In addition, we found that in DBLP the number of incoming citations is considerably smaller than the number of outgoing citations. At first glance, this might seem paradoxically, but it is simply explained by the fact that DBLP contains many untargeted citations. Combined with the previous observation that only a fraction of all publications have outgoing citations, we conclude that the DBLP citation system is very incomplete, although in some sense natural in that it follows natural distributions such as power law distribution (w.r.t. incoming citations) or the Gaussian distribution (w.r.t. outgoing references, cf. Sect. 16.3.1.1).

16.3.2 Data Generator Implementation and RDF Scheme

All the characteristics discussed throughout Sect. 16.3.1 are implemented in the SP²Bench data generator. The implementation is written in C++ and offers two parameters, to fix either a triple count limit or the year up to which data will be generated. The generation process is simulation-based, which, among others, means that we assign life times to authors and individually estimate their future behavior, taking into account global publication and coauthor constraints and characteristics, as well as the number of distinct and new authors per year (cf. Sect. 16.3.1.3).

All random functions (which, for example, are used to assign the attributes according to Table 16.1, or to sample data according to the approximation functions in Fig. 16.1) base on a fixed seed. This makes data generation deterministic, i.e., the parameter setting uniquely identifies the outcome. In addition, the generator is implemented in plain ANSI C++, which asserts platform-independence. The fixed random seed and the platform-independent implementation ensure that documents generated under different platforms are always identical, so experimental results from different platforms remain (at least to a certain degree) comparable.

We next survey selected data generator and output document characteristics for documents containing up to 25M RDF triples that have been generated with the SP²Bench data generator implementation. Table 16.2 lists the size of the output file, the year up to which data was generated, the counts of the document class instances (cf. Sect. 16.3.1.2), and the number of total authors and distinct authors contained in the data set (cf. Sect. 16.3.1.3). One can observe superlinear growth for the number of authors relative to the number of triples in the data set, which is primarily caused by the increasing average number of authors per publication, as discussed in Sect. 16.3.1.1. The growth rate of proceedings and inproceedings is also superlinear, while the number of journals and articles increases sublinear. These observations reflect the development of proceedings, inproceedings, journals, and articles sketched in Fig. 16.1(b). Note that the number of inproceedings and articles in the data set clearly dominates the remaining document classes. Finally,

Table 16.2 Characteristics of generated documents

#Triples	10k	50k	250k	1M	5M	25M
file size [MB]	1.0	5.1	26	106	533	2694
data up to	1955	1967	1979	1989	2001	2015
`#Tot.Auth.`	1.5k	6.8k	34.5k	151.0k	898.0k	5.4M
`#Dist.Auth.`	0.9k	4.1k	20.0k	82.1k	429.6k	2.1M
`#Journals`	25	104	439	1.4k	4.6k	11.7k
`#Articles`	916	4.0k	17.1k	56.9k	207.8k	642.8k
`#Proc.`	6	37	213	903	4.7k	24.4k
`#Inproc.`	169	1.4k	9.2k	43.5k	255.2k	1.5M
`#Incoll.`	18	56	173	442	1.4k	4.5k
`#Books`	0	0	39	356	973	1.7k
`#PhD Th.`	0	0	0	101	237	365
`#Mast.Th.`	0	0	0	50	95	169
`#WWWs`	0	0	0	35	92	168

we remark that—like in the original DBLP database—in the early years instances of some document classes are missing, e.g., there are no BOOK or WWW documents for these years.

The SP²Bench RDF Scheme for DBLP Having established the basic knowledge of structural aspects of DBLP, we are now ready to describe the RDF scheme for the DBLP data set that is implemented in the SP²Bench data generator. The scheme basically follows the approach in [5], an existing XML-to-RDF mapping of the original DBLP database. However, with the goal to generate arbitrarily-sized documents, the SP²Bench data generator uses lists of first and last names, publishers, and random words, rather than real author, publications and conference names. The generated SP²Bench conference and journal names are always strings of the form "*Conference $i ($year)*" and "*Journal $i ($year)*", where *$i* is a unique conference (respectively journal) number in year *$year*. Furthermore, predefined lists of random words are used to generate string content, such as titles or abstracts. Concerning person names, the generator relies on lists of first and last names to create fresh random names. Finally, domain-specific string-content, such as the pages specification or the ISBN number of documents are filled with random strings of a reasonable domain (for instance, ISBN-like random strings).

Following [5], SP²Bench uses existing RDF vocabularies to describe resources in a uniform way. It borrows vocabulary from FOAF (namespace `foaf`) for describing persons, and from SWRC (namespace `swrc`) and Dublin Core (namespace `dc`) for

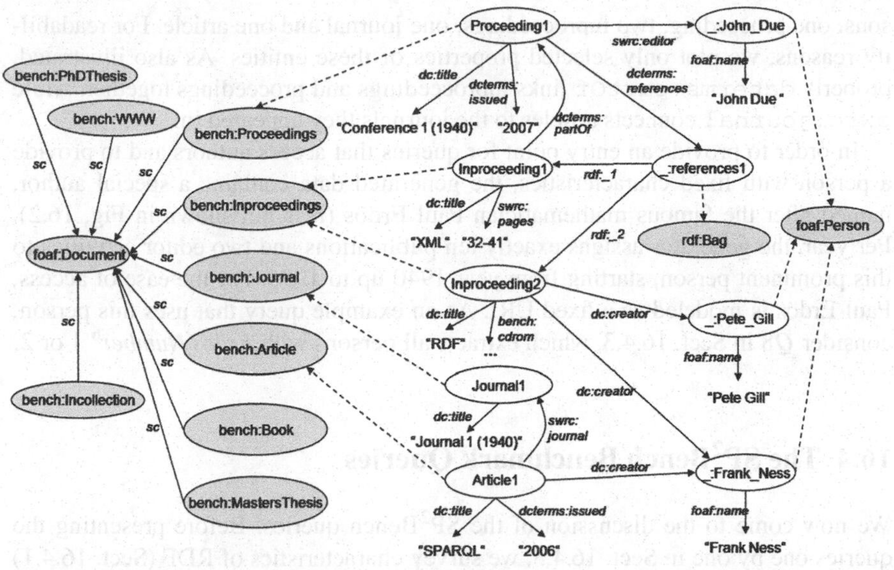

Fig. 16.2 Sample RDF database that illustrates the structure of generated SP²Bench data

describing scientific resources.[5] Additionally, the fresh namespace `bench` defines DBLP-specific document classes, such as `bench:Book` and `bench:WWW`.

Unfortunately, the XML-to-RDF translation of DBLP presented in [5] neither contains blank nodes nor RDF containers. With the goal to contribute a comprehensive benchmark, though, SP²Bench requires such RDF-specific constructs. For this reason, persons in the data set are modeled as (unique) blank nodes "*_:firstname_lastname*" (using the lists of first- and lastnames mentioned above), instead of URIs. Moreover, to have RDF containers available, the SP²Bench data generator models outgoing citations of documents using standard `rdf:Bag` containers. As a further modification, we enrich a small fraction of ARTICLE and INPROCEEDINGS documents with the property `bench:abstract`, which carries comparably large string content (the original DBLP data set does not contain abstracts).

Figure 16.2 illustrates a sample DBLP instance in RDF format, as it might be generated by the SP²Bench data generator. Dashed edges are typing edges (i.e., `rdf:type`) and `sc` stands as an abbreviation for `rdfs:subClassOf`. On the logical level, we distinguish between the *schema* layer (gray) and the *instance* layer (white). As discussed before, reference lists are modeled as blank nodes of type `rdf:Bag` (see e.g., node *_:references1*), while both authors and editors are modeled as blank nodes of type `foaf:Person`. On the schema level, class `foaf:Document` splits up into the DBLP document classes `bench:Journal`, `bench:Article`, and so on. In summary, the sample graph defines three per-

[5] See http://www.foaf-project.org/, http://ontoware.org/projects/swrc/, and http://dublincore.org/, respectively.

sons, one proceeding, two inproceedings, one journal and one article. For readability reasons, we plot only selected properties of these entities. As also illustrated, property `dcterms:partOf` links inproceedings and proceedings together, while `swrc:journal` connects articles to the journals they appeared in.

In order to provide an entry point for queries that access authors and to provide a person with fixed characteristics, the generated data contains a special author, named after the famous mathematician Paul Erdös (it is not shown in Fig. 16.2). Per year, the generator assigns exactly ten publications and two editor activities to this prominent person, starting from year 1940 up to 1996. For the ease of access, Paul Erdös is modeled as a fixed URI. As an example query that uses this person, consider *Q*8 in Sect. 16.4.3, which extracts all persons with *Erdös Number*[6] 1 or 2.

16.4 The SP^{2}Bench Benchmark Queries

We now come to the discussion of the SP^{2}Bench queries. Before presenting the queries one by one in Sect. 16.4.3, we survey characteristics of RDF (Sect. 16.4.1) and SPARQL (Sect. 16.4.2) that were of particular interest for query design.

16.4.1 RDF Characteristics

Decisions on how RDF data is stored and accessed by SPARQL engines might heavily influence the performance of the engine (see for instance the discussions in [1, 26, 36]). Consequently, any reasonable SPARQL benchmark should consider the specifics of the underlying RDF data representation language.

The first aspect that is interesting with respect to the RDF data format is that RDF constitutes elements from three different domains, namely URIs, blank nodes, and literals. SPARQL engines might represent elements from these domains differently (e.g., it might make sense to have a special index for literals to accelerate text search). The SP^{2}Bench queries therefore access all three entities and different combinations thereof; line 1 in Table 16.3 surveys this characteristic for the SP^{2}Bench queries, where abbreviations are indicated by bold font, e.g., using **B** as a shortcut for **B**LANK NODES.[7] Line 1 also indicates queries that access comparably large literals (namely the abstracts of documents) and RDF containers (i.e., the outgoing references, which are of type `rdf:Bag`). Containers are of particular interest due to their special semantics and the fact that they induce a (possibly large) set of membership properties `rdf:_1`, `rdf:_2`, `rdf:_3`, ... As argued in [26], this may induce problems for some RDF storage schemes like Vertical Partitioning [1].

---

[6] See http://www.oakland.edu/enp/.

[7] As we shall see in Sect. 16.4.3, *Q*12*a* and *Q*12*b* are ASK-counterparts of the SELECT queries *Q*5*a* and *Q*8, respectively. The ASK versions of these queries are not explicitly listed in the table.

Table 16.3 Selected properties of the SP²Bench queries

Query	1	2	3abc	4	5ab	6
1 Data Access: **B**LANK NODES, **L**ITERALS, **U**RIS, **L**a**R**GE LITERALS, **C**ONTAINERS	`L,U`	`L,U,La`	`L,U`	`B,L,U`	`B,L,U`	`B,L,U`
2 Access Pattern: **S**UBJ., **P**RED., **O**BJ., **N**ONE	`P,PO`	`P,PO`	`N,PO`	`P,PO`	`P,PO`	`P,PO`
3 Operators: **A**ND, **F**ILTER, **U**NION, **O**PTIONAL	`A`	`A,O`	`A,F`	`A,F`	`A,F`	`A,F,O`
4 Modifiers: **D**ISTINCT, **L**IMIT, **O**f**F**SET, **O**RDER **b**Y	–	`Ob`	–	`D`	`D`	
5 Filter Pushing Possible?	–	–	✓	–	✓/–	✓
6 Reusing of Graph Patterns Possible?	–	–	–	✓	–	✓

Query	7	8	9	10	11	12c
1 Data Access: **B**LANK NODES, **L**ITERALS, **U**RIS, **L**a**R**GE LITERALS, **C**ONTAINERS	`L,U,C`	`B,L,U`	`B,L,U`	`U`	`L,U`	`U`
2 Access Pattern: **S**UBJ., **P**RED., **O**BJ., **N**ONE	`P,PO`	`P,PO`	`N,PO`	`O`	`P`	`SPO`
3 Operators: **A**ND, **F**ILTER, **U**NION, **O**PTIONAL	`A,F,O`	`A,F,U`	`A,U`	–	–	–
4 Modifiers: **D**ISTINCT, **L**IMIT, **O**f**F**SET, **O**RDER **b**Y	`D`	`D`	`D`	–	`L,Ob,Of`	–
5 Filter Pushing Possible?	✓	✓	–	–	–	–
6 Reusing of Graph Patterns Possible?	✓	✓	✓	–	–	–

A second important requirement in the context of RDF data is to test different data access paths at triple pattern level. Triple patterns in SPARQL queries may contain variables in any position and the efficient evaluation of single triple patterns forms the basis for the fast evaluation of more complex queries. On the one hand, it seems reasonable to assume that in most triple patterns the predicate is fixed, such as is the case in patterns like `(?book,dc:creator,?name)` or `(bench:Book1,dc:creator,?name)`, asking for authors of all or a fixed book, respectively. Such patterns are natural counterparts of SQL queries, which select a fixed set of properties from entities, by accessing exactly those table attributes that contain the desired properties. On the other hand, as also argued in [29, 36], one strength of RDF querying is the flexibility of having variables in predicate position, which allows for patterns like `(Book1,?prop,?val)`, to obtain a compact description of a certain resource, or `(?subj,?prop,Person1)`, to extract all entities that stand in direct relation to `Person1`. We survey the use of data access patterns in the SP²Bench queries in Table 16.3, Line 2, where e.g. the shortcut `PO` denotes that the query contains triple patterns with fixed predicate and object position and a variable in subject position. While, in most triple patterns the predicate position is fixed, the SP^{2}Bench queries cover also other patterns, such as triple patterns containing only variables (*Q*3*a*, *Q*3*b*, *Q*3*c*, and *Q*9), patterns where only the object is bound (*Q*10), and variable-free triple patterns (*Q*12*c*).

16.4.2 SPARQL Characteristics

Next, we turn towards a discussion of SPARQL characteristics that were of particular interest in query design. Rows 3 and 4 in Table 16.3 survey the operators and solution modifiers that are used in the benchmark queries. As can be seen, the queries cover various operator constellations, combined with selected solution modifier combinations. Special care in query design was taken in operator OPTIONAL, arguably the most complex operator in the SPARQL query language [23, 27], which can be used to encode (closed-world) negation in SPARQL [3] (cf. *Q*6 and *Q*7).

Another important objective of SP^{2}Bench was to design queries that are amenable to a wide range of SPARQL optimization approaches. One promising approach to SPARQL optimization is the reordering of triple patterns based on selectivity estimation [22, 30], similar by idea to join reordering in Relational Algebra optimization. A beneficial ordering of triple patterns depends on both the selectivity of triple patterns and data access paths that are provided by the engine. Actually, most SP^{2}Bench queries might benefit from such an optimization, because most of them contain large AND-connected blocks and require series of joins. Closely related to triple reordering is filter pushing, which aims at an early evaluation of filter conditions (see e.g., [27]). Like triple pattern reordering, filter pushing might speed up the evaluation by decreasing the size of intermediate results. Row 5 in Table 16.3 identifies the SP^{2}Bench queries that are amenable to filter pushing techniques.

Another reasonable idea is to reuse evaluation results of graph pattern evaluation (or even of whole subqueries). This strategy is applicable whenever the same pattern or subquery is used multiple times in the same query. As a simple example, consider *Q*4 in Sect. 16.4.3. In that query, `?article1` and `?article2` in the first and second triple pattern will be bound to exactly the same nodes of the input RDF graph, so it suffices to evaluate this pattern only once and use this result for both triple patterns. We survey the applicability of graph pattern reusing in Table 16.3, row 6. We will sketch more optimization approaches, such as Semantic Query Optimization (cf. [27]), when discussing the individual queries in the following section.

16.4.3 Discussion of Benchmark Queries

We now come to a one by one presentation of the SP^{2}Bench queries, covering the challenges and the characteristics of the individual queries. In the following discussion, we distinguish between *in-memory* engines, which load the document from file and process queries in main memory, and *native* engines, which rely on a physical

Table 16.4 Number of query results for SELECT queries on documents up to 25 million RDF triples

	$Q1$	$Q2$	$Q3a$	$Q3b$	$Q3c$	$Q4$	$Q5a$	$Q5b$	$Q6$	$Q7$	$Q8$	$Q9$	$Q10$	$Q11$
10k	1	147	846	9	0	23226	155	155	229	0	184	4	166	10
50k	1	965	3647	25	0	104746	1085	1085	1769	2	264	4	307	10
250k	1	6197	15853	127	0	542801	6904	6904	12093	62	332	4	452	10
1M	1	32770	52676	379	0	2586733	35241	35241	62795	292	400	4	572	10
5M	1	248738	192373	1317	0	18362955	210662	210662	417625	1200	493	4	656	10
25M	1	1876999	594890	4075	0	n/a	696681	696681	1945167	5099	493	4	656	10

database system. When discussing the challenges for native engines, we always assume that the document has been loaded into the database prior to query processing.

Before starting our discussion, we survey the result sizes of the individual queries on RDF documents of different size in Table 16.4. The overview shows that the queries vary in their result size (e.g., we have queries with increasing, constant and empty result size). The survey forms the basis for the subsequent discussion.

Benchmark Query $Q1$: *Return the year of publication of "Journal 1 (1940)".*

```
SELECT ?yr
WHERE {
  ?journal rdf:type bench:Journal.
  ?journal dc:title ''Journal 1 (1940)''^^xsd:string.
  ?journal dcterms:issued ?yr }
```

Benchmark query $Q1$ returns exactly one result (for arbitrarily large documents). Native engines might use index lookups to answer this query in (almost) constant time, i.e., execution time should be independent from document size. In-memory engines must scan the whole document and should scale linearly to document size.

Benchmark Query $Q2$: *Extract all inproceedings with properties* dc:creator, bench:booktitle, dcterms:issued, dcterms:partOf, rdfs:seeAlso, dc:title, swrc:pages, foaf:homepage, *and optionally* bench:abstract, *including the respective values.*

```
SELECT ?inproc ?author ?booktitle ?title
       ?proc ?ee ?page ?url ?yr ?abstract
WHERE {
  ?inproc rdf:type bench:Inproceedings.
  ?inproc dc:creator ?author.
  ?inproc bench:booktitle ?booktitle.
  ?inproc dc:title ?title.
  ?inproc dcterms:partOf ?proc.
  ?inproc rdfs:seeAlso ?ee.
  ?inproc swrc:pages ?page.
  ?inproc foaf:homepage ?url.
  ?inproc dcterms:issued ?yr
  OPTIONAL { ?inproc bench:abstract ?abstract }
} ORDER BY ?yr
```

This query implements a large star-join pattern, where different properties of inproceedings (variable `?inproc`) are requested. It contains a simple OPTIONAL clause, and accesses large strings (i.e., the abstracts). Result size grows with database size, and a final result ordering is necessary due to operator ORDER BY. Both native and in-memory engines might reach evaluation times almost linear to the document size.

Benchmark Queries *Q3abc*: *Select all articles with property* (a) swrc:pages, (b) swrc:month, *or* (c) swrc:isbn.

```
(a) SELECT ?article
    WHERE { ?article rdf:type bench:Article.
            ?article ?property ?value
    FILTER (?property=swrc:pages) }

(b) Q3a, but "swrc:month" instead of "swrc:pages"

(c) Q3a, but "swrc:isbn" instead of "swrc:pages"
```

These three queries test FILTER expressions with varying selectivity. According to Table 16.1, the FILTER expression in *Q3a* is not very selective (i.e., retains about 92.61% of all articles). Data access through a secondary index for *Q3a* is probably not very efficient, but might work well for *Q3b*, which selects only 0.65% of all articles. The filter condition in *Q3c* is never satisfied, because no articles have swrc:isbn predicates. Native engines might use statistics to answer *Q3c* in constant time.

Benchmark Query *Q4*: *Select all distinct pairs of article author names for authors that have published in the same journal.*

```
SELECT DISTINCT ?name1 ?name2
WHERE { ?article1 rdf:type bench:Article.
        ?article2 rdf:type bench:Article.
        ?article1 dc:creator ?author1.
        ?author1 foaf:name ?name1.
        ?article2 dc:creator ?author2.
        ?author2 foaf:name ?name2.
        ?article1 swrc:journal ?journal.
        ?article2 swrc:journal ?journal
        FILTER (?name1<?name2) }
```

Q4 contains a rather long graph chain, i.e. variables `?name1`, and `?name2` are linked through the articles that different authors have published in the same journal. As one might expect, the result is very large (cf. Table 16.4). Instead of evaluating the outer pattern block and applying the FILTER afterwards, engines might embed the FILTER expression in the computation of the block, e.g., by exploiting indices on author names. The DISTINCT modifier further complicates the query. We shall expect superlinear behavior for this query, even for native engines.

Benchmark Queries *Q5ab*: *Return the names of all persons that occur as author of at least one inproceeding and at least one article.*

```
(a) SELECT DISTINCT ?person ?name
    WHERE { ?article rdf:type bench:Article.
            ?article dc:creator ?person.
            ?inproc rdf:type bench:Inproceedings.
            ?inproc dc:creator ?person2.
            ?person foaf:name ?name.
            ?person2 foaf:name ?name2
            FILTER(?name=?name2) }

(b) SELECT DISTINCT ?person ?name
    WHERE { ?article rdf:type bench:Article.
            ?article dc:creator ?person.
            ?inproc rdf:type bench:Inproceedings.
            ?inproc dc:creator ?person.
            ?person foaf:name ?name }
```

Q5a and *Q5b* test different join variants: *Q5a* implements an implicit join on author names (encoded in the FILTER condition), while *Q5b* explicitly joins the authors on variable ?name. Although in general the queries are not equivalent, the one-to-one mapping between authors and their names (i.e., author names constitute primary keys) in the SP²Bench scenario implies equivalence. In [18, 27], semantic optimization using such keys for RDF has been proposed. Such approaches might detect the equivalence of *Q5a* and *Q5b* in and choose the more efficient variant.

Benchmark Query *Q6*: *Return, for each year, the set of all publications authored by persons that have not published in years before.*

```
SELECT ?yr ?name ?doc
WHERE {
?class rdfs:subClassOf foaf:Document.
?doc rdf:type ?class.
?doc dcterms:issued ?yr.
?doc dc:creator ?author.
?author foaf:name ?name
OPTIONAL {
  ?class2 rdfs:subClassOf foaf:Document.
  ?doc2 rdf:type ?class2.
  ?doc2 dcterms:issued ?yr2.
  ?doc2 dc:creator ?author2
  FILTER (?author=?author2 && ?yr2<?yr) }
FILTER (!bound(?author2)) }
```

This query implements closed world negation (CWN), expressed through a combination of operators OPTIONAL, FILTER, and BOUND. The idea of the construction is that the block outside the OPTIONAL expression computes all publications, while the inner one constitutes earlier publications from authors that appear outside. The outer FILTER expression then retains publications for which ?author2 is unbound, i.e., those publications of authors without publications in earlier years. For this query, SPARQL-specific optimization like the algebraic rewriting of closed-world negation proposed in [27], might be beneficial.

Benchmark Query $Q7$: *Return the titles of all publications that have been cited at least once, but not by any paper that has not been cited itself.*

```
SELECT DISTINCT ?title
WHERE {
  ?class rdfs:subClassOf foaf:Document.
  ?doc rdf:type ?class.
  ?doc dc:title ?title.
  ?bag2 ?member2 ?doc.
  ?doc2 dcterms:references ?bag2
  OPTIONAL {
    ?class3 rdfs:subClassOf foaf:Document.
    ?doc3 rdf:type ?class3.
    ?doc3 dcterms:references ?bag3.
    ?bag3 ?member3 ?doc
    OPTIONAL {
      ?class4 rdfs:subClassOf foaf:Document.
      ?doc4 rdf:type ?class4.
      ?doc4 dcterms:references ?bag4.
      ?bag4 ?member4 ?doc3
    } FILTER (!bound(?doc4))
  } FILTER (!bound(?doc3))
}
```

This query tests double negation, which requires the encoding of nested closed-world negation. Recalling that the citation system of DBLP is rather incomplete (cf. Sect. 16.3.1.3), this query returns only few results (cf. Table 16.4). However, the query is challenging due to the double negation. Engines might reuse graph pattern evaluation results. For instance, the AND-connected triple pattern block `$1 rdfs:subClassOf foaf:Document. $2 rdf:type $1` occurs three times, for (i) `$1:=?class`, `$2:=?doc`, (ii) `$1:=?class3`, `$2:= ?doc3`, and (iii) `$1:=?class4`, `$2:=?doc4`.

Benchmark Query $Q8$: *Compute authors that have published with Paul Erdös or with an author that has published with Paul Erdös.*

```
SELECT DISTINCT ?name
WHERE {
  ?erdoes rdf:type foaf:Person.
  ?erdoes foaf:name "Paul Erdoes"^^xsd:string.
  { ?doc dc:creator ?erdoes.
    ?doc dc:creator ?author.
    ?doc2 dc:creator ?author.
    ?doc2 dc:creator ?author2.
    ?author2 foaf:name ?name
    FILTER (?author!=?erdoes &&
            ?doc2!=?doc &&
            ?author2!=?erdoes &&
            ?author2!=?author)
  } UNION {
    ?doc dc:creator ?erdoes.
    ?doc dc:creator ?author.
    ?author foaf:name ?name
    FILTER (?author!=?erdoes) }
}
```

Here, the evaluation of the second UNION part is basically "contained" in the evaluation of the first part. Hence, techniques like graph pattern (or subexpression) reusing are applicable. Another promising strategy is to decompose the filter expressions and push its components down in the operator tree (cf. [27]), in order to apply filter subexpressions early and to decrease the size of intermediate results.

Benchmark Query *Q*9**:** *Return incoming and outgoing properties of persons.*

```
SELECT DISTINCT ?predicate
WHERE {
  { ?person rdf:type foaf:Person.
    ?subject ?predicate ?person } UNION
  { ?person rdf:type foaf:Person.
    ?person ?predicate ?object } }
```

*Q*9 has been primarily designed to test nonstandard data access patterns. Naive implementations would compute the triple patterns of the UNION subexpressions separately, thus evaluating patterns where no component is bound. Then, pattern `?subject ?predicate ?person` selects all graph triples, which is rather inefficient. Another idea is to evaluate the first triple in each UNION subexpression, afterwards using the bindings for variable `?person` to evaluate the second pattern efficiently. Note that the result size is exactly 4 for sufficiently large documents (see Table 16.4). RDF-specific statistics about incoming and outgoing properties of *Person*-typed objects (in native engines) might help to answer this query in constant time, even without data access. In-memory engines, however, must always load the whole document and therefore should scale linearly to document size.

Benchmark Query *Q*10**:** *Return all subjects that stand in some relation to person* "Paul Erdös"*, including the type of their relation.*

```
SELECT ?subj ?pred
WHERE { ?subj ?pred person:Paul_Erdoes }
```

In the SP²Bench scenario, this query can be reformulated as: *Return publications and venues in which* "Paul Erdös" *is involved as author or as editor.* It implements an object bound-only access pattern. In contrast to *Q*9, statistics are not immediately useful, because the result includes the subjects (which must be extracted from the data set). Recalling that "Paul Erdös" is active only between 1940 and 1996 (cf. the discussion in Sect. 16.3.2), the result size stabilizes for large documents. Native engines that exploit indices might reach (almost) constant execution time.

Benchmark Query *Q*11**:** *Return (up to) 10 electronic edition URLs starting from the 51th publication, in lexicographical order.*

```
SELECT ?ee
WHERE { ?publication rdfs:seeAlso ?ee }
ORDER BY ?ee LIMIT 10 OFFSET 50
```

The focus of this query lies on the combination of solution modifiers ORDER BY, LIMIT and OFFSET. In-memory engines have to read, process and sort electronic editions prior to application of the LIMIT and OFFSET modifiers. In contrast, native engines might exploit indices to access only a fraction of all electronic editions and, as the result size is limited to 10 due to the LIMIT modifier, would optimally reach constant runtime, independent from the size of the input document.

Benchmark Query $Q12$**:** (a) *Return yes if a person occurs as author of at least one inproceeding and article, no otherwise;* (b) *Return yes if an author has published with Paul Erdös or with an author that has published with* "Paul Erdös", *and no otherwise;* (c) *Return yes if person* "John Q. Public" *is present in the database.*

```
(Q12a) Q5a as ASK query

(Q12b) Q8 as ASK query

(Q12c) ASK {person:John_Q_Public rfd:type foaf:Person}
```

All three queries are boolean queries, designed to test the efficient implementation of the SPARQL ASK query form. $Q12a$ and $Q12b$ share the properties of their SELECT counterparts $Q5a$ and $Q8$, respectively. They always return *yes* for sufficiently large documents. When evaluating ASK queries, engines should stop the evaluation process as soon as a solution has been found. A reasonable optimization approach would be to adapt the query execution plan, trying to efficiently locate a witness. For instance, based on execution time estimations it might be favorable to evaluate the (simpler) second part of the UNION in $Q12b$ first. $Q12c$ asks for a single triple that is not present in the database. With indices, native engines might answer $Q12c$ in constant time. Again, in-memory engines must read and scan the whole document.

16.5 Benchmark Metrics

In this section, we propose several benchmark metrics that cover different aspects of the evaluation process. These metrics reflect the scope and design decisions of SP^{2}Bench and can be used to systematically evaluate benchmark results.

We propose to perform three runs over documents comprising 10k, 50k, 250k, 1M, 5M and 25M RDF triples, using a fixed timeout of 30 min per query and document. The reported time should include the average value over all three runs and, if significant, the errors within these runs. This setting was tested in [26, 28] and, for state-of-the-art engines, can be evaluated in reasonable time (typically within few days). If the tested engine is fast enough, nothing prevents the user from adding larger documents. In the following, we shortly describe a set of interesting metrics.

1. SUCCESS RATE: As a first indicator, we propose to survey the success rates for the engine on top of all document sizes, distinguishing between Success, Timeout (e.g., an execution time > 30 min), Memory Exhaustion (if an additional memory limit was set) and general Errors. This metric gives a good survey over scaling properties and might give first insights into the engine's overall behavior.
2. LOADING TIME: The loading time for documents of different sizes is interesting to get insights into the efficiency and, particularly, to see how document loading scales with document size. This metric primarily applies to engines with a physical database backend and might be irrelevant for in-memory engines, where document loading is usually part of the query evaluation process.
3. PER-QUERY PERFORMANCE: Individual performance results for all queries over all document sizes give more detailed insights into the behavior than the SUCCESS RATE metric discussed before. The PER-QUERY PERFORMANCE metric forms the basis for a deep study of the results and allows to investigate strengths, weaknesses and scaling of the tested implementation based on a one by one discussion of the engine result for the individual benchmark queries.
4. GLOBAL PERFORMANCE: This metric integrates the individual per-query results into a global performance measure. It contains, for each tested document size, the arithmetic and the geometric mean[8] of the engine's average execution time over all queries. We propose to penalize timeouts and other errors with 3600 s (i.e., twice the evaluation time limit). GLOBAL PERFORMANCE is well-suited to investigate the overall scaling properties of engines and to compare the performance of different evaluation approaches. Note that the arithmetic mean imposes a stronger penalty on outlier queries than the geometric mean. Generally speaking, the geometric mean better reflects the average behavior, while the arithmetic mean gives good insights in the worst-case behavior.
5. MEMORY CONSUMPTION: In particular, for engines with a physical backend, the main memory consumption for the individual queries and also the average memory consumption over all queries might be of interest. Optimally, physical backend database engines should get by with a constant main memory consumption, independent from the size of the input document.

We refer the interested reader to [26, 28] for example discussions of SP²Bench evaluation results based on the metrics presented above.

16.6 Conclusion

In this chapter, we presented the SP²Bench performance benchmark for SPARQL, which constitutes a methodical approach for testing the performance of engines

[8]The geometric mean is defined as the nth root of the product over n numbers.

w.r.t. different operator constellations, RDF access paths, typical RDF constructs and a variety of possible optimization approaches. SP^{2}Bench allows to assess the performance of SPARQL engines in a general, comprehensive way and to identify weaknesses and strengths of evaluation approaches. In this line, the SP^{2}Bench framework is a useful tool for both industrial and research quality assessment.

The SP^{2}Bench data generator supports the creation of arbitrarily large DBLP-style documents, which implement various real-world distributions, accounting for the social-world character of the Semantic Web. While, in the context of SP^{2}Bench, this data forms the basis for the design of challenging and predictable benchmark queries, the data generator might also be useful in other Semantic Web projects, i.e., whenever large amounts of test data with natural distributions are needed.

References

1. Abadi, D.J., Marcus, A., Madden, S., Hollenbach, K.J.: Scalable Semantic Web data management using vertical partitioning. In: VLDB, pp. 411–422 (2007)
2. Abadi, D.J., Marcus, A., Madden, S., Hollenbach, K.J.: Using the Barton libraries dataset as an RDF benchmark. Technical Report, MIT-CSAIL-TR-2007-036, MIT (2007)
3. Angles, R., Gutiérrez, C.: The expressive power of SPARQL. In: ISWC, pp. 114–129 (2008)
4. Alexaki, S., Christophides, V., Karvounarakis, G., Plexousakis, D.: On storing voluminous RDF descriptions: the case of web portal catalogs. In: WebDB, pp. 43–48 (2001)
5. Bizer, C., Cyganiak, R.: D2R Server publishing the DBLP Bibliography Database. http://www4.wiwiss.fu-berlin.de/dblp/
6. Bizer, C., Schultz, A.: The Berlin SPARQL benchmark. Int. J. Semant. Web Inf. Syst., Special Issue on Scalability and Performance of Semantic Web Systems (2009)
7. Broekstra, J., Kampman, A., van Harmelen, F.: Sesame: A generic architecture for storing and querying RDF and RDF schema. In: ISWC, pp. 54–68 (2002)
8. Carey, M.J., DeWitt, D.J., Naughton, J.F.: The OO7 benchmark. In: SIGMOD, pp. 12–21 (1993)
9. Chebotko, A., Lu, S., Jamil, H.M., Fotouhi, F.: Semantics preserving SPARQL-to-SQL query translation for optional graph patterns. Technical Report, TR-DB-052006-CLJF (2006)
10. Cyganiac, R.: A relational algebra for SPARQL. Technical Report, HP Laboratories Bristol (2005)
11. Elmacioglu, E., Lee, D.: On six degrees of separation in DBLP-DB and more. SIGMOD Rec. **34**(2), 33–40 (2005)
12. Gray, J.: The Benchmark Handbook for Database and Transaction Systems. Morgan Kaufmann, San Mateo (1993)
13. Groppe, S., Groppe, J., Linnemann, V.: Using an index of precomputed joins in order to speed up SPARQL processing. In: ICEIS, pp. 13–20 (2007)
14. Guo, Y., Pan, Z., Heflin, J.: LUBM: a benchmark for OWL knowledge base systems. In: Web Semantics: Science, Services and Agents on the WWW, vol. 3(2–3), pp. 158–182 (2005)
15. Harris, S., Gibbins, N.: 3store: efficient bulk RDF storage. In: PSSS (2003)
16. Harth, A., Decker, S.: Optimized index structures for querying RDF from the web. In: LA-WEB, pp. 71–80 (2005)
17. Hartig, O., Heese, R.: The SPARQL query graph model for query optimization. In: ESWC, pp. 564–578 (2007)
18. Lausen, G., Meier, M., Schmidt, M.: SPARQLing constraints for RDF. In: EDBT, pp. 499–509 (2008)
19. Ley, M.: DBLP Database. http://www.informatik.uni-trier.de/~ley/db/

20. Lotka, A.J.: The frequency distribution of scientific production. J. Wash. Acad. Sci. **16**, 317–323 (1926)
21. Magkanaraki, A., Alexaki, S., Christophides, V., Plexousakis, D.: Benchmarking RDF schemas for the Semantic Web. In: ISWC, pp. 132–146 (2002)
22. Neumann, T., Weikum, G.: RDF-3X: a RISC-style engine for RDF. In: PVLDB, pp. 647–659 (2008)
23. Pérez, J., Arenas, M., Gutiérrez, C.: Semantics and complexity of SPARQL. In: ICSW, pp. 30–43 (2006)
24. Polleres, A.: From SPARQL to rules (and back). In: WWW, pp. 787–796 (2007)
25. Schmidt, A., Waas, F., Kersten, M.L., Carey, M.J., Manolescu, I., Busse, R.: XMark: A benchmark for XML data management. In: VLDB, pp. 974–985 (2002)
26. Schmidt, M., Hornung, T., Küchlin, N., Lausen, G., Pinkel, C.: An experimental comparison of RDF data management approaches in a SPARQL benchmark scenario. In: ISWC, pp. 82–97 (2008)
27. Schmidt, M., Meier, M., Lausen, G.: Foundations of SPARQL query optimization. Technical Report, Corr cs.DB 0812.3788 (2008)
28. Schmidt, M., Hornung, T., Lausen, G., Pinkel, C.: SP²Bench: a SPARQL performance benchmark. In: ICDE, pp. 222–233 (2009)
29. Sidirourgos, L., Goncalves, R., Kersten, M.L., Nes, N., Manegold, S.: Column-store support for RDF data management: not all swans are white. In: PVLDB, pp. 1553–1563 (2008)
30. Stocker, M., Seaborne, A., Bernstein, A., Kiefer, C., Reynolds, D.: SPARQL basic graph pattern optimization using selectivity estimation. In: WWW, pp. 505–604 (2008)
31. Theoharis, Y., Christophides, V., Karvounarakis, G.: Benchmarking RDF representations of RDF/S stores. In: ISWC, pp. 685–701 (2005)
32. Theoharis, Y., Tzitzikas, Y., Kotzinos, D., Christophides, V.: On graph features of Semantic Web schemas. IEEE Trans. Knowl. Data Eng. **20**(5), 692–702 (2008)
33. W3C: Web Ontology Language (OWL). http://www.w3.org/2004/OWL/
34. W3C: Resource Description Framework (RDF). http://www.w3.org/RDF/
35. W3C: SPARQL Query Language for RDF. W3C Recommendation, 15 January 2008. http://www.w3.org/TR/2008/REC-rdf-sparql-query-20080115/
36. Weiss, C., Karras, P., Bernstein, A.: Hexastore: sextuple indexing for Semantic Web data management. In: VLDB, pp. 1008–1019 (2008)

Part IV
Semantic Web Applications

Chapter 17
Using OWL in Data Integration

Diego Calvanese, Giuseppe De Giacomo, Domenico Lembo, Maurizio Lenzerini, Riccardo Rosati, and Marco Ruzzi

Abstract One of the outcomes of the research work carried out on data integration in the last years is a clear architecture, comprising a global schema, the source schema and the mapping between the source and the global schema. In this chapter, we study data integration under this framework when the global schema is specified in OWL, the standard language for the Semantic Web and discuss the impact of this choice on computational complexity of query answering under different instantiations of the framework in terms of query language and form and interpretation of the mapping. We show that query answering in the resulting setting is computationally too complex, and discuss in detail the various sources of complexity. Then, we show how to limit the expressive power of the various components of the framework in order to have efficient query answering, in principle as efficient as query processing in relational DBMSs. In particular, we adopt OWL 2 QL as the ontology language used to express the global schema. OWL 2 QL is one of the tractable profiles of OWL 2, and essentially corresponds to a member of the *DL-Lite* family, a family of Description Logics designed to have a good trade-off between expressive power of the language and computational complexity of reasoning.

D. Calvanese (✉)
KRDB Research Centre, Free University of Bozen-Bolzano, Piazza Domenicani 3, 39100 Bolzano, Italy
e-mail: calvanese@inf.unibz.it

G. De Giacomo · D. Lembo · M. Lenzerini · R. Rosati · M. Ruzzi
Dip. di Informatica e Sistemistica, SAPIENZA Università di Roma, Via Ariosto 25, 00185 Rome, Italy

G. De Giacomo
e-mail: degiacomo@dis.uniroma1.it

D. Lembo
e-mail: lembo@dis.uniroma1.it

M. Lenzerini
e-mail: lenzerini@dis.uniroma1.it

R. Rosati
e-mail: rosati@dis.uniroma1.it

M. Ruzzi
e-mail: ruzzi@dis.uniroma1.it

R. De Virgilio et al. (eds.), *Semantic Web Information Management*,
DOI 10.1007/978-3-642-04329-1_17,

17.1 Introduction

Data integration is the problem of combining data from different sources, and to provide a single interface for the consumers of information. The main purpose of such an interface is to free the client from the knowledge about where the source data are, and how they can be accessed. Data integration is considered one of the main challenges that Information Technology (IT) currently faces [10]. It is highly relevant in classical IT applications, such as enterprise information management and data warehousing, as well as in scenarios like scientific computing, e-government and web data management.

The need of integrating data arises not only within a single organization, but also when different organizations interoperate (inter-organization integration), like in supply-chain scenarios, or in industrial districts. One of the reasons for such a need is that, on the one hand, large amounts of heterogeneous data, often collected and stored by different applications and systems, are nowadays available, and on the other hand, the need of accessing such data by means of unified mechanisms is becoming more and more crucial, both within and outside the organization boundaries.

In the last two decades, the research on data integration has produced many significant results. One important outcome of this research work is a clear architecture for data integration [63, 70]. According to this architecture, the main components of a data integration system are the global schema, the sources, and the mapping between the two. The sources represent the repositories where the data are, the global schema, also called mediated schema, represents the unified structure presented to the client, and the mapping relates the source data with the global schema. A typical service provided by the system is query answering, i.e., computing the answer to a query posed to the global schema by accessing the sources, collecting the relevant data, and packaging such data in the final answer. Much of the work carried out by the scientific community has concentrated on this task. Many surveys indicate that the market for information integration software is expected to grow considerably in the next years, and to reach about 4 billion US dollars in 2012. Despite the above-mentioned research work, and despite the urgent need for effective solutions, information integration is still largely unresolved. Each commercial data integration tool covers only one of the aspects of the problem, e.g., extraction and loading of data, wrapping data sources or answering federated queries. The result is that a comprehensive solution to the problem is very difficult to achieve with the current technology. There are several reasons why the current methods and techniques for information integration are still far from providing such a solution. We argue that one of the most important reasons is that current tools express the global schema in terms of a so-called logical database model, typically the relational data model. The term logical model refers to the data models of current Data Base Management Systems (DBMSs), and it is well-known that the abstractions and the constructs provided by these models are influenced by implementation issues. It follows that the global schema represents a sort of unified data structure accommodating the various data at the sources, and the client, although freed from physical aspects of the source data (where they are, and how they can be accessed), is still exposed to logical aspects of such data, i.e., how they are packed into specific data structures.

In this chapter, we discuss a different approach, which is based on the idea of posing the semantics of the application domain at the center of the scene. According to this approach, the usual global schema of traditional data integration systems is replaced by the conceptual model of the application domain, and such a conceptual schema is expressed through OWL, the logic-based ontology language used in the Semantic Web. With this approach, the integrated view that the system provides to information consumers is not merely a data structure accommodating the various data at the sources, but a semantically rich description of the relevant concepts in the domain of interest. The distinction between the conceptual model and the data sources reflects the separation between the conceptual level, the one presented to the client, and the logical/physical level of the information system, the one stored in the sources, with the mapping acting as the reconciling structure between the two levels. By using OWL, the global schema of the integration system becomes a declarative, formal specification of the domain of interest, i.e., a logic-based conceptualization of the relevant concepts in the domain, and the relevant relationships among these concepts.

There are several crucial advantages in the semantic approach we pursue in our proposal. First, the conceptual layer in the architecture is the obvious means for pursuing a declarative approach to information integration. By making the representation of the domain explicit, we gain *reusability* of the acquired knowledge, which is not achieved when the global schema is simply a unified description of the underlying data sources. This may also have consequences on the design of user interfaces, since conceptual models are close to the user perception of the domain. Second, the mapping layer explicitly specifies the relationships between the domain concepts on the one hand and the data sources on the other hand. Such a mapping is not only used for the operation of the information system, but also for *documentation purposes*. The importance of this aspect clearly emerges when looking at large organizations where the information about data is widespread into separate pieces of documentation that are often difficult to access and non-necessarily conforming to common standards. The conceptual model built for data integration can thus provide a common ground for the documentation of the organization data, with obvious advantages in the maintenance phase of the system. A third advantage has to do with the *extensibility* of the system. One criticism that is often raised to data integration is that it requires merging and integrating the source data in advance, and this merging process can be very costly. However, the conceptual approach we advocate does not impose to fully integrate the data sources at once. Rather, after building even a rough skeleton of the domain model, one can incrementally add new data sources or new elements therein, when they become available, or when needed, thus amortizing the cost of integration. Therefore, the overall design can be regarded as the incremental process of understanding and representing the domain, the available data sources, and the relationships between them.

The adoption of an expressive ontology language for specifying the global schema comes, however, at a price. Indeed, it is not hard to see that query answering in the resulting framework for data integration is computationally too complex. Starting from this observation, the goals of this chapter are as follows:

- We provide the formal definition (syntax and semantics) of a data integration framework where the global schema is an ontology expressed in OWL (Sect. 17.2).
- We discuss in detail the various sources of complexity in such a data integration framework (Sect. 17.3).
- We show how to limit the expressive power of the various components of the framework in such a way that query answering becomes tractable (Sect. 17.4). In particular, in order to achieve efficient query answering, in principle as efficient as query processing in relational DBMSs, we adopt a language of the *DL-Lite* family [19] as the ontology language used to express the global schema. More precisely, we consider OWL 2 QL, one of the tractable profiles of OWL 2.

We end the chapter by discussing related in Sect. 17.5, and by presenting some final observations in Sect. 17.6.

17.2 The Data Integration Framework

As pointed out in the Introduction, one of the major outcomes of the research in information integration [70, 85] is a conceptual architecture for a data integration system formed by a *global schema*, which provides a representation of the domain of interest, a *source schema*, which describes the set of sources involved in the integration process, and a *mapping*, which establishes the semantic relationship between the global and the source schema. In such a scenario, the user accesses the global schema asking her queries, which will be automatically processed taking into account the knowledge specified by the global schema, the mapping, and the data at the sources, which are suitably accessed to retrieve the data that form the answer for the user's query.

Following the idea, that the domain of interest should be represented through a conceptual model, we find it natural to specify the global schema as an ontology. The ontology language we consider is OWL, the Web Ontology Language, in its forthcoming version, called OWL 2,[1] which is currently being standardized by the World Wide Web Consortium (W3C).[2] More precisely, we adopt OWL 2 DL, the fragment of OWL 2 that is based on Description Logics (DLs) [8]. DLs are logics specifically designed to represent structured knowledge and to reason upon it, and as such are perfectly suited as languages for representing ontologies. DLs are based on the idea that the knowledge in the domain to represent should be structured by grouping into classes objects of interest that have properties in common, and explicitly representing those properties through the relevant relationships holding among

[1] http://www.w3.org/TR/owl2-overview/.

[2] http://www.w3c.org/.

such classes. It follows that the global schema is given in terms of *classes*, each representing a set of objects, *object properties*, i.e., binary relations between classes, and *data properties*, i.e., binary relations between classes and data-types.

From atomic classes and properties, it is possible to construct complex classes and properties. Then, the domain is modeled through assertions involving atomic and complex classes and properties (such as ISA relations, cardinality restrictions, specifications of domain and range of properties, etc.). We do not provide here the detailed syntax and semantics of OWL 2 DL, and refer the reader to the W3C technical report on the subject.[3] It is however worth noticing that OWL 2 DL is essentially a variant of *SROIQ*(*D*), a DL that extends the basic DL *ALC* with transitive roles, regular hierarchies, inverse rules, functionalities of roles, data types and qualified number restrictions [65]. Therefore, OWL 2 DL has a rigorous logical underpinning and a formal semantics, which essentially corresponds to the semantics of *SROIQ*(*D*).

It is important to point out that the global schema only represents intensional knowledge and therefore for its specification we only allow for the use of OWL intensional constructs. In other words, the only instances available for the global schema are the instances retrieved from the sources through the mappings and no additional extensional knowledge is specified for it. Using the DL terminology, we say that the global schema is a TBox, and that no ABox is explicitly specified.

As for the source schema, we assume it is specified as a relational schema. Indeed, very many data sources are available that store data using relational DBMSs. Furthermore, several software companies provide a variety of wrapper based tools enabling a database-like access to non-relational data sources. Therefore, we will describe the sources as a set of relational tables managed by the same relational DBMS and refer to them as if they were stored locally rather than distributed. This is indeed a situation that is always possible to achieve, by making use of capabilities provided by commercial relational data federation tools, which wrap heterogeneous and distributed data sources and present them as if they were a single relational database. We also assume that no integrity constraints are imposed over data sources, that is, each data source is responsible for maintaining its data correct with respect to its own constraints.

The mapping establishes the relationship between the source schema and the global schema, thus specifies how data stored at the sources are linked to the instances of the classes and the properties in the global schema.

Two basic approaches for specifying the mapping have been proposed in the literature. In the first approach, called *global-as-view* (GAV), a query over the source schema is associated with an element of the global schema, so that its meaning is specified in terms of the data residing at the sources. Conversely, the second approach, called *local-as-view* (LAV), requires every relation of the source schema to be defined as a query over the global schema. More recently, a further approach has been considered, which allows for specifying mapping assertions in which a query over the global schema is put in correspondence with a query over the source

[3] www.w3.org/TR/owl2-syntax/.

schema [70]. Such an approach, called (generalized) *global-local-as-view* (GLAV), since it generalizes both the LAV and the GAV approaches [70], is the one we adopt in this paper.

In the data integration settings, described above, the mapping specification has to take into account the *impedance mismatch problem*, i.e., the mismatch between the way in which data is (and can be) represented in a data source, and the way in which the corresponding information is rendered through the global schema. Specifically, the impedance mismatch problem arises from the fact that instances of the source relations are tuples of values, whereas instances of the classes and properties in the global schema are objects, each one denoted by an ad hoc identifier (e.g., a constant in logic), not to be confused with any value item.

More in detail, mapping assertions keep data values separate from object identifiers, and construct identifiers as (logic) terms over values. Each such object identifier has the form $f(d_1, \ldots, d_n)$, where f is a function symbol of arity $n > 0$, and $d_1, \ldots, d_n$ are values retrieved from the sources.

We now present in detail how mapping assertions are specified. Given a source schema $\mathcal{S}$ and a global schema $\mathcal{G}$, a *mapping assertion* from $\mathcal{S}$ to $\mathcal{G}$ is an expression of the form

$$\Phi(\mathbf{v}) \rightsquigarrow_t \Psi(\mathbf{w}),$$

where

- $\Phi(\mathbf{v})$, called the *body* of the mapping, is a first-order logic (FOL) query of arity $n > 0$, with distinguished variables (i.e., free variables) $\mathbf{v}$, over the source schema $\mathcal{S}$;
- $\Psi(\mathbf{w})$, called the *head*, is a first-order query over the global schema $\mathcal{G}$, whose distinguished variables $\mathbf{w}$ appear in the body, i.e., are variables in $\mathbf{v}$. The atoms in $\Psi(\mathbf{w})$ are built over the variables $\mathbf{w}$ and over terms, each one of the form $f(w_1, \ldots, w_n)$ where f is a function symbol of arity $n > 0$ and $w_1, \ldots, w_n$ are variables in $\mathbf{w}$;
- the subscript t stands for the *type* of the mapping assertion, which specifies the underlying semantic assumption. We distinguish the following types of mapping assertions:
  - $\rightsquigarrow_s$, denoting a *sound* mapping assertion, with the intended meaning that the data in the answer to the query over the sources, modulo the construction of object identifiers by means of function symbols, are a subset of the data in the answer to the query over the global schema;
  - $\rightsquigarrow_c$, denoting a *complete* mapping assertion, whose intended meaning is the converse of that of a sound assertion;
  - $\rightsquigarrow_e$, denoting an *exact* mapping assertion, whose intended meaning is that of an assertion that is both sound and complete.

For specifying the two queries in a mapping assertion, we use the languages that are commonly used for querying respectively relational databases and OWL ontologies, and that capture the expressive power of FOL queries. More precisely, we

SubClassOf(*Dean Professor*)
DisjointClasses(*Student Professor*)
SubClassOf(*University Organization*)
SubClassOf(*College Organization*)
ObjectPropertyDomain(*advisor Student*)
ObjectPropertyRange(*advisor Professor*)
ObjectPropertyDomain(*headOf Dean*)
ObjectPropertyRange(*headOf College*)
ObjectPropertyDomain(*takesCourse Student*)
ObjectPropertyRange(*takesCourse Course*)
FunctionalObjectProperty(*headOf*)
EquivalentClasses(*Person* ObjectUnionOf(*Student Professor*))
SubClassOf(*Student* ObjectSomeValuesFrom(*takesCourse Course*))
SubClassOf(*Professor* ObjectSomeValuesFrom(*worksFor University*))
SubClassOf(*Professor* ObjectSomeValuesFrom(*teacherOf Course*))
SubClassOf(*Dean* ObjectSomeValuesFrom(*headOf College*))
DisjointClasses(*Dean* ObjectSomeValuesFrom(*teacherOf Course*))

Fig. 17.1 Global schema of Example 17.1

specify the body of the mapping in SQL, whereas for the head we use the SPARQL syntax.[4]

In the following, we will denote a *data integration system* $\mathcal{I}$ as a tuple $\langle \mathcal{G}, \mathcal{S}, \mathcal{M} \rangle$, where $\mathcal{G}$ denotes the global schema, $\mathcal{S}$ denotes the source schema, and $\mathcal{M}$ denotes the *mapping*, which is a set of mapping assertions between $\mathcal{S}$ and $\mathcal{G}$.

Example 17.1 We now present an example of data integration system extracted from a real integration experiment involving data from different sources in use at SAPIENZA University of Rome. The global schema that we adopt is defined by means of the OWL 2 assertions shown in Fig. 17.1. It is in fact a portion of the Lehigh University Benchmark (LUBM) ontology,[5] an ontology that is commonly used for testing ontology-based applications in the Semantic Web. In particular, the global schema contains the classes *Person*, *Student*, *Professor*, *Organization*, *College*, *Dean* and *Course*, and the object properties *headOf*, *worksFor*, *takesCourse* and *advisor*. For the sake of simplicity, we do not report in this example assertions involving data properties, but they are obviously allowed in our framework.

The source schema is a set of relational tables resulting from the federation of several data sources of the School of Engineering of the SAPIENZA University of Rome, and the portion that we consider in this example is constituted by the relational tables shown in Fig. 17.2.

As for the mapping, referring to the global and source schemas presented above, we provide in Fig. 17.3 some sample mapping assertions.[6]

The mapping assertion M_1 specifies that the tuples from the source table students provide the information needed to build the instances of the class *Student*. In par-

---

[4] http://www.w3.org/TR/rdf-sparql-query/.

[5] http://swat.cse.lehigh.edu/projects/lubm/.

[6] With some abuse of notation we make use, in the SPARQL query in the head of the mapping assertions, of the logical terms that construct object identifiers, that is, **st**(`ID`), **pr**(`PROF_ID`) and **st**(`STUD_ ID`), which have to be considered as simple SPARQL variables.

faculty(*UNIVERSITY_CODE, CODE, DESCRIPTION*)
students(*ID, FNAME, SNAME, DOB, ADDRESS*)
course(*FACULTY_CODE, CODE, DESCRIPTION*)
assignment(*COURSE_CODE, PROFESSOR, YEAR*)
professor(*CODE, FNAME, SNAME, ADDRESS, PHONE*)
exam(*STUD_ID, COURSE_CODE, DATE, RATING*)
career(*STUD_ID, ACADEMIC_YEAR, FACULTY_CODE*)
degree(*STUD_ID, YEAR, PROF_ID, TITLE*)

Fig. 17.2 Relational tables of the source schema of Example 17.1

```
M1: SELECT ID                        ~>s  SELECT ?st(ID) {
    FROM STUDENTS                           ?st(ID) rdf:type Student
    WHERE DOB <= '1990/01/01'             }

M2: SELECT STUD_ID,PROF_ID           ~>e  SELECT ?st(STUD_ID) ?pr(PROF_ ID){
    FROM DEGREE                             ?st(STUD_ID) advisor ?pr(PROF_ID)
    WHERE YEAR > 2000                     }

M3: SELECT STUD_ID                   ~>s  SELECT ?st(STUD_ID) {
    FROM EXAM                               ?st(STUD_ID) advisor ?X
    WHERE COURSE_CODE NOT IN              }
      (SELECT COURSE_CODE
       FROM ASSIGNMENT
       WHERE YEAR < 1990)
```

Fig. 17.3 Mapping assertions of Example 17.1

ticular, the query in the body of M_1 retrieves the code for the students whose date of birth is before 1990; each such code is then used to build the object identifier for the student by means of the unary function symbol **st**. Similarly, the mapping M_2 extracts data from the table degree, containing information on the student's master degree, such as the year of the degree, the title of the thesis and the code of the advisor. The tuples retrieved by the query in the body of M_2, involving only degree titles earned after 2000, are used to build instances for the object property *advisor*: the instances are constructed by means of the function symbols **pr** and **st**. Finally, the mapping assertion M_3 contributes to the construction of the domain of *advisor*, taking from the source table exam only codes of students that have passed the exam of courses that have never been assigned to some professor before 1990. Notice that M_1 and M_3 are sound mapping assertions, whereas M_2 is an exact mapping assertion.

The semantics of a data integration system $\mathcal{I} = \langle \mathcal{G}, \mathcal{S}, \mathcal{M} \rangle$ is defined with respect to a database instance D for the source schema $\mathcal{S}$, and is given in terms of first-order interpretations of the global schema $\mathcal{G}$: an interpretation $I = (\Delta^I, \cdot^I)$ is a *model* for the data integration system $\mathcal{I}$, if it satisfies all the assertions in $\mathcal{G}$, i.e., it is a model of $\mathcal{G}$, and it satisfies the mapping assertions in $\mathcal{M}$ with respect to D. As for the notion of satisfying global assertions, we adopt the standard OWL semantics,[7] whereas to give the precise definition of mapping satisfaction, we need to introduce some preliminary notions.

Let γ be a FOL formula with free variables $\mathbf{x} = (x_1, \ldots, x_n)$, and let $\mathbf{s} = (s_1, \ldots, s_n)$ be a tuple of values. A ground instance $\gamma[\mathbf{x}/\mathbf{s}]$ of γ is obtained from γ by substituting every occurrence of x_i with s_i, for $i \in \{1, \ldots, n\}$.

Now, we are ready to formally define the semantic interpretation of mapping assertions, which reflects the different semantic assumptions that one wants to adopt and that influence the meaning of mapping satisfaction. Specifically: (i) a *sound* mapping assertion corresponds to a first-order logic implication from the sources to the global schema (intuitively, the body of the assertion logically implies its head); (ii) a *complete* mapping assertion corresponds to a first-order logic implication from the global schema to the sources (intuitively, the head of the assertion logically implies its body); finally (iii) an *exact* mapping assertion is both sound and complete, i.e., logical implication is in both directions.

Formally, we say that an interpretation $I = (\Delta^I, \cdot^I)$ *satisfies* the mapping assertion

$$\Phi(\mathbf{v}) \rightsquigarrow_t \Psi(\mathbf{w})$$

with respect to D, if for every ground instance $\Phi[\mathbf{v}/\mathbf{s}] \rightsquigarrow_t \Psi[\mathbf{v}/\mathbf{s}]$ of the mapping we have that

- $\Phi[\mathbf{v}/\mathbf{s}]^D = true$ implies $\Psi[\mathbf{v}/\mathbf{s}]^I = true$, if the mapping is sound, i.e., $t = s$,
- $\Psi[\mathbf{v}/\mathbf{s}]^I = true$ implies $\Phi[\mathbf{v}/\mathbf{s}]^D = true$, if the mapping is complete, i.e., $t = c$,
- $\Phi[\mathbf{v}/\mathbf{s}]^D = true$ if and only if $\Psi[\mathbf{v}/\mathbf{s}]^I = true$, if the mapping is exact, i.e., $t = e$,

where $\Psi[\mathbf{v}/\mathbf{s}]^I$ (resp., $\Phi[\mathbf{v}/\mathbf{s}]^D$), denotes the evaluation of a (ground) FOL formula over the interpretation I (resp., database D) [2].

In our framework, we allow mapping assertions to be either sound or exact, which are the two semantic assumptions most commonly adopted and more thoroughly studied in data integration.

Finally, queries posed by users over the global schema are FOL queries (specified in the SPARQL syntax). Given a FOL query q, with free variables $\mathbf{x}$, expressed over a data integration system $\mathcal{I}$, the set of *certain answers* to q over $\mathcal{I}$ with respect to a source database D is the set of tuples $\mathbf{c}$ of constants from D such that $q[\mathbf{x}/\mathbf{c}]^I = true$ for every model I of $\mathcal{I}$, i.e., $\mathbf{c}$ is in the answer to q in every model I of $\mathcal{I}$.

Example 17.2 To see the different semantic behavior of sound and exact mappings, we refer again to the data integration system presented in Example 17.1, and consider the sample source database D given in Fig. 17.4 (notice that we are assuming that all nonmentioned source tables are empty).

It is easy to see that no interpretation of the global schema satisfies the mapping. Intuitively, this is caused by the fact that mapping assertion M_3 forces $\mathbf{st}(1002)$ to be someone for which an advisor exists, but this contradicts the exact assumption on

[7] http://www.w3.org/TR/owl2-semantics/.

DEGREE			
STUD_ID	**YEAR**	**PROF_ID**	**TITLE**
1001	2003	P12	Handling Incomplete Information in Data Integration

EXAM			
STUD_ID	**COURSE_CODE**	**DATE**	**RATING**
1002	B15	1999-10-10	27

Fig. 17.4 Source database of Example 17.2

the mapping assertion M_2, which then implies that 1002 must be a *STUD_ID* of any tuple in the extension of the relational table degree, but this tuple does not exist in the source database D. Since there is no interpretation satisfying the mapping, there is no model for the data integration system, thus the system is considered inconsistent. Conversely, if we assume that M_2 is a sound mapping, we have that the system is no longer inconsistent, since M_2 is no longer contradicted by the fact that **st**(1002) has an advisor.

Let us now consider the following query over the system (in which M_2 is assumed to be sound).

```
SELECT ?S {
    ?S rdf:type Student
}
```

Intuitively, the query is asking for all the students. Now, since everyone that has an advisor is a student (according to the assertion ObjectPropertyDomain(*advisor Student*)), we can easily conclude (according to the mapping) that the set of certain answers to the query with respect to the source database D is {**st**(1001), **st**(1002)}.

17.3 Computational Characterization of Query Answering

The framework we have presented in the above section explains how Semantic Web languages like OWL or SPARQL can be used for data integration. The resulting setting turns out to be really expressive, since it allows for very expressive mappings (GLAV) that can be interpreted under different semantic assumptions (sound and exact), an expressive global schema (OWL), and expressive query languages, both over the global schema and over the sources. This expressiveness is useful for modelling purposes: however, it makes reasoning in such a framework problematic from a computational point of view.

In this section, we study computational issues connected to query answering, with the aim of showing which are the sources of complexity in the given framework that make this task difficult to deal with (or even impossible, with a sound and complete procedure). What we want to highlight here is that the use in ontology-based data integration systems of standard or common languages and assumptions adopted in Semantic Web, Knowledge Representation and Database applications, requires careful attention. Indeed, reasoning over ontologies and data integration systems means reasoning over incomplete information, which is in general a hard task. As we will see in the following, in order to keep the complexity of query answering low, several limitations need to be imposed over the framework given in Sect. 17.2. Ideally, the complexity we aim at is the one required for evaluation of SQL queries over relational databases. This complexity, indeed, would allow us to rely over relational database technology that is nowadays the only available technology for dealing with the large amounts of data (e.g., of the order of millions of instances) typical of data integration applications. In other words, we aim at rightsizing the framework in such a way that query answering is reducible to plain evaluation of an SQL query posed over a relational DBMS or data federation tool which is in charge of managing the data sources. Formally, such a property is called *FOL-reducibility* of query answering (since FOL queries can be straightforwardly expressed in SQL) [19]. In terms of computational complexity, this means that the whole query answering process is in AC^0 in data complexity, i.e., the complexity measured only in the size of the data [2].[8]

We proceed as follows:

1. We first show that query answering in the general framework is undecidable, and that the cause of undecidability resides in the use of FOL as user query language and mapping language. We then renounce to having FOL queries over the global schema, both as users' queries and as mapping queries, and adopt Unions of Conjunctive Queries (UCQs), i.e., FOL queries expressible as a union of select-project-join SQL queries.
2. We then show that, even if the global schema is a flat schema (i.e., a set of predicates, without any terminological axiom over them), query answering of UCQs is intractable. There are two independent sources of complexity for this intractability: the presence of exact mappings, and the use of UCQs over the global schema in the head of GLAV mappings.
3. We finally show that, even if we do not allow for exact mappings and UCQs in the head of mapping assertions, when the global schema is specified in OWL, query answering is intractable as well. Therefore, OWL as global schema language turns out to be a third source of complexity for intractability.

Undecidability of query answering mentioned at the first point is a straightforward consequence of the undecidability of the validity problem in FOL, i.e., checking wether a FOL sentence evaluates to true in every interpretation. Indeed, a reduction can be constructed from such a problem to a query answering problem in data integration, exploiting the fact that the user query language is FOL. Furthermore, even if the user may only ask atomic queries (i.e., we disallow FOL as user query language), it is still possible to reduce FOL validity to query answering in data integration by exploiting the fact that the query in the head of mapping assertions is a

[8] The complexity class AC^0 is essentially the one that corresponds to the data complexity of evaluating a first-order (i.e., an SQL) query over a relational database.

FOL query. Notice that this holds even if the global schema is simply a set of concept and property predicates, and mappings are sound LAV mappings. Therefore, to have decidable query answering, queries over the global schema (both user queries and head mapping queries) cannot be expressed in FOL.

We therefore decide to limit the expressive power of the query language in order to have decidable query answering. At the same time, however, we need flexible mechanisms for extracting data from an integration system, such as those ensured by database query languages. Traditional DL inference tasks, like instance checking and instance retrieval [42, 81], are indeed not suited for this purpose, since they cannot refer to the same object via multiple navigation paths in the ontology, i.e., they allow only for a limited form of join, namely chaining. UCQs provide a good trade-off between expressive power and nice computational properties. They are also the most expressive fragment of FOL for which query answering over expressive DLs has been shown to be decidable [8, 23].

Even though it is open whether answering UCQs over ontologies specified in OWL 2 DL (or in its DL counterpart $\mathcal{SROIQ}(\mathcal{D})$) is decidable, we will see in the following that such a choice causes intractability of query answering already for ontologies expressed in fragments of OWL 2 DL, and therefore some further right-sizing of the framework is needed to achieve our ultimate goal of having query answering in AC^0.

Before delving into this aspect, however, we first notice that having UCQs as the language for expressing the query in the head of mapping assertions has a bad computational impact, even when the global schema is a plain theory, i.e., without axioms. Indeed, as shown in [1], answering UCQs is coNP-hard in data complexity in the presence of (either exact or sound) LAV mappings under a global schema that is a flat relational schema. For the case of sound mappings only, the intractability holds if queries over the global schema in the mapping assertions are UCQs, while for the case of exact mappings, the intractability holds even if such queries are Conjunctive Queries (CQs), i.e., disjunction is not allowed. This obviously implies that query answering in our framework, independently from the language adopted for the global schema, is coNP-hard in the size of the data. As further shown in [1], the combination of sound mappings and mapping queries over the global schema that are CQs leads to membership of query answering in PTIME. For modeling reasons, we do not want to renounce to the expressive power of CQs over the global schema in mapping assertions, thus the above results force us to discard exact mappings and to rely on sound mappings only.

Finally, we turn back to UCQs as user query language over the OWL 2 DL global schema. Recent studies on DLs have in fact shown that query answering of UCQs is coNP-complete in data complexity for fragments of OWL 2 DL that correspond to expressive DLs of the $\mathcal{SH}$ family, which constitutes the logical underpinning of the OWL languages [52, 78]. In fact, in [18] it was already shown that query answering of CQs is coNP-hard already for very simple ontology languages (fragments of OWL 2 DL) allowing for some basic ontology constructs, such as covering (which allows to say, for instance, that the set of persons is the union of men and women). Therefore, there is no hope to have tractable query answering in a framework in which the global schema is specified in OWL 2 DL. To overcome this problem, in the next section, we present a suitable fragment of OWL 2 DL characterized by a good trade-off between expressive power and complexity of reasoning, and for which query answering turns out to be tractable (in fact in AC^0) in data complexity.

17.4 Data Integration Using OWL 2 QL

In this section, we analyze data integration under global schemas expressed in OWL 2 QL, a tractable profile[9] of OWL 2, which is essentially based on the description logic *DL-Lite*$_R$ [19]. We will show that expressing the global schema in OWL 2 QL allows for efficient query answering. More precisely query answering is first-order rewritable, i.e., it can be reduced to evaluation of a first-order query (directly expressible in SQL) over a database instance, provided that the user's query is a UCQ, each mapping assertion is sound, and it has a FOL query over the source schema in its head and a CQ over the global schema in its body (cf. Sects. 17.2 and 17.3).

To ease exposition, we will focus here on *DL-Lite*$_R$, the DL on which OWL 2 QL is essentially based, but we remark that all the results and the techniques for *DL-Lite*$_R$ presented here also hold when the global schema is expressed instead in OWL 2 QL. For a more detailed description of OWL 2 QL, we refer the reader to the W3C technical report on the OWL 2 profiles.

To introduce *DL-Lite*$_R$, we use the following notation:

- A denotes an *atomic concept*, B a *basic concept*, and C a *general concept*;
- P denotes an *atomic role*, Q a *basic role*, and R a *general role*.

Then, *DL-Lite*$_R$ expressions are defined as follows.[10]

- Basic and general *concept expressions*:

$$B ::= A \mid \exists Q, \qquad C ::= \top \mid B \mid \neg B \mid \exists Q.C$$

  where the concept $\top$ is the universal concept, and corresponds to the OWL class `owl:Thing`, which denotes the set of all individuals; $\neg B$ denotes the negation of a basic concept B; the concept $\exists Q$ is the unqualified existential restriction, which denotes the domain of a role Q, i.e., the set of objects that Q relates to some object, and corresponds to the OWL expression ObjectSomeValuesFrom(Q, `owl:Thing`); the concept $\exists Q.C$, also called qualified existential restriction, denotes the qualified domain of Q w.r.t. C, i.e., the set of objects that Q relates to some instance of C, and corresponds to the OWL expression ObjectSomeValuesFrom(Q, C).

---

[9] http://www.w3.org/TR/owl2-profiles/.

[10] *DL-Lite*$_R$ can be easily extended with attribute expressions, i.e., assertions involving data properties (cf. [79]). For the sake of simplicity we do not introduce such expressions here (they are however available in OWL 2 QL).

- Basic and general *role expressions*:

$$Q ::= P \mid P^-, \qquad R ::= Q \mid \neg Q$$

  where P^- denotes the inverse of an atomic role, and $\neg Q$ denotes the negation of a basic role.

A *DL-Lite$_R$ TBox* allows one to represent intensional knowledge by means of *inclusion assertions*, i.e., expressions of the following forms:

$$B \sqsubseteq C \quad \textit{concept inclusion assertion}$$
$$Q \sqsubseteq R \quad \textit{role inclusion assertion}$$

A concept inclusion assertion expresses that a (basic) concept B is subsumed by a (general) concept C. Analogously for role inclusion assertions.

For the semantics of *DL-Lite$_R$* knowledge bases (constituted by a TBox and an ABox, which specifies the instances of concept and roles) we refer the reader to [19]. As shown in [19], reasoning over a *DL-Lite$_R$* knowledge base is tractable. More precisely, TBox reasoning is in NLOGSPACE and answering unions of conjunctive queries is FOL-reducible, and hence in AC^0 w.r.t. data complexity. Thus, *DL-Lite$_R$* appears particularly suited for integration of large amounts of data.

We now analyze data integration systems of the form $\mathcal{I} = \langle \mathcal{G}, \mathcal{S}, \mathcal{M} \rangle$ in which $\mathcal{G}$ is a *DL-Lite$_R$* TBox, $\mathcal{S}$ is a relational schema, and $\mathcal{M}$ is a set of sound GLAV mappings from $\mathcal{S}$ to $\mathcal{G}$, with a FOL query over $\mathcal{S}$ in the body and a UCQ over $\mathcal{G}$ in the head. More precisely, given such a system $\mathcal{I}$, a database instance D for the source schema $\mathcal{S}$, and a UCQ q over $\mathcal{G}$, we want to compute the certain answers to q over $\mathcal{I}$ w.r.t. D. We assume that $\mathcal{I}$ is satisfiable with respect to D, i.e., there exists a model for $\mathcal{I}$ and D.

The query answering algorithm is constituted by the following four steps, which we describe in the following:

1. *Schema-Rewriting*
2. *LAV-Rewriting*
3. *GAV-Rewriting*
4. *Source-Evaluation*

Schema-Rewriting Given a UCQ Q over a data integration system $\mathcal{I} = \langle \mathcal{G}, \mathcal{S}, \mathcal{M} \rangle$, and a source database D for $\mathcal{I}$, the Schema-Rewriting step computes a new UCQ Q' over $\mathcal{I}$, where the assertions of $\mathcal{G}$ are compiled in. In computing the rewriting, only inclusion assertions of the form $B_1 \sqsubseteq B_2$, and $Q_1 \sqsubseteq Q_2$ are taken into account, where B_1 and B_2 are basic concepts, and Q_1 and Q_2 are basic roles. Intuitively, the query Q is rewritten according to the knowledge specified in $\mathcal{G}$ that is relevant for answering Q, in such a way that the rewritten query Q' is such that the certain answers to Q over $\mathcal{I}$ and D are equal to the certain answers to Q' over $\mathcal{I}' = \langle \emptyset, \mathcal{S}, \mathcal{M} \rangle$ and D, i.e., the Schema-Rewriting step allows to get rid of $\mathcal{G}$.

We refer the reader to [19] for a formal description of the Schema-Rewriting algorithm and for a proof of its soundness and completeness. We only notice here that the Schema-Rewriting step does not depend on the source database D, runs in polynomial time in the size of $\mathcal{G}$, and returns a query Q' whose size is at most exponential in the size of Q.

LAV-Rewriting Given the UCQ Q' over $\mathcal{I}$ computed by the Schema-Rewriting step, the LAV-Rewriting step considers the "LAV-part" of the mapping $\mathcal{M}$, denoted by $LAV(\mathcal{M})$ in the following.

First, we define the "LAV part" and the "GAV part" of a GLAV mapping $\mathcal{M}$ as follows. Let $\mathcal{M} = \{M_1, \ldots, M_k\}$ be a set of k mapping assertions.[11] Suppose the GLAV mapping assertion M_i is of the form

$$SQL_s(x_1, \ldots, x_n) \rightsquigarrow_s CQ_g(x_1, \ldots, x_n)$$

where $SQL_s(x_1, \ldots, x_n)$ is an SQL query over $\mathcal{S}$ and $CQ_g(x_1, \ldots, x_n)$ is a conjunctive query over $\mathcal{G}$, both with distinguished variables $x_1, \ldots, x_n$. Then, we define M_i' as the LAV mapping assertion

$$aux_i(x_1, \ldots, x_n) \rightsquigarrow_s CQ_g(x_1, \ldots, x_n)$$

where aux_i is a new auxiliary relation symbol of arity n, and define M_i'' as the GAV mapping assertion

$$SQL_s(x_1, \ldots, x_n) \rightsquigarrow_s aux_i(x_1, \ldots, x_n)$$

Then, we denote by $LAV(\mathcal{M})$ the set of LAV mappings $\{M_1', \ldots, M_k'\}$, and we denote by $GAV(\mathcal{M})$ the set of GAV mappings $\{M_1'', \ldots, M_k''\}$. Notice that each $\mathcal{M}'$ is a set of LAV mappings from the set of relations $aux_1, \ldots, aux_k$ to $\mathcal{G}$. In other words, such auxiliary relations play the role of source predicates in $\mathcal{M}'$, whereas has to be considered global predicates in M_i''.

Now, the LAV-Rewriting step reformulates the UCQ Q' to a UCQ Q'' over the set $AUX = \{aux_1, \ldots, aux_k\}$ of auxiliary relations in such a way that, for every database instance D_{aux} for the schema AUX, the set of certain answers to Q' over $\langle \emptyset, AUX, LAV(\mathcal{M}) \rangle$ w.r.t. D_{aux} is equal to the evaluation of the query Q'' over D_{aux}. This is realized by applying any of the well-known methods that are able to rewrite a union of conjunctive queries with respect to a set of LAV mappings (e.g., the inverse rules algorithm [1] or the Minicon algorithm [80]). Moreover, the LAV-Rewriting procedure does not depend on D and runs in polynomial time in the size of $LAV(\mathcal{M})$ (i.e., in the size of $\mathcal{M}$).

GAV-Rewriting Given the UCQ Q'' over the auxiliary schema AUX computed by the previous step, and the set of GAV mappings $GAV(\mathcal{M})$, the GAV-Rewriting step computes, by using logic programming technology, an SQL query Q''' over the source schema $\mathcal{S}$. It can be shown (see [79], where this step is called the *unfolding*

[11] To ease the exposition, we do not consider in the following the presence in the mapping of logical terms that construct object identifiers. The treatment can be easily generalized to this case.

step) that Q''' is such that, for every database instance D for the schema $\mathcal{S}$, the set of certain answers to Q'' over $\langle \emptyset, \mathcal{S}, GAV(\mathcal{M})\rangle$ w.r.t. D is equal to the evaluation of the query Q''' over D. Moreover, the GAV-Rewriting step does not depend on D, runs in polynomial time in the size of $GAV(\mathcal{M})$ (i.e., in the size of $\mathcal{M}$), and returns a query whose size is polynomial in the size of Q''.

Source-Evaluation The final step consists in simply evaluating the SQL query Q''', produced by the GAV-Rewriting step, over D. Notice that, to actually perform such an evaluation, a data federation tool managing the data sources is needed, because the query Q''' is distributed over several autonomous data sources.

It can be shown that the query answering procedure described above correctly computes the certain answers to UCQs, i.e., for every database instance D for the schema $\mathcal{S}$, the set of certain answers to Q over $\langle \mathcal{G}, \mathcal{S}, \mathcal{M}\rangle$ w.r.t. D is equal to the evaluation of the query Q''' over D. Based on the computational properties of such an algorithm, we can then characterize the complexity of our query answering method.

Theorem 17.1 *Let $\mathcal{I} = \langle \mathcal{G}, \mathcal{S}, \mathcal{M}\rangle$ be a data integration system where $\mathcal{G}$ is a DL-Lite$_R$ TBox and $\mathcal{M}$ is a set of GLAV mappings of the limited form described above, and let D be a source database for $\mathcal{I}$. Answering a UCQ over $\mathcal{I}$ with respect to D can be reduced to the evaluation of an SQL query over D, i.e., it is FOL-reducible, and it is in AC^0 in the size of D.*

Finally, we remark that, as we said at the beginning of this section, we have assumed that the data integration system $\mathcal{I}$ is satisfiable with respect to the database D. Notably, it can be shown that all the machinery we have devised for query answering can also be used for checking satisfiability of $\mathcal{I}$ with respect to D. Therefore, checking satisfiability can also be reduced to sending appropriate SQL queries to the source database [79].

Example 17.3 Consider again Example 17.1. According to what has been said in Sect. 17.3 and in this section, we have to renounce to some of the modeling choices initially adopted. To this aim, we substitute M_2 with the mapping assertion

M_2':
```
SELECT STUD_ID, PROF_ID   ~>s   SELECT ?st(STUD_ID) ?pr(PROF_ ID){
FROM DEGREE                            ?st(STUD_ID) advisor ?pr(PROF_ID)
WHERE YEAR > 2000                      }
```

which is analogous to M_2 but is sound rather than exact. Furthermore, we adapt the global schema described in Fig. 17.1 in such a way to obtain its OWL 2 QL approximation. In particular, we eliminate the assertion FunctionalObjectProperty(*headOf*), since functionality is not allowed in OWL 2 QL, and approximate EquivalentClasses(*Person* ObjectUnionOf(*Student Professor*)) with the two assertions SubClassOf(*Student Person*) and SubClassOf(*Professor Person*), since the use of the union in the right-hand side of inclusion assertions is not allowed in OWL 2 QL. In Fig. 17.5, we give the refined global schema expressed in the *DL-Lite$_R$* syntax.

$$
\begin{array}{ll}
\mathit{Dean} \sqsubseteq \mathit{Professor} & \mathit{Student} \sqsubseteq \neg\mathit{Professor} \\
\mathit{University} \sqsubseteq \mathit{Organization} & \mathit{College} \sqsubseteq \mathit{Organization} \\
\exists \mathit{advisor} \sqsubseteq \mathit{Student} & \exists \mathit{advisor}^- \sqsubseteq \mathit{Professor} \\
\exists \mathit{headOf} \sqsubseteq \mathit{Dean} & \exists \mathit{headOf}^- \sqsubseteq \mathit{College} \\
\exists \mathit{takesCourse} \sqsubseteq \mathit{Student} & \exists \mathit{takesCourse}^- \sqsubseteq \mathit{Course} \\
\mathit{Student} \sqsubseteq \mathit{Person} & \mathit{Professor} \sqsubseteq \mathit{Person} \\
\mathit{Student} \sqsubseteq \exists \mathit{takesCourse}.\mathit{Course} & \\
\mathit{Professor} \sqsubseteq \exists \mathit{worksFor}.\mathit{University} & \\
\mathit{Professor} \sqsubseteq \exists \mathit{teacherOf}.\mathit{Course} & \\
\mathit{Dean} \sqsubseteq \exists \mathit{headOf}.\mathit{College} & \\
\mathit{Dean} \sqsubseteq \neg\exists \mathit{teacherOf}.\mathit{Course} &
\end{array}
$$

Fig. 17.5 Global schema of Example 17.3 in the *DL-Lite*$_R$ syntax

Then, consider again the query asking for all students

```
SELECT ?S {
  ?S rdf:type Student
}
```

and process it according to the query answering algorithm described above. After the schema-rewriting step, we obtain the following query.

```
SELECT ?S {
  ?S rdf:type Student
}
UNION
SELECT ?S {
  ?S advisor ?X
}
UNION
SELECT ?S {
  ?S takesCourse ?X
}
```

To get the intuition behind the schema-rewriting step, consider that, in this example, the global schema specifies that everyone that has an advisor is a student ($\exists advisor \sqsubseteq Student$), and that everyone that takes a course is a student ($\exists takesCourse \sqsubseteq Student$). After the schema rewriting step, this knowledge is compiled in the query, which now, besides asking for (explicit) students, asks also for those that have an advisor and those that take a course. This rewritten query can be now evaluated over the system in which the global schema is considered empty.

Let us now consider the mapping. We notice that in this example the "GAV part" of the mapping is constituted by the two GAV assertions M_1 and M_2 and the "LAV part" is constituted by the LAV assertion M_3.[12] Therefore, there is no need to introduce auxiliary predicates. Then, in the LAV-rewriting step we rewrite the query according to M_3, whereas in the GAV-rewriting step we rewrite it on the basis of M_1 and M_2. We thus obtain the following query, which we express in SQL.[13]

```
SELECT st(ID) FROM STUDENTS
WHERE DOB <= '1990/01/01'
  UNION
SELECT st(STUD_ID) FROM DEGREE
WHERE YEAR > 2000
  UNION
SELECT st(STUD_ID) FROM EXAM
WHERE COURSE_CODE NOT IN
  ( SELECT COURSE_CODE FROM ASSIGNMENT
    WHERE YEAR < 1990)
```

It is easy to see that the evaluation of such a query over the source database D given in Fig. 17.4 returns the set of certain answers $\{\mathbf{st}(1001), \mathbf{st}(1002)\}$.

17.5 Related Work

Research in information integration has been very active in the last fifteen years, and has produced a number of results and technical contributions, from both the theoretical and practical points of view [62, 68, 70, 85].

The setting that has been more deeply investigated is the traditional centralized (as known as mediator-based) data integration setting, where the integration is performed through a centralized global schema connected to sources via semantic mappings. As already said, this is also the setting considered in the present chapter.

Among the various problems related to data integration, the problem of answering queries posed over the global schema is the one that has been addressed most intensively. The first proposals, developed in the middle 90s, faced such a problem in a procedural way, thus not providing the users with a real declarative support to data integration. Systems like TSIMMIS (The Stanford-IBM Manager of Multiple Information Sources) [33], or Garlic [31] are essentially hierarchies of wrappers (cf. Sect. 17.2) and mediators, which are in charge of triggering the right wrappers and putting together the data that they return into the final answers to users' queries (or feeding in turn other mediators). Both TSIMMIS and Garlic can be considered

[12] M_3 is a LAV assertion since not all the variables occurring in the head are mapped to distinguished variables in the body, i.e., M_3 has existentially quantified variables in the head.

[13] In the SELECT clause, with some abuse of notation, we make use of the logical terms that construct object identifiers. These logical terms can be easily obtained resorting to SQL functions for string manipulation, as suggested in [79].

primitive forms of systems adopting GAV mapping, but, since each mediator works in an independent manner, it turns out that no real integration is ever achieved.

A different (declarative) approach to the problem of query answering in data integration has been instead followed in the setting in which LAV mapping is considered. In such setting, query answering calls for facing the issue of query processing using views [27, 70, 73, 85], i.e., the issue of how to use the information about the global schema, the mappings, and the data stored at the sources, to answer the users' queries posed over the global schema. Two notable examples of systems following such approach in a relational context are Information Manifold (IM) [74, 75], and INFOMASTER [1, 43, 51]. For query answering, both systems propose query rewriting procedures, called the bucket algorithm and the inverse rules algorithm, respectively. Such algorithms have been originally designed for the case in which both the users' and the mapping queries are CQs, but some extensions have been proposed that consider also more expressive settings (see, e.g., [43] and [59]). An interesting optimization for the bucket algorithm, called the Minicon algorithm, can be found in [80], where it is shown that Minicon significantly speeds up query processing with respect to previously proposed procedures. It is worth noticing that all the above mentioned algorithms in principle can be used in the LAV-Rewriting step of the query answering procedure presented in Sect. 17.4.

Many other studies have considered the query answering problem in data integration systems in various settings. For example, the relational setting (under various assumptions on the languages used for the mapping and the queries) has been analyzed in [55, 72], whereas the impact on query answering of specifying different forms of integrity constraints on a relational global schema has been considered in [43, 59] for LAV mappings, and in [15, 16] for GAV mappings. Also, query answering in the presence of semistructured data sources and global schemas has been considered in [28–30], and is still the subject of intensive investigations.

Despite the intensive research of the last years described so far, only few efforts have been dedicated to the study of data integration through conceptual models, and in particular through ontologies. This problem has been considered for example in [22], where the authors propose a formal framework for Ontology Integration Systems (OISs). Their view of a formal framework deals with a situation where there are various local ontologies, developed independently from each other, assisting the task to build an integrated, global ontology as a means for extracting information from the local ones. Ontologies in their framework are expressed as DL knowledge bases, and mappings between ontologies are expressed through suitable mechanisms based on queries, which actually correspond to the GAV and LAV approaches adopted in data integration.

We point out that most of the work carried out so far on ontology-based information integration is on which language or which method to use to build a global ontology on the basis of the local ones [13, 40], whereas the problem of querying an integrated ontology, i.e., a global schema of a mediator-based data integration system expressed in terms of an ontology, still needs further investigation. Among the first studies on this problem, we mention [14, 24, 25]. In particular, in [14], global schemas specified as UML class diagrams, translated into simple DL theories, are considered, and reasoning (i.e., query processing) over them is studied (in fact, the mediator-based integration framework is only envisaged in the paper, but the proposed techniques are easily extendible to GAV data integration systems). In [24], the use in data integration systems of logic theories expressed in *DLR*, an expressive DL allowing for the use of n-ary relationships, is investigated, but no complete query answering processing algorithms are provided. In [25], the above theoretical studies are applied to a data warehouse context.

When the global schema of a data integration system is specified in terms of a DL ontology, it is natural to look at the research carried out in the DL field and at the tools developed for specifying and reasoning over DL knowledge bases, and investigate if and how they can be applied in a data integration setting.

In this respect, it is worth noticing that current reasoners for expressive DLs perform indeed well in practice, and show that even procedures that are exponential in the size of the knowledge base might be acceptable under suitable conditions. This has been achieved during the years, thanks to the intensive research aimed at understanding the frontier between tractability (i.e., solvable by a polynomial time algorithm) and intractability of reasoning over concept expressions. The maximal combinations of constructs (among those most commonly used) that still guarantee polynomial time inference procedures were identified, which allowed to exactly characterize the tractability frontier [8, 41]. It should be noted that the techniques and technical tools that were used to prove such results, namely tableaux-based algorithms, are at the basis of the modern state of the art DL reasoning systems [77], such as Fact [64], Racer [60] and Pellet [83, 84]. However, such reasoners have not specifically been tailored to deal with large amounts of data, which is a critical issue in all those settings in which ontologies are used as a high-level, conceptual view over data repositories, as in data integration.

In data integration, data are typically very large and dominate the intensional level of the ontologies. Hence, while one could still accept reasoning that is exponential on the intensional part, it is mandatory that reasoning is polynomial in the data (i.e., in data complexity). Traditionally, research carried out in DLs has not paid much attention to the data complexity of reasoning, and only recently efficient management of large amounts of data [34, 66] has become a primary concern in ontology reasoning systems, and data complexity has been studied explicitly [6, 7, 18, 67, 69, 78]. Unfortunately, research on the trade-off between expressive power and computational complexity of reasoning has shown that many DLs with efficient reasoning algorithms lack the modeling power required for capturing conceptual models and basic ontology languages. An interesting line of research, followed, e.g., in [18, 19, 79], is therefore the one that is aimed at defining ontology languages which allow for both efficient reasoning, and in particular answering of complex queries as CQs, and good modeling power, that means enabling the specification of basic ontology constructs. The OWL2 QL profile described in Sect. 17.4 is indeed one of such languages.

It is worth noticing that all the above mentioned approaches to data integration do not consider the problem of data that may result inconsistent with respect to integrity constraints specified over the global schema. This is in fact a quite common situation, since data stored at autonomous sources in general are not required to be compliant with global integrity constraints. This problem is even more evident when the global schema is given in terms of an ontology, which provides the conceptualization of the domain of interest, constructed separately, and in principle independently, from the sources to be integrated.

In the cases in which data may contradict global integrity constraints, the main problem that arises is how to obtain significant answers from inconsistent systems. Traditionally, the approach adopted to remedy this problem has been through data cleaning [11]. This approach is procedural in nature, and is based on domain-specific transformation mechanisms applied to the data retrieved from the sources. Only very recently, the first academic prototype implementations have appeared, which provide declarative approaches to the treatment of inconsistency of data, in the line of the studies on consistent query answering [4]. In such approaches, the common basic idea is that inconsistency might be eliminated by modifying the database representing the extension of the system (e.g., the models of the data integration system), and reasoning on the "repaired" database. Since several repairs are possible, the "consistent answers" are the answer to users' query returned by the evaluation of the query in every repair. In many papers, it has been proposed to formalize repair semantics by using logic programs [12, 16, 56]. The common idea is to encode the constraints of the global schema into a logic program, using unstratified negation or disjunction, such that the stable models of this program [50] yield the repairs of the global database, and the user query can be compiled in this program in such a way that its evaluation returns the consistent answers. This is for example the approach followed by the INFOMIX system [71]. INFOMIX processes users' queries (expressed in Datalog) posed over a relational global schema with key, inclusion, and exclusion dependencies, in a GAV setting, by means of a query rewriting technique that produces a Datalog program enriched with negation, under stable model semantics [16, 58].

Other interesting proposals on inconsistency management are the Hippo system [35, 36], and the ConQuer system [47, 49], which are focused on identifying cases in which computing consistent answers is tractable. However, such proposals have been essentially developed in the context of a single database system, and therefore do not deal with all aspects of a complex data integration environment.

A different approach in mediator-based information integration looks at data management under the perspective of exchanging data between the sources and the global schema, called the target schema in data exchange terminology. Data exchange has similar logical foundations to those of virtual mediator-based data integration discussed in the present paper. The basic notions of data exchange and its first formalization were given in [44]. In particular, a *solution* to the data exchange problem for a given source instance is a finite target instance that, together with the source instance, satisfies both *target dependencies*, i.e., constraints specified over the target schema, and *source-to-target dependencies*, i.e., mappings between the source and the target schema. A *universal solution* is a special solution that is homomorphic to every possible solution. Universal solutions are particularly important in data exchange, since, as shown in [44], the certain answers to a union of conjunctive queries q can be obtained by evaluating q over any universal solution.

Among all universal solutions, the *core* assumes a crucial importance, for being it the "smallest" one, and therefore in principle the best universal solution to compute [45]. The problem of computing the core is studied in [45, 53, 54], under different forms of target dependencies. In particular, in [54] a polynomial-time procedure for computing the core under classical data exchange constraints is provided.

Other works on data exchange studied, respectively, query answering (by first-order rewriting) for first-order logic (FOL) queries [3], schema mapping compositions [46], exchange of XML documents when both the source and the target schemas are XML DTDs [5], and relationship between data exchange and incomplete information [76].

Even if all the above studies are of great interest for ontology-based data integration, the role of ontologies in data exchange has not been investigated so far. Therefore, materialized data integration in the Semantic Web is a subject that still needs to be taken into account.

More recently, the issue of data integration has been considered in the more dynamic context of Peer-to-Peer (P2P) data management [61]. In a nutshell, a P2P system is characterized by an architecture constituted by various autonomous nodes that hold data and that are linked to other nodes by means of mappings.

Opposed to the first, "semantic-less" approaches, focused essentially on file sharing, data-oriented approaches to P2P have been proposed recently [9, 57, 61]. Differently from the traditional mediator-based setting, integration in data-oriented P2P systems is not based on a global schema. Instead, each peer represents an autonomous information system, and information integration is achieved by establishing P2P mappings, i.e., mappings among the various peers. Queries are posed to one peer, and the role of query processing is to exploit both the data that are internal to the peer, and the mappings between the peer and the other peers in the system.

While techniques for query answering and data exchange have been studied and developed extensively in the mediator-based setting, there is still a fundamental lack of understanding behind the basic issues of data integration in P2P systems. In particular, it needs to be investigated whether the usual approach of resorting to a first-order logic interpretation of P2P mappings (followed, e.g., by [9, 32, 61]), is still appropriate in the presence of possibly cyclic mappings, or whether alternative semantic characterizations should be adopted [20, 26]. Also, data exchange in a P2P setting still remains largely unexplored. Two exceptions are [48], where the problem is studied in a setting in which only two peers interact with different roles and capabilities, and [37], where a preliminary investigation of data exchange in a full-fledged P2P setting is proposed.

The case in which peers export an ontology (rather than a simple relational schema), has been studied in [17, 82]. In these papers, it is shown that query answering in this setting is a very complex task, and to have tractable cases, very severe limitations have to be imposed on the expressivity of the ontology language and the form of P2P mappings, even in very simple settings, e.g., when the whole system is constituted by two peers, as in [17].

17.6 Conclusion

In this paper, we have shown the impact on the computational complexity of query answering of adopting the OWL language (more precisely OWL 2 DL) for specifying the global schema of a data integration system. To precisely characterize this impact, we have chosen very expressive formalisms for instantiating the various components of a data integration system (GLAV sound and exact mappings, FOL queries over the global schema, both for the users' queries and head queries in mapping assertions). Even though interesting from a modeling point of view, we have shown that such choices soon lead to undecidability of query answering or, under some limitations, to intractability of query answering. We have identified the various sources of complexity, and have eliminated them by rightsizing the overall framework, in such a way that query answering turns out to be in principle as efficient as standard query processing in relational DBMSs. At the core of the new framework, we have OWL 2 QL, a tractable fragment of OWL 2, which we use for specifying the global schema of data integration systems. OWL 2 QL is essentially a variant of $DL\text{-}Lite_R$ and presents the same nice computational behavior typical of all DLs of the *DL-Lite* family.

The approach illustrated in this paper is under development in a prototype system called MASTRO-I, a tool for ontology-based data integration supporting global schemas specified in the *DL-Lite* family (and therefore in OWL 2 QL), which makes use of the QUONTO[14] reasoner for *DL-Lite*. Such a tool is in fact able to deal with ontologies even more expressive than OWL 2 QL, allowing for the specification, in a controlled way, of functionality assertions and complex forms of identification constraints (see [21]), and is also able to answer full SQL queries, under a suitable semantic approximation.

Other aspects, which are important for the problem of semantic data integration, have not been addressed yet in the development of the system, but are under investigation. Among them we mention the problem of handling inconsistencies in the data, possibly using a declarative, rather than an ad-hoc procedural approach, in the line of the work on consistent query answering (cf. Sect. 17.5). A second interesting problem for further work is looking at "write-also" data integration, i.e., allowing support also for updates expressed on the global schema (e.g., in the line of the work described in [38, 39]). How to express an update formulated over the global ontology in terms of series of insert and delete operations executed over the underlying data sources is a challenging issue in this context.

References

1. Abiteboul, S., Duschka, O.: Complexity of answering queries using materialized views. In: Proc. of the 17th ACM SIGACT SIGMOD SIGART Symp. on Principles of Database Systems (PODS'98), pp. 254–265 (1998)

[14] http://www.dis.uniroma1.it/quonto/.

2. Abiteboul, S., Hull, R., Vianu, V.: Foundations of Databases. Addison-Wesley, Reading (1995)
3. Arenas, M., Barcelo, P., Fagin, R., Libkin, L.: Locally consistent transformations and query answering in data exchange. In: Proc. of the 23rd ACM SIGACT SIGMOD SIGART Symp. on Principles of Database Systems (PODS 2004), pp. 229–240 (2004)
4. Arenas, M., Bertossi, L.E., Chomicki, J.: Consistent query answers in inconsistent databases. In: Proc. of the 18th ACM SIGACT SIGMOD SIGART Symp. on Principles of Database Systems (PODS'99), pp. 68–79 (1999)
5. Arenas, M., Libkin, L.: XML data exchange: Consistency and query answering. In: Proc. of the 24rd ACM SIGACT SIGMOD SIGART Symp. on Principles of Database Systems (PODS 2005), pp. 13–24 (2005)
6. Artale, A., Calvanese, D., Kontchakov, R., Zakharyaschev, M.: DL-Lite in the light of first-order logic. In: Proc. of the 22nd Nat. Conf. on Artificial Intelligence (AAAI 2007), pp. 361–366 (2007)
7. Artale, A., Calvanese, D., Kontchakov, R., Zakharyaschev, M.: The *DL-Lite* family and relations. Tech. Rep. BBKCS-09-03, School of Computer Science and Information Systems, Birbeck College, London (2009). Available at http://www.dcs.bbk.ac.uk/research/techreps/2009/bbkcs-09-03.pdf
8. Baader, F., Calvanese, D., McGuinness, D., Nardi, D., Patel-Schneider, P.F. (eds.): The Description Logic Handbook: Theory, Implementation and Applications. Cambridge University Press, Cambridge (2003)
9. Bernstein, P.A., Giunchiglia, F., Kementsietsidis, A., Mylopoulos, J., Serafini, L., Zaihrayeu, I.: Data management for peer-to-peer computing: A vision. In: Proc. of the 5th Int. Workshop on the Web and Databases (WebDB 2002) (2002)
10. Bernstein, P.A., Haas, L.: Information integration in the enterprise. Commun. ACM **51**(9), 72–79 (2008)
11. Bouzeghoub, M., Lenzerini, M.: Introduction to the special issue on data extraction, cleaning, and reconciliation. Inf. Syst. **26**(8), 535–536 (2001)
12. Bravo, L., Bertossi, L.: Logic programming for consistently querying data integration systems. In: Proc. of the 18th Int. Joint Conf. on Artificial Intelligence (IJCAI 2003), pp. 10–15 (2003)
13. Broekstra, J., Klein, M., Fensel, D., Horrocks, I.: Adding formal semantics to the Web: building on top of RDF Schema. In: Proc. of the ECDL 2000 Workshop on the Semantic Web (2000)
14. Calì, A., Calvanese, D., De Giacomo, G., Lenzerini, M.: Reasoning on UML class diagrams in description logics. In: Proc. of IJCAR Workshop on Precise Modelling and Deduction for Object-oriented Software Development (PMD 2001) (2001)
15. Calì, A., Calvanese, D., De Giacomo, G., Lenzerini, M.: Data integration under integrity constraints. Inf. Syst. **29**, 147–163 (2004)
16. Calì, A., Lembo, D., Rosati, R.: Query rewriting and answering under constraints in data integration systems. In: Proc. of the 18th Int. Joint Conf. on Artificial Intelligence (IJCAI 2003), pp. 16–21 (2003)
17. Calvanese, D., De Giacomo, G., Lembo, D., Lenzerini, M., Rosati, R.: What to ask to a peer: Ontology-based query reformulation. In: Proc. of the 9th Int. Conf. on the Principles of Knowledge Representation and Reasoning (KR 2004), pp. 469–478 (2004)
18. Calvanese, D., De Giacomo, G., Lembo, D., Lenzerini, M., Rosati, R.: Data complexity of query answering in description logics. In: Proc. of the 10th Int. Conf. on the Principles of Knowledge Representation and Reasoning (KR 2006), pp. 260–270 (2006)
19. Calvanese, D., De Giacomo, G., Lembo, D., Lenzerini, M., Rosati, R.: Tractable reasoning and efficient query answering in description logics: The *DL-Lite* family. J. Autom. Reason. **39**(3), 385–429 (2007)
20. Calvanese, D., De Giacomo, G., Lembo, D., Lenzerini, M., Rosati, R.: Inconsistency tolerance in P2P data integration: An epistemic logic approach. Inf. Syst. **33**(4), 360–384 (2008)
21. Calvanese, D., De Giacomo, G., Lembo, D., Lenzerini, M., Rosati, R.: Path-based identification constraints in description logics. In: Proc. of the 11th Int. Conf. on the Principles of Knowledge Representation and Reasoning (KR 2008), pp. 231–241 (2008)

22. Calvanese, D., De Giacomo, G., Lenzerini, M.: 2ATAs make DLs easy. In: Proc. of the 2002 Description Logic Workshop (DL 2002), CEUR Electronic Workshop Proceedings, vol. 53, pp. 107–118 (2002). http://ceur-ws.org/
23. Calvanese, D., De Giacomo, G., Lenzerini, M.: Conjunctive query containment and answering under description logics constraints. ACM Trans. Comput. Log. **9**(3), 22.1–22.31 (2008)
24. Calvanese, D., De Giacomo, G., Lenzerini, M., Nardi, D., Rosati, R.: Description logic framework for information integration. In: Proc. of the 6th Int. Conf. on the Principles of Knowledge Representation and Reasoning (KR'98), pp. 2–13 (1998)
25. Calvanese, D., De Giacomo, G., Lenzerini, M., Nardi, D., Rosati, R.: Data integration in data warehousing. Int. J. Coop. Inf. Syst. **10**(3), 237–271 (2001)
26. Calvanese, D., De Giacomo, G., Lenzerini, M., Rosati, R.: Logical foundations of peer-to-peer data integration. In: Proc. of the 23rd ACM SIGACT SIGMOD SIGART Symp. on Principles of Database Systems (PODS 2004), pp. 241–251 (2004)
27. Calvanese, D., De Giacomo, G., Lenzerini, M., Vardi, M.Y.: What is query rewriting? In: Proc. of the 7th Int. Workshop on Knowledge Representation Meets Databases (KRDB 2000), CEUR Electronic Workshop Proceedings, vol. 29, pp. 17–27 (2000). http://ceur-ws.org/
28. Calvanese, D., De Giacomo, G., Lenzerini, M., Vardi, M.Y.: Rewriting of regular expressions and regular path queries. J. Comput. Syst. Sci. **64**(3), 443–465 (2002)
29. Calvanese, D., De Giacomo, G., Lenzerini, M., Vardi, M.Y.: View-based query processing: On the relationship between rewriting, answering and losslessness. In: Proc. of the 10th Int. Conf. on Database Theory (ICDT 2005). Lecture Notes in Computer Science, vol. 3363, pp. 321–336. Springer, Berlin (2005)
30. Calvanese, D., De Giacomo, G., Vardi, M.Y.: Decidable containment of recursive queries. Theor. Comput. Sci. **336**(1), 33–56 (2005)
31. Carey, M.J., Haas, L.M., Schwarz, P.M., Arya, M., Cody, W.F., Fagin, R., Flickner, M., Luniewski, A., Niblack, W., Petkovic, D., Thomas, J., Williams, J.H., Wimmers, E.L.: Towards heterogeneous multimedia information systems: The Garlic approach. In: Proc. of the 5th Int. Workshop on Research Issues in Data Engineering—Distributed Object Management (RIDE-DOM'95), pp. 124–131. IEEE Computer Society, Los Alamitos (1995)
32. Catarci, T., Lenzerini, M.: Representing and using interschema knowledge in cooperative information systems. J. Intell. Coop. Inf. Syst. **2**(4), 375–398 (1993)
33. Chawathe, S.S., Garcia-Molina, H., Hammer, J., Ireland, K., Papakonstantinou, Y., Ullman, J.D., Widom, J.: The TSIMMIS project: Integration of heterogeneous information sources. In: Proc. of the 10th Meeting of the Information Processing Society of Japan (IPSJ'94), pp. 7–18 (1994)
34. Chen, C., Haarslev, V., Wang, J.: LAS: extending racer by a large ABox store. In: Proc. of the 2005 Description Logic Workshop (DL 2005), CEUR Electronic Workshop Proceedings, vol. 147 (2005). http://ceur-ws.org/
35. Chomicki, J., Marcinkowski, J., Staworko, S.: Computing consistent query answers using conflict hypergraphs. In: Proc. of the 13th Int. Conf. on Information and Knowledge Management (CIKM 2004), pp. 417–426 (2004)
36. Chomicki, J., Marcinkowski, J., Staworko, S.: Hippo: a system for computing consistent query answers to a class of SQL queries. In: Proc. of the 9th Int. Conf. on Extending Database Technology (EDBT 2004), pp. 841–844. Springer, Berlin (2004)
37. De Giacomo, G., Lembo, D., Lenzerini, M., Rosati, R.: On reconciling data exchange, data integration, and peer data management. In: Proc. of the 26th ACM SIGACT SIGMOD SIGART Symp. on Principles of Database Systems (PODS 2007), pp. 133–142 (2007)
38. De Giacomo, G., Lenzerini, M., Poggi, A., Rosati, R.: On the update of description logic ontologies at the instance level. In: Proc. of the 21st Nat. Conf. on Artificial Intelligence (AAAI 2006), pp. 1271–1276 (2006)
39. De Giacomo, G., Lenzerini, M., Poggi, A., Rosati, R.: On the approximation of instance level update and erasure in description logics. In: Proc. of the 22nd Nat. Conf. on Artificial Intelligence (AAAI 2007), pp. 403–408 (2007)

40. Decker, S., Fensel, D., van Harmelen, F., Horrocks, I., Melnik, S., Klein, M., Broekstra, J.: Knowledge representation on the web. In: Proc. of the 2000 Description Logic Workshop (DL 2000), CEUR Electronic Workshop Proceedings, vol. 33, pp. 89–97 (2000). http://ceur-ws.org/
41. Donini, F.M., Lenzerini, M., Nardi, D., Nutt, W.: The complexity of concept languages. Inf. Comput. **134**, 1–58 (1997)
42. Donini, F.M., Lenzerini, M., Nardi, D., Schaerf, A.: Deduction in concept languages: From subsumption to instance checking. J. Log. Comput. **4**(4), 423–452 (1994)
43. Duschka, O.M., Genesereth, M.R., Levy, A.Y.: Recursive query plans for data integration. J. Log. Program. **43**(1), 49–73 (2000)
44. Fagin, R., Kolaitis, P.G., Miller, R.J., Popa, L.: Data exchange: Semantics and query answering. Theor. Comput. Sci. **336**(1), 89–124 (2005)
45. Fagin, R., Kolaitis, P.G., Popa, L.: Data exchange: Getting to the core. ACM Trans. Database Syst. **30**(1), 174–210 (2005)
46. Fagin, R., Kolaitis, P.G., Popa, L., Tan, W.C.: Composing schema mappings: Second-order dependencies to the rescue. ACM Trans. Database Syst. **30**(4), 994–1055 (2005)
47. Fuxman, A., Fazli, E., Miller, R.J.: ConQuer: Efficient management of inconsistent databases. In: Proc. of the ACM SIGMOD Int. Conf. on Management of Data, pp. 155–166 (2005)
48. Fuxman, A., Kolaitis, P.G., Miller, R.J., Tan, W.C.: Peer data exchange. ACM Trans. Database Syst. **31**(4), 1454–1498 (2005)
49. Fuxman, A., Miller, R.J.: First-order query rewriting for inconsistent databases. J. Comput. Syst. Sci. **73**(4), 610–635 (2007)
50. Gelfond, M., Lifschitz, V.: The stable model semantics for logic programming. In: Proc. of the 5th Logic Programming Symposium, pp. 1070–1080. MIT Press, Cambridge (1988)
51. Genereseth, M.R., Keller, A.M., Duschka, O.M.: Infomaster: An information integration system. In: Proc. of the ACM SIGMOD Int. Conf. on Management of Data, pp. 539–542 (1997)
52. Glimm, B., Horrocks, I., Lutz, C., Sattler, U.: Conjunctive query answering for the description logic $\mathcal{SHIQ}$. J. Artif. Intell. Res. **31**, 151–198 (2008)
53. Gottlob, G.: Computing cores for data exchange: New algorithms and practical solutions. In: Proc. of the 24rd ACM SIGACT SIGMOD SIGART Symp. on Principles of Database Systems (PODS 2005), pp. 148–159 (2005)
54. Gottlob, G., Nash, A.: Data exchange: Computing cores in polynomial time. In: Proc. of the 25th ACM SIGACT SIGMOD SIGART Symp. on Principles of Database Systems (PODS 2006), pp. 40–49 (2006)
55. Grahne, G., Mendelzon, A.O.: Tableau techniques for querying information sources through global schemas. In: Proc. of the 7th Int. Conf. on Database Theory (ICDT'99). Lecture Notes in Computer Science, vol. 1540, pp. 332–347. Springer, Berlin (1999)
56. Greco, G., Greco, S., Zumpano, E.: A logical framework for querying and repairing inconsistent databases. IEEE Trans. Knowl. Data Eng. **15**(6), 1389–1408 (2003)
57. Gribble, S., Halevy, A., Ives, Z., Rodrig, M., Suciu, D.: What can databases do for peer-to-peer? In: Proc. of the 4th Int. Workshop on the Web and Databases (WebDB 2001) (2001)
58. Grieco, L., Lembo, D., Ruzzi, M., Rosati, R.: Consistent query answering under key and exclusion dependencies: Algorithms and experiments. In: Proc. of the 14th Int. Conf. on Information and Knowledge Management (CIKM 2005), pp. 792–799 (2005)
59. Gryz, J.: Query rewriting using views in the presence of functional and inclusion dependencies. Inf. Syst. **24**(7), 597–612 (1999)
60. Haarslev, V., Möller, R.: RACER system description. In: Proc. of the Int. Joint Conf. on Automated Reasoning (IJCAR 2001). Lecture Notes in Artificial Intelligence, vol. 2083, pp. 701–705. Springer, Berlin (2001)
61. Halevy, A., Ives, Z., Suciu, D., Tatarinov, I.: Schema mediation in peer data management systems. In: Proc. of the 19th IEEE Int. Conf. on Data Engineering (ICDE 2003), pp. 505–516 (2003)
62. Halevy, A.Y.: Answering queries using views: A survey. Very Large Database J. **10**(4), 270–294 (2001)

63. Halevy, A.Y., Rajaraman, A., Ordille, J.: Data integration: The teenage years. In: Proc. of the 32nd Int. Conf. on Very Large Data Bases (VLDB 2006), pp. 9–16 (2006)
64. Horrocks, I.: Using an expressive description logic: FaCT or fiction? In: Proc. of the 6th Int. Conf. on the Principles of Knowledge Representation and Reasoning (KR'98), pp. 636–647 (1998)
65. Horrocks, I., Kutz, O., Sattler, U.: The even more irresistible $\mathcal{SROIQ}$. In: Proc. of the 10th Int. Conf. on the Principles of Knowledge Representation and Reasoning (KR 2006), pp. 57–67 (2006)
66. Horrocks, I., Li, L., Turi, D., Bechhofer, S.: The Instance Store: DL reasoning with large numbers of individuals. In: Proc. of the 2004 Description Logic Workshop (DL 2004), CEUR Electronic Workshop Proceedings, vol. 104 (2004). http://ceur-ws.org/
67. Hustadt, U., Motik, B., Sattler, U.: Data complexity of reasoning in very expressive description logics. In: Proc. of the 19th Int. Joint Conf. on Artificial Intelligence (IJCAI 2005), pp. 466–471 (2005)
68. Kolaitis, P.G.: Schema mappings, data exchange, and metadata management. In: Proc. of the 24th ACM SIGACT SIGMOD SIGART Symp. on Principles of Database Systems (PODS 2005), pp. 61–75 (2005)
69. Krisnadhi, A., Lutz, C.: Data complexity in the $\mathcal{EL}$ family of description logics. In: Proc. of the 14th Int. Conf. on Logic for Programming, Artificial Intelligence, and Reasoning (LPAR 2007), pp. 333–347 (2007)
70. Lenzerini, M.: Data integration: A theoretical perspective. In: Proc. of the 21st ACM SIGACT SIGMOD SIGART Symp. on Principles of Database Systems (PODS 2002), pp. 233–246 (2002)
71. Leone, N., Eiter, T., Faber, W., Fink, M., Gottlob, G., Greco, G., Kalka, E., Ianni, G., Lembo, D., Lenzerini, M., Lio, V., Nowicki, B., Rosati, R., Ruzzi, M., Staniszkis, W., Terracina, G.: The INFOMIX system for advanced integration of incomplete and inconsistent data. In: Proc. of the ACM SIGMOD Int. Conf. on Management of Data, pp. 915–917 (2005)
72. Levy, A.Y.: Logic-based techniques in data integration. In: Minker, J. (ed.) Logic Based Artificial Intelligence. Kluwer Academic, Dordrecht (2000)
73. Levy, A.Y., Mendelzon, A.O., Sagiv, Y., Srivastava, D.: Answering queries using views. In: Proc. of the 14th ACM SIGACT SIGMOD SIGART Symp. on Principles of Database Systems (PODS'95), pp. 95–104 (1995)
74. Levy, A.Y., Rajaraman, A., Ordille, J.J.: Querying heterogenous information sources using source descriptions. In: Proc. of the 22nd Int. Conf. on Very Large Data Bases (VLDB'96) (1996)
75. Levy, A.Y., Srivastava, D., Kirk, T.: Data model and query evaluation in global information systems. J. Intell. Inf. Syst. **5**, 121–143 (1995)
76. Libkin, L.: Data exchange and incomplete information. In: Proc. of the 25th ACM SIGACT SIGMOD SIGART Symp. on Principles of Database Systems (PODS 2006), pp. 60–69 (2006)
77. Möller, R., Haarslev, V.: Description logic systems. In: Baader, F., Calvanese, D., McGuinness, D., Nardi, D., Patel-Schneider, P.F. (eds.) The Description Logic Handbook: Theory, Implementation and Applications, pp. 282–305. Cambridge University Press, Cambridge (2003), Chap. 8
78. Ortiz, M., Calvanese, D., Eiter, T.: Data complexity of query answering in expressive description logics via tableaux. J. Autom. Reason. **41**(1), 61–98 (2008)
79. Poggi, A., Lembo, D., Calvanese, D., De Giacomo, G., Lenzerini, M., Rosati, R.: Linking data to ontologies. J. Data Semant. **X**, 133–173 (2008)
80. Pottinger, R., Levy, A.Y.: A scalable algorithm for answering queries using views. In: Proc. of the 26th Int. Conf. on Very Large Data Bases (VLDB 2000), pp. 484–495 (2000)
81. Schaerf, A.: On the complexity of the instance checking problem in concept languages with existential quantification. J. Intell. Inf. Syst. **2**, 265–278 (1993)
82. Serafini, L., Ghidini, C.: Using wrapper agents to answer queries in distributed information systems. In: Proc. of the 1st Int. Conf. on Advances in Information Systems (ADVIS-2000). Lecture Notes in Computer Science, vol. 1909. Springer, Berlin (2000)

83. Sirin, E., Parsia, B.: Pellet system description. In: Proc. of the 2006 Description Logic Workshop (DL 2006), CEUR Electronic Workshop Proceedings, vol. 189 (2006). http://ceur-ws.org/
84. Sirin, E., Parsia, B., Cuenca Grau, B., Kalyanpur, A., Katz, Y.: Pellet: a practical OWL-DL reasoner. Tech. Rep., University of Maryland Institute for Advanced Computer Studies (UMIACS) (2005)
85. Ullman, J.D.: Information integration using logical views. Theor. Comput. Sci. **239**(2), 189–210 (2000)

Chapter 18
Service Knowledge Spaces for Semantic Collaboration in Web-based Systems

Devis Bianchini, Valeria De Antonellis, and Michele Melchiori

Abstract Semantic Web technologies have been applied to enable collaboration in open distributed systems, where interoperability issues raise due to the absence of a global view of the shared resources. Adoption of service-oriented technologies has improved interoperability at the application level by exporting systems functionalities as Web services. In fact, Service Oriented Architecture (SOA) constitutes an appropriate platform-independent approach to implement collaboration activities by means of automatic service discovery and composition. Recently, service discovery has been applied to collaborative environments such as the P2P one, where independent partners need cooperate through resource sharing without a stable network configuration and adopting different semantic models. Model-based techniques relying on Semantic Web need be defined to generate semantic service descriptions, allowing collaborative partners to export their functionalities in a semantic way. Semantic-based service matchmaking techniques are in charge of effectively and efficiently evaluating similarity between service requests and service offers in a huge, dynamic distributed environment. The result is an evolving service knowledge space where collaborative partners that provide similar services are semantically related and constitute synergic service centres in a given domain. Specific modeling requirements related to Semantic Web, service-oriented and P2P technologies must be considered.

18.1 Introduction

Semantic Web technologies have been applied to enable collaboration in open distributed systems, where interoperability issues raise due to the absence of a global

D. Bianchini (✉) · V. De Antonellis · M. Melchiori
Department of Electronics for Automation, University of Brescia, via Branze 38,
25123 Brescia, Italy
e-mail: bianchin@ing.unibs.it

V. De Antonellis
e-mail: deantone@ing.unibs.it

M. Melchiori
e-mail: melchior@ing.unibs.it

R. De Virgilio et al. (eds.), *Semantic Web Information Management*,
DOI 10.1007/978-3-642-04329-1_18, © Springer-Verlag Berlin Heidelberg 2010

view of the shared resources. Adoption of service-oriented technologies has improved interoperability at the application level by exporting systems functionalities as Web services. In fact, Service Oriented Architecture (SOA) constitutes an appropriate platform-independent approach to implement collaboration activities by means of automatic service discovery and composition. Recently, service discovery has been applied to collaborative environments such as the P2P one, where independent partners need cooperate through resource sharing without a stable network configuration and adopting different semantic models. Model-based techniques relying on Semantic Web need be defined to generate semantic service descriptions, allowing collaborative partners to export their functionalities in a semantic way. Semantic-based service matchmaking techniques are in charge of effectively and efficiently evaluating the similarity between service requests and service offers in a huge, dynamic distributed environment. The result is an evolving service knowledge space where collaborative partners that provide similar services are semantically related and constitute synergic service centres in a given domain. Specific modeling requirements related to Semantic Web, service-oriented and P2P technologies must be considered.

This chapter is organized as follows. In Sect. 18.2, we point out requirements for semantic collaboration in networked Web-based systems. In Sect. 18.3, we show how to implement this collaboration through Web Services and we provide a model-based semantic description of Web services in a P2P environment. Section 18.4 presents the architecture of a Distributed Service Registry (DSR) that implements the requirements previously introduced and the maintenance strategies of the DSR in the considered collaborative scenario will be described. In Sect. 18.5, semantic collaboration through Web services registered in the DSR will be explained. Finally, Sect. 18.7 closes the chapter.

18.2 Semantic Collaboration in Networked Web-based Systems

Collaborative Web-based systems in P2P networks should reflect a set of requirements that are directly related to the inner properties of P2P environments, that is, technological and semantic heterogeneity, high dynamicity, autonomy of collaborative partners. In past years, traditional distributed collaboration systems were featured by resource sharing among a fixed/limited number of different partners, with a priori knowledge about each other, mainly obtained through mediator-based architectures. In that scenario, collaboration constraints change quite rarely and partners are statically connected one to another. The collaboration environments we consider here have different requirements, that we will shortly present in the following. In particular, in the considered collaborative scenario different organizations join a P2P network and aim at providing and finding useful services to perform their business activities. To improve the efficacy and efficiency of service discovery, we propose a distributed and dynamic *service knowledge space* with supporting tools, where peers storing similar services are connected by means of semantic links. The service knowledge space has been designed to support peers that receive a service request in:

- *local service provisioning*, to search for locally available services apt to fulfill the request;
- *alternative service provisioning*, to search on the network for services that provide equivalent functionalities with respect to those provided locally; this kind of collaboration is made available to retrieve alternative search results when local services are not currently working or are not able to guarantee the required Quality of Service (QoS);
- *complementary service provisioning*, to search on the network for services that add functionalities with respect to those locally provided; this kind of collaboration is made available to extend search results when locally available services are not able to completely satisfy the service request.

Typically, in P2P networks the collaboration among partners takes place in a dynamic way. Partners have their own knowledge and loosely connect one to another (in general, only when there is a knowledge sharing need). Partners can join and leave at any moment the P2P network and the collaboration constraints may frequently change. Moreover, strong technological and semantic heterogeneity impose additional constraints, such as platform independence and semantic interoperability. XML-based technologies enable data exchange and Web Services ensure platform-independence. However, the adoption of Web Services for collaboration purposes requires innovative solutions, to enable effective functionality sharing between collaborative partners. In particular, semantic modeling of Web service functionalities must be provided. With the advent of the Semantic Web, the use of ontologies for semantic modeling has been widely suggested and, in particular, ontology-based techniques have been defined for service description and matchmaking. Specifically, ontologies and Semantic Web technologies are adopted as key solutions to actually define the fundamental components of semantic collaborative platforms. Semantic service description in P2P networks cannot constrain to a unique shared ontology. Moreover, a semantic model to represent knowledge about available services over the network must be defined; efficient and effective exploitation of such knowledge to implement collaboration scenarios must be provided, taking into account the scalability and high dynamicity of open P2P environments.

Main limitations in many existing infrastructures and approaches for semantic collaboration in open, P2P environments through Web services sharing, are due to the assumption of a common ontology and to the absence of strategies apt to prune the set of peers to which forward the request for efficiency purposes. Instead, it is essential to assume that each peer has its local service registry and its own ontology; there is no common ontology to which peers are committed. As a consequence, a priori agreement among the peers is not required and there is not the need for peers acting as coordinators, thus increasing the robustness of the approach. We aim at addressing these open issues with an innovative organization of semantic service descriptions throughout the network of registries and with flexible service retrieval techniques.

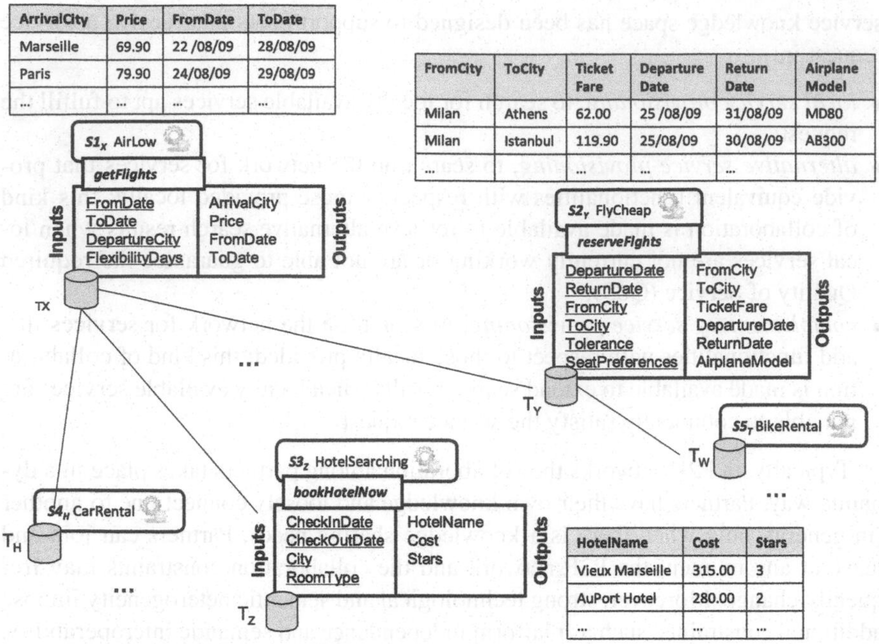

Fig. 18.1 Running example

The following scenario exemplifies the problem to be solved. Consider a P2P network in the travel domain, where travel agencies join to collaborate by providing travel services to potential clients. Suppose that a traveller wants to organize a week holiday in one of the European cities with low-cost flights. The traveller has not chosen the destination yet and his/her constraints regard the cost of the holiday and the departure and return dates. Firstly, he/she looks for available low-cost flights and, on the basis of the offers, decides which city to visit. Secondly, he/she has to find a cheap accommodation for the final destination of the journey. In Fig. 18.1, a set of travel agencies is shown that collaboratively provide search services apt to find flight reservation and hotel booking facilities and display search results ordered by price. Samples of possible search services are depicted in the figure, where examples of search results are also shown. Agencies T_X, T_Y provide alternative low-cost flight services. For example, service `AirLow` on peer T_X provides, as outputs, the price and arrival city of a low-cost flight for the departure and return dates, given in input the departure city and the admitted flexibility. Other agencies, namely, T_Z, T_H, T_W, provide additional functionalities, such as hotel booking, car and bike rental facilities. Service `HotelSearching` of the travel agency T_Z (to which T_X is connected in the P2P network) provides the name, cost and stars of hotels in a specified city for which a given type of room is available, from a check-in to a check-out date.

The service knowledge space across the travel agencies, as proposed in this chapter, could support the user in three ways: (i) given a low-cost flight search request submitted to the T_X agency, T_X is able to suggest the local service `AirLow`; (ii) it can also suggest services with similar interfaces, provided by different agencies (for example, service `FlyCheap` of T_Y) that can be invoked if T_X local search results are not satisfying; (iii) once selected a low-cost flight booking service, say `AirLow`, the travel agency is able to suggest possible related services (accepting as INPUT what is OUTPUT of `AirLow`), such as hotel booking facilities (for example, service `HotelSearching` provided by the T_Z partner).

18.3 Service Knowledge Space

18.3.1 Preliminary Notions

In this section, we first provide basic notions for introducing the service-oriented collaboration infrastructure, then we focus on our approach for model-based service description. In the Service-Oriented Architecture (SOA), each actor/peer can play different roles. A peer acts as a *requester*, formulating a service request to search for available functionalities on the network. A peer can also act as a service *provider*, exporting its own functionalities as Web Services on the network. Finally, a peer can also act as a *broker*, maintaining the descriptions of locally available services.

We model Web services as functional facilities that are made available and are invocable via their interfaces [19, 20], described through operations and I/O parameters. To be compliant with existing and widely accepted standards, we represent service functional interfaces by means of the WSDL document [11], that distinguishes among the abstract service interface (operations and I/O messages, in turn containing I/O parameters) and concrete bindings for service execution. Services that are supplied on the network are executed via the concrete bindings, but their abstract interface is exported to enable service discovery. A service abstract interface may correspond to several concrete bindings.

Acting as a broker, the peer is equipped with a service registry, where services are registered together with provider's contact information. Services are registered into UDDI registries [22], where they are identified through their `serviceKey` and are associated to the corresponding WSDL interface specification through the `tModel` mechanism. According to the UDDI standard, published services are categorized through service categories, extracted from available standard taxonomies (e.g., UNSPSC, NAiCS). Categorization of services in the registry is obtained through the `CategoryBag` structure provided by the UDDI standard. The registry APIs include facilities for service searching, publication and maintenance. In the classical SOA vision, there exists only one service repository (possibly mirrored), where service providers register their own services and requesters are able to find them.

18.3.2 Model-based Service Description

WSDL abstract interface only provides service functional description from a syntactic viewpoint, but to automate service discovery semantic ambiguities must be solved. To this purpose, we adopt an OWL-DL *peer ontology* to conceptualize domain concepts used in service interface description. Details about the peer ontology will be given below. Thus, from the WSDL abstract service interface a semantic service description is generated, where the operations and I/O parameters are mapped to concepts of the peer ontology. Moreover, available standard taxonomies (e.g., UNSPSC, NAiCS) are used to classify semantic service descriptions stored in the underlying UDDI registry. The semantic service description of a service S is defined as the following pair:

$$\langle CAT(S), OP(S) \rangle \tag{18.1}$$

where:

- $CAT(S)$ is a set of service categories extracted from standard taxonomies (e.g., UNSPSC, NAiCS);
- $OP(S)$ is a set of service operations; each operation $op_i \in OP(S)$ is in turn defined as a 3-uple

$$\langle name\_op_i, IN(op_i), OUT(op_i) \rangle \tag{18.2}$$

  where:
  - $name\_op_i$ is a concept from the OWL-DL peer ontology representing the operation name;
  - $IN(op_i)$ is a set of concepts from the OWL-DL peer ontology representing the input parameters of the operation op_i;
  - $OUT(op_i)$ is a set of concepts from the OWL-DL peer ontology representing the output parameters of the operation op_i.

The semantic service descriptions constitute the annotated version of the WSDL specification and are serialized according to recently proposed languages for semantic annotation of the service functional interface (e.g., WSDL-S [2]). Service concrete bindings published into the peer UDDI registry are associated to their semantic service description through the `tModel` mechanism, as shown in Fig. 18.2. In the figure, the `AirLow` service in the UDDI registry of T_X travel agency is associated to a WSDL-S specification where, for example, `ArrivalCity` output is annotated with the `Destination` concept and the `getFlights` operation is annotated with the `FlightBooking` concept defined in the T_X peer ontology. Finally, the service is associated to the `Travel Facilitations` category of the NAICS taxonomy by means of the `CategoryBag` structure made available in the UDDI standard.

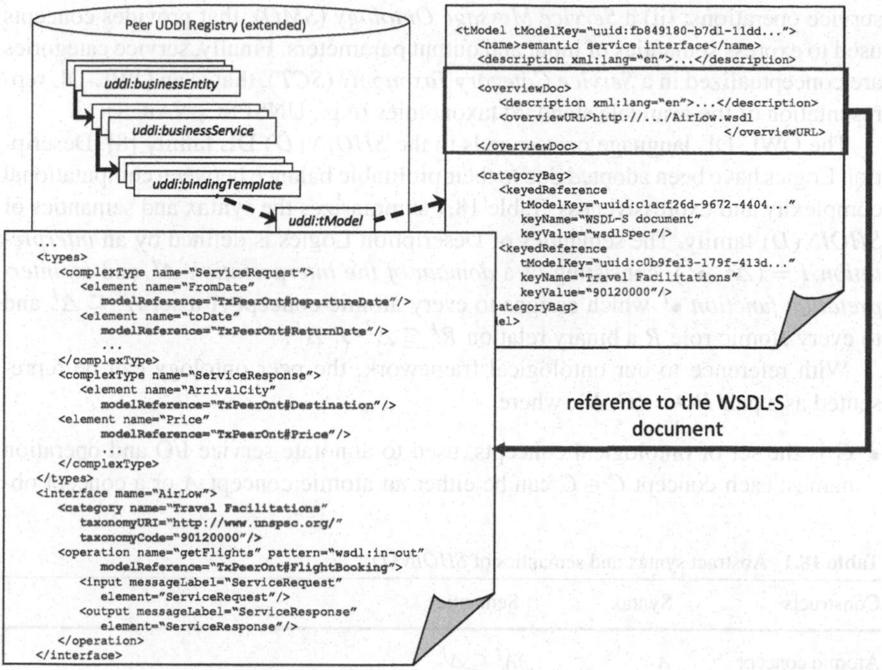

Fig. 18.2 Publication of a semantic service description inside the semantically-enriched UDDI Registry

18.3.3 Ontological Infrastructure

The proposed ontological infrastructure aims at providing a semantic-enriched representation of service functionalities in order to facilitate collaborative activities. In particular, we consider two kinds of service knowledge: (i) a *local service knowledge* representation, to enable the definition of the semantic service descriptions introduced in the previous section; (ii) a *network service knowledge*, to conceptualize the notion of *semantic links* between peers with similar services, to improve service request forwarding throughout the P2P network. The ontological infrastructure is the core of the Distributed Service Registry discussed in Sect. 18.4, that provides capabilities to exploit both the local and the network service knowledge and to properly maintain them.

18.3.3.1 Local Service Knowledge

Each collaborative partner, that acts as a service broker, is equipped with an OWL-DL peer ontology whose concepts are used to build the semantic descriptions of services stored locally. In particular, the peer ontology is composed of: (i) a *Service Functionality Ontology* (*SFO*), that provides concepts used to express semantics of service operations; (ii) a *Service Message Ontology* (*SMO*), that provides concepts used to express semantics of input and output parameters. Finally, service categories are conceptualized in a *Service Category Taxonomy* (*SCT*), that is an OWL-DL representation of the available standard taxonomies (e.g., UNSPSC, NAiCS).

The OWL-DL language corresponds to the $SHOIN(D)$ DL family [8]. Description Logics have been adopted due to their profitable balance between computational complexity and expressiveness. Table 18.1 summarizes the syntax and semantics of $SHOIN(D)$ family. The semantics of Description Logics is defined by an *interpretation* $I = (\Delta^I, \bullet^I)$, consisting of a *domain of the interpretation* Δ^I and an *interpretation function* $\bullet^I$ which assigns to every atomic concept A a set $A^I \subseteq \Delta^I$ and to every atomic role R a binary relation $R^I \subseteq \Delta^I \times \Delta^I$.

With reference to our ontological framework, the peer ontology can be represented as a pair $PO = \langle \mathcal{C}, \mathcal{R} \rangle$, where:

- $\mathcal{C}$ is the set of ontological concepts, used to annotate service I/O and operation names; each concept $C \in \mathcal{C}$ can be either an atomic concept A or a concept ob-

Table 18.1 Abstract syntax and semantics of $SHOIN(D)$

Constructs	Syntax	Semantics
Atomic concept	A	$A^I \subseteq \Delta^I$
Role name	R	$R^I \subseteq \Delta^I \times \Delta^I$
Individuals	i	$i^I \in \Delta^I$
Enumeration	$\{i_1, i_2, \ldots, i_n\}$	$(\{i_1, i_2, \ldots, i_n\})^I = \{(i_1)^I, (i_2)^I, \ldots, (i_n)^I\}$
Intersection	$C_1 \sqcap C_2$	$(C_1 \sqcap C_2)^I = (C_1)^I \cap (C_2)^I$
Union	$C_1 \sqcup C_2$	$(C_1 \sqcup C_2)^I = (C_1)^I \cup (C_2)^I$
Negation	$\neg C$	$(\neg C)^I = \Delta^I - C^I$
Existential role restriction	$\exists R.C$	$(\exists R.C)^I = \{c \in \Delta^I \mid \exists d \in \Delta^I \ s.t.\ (c,d) \in R^I \wedge d \in C^I\}$
Universal role restriction	$\forall R.C$	$(\forall R.C)^I = \{c \in \Delta^I \mid \forall d \in \Delta^I \ s.t.\ (c,d) \in R^I \Rightarrow d \in C^I\}$
Universal concept	$\top$	$(\top)^I = \Delta^I$
Empty concept	$\bot$	$(\bot)^I = \emptyset$
Equivalence	$C_1 \equiv C_2$	$(C_1)^I = (C_2)^I$
Subsumption	$C_1 \sqsubseteq C_2$	$(C_1)^I \subseteq (C_2)^I$
Inverse role	R^-	$(R^-)^I = (R^I)^-$
Role transitivity	$(Tr(R))$	$(Tr(R))^I = (R^I)^+$
Role hierarchy	$R_1 \sqsubseteq R_2$	$(R_1)^I \subseteq (R_2)^I$
At-most cardinality constraint	$\leq nR$	$(\leq nR)^I = \{x \in \Delta^I \mid \#(\{y \ s.t.\ (x,y) \in R^I\}) \leq n\}$
At-least cardinality constraint	$\geq nR$	$(\geq nR)^I = \{x \in \Delta^I \mid \#(\{y \ s.t.\ (x,y) \in R^I\}) \geq n\}$
Exactly cardinality constraint	$= nR$	$(= nR)^I = \{x \in \Delta^I \mid \#(\{y \ s.t.\ (x,y) \in R^I\}) = n\}$

tained through enumeration, intersection, union, negation, existential and universal role restriction;

- R is the set of semantic relationships between concepts, conceptualized through role names R, on which inverse role, role transitivity, role hierarchy and cardinality constraints hold.

Moreover, equivalence and subsumption constraints are defined between concepts and will be exploited in a deductive service matchmaking model as show in Sect. 18.3.3.2.

In the collaborative environment, each peer has its own ontology. In fact, concepts and relationships contained in the OWL-DL peer ontology of a travel agency/peer T_X are not necessarily defined with the same terms as the concepts and relationships in the OWL-DL ontology of another collaborative agency/peer. They can present terminological discrepancies (e.g., synonymies, homonymies) that must be solved to enable effective comparison between semantic service descriptions on different peers. To solve these terminological heterogeneities, the OWL-DL peer ontology is extended with a Thesaurus, extracted from an underlying lexical system (e.g., WordNet [14]), where terms are related each other and with the names of ontological concepts by means of terminological relationships. In [6], the combined use of a Thesaurus and an OWL-DL ontology is detailed. A weight $\sigma_{\text{rel}} \in (0,1]$ is associated with each kind of relationship, to establish the affinity between names. The following terminological relationships are defined: (i) synonymy (SYN), with $\sigma_{\text{SYN}} = 1.0$, established between two terms that can be used in an interchangeable way (e.g., `Price` SYN `Cost`); (ii) narrower/broader term (BT/NT), with $\sigma_{\text{BT/NT}} = 0.8$, established between a term n_1 and another term n_2, where n_1 has a more generic (resp., specific) meaning than n_2 (e.g., `DepartureCity` NT `City`); (iii) related term (RT), with $\sigma_{\text{RT}} = 0.5$, established between two terms whose meaning is related in the considered application scenario (e.g., `Payment` RT `ElectronicTicket`). For example, $\sigma_{\text{SYN}} = 1.0$ because synonymy relationship is generally considered a more precise indicator of the affinity between names. In [10], techniques apt to guide the process designer in the construction of the Thesaurus are explained. The Thesaurus constitutes a fundamental asset to extend semantic service descriptions annotated with the OWL-DL peer ontology. Specifically, terminological relationships are used to quantify the name affinity between different concept names as follows.

Definition 18.1 (Name Affinity) Two generic terms n_1 and n_2 can be related by one or more chains of relationships: we call *path* of length m between two terms n_1 and n_2, denoted with $n_1 \rightarrow^m n_2$, a finite ordered sequence of m relationships. The *strength* of $n_1 \rightarrow^m n_2$ is the product of the weights of all the relationships belonging to the path, that is, $\rho(n_1 \rightarrow^m n_2) = \prod_{k=1}^{m}(\sigma_k) \in (0,1]$. Since between two terms there can exist more than one path, the one with the highest strength is chosen. The *Name Affinity* coefficient between n_1 and n_2, denoted by $NAff(n_1, n_2)$, is defined as follows:

$$NAff(n_1, n_2) = \begin{cases} 1 & \text{if } n_1 = n_2 \\ \max_m(\rho(n_1 \to^m n_2)) & \text{if } n_1 \neq n_2 \wedge \max_m(\rho(n_1 \to^m n_2)) \geq \alpha \\ 0 & \text{otherwise} \end{cases} \tag{18.3}$$

Only name affinities that are equal or greater than an affinity threshold α are considered, where α is set to filter out not relevant affinity values. Name Affinity coefficient is used to extend traditional Description Logic subsumption test as follows.

Definition 18.2 (Affinity-based subsumption test) Given an atomic concept C in the peer ontology PO, we define the set of terms in the Thesaurus that have name affinity with the concept C as $C_{TH} = \{T \in TH \mid T \sim C\}$. By analogy, we define the set of concepts of PO that have name affinity with a term T in TH as $T_{PO} = \{C \in PO \mid T \in C_{TH}\}$.

Given the peer ontology PO, the thesaurus TH and a pair of terms T^1 and T^2 used in service descriptions to denote service elements, T^1 is subsumed by T^2 with respect to TH, denoted by $T^1 \sqsubseteq_{TH} T^2$, if and only if there exists $C \in T^1{}_{PO}$ and $D \in T^2{}_{PO}$ such that $C \sqsubseteq D$ is satisfied in PO.

Note that we pose $T^1 \equiv_{TH} T^2$ if both $T^1 \sqsubseteq_{TH} T^2$ and $T^2 \sqsubseteq_{TH} T^1$ hold.

18.3.3.2 Network Service Knowledge

Network service knowledge on each peer is constituted by a set of *semantic links* towards similar or related services stored on different peers of the collaborative network. Two kinds of semantic links are defined:

functional similarity links, denoted with $S_1 \approx S_2$, that relate similar semantic service descriptions S_1 and S_2 registered on two different peers, that is, services with similar functionalities working on similar I/O parameters;

coupling similarity links, denoted with $S_1 \to S_2$, to assert that outputs of S_1 are semantically related to the inputs of S_2; S_1 and S_2 are defined as coupled and can be taken into account as suitable for composition.

The building block to define semantic links is the notion of similarity between semantic service descriptions. In [6], we have proposed a hybrid matchmaking model (named FC-MATCH) to compare semantic service descriptions based on the peer ontology and the Thesaurus. In the hybrid model, service inputs and outputs are separately compared according to distinct matching models: a deductive matching model, exploiting semantic relationships in the peer ontology and a similarity-based matching model, based on the name affinity evaluation between terms used in the semantic service descriptions. Matching techniques are applied to evaluate: (i) the degree of matching between services, to establish functional similarity links, (ii) the degree of interdependency between services, to establish coupling similarity links. A prefiltering step is applied on the basis of service category taxonomy to avoid service matchmaking in case of mismatching categories.

First, a deductive model is used to qualify the kind of match `MatchType`(S_1, S_2) between two semantic service descriptions S_1 and S_2. The deductive matching model applies the affinity-based subsumption test, defined in the previous section, to service description elements considered separately (operations, input parameters, output parameters) to classify the match between S_1 and S_2. In [6], a formal definition of the following kinds of match has been given.

EXACT to denote that S_1 and S_2 have the same capabilities, that is, for each operation in S_1 there exists an operation in S_2 that has: (i) an equivalent name; (ii) equivalent output parameters; (iii) equivalent input parameters.

EXTENDS to denote that S_2 offers at least the same capabilities of S_1, that is, for each operation in S_1 there exists an operation in S_2 that has: (i) an equivalent or more specific operation name; (ii) an equivalent or more specific output parameter for each output parameter of the S_1 operation; (iii) a set of input parameters, each of them is equivalent or more generic than an input parameter of the S_1 operation; the inverse kind of match is denoted as RESTRICTS; the rationale behind the EXTENDS match is that S_2 at least fulfills the functionalities of S_1 if it provides all the S_1 outputs, but, on the other hand, S_1 must be able to provide all the inputs needed for the S_2 execution.

INTERSECTS to denote that S_1 and S_2 have some common capabilities, that is, there exists an operation in S_2 and an operation in S_1 such that: (i) their names are related in any generalization hierarchy; (ii) there exists a pair of I/O parameters, one from S_1 and one from S_2, that are related in any generalization hierarchy.

MISMATCH otherwise.

In case of partial match (S_2 RESTRICTS|INTERSECTS S_1), a similarity-based matching model is used to quantify the degree of match $GSim(S_1, S_2)$ between semantic service descriptions through coefficients properly defined to deal with service functional interfaces. A detailed description of similarity coefficients and their application is given in [6]. Basically, we distinguish among the *Entity-based similarity* coefficient (*ESim*), that evaluates the similarity of all the I/O parameters of the compared services to measure how much they are based on the same information, and the *Functionality-based similarity* coefficient (*FSim*), that compares pairs of operations together with their corresponding I/O parameters to measure how much the two services perform the same functionalities. *ESim* and *FSim* are normalized into the [0, 1] range and combined in the *Global similarity* coefficient *GSim*, according to the following formula:

$$GSim(S_1, S_2) = w_1 \cdot NormESim(S_1, S_2) + w_2 \cdot NormFSim(S_1, S_2) \in [0, 1] \tag{18.4}$$

where w_1, w_2 are weights introduced to assess the relevance of each kind of similarity ($w_1 \in [0, 1]$ and $w_2 = 1 - w_1$). EXACT and EXTENDS match correspond to the case $GSim(S_1, S_2) = 1.0$, while $GSim(S_1, S_2) = 0.0$ in case of MISMATCH. A match is recognized between S_1 and S_2 if the kind of match is not MISMATCH and the global similarity degree is equal or greater than a threshold δ. In [6], experimentations performed to identify the best threshold value have been presented. Service categories are initially exploited to filter out not matching services: if there is not at least a category of S_1 that is equivalent to or more specific than a category of S_2 in the Service Category Taxonomy (or viceversa), the FC-MATCH algorithm is not applied at all, the kind of match is directly set to MISMATCH and $GSim(S_1, S_2) = 0.0$. If a match is recognized between S_1 and S_2, a *functional similarity link* is defined from S_1 to S_2 as a 4-uple:

$$\langle S_1, S_2, \texttt{MatchType}(S_1, S_2), GSim(S_1, S_2)\rangle \tag{18.5}$$

If a match between S_1 and S_2 is not recognized, services are analyzed with respect to the degree of interdependency between them. On the basis of the number of output parameters in the first service that can be recognized to have semantic correspondences with the input ones of the second service, their degree of coupling is measured. The evaluation relies on the following coupling coefficient:

$$Coupl(S_1, S_2) = \left[2 \cdot \frac{\sum_{i,j} NAff(out_i, in_j)}{|OUT(S_1)| + |IN(S_2)|}\right] \in [0, 1]$$

where: $OUT(S_1)$ (resp., $IN(S_1)$) is the set of overall output (resp., input) parameters of S_1, $out_i \in OUT(S_1)$, $in_j \in IN(S_2)$. S_1 and S_2 are recognized as coupled if $Coupl(S_1, S_2)$ is equal or greater than a pre-defined threshold and a *coupling similarity link* is defined from S_1 to S_2 as a 3-uple:

$$\langle S_1, S_2, Coupl(S_1, S_2)\rangle \tag{18.6}$$

When either a functional or a coupling similarity link is established between two collaborative partners, the latter are defined as semantic neighbors.

Example In Fig. 18.3, semantic links starting from the `AirLow` service provided by the T_X travel agency are shown. Services `AirLow` and `FlyCheap` are related through a functional similarity link. Indeed, we see that the input `Seat-Preferences` of `FlyCheap` does not correspond to any input in `AirLow`. As a consequence, EXACT and EXTENDS match conditions cannot be satisfied (since $IN(\texttt{FlyCheap}) \not\subseteq IN(\texttt{AirLow})$). On the other hand, `FlyCheap` provides outputs `FromCity` and `AirplaneModel` that are not provided by `AirLow`. Semantic correspondences between all the other I/O parameters of the two services are recognized, so `FlyCheap` INTERSECTS `AirLow` (partial match) is established. Similarity based evaluation is therefore performed to obtain the *GSim* value. Moreover, `AirLow` and `HotelSearching` do not provide matching functionalities, but there is a relevant overlapping between the outputs of `AirLow` and the inputs of `HotelSearching`: a coupling similarity link is established between these two semantic service descriptions.

Each peer maintains an OWL-DL representation of its network knowledge, as shown in Fig. 18.4. For each semantic service description Si_X owned by T_X the semantic links starting from Si_X are represented in the OWL-DL document and

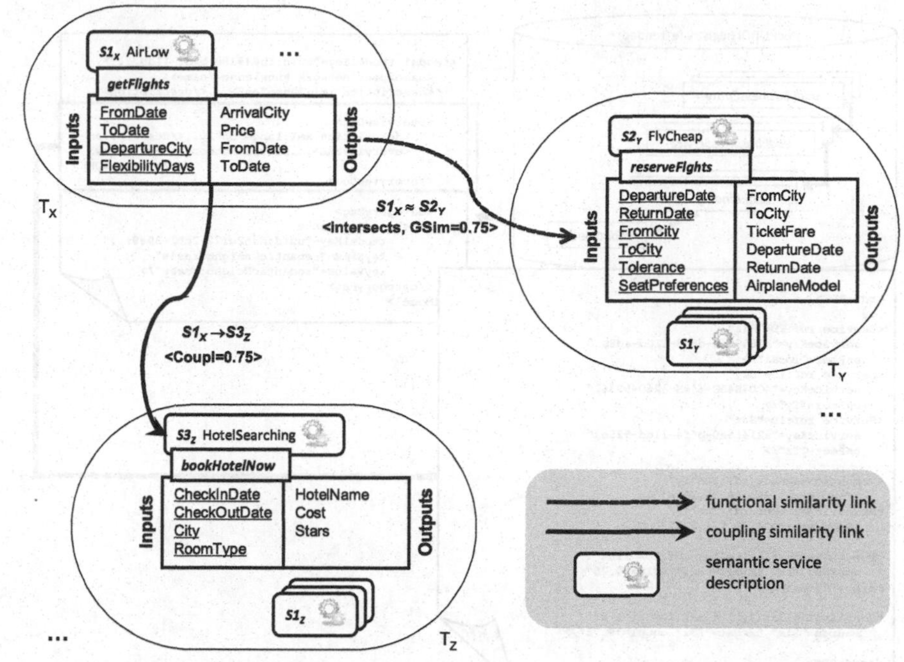

Fig. 18.3 Service network knowledge of T_X travel agency

are associated to Si_X through `tModel` mechanism. Local and network knowledge constitute a semantic overlay built and maintained over the underlying logical P2P network.

18.4 Distributed Semantic Service Management

The service knowledge space described in the previous sections must be properly maintained to face the inner dynamism of P2P network and can be efficiently and effectively exploited to enable collaboration scenarios presented in Sect. 18.2. To this aim, we propose a virtual Distributed Service Registry (DSR) and a reference architecture to support semantic search over P2P networks. The proposed reference architecture for each peer is based on:

- the local portion of the virtual Distributed Service Registry (DSR), where available services are registered and local and network service knowledge are organized on two layers;
- a semantic search assistant, that exploits the two-layer organization of the DSR to satisfy requested user's searches, also suggesting possible alternative services or related services suitable for composition;

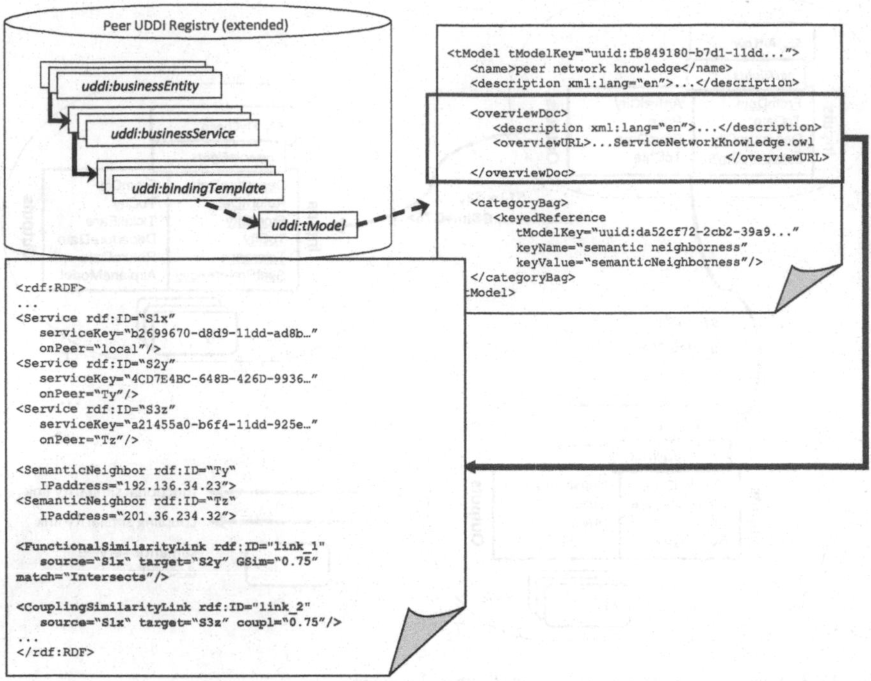

Fig. 18.4 OWL-DL representation of the T_X service network knowledge

- a service knowledge evolution manager, that updates peer local knowledge through local interactions with other peers.

The purpose of this section and the next one is to present the capabilities of the proposed architecture, highlighting how it enables the semantic collaboration in Web-based systems.

18.4.1 Distributed Service Registry Structure

The DSR is organized on two layers, as shown in Fig. 18.5:

- a *logical layer*, in which UDDI registries of collaborative partners are connected as peers in a P2P network; at this layer, each registry maintains the functional interfaces of local services; in Fig. 18.5, registries of the three travel agencies T_X, T_Y and T_Z are highlighted, connected through logical links;
- a *semantic layer*, where peer registries are semantic-enriched (local knowledge) and semantic links between peer registries holding similar services are established (network knowledge); at this layer, the service knowledge evolution manager is in charge of maintaining the local and network knowledge given the high

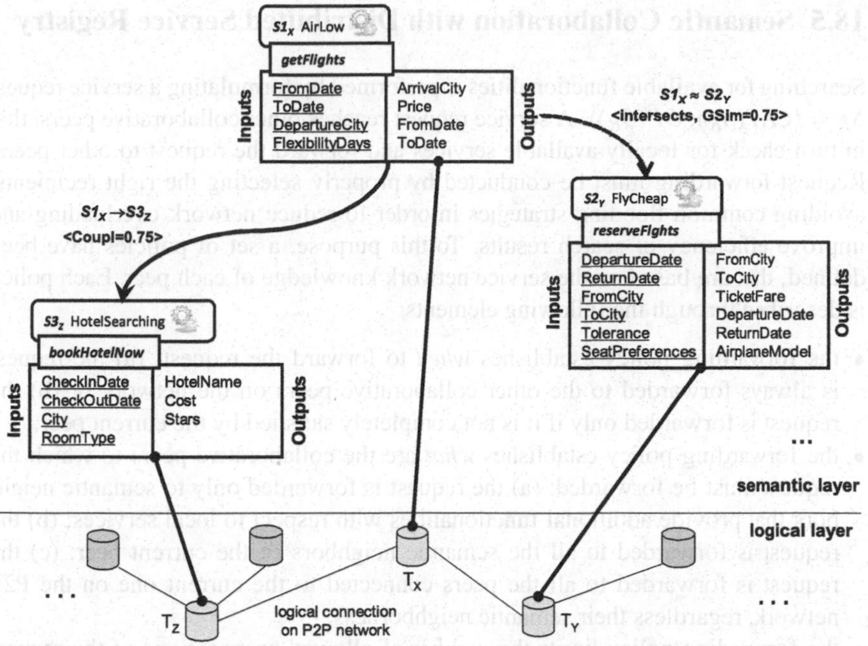

Fig. 18.5 Semantic organization of services in the running example, organized on the two-layer DSR

dynamism of the underlying P2P network; knowledge maintenance is obtained through point-to-point local interactions between peers, as shown in Sect. 18.4.2.

18.4.2 Distributed Service Registry Maintenance

The knowledge evolution manager is responsible of setting semantic links by applying service matchmaking techniques introduced in Sect. 18.3.3.2. To this aim, a knowledge harvesting process is adopted. Specifically, at predefined time intervals, the knowledge evolution manager of a peer, e.g., T_X, sends a probe request for each locally available service that is not yet source of a semantic link. The probe request contains the semantic description of the service. Another peer, say T_Y, receiving the request, applies through its knowledge evolution manager the matching techniques between the probe request and each local semantic service description and a reply is sent back to T_X containing: (i) a reference to the matching service, (ii) the corresponding matching information, that is, the kind of match and the value of *GSim* coefficient for functional similarity links or the value of *Coupl* coefficient for coupling similarity links. T_X collects received information and establishes a semantic link towards T_Y. Semantic links from T_X to T_Y are removed if a given number of service requests sent to T_Y are not answered.

18.5 Semantic Collaboration with Distributed Service Registry

Searching for available functionalities is performed by formulating a service request $S_R = \langle CAT(S_R), OP(S_R)\rangle$. A service request reaches other collaborative peers, that in turn check for locally available services and forward the request to other peers. Request forwarding must be conducted by properly selecting the right recipients, avoiding common flooding strategies in order to reduce network overloading and improve efficiency of search results. To this purpose, a set of policies have been defined, that are based on the service network knowledge of each peer. Each policy is described through the following elements:

- the forwarding policy establishes *when* to forward the request: (a) the request is always forwarded to the other collaborative peers on the network or (b) the request is forwarded only if it is not completely satisfied by the current peer;
- the forwarding policy establishes *what* are the collaborative peers to which the request must be forwarded: (a) the request is forwarded only to semantic neighbors that provide additional functionalities with respect to local services; (b) the request is forwarded to all the semantic neighbors of the current peer; (c) the request is forwarded to all the peers connected to the current one on the P2P network, regardless their semantic neighborness;
- the forwarding policy limits the *number* of allowed propagations of the request in order to avoid cycles and further reduce network overload; this is obtained by means of a TTL (Time-To-Live) mechanism; each time a peer forwards a request, the TTL is decreased by 1; when the TTL = 0, the request cannot be further propagated.

The service discovery task, on which collaboration is based, is performed according to the following steps.

Selection of semantic neighbors The search request S_R submitted to the peer T_X is matched against the local semantic service descriptions and a list $MS(S_R)$ of matching service descriptions is obtained. The request S_R can be forwarded to the other nodes of the DSR to extend the list of matching services. To prune the set of nodes to be investigated, thus avoiding time-consuming distributed service search, semantic neighbors that are related to services $Si_X \in MS(S_R)$ through functional similarity links are selected as request recipients. Moreover, candidate semantic neighbors can be filtered according to the forwarding policies, that are based on the matching information labeling the semantic links. First, for each semantic link sl starting from a service $Si_X \in MS(S_R)$, the harmonic mean is evaluated to combine the similarity $GSim()$ on sl with the similarity between S_R and Si_X, that is:

$$r_{sl} = \frac{2 * GSim^{sl} * GSim(S_R, Si_X)}{GSim^{sl} + GSim(S_R, Si_X)}$$

where r_{sl} is the relevance value associated to the semantic link sl and $GSim^{sl}$ is the similarity value labeling sl. Second, the list of candidate semantic links ranked with respect to the r_{sl} value is filtered according to a threshold-based mechanism. Finally, two different forwarding policies are applied.

According to a *minimal policy*, search over the network stops when matching services which fully satisfy the request have been found. In *exhaustive policies*, the search does not stop when matching services that fully satisfy the request are found: the request S_R is forwarded to semantic neighbors to find other services that could present, for example, better non functional features. In [7] a detailed presentation of different forwarding rules based on functional similarity semantic links is provided. It is important to stress that without the organization of services through semantic links, the discovery process would rely on conventional P2P infrastructures and associated routing protocols for query propagation in the network (e.g., flooding). Exploiting the semantic links, it is possible to enforce query forwarding according to content similarities rather than to the mere network topology. Note that in this step, depending on the selected forwarding policy, a complementary service provisioning or an alternative service provisioning collaboration scenario is implemented.

Request forwarding and collection of search results Once the candidate semantic neighbors have been selected, the search request S_R is forwarded towards them in order to obtain required search results on the DSR. A token-based strategy is adopted to avoid cycles and network overloading. Each semantic neighbor receiving the request checks for locally available matching services: if matches have been found, the semantic neighbor replies to the registry R_X, from which the request started, it consumes a token and, if the remaining number of tokens is not zero, it repeats the forwarding procedure based on its semantic neighbors and the current token value.

Extending the search results through related services Once the user selects one of the search results, coupling similarity links are exploited to propose to the user additional results collecting those services that can offer additional functionalities with respect to the user request (since their inputs are related to the outputs of the selected services). In the running example, if $S1_X$ is selected, the system exploits the semantic link ($S1_X \rightarrow S3_Z$) to propose the $S3_Z$ service to the user as a service complementary to $S1_X$.

Figure 18.6 displays the Web interface that assists a travel agent during semantic search on each registry in the DSR for the considered application scenario. In the "Search for" area of the Web interface, the travel agent of T_X agency searches for local services that provide information about the available destinations and corresponding fares of low-cost flights, given the departure and return dates and the departure city (first phase in the figure). Locally available services with corresponding inputs and outputs, the kind of match and the similarity degree with respect to the request are displayed. In the "Search for" area, the agent can also specify a similarity threshold to filter out not relevant services. In the running example, only the `FlyCheap` service is listed among the local results. Note that I/O names in the list of the retrieved services are displayed together with (possible) corresponding terms used while compiling the search form (e.g., `FromCity` and `DepartureCity` in

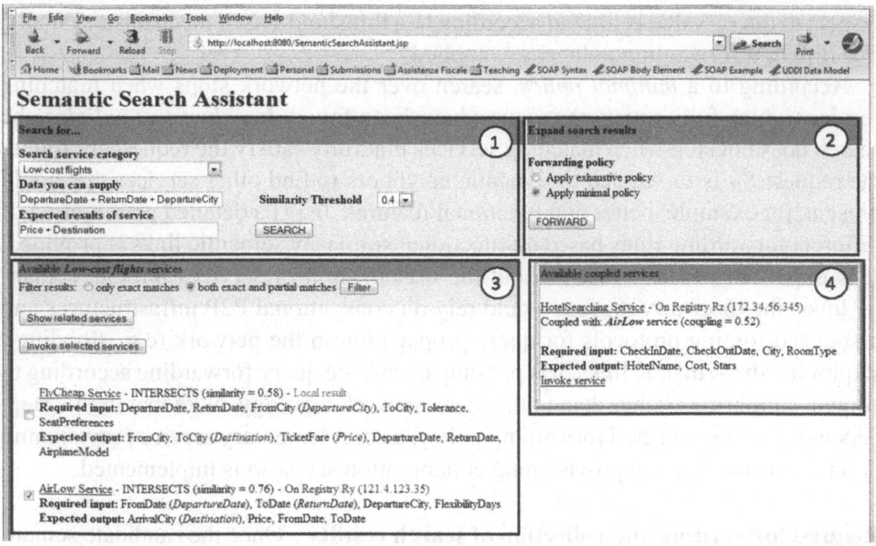

Fig. 18.6 Semantic search assistant Web interface

figure). At this point, one of the available forwarding policies (exhaustive or minimal) can be applied to propagate the service request to the other collaborative agencies following functional semantic links, to find additional similar services (second phase). In the example, the `AirLow` service provided by the T_Y agency is added to the retrieved ones. The collected services are listed on the interface (third phase). After selecting one or more retrieved services, the agent can visualize (through the "`Show related services`" button) a list of services that are related to the selected ones by means of coupling similarity links (fourth phase).

18.5.1 Experimental Evaluation

The presented approach is based on previous work on semantic service matchmaking and P2P semantic-driven service discovery [7]. Experimentations on semantic service matchmaking have been presented in [6], respectively. To test P2P semantic-driven service discovery we performed a set of simulations by implementing a DSR simulator designed on the basis of the Neurogrid P2P simulator.[1]

The simulator is able to build the DSR semantic layer, run over it the service discovery process according to the minimal and exhaustive forwarding policies and collect statistics useful for the evaluation of the approach. Performed simulations are in particular devoted to evaluate: (i) DSR scalability; (ii) performances of DSR forwarding mechanism. In Fig. 18.7(a), recall evaluation is plotted as the number of

[1] http://www.neurogrid.net.

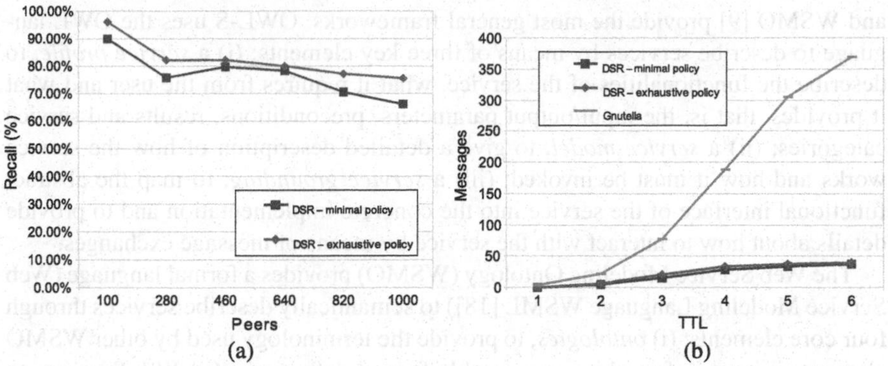

Fig. 18.7 Experimental evaluation: (**a**) DSR recall, (**b**) comparison of generated traffic

peers in the DSR grows. Recall varies in the range [0.66–0.90] for minimal policy and in [0.76–0.99] for exhaustive and decreases smoothly as the number of peers grows showing that the approach scales quite well.

The simulations we have run also compares the DSR forwarding policy with the well known Gnutella P2P protocol both in terms of efficiency and scalability. Actually, Gnutella is oriented to document discovery, but we have implemented in the simulations a service discovery process that exploits the Gnutella forwarding policy in order to compare it with DSR. The choice of a comparison with Gnutella is due to the fact that both DSR and Gnutella define an overlay network built on top of a P2P network and that Gnutella message forwarding policy is well-known and frequently considered as a reference example. In particular, DSR and Gnutella forwarding policies have been compared on the generated messages as the scope of the request, that is the TTL parameter, grows. As TTL increases, the number of peers reached by the request grows, so better recall is generally expected. On the other hand, also the traffic increases. In Fig. 18.7(b), the results for generated traffic of DSR minimal, exhaustive and Gnutella policies are shown and compared. We can note the better performances for both DSR semantic forwarding policies with respect to non semantic one.

18.6 Related Work

Research areas relevant to semantic collaboration in Web-based systems are related to the use of ontologies for semantic service description, service discovery and matchhmaking, P2P semantic collaboration.

Ontology-based Service Description Semantic Web technologies, in particular ontology-based techniques and tools, are exploited to add semantics to service descriptions and to support location of services that fulfill a given user request in highly dynamic environments. In particular, for service semantic description, OWL-S [21] and WSMO [9] provide the most general frameworks. OWL-S uses the OWL language to describe services by means of three key elements: (i) a *service profile*, to describe the functionalities of the service, what it requires from the user and what it provides, that is, the input/output parameters, preconditions, results and service categories; (ii) a *service model*, to give a detailed description of how the service works and how it must be invoked; (iii) a *service grounding*, to map the abstract functional interface of the service into the concrete implementation and to provide details about how to interact with the service by means of message exchanges.

The Web Service Modeling Ontology (WSMO) provides a formal language (Web Service Modeling Language WSML [18]) to semantically describe services through four core elements: (i) *ontologies*, to provide the terminology used by other WSMO elements in terms of machine-processable formal definitions; (ii) *Web Services*, to describe *non functional properties*, *capabilities* and *interfaces*; (iii) *goals*, to represent the user's requirements in terms of expected outputs and effects; (iv) *mediators*, to deal with interoperability problems between different WSMO elements; a WSMO mediator serves as a third party component connecting heterogeneous elements.

Both OWL-S and WSMO require an high expressiveness of the description language with high computational complexity in reasoning. Both of the approaches use domain ontologies to express semantics of service description elements, while the organization of services themselves into service ontologies is not completely addressed to improve the efficiency of the discovery process as in our service knowledge space. The only effort in this sense has been made by the OWL-S approach, that aims at organizing Service Profiles into profile hierarchies and at classifying them by means of service categories.

Service Discovery and Matchmaking Different service matchmaking approaches have been developed aiming at improving keyword-based techniques provided by UDDI registry. In general, service matchmaking strategies that are based on purely logic reasoning [17] present high precision and recall and are characterized by a good trade-off between expressiveness and computational complexity, but are often characterized by low flexibility. By flexibility, it is meant that the matchmaker is able to recognize not only exact matches but also the degree of similarity between a service request and a service advertisement that do not match exactly. Moreover, these approaches usually suffer from scalability problems. In [17], a service matchmaking strategy based on the OWL-S service profile and on a DL reasoner is proposed. The overall DAML + OIL expression representing a service profile is consistently mapped into a single DL expression and DL-based reasoning facilities are applied to check if the request description is equivalent, subsumed or consistent with the descriptions of service advertisements.

On the contrary, with respect to logic-based approaches, similarity-based approaches are characterized by high flexibility, but also limited precision and recall, because, for example, if a partial match is found, there is no way to know if it is due to the fact that the required functionalities are more than the provided ones or viceversa. In [12], a Web Service description is expressed through Web Service name with its textual description, names of operations and their textual descriptions, input/output parameter descriptions, that is, their name, data type and cardinality, as contained in the corresponding WSDL file. The proposed algorithm evaluates the similarity of a pair of Web Service operations by exploiting a novel clustering procedure that groups parameter names into semantically meaningful concepts.

A comparison of deductive and similarity-based approaches shows that the former ones are able to distinguish between the service request and the service advertisement, but do not provide a quantification of how much the advertisement matches with the request, while the latter approaches are symmetric, not distinguishing between the request and the advertisement, but provide a quantification of the degree of match. In our DSR, a hybrid matchmaking model is used to combine advantages from deductive and similarity-based models.

Also in [15], a mixed service matchmaking approach, called OWLS-MX, has been proposed. Services are described using OWL-S Service Profiles and the degree of match of a service advertisement *S* with a service request *R* is based not only on the semantic relationships between DL constructs that express service description elements, but also on frequencies of indexed terms of these descriptions, that are evaluated through traditional Information Retrieval metrics. We note that the similarity-based part of this approach exploits IR techniques that are not tailored to service description comparisons and do not use lexical knowledge to enhance matchmaking effectiveness.

P2P Service-based Semantic Collaboration P2P semantic-driven service discovery has attracted much attention from Web services and Semantic Web area and relies on several efforts in related research fields, such as data integration and emergent semantics in P2P environments [1, 5, 16] to go beyond limitations of centralized service-oriented architectures. In METEOR-S [23] service descriptions are kept in UDDI Registries semantically enhanced with local domain ontologies, while a centralized registries ontology is used to classify peer registries. During the discovery process, registries ontology is browsed to find the proper registry to which submit the request. The registries ontology is predefined and must be manually developed or updated. The system provides a support for the semantic annotation of published services. However, this kind of approach is not well suited for P2P environment, since it is not completely decentralized and high dynamism of P2P requires a better support for registry evolution.

WSPDS [3] describes a P2P network where peers have local DAML-S ontologies to provide service semantics and links with other peers based on similarity between services they provide. When a request is submitted to a peer, it searches for local matching results and forwards the request to all peers where similar services are stored, independently from the current request or the local results of matchmaking. In this work, mechanisms apt to keep the distributed registry up-to-date are not developed.

In [4], a P2P-based system to support efficient access to e-catalogs resident data is provided, where scalability issues are solved by organizing information space in communities that are interrelated using peer relationships, defined as mappings between ontologies. Selection of relevant peers to which queries must be forwarded is established on that basis of community descriptions and peer relationships to identify the catalogs that more relevant to users queries. A query rewriting algorithm is adopted to translate the query into the recipient language. Efficient peer selection strategies for query forwarding are not developed in the cited work.

A proposal for a three-layer distributed UDDI-based registry, called ad-UDDI, is described in [13]. The middle layer is composed of ad-UDDI registries that are associated to one or more categories taken from the Global Industry Classification Standard (GICS). Each ad-UDDI registry is manually associated to one or more categories in the considered classification. This approach is not completely decentralized since all ad-UDDI registries should be registered at the top level in a special ad-UDDI root registry that collects all the information about single registries. Neighboring relationships between two ad-UDDI registries at the middle layer are established if the registries have at least one GICS category in common. Services are positioned at the bottom layer of the architecture and are stored in one or more ad-UDDI registries depending on the GICS categories in which services must be classified. The ad-UDDI architecture is therefore based on a partially centralized organization to keep information about single registries and neighbouring relationships among registries. An innovative aspect of the ad-UDDI approach with respect to traditional implementations is the adoption of an active monitoring mechanism that keeps updated the information about services stored in the ad-UDDI registries. A weak aspect of this approach is therefore the presence of centralized Root Registry that represents a single point of failure.

18.7 Conclusion

In this chapter, we presented a model-based approach to enable semantic collaboration in Web-based systems based on a service-oriented architecture, where shared functionalities are made available through Web service functional interfaces. In such a scenario, collaborative partners act as peers in a P2P network, equipped with their own repositories, where exported services are published together with an ontological infrastructure to provide semantic-enriched representation of service functionalities in order to facilitate collaborative activities. Moreover, we also considered the representation of a network service knowledge, to conceptualize the notion of semantic links between peers that store similar services, thus enabling the application of novel service request forwarding policies throughout the P2P network.

The proposed approach aims at overcoming open issues related to the collaboration in open, P2P environments: a common resource conceptualization is not feasible, due to the presence of many autonomous collaborative peers that assume their own ontologies to represent shared services; a centralized structure for management of service retrieval and update should be avoided to face with high dynamicity of the considered environments; efficient strategies apt to prune service requests for efficiency purposes are required. A Distributed Service Registry (DSR) infrastructure that implements the proposed approach has been also presented.

Future efforts will be devoted to complete the proposed architecture with the refinement and testing of knowledge evolution and request forwarding strategies and to evaluate the effectiveness of the DSR in supporting the user to define mappings between heterogeneous functionalities provided by different peers in order to implement automatic service discovery under the considered Web-based collaborative systems requirements. The resulting application will be validated on real case scenarios.

References

1. Aberer, K., Cudre-Mauroux, P., Hauswirth, M.: The chatty Web: emergent semantics through gossiping. In: Proc. of the 12th International World Wide Web Conference (WWW'03), Budapest, Hungary, pp. 197–206 (2003)
2. Akkiraju, R., Farrell, J., Miller, J., Nagarajan, M., Schmidt, M., Sheth, A., Verma, K.: Web Service Semantics—WSDL-S. A joint UGA-IBM Technical Note, Version 1.0 (2005). http://lsdis.cs.uga.edu/Projects/METEOR-S/WSDL-S
3. Banaei-Kashani, F., Chen, C., Shahabi, C.: WSPDS: Web services peer-to-peer discovery service. In: Proc. of the 5th Int. Conference on Internet Computing (IC'04), Las Vegas, Nevada, USA, pp. 733–743 (2004)
4. Benatallah, B., Hacid, M., Paik, H., Rey, C., Toumani, F.: Towards semantic-driven, flexible and scalable framework for peering and querying e-catalog communities. Inf. Syst. **31**(4–5), 266–294 (2006)
5. Bernstein, P., Giunchigiloa, F., Kementsietsidis, A., Mylopoulos, J., Serafini, L., Zaihrayeu, I.: Data management for peer-to-peer computing: a vision. In: Proc. of the 5th International Workshop on the Web and Databases (WebDB'02), Madison, Wisconsin, pp. 177–186 (2002)
6. Bianchini, D., Antonellis, V.D., Melchiori, M.: Flexible semantic-based service matchmaking and discovery. World Wide Web J. **11**(2), 227–251 (2008)
7. Bianchini, D., Antonellis, V.D., Melchiori, M., Salvi, D.: A semantic overlay for service discovery across Web information systems. In: Proc. of 9th Int. Conference on Web Information Systems Engineering (WISE'08), Auckland, New Zealand, pp. 292–306 (2008)
8. de Bruijn, J., Polleres, A., Lara, R., Fensel, D.: OWL-DL vs. OWL flight: conceptual modeling and reasoning for the Semantic Web. In: Proc. Forum of the 14th Int. World Wide Web Conference (WWW 2005), Chiba, Japan (2005)
9. Bussler, C., de Bruijn, J., Feier, C., Fensel, D., Keller, U., Lara, R., Lausen, H., Polleres, A., Roman, D., Stollberg, M.: Web service modeling ontology. In: Applied Ontology, vol. 1, pp. 77–106. IOS Press, Amsterdam (2005)
10. Castano, S., Antonellis, V.D., diVimercati, S.D.C.: Global viewing of heterogeneous data sources. IEEE Trans. Knowl. Data Eng. **13**(2) (2001)
11. Chinnici, R., Moreau, J., Ryman, A., Weerawarana, S.: Web Services Description Language (WSDL) Version 2.0. World Wide Web Consortium (W3C) Recommendation (2007). http://www.w3.org/TR/2007/REC-wsdl20-20070626/
12. Dong, X., Halevy, A.Y., Madhavan, J., Nemes, E., Zhang, J.: Similarity search for Web services. In: Proc. of the 30th Int. Conference on Very Large Data Bases (VLDB2004), Toronto, Canada, pp. 372–383 (2004)
13. Du, Z., Huai, J., Liu, Y.: Ad-UDDI: An active and distributed service registry. In: Proc. of 6th Int. Workshop on Technologies for E-Services (TES'05), Trondheim, Norway, pp. 58–71 (2005)
14. Fellbaum, C.: Wordnet: An Electronic Lexical Database. MIT Press, Cambridge (1998)
15. Fries, B., Khalid, M., Klusch, M., Sycara, K.: OWLS-MX: Hybrid OWL-S service matchmaking. In: Proc. of First International AAAI Symposium on Agents and Semantic Web, Arlington, VA, USA (2005)

16. Halevy, A., Ives, Z., Suciu, D., Tatarinov, I.: Schema mediation in peer data management systems. In: Proc. of the 19th International Conference on Data Engineering (ICDE'03), Bangalore, India, pp. 505–516 (2003)
17. Horrocks, I., Li, L.: A software framework for matchmaking based on Semantic Web technology. Special Issue on Semantic Web Services and Their Role in Enterprise Application Integration and E-Commerce. M. Wellman, J. Riedl (eds.) Int. J. Electron. Commer. (IJEC 2004) (2004)
18. Lausen, H., de Bruijn, J., Polleres, A., Fensel, D.: Wsml—a language framework for Semantic Web services (2005). Position Paper for the W3C rules workshop, Washington DC, USA, April 2005
19. Paolucci, M., Sycara, K., Nishimura, T., Srinivasan, N.: Using DAML-S for P2P discovery. In: Proceedings of the Int. Conference on Web Services (ICWS2003), pp. 203–207 (2003)
20. Stollberg, M., Keller, U., Lausen, H.: Two-phase Web service discovery based on rich functional descriptions. In: Proc. of the 4th European Semantic Web Conference (ESWC2007), Innsbruck, Austria, pp. 99–113 (2007)
21. The OWL Service Coalition. OWL-S 1.1 release (2004). http://www.daml.org/services/owl-s/1.1/
22. UDDI Technical White Paper. http://www.uddi.org/pubs/lru_UDDI_Technical_Paper.pdf (2001)
23. Verma, K., Sivashanmugam, K., Sheth, A., Patil, A., Oundhakar, S., Miller, J.: METEOR-S WSDI: A scalable infrastructure of registries for semantic publication and discovery of Web services. J. Inf. Technol. Manag., Special Issue on Universal Global Integration **6**(1), 17–39 (2005)

Chapter 19
Informative Top-k Retrieval for Advanced Skill Management

Simona Colucci, Tommaso Di Noia,
Azzurra Ragone, Michele Ruta,
Umberto Straccia, and Eufemia Tinelli

Abstract The paper presents a knowledge-based framework for skills and talent management based on an advanced matchmaking between profiles of candidates and available job positions. Interestingly, informative content of top-k retrieval is enriched through semantic capabilities. The proposed approach allows to: (1) express a requested profile in terms of both hard constraints and soft ones; (2) provide a ranking function based also on qualitative attributes of a profile; (3) explain the resulting outcomes (given a job request, a motivation for the obtained score of each selected profile is provided). Top-k retrieval allows to select most promising candidates according to an ontology formalizing the domain knowledge. Such a knowledge is further exploited to provide a semantic-based explanation of missing or conflicting features in retrieved profiles. They also indicate additional profile characteristics emerging by the retrieval procedure for a further request refinement. A concrete case study followed by an exhaustive experimental campaign is reported to prove the approach effectiveness.

S. Colucci · T. Di Noia · A. Ragone · M. Ruta · E. Tinelli (✉)
Politecnico di Bari, via E. Orabona 4, 70125 Bari, Italy
e-mail: e.tinelli@poliba.it

S. Colucci
e-mail: s.colucci@poliba.it

T. Di Noia
e-mail: t.dinoia@poliba.it

A. Ragone
e-mail: a.ragone@poliba.it

M. Ruta
e-mail: m.ruta@poliba.it

S. Colucci
Data Over Ontological Models—D.O.O.M. srl, via N. Paganini 7, 75100 Matera, Italy
e-mail: simona.colucci@doom-srl.it

U. Straccia
ISTI-CNR, Via G. Moruzzi 1, 56124 Pisa, Italy
e-mail: straccia@isti.cnr.it

R. De Virgilio et al. (eds.), *Semantic Web Information Management*,
DOI 10.1007/978-3-642-04329-1_19, © Springer-Verlag Berlin Heidelberg 2010

19.1 Introduction

Human resources retrieval can be a very complex process due to the difficulties for recruiters in properly expressing their requirements. Given the increasing competitiveness in job market, e-recruitment systems should provide more complex and articulated procedures in order to avoid the money loss caused by a wrong—or simply nonoptimal—assignment. Hence, there is the need to face a change in the old paradigms and techniques for managing talents and skills. Currently, recruiters describe vacant job positions exploiting traditional recruiting methods, such as advertisements and referral systems. More recently, on-line recruitment websites (see http://www.monster.com/, http://www.careerbuilder.com to cite a few) have been employed, which mainly build their retrieval techniques on a keyword-based search. In spite of the speed-up reached in profile collection, such systems require a considerable engagement for the recruiter often producing unsatisfactory results. The process of describing the vacancy has to be particularly accurate to produce adequate results, turning into a very time-consuming task. Furthermore, the recruiter is not fully aware of retrieval and ranking criteria (if any) and he/she receives as output a list of possible candidates not following any explicit set criteria. So the choice of a particular profile in the returned set is made according to a further manual selection of the returned profiles. Moreover, considering that the system interrogation is keyword-based, the recruiter can express only mandatory requirements. On the other hand, a job offer is usually characterized by some features which are strictly required and some other ones which are only preferred, possibly with a preference degree. A system flexible enough to reflect such a diversification would allow a relevant distinction in job vacancy descriptions. In addition, having a ranked list of candidates (and not trivially a set of candidates) represents a significant added value, especially if the recruiter may choose the ranking criterion. Finally, after selecting a profile, a guided comparison between the required job position and the returned candidate description which explains the resulting match, would be very useful for a further request refinement step. Semantic-based techniques and technologies allow for making more efficient and flexible the recruitment process. The approach presented here is based on an automatic matchmaking process between available candidate profiles and vacant job positions according to mandatory requirements and preferences provided by the recruiter. Both, candidates and job vacancies, are described in a formal language suitable for data intensive applications allowing a good trade-off between expressiveness and computational complexity. The proposed system combines flexibility in query formulation with an explanation of solutions. The matchmaking between job positions and candidates profiles exploits top-k retrieval techniques [20] by using a matching engine which performs top-k queries over a DLR-Lite [4] Knowledge Base (KB). It returns a ranked list of candidates managing also non-exact matches. Furthermore, the informative content of resulting outcomes is enriched with additional information explaining results of comparison of each retrieved candidate with respect to the job offer. The remainder of the chapter is organized as follows: in the next section, we report on the formal background underlying the approach; in Sect. 19.3, the proposed framework is outlined, whereas in Sect. 19.4 its effectiveness is proved through an exhaustive experimentation. A comparison with available tools and approaches to human resources retrieval is presented in Sect. 19.5. Conclusions and future work close the chapter.

19.2 Preliminaries

A logic-based approach is combined with a relational model to fully characterize the application field. On the one hand, Description Logics (DLs) are exploited to define proper axioms related to the knowledge domain. On the other hand, data related to candidate profiles are stored within a database so that conjunctive queries can be used to describe requests and to rank answers according to a scoring function. In this way, the *Top-k* scored tuples satisfying the query are provided (the interested reader may refer to *Top-k query answering* [15, 18–21] for a more detailed description).

Reference Formalism The specific DL we adopt is based on an extension of DLR-Lite [4], namely *top-k DLR-Lite*, not including negation operator but including built-in predicates. Differently from usual DLs, DLR-Lite supports also n-ary relations ($n \geq 1$).

A *knowledge base* $\mathcal{K} = \langle \mathcal{F}, \mathcal{O}, \mathcal{A} \rangle$ stores the domain knowledge. Basically, it consists of three components: *facts* $\mathcal{F}$, *Ontology* $\mathcal{O}$ and *Abstraction* $\mathcal{A}$, which are defined as in the following:

- *facts Component*: $\mathcal{F}$ is a finite set of expressions in the form $R(c_1, \ldots, c_n)$, where R is an n-ary relation and every c_i is a constant. For each R, we represent the facts $R(c_1, \ldots, c_n)$ in $\mathcal{F}$ by means of a relational n-ary table T_R, containing the records $\langle c_1, \ldots, c_n \rangle$.
- *ontology Component*: $\mathcal{O}$ is used to define relevant axioms of the application domain involving concept classes and relationships among them. Given an alphabet of n-ary relations (denoted as R), and an alphabet of unary relations, namely *atomic concepts* (denoted as A), the component $\mathcal{O}$ is a finite set of *axioms* having the form $Rl_1 \sqcap \cdots \sqcap Rl_m \sqsubseteq Rr$ where $m \geq 1$, all Rl_i and Rr have the same *arity*. Rl_i is a *left-hand relation* and Rr is a *right-hand relation*. The syntax of the relations appearing on the left-hand and right-hand side of ontology axioms is specified below:

$$Rr \to A \mid \exists[i_1, \ldots, i_k]R$$

$$Rl \to A \mid \exists[i_1, \ldots, i_k]R \mid \exists[i_1, \ldots, i_k]R.(Cond_1 \sqcap \cdots \sqcap Cond_h)$$

$$Cond \to \big([i] \leq v\big) \mid \big([i] < v\big) \mid \big([i] \geq v\big) \mid \big([i] > v\big) \mid \big([i] = v\big) \mid \big([i] \neq v\big)$$

where A is an atomic concept, R is an n-ary relation with $1 \leq i_1, i_2, \ldots, i_k \leq n$, $1 \leq i \leq n$, v is a reference value for the concrete domain interpretation and $h \geq 1$. Here, $\exists[i_1, \ldots, i_k]R$ is the projection of the relation R on the columns $i_1, \ldots, i_k$.

Hence, $\exists[i_1, \ldots, i_k]R$ has arity k. On the other hand, $\exists[i_1, \ldots, i_k]R.(Cond_1 \sqcap \cdots \sqcap Cond_l)$ further restricts the projection $\exists[i_1, \ldots, i_k]R$ according to the conditions specified in $Cond_i$. For instance, $([i] \leq v)$ specifies that the values of the i-th column have to be less or equal than the value v. Besides other constructs, *top-k DLR-Lite* supports concrete domains which are defined as pairs $\langle \Delta_{\mathrm{d}}, \Phi_{\mathrm{d}} \rangle$, where Δ_{d} is an interpretation domain and Φ_{d} is the set of n-ary *domain predicates d* and an interpretation $d^{\mathrm{d}}\colon \Delta_{\mathrm{d}}^n \to \{0, 1\}$.

– *Abstraction Component*: a set of "abstraction statements" allowing to connect atomic concepts and relations to physical relational tables. Basically, this component is a wrapper for the underlying database and thus, it prevents that relational table names occur in the ontology. Let R_1 be a relation symbol and let R_2 be an m-ary table in the database. Let $c_1, \ldots, c_n$ be $n \leq m$ column names of relation R_2 of type t_i. Hence, a *simple abstraction statement* is in the form $R_1 \mapsto R_2(c_1[t_1], \ldots, c_n[t_n])$ stating that R_1 is an n-ary relation of the ontology component mapped into the projection on columns $c_1, \ldots, c_n$ of R_2. We assume that R_1 occurs in $\mathcal{O}$, while R_2 occurs in $\mathcal{F}$. The retrieval of facts from the KB requires a proper query language. In what follows, both language syntax and semantics are detailed.

Query Language Queries are in a conjunctive form and enable a scoring function to rank answers. Each *query* is structured as reported hereafter:

$$q(\mathbf{x})[s] \leftarrow \exists \mathbf{y}\ R_1(\mathbf{z}_1), \ldots, R_l(\mathbf{z}_l), \mathsf{OrderBy}\big(s = f\big(p_1(\mathbf{z}'_1), \ldots, p_h(\mathbf{z}'_h)\big)\big) \quad (19.1)$$

where (1) q is an n-ary relation (every R_i is an n_i-ary relation) whereas $\mathbf{x}$ are the related n variables (*distinguished variables*); (2) $\mathbf{y}$ are the so-called *non-distinguished variables*; (3) $\mathbf{z_i}$, $\mathbf{z'_j}$ are tuples of constant or variable values in $\mathbf{x}$ or $\mathbf{y}$. Any variable in $\mathbf{x}$ occurs in some $\mathbf{z_i}$. Any variable in $\mathbf{z'_j}$ occurs in some $\mathbf{z_i}$; (4) p_j is an n_j-ary *fuzzy predicate* assigning to each n_j-ary tuple $\mathbf{c}_j$ a *score* $p_j(\mathbf{c}_j) \in [0, 1]_m$. Such predicates have been named *expensive predicates* in [5] as the related score is not precomputed offline, but it is calculated at runtime during query execution. Notice that the n-ary fuzzy predicate p is required to be *safe*, that is, no m-ary fuzzy predicates p' such that $m < n$ and $p = p'$ must be present; (5) f is a *scoring* function $f\colon ([0, 1]_m)^h \to [0, 1]_m$, which combines the scores of the h fuzzy predicates $p_j(\mathbf{c}''_j)$ into an overall *score* to be assigned to the rule head $q(\mathbf{c})$. We assume that f is *monotone*, i.e., for each $\mathbf{v}, \mathbf{v}' \in ([0, 1]_m)^h$ such that $\mathbf{v} \leq \mathbf{v}'$, $f(\mathbf{v}) \leq f(\mathbf{v}')$ holds, where $(v_1, \ldots, v_h) \leq (v'_1, \ldots, v'_h)$ iff $v_i \leq v'_i$ for all i.

Finally, a *disjunctive query* $\mathbf{q}$ is, as usual, a finite set of conjunctive queries where all the rules have the same head. We omit to specify $\exists \mathbf{y}$ when $\mathbf{y}$ can be clearly elicited from the context. $R_i(\mathbf{z_i})$ may also be a concrete unary predicate in the form $(z \leq v)$, $(z < v)$, $(z \geq v)$, $(z > v)$, $(z = v)$, $(z \neq v)$, where z is a variable, and v is a concrete domain proper value. We call $q(\mathbf{x})[s]$ its *head*, $\exists \mathbf{y}.R_1(\mathbf{z}_1), \ldots, R_l(\mathbf{z}_l)$ its *body* and $\mathsf{OrderBy}(\ldots)$ the *scoring atom*. The informal meaning of such a query is: if $\mathbf{z}_i$ is an instance of R_i, then $\mathbf{x}$ is an instance of q with a degree less or equal to $f(p_1(\mathbf{z}'_1), \ldots, p_h(\mathbf{z}'_h))$. Also the scoring atom can be omitted. In this case, we assume $s = 1$.

Top-k Retrieval Given a KB $\mathcal{K}$, and a disjunctive query $\mathbf{q}$, we denote with $ans_k(\mathcal{K}, \mathbf{q})$ the k tuples $\langle \mathbf{c}, s \rangle$ instantiating the query relation q with a maximal score (if such k tuples exist), and ranked in decreasing order w.r.t. the score s.

From a query answering standpoint, top-k retrieval extends the DL-Lite/DLR-Lite reasoning approach [4] to the fuzzy case. The reasoning algorithm is an extension of the one described in [4, 18, 20]. Given a query $q(\mathbf{x})[s] \leftarrow \exists \mathbf{y} \phi(\mathbf{x}, \mathbf{y})$, the algorithm proceeds as reported hereafter:

1. by considering $\mathcal{O}$, the original query $\mathbf{q}$ is *reformulated* into a set of conjunctive queries $r(\mathbf{q}, \mathcal{O})$. Basically, the reformulation procedure closely resembles to a top-down resolution procedure for logic programming, where each axiom is seen as a logic programming rule;
2. we remove redundant ones from $r(\mathbf{q}, \mathcal{O})$;
3. the reformulated queries $q' \in r(\mathbf{q}, \mathcal{O})$ are translated into ranked SQL queries and evaluated. The query evaluation of each ranked SQL query returns the top-k answer set for that query. Specifically, the RankSQL [14] system is exploited for this purpose;
4. all the $n = |r(\mathbf{q}, \mathcal{O})|$ top-k answer sets have to be merged into the final top-k answer set $ans_k(\mathcal{K}, \mathbf{q})$. As $k \cdot n$ may be large, we apply a *Disjunctive Threshold Algorithm* (DTA, see for example [20]) to collect all the answer sets.

A detailed description of the top-k retrieval algorithm is beyond the scope of this work. An implementation of it is part of the SoftFacts system.[1]

19.3 Human Resources Retrieval

The top-k retrieval approach described above can be targeted to several discovery problems. In this paper, we describe its application to a Human Resources Management. The theoretical framework has been implemented into `I.M.P.A.K.T.` [22], a system for skills management developed by *Data Over Ontological Models s.r.l.*[2] as a commercial solution implementing the skill matching framework designed in [6]. In what follows, the general features of the system as well as a description of the components architecture will be provided. The retrieval process starts by *querying* a *knowledge base* where candidate profiles (*f*acts expressed trough a domain-independent framework) are stored in a relational database. The reference vocabulary is provided by an *ontology*, representing main concepts and relations among them in the knowledge domain (see Appendix A). In what follows, each system component will be explained in depth. The information in the ontology (Sect. 19.3.1) is exploited to compose queries (Sect. 19.3.3) addressed to the database component (Sect. 19.3.2). The final goal is to obtain a top-k retrieval answer set (Sect. 19.3.4) enriched by information useful for outcomes explanation. The whole process is depicted in Fig. 19.1 and summarized hereafter.

---

[1] http://gaia.isti.cnr.it/~straccia/software/SoftFacts/SoftFacts.html.

[2] http://www.doom-srl.it/.

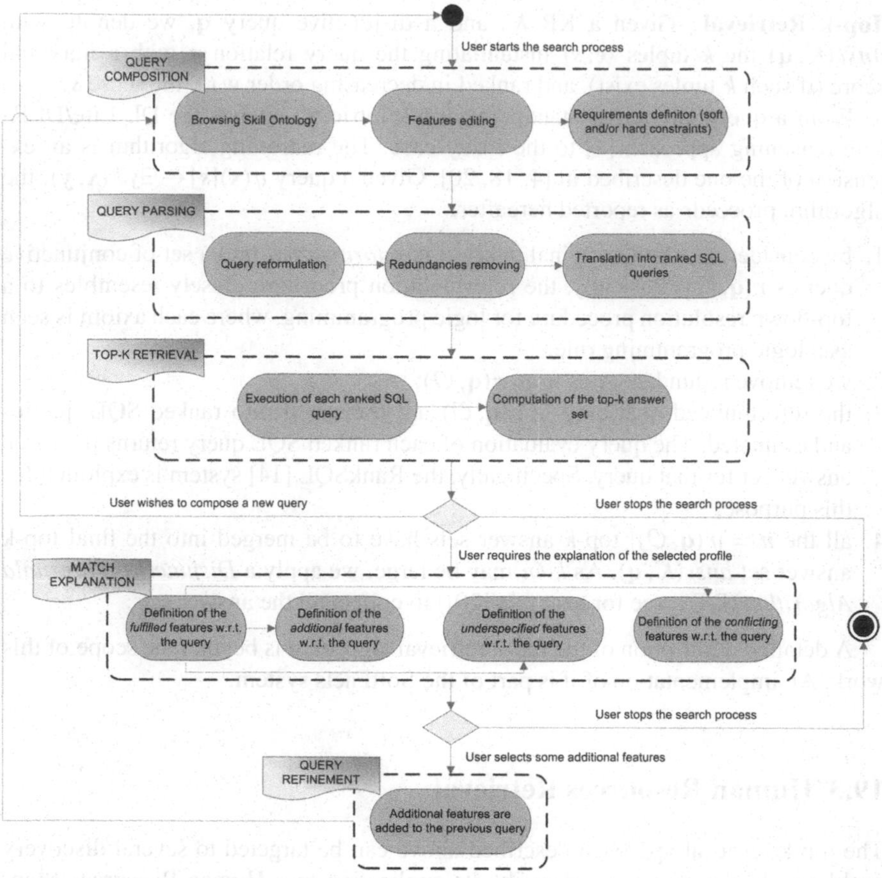

Fig. 19.1 The informative top-k retrieval process

– **Storage Phase**
  - *Knowledge modeling*. A candidate's CV includes personal and employer information. They are modeled according to an ontology $\mathcal{O}$ and, after a preprocessing phase, they are stored in a relational DBMS.
  - *Knowledge pre-processing*. The semantic annotation of a CV is parsed to group in the same collection features related to the same area e.g., *Job Title* or *Education Level*. We denote with p (for profile) the resulting description of a candidate. For each feature in a collection, the system will build a normalized version taking into account ontology $\mathcal{O}$ axioms so producing a normalized version of the profile description denoted as p_{norm}.
  - *Knowledge storage*. The system stores both p and p_{norm} in a relational database. Notice that p and p_{norm} will be maintained in different tables and for each feature collection there will be a specific table. The need to have two differently parsed description of the same candidate—and consequently a different relational representation—will be clarified in the following *query phase*.

- **Query phase**
  - *Query composition*. The recruiter expresses information useful to describe the profile to search for according to the ontology $\mathcal{O}$. Hence, the user query can be considered as a set of features grouped by area of interest. Each feature can be settled as either a strict requirement or a preference (hard or soft constraints, respectively).
  - *Top-k retrieval*. The query composed by the user is reformulated according to the rules in Sect. 19.2 and the top-k retrieval process starts considering only the *non-normalized* profiles p stored in the relational database.
  - *Match explanation*. Once top-k resources have been retrieved, their formal representation w.r.t. the ontology $\mathcal{O}$ may be exploited for explaining results. We name *match explanation* a semantic-based comparison between each feature of retrieved candidate and the corresponding request in the user query. By exploiting the *normalized* profiles p_{norm} stored in the relational database, the system provides the comparison outcomes classifying each candidate feature in the following classes: (1) fulfilled; (2) additional; (3) underspecified and (4) conflicting.

19.3.1 Ontology Component

The skill ontology underlying `I.M.P.A.K.T.` mainly focuses on ICT domain and contains 3341 `rdfs:class` classes representing both candidate's knowledge and her complementary skills. The former refer to the candidate background knowledge about specific technologies and tools, the latter represent personal and social characteristics. An upper level sketch of the ontology is shown in Fig. 19.2. The whole ontology has been developed by two domain experts working full time for 10 months following Methontology [11] specifications. The root class of the `I.M.P.A.K.T.` ontology is `Profile`. Every CV description is an instance of it. `Profile` class also is the domain of `rdf:Property` roles needed to represent both personal information (i.e., first/second name, address, telephone)[3] and "ontological" characteristics modeling skills, knowledge and competencies. Main ontology roles are reported hereafter:

- `hasKnowledge`. Its range classes are, for instance, `Functional Programming`, `XML` to cite a few. Along with the skill representation, it is allowed to specify the related experience and competence expressed in years.
- `hasJobTitle`. It is exploited to model job positions as `Teacher Assistant` or `Database Administrator`. All the job positions represented in the ontology are subclasses of `Job Title`. Also in this case it is possible to specify the job experience (in years).

[3] Many properties are obtained with a mapping of `vcard` [12] and `foaf` [8] specifications.

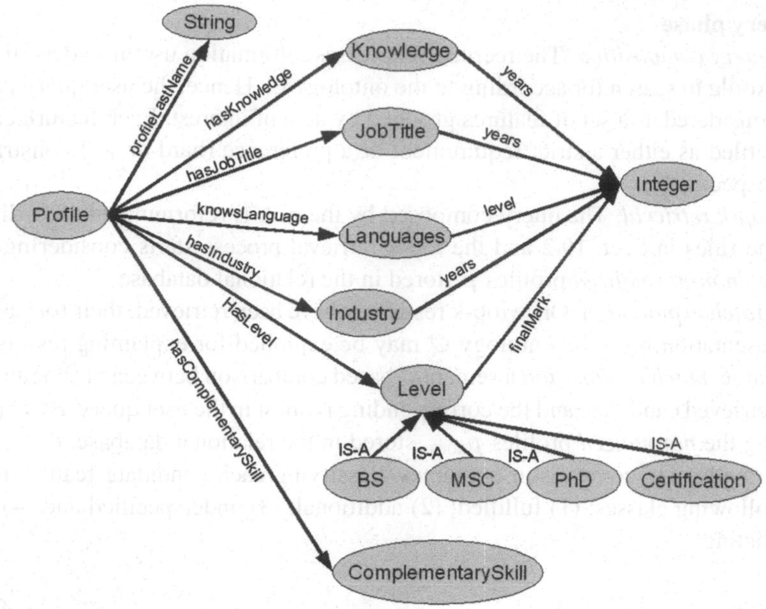

Fig. 19.2 A graphical sketch of the ontology structure

- `hasLanguage`. The knowledge of a specific `Language` may be further specified and classified in `verbal knowledge`, `reading knowledge` and `writing knowledge` followed by the reference level `Basic`, `Good` or `Excellent`.
- `hasIndustry`. It is used, along with its reference range `Industry`, to model institute areas, research laboratories, company departments where a candidate works or worked. Years of work experience in a specific field may be specified.
- `hasLevel`. It is adopted to represent everything related to candidate education and training. From basic education to `Master Degree`, the whole candidate's qualifications can be specified including specific `Certifications` she gained.
- `hasComplementarySkills`. It models complementary attitudes (namely soft skills) such as `Cooperation`, `Stress Tolerance`, and `Leadership` which complete CV's basic information about knowledge, technical skills and competence and which often are very useful to correctly evaluate a candidate profile.

In its current implementation, the ontology does not report disjunction axioms. Reasonably, in the recruitment field it is quite rare to assert that *if you know* "*A*" *then you do not know* "*B*". The above described properties represent what will be defined *entry points* in the domain ontology while their range represents what will be defined *main categories*. To help the reader in better understanding the case study reported later on, an ontology axioms excerpt is reported in Appendix A.

19.3.2 Database Component

In order to perform the top-k retrieval, candidates must be stored as *facts* in a relational database. If additional ontological information underlying each profile are added in the database, a match explanation can be enabled to make the recruiter aware of the retrieval results and to perform a possible query refinement. The Entity-Relationship (ER) model designed to this aim is shown in Fig. 19.3. The slightly redundant relational structure is needed to separately optimize the above processes: top-k retrieval of candidates (Fig. 19.3(a)) and match explanation (Fig. 19.3(b)).

The main entity is `profile` which bridges (a) and (b) model components. `profile` contains the so called *structured info* such as personal information (i.e., last and first name, birth date—see `profile` table map-role in Fig. 19.4 for more details) and employer information (i.e., preferred working hours, car availability). With respect to Fig. 19.3(a), notice that the model reproduces the structure of the ontology component (see Fig. 19.2): for each main category in the ontology, one entity in a *many-to-many* relation with `profile` is modeled. The ontology is mapped into the relational tables in (a) using the abstraction component $\mathcal{A}$ of the underlying DLR-Lite KB (see Sect. 19.2) represented in Fig. 19.4. Attributes as `years`, `mark`, `reading level`, `writing level` and `verbal level` are modeled in specific tables (main categories) in order to maintain the corresponding data property values.

The model in part (a) of Fig. 19.3 allows to perform a classical top-k retrieval problem over a knowledge base, whereas part (b) of the model has been properly

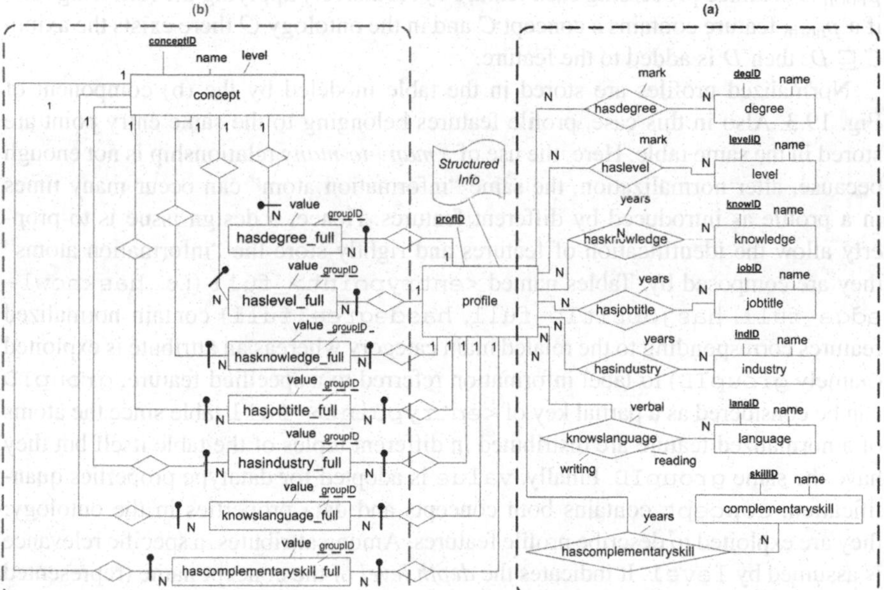

Fig. 19.3 Entity-Relationship model underlying the case study

```
(MAP-ROLE Profile profile (profID, FirstName, LastName, Genre,
 BirthDate, CityOfBirth, Address, City, ZipCode, Country, IdentityCode,
 PhoneNumber, Email, WebPage, Nationality, ResidentIn,
 SuddenJobAvailability, JobLocation, FlexibleWorkHours,
 TravelingAvailability, CertificationInstitute, Salary, CarAvailability))
(MAP-ROLE degreeName degree (degID, name))
(MAP-ROLE levelName level (levelID, name))
(MAP-ROLE industryName industry (indID,name))
(MAP-ROLE jobName jobtitle (jobID, Name))
(MAP-ROLE knowledgeName knowledge (knowID, name))
(MAP-ROLE languageName language (langID, name))
(MAP-ROLE skillName complementaryskill (skillID, name))
(MAP-ROLE hasDegree hasdegree (profID, classID, mark))
(MAP-ROLE hasLevel haslevel (profID, classID, mark))
(MAP-ROLE hasIndustry hasindustry (profID, classID, years))
(MAP-ROLE hasJobTitle hasjobtitle (profID, classID, years))
(MAP-ROLE hasKnowledge hasknowledge (profID, classID, years))
(MAP-ROLE knowsLanguage knowslanguage (profID, classID, reading, verbal,
 writing))
(MAP-ROLE hasComplementarySkill hascomplementaryskill (profID, classID,
 years))
```

Fig. 19.4 Relational tables deriving from ontology mapping

designed to enable an ontology-based classification of profiles for making explicit differences between each retrieved candidate and submitted query. To this aim, a normalization procedure on each profile must be performed in order to put in evidence all the "information atoms" a single feature is made of. The normalized profile p_{norm} is obtained processing each feature by recursively applying the following rule: if a p_{norm} feature contains a concept C and in the ontology $\mathcal{O}$ there exists the axiom $C \sqsubseteq D$, then D is added to the feature.

Normalized profiles are stored in the table modeled by the (b) component of Fig. 19.3. Also in this case, profile features belonging to the same entry point are stored in the same table. Here, the use of a *many-to-many* relationship is not enough because, after normalization, the same "information atom" can occur many times in a profile as introduced by different features. Hence, a design issue is to properly allow the identification of features and rightly store the "information atoms" they are composed by. Tables named `<entrypoint>_full` (i.e., `hasknowledge_full`, `hasjobtitle_full`, `hasdegree_full`) contain normalized features corresponding to the related main category whereas an attribute is exploited (namely `groupID`) to label information referred to a specified feature. `groupID` can be considered as a partial key of `<entrypoint>_full` table since the atoms of a normalized feature are distributed in different tuples of the table itself but they have the same `groupID`. Finally, `value` is adopted for datatype properties quantification. `concept` contains both concepts and data properties in the ontology; they are exploited to describe profile features. Among attributes, a specific relevance is assumed by `level`. It indicates the *depth level* of the concept name (represented by one tuple) in the ontology (taxonomy). This attribute is needed for match explanation to more efficiently detect the most specific concept in a concept set (i.e., a set of features sharing the same `groupID`). Note that `level` is meaningful only when `conceptID` corresponds to a concept name.

In order to better clarify both usefulness and effectiveness of the previous E-R modeling w.r.t. skill and talent management domain, a toy profile description is proposed hereafter. Let us suppose *Jack* is searching for a job; his profile can be described as: "*Jack speaks English with a scholar level whereas he's doing better with written English. He has a degree in Computer Science Engineering, with mark equal to 110 (out of 110), an excellent experience in Java programming (5 years) and he is one year experienced in Web Design, ...*". *Jack*'s profile can be represented according to both *entry points* and *main categories* in Fig. 19.2:

- **hasDegree**: Computer Science Engineering (final mark = 110)
- **hasKnowledge**: Java (years of experience = 5); Web design (years of experience = 1)
- **knowsLanguage**: English (verbalLevel = 1, writingLevel = 2)

The previous profile will be normalized and split in components. So it is stored in proper tables. With reference to the model in Fig. 19.3, storage details are reported hereafter:

- *part* (a): a tuple is added to `hasdegree`, `hasknowledge`, `knowslanguage` tables, respectively. It contains a concept name and one or more data property values. Tuple stored in the `hasdegree` table is shown in Fig. 19.5;
- *part* (b): some tuples (the exact value depends on the depth of concept in the ontology) are added to tables `hasdegree_full`, `hasknowledge_full` and `knowslanguage_full`, respectively. Furthermore, a tuple is added for each information atom and data property value. Tuples stored in `hasdegree_full` table are reported in Fig. 19.6.

For the sake of clarity, in Fig. 19.3 we do not represent tables needed to store intermediate match results for computing the final explanation. After top-k retrieval, given a profile (labeled by a `profID`), denoting as i the i-th feature of the *reformulated* top-k query, i belongs to a specific entry point. Hence, the system stores all

profile			
profID	*FirstName*	*LastName*	...
1	Jack	Sparrow	...

hasdegree		
profID	*classID*	*mark*
1	29	110
...	...	...

degree	
degID	*name*
29	Computer_Science_Engineering
...	...

Fig. 19.5 `profile`, `hasdegree` and `degree` tables for Jack's profile

hasdegree_full			
profID	*groupID*	*conceptID*	*value*
1	1	30	null
1	1	56	null
1	1	16	null
1	1	4	110
...	...	...	...

concept		
concepID	*name*	*level*
4	mark	null
16	Degree	1
30	Computer_Science_Engineering	3
56	Engineering_Degree	2
...	...	...

Fig. 19.6 `hasdegree_full` and `concept` tables for Jack's normalized profile

the *normalized* profile tuples containing at least the concept name in *i* in a proper auxiliary table just named `<entrypoint>_full_i`. For example, if the recruiter is looking for "a candidate having an Engineering Degree with a final mark equal or higher than 103 (out of 110)" and she selects a profile from the top-k answer set for the explanation, then the system will retrieve all the tuples satisfying the query feature for the specific `profID` from the `hasdegree_full` table. Those tuples will be materialized in the `hasdegree_full_1` table created at runtime.

Given a `profID`, considering each feature *i* in the *reformulated* top-k query and the corresponding `<entrypoint>_ full` and `<entrypoint>_full_i` tables, the system will compute the following classes of features:

1. **fulfilled**: all the features in `<entrypoint>_full_i` table are de-normalized according to `level` value of concepts sharing a `groupID`. The resulting tuples represent the so called *fulfilled features*. In this class, duplicate features can exist so the class has to be preprocessed before showing it to the user (see `Object Oriented Programming` feature in Fig. 19.10 for a concrete example);
2. **additional**: given a `groupID` collection, if there exists a concept in the related `<entrypoint>_full` table with a `level` higher than the one in the query and/or if there is a data property not specified in the query itself, these "information atoms" are classified as *additional features*. Features not required by the user but considered as significant for the skill domain also belong to this set of features. Particularly, all the features stored in `<hasknowedge>_full` table not required in the whole user query (i.e., not only in a query feature) are also presented as additional features. However, the system distinguishes between these two different kind of additional features (see Fig. 19.9);
3. **conflicting**: given a `groupID` collection, if there exists a data property in the `<entrypoint>_full_i` table lower than the one required by a query feature, that "information atoms" are classified as *conflicting features*;
4. **underspecified**: if all the concept names and/or data properties required by the query are lacking in the corresponding `<entrypoint>_full_i` table, the missing "information atoms" are classified as *underspecified features*.

Obviously, in case of query features settled as "strict requirements" only *fulfilled features* have to be considered whereas *additional* ones are optional.

19.3.3 Query Process (by Example)

Let us consider a recruiter looking for "*a candidate having an Engineering Degree* (*possibly with a final mark equal or higher than 103* (*out of 110*)). *A Ph.D. is preferred and a good ability to write in English is required. She should be at least six years experienced in Java and she should have complex problem solving capabilities*". Such a job request, can be summarized as:

1. Strictly required constraints:
   a. Engineering degree;

2. Preferences:
   a. Engineering degree final mark ≥ 103;
   b. Doctoral Degree;
   c. Java programming and experience ≥ 6 years;
   d. Complex problem solving capabilities;
   e. Good written English.

In the following, we show how the approach we propose can provide an answer to the above request w.r.t. to the data-set in Appendix B, made up by ten candidates whose profile has been chosen to evidence peculiarities of our approach:

- 8 out of 10 selected profiles include features covering all introduced categories in order to show how the proposed modeling allows to convey most information needed in real-world recruitment;
- two candidates (*Carla Buono* and *Marcello Cannone*) do not fulfill strict requirements specified in the query and then they will not be part of the final result set;
- a small subset of candidate sample is made up by people (*Mario Rossi*, *Daniela Bianchi* and *Elena Pomarico*) with similar profiles: their CVs only differ by experience years associated to job titles, enterprise working or exploitation of a given competence. Such a choice allows us to make clear how these differences, even slight, cause profiles to be differently ranked by the scoring mechanism and evaluated by the match explanation facilities;
- three candidates (*Lucio Battista*, *Mariangela Porro* and *Nicola Marco*) satisfy only a few characteristics other than strict requirements. The scoring mechanism will rank them lower than profiles better filling query preferences (*Domenico De Palo* and *Carmelo Piccolo*);
- two profiles (*Mario Rossi* and *Carmelo Piccolo*) include features slightly conflicting with query preferences. In the match explanation phase they will be automatically highlighted;
- many selected profiles have additional features w.r.t. the query. They will be presented in the match explanation.

`I.M.P.A.K.T.` provides a graphical interface to compose the recruiter's requests: Fig. 19.7 shows such a GUI reporting the example query description. In the menu (a), all the entry points are listed; panel (b) allows to search for ontology concepts according to their meaning; section (c) enables the user to explore both taxonomy and properties of a selected concept. Entry points in menu (a) represent main classes and relationships in Fig. 19.2. Once an item is selected in panel (c), the corresponding menu is dynamically filled and added to panel (d) enumerating the features requested in the query. For each of them, the GUI allows: (1) to define if the feature is a strict one—panel (f)—or if it is a preference—panel (c); (2) to delete the whole feature; (3) to complete the description showing all the elements (concepts, object properties and data properties) that could be added to the selected feature; (4) to edit either each feature atom or existing data property values. In what fol-

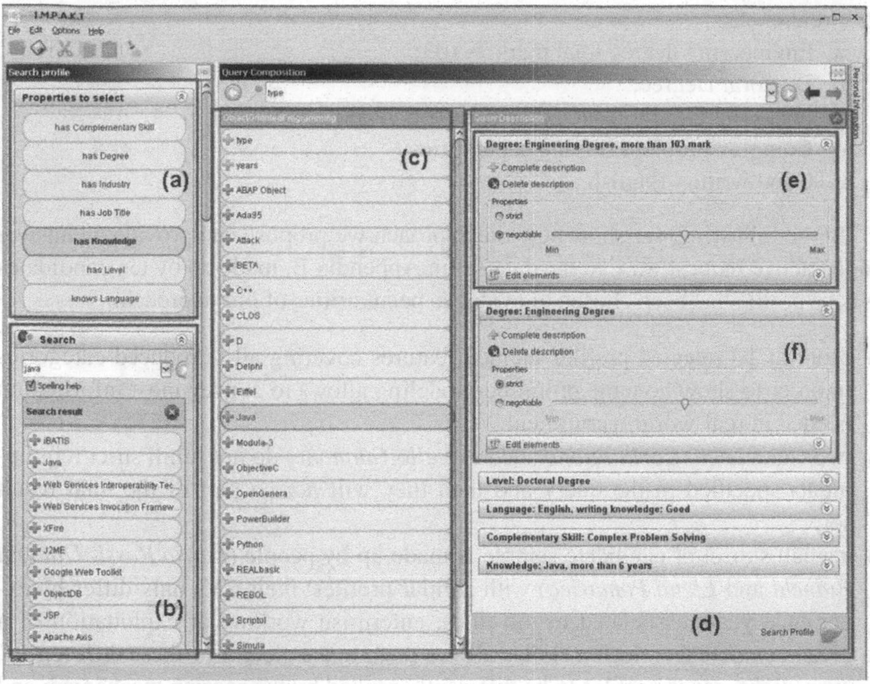

Fig. 19.7 Query composition GUI

lows, we report the formalization of the job request according to the query language introduced in Sect. 19.2, aimed at top-k retrieval:

```
q(id, lastName)
←
profileLastName(id, lastName),
hasDegree(id, degreeId, mark), degreeName(degreeId, degreeName), Engineering_Degree(degreeId),
hasLevel(id, levelId, levelmark), levelName(levelId, levelName),
knowsLanguage(id, lanID, Reading, Verbal, Writing), languageName(langID, langName),
hasKnowledge(id, classID, years, type, level), knowledgeName(classID, hasKnowledge),
hasComplementarySkill(id, classID2)skillName(classID2, capabilities)

OrderBy(s = rs(mark; 102, 110) · 0.166 + pref1(levelName; Doctoral_Degree) · 0.166+
pref1(langName; English) · pref4(Writing; NotSpecified/1.0, Basic/3.0, Good/6.0, Excellent/9.0) · 0.166+
rs(years; 5, 10) · pref1(hasKnowledge; Java) · 0.166+
pref1(capabilities; Complex_Problem_Solving) · 0.166)
```

19.3.4 Match Explanation

Figure 19.8(a) shows how the I.M.P.A.K.T. GUI renders match explanation result. Candidates are sorted by their score. Noteworthy, only eight candidates are

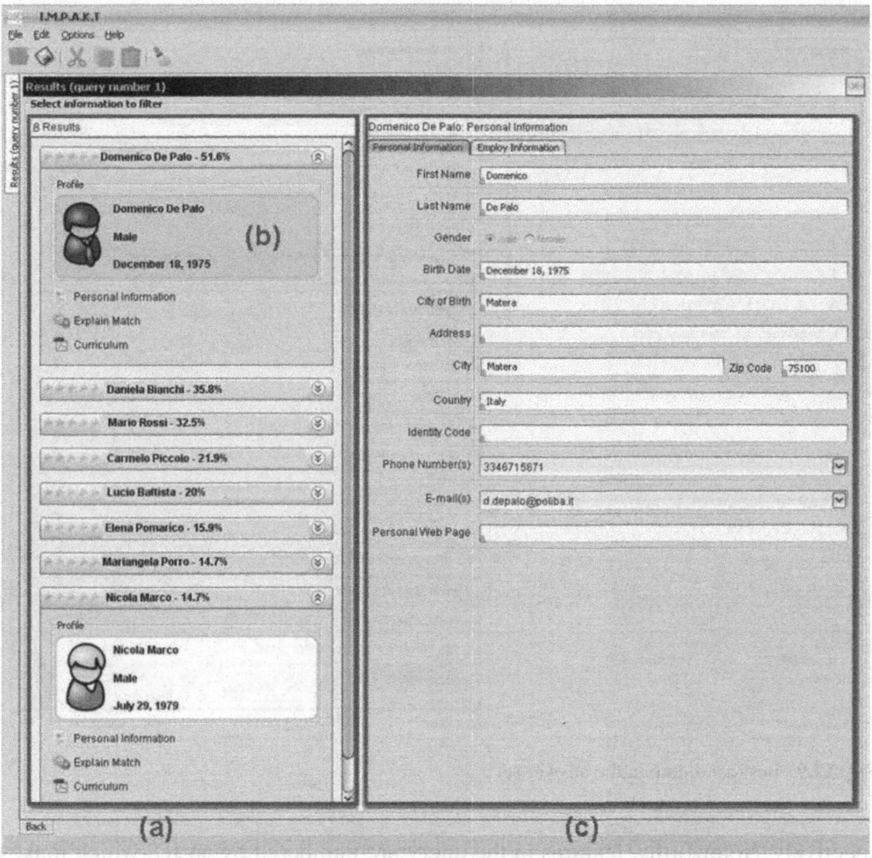

Fig. 19.8 Informative top-k retrieval answer set

retrieved, given that neither *Carla Buono* nor *Marcello Cannone* have an Engineering Degree, which is strictly required by the query. Detailed information about the two candidates can be shown expanding related panels as in Fig. 19.8(b). Three options are made available for each retrieved candidate: (i) *personal information*, (ii) *textual CV*, (iii) *explain match*.

By selecting view (i), the panel displayed in Fig. 19.8(c) is shown on the right side of the GUI. It gathers both personal and employ information related to the selected candidate. View (ii) allows the rendering of textual CV of the selected candidate. In view (iii), query and selected profiles are graphically compared. In Fig. 19.9, the best (*Domenico De Palo*) retrieved profile in the answer set is examined, in order to explain the retrieval results. On the contrary, Fig. 19.10 shows a comparison between *Mario Rossi*'s profile and the example query. Here, conflicting features are identified and shown to the end user.

We explain how query/result comparison behaves with the aid of Fig. 19.9. Panels (a) and (b) sum up strict requirements and preferences in the original query, re-

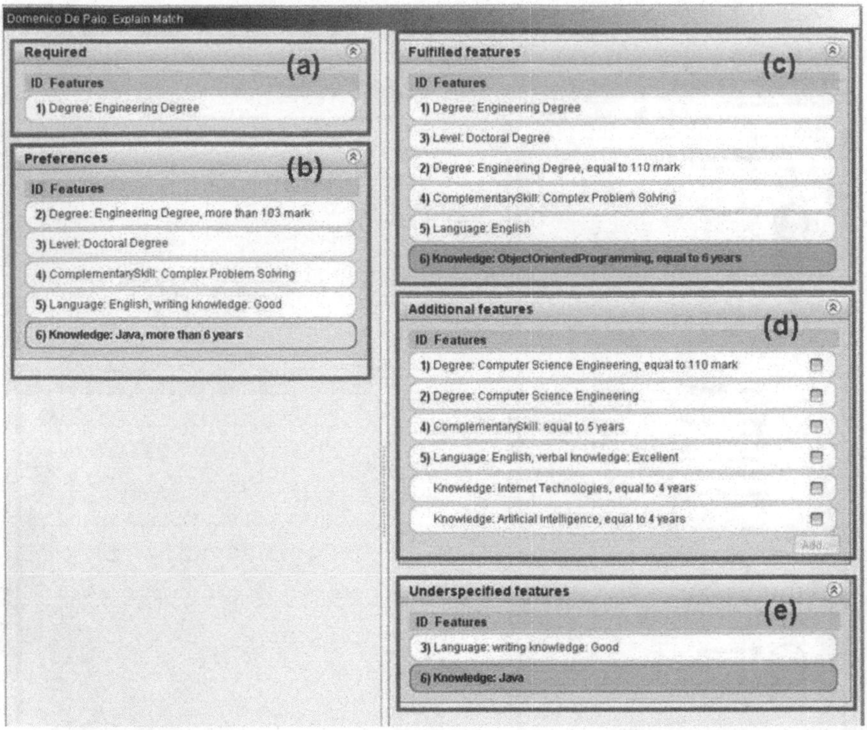

Fig. 19.9 Best candidate in the answer set

spectively. Noteworthy, features in the query are numbered by an ID, which makes easier to identify them while comparing the retrieved profiles. The remaining of the GUI shows the following information:

- Panel (c) shows *fulfilled features*, i.e., features required with the query and either perfectly matched by the candidate or slightly conflicting in her profile;
- Panel (d) provides *additional features*, i.e., technical skills in the candidate CV not required at all by the query or more specific than the required ones;
- Panel (e) gathers *underspecified features*, i.e., parts of the query not explicitly specified in the retrieved CV.

The presentation of comparison results makes use of feature IDs: the ID of the related feature in the query is assigned to each fulfilled and underspecified characteristic in the profile; the same presentation is provided in case of additional characteristics. For example, by looking at Fig. 19.9(c), we can assert that *Domenico De Palo* almost completely fulfills query features from 1 to 6, even though preference 3 (Java Programming) and preference 5 (good writing English knowledge) result underspecified (see panel (e)). In fact, *Domenico De Palo* has 6 years experience in object oriented programming (a direct ancestor of Java programming in the reference ontology), and he knows English, even though nothing is specified within

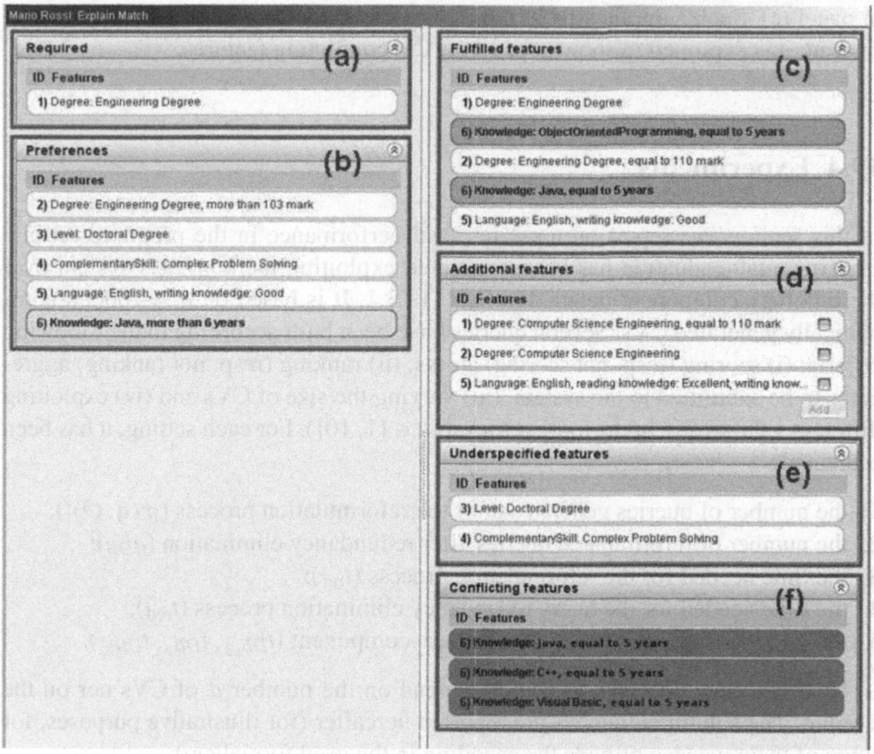

Fig. 19.10 Candidate in the answer set with conflicting features

his CV about competence in writing English documents. It is noteworthy that by clicking on a query feature in (a) or (b), the GUI automatically highlights all characteristics labeled by the same ID in panels (c), (d) and (e). Finally, let us have a look to panel (d). *Domenico De Palo* has several additional features w.r.t. the query, either related to elicited preferences and requirements (numbered features in (d)) or to other profile competencies (not numbered features in (d)). By looking at feature 1 in (d), for example, it can be noticed that the candidate is not only an Engineer, as required by the recruiter, but he is a Computer Science Engineer with full marks. Moreover, he has 4 years of knowledge in *Internet Technologies* and *Artificial Intelligence*, and this could be an added value for the recruiter, even if it was not explicitly asked for. Figure 19.10 represents an explanation of the match between *Mario Rossi*'s CV and the example query. Let us consider feature 6 in the query: "*at least six years of Java experience*". By looking at Fig. 19.10(c), it can be noticed that *Mario Rossi* is 5 years experienced in Java and Object Oriented Programming. Such a conflict is highlighted in the GUI as shown in Fig. 19.10(f) so making the recruiter aware of profile features slightly conflicting with the query. Notice that the same preference (i.e., the one identified by ID 6) generates two information atoms in panel (c). Such a duplication in fulfilled features does not introduce redundancy. Instead, it is exploited to show in panel (f) CV conflicting features.

19.4 Experiments

In this section, we report on top-k retrieval performance in the proposed setting. Experimental evaluation has been conducted exploiting the *SoftFacts* system over the ontology component detailed in Sect. 19.3.1. It is based on $d = 100000$ automatically generated CVs. Several queries have been built according to the following criteria: (i) scoring (resp. not scoring) atoms, (ii) ranking (resp. not ranking) aggregates to be submitted to the system, (iii) varying the size of CVs and (iv) exploiting different values for k in the top-k retrieval ($k \in \{1, 10\}$). For each setting, it has been evaluated:

1. the number of queries generated after the reformulation process ($|r(\mathbf{q}, \mathcal{O})|$);
2. the number of reformulated queries after redundancy elimination (q_{DB});
3. the time needed for the reformulation process (t_{ref});
4. the time needed for the query redundancy elimination process (t_{red});
5. the query answering time of the database component ($t_{DB_{\text{all}}}, t_{DB_1}, t_{DB_{10}}$).

Note that measures in 1–4 neither depend on the number d of CVs nor on the k value. The submitted queries are reported hereafter (for illustrative purposes, for some of them we also provide the encoding in the used formalism):

1. Retrieve CV referred to candidates with some competences about Engineering Technology.

```
q(id, lastName, hasKnowledge, Years)
← profileLastName(id, lastName),
   hasKnowledge(id, classID, Years, Type, Level),
   knowledgeName(classID, hasKnowledge),
   Engineering_and_Technology(classID)
```

2. Retrieve CV referred to candidates with an Engineering degree.
3. Retrieve CV referred to candidates with a competence in Artificial Intelligence, having a degree with final mark greater than 100/110.
4. Retrieve CV referred to candidates with a competence in Artificial Intelligence, having an Engineering degree with final mark greater than 100/110.
5. Retrieve CV referred to candidates experienced in Information Systems (at least 15 years), having a degree with final mark greater than 100.
6. Retrieve top-k CV referred to candidates with a competence in Artificial Intelligence, having a degree with final mark scored according to a right-shoulder fuzzy function $rs(mark; 100, 110)$.

```
q(id, lastName, degreeName, mark, hasKnowledge, years)
← profileLastName(id, lastName), hasDegree(id, degreeId, mark), degreeName(degreeId, degreeName),
   hasKnowledge(id, classID, years, type, level), knowledgeName(classID, hasKnowledge),
   Artificial_Intelligence(classID), OrderBy(s = rs(mark; 100, 110))
```

7. Retrieve CV referred to candidates having an Engineering degree with final mark scored according to $rs(mark; 100, 110)$.
8. Retrieve top-k CV referred to candidates with a competence in Artificial Intelligence, having an Engineering degree with final mark scored according to $rs(mark; 100, 110)$.
9. Retrieve CV referred to candidates with a competence in Information Systems, having an Engineering degree with final mark and years of experience both scored according to $rs(mark; 100, 110) \cdot 0.4 + rs(years; 15, 25) \cdot 0.6$.
10. Retrieve CV referred to candidates with a good competence in Artificial Intelligence. Final mark, years and experience level are scored according to the function $rs(mark; 100, 110) \cdot 0.4 + rs(years; 15, 25) \cdot pref(level; Good/0.6, Excellent/1.0) \cdot 0.6$.

```
q(id, lastName, degreeName, mark, hasKnowledge, years, kType)
← profileLastName(id, lastName), hasDegree(id, degreeId, mark), degreeName(degreeId, degreeName),
   hasKnowledge(id, classID, years, type, level), knowledgeLevelName(level, kType), Good(level),
   knowledgeName(classID, hasKnowledge), Artificial_Intelligence(classID),
   OrderBy(s = rs(mark; 100, 110) · 0.4 + rs(years; 15, 25) · pref(level; Good/0.6, Excellent/1.0) · 0.6)
```

11. Retrieve CV referred to candidates with a competence in Artificial Intelligence, grouped by $MAX[rs(mark; 100, 110) \cdot 0.4 + rs(years; 15, 25) \cdot 0.6]$.

```
q(id, lastName)
← profileLastName(id, lastName), hasDegree(id, degreeId, mark),
   hasKnowledge(id, classID, years, type, level), Artificial_Intelligence(classID),
   GroupBy(id, lastname), OrderBy(s = MAX[rs(mark; 100, 110) · 0.4 + rs(years; 15, 25) · 0.6])
```

12. Retrieve CV referred to candidates with a competence in Artificial Intelligence, having an Engineering degree, grouped by $AVG(rs(mark; 100, 110) \cdot 0.4 + rs(years; 15, 25) \cdot 0.6)$.

Queries 1–5 are *crisp* since they do not involve any fuzzy predicate. As each answer scores 1.0, we would like to verify whether there is a difference between the retrieval time of all records and the one of just the best k. The remaining queries are top-k ones. In query 9, an example of score combination is shown, with a preference on the experience years. In query 10, we use the following preference scoring function: $pref(level; Good/0.6, Excellent/1.0)$, which returns either 0.6 if *level* is *Good* or 1.0 if *level* is *Excellent*. Queries 11 and 12 use ranking aggregates.

Table 19.1 Retrieval statistics

Size 100000

Query	All	top-1	top-10	$\|ans(\mathcal{K}, q)\|$	$\|r(\mathbf{q}, \mathcal{O})\|$	q_{DB}	t_{ref}	t_{red}	$t_{DB_{\text{all}}}$	t_{DB_1}	$t_{DB_{10}}$
1	7.507	2.489	2.581	3985	1599	1066	1.723	0.010	5.738	0.203	0.258
2	0.193	0.036	0.037	445	69	46	0.016	0.001	0.137	0.017	0.039
3	0.164	0.030	0.066	19	18	12	0.006	0.001	0.126	0.015	0.057
4	3.194	2.143	3.155	8	1242	552	2.072	0.015	1.075	0.106	0.875
5	0.348	0.067	0.186	19	75	50	0.027	0.001	0.300	0.021	0.141
6	0.114	0.052	0.102	93	18	12	0.005	0.001	0.088	0.036	0.082
7	0.207	0.053	0.146	445	69	46	0.013	0.001	0.166	0.014	0.118
8	3.090	2.353	3.080	21	1242	552	1.242	0.013	1.306	0.512	1.125
9	22.764	22.702	22.754	91	5175	2300	17.850	0.058	4.819	4.604	4.766
10	0.759	0.378	0.369	40	108	48	0.229	0.003	0.498	0.159	0.145
11	0.105	0.100	0.101	37	18	12	0.004	0.001	0.075	0.072	0.074
12	2.2	2.038	2.128	15	828	552	0.794	0.005	1.370	1.296	1.128
Average	3.834	3.0303	3.248	516.6	961.5	468.4	2.318	0.01	1.4053	0.601	0.761
Median	0.0554	0.223	0.278	65.5	91.5	49	0.128	0.002	0.399	0.133	0.143

Tests have been performed on a MacPro PC equipped with a 2×3 GHz Dual-Core processor and 9 GB RAM with Mac OS X 10.5.5 onboard. Results are shown in Table 19.1 (time is expressed in seconds). Some consideration can be made about experimental outcomes:

- the response time is always acceptable if one takes into account the non negligible ontology size, the relevant number of CVs and the lacking of any indexation for relational tables;
- if the answer set is large (as in the case of query 1), there is a significant drop in response time for the top-k case;
- for each query, the response time increases while the retrieved records increase;
- the set size of reformulated queries $|r(\mathbf{q}, \mathcal{O})|$ may be non negligible, hence the redundancy elimination could remove almost one-third of the original set. Nevertheless the time needed for reduction phase is negligible;
- the database answering time increases with the number of top-k results to be retrieved.

Note that for query 9, most of time is spent for query reformulation phase.

19.5 Related Work

In this section, we gather approaches to Human Resources retrieval related to our proposal, both in terms of research investigations and prototype tools.

19.5.1 Research Approaches

Several approaches have been presented, where databases allow users and applications to access both ontologies and other structured data in a seamless way. Das et al. [7] developed a system that stores OWL-Lite and OWL-DL ontologies in Oracle RDBMSs, and that provides a set of SQL operators for ontology-based matching. *Jena 2 Ontology Stores* [23], *Sesame* [2] and *Oracle RDF Store* use a three columns relational table $\langle Subject, Property, Object \rangle$ to memorize RDF triples. In spite of the same storing model, these systems present different inference capabilities among them. Other ontology storage systems—such as *DLDB* [17] and *Sesame on PostgreSQL* [2]—adopt binary tables. They create a table for each class in an ontology. A possible optimization is to cache the classification hierarchy in the database and to provide tables maintaining all the subsumption relationships between primitive concepts. This happens for example in *Instance Store* (***iS***) [1], a system for reasoning over OWL KBs specifically adopted in biomedical-informatics domains. ***iS*** is also able—by means of a hybrid reasoner/database approach—to reply to instance retrieval queries w.r.t. an ontology, given a set of axioms asserting class-instance relationships. A comparison between ***iS*** and the approach we present here show the former reduces instance retrieval to pure TBox reasoning and it is able to return only exact matches whilst we use an enriched relational schema storing only the ABox (i.e., facts) in order to provide a logic-based ranked list of results and the not classified ontology. Other systems using RDBMS to deal with large amounts of data are *QuOnto*[4] and *Owlgres*.[5] They are DL-Lite reasoners providing consistency checking and conjunctive query services. Neither QuOnto nor OWLgres returns a ranked list of results. SHER ([9, 10]) is a highly-scalable OWL reasoner performing both membership and conjunctive query answering over large relational datasets using ontologies modeled in a subset of OWL-DL without nominals. It relies on an indexing technique summarizing database instances into a compact representation used for reasoning. It works by selectively uncompressing portions of the summarized representation relevant for the query, in a process called refinement. SHER uses Pellet to reason over the summarized data it enables motivations for data inconsistency. SHER allows for getting fast incomplete answers to queries, but it does not provide a ranked list of results.

Top-k queries [3] ensure an efficient ranking support in RDBMSs letting the system to provide only a subset of query results, according to a user-specified ordering function (which generally aggregates multiple ranking criteria). The algebra is implemented by means of both an efficient query execution model [3] and new physical rank-aware operators [13] where rank relations are processed incrementally. RankSQL [14] is the first RDBMS that fully integrates a ranking support as a first-class functionality. In other systems, basically the user adopts terms like *ideal*, *good* for expressing her preferences and *high*, *medium* for setting the relevance she

---

[4] http://www.dis.uniroma1.it/~quonto/.

[5] http://pellet.owldl.com/owlgres/.

assigns to a ranking criterion. SQLf [16] is another SQL extension to cope with user preferences. It allows to formulate queries on atomic conditions defined by fuzzy sets. Each attribute of a tuple is associated to a satisfaction degree μ in [0, 1].

19.5.2 Commercial Tools

Currently, several commercial tools for talent management and e-recruitment are available. Most of them are enterprise suites supporting human resource management, including solutions that, even though improving the recruitment process by means of innovative media and tools, do not have a significant novelty charge. Available solutions in fact exploit databases to store candidate's personal and employment information, and do not ground on a logic-based structure. To the best of our knowledge, one of the few logic-based solutions for recruitment and referral process is STAIRS, a system in use at US Navy Department allowing to retrieve referral lists of best qualified candidates w.r.t. a specific mansion, according to the number of required skills they match. The commercial software supporting STAIRS is RESUMIX[6] an automated staffing tool making use of artificial intelligence techniques and adopted only as an internal tool. The system allows also to distinguish skills in *required* and *desired* ones in the query formulation: all required skills must be matched by the retrieved candidate, differently from *desired* ones. Among semantic-based tools for recruitment, noteworthy are products offered by Sovren,[7] which provide solutions for parsing both CV and job requests starting from several text formats to HR-XML schema. A semantic-based matchmaking engine automatically returns a ranked list of best candidates given a job vacation, posted in any textual format. The matching process is by the way completely hidden to the recruiter, which does not receive any explanation about retrieved results. Sovren tools also manage the distinction between required and preferred skills in job offers posting.

Appendix A: Ontology Axioms Excerpts

Excerpt of Degree and Level classes hierarchy

```
(IMPLIES Engineering_Degree Degree)
(IMPLIES Computer_Science_Engineering Engineering_Degree)
(IMPLIES Managerial_Engineering Engineering_Degree)
(IMPLIES Electronics_Engineering Engineering_Degree)
```

[6]http://www.cpol.army.mil.

[7]http://www.sovren.com/default.aspx.

```
(IMPLIES Mechanical_Engineering Engineering_Degree)
(IMPLIES Statistics Mathematical_Sciences)
(IMPLIES Mathematical_Sciences Degree)
(IMPLIES Management_degree Social_Studies)
(IMPLIES Social_Studies Degree)

(IMPLIES Doctoral_Degree Level)
(IMPLIES Master_Degree Level)
(IMPLIES Master_after_master Level)
(IMPLIES Secondary_School)
(IMPLIES Bachelor Level)
(IMPLIES CCDP Design_Certification)
(IMPLIES Design_Certification Cisco)
(IMPLIES Cisco Certification)
(IMPLIES Certification Level)
```

Excerpt of Job Title and Industry classes hierarchy

```
(IMPLIES Database_Administrator Computer_Specialist)
(IMPLIES Network_and_Computer_Systems_Administrator Computer_Specialist)
(IMPLIES Computer_Specialist Computer_and_Mathematical_Occupation)
(IMPLIES Computer_and_Mathematical_Occupation Job_Title)
(IMPLIES Training_and_Development_Manager Human_Resources_Manager)
(IMPLIES Human_Resources_Manager Manager)
(IMPLIES Project_Manager Manager)
(IMPLIES Manager Job_Title)
(IMPLIES Cost_Estimators Business_Operation_Specialist)
(IMPLIES Business_Operation_Specialist
                              Business_and_Financial_Operations_Occupation)
(IMPLIES Business_and_Financial_Operations_Occupation Job_Title)
(IMPLIES Budget_Analysts Financial_Specialist)
(IMPLIES Financial_Specialist Business_and_Financial_Operations_Occupation)
(IMPLIES Patternmaker_Metal_and_Plastic
                              Model_Makers_and_Patternmakers_Metal_and_Plastic)
(IMPLIES Model_Makers_and_Patternmakers_Metal_and_Plastic
                              Metal_Workers_and_Plastic_Workers)
(IMPLIES Metal_Workers_and_Plastic_Workers Production_Occupation)
(IMPLIES Production_Occupation Job_Title)
(IMPLIES ProcessPlanner Job_Title)
(IMPLIES Teachers Job_Title)

(IMPLIES Banking_and_Consumer_Lending Banking)
(IMPLIES Banking Industry)
(IMPLIES IT_and_Telematics_Applications Industry)
(IMPLIES Business_Strategic_Management Business)
(IMPLIES Business Socio-economic_development_models_economic_aspects)
(IMPLIES Socio-economic_development_models_economic_aspects
                              Social_and_Economics)
(IMPLIES Social_and_Economics Industry)
(IMPLIES Finance_Banking Financial_Services)
(IMPLIES Financial_Services Socio-economic_development_models_economic_aspects)
(IMPLIES Sales Industry)
(IMPLIES Engineering_Services Industry)
(IMPLIES Clothing_and_Textile_Manufacturing Industrial_Manufacture)
(IMPLIES Industrial_Manufacture
                              Industrial_Manufacturing_Material_and_Transport)
(IMPLIES Industrial_Manufacturing_Material_and_Transport Industry)
```

Excerpt of Knowledge classes hierarchy

```
(IMPLIES Engineering_and_Technology Knowledge)
(IMPLIES Computer_Science_Skill Engineering_and_Technology)
(IMPLIES Artificial_Intelligence Computer_Science_Skill)
(IMPLIES Information_Systems Computer_Science_Skill)
(IMPLIES Java Object_Oriented_Programming)
(IMPLIES Cplusplus Object_Oriented_Programming)
(IMPLIES Visual_Basic Object_Oriented_Programming)
(IMPLIES Object_Oriented_Programming Programming_Languages)
(IMPLIES Programming_Languages Software_Development)
(IMPLIES Software_Development Computer_Science_Skill)
(IMPLIES Fuzzy Artificial_Intelligence)
(IMPLIES Data_Mining Artificial_Intelligence)
(IMPLIES Machine_Learning Artificial_Intelligence)
(IMPLIES Knowledge_Representation Artificial_Intelligence)
(IMPLIES Natural_Language Artificial_Intelligence)
(IMPLIES DBMS Information_Systems)
(IMPLIES Information_Systems Computer_Science_SKill)
(IMPLIES Internet_Technologies Computer_Science_SKill)
(IMPLIES Web_Technologies Development_Technologies)
(IMPLIES Workflow_Management Engineering_and_Technology)
(IMPLIES VBScript Script_Languages)
(IMPLIES Script_Languages Programming_Languages)
(IMPLIES Development_Technologies Software_Developmnent)
(IMPLIES Sales_and_Marketing Business_and_Management)
(IMPLIES Business_and_Management Knowledge)
(IMPLIES Administration_and_Management Business_and_Management)
(IMPLIES Economics_and_Accounting Business_and_Management)
(IMPLIES ProcessPerformanceMonitoring Managerial_Skill)
(IMPLIES Managerial_Skill Business_and_Management)
(IMPLIES Mathematics Mathematics_and_Science)
(IMPLIES Mathematics_and_Science Knowledge)
```

Excerpt of Complementary Skills and Language knowledge hierarchy

```
(IMPLIES Complex_Problem_Solving_Skills Cross_Functional_Skills)
(IMPLIES Cross_Functional_Skills Worker_Requirements)
(IMPLIES Worker_Requirements Skill)
(IMPLIES Cooperation Interpersonal_Orientation)
(IMPLIES Interpersonal_Orientation Work_Styles)
(IMPLIES Work_Styles Worker_Characteristics)
(IMPLIES Worker_Characteristics Skill)
(IMPLIES Leadership Social_Influence)
(IMPLIES Social_Influence Work_Styles)
(IMPLIES Learning_Strategies Process)
(IMPLIES Process Basic_Skills)
(IMPLIES Basic_Skills Worker_Requirements)
(IMPLIES Critical_Thinking Process)
(IMPLIES Monitoring Process)
(IMPLIES Visualization Spatial_Abilities)
(IMPLIES Spatial_Abilities Cognitive_Abilities)
(IMPLIES Cognitive_Abilities Abilities)
(IMPLIES Abilities Worker_Characteristics)
(IMPLIES Spatial_Orientation Spatial_Abilities)
(IMPLIES Verbal_Abilities Cognitive_Abilities)
(IMPLIES Systems_Skills Cross_Functional_Skills)
(IMPLIES Visual_Color_Discrimination Visual_Abilities)
(IMPLIES Visual_Abilities Sensory_Abilities)
(IMPLIES Sensory_Abilities Psychomotor_Abilities)
(IMPLIES Psychomotor_Abilities Worker_Characteristics)
```

```
(IMPLIES English Language)
(IMPLIES French Language)
(IMPLIES German Language)
```

Appendix B: Example Candidate Profiles Set

1. **Mario Rossi**
    - *Degree*: Computer Science Engineering, mark 110
    - *Level*: Secondary School (mark 60), Master Degree
    - *JobTitle*: Database Administrator (4 years), Project Manager (2 years)
    - *Industry*: Banking (4 years), IT and Telematics Applications (2 years)
    - *Knowledge*: Cplusplus (5 years), Java (5 years), Visual Basic (5 years)
    - *ComplementarySkill*: Cooperation (5 years), LeaderShip (5 years)
    - *Language*: English (excellent writing, verbal and reading), French (good writing)
2. **Daniela Bianchi**
    - *Degree*: Computer Science Engineering (mark 110)
    - *Level*: Secondary School (mark 60), Bachelor
    - *JobTitle*: Database administrator (4 years), Project Manager (2 years)
    - *Industry*: Banking (4 years), IT and Telematics Applications (2 years)
    - *Knowledge*: Cplusplus (2 years), Java (6 years), Visual Basic (1 years)
    - *ComplementarySkill*: Cooperation (5 years), LeaderShip (5 years)
    - *Language*: English (excellent verbal, writing and reading), French (good writing)
3. **Lucio Battista**
    - *Degree*: Managerial Engineering (mark 104)
    - *Level*: Secondary School (mark 60), Master Degree, CCDP
    - *JobTitle*: Database Administrator (4 years), Project Manager (2 years)
    - *Industry*: Banking (4 years), IT and Telematics Applications (2 years)
    - *Knowledge*: DBMS (2 years)
    - *ComplementarySkill*: Cooperation (5 years), LeaderShip (5 years)
    - *Language*: English (excellent verbal, writing and reading), French (good writing)
4. **Mariangela Porro**
    - *Degree*: Managerial Engineering (mark 104)
    - *Level*: Secondary School (mark 60), Master Degree, Master after master
    - *JobTitle*: Database Administrator (4 years), Network computer systems Administrator (4 years)
    - *Industry*: Banking (4 years), IT and Telematics Applications (2 years)

- *Knowledge*: DBMS (2 years), Web Technologies (2 years)
- *ComplementarySkill*: Learning Strategy (8 years)
- *Language*: English (good verbal, writing and reading)

5. **Nicola Marco**
   - *Degree*: Electronics Engineering (mark 104)
   - *Level*: Bachelor, Master after Master
   - *JobTitle*: Database Administrator (2 years), Network computer systems Administrator (2 years)
   - *Industry*: Banking (4 years), IT and Telematics Applications (2 years)
   - *Knowledge*: DBMS (5 years), Web Technologies (5 years)
   - *ComplementarySkill*: Learning Strategy (8 years)
   - *Language*: English (good writing, verbal and reading)
6. **Carla Buono**
   - *Degree*: Statistics (mark 106)
   - *Level*: Master Degree, Master after Master
   - *JobTitle*: Cost Estimator (4 years), Budget Analysts (10 years)
   - *Industry*: Banking (4 years), Business Strategic Management (2 years), Finance Banking (1 years)
   - *Knowledge*: Sales and Marketing (2 years), Administration and Management (4 years), Mathematics (10 years)
   - *ComplementarySkill*: Critical thinking (8 years), monitoring (8 years)
   - *Language*: English (excellent writing, verbal and reading knowledge), French (good writing knowledge)
7. **Marcello Cannone**
   - *Degree*: Management Degree (mark 106)
   - *JobTitle*: Training and Development Manager (2 years)
   - *Industry*: Sales, Banking and Consumer Lending
   - *Knowledge*: Economics and Accounting (4 years), WorkflowManagement
   - *ComplementarySkill*: Visualization, Spatial orientation, Verbal abilities
   - *Language*: English, German (excellent writing and reading knowledge, basic verbal knowledge)
8. **Carmelo Piccolo**
   - *Degree*: Mechanical Engineering (mark 79)
   - *JobTitle*: Patternmaker Metal and Plastic, Process Planner (6 years)
   - *Industry*: Engineering Services (14 years), Clothing and Textile Manufacturing (11 years)
   - *Knowledge*: VBScript, Process Performance Monitoring
   - *ComplementarySkill*: Systems Skills, Complex problem solving (10 years), Visual Color Discrimination (14 years)
   - *Language*: English (basic writing knowledge), French (excellent reading knowledge)

9. **Elena Pomarico**
    - *Degree*: Computer Science Engineering
    - *Level*: Secondary School, Bachelor
    - *JobTitle*: Database Administrator, Project Manager
    - *Industry*: Banking, IT and Telematics Applications
    - *Knowledge*: CplusPlus, Java, Visual Basic
    - *ComplementarySkill*: Cooperation, Leadership
    - *Language*: English (excellent writing, reading and verbal knowledge), French (good writing knowledge)

10. **Domenico De Palo**
    - *Degree*: Computer Science Engineering (mark 110)
    - *Level*: Doctoral Degree
    - *JobTitle*: Project Manager (4 years), Teachers (4 years), Database Administrator (4 years)
    - *Knowledge*: OOprogramming (6 years), Artificial intelligence (4 years), Internet technologies (4 years)
    - *ComplementarySkill*: Cooperation (6 years), Complex problem solving (5 years)
    - *Language*: English (excellent verbal knowledge)

References

1. Bechhofer, S., Horrocks, I., Turi, D.: The OWL instance store: system description. In: The 20th International Conference on Automated Deduction (CADE '05), pp. 177–181 (2005)
2. Broekstra, J., Kampman, A., van Harmelen, F.: Sesame: a generic architecture for storing and querying RDF and RDF schema. In: The First International Semantic Web Conference (ISWC '02), pp. 54–68. Springer, Berlin (2002)
3. Li, C., Chang, K.C.-C., Ilyas, I.F., Song, S.: RankSQL: Query Algebra and Optimization for Relational Top-k Queries, pp. 131–142. ACM, New York (2005)
4. Calvanese, D., De Giacomo, G., Lembo, D., Lenzerini, M., Rosati, R.: Data complexity of query answering in description logics. In: Proceedings of the Tenth International Conference on Principles of Knowledge Representation and Reasoning (KR-06), pp. 260–270 (2006)
5. Chang, K.C.C., won Hwang, S.: Minimal probing: Supporting expensive predicates for top-k queries. In: SIGMOD Conference (2002). citeseer.ist.psu.edu/ands02minimal.html
6. Colucci, S., Di Noia, T., Di Sciascio, E., Donini, F.M., Ragone, A.: Semantic-based skill management for automated task assignment and courseware composition. J. Univers. Comput. Sci. **13**(9), 1184–1212 (2007)
7. Das, S., Chong, E.I., Eadon, G., Srinivasan, J.: Supporting ontology-based semantic matching in RDBMS. In: The 30th International Conference on Very Large Data Bases (VLDB'04), pp. 1054–1065. VLDB Endowment (2004)
8. Dodds, L.: An introduction to foaf (2004). http://www.xml.com/pub/a/2004/02/04/foaf.html
9. Dolby, J., Fokoue, A., Kalyanpur, A., Kershenbaum, A., Schonberg, E., Srinivas, K., Ma, L.: Scalable semantic retrieval through summarization and refinement. In: Proceedings of the Twenty-Second AAAI Conference on Artificial Intelligence (AAAI 2007) (2007)
10. Fokoue, A., Kershenbaum, A., Ma, L., Schonberg, E., Srinivas, K.: The summary abox: Cutting ontologies down to size. In: Proceedings of 5th International Semantic Web Conference (ISWC 2006), pp. 343–356 (2006)

11. Gomez-Perez, A., Corcho, O., Fernandez-Lopez, M.: Ontological Engineering: With Examples from the Areas of Knowledge Management, e-Commerce and the Semantic Web, 1st edn. Advanced Information and Knowledge Processing. Springer, Berlin (2004)
12. Iannella, R.: Representing vcard objects in rdf/xml (2001). http://www.w3.org/TR/vcard-rdf
13. Ilyas, I.F., Aref, W.G., Elmagarmid, A.K.: Supporting top-k join queries in relational databases. Very Large Database J. **13**(3), 207–221 (2004)
14. Li, C., Soliman, M.A., Chang, K.C.C., Ilyas, I.F.: RankSQL: Supporting Ranking Queries in Relational Database Management Systems, pp. 1342–1345. VLDB Endowment (2005)
15. Lukasiewicz, T., Straccia, U.: Top-k retrieval in description logic programs under vagueness for the Semantic Web. In: Proceedings of the 1st International Conference on Scalable Uncertainty Management (SUM-07). Lecture Notes in Computer Science, vol. 4772, pp. 16–30. Springer, Berlin (2007)
16. Bosc, P., Pivert, O.: SQLf: a relational database language for fuzzy querying. IEEE Trans. Fuzzy Syst. **3**(1), 1–17 (1995)
17. Pan, Z., Heflin, J.: DLDB: extending relational databases to support Semantic Web queries. In: The First International Workshop on Practical and Scalable Semantic Systems (PSSS1), vol. 89, pp. 109–113 (2003). CEUR-WS.org
18. Straccia, U.: Answering vague queries in fuzzy DL-Lite. In: Proceedings of the 11th International Conference on Information Processing and Managment of Uncertainty in Knowledge-Based Systems, (IPMU-06), pp. 2238–2245. E.D.K., Paris (2006)
19. Straccia, U.: Towards top-k query answering in deductive databases. In: Proceedings of the 2006 IEEE International Conference on Systems, Man and Cybernetics (SMC-06), pp. 4873–4879. IEEE, New York (2006)
20. Straccia, U.: Towards top-k query answering in description logics: the case of DL-Lite. In: Proceedings of the 10th European Conference on Logics in Artificial Intelligence (JELIA-06). Lecture Notes in Computer Science, vol. 4160, pp. 439–451. Springer, Berlin (2006)
21. Straccia, U.: Towards vague query answering in logic programming for logic-based information retrieval. In: World Congress of the International Fuzzy Systems Association (IFSA-07). Lecture Notes in Computer Science, vol. 4529, pp. 125–134. Springer, Berlin (2007)
22. Tinelli, E., Cascone, A., Ruta, M., Di Noia, T., Di Sciascio, E., Donini, F.M.: I.M.P.A.K.T.: an innovative, semantic-based skill management system exploiting standard SQL. In: 11th International Conference on Enterprise Information Systems (ICEIS'09), vol. AIDSS, pp. 224–229
23. Wilkinson, K., Sayers, C., Kuno, H.A., Reynolds, D.: Efficient RDF storage and retrieval in Jena2. In: The first International Workshop on Semantic Web and Databases (SWDB'03), pp. 131–150 (2003)

Part V
Engineering Semantic Web Systems

Chapter 20
MIDST: Interoperability for Semantic Annotations

Paolo Atzeni, Pierluigi Del Nostro, and Stefano Paolozzi

Abstract In the last years, interoperability of ontologies and databases has received a lot of attention. However, most of the work has concentrated on specific problems (such as storing an ontology in a database or making database data available to ontologies) and referred to specific models for each of the two. Here, we propose an approach that aims at being more general and model independent. In fact, it works for different dialects for ontologies and for various data models for databases. Also, it supports translations in both directions (ontologies to databases and vice versa) and it allows for flexibility in the translations, so that customization is possible. The proposal extends recent work for schema and data translation (the MIDST project, which implements the ModelGen operator proposed in model management), which relies on a metamodel approach, where data models and variations thereof are described in a common framework and translations are built as compositions of elementary ones.

20.1 Introduction

Metadata is descriptive information about data and applications, used to specify how data is represented, stored and transformed, or may describe interfaces and behaviour of software components.

Leveraging on the concept of metadata, many activities arise in the management of data, Web site and portals, network and in various fields of computer-aided engineering.

Data integration can also be considered one of the metadata related activities, since solving a data integration problem requires the manipulation of metadata that

P. Atzeni (✉) · P. Del Nostro · S. Paolozzi
Università Roma Tre, Via della Vasca Navale 79, 00146 Rome, Italy
e-mail: atzeni@dia.uniroma3.it

P. Del Nostro
e-mail: pdn@dia.uniroma3.it

S. Paolozzi
e-mail: stefano.paolozzi@gmail.com

R. De Virgilio et al. (eds.), *Semantic Web Information Management*,
DOI 10.1007/978-3-642-04329-1_20,

describe the elements involved in the integration process. Works on metadata issues goes back to the early 1970s, when data translation was already a hot database research topic. However, there is still a lack of standardization in this field.

The problem of translating schemas between data models is acquiring progressive significance in heterogeneous environments. Applications are usually designed to deal with information represented according to a specific data model, while the evolution of systems (in databases as well as in other technology domains, such as the Web) led to the adoption of many representation paradigms.

Heterogeneity raises because data sources are independently developed by different people and for different purposes and subsequently need to be integrated. The data sources may use different data models, different schemas and different dialects.

A typical example of such "rich" data sources are semantic annotations. Semantic annotation is the creation of metadata and relations between them with the task of defining new methods of access to information and enriching the potentialities of the ones already existent. The main goal is to have information on the Web, defined in such a way that its meaning could be explicitly interpreted also by automatic systems, not just by human beings.

A key objective of data integration is to provide a uniform view covering a number of this kind of heterogeneous data sources.

Using such a view, data that resides at the sources can be accessed in a uniform way. This data is usually described using database schemas, such as relational, or XML schemas. To construct a uniform view, source schemas are matched to identify their similarities and discrepancies. The relevant portions of schemas are extracted and integrated into a uniform schema. The *translation* of data from the representation used at the sources into the representation conforming to the uniform schema is specified using database transformations.

An interesting research area that has been recently exploited to address these issues is called *model management*.

A central concept in generic model management is that of a *model*. A model is a formal description of a metadata artifact. Examples of models include relational database models, ontologies, interface definitions, object diagrams, etc. The manipulation of models usually involves designing *transformations* between models. Formal descriptions of such transformations are called mappings. Examples of mappings are SQL views, XSL transformations, ontology articulations, mappings between class definitions and relational schemas, mappings between two versions of a model, etc. The key idea behind model management is to develop a set of algebraic operators that generalize the transformation operations utilized across various metadata applications. These operators are applied to models and mappings as a whole rather than to their individual elements, and simplify the programming of metadata applications.

We remark that in this paper we use the terms schema and data model as common in the database literature, though a recent trend in model management follows a different terminology (and uses model instead of schema and metamodel instead of data model [9]).

An ambitious goal is to consider translations in a model generic setting [6, 8], where the main problem can be formulated as follows: given two data models M_1

and M_2 (from a set of models of interest) and a schema S_1 of M_1, translate S_1 into a schema S_2 of M_2 that properly represents S_1.

Our first work was specifically oriented to database model transformations [1, 2]. However the never-ending spread of Semantic Web models is bringing new integration problems.

The Semantic Web comes from the idea of Tim Berners-Lee [7] that the Web as a whole can be made more intelligent and perhaps even intuitive about how to serve a users needs. Although search engines index much of the Web's content, they have little ability to select the pages that a user really wants or needs. Berners-Lee foresees a number of ways in which developers and authors, singly or in collaborations, can use self-descriptions and other techniques so that the context-understanding programs can selectively find what users want. The Semantic Web is specifically a Web of machine-readable information whose meaning is well-defined by standards: it absolutely needs the interoperable infrastructure that only global standard protocols can provide.

This need of interoperability convinces us to extend our first proposal, that was strictly related to database models, to address also Semantic Web models and in particular those models related to the wide research area of semantic annotations. For the sake of this chapter, we explain how our approach can be extended to manage the integration of semantic annotation, defined by means of ontologies, with (relational) databases.

In particular, the main contributions of this chapter are:

- the adoption of a general model to properly represent a broad range of data models. The proposed general model is based on the idea of *construct*: a construct represents a "structural" concept of a data model. We find out a construct for each "structural" concept of every considered data model and, hence, a data model can be completely represented by means of its constructs set.
- the extension of the general model approach to properly represent all (ideally) Semantic Web data models with particular attention to semantic annotation models.
- the implementation of a flexible framework that allows to validate the concepts of the approach and to test their effectiveness. The main components of the tool, include a set of modules to support users in defining and managing models, schemas, Skolem functions, translations, import and export of schemas.

20.2 State of the Art

Starting from the analysis of the available approaches that propose to face the problem of the translations of schemes and data between ontologies and databases, it is possible to underline several aspects that motivate our research.

20.2.1 From Database to Ontology

First of all, we can consider the problem of integration of heterogeneous sources of information. Ontologies play a key role in this process. The term "ontology" is borrowed from philosophy, where *Ontology* is a systematic account of *Existence*. In computer science, an ontology is formally a defined system of concepts. An ontology is "a formal, explicit specification of a shared conceptualization" [13]. Conceptualization corresponds to an abstract model of a domain which identifies the relevant concepts and their relationships. Explicitly it means that the used concepts are unique and their usage is formally confined. Formal refers to the fact that ontologies should be machine-readable. Shared indicates that an ontology is accepted by a group of people and used cooperatively.

Ontologies can be used to define semantic mapping between different information sources. A typical example is the integration of data coming from old legacy systems. Autonomous database systems usually have incompatible schemas making interoperability among them difficult. For a long time, this has been recognized as a schema mapping and data integration problem [19]. In simplest terms, database integration requires (i) mapping systems that define the relationships (mappings) among database schemas and (ii) integration systems that use those mappings to answer queries or translate data across database sources. In addition to the more expressive representations offered by ontologies, they allow integration to cover a larger variety of structured data in theory, although it raises the question of adequate performance in real systems.

Another important aspect to consider is the acquiring of domain ontology that still requires great efforts. Therefore, it is necessary to develop methods and techniques that allow reducing the effort necessary for the knowledge acquisition process. Database schemata, in particular the conceptual schemata modeled in semantic data models such as the Entity-Relationship (ER) model contains (implicitly) abundant domain knowledge. Extracting the knowledge from them can thus profitably support the development of Web ontologies.

Also the so called *Deep Web* arises similar problems. Nowadays, indeed, a large percentage of Web pages are not static documents. On the contrary, the majority of Web pages are dynamic. Therefore the majority of information on the Web is generated from underlying databases (i.e. the deep Web [10]). To discover content on the Web, search engines use Web crawlers that follow hyperlinks. This technique is ideal for discovering resources on the surface Web but is often ineffective at finding deep Web resources. Moreover, it is not possible to semantically annotate the dynamic pages generated from the data sources. Existing tools can only produce semantic annotations for static Web pages and how to annotate dynamic Web pages that are generated from the underlying databases when the clients request the pages is still an open problem [22]. This problem has been referred to as *deep annotation* [15, 26] that means the process of creating ontological instances for the database-based, dynamic contents by reaching out to the Deep Web and directly annotating the underlying database of the dynamic Web site.

One of the research fields which has recently gained much scientific interest within the database community are Peer-to-Peer databases, where peers have the autonomy to decide whether to join or to leave an information sharing environment at any time. The principle is: data stored on one single peer has to be made accessible to other remote peers and vice versa. Afterwards, this data can be requested, queried, replicated or integrated depending on the purpose of the remote system. As a result, sharing relational data within a Peer-to-Peer environment means to distribute not only data items themselves, but also their schemas among multiple previously unknown peers. We thus need an exchange format, which on the one side can be understood by a broad community of peers without being explicitly arranged beforehand and which on the other side has to be suitable for representing relational schemas and their corresponding data instances. This can be suitably achieved through the use of ontologies without having to define a schema and data exchange format explicitly.

20.2.2 From Ontology to Database

The ontologies are important for the integration of data and of applications, besides they facilitate the communication between human beings and informative systems. However, to benefit from the large amount of information stored in ontologies it is necessary to have efficient and effective ways to manage and query those data.

Large ontologies are often stored in database repositories in order to exploit their ability to handle secondary storage and to answer queries in efficient ways. Actually, several tools for managing (building, inferring, querying, etc.) ontology data and ontology-based metadata are available (e.g., Protégé [21]). Usually, ontology-based data manipulated by these tools are stored in the main memory. Thus, for applications manipulating a large amount of ontology-based data, query performance becomes a new issue. Therefore, due to the maturity of database systems, it is possible to efficiently store large ontologies (with million of instances) getting benefit from the functionalities offered by DBMSs (i.e., query performance, efficient storage, transaction management, etc.).

20.2.3 Translation Between Ontologies and Databases

As stated in the previous section, we are interested in semantic annotations that have a high level of formality, i.e., those annotations that can be represented by means of ontologies.

Various proposals have been conceived to describe the translation between ontologies and databases, but the majority of these approaches study only one-way transformations (i.e., ontology to database or database to ontology).

We can classify the different approaches in two main branches: (i) *dictionary-based* and (ii) *dictionary-independent*.

In the first kind of approach, a sort of dictionary is used to define the guideline of the transformations between ontology and database. To represent a relational schema and its instances, ad-hoc ontologies are created as in [18] and [24]. Both approaches describe the database schema and instances by means of a suitable dictionary used in an ontology.

In [24], the authors propose an approach that helps the domain experts to quickly generate and publish OWL ontologies describing the underlying relational database systems while preserving their structural constraints. The generated ontologies are constructed using a set of vocabularies and structures defined in schema that describes relational database systems on the Web so they guarantees that user applications can work with data instances that conformed to a set of known vocabularies and structures. Handschuh et al. [15] apply a similar approach for annotating data intensive websites. In these works, mappings are managed referring to specific ontologies that describe the source relational model. Das et al. [12] proposed a solution for extracting data from the OWL document, and then storing data in relational database. It uses a *reference ontology* as a dictionary. It also enables users to reference ontology data directly from SQL using the semantic match operators.

Dictionary-independent approaches do not use a prefixed dictionary to perform the translations. These include approaches that use Description Logics or machine learning techniques such as [14]. These kind of approaches do not use ad hoc ontologies but aim at representing the semantics of the information in the relational database source. Cullot et al. [11] and Shen et al. [23] are representative examples.

In [11], the DB2OWL tool is described. It looks for some particular cases of database tables to determine which ontology component has to be created from which database component. The created ontology is expressed in OWL-DL language[1] which is based on Description Logics.

Shen et al. [23] propose mapping rules from relational model to OWL for the data integration and they are classified as concepts, properties, restrictions and instances. These rules can be applied to mapping relational database to ontologies in OWL, whereby the mapping and transferring can be performed (semi-)automatically. The rules for concepts, properties and restrictions depict the correspondence at metadata level, which avoid migrating the large amount of data. The rules for instances are applied to create data for exchanging at running time. All the rules can also be applied to learning ontologies from relational database.

A number of formal approaches based on Description Logics exist (see for example [27] and [20]). These cannot be compared with our work, as we concentrate on structural aspects and so we do not refer to reasoning capabilities. Moreover, these pieces of work refer to one specific data model, ER or relational, whereas our approach applies to many different data models, belonging to many families, including relational, ER, object-oriented and object-relational.

While the dictionary-based approaches are preferable in case of ontologies creation as an interchange format, the dictionary-independent approaches find their

[1] http://www.w3.org/TR/owl-features/.

greatest application in sharing knowledge, extrapolated from relational databases, on a particular domain of interest.

20.3 Model Independent Schema and Data Translation

To allow the definition of translations between heterogeneous models, exploiting a model-independent approach, MIDST implements the concepts described in the introductory chapter *Data and Metadata management*, with enhancements for the applicability in the context of Semantic Web. Let us briefly recall the main concepts of the adopted model management approach. To provide descriptions of models, we use *metamodels*. A metamodel is defined as a set of generic constructs that can be used to define models, which are instances of the metamodel. This idea is based on the Hull and King's observation [16] that the constructs used in most known models can be expressed by a limited set of generic (i.e., model-independent) *metaconstructs*: lexical, abstract, aggregation, generalization, function. In fact, we define a metamodel by means of a set of generic metaconstructs [5]. Each model is represented by its constructs and the metaconstructs they refer to. The various constructs are related to one another by means of references (for example, each attribute of an abstract has a reference to the abstract it belongs to) and have properties that specify details of interest (for example, for each attribute we specify whether it is part of the identifier and for each aggregation of abstracts we specify its cardinalities). A major concept in our approach is the *supermodel*, a model that has constructs corresponding to all the metaconstructs known to the system. Thus, each model is a specialization of the supermodel and a schema in any model is also a schema in the supermodel, apart from the specific names used for constructs.

The supermodel gives us two interesting benefits. First of all, it acts like a "pivot" model, so that it is sufficient to have translations from each model to and from the supermodel, rather than translations for every couple of models. Therefore, a linear, and not a quadratic, number of translations is needed. Indeed, since every schema in any model is also a schema of the supermodel (without considering constructs renaming), the only needed translations are those within the supermodel with the target model in mind. A translation is composed of (i) a "copy" (with construct renaming) from the source model into the supermodel; (ii) an actual transformation within the supermodel, whose output includes only constructs allowed in the target model; (iii) another copy (again with renaming into the target model). The second advantage is related to the fact that the supermodel emphasizes the common features of models. Therefore, if two source models share a construct, then their translations towards similar target models could share a portion of the translation as well. In our approach, we follow this observation by defining elementary (or basic) translations that refer to single constructs (or even specific variants thereof). Then actual translations are specified as compositions of basic ones, with significant reuse of them.

It is important to observe that our approach is independent of the specific supermodel that is adopted, as new metaconstructs and can be added. All the information about models and schemas is maintained in a dictionary that we have defined in a relational implementation, that we call *relational dictionary*. The supermodel is the core of the dictionary; it is predefined (but can be extended) and used as the basis for the definition of specific models. Essentially, the dictionary is initialized with the available supermodel constructs, with their properties and references.

20.3.1 Basic Translations

In the current implementation of MIDST tool, translations are implemented by means of Datalog-variant rules with OID invention, where the latter feature is obtained through the use of Skolem functions [17]. This technique has several advantages:

- rules are independent of the main engine that interprets them, enabling rapid development of translations;
- the system itself can verify basic properties of sets of transformations (e.g., some form of correctness) by reasoning about the bodies and heads of Datalog rules [4];
- transformations can be easily customized. For example, it is possible to add "selection condition" that specifies the schema elements to which a transformation is applied.

Another benefit of using Skolem functions is that their values can be stored in the dictionary and used to represent the mappings from a source to a target schema. Each translation is usually concerned with a very specific task, such as eliminating a certain variant of a construct (possibly introducing another construct), with most of the constructs left unchanged. Therefore, in our programs only a few of the rules concerns real translations, whereas most of them just copy constructs from the source schema to the target one. We use a nonpositional notation for rules, so we indicate the names of the fields and omit those that are not needed (rather than using anonymous variables). Our rules generate constructs for a target schema (*tgt*) from those in a source schema (*src*). We may assume that variables *tgt* and *src* are bound to constants when the rule is executed. Each predicate has an OID argument. For each schema we have a different set of identifiers for the constructs. So, when a construct is produced by a rule, it has to have a "new" identifier. It is generated by means of a Skolem function, denoted by the # sign in the rules. An example of the rule is presented in Fig. 20.1. This rule generates a new ABSTRACT for each ABSTRACT in the source schema.

We have the following restrictions on our rules. First, we have the standard "safety" requirements [25]: the literal in the head must have all fields, and each of them with a constant or a variable that appears in the body (in a positive literal) or a Skolem term. Similarly, all Skolem terms in the head or in the body have arguments that are constants or variables that appear in the body. Moreover, our Datalog programs are assumed to be coherent with respect to referential constraints: if there is a rule that produces a construct *C* that refers to a construct *CO*, then there is another rule that generates a suitable *CO* that guarantees the satisfaction of the constraint.

Fig. 20.1 A simple Datalog rule

ABSTRACT(
    OID:#abstract_0(*absOid*),
    Abs-Name: *name*
    Schema: *tgt*)
←
ABSTRACT(
    OID: *absOid*,
    Abs-Name: *name*
    Schema: *src*)

Most of our rules are *recursive* according to the standard definition. However, recursion is only "apparent". A really recursive application happens only for rules that have atoms that refer to the target schema also in their body. In our experiments, we have developed a set of basic translations to handle the models that can be defined with our current metamodel.

20.3.2 More Complex Translations

Intuitively, complex translations can be performed by means of composition of basic rules as clearly described in [3]. However, with many possible models and many basic translations, it becomes important to understand how to find a suitable translation given a source and a target model. In this context we can find two main problems. The first one is how to verify what target model is generated by applying a basic step to a source model. The second problem is related to the "size" of the translations: due to the number of constructs and properties, we have too many models (a combinatorial explosion of them, if the variants of constructs grow) and it would be inefficient to find all associations between basic translations and pairs of models.

We propose a complete solution to the first issue, as follows. We associate a concise description with each model, by indicating the constructs it involves with the associated properties (described in terms of propositional formulas), and a signature with each basic translation. Then a notion of application of a signature to a model description allows us to obtain the description of the target model. With our basic translations written in a Datalog dialect with OID-invention, as we will see shortly, it turns out that signatures can be automatically generated and the application of signatures gives an exact description of the target model. With respect to the second issue, the complexity of the problem cannot be completely avoided, but we have defined algorithms that, under reasonable hypotheses, efficiently find a complex translation given a pair of models (source and target) (for more detail about complex translations see [3]).

20.4 OWL and Relational Database Interoperability

As we said, the starting point of our approach is the idea that a *metamodel* is a set of constructs (called *metaconstructs*) that can be used to define models, which are instances of the metamodel. Therefore, we actually define a model as a set of constructs, each of which corresponds to a metaconstruct. An even more important notion, is the *Supermodel*: it is a model that has a construct for each metaconstruct, in the most general version. Each model can be seen as a specialization of the supermodel, except for renaming of constructs. In order to achieve the complex tasks of interoperability and integration of databases and ontologies, it is necessary to firstly define each model in term of supermodel metaconstructs. In the following, we show our representations of (relational) database and ontology data models by means of metaconstructs. The first one is already present in the previous version of the MIDST project, the second is completely new and it belongs to the work of extending our approach to Semantic Web and in particular to Semantic Annotation defined by means of ontologies.

20.4.1 Relational Data Model

The relational data model is the standard model for logical design of databases. The most important construct is the relation, which consists of a heading and a body. A heading is a set of attributes, while a body (of an n-ary relation) is a set of n-tuples. Each relation is a table, therefore we consider a relational model with tables constituted by columns of a specified type; each column could allow `null` value or be part of the primary key of the table. Moreover, we can specify foreign keys between tables involving one or more columns. The Fig. 20.2 shows the constructs of the relational metamodel in a UML-like class diagram.

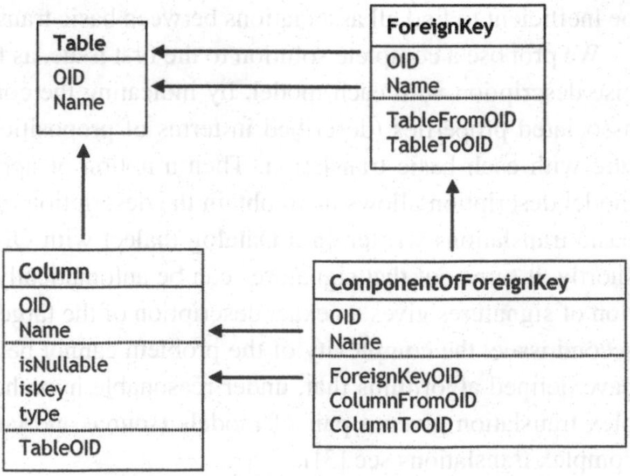

Fig. 20.2 Relational metamodel

Following the MIDST conventions each construct is made of four parts:

- the construct name, that is unique in the model;
- a list of required attributes. Generally we have:

OID that is the unambiguous identifier of each instance of the construct
Name the name that identifies the instance of the construct

- a list of properties that defines the characteristics of the construct;
- a list of references to other constructs that establishes the relationships between the different constructs in the model.

In the following description, for each construct we show the correspondent representation in terms of supermodel metaconstruct.

Table SM-AGGREGATION. Each table in the relational model can be seen as a set (or "aggregation") of columns. Therefore, we map tables with aggregations of lexicals.

Column SM-LEXICAL. We can specify the data type of the column (`type`) and whether it is part of the primary key (`isIdentifier`) or it allows null value (`isNullable`). It has a reference toward an SM-AGGREGATION.

Foreign Key SM-FOREIGNKEY and SM-COMPONENTOFFOREIGNKEY. With the first construct (referencing two SM-AGGREGATIONs), we specify the existence of a foreign key between two tables; with the second construct (referencing one SM-FOREIGNKEY and two SM-LEXICALs), we specify the columns involved in a foreign key.

The relational metamodel is shown in Fig. 20.3.

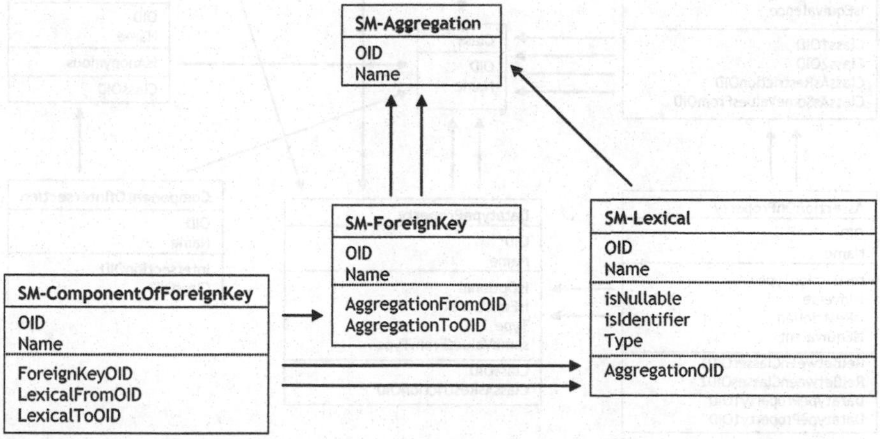

Fig. 20.3 Relational metamodel in terms of supermodel metaconstructs

20.4.2 OWL Data Model

The most important construct of the OWL data model is CLASS that represents the concept of class. In Fig. 20.4, the metamodel of OWL Lite is shown.

The construct CLASS represents classes both named or restricted: to know what type of class is identified by an instance of the construct, it is necessary to take into account the references to other constructs. For example, a class defined as a restriction on a property, will be referenced from the CLASSASRESTRICTIONOID of RELATIONSHIPBETWEENCLASSES construct, which represents relations between classes (both ObjectProperty and DatatypeProperty). A class defined as a finite intersection of other classes will be referenced from `ClassOID` of the INTERSECTION construct. A class definition defined by identifier instead is simply represented by its name valued in the name of the CLASS construct.

The construct RELATIONSHIPBETWEENCLASSES is used to represent an *objectProperty* and the equivalence between classes. In the case of an equivalence relation, the instance of this construct should have:

- the property `isEquivalence` set to `TRUE`;
- the property `isDirected` set to `FALSE` (because the direction of an equivalence relation is not important);

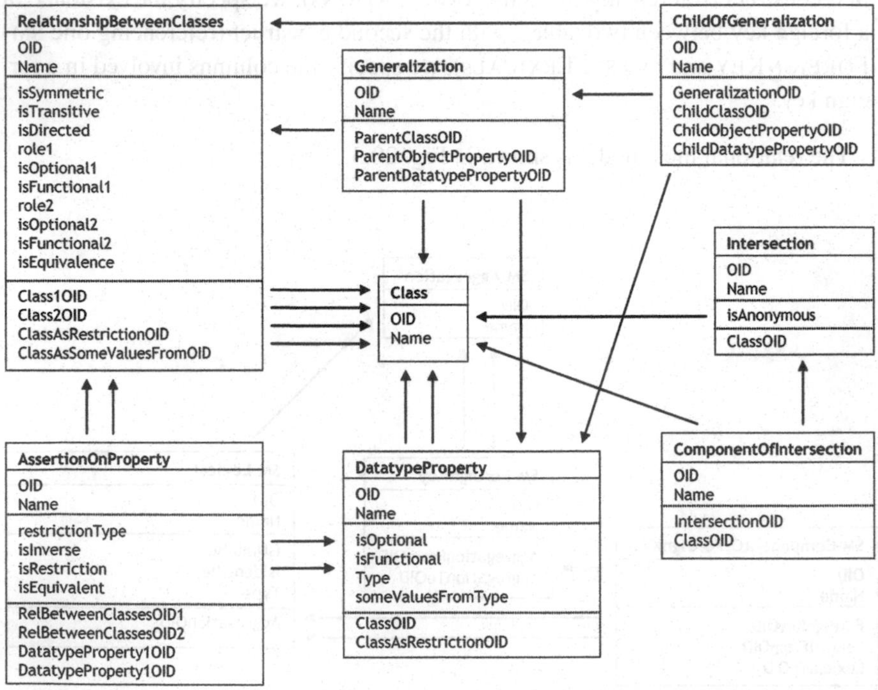

Fig. 20.4 OWL Lite metamodel

- references class1OID and class2OID refer to the two classes involved in the equivalence relationship;
- other properties and references are not considered.

In the case of an object property, the instance of this construct should have:

- the property isSymmetric is set to TRUE if the object property that we are representing is an owl:SymmetricProperty;
- the property isTransitive is set to TRUE if the object property that we are representing is an owl:TransitiveProperty;
- the property isDirected set to TRUE (because the direction of the property is established by the domain and range global restrictions);
- the property isFunctional1 is set to TRUE if the object property is an owl:FunctionalProperty or the maximum cardinality is 1;
- the property isFunctional2 is set to TRUE if the object property is an owl:InverseFunctionalProperty;
- references class1OID and class2OID refer respectively to the domain class and to the range class.

The different kinds of restriction modify the instance of the RELATIONSHIPBETWEENCLASSES construct. The possibilities are summarized in Fig. 20.5.

Datatype properties are represented by the DATATYPEPROPERTY construct. Each instance of this construct should have:

- the property isFunctional is set to TRUE if the object property is an owl:FunctionalProperty;
- the property Type contains the data type of the property (e.g., int, bool, etc.);
- reference class1OID refers to the domain class.

The construct ASSERTIONONPROPERTY is used to represent the characteristics of a property (object property or datatype property). Let P_1 and P_2 two properties, with our construct it is possible to represent the following situations:

- P_1 is the inverse of P_2;
- P_1 is a restriction of P_2, with the type of restriction;
- P_1 is equivalent to P_2.

Restriction Type	Attribute	Value
owl:AllValuesFrom	Class2OID	Refers to range class
owl:someValuesFrom	ClassAsSomeValuesFromOID	Refers to the class thast indicates the value of the OWL construct
owl:MinCardinality	isOptional1	FALSE if the minimum cardinality is 1; TRUE otherwise
owl:MaxCardinality	isFunctional1	TRUE if the minimum cardinality is 1; FALSE otherwise
owl:Cardinality	isOptional1, isFunctional1	The combinations of the two above situations

Fig. 20.5 OWL Restriction for RELATIONSHIPBETWEENCLASSES construct

The ASSERTIONONPROPERTY construct has a boolean attribute for each of the previous assertions, namely: `isInverse`, `isRestriction`, `isEquivalent`.

Through INTERSECTION and COMPONENTOFINTERSECTION constructs, we model the intersection of two or more OWL classes.

Let be C a class that is the intersection of the classes C_1 and C_2, in order to represent this situation we need:

- to create an instance I of the construct INTERSECTION in which `ClassOID` is related to the class C;
- to create an instance of the construct COMPONENTOFINTERSECTION for each class that is a component of the intersection. In our case I_1 that is related to C_1 and I_2 that is related to C_2. Both I_1 and I_2 must be related to the intersection I by means of the reference `IntersectionOID`.

The attribute `isAnonymous` in COMPONENTOFINTERSECTION construct is set to `FALSE` value if the class defined as intersection is also defined by an URI. The two kinds of OWL generalizations, referring to classes and properties (i.e. `rdfs:subClassOf` and `rdfs:subPropertyOf`), are represented through GENERALIZATION and CHILDOFGENERALIZATION constructs.

GENERALIZATION holds:

- the reference `ParentClassOID`, used to point to the CLASS construct representing the parent class, for the class generalization (`rdfs:subClassOf`);
- the reference `ParentObjectPropertyOID`, which referenced the RELATIONSHIPBETWEENCLASSES construct, in the case of generalization of an object property (`rdfs:subPropertyOf`);
- the reference `ParentDatatypeProperty`, which referenced the DATATYPEPROPERTY construct, in the kind of the generalization we are representing is between datatype property (`rdfs:subPropertyOf`).

CHILDOFGENERALIZATION refers to the elements (children) of the generalization. For example, let C_1 a sub-class of class C_2, we have:

- an instance G of the GENERALIZATION construct in which the reference attribute `ParentClassOID` belongs to the class C_2;
- the instance C_G of the construct CHILDOFGENERALIZATION in which the attribute `ChildClassOID` belongs to the class C_1.

20.5 An Extended Supermodel

In the previous section, we introduced both relational and OWL metamodels. Relational metamodel is already included in the previous work, and the reader can find more details about it in [2, 3]. Here, we want to analyze the extension of the supermodel in order to consider also ontologies (in particular OWL-compliant ontologies) and in general to address semantic annotation. In order to show the generality of the approach, we show how the supermodel can be modified and enhanced to represent

Fig. 20.6 Correspondences between OWL model and the supermodel

OWL Model	Supermodel
CLASS	SM-ABSTRACT
RELATIONSHIPBETWEENCLASSES	SM-BINARYAGGREGATIONOFABSTRACTS
DATATYPEPROPERTY	SM-LEXICAL
GENERALIZATION	SM-GENERALIZATION
CHILDOFGENERALIZATION	SM-CHILDOFGENERALIZATION

those semantic Web elements. Due to the complexity of the whole supermodel, we consider only the constructs that are involved in the translation between semantic annotations and databases. In the following, we briefly describe some of the major extensions made to the supermodel.

The extensibility of the supermodel allows us to reuse some of the available constructs. Some of the most clear correspondences between the OWL model constructs and the supermodel metaconstructs are shown in Fig. 20.6.

As we can see in Fig. 20.6, the SM-ABSTRACT can be used to represent the CLASS construct of OWL. Indeed, SM-ABSTRACT is used to represent abstract entities as it models, for example, the ENTITY construct of the Entity-Relationship model or the ROOTELEMENT construct of XML.

The SM-BINARYAGGREGATIONOFABSTRACTS metaconstruct is used to represent the concept of binary relationship between two different abstract entities (SM-ABSTRACT). It includes the attributes `isOptional1`, `isOptional2`, `isFunctional1` and `isFunctional2`) that allow the definition of relationship cardinality in both sides. The attribute `isDirected` allows the definition of the relationship direction, while `Abstract1OID` and `Abstract2OID` belong to the SM-ABSTRACTs participating in the relation, whose roles are defined by `role1` and `role2` attributes.

The SM-LEXICAL metaconstruct represents the concept of lexical, i.e., a property with a primitive type value. The `isOptional` attribute allows to specify the minimum cardinality, the attribute `isNullable` specifies if it is allowed or not to have a `NULL` value. Obviously, `AbstractOID` belongs to the SM-ABSTRACT that owns the SM-LEXICAL.

Both SM-GENERALIZATION and SM-CHILDOFGENERALIZATION are used to represent the concept of generalization of SM-ABSTRACTs.

A more careful analysis of the supermodel shows how some of the constructs of the OWL model do not have a direct correlation with its constructs. Moreover, some of the constructs for which that correspondence is present, do not contain sufficient attributes to the representation of whole information. In the following, we describe new constructs and how to extend the available ones.

20.5.1 Management of Intersections

To manage the intersections, we introduce an SM-SET metaconstruct representing a generic set of abstracts. In order to consider also other sets (like OWL DL unions or RDF collections), we add the Type attribute to determine the kind of set we are considering. Elements of SM-SET (for example the classes which participate to an OWL intersection) are represented by means of an SM-COMPONENTOFSET metaconstruct. A set of SM-ABSTRACT is an abstract itself so we also introduce a reference to SM-ABSTRACT (e.g., an intersection of classes is a class itself in OWL).

20.5.2 Management of Restrictions

As we previously described, in the OWL model the restrictions on object properties can be represented through the RELATIONSHIPBETWEENCLASSES construct, while restrictions on datatype properties are dealt with the construct DATATYPEPROPERTY. The two corresponding metaconstructs in the supermodel are respectively, SM-BINARYAGGREGATIONOF ABSTRACTS and SM-LEXICAL (see Fig. 20.6). However, the old versions of those constructs must be revised in order to properly handle the additional information defined by the restrictions.

Recalling that a restriction in OWL is considered as a class, it is necessary to add, to the SM-BINARYAGGREGATIONOFABSTRACTS metaconstruct, a reference to the class that represents the restriction.

Moreover, in order to manage the `owl:someValuesFrom` constraint we add a reference `AbstractAsSomeValuesFromOID` that points to an SM-ABSTRACT. For the SM-LEXICAL metaconstruct, we have a similar situation except for the fact that the `owl:someValuesFrom` constraint cab be represented as a simple attribute (`someValuesFromType`). Finally, we must add a completely new metaconstruct to indicate when an SM-BINARYAGGREGATIONOFABSTRACTS is a restriction of a different SM-BINARYAGGREGATIONOFABSTRACTS (the same for two SM-LEXICALs) and the kind of the restriction.

20.5.3 Classes Equivalence

The equivalence relation between classes can be seen as a binary relationship. For this reason, the SM-BINARYAGGREGATIONOFABSTRACTS metaconstruct is used to represent it within the supermodel. The `isEquivalence` boolean attribute, is added in this construct, in order to specify whether the relationship is an equivalence or not.

20.5.4 Properties Equivalence

The equivalence between properties (both object and datatype) is represented by the metaconstruct SM-ASSERTIONONPROPERTY. In this metaconstruct we have added the `isEquivalent` attribute that determines whether a property is considered equivalent to another or not.

20.5.5 Object and Datatype Properties Generalization

The previous version of the supermodel was able to manage only generalization between SM-ABSTRACTs. In order to also manage the OWL properties generalizations, we have enhanced the two generalization metaconstructs, i.e., SM-GENERALIZATION and SM-CHILDOFGENERALIZATION. For this purpose, we have introduced two reference attributes in SM-GENERALIZATION, namely they are `ParentBinAggrOID` and `ParentLexicalOID`. The last reference belongs to SM-LEXICAL, the other one to SM-BINARYAGGREGATIONOFABSTRACTS. Similarly, we add two other references to SM-CHILDOFGENERALIZATION: that is `ChildBin AggrOID` in case of object property generalizations and `LexicalOID` in case of datatype property generalizations.

20.5.6 Functional Datatype Properties

In OWL, we can define *functional* datatype properties. This is managed adding the boolean attribute `isFunctional` in the `sm-Lexical` metaconstruct.

20.5.7 Symmetric, Transitive and Inverse Object Properties

Symmetric and transitive properties are easily managed in the supermodel adding the boolean attributes `isSymmetric` and `isTransitive` to the metaconstruct SM-BINARY AGGREGATIONOFABSTRACTS.

For the inverse of a property, we exploit the SM-ASSERTIONONPROPERTY metaconstruct again, adding to it the boolean attribute `isInverse`.

In Fig. 20.7, we show the portion of interest (for ontology and database transformation) of the extended supermodel.

20.6 Translation Rules

In this section, we will briefly illustrate how the translations between OWL ontologies to Relational database (in both directions) can be performed, exploiting a set of Datalog rules with OID invention. Due to space limitation, we only report the most significative portion of this set. When defining rules for a translation process, basic rules with specific purpose can be combined into macro rules that execute them in a specific order.

Let us start with the case of translating from a Relational Database to an OWL ontology. The overall translation can be seen as a macro rule built on the following steps:

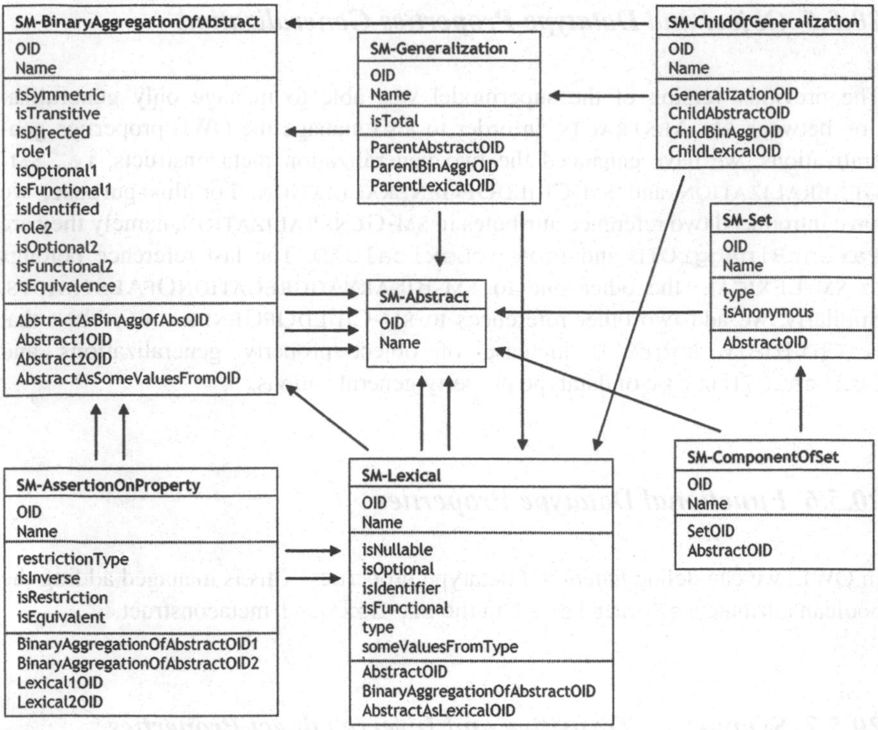

Fig. 20.7 A portion of the extended supermodel

1. Replace SM-AGGREGATIONs with ABSTRACTs;
2. Generalizations for SM-AGGREGATIONs which have SM-LEXICALs referencing only one table;
3. Replace SM-AGGREGATIONs with LEXICALs referencing two different tables with two SM-BINARYAGGREGATIONOFABSTRACTSs;
4. Replace SM-AGGREGATIONs which have only one foreign key with two SM-BINARYAGGREGATIONOFABSTRACTSs;
5. Replace SM-AGGREGATIONs which do not have only one foreign key with two SM-BINARYAGGREGATIONOFABSTRACTSs;
6. Creation of SM-ASSERTIONONPROPERTY to address inverse relations;
7. Management of restriction for SM-LEXICALs (Datatype properties) which are not foreign keys;
8. Management of restrictions for SM-LEXICALs (Object properties) which are foreign keys.

Due to space limitation, we will illustrate the basic rules related to the first two steps. The rule below transforms SM-AGGREGATIONs (corresponding to tables) into SM-ABSTRACTs (corresponding to OWL concepts). The rule with prefix TMP filter the tables that implement the relation many to many.

```
SM_Abstract (OID: #AbstractOID_3*(oid), Name: name)
<-
SM_Aggregation (OID: oid, Name: name),
!TMP_AggWithTwoKeyReferencesWithoutOtherLexicals(OID: oid) ;
```

The following rules create a SM-GENERALIZATION for the SM-AGGREGATIONs (parents) that are referred by other SM-AGGREGATIONs (children) by means of a single foreign key.

```
SM_Generalization (OID: #GeneralizationOID_1*(aggToOID),
Name: aggToName, ParentAbstractOID: #AbstractOID_3(aggToOID))
<-
TMP_AggWithSingleKeyReference(OID: aggOID),
SM_Lexical(OID: lexOID, isIdentifier: "true", AggregationOID: aggOID),
SM_ComponentOfForeignKey(LexicalFromOID: lexOID, ForeignKeyOID: fkOID),
SM_ForeignKey(OID: fkOID, AggregationFromOID: aggOID,
              AggregationToOID: aggToOID),
SM_Aggregation (OID: aggToOID, Name: aggToName);

SM_ChildOfGeneralization (OID: #ChildOfGeneralizationOID_1*(aggOID),
    Name: aggName, GeneralizationOID: #GeneralizationOID_1(aggToOID),
    ChildAbstractOID: #AbstractOID_3(aggOID))
<-
TMP_AggWithSingleKeyReference(OID: aggOID),
SM_Lexical(OID: lexOID, isIdentifier: "true", AggregationOID: aggOID),
SM_ComponentOfForeignKey(LexicalFromOID: lexOID, ForeignKeyOID: fkOID),
SM_ForeignKey(OID: fkOID, AggregationFromOID: aggOID,
              AggregationToOID: aggToOID),
SM_Aggregation (OID: aggOID, Name: aggName),
SM_Aggregation (OID: aggToOID, Name: aggToName);
```

To perform the translation from OWL to a relational representation, the macro rule implementing the overall translation is composed as follows.

1. Preliminary selections. In this phase. the system finds the named classes, object property restrictions, datatype restrictions and inverse object properties. These are the elements that can be translated with simple translations.
2. Object properties hierarchy computation. Here, we capture the structure of object properties hierarchy, searching the parent-child relationships between each object property.
3. Datatype properties hierarchy computation. This step is similar to the previous but related to datatype properties.
4. Class hierarchy computation. As the previous two steps, here the relationships parent-child between classes are computed.
5. Selection of object properties that can be translated in the relational model. Not all the object properties have a correspondence in the relational model. For example, object properties with NULL range are filtered in this step, because in the relational model it would mean having a relationship with everything and it is not allowed.

6. Translation to relational model. All the elements that result from the previous steps are translated directly into the relational model.

The next rule illustrates how we can extract *named classes* from the OWL document.

```
TMP_NamedClass [SOURCE](OID: oid)
<-
SM_Abstract(OID: oid),
!SM_BinaryAggregationOfAbstracts(
    AbstractAsBinAggOfAbsOID: oid),
!SM_Lexical (
    abstractAsLexicalOID: oid),
!SM_Set(
    AbstractOID: oid,
    isAnonymous: "true") ;
```

In the following rule, a temporary element is built to store the object property hierarchy, exploiting the generalization between binary aggregation of abstracts.

```
TMP_ObjectPropertyHierarchy [SOURCE] (
    ParentOID: parentOID,
    ChildOID: childOID
)
<-
SM_Generalization (OID: genOID, parentBinAggrOID: parentOID),
SM_ChildOfGeneralization (generalizationOID: genOID,
                          childBinAggrOID: childOID),
SM_BinaryAggregationOfAbstracts (OID: parentOID, isEquivalence:"false"),
SM_BinaryAggregationOfAbstracts (OID: childOID, isEquivalence:"false");
```

20.7 Conclusion

Semantic annotation is the creation of metadata and relations between them with the task of defining new methods of access to information and enriching the potentialities of the ones already existent. Therefore, semantic annotations are used to enrich the informative content of Web documents and to express in more formal way the meaning of a resource.

A remarkable issue in the context of semantic annotations is represented by semantic interoperability, because it introduces notable challenges. The semantic interoperability is, in general, the ability to share the "meaning" of available information and of the applications built on them. From the point of view, this opens the possibility of operating with heterogenous resources by providing a bridge of common techniques and methods.

In this chapter, we focused on "model-generic" interoperability by means of translation of schemas and data. We discussed our recent results and our contributions to the development of the MIDST platform that allows the specification of the models of interest (mainly semantic annotation formalism and database), with all relevant details, and the generation of translations of their schemas from one model to another.

The usefulness of the MIDST proposal relies on the expressive power of its supermodel, that is the set of models handled and accuracy and precision of such models representation. In order to improve the expressive power of the supermodel, we extended it with more complex structured elements (such as collections) in order to properly represent semantic annotation data models. In particular, we show how our approach can be suitable to perform translation from relational databases to OWL ontologies and viceversa.

References

1. Atzeni, P., Cappellari, P., Bernstein, P.A.: A multilevel dictionary for model management. In: ER, pp. 160–175 (2005)
2. Atzeni, P., Cappellari, P., Bernstein, P.A.: Model-independent schema and data translation. In: EDBT, pp. 368–385 (2006)
3. Atzeni, P., Cappellari, P., Torlone, R., Bernstein, P.A., Gianforme, G.: Model-independent schema translation. VLDB J. **17**(6), 1347–1370 (2008)
4. Atzeni, P., Gianforme, G., Cappellari, P.: Reasoning on data models in schema translation. In: Hartmann, S., Kern-Isberner, G. (eds.) FoIKS. Lecture Notes in Computer Science, vol. 4932, pp. 158–177. Springer, Berlin (2008)
5. Atzeni, P., Torlone, R.: A metamodel approach for the management of multiple models and translation of schemes. Inf. Syst. **18**(6), 349–362 (1993)
6. Atzeni, P., Torlone, R.: Management of Multiple Models in an Extensible Database Design Tool, pp. 79–95. Springer, Berlin (1996)
7. Berners-Lee, T., Hendler, J., Lassila, O.: The Semantic Web. Scientific American, New York (2001)
8. Bernstein, P.A.: Applying model management to classical meta data problems. In: CIDR (2003)
9. Bernstein, P.A., Ho, H.: Model management and schema mappings: theory and practice. In: VLDB, pp. 1439–1440 (2007)
10. Chang, K.C.C., He, B., Li, C., Patel, M., Zhang, Z.: Structured databases on the web: observations and implications. SIGMOD Rec. **33**(3), 61–70 (2004)
11. Cullot, N., Ghawi, R., Yétongnon, K.: Db2owl: a tool for automatic database-to-ontology mapping. In: Ceci, M., Malerba, D., Tanca, L. (eds.) SEBD, pp. 491–494 (2007)
12. Das, S., Chong, E.I., Eadon, G., Srinivasan, J.: Supporting ontology-based semantic matching in rdbms. In: VLDB '04: Proceedings of the Thirtieth International Conference on Very Large Data Bases, pp. 1054–1065. VLDB Endowment (2004)
13. Gruber, T.R.: Toward principles for the design of ontologies used for knowledge sharing. Int. J. Hum.-Comput. Stud. **43**(5–6), 907–928 (1995)
14. Habegger, B.: Mapping a database into an ontology: an interactive relational learning approach. In: ICDE, pp. 1443–1447 (2007)
15. Handschuh, S., Staab, S., Volz, R.: On deep annotation. In: WWW, pp. 431–438 (2003)
16. Hull, R., King, R.: Semantic database modeling: survey, applications, and research issues. ACM Comput. Surv. **19**(3), 201–260 (1987)
17. Hull, R., Yoshikawa, M.: Ilog: declarative creation and manipulation of object identifiers. In: Proceedings of the Sixteenth International Conference on Very Large Databases, pp. 455–468. Morgan Kaufmann, San Mateo (1990)

18. de Laborda, C.P., Conrad, S.: Relational.owl: a data and schema representation format based on owl. In: APCCM '05: Proceedings of the 2nd Asia-Pacific Conference on Conceptual Modelling, pp. 89–96. Australian Computer Society, Darlinghurst (2005)
19. Lenzerini, M.: Data integration: a theoretical perspective. In: PODS '02: Proceedings of the Twenty-First ACM SIGMOD-SIGACT-SIGART Symposium on Principles of Database Systems, pp. 233–246. ACM, New York (2002)
20. Motik, B., Horrocks, I., Sattler, U.: Bridging the gap between owl and relational databases. In: WWW '07: Proceedings of the 16th International Conference on World Wide Web, pp. 807–816. ACM, New York (2007)
21. Noy, N., Fergerson, R., Musen, M.: The knowledge model of protégé-2000: Combining interoperability and flexibility. Lect. Notes Comput. Sci. **1937**, 69–82 (2000)
22. Reeve, L., Han, H.: Survey of semantic annotation platforms. In: SAC '05: Proceedings of the 2005 ACM Symposium on Applied Computing, pp. 1634–1638. ACM, New York (2005)
23. Shen, G., Huang, Z., Zhu, X., Zhao, X.: Research on the rules of mapping from relational model to owl. In: Grau, B.C., Hitzler, P., Shankey, C., Wallace, E. (eds.) Proceedings of the OWLED '06 Workshop on OWL: Experiences and Directions, pp. 21–29 (2006)
24. Trinh, Q., Barker, K., Alhajj, R.: Rdb2ont: a tool for generating owl ontologies from relational database systems. In: AICT-ICIW '06: Proceedings of the Advanced Int'l Conference on Telecommunications and Int'l Conference on Internet and Web Applications and Services, p. 170. IEEE Computer Society, Los Alamitos (2006)
25. Ullman, J.D., Widom, J.: A First Course in Database Systems (1997)
26. Volz, R., Handschuh, S., Staab, S., Stojanovic, L., Stojanovic, N.: Unveiling the hidden bride: deep annotation for mapping and migrating legacy data to the Semantic Web. J. Web Semant. **1**(2), 187–206 (2004)
27. Xu, Z., Cao, X., Dong, Y., Su, W.: Formal approach and automated tool for translating er schemata into owl ontologies. In: PAKDD, pp. 464–475 (2004)

Chapter 21
Virtuoso: RDF Support in a Native RDBMS

Orri Erling and Ivan Mikhailov

Abstract RDF (Resource Description Framework) is seeing rapidly increasing adoption, for example, in the context of the Linked Open Data (LOD) movement and diverse life sciences data publishing and integration projects. This paper discusses how we have adapted OpenLink Virtuoso, a general purpose RDBMS, for this new type of workload. We discuss adapting Virtuoso's relational engine for native RDF support with dedicated data types, bitmap indexing and SQL optimizer techniques. We further discuss scaling out by running on a cluster of commodity servers, each with local memory and disk. We look at how this impacts query planning and execution and how we achieve high parallel utilization of multiple CPU cores on multiple servers. We present comparisons with other RDF storage models as well as other approaches to scaling out on server clusters. We present conclusions and metrics as well as a number of use cases, from DBpedia to bio informatics and collaborative web applications.

21.1 Introduction

Virtuoso is a multi-protocol server providing ODBC/JDBC access to relational data stored either within Virtuoso itself or any combination of external relational databases. Besides catering for SQL clients, Virtuoso has a built-in HTTP server providing a DAV repository, SOAP and WS* protocol end points and dynamic web pages in a variety of scripting languages. Given this background and the present emergence of the Semantic Web, incorporating RDF functionality into the product is a logical next step. RDF data has been stored in relational databases since the inception of the model [3, 14]. Performance considerations have however led to the development of custom RDF engines, e.g., RDF Gateway [13], Kowari [15] and others. Other vendors such as Oracle and OpenLink have opted for building a degree of native RDF support into an existing relational platform.

For a production strength DBMS, we need a balanced set of capabilities. Failure with any of the below may cost orders of magnitude in performance.

O. Erling (✉) · I. Mikhailov
OpenLink Software, 10 Burlington Mall Road, Suite 265, Burlington, MA 01803, USA
e-mail: oerling@openlinksw.com
url: http://www.openlinksw.com

I. Mikhailov
e-mail: imikhailov@openlinksw.com

R. De Virgilio et al. (eds.), *Semantic Web Information Management*,
DOI 10.1007/978-3-642-04329-1_21, © Springer-Verlag Berlin Heidelberg 2010

- Doing the right things—A bad query plan can destroy any possibility of performance, no matter how good the rest is.
- Doing things in the right place—Processing must take place close to the data. For example, if an unmodified RDBMS is used as back end for SPARQL, impedance mismatch between type systems may cause the SPARQL front end to do things that belong to the back end. If SPARQL is mapped to SQL, we must get a single SQL statement with all joins inside, so that the back end database can optimize the query. Failure to do either will kill performance by requiring client-server round trips.
- Doing things in memory—A single disk read takes the time of thousands of table lookups in memory. Inefficient use of space leads to needless disk access. This is specially bad with RDF, where the data model is not geared to application specific disk layout.
- Scale—If RDF is the means of turning the web into a database, then scale is important. This means that a scale out approach becomes inevitable at some point. When we move from a single server to multiple servers, performance dynamics change qualitatively.

We shall discuss our response to all these challenges in the course of this chapter.

21.2 State of the Art

We will compare Virtuoso in terms of database layout and clustering features to different commercial and research work.

Vertical Layouts Column oriented stores like Vertica [21] and [1] approach storing triples by making a two-column table for each distinct predicate in the corpus of data. This offers attractive data compression and performance for workloads where both predicate and graph are fixed at query preparation time. The graph and predicate serve to select the tables that the query will access. Situations where the graph or predicate are unknown will lead to having to look at all tables, creating very large unions inside the query plan. Implementing column oriented storage for a table of quads with `G`, `S`, `P` and `O` has been tried by us but the performance was found to be less than that of our approach with covering multi-part indices. We have not tried the table per predicate approach because our target workloads involve queries where graph and predicate are variable.

Triples Indexed with Sorted Lists Hexastore is a triple store storage scheme aiming at uniform access performance regardless of which combination of `S`, `P` and `O` are specified in a query. Hexastore also makes extensive use of merge joins; For each combination of any two of `S`, `P`, `O`, there is a sorted list of the values of the third key part. Further, the list of `O`'s is shared between the indices of `S`, `P` and `P`, `S`. These lists can then be efficiently merge joined. Hexastore does not however include a graph in the index. Adding a graph would be possible, but would need extra storage. Virtuoso could also share structure between indices, as Hexastore does, but elects not to do this in order to save a random access and in order to keep the indices independently partitionable.

Clustered Quad Stores YARS2 from Deri is a cluster based quad store. The basic philosophies and target workloads are similar but Virtuoso is further engineered. The difference in storage is that YARS2 does not assign fixed length identifiers to URI's but stores them as text in indices. On top of this, YARS2 applies a page level compression, resulting in about 90% space savings. Virtuoso uses fixed length identifiers and elimination of shared leading key parts but does not do stream compression. When we measured the performance of gzip compression, on Virtuoso pages, which were already fairly compact, we found that 90% of pages dropped to under half size. There are no actual numbers on data sizes with Virtuoso and YARS2.

The data partitioning schemes in YARS2 and Virtuoso are similar. Virtuoso has a more sophisticated query optimizer, drawing on real time samples of data for cardinality estimates and generating permutations for join order. YARS has a simpler query planning model which does not evaluate costs of different join order permutations.

For full text index, Virtuoso integrates its own text index whereas YARS2 uses Lucene. Virtuoso is written in C whereas YARS2 and Lucene are in Java.

Oracle RAC [17] can be compared with Virtuoso in terms of its cluster support. Most clustered databases, including Virtuoso partition data according to the values of partitioning columns. Oracle RAC does not partition data, being based on a shared disk image served by multiple servers, each with its own cache of the data. The servers then implement a cache consistency protocol called cache fusion in order to manage consistency of concurrent read and update. Cache fusion has the advantage of requiring no reshuffling of the database when servers are added or removed and does not require the database administrator to specify partitioning, which may be difficult with databases of thousands of tables.

We chose not to implement cache fusion and went the partitioning route for the following reasons:

- Latency—When data is partitioned, only one server will have a cached copy of the data and needs no synchronization out of process for reading the page into cache or updating it. To absorb the latency, cache fusion has data migrate to the cache of the node that last needed the data, so that when the working set has settled, data is already cached on the node that needs it. This works when there is high affinity between data and the client using the data. For OLTP this may indeed be so. For our target workload of web-scale inference and analysis, we cannot assume such affinity. Also, if we implemented cache fusion, we would have to allow multiple cached copies of a page on different server so as to eliminate the snoop traffic for reading. This would result in inefficient use of RAM, all nodes ending up with overlapping caches. Optimizing use of RAM, so that all servers had distinct caches and required no synchronization for reading was another reason for not doing cache fusion. Thus, instead of cluster traffic in relation to index lookups and updates, we have cluster traffic for higher level operations,

such as batches of index lookups and whole subqueries. By shipping larger functions, we achieve higher latency tolerance and smaller amount of data movement between nodes, thus being less dependent on the quality of the network. Indeed, for TPC H, Oracle RAC is usually measured with Infiniband interconnects [16] when other cluster databases are measured with dual 1 Gbit Ethernet.
- Flexibility of deployment—In order to run well on clouds, one cannot rely on having a storage are network (SAN) shared among servers. Further, local disk offers lower cost than a SAN. On the network side, the cloud interconnects we have seen are probably 1 Gbit Ethernet but perform under the level of a private dual 1 Gbit segment.

SPARQL Processor Without Local Data Storage D2RQ is the most commonly mentioned tool for running SPARQL queries against SQL databases. It is similar in function to the Virtuoso RDF views. The difference is that Virtuoso offers higher performance [5] and has more optimization logic for mappings where an RDF triple may be generated from multiple sources. Also, Virtuoso RDF views take advantage of always generating Virtuoso SQL, which allows for more optimization. If the relational data is not in Virtuoso, the Virtuoso SQL compiler will generate a distributed query plan. With D2RQ, the distributed evaluation is done in the D2RQ engine and to our knowledge D2RQ does not exploit statistics of the remote databases for distributed query optimization, as Virtuoso SQL does.

21.3 Triple Storage

The RDF data model consists of triples composed of a subject, predicate and object. Triples are further grouped into graphs. The graph, subject and predicate are URI's and the object may be a URI or a member of any XML schema data type, i.e., any scalar or XML fragment. URI's are internally given fixed length identifiers, since storing the text of a URI in the quad table would take prohibitive space. In the following, we use URI (Universal Resource Identifier) and IRI (Internationalized Resource Identifier) interchangeably. Virtuoso's RDF storage solution is fairly conventional: a single table of four columns holds one quad, i.e. triple plus graph per row. The columns are `G` for graph, `P` for predicate, `S` for subject and `O` for object. `P`, `G` and `S` are IRI ID's, for which we have a custom data type, a 64 bit number distinguishable at run time from integer. The `O` column is of SQL type ANY, meaning any serializable SQL object, from scalar to array or user defined type instance. Indexing supports a lexicographic ordering of type ANY, meaning that with any two elements of compatible type, the order is that of the data type(s) in question with default collation. This means that normal range lookups are supported by the index.

Since `O` is a primary key part, we do not wish to have long `O` values repeated in the index. Hence `O`'s of string type that are longer than 12 characters are assigned a unique ID and this ID is stored as the `O` of the quad table. For example, Oracle [18] has chosen to give a unique ID to all distinct `O`'s, regardless of type. We however store short `O` values inline and assign ID's only to long ones.

RDF workloads may in principle access data based on any combination of columns of the quad table. Even though this is not mandated by the RDF model, we find it valuable to be able to issue queries which leave the graph unspecified. Queries like "how and where are S and O related" are entirely possible, unlike in the relational world where tables and columns cannot be variable at query time. To support such access patterns, we find that 4 indices over the quad table are needed, representing 4 out of the 24 permutations of G, S, P and O. If we could always assume that the graph were a constant supplied in the query, then 2 indices would suffice.

The default index layout consists of four covering indices, i.e., 4 indices of which each contains all the columns of the table. These are SPOG, OPGS, POGS and GPOS.

We note that since `S` is the last key part of `P, G, O, S` and it is an integer-like scalar, we can represent it as a bitmap, one bitmap per distinct `P, G, O`. With the Dbpedia data set, this causes the space consumption of a bitmap index to drop to about a third of the equivalent non-bitmap index.

Bitmap indices have a further advantage, in answering queries like

```
graph <my-friends> {
    ?s foaf:knows people:John , people:Mary }
```

the index structure allows the AND of the conditions to be calculated as a merge intersection of two sparse bitmaps. The people who know both John and Mary are given by the bitwise and of the bitmap of those who know John and those who know Mary. With the LUBM [9] queries, we find that enabling bitmap intersections doubles the speed compared with a model that does loop joins exclusively.

The mapping between an IRI ID and the IRI is represented in two tables, one for the namespace prefixes and one for the local part of the name. The mapping between ID's of long `O` values and their full text is kept in a separate table, with the full text or its MD5 check-sum as one key and the ID as primary key. A separate table holds an optional full text index of all the O values. Even though not required by RDF or SPARQL, a full text index on all literals is usually desirable.

The type cast rules for comparison of data are different in SQL and SPARQL. SPARQL will silently fail where SQL signals an error. This is supported in the query execution engine and enabled with a special query hint. Other RDF oriented accommodations include typed and language tagged strings as a native data type and numerous SQL optimizer special cases.

Compression We have implemented compression at two levels. Within each database page, we store distinct values only once and eliminate common prefixes of strings. Using 2 indices and 32 bit IRI id's, Without key compression, we get 75 bytes per triple with a billion-triple LUBM data set (LUBM scale 8000). With compression, we get 35 bytes per triple. Thus, key compression doubles the working set while sacrificing no random access performance. A single triple out of a billion can be located in less than 5 microseconds with or without key compression.

When applying gzip to database pages, we see a typical compression to 40% of original size, even after key compression. This is understandable since indices are by nature repetitive, even if the repeating parts are shortened by key compression. Over 99% of 8K pages filled to 90% compress to less than 3K with gzip at default compression settings. This does not improve working set but saves disk. Detailed performance impact measurement is yet to be made.

Using a four index layout plus full text index on all literals, The Billion Triples Challenge data set, 1150M triples, including DBpedia, Freebase, US Census and numerous web crawls took 120 GB of allocated database pages, with 64 bit ID's and key compression but no gzip [8].

Alternative Index Layouts Storage layouts based on multi-part indices always favor some access pattern over another. To support flat performance, regardless of which combination of columns were specified, we have experimented with a table holding `G`, `S`, `P`, `O` as a dependent part of a row id and made 4 single column bitmap indices for `G`, `S`, `P` and `O`. In this way, no combination of criteria is penalized. However, performing the bitmap AND of 4 given parts to check for existence of a quad takes 2.5 times longer than the same check from a single 4 part index. We have therefore kept to using multipart indices. In practice, we find it preferable to use many covering indices.

21.4 SPARQL and SQL

Virtuoso offers SPARQL inside SQL, somewhat similarly to Oraclés RDF_MATCH table function. A SPARQL subquery or derived table is accepted either as a top level SQL statement of wherever a subquery or derived table is accepted. Thus, SPARQL inherits all the aggregation and grouping functions of SQL, as well as any built-in or user defined functions. Another benefit of this is that all supported CLI's work directly with SPARQL, with no modifications. For example, one may write a PHP web page querying the triple store using the PHP to ODBC bridge. The SPARQL text simply has to be prefixed with the SPARQL keyword to distinguish it from SQL. A SPARQL end point for HTTP is equally available. We have further implemented Virtuoso drivers for the popular Jena, Sesame and Redland RDF frameworks. Thus applications written in these can transparently use Virtuoso as the storage and query processor.

Internally, SPARQL is translated into SQL at the time of parsing the query. If all triples are in one table, the translation is straightforward, with union becoming a SQL union and optional becoming a left outer join. The translator optimizes the data transferred between parts of the queries, so that variables needed only inside a derived table are not copied outside of it. If cardinalities are correctly predicted, the resulting execution plans are sensible. SPARQL features like construct and describe are implemented as user defined aggregates.

SQL Cost Model and RDF Queries When all triples are stored in a single table, correct join order and join type decisions are difficult to make given only the table and column cardinalities for the RDF quad table. Histograms for ranges of `P`, `G`, `O` and `S` are also not useful. Our solution for this problem is to go look at the data itself when compiling the query. Since the SQL compiler is in the same process as the index hosting the data, this can be done whenever one or more leading key parts of an index are constants known at compile time. For example, in the previous example, of people knowing both John and Mary, the `G`, `P` and `O` are known for two triples. A single lookup in log(n) time retrieves the first part of the bitmap for

```
((G = <my-friends>) and (P = foaf:knows) and
  (O = <http://people.com/people#John>) )
```

The entire bitmap may span multiple pages in the index tree but reading the first bits and knowing how many sibling leaves are referenced from upper levels of the tree with the same `P`, `G`, `O` allows calculating a ballpark cardinality for the `P`, `G`, `O` combination. The same estimate can be made either for the whole index, with no key part known, using a few random samples or any number of leading key parts given. While primarily motivated by RDF, the same technique works equally well with any relational index.

Basic RDF Inferencing Much of basic T box (terminology box, akin to schema) inferencing such as subclasses and subproperties can be accomplished by query rewrite. We have integrated this capability directly in the Virtuoso SQL execution engine. With a query like

```
select ?person where { ?person a lubm:Professor }
```

we add an extra query graph node that will iterate over the subclasses of class `lubm:Professor` and retrieve all persons that have any of these as `rdf:type`. When asking for the class of an IRI, we also return any superclasses. Thus, the behavior is indistinguishable from having all the implied classes explicitly stored in the database.

For reasoning over instance data, Virtuoso has special support for `owl:sameAs`. When either an `O` or `S` is compared with equality with an IRI, the IRI is expanded into the transitive closure of its `owl:sameAs` synonyms and each of these is tried in turn. Thus, when `owl:sameAs` expansion is enabled, the SQL query graph is transparently expanded to have an extra node joining each `S` or `O` to all synonyms of the given value. Thus,

```
select ?lat where { <Berlin> has_latitude ?lat }
```

will give the latitude of Berlin even if `<Berlin>` has no direct latitude but `geo:Berlin` does have a latitude and is declared to be synonym of `<Berlin>`.

The `owl:sameAs` predicate applied to classes and properties can be handled through the same mechanism as subclasses and sub-properties.

Virtuoso has SPARQL extensions for subqueries, including a transitive subquery feature. For example, the pattern `<john> foaf:knows ?person option (transitive)` will bind `?person` to everybody `<john>` knows plus everybody they know and so on up to full transitive closure. There are further options for limiting the depth and returning the path leading to each binding and so forth. The query

```
select ?p2 where {
  {  select ?p1 ?p2 where {
       ?p1 foaf:knows ?p2 . ?p2 foaf:knows ?p1 }
     } option transitive (in (?p1) out (?p2)) .
filter (?p1 = <john>) }
```

would only consider reciprocal `foaf:knows` relations. Thus, the step in the transitivity can be complex. If both ends of a transitive relation are given, then this feature can be used for obtaining the paths that connect the two ends. More examples are at [8].

Data Manipulation Virtuoso supports the SPARUL SPARQL extension, compatible with JENA [14]. Updates can be run either transactionally or with automatic commit after each modified triple.

Full Text All or selected string valued objects can be full text indexed. Queries like

```
select ?person from <people> where {
    ?person a person ; has_resume ?r .
    ?r bif:contains 'SQL and "semantic web"' }
```

will use the text index for resolving the pseudo-predicate `bif:contains`.

Aggregation Basic SQL style aggregation is supported through queries like

```
select ?product sum (?value) from <sales> where {
    <ACME> has_order ?o .  ?o has_line ?ol .
    ?ol has_product ?product ; has_value ?value }
```

This returns the total value of orders by ACME grouped by product.

RDF Sponge The Virtuoso SPARQL run-time can retrieve external resources for querying. This functionality is referred to as "RDF Sponge". Having retrieved an initial resource, it can automatically follow selected IRI's for retrieving additional resources. Several modes are possible: follow only selected links, such as `sioc:see_also` or try dereferencing any intermediate query results, for example. Resources thus retrieved are kept in their private graphs or they can be merged into a common graph. When they are kept in private graphs, HTTP caching headers are observed for caching, the local copy of a retrieved remote graph is usually kept for some limited time. The sponge procedure is extensible so it can extract RDF data from non-RDF resources with pluggable RDF-izers called cartridges. Over 30 such cartridges exist to date, covering GRDDL, RDF, microformats, many XML formats such as XBRL [22] and more. This provides a common tool for traversing sets of interlinked documents such as personal FOAFs that refer to each other.

21.5 Clustering and Scalability

For the entire history of RDF and the Semantic Web, one of the dominant themes of the discourse has been scalability. The data web can be said to be one of the frontiers of databasing, as data volumes are easily very large and since there is generally no application-specific table layout and index structure, things take more space than with the corresponding relational representation. This section discusses the work done in scale-out clustering in Virtuoso. At the time of writing, Virtuoso has a cluster edition that runs on shared nothing clusters of commodity servers. This is being used for hosting large parts of the linked open data cloud.

As we move in the direction of parallelism, dynamics of performance change significantly: when moving from a single CPU to multiple CPU's or cores, the cost of resource contention between threads jumps significantly. Thus, if special care is not taken, a thread blocking to wait for another is so expensive that any gains from parallelism may be entirely lost. A single wait may cost whole microseconds. When we move from one multithreaded process to multiple multithreaded server processes connected by a network, the network latency becomes the dominant cost factor. Within a single machine, a message round trip with empty message and no processing costs about 50 microseconds, including thread switching at both ends. With a 1 Gbit Ethernet added to the mix, the cost goes to about 150 microseconds, assuming no contention on the network.

These basic facts dictate the architecture of any DBMS for server clusters. The issues of query optimization are largely the same as for single servers but the execution engine has entirely different priorities.

The cost of finding a single quad from 100 million is about 5 microseconds. This is a tiny fraction of the overhead of doing any operation involving any inter-process communication. For this reason, it is vital to group as many operations as possible within a single message.

Clustered databases usually use some partitioning scheme, where the values of one or more key columns dictate which server will store the row. Also nonpartitioned cluster systems such as Oracle RAC exist. With Virtuoso, we decided to use hash partitioning according to the subject or object of a quad. Thus, a single quad is indexed many ways and each index may be partitioned differently, there is no need for all the entries of a single quad to be on the same server. Also in relational applications, Virtuoso allows specifying partitioning index by index. We do not use the graph or predicate of a quad for partitioning since these may have very uneven distributions.

21.5.1 Query Execution Model

When the network latency is the main cost factor, having a maximally asynchronous and non-blocking message flow between the processes participating in a query is necessary. A query is addressed to an arbitrary node of the cluster. This node is called the *query coordinator* and it is responsible for dispatching the query to the relevant cluster nodes and assembling the response.

The basic query is a set of nested loops. Take for example

```
select * where {
    <john> foaf:knows ?person .
    ?person foaf:mbox ?mbox ; foaf:nick ?nick }
```

This can be seen as a pipeline of 3 stages. The first produces all the friends of `<john>`. The second takes the set of friends and adds the `foaf:mbox` for each. The third adds the `foaf:nick` to the result row. The results from the 3rd stage can be returned to the client.

Suppose the index from subject to object is partitioned by subject, which is quite natural. For the first, we know the subject, so we know which partition has the friends of `<john>`. We ask for them and get them in a single message exchange, unless there are megabytes worth of them in which case we would ask for the next batch when near the end of the first batch. Each of these is a subject in its turn, thus for each friend we know which partition has the `foaf:mbox`. We group all messages headed for each partition together and send them and again gather the results. The same process is repeated for the `foaf:nick`.

This is the naive way of evaluating the query. Even this produces fair parallelism through bundling messages in sufficiently large batches. We first note that the subject for the `foaf:mbox` and `foaf:nick` patterns is the same, hence they are always in the same partition since the index is partitioned by subject. Thus, we get the two in a single operation: we send to each partition that has a friend of `<john>` the query fragment

```
{ ?person foaf:mbox ?mbox ; foaf:nick ?nick }
```

If there were other conditions such as `filter (?nick != "Alice")`, we could bundle these in as well. This removes a whole message round trip and nearly halves the network traffic for the query.

Next, we see that the partition that evaluates

```
{ <john> foaf:knows ?person }
```

does not have to return the set of friends to the query coordinator but can by itself dispatch these to the appropriate partition for each. This eliminates yet another round trip. Now the query runs in 3 message steps: 1. ask for friends of `<john>`

2. each partition that can have one of the friends gets all the friends in its range and gets their nicks and mailboxes and 3. all completed bindings are returned to the coordinator.

This last optimization is applicable when the results do not have to be returned in any given order. Adding an *order by* at the end of the query takes care of this. In this way, each partition sorts the bindings it produces and the query coordinator only needs to merge ordered streams of bindings from the partitions. The cost of the final *order by* is negligible compared to the latency and data transfer savings.

When the query involves aggregation, sorting or grouping, the aggregation takes place on each involved partition separately and is collected to the coordinator at the end in one message round trip.

Consider

```
base <http://myopenlink.net/dataspace/>
select ?o ?distance
  ((select count (*) where {?o foaf:knows ?xx}))
where {
    { select ?s ?o where { ?s foaf:knows ?o }
      } option (transitive, t_in(?s), t_out(?o),
      t_min (1), t_max (4), t_distinct,
      t_step ('step_no') as ?distance) .
    filter (?s = <person/kidehen#this>)
  } order by ?distance desc 3 limit 50
```

This starts with `<http://myopenlink...kidehen#this>` and gets all the distinct subjects related to this by 1 to 3 consecutive `foaf:knows` steps. For each such person, the people this person `foaf:knows` are counted. The results are returned sorted by distance and descending count of friends.

This is 3 round trips for the transitive `foaf:knows` up to 3 deep. Each step must return results to the coordinator for handling the distinctness. Then there is one round trip for the friend counts of each person, since

```
select count (*) where {?o foaf:knows ?xx}
```

can be evaluated within one partition for each `?o`. Thus, the count subquery in the selection is also parallelized. The rest is local processing on the coordinator.

Since the coordinator is an arbitrary node of the cluster, it will itself handle the bindings that fall into its partition in addition to overall query coordinating.

21.5.2 Performance

With the Billion Triples Challenge data set, we have 25 million `foaf:knows` triples. Of these, 92K are such that for `?x foaf:knows ?y` there is a `?y foaf:knows ?x` in some graph. The query is

```
select count (*) where {
  ?x foaf:knows ?y . ?y foaf:knows ?x }
```

This runs in 7.7 seconds on two dual 4 core Xeon machines, for a total of 3.4 million random triple lookups per second. The database is partitioned in 12, 6 partitions per machine. We have 11.5 of the 16 cores busy for the query, where 12 cores would be the maximum. The interconnect traffic is only 19 MB/s, meaning that we are using a fraction of the total interconnect bandwidth of dual 1 Gb Ethernets.

In this situation, each partition directly sends the `(?x, ?y)` pairs to the partition that holds the possibly existing `(?y, ?x)` pair. If instead we pass these through a single coordinator node, the execution time jumps to 35 seconds and the interconnect traffic to 39 MB/s.

Experience shows that series of simple joins, single triple OPTIONALs or existence tests followed by aggregation or sorting will scale near linearly with the addition of hardware. More complex query structures require passing data through the coordinator at least part of the time, for example between steps of a transitive subquery or for DISTINCTs and complex existence subqueries. Even then, between 4 to 6 cores can be busy for a single query. Disk performance always increases linearly with clustering, since even the most naive message pattern will deliver tasks over an order of magnitude faster than a disk bound process can handle them. Since each node of the cluster caches its partition of the data and nothing else, any added nodes linearly add to the main memory, which is the most determining resource in any DBMS that is primarily doing random access.

21.6 Mapping Relational Data into RDF for SPARQL Access

RDF and ontologies form the final completing piece of the enterprise data integration puzzle. Many disparate legacy systems may be projected onto a common ontology using different rules, providing instant content for the Semantic Web. One example of this is OpenLink's ongoing project of mapping popular Web 2.0 applications such as Wordpress, Mediawiki, PHP BB and others onto SIOC [19] through Virtuoso's RDF Views system.

Most data integration done with RDF to date is based on extracting triples from different relational databases and importing these into a triple store. However, when the data volumes are very large or the data is rapidly changing, this becomes impractical. Also, RDBMS's are generally more efficient than triple stores for analytic queries. Maintaining a separate RDF warehouse is extra work. For these reasons, exposing RDB assets as RDF without extract-transform-load (ETL) is desirable.

On the other hand, if the number of distinct data sources is very large, if there is high cost of access or if complex inference and post-processing of the data is needed, then a degree of RDF warehousing is appropriate.

The problem domain is well recognized, with work by D2RQ [4], SPASQL [11], DBLP [7] among others. Virtuoso differs from these primarily in that it combines the mapping with native triple storage and may offer better distributed SQL query optimization through its long history as a SQL federated database.

In Virtuoso, an RDF mapping schema consists of declarations of one or more quad storages. The default quad storage declares that the system table `RDF_QUAD` consists of four columns (`G`, `S`, `P` and `O`) that contain fields of stored triples, using special formats that are suitable for arbitrary RDF nodes and literals. The storage can be extended as follows.

An IRI class defines that an SQL value or a tuple of SQL values can be converted into an IRI in a certain way, e.g., an IRI of a user account can be built from the user ID, a permalink of a blog post consists of host name, user name and post ID etc. A conversion of this sort may be declared as bijection so an IRI can be parsed into original SQL values. The compiler knows that a join on two IRIs calculated by same bijection IRI class can be replaced with join on raw SQL values that can efficiently use native indexes of relational tables. It is also possible to declare one IRI class `A` as `subClassOf` other class `B` so the optimizer may simplify joins between values made by `A` and `B` if `A` is bijection.

Most of IRI classes are defined by format strings similar to one used in standard C `sprintf` function. Complex transformations may be specified by user-defined functions. In any case, the definition may optionally provide a list of sprintf-style formats such that any IRI made by the IRI class always matches one of these formats. The SPARQL optimizer pays attention to formats of created IRIs to eliminate joins between IRIs created by totally disjoint IRI classes. For two given `sprintf` format strings, the SPARQL optimizer can find a common sub-format of these two or try to prove that no one IRI may match both formats.

```
prefix : <http://www.openlinksw.com/schemas/oplsioc#>
create iri class :user-iri "http://myhost/users/%s"
  ( in login_name varchar not null ) .
create iri class :blog-home "http://myhost/%s/home"
  ( in blog_home varchar not null ) .
create iri class :permalink "http://myhost/%s/%d"
  ( in blog_home varchar not null,
    in post_id integer not null ) .
make :user_iri subclass of :grantee_iri .
make :group_iri subclass of :grantee_iri .
```

IRI classes describe how to format SQL values but do not specify the origin of those values. This part of mapping declaration starts from a set of table aliases, similar to FROM and WHERE clauses of an SQL SELECT statement.

The mapping consists of quad patterns which declare how a quad (triple + graph) can be constructed from relational data. The pattern has typically a constant for the graph and the predicate and columns or groups of columns for the subject and object. The quad pattern may contain additional SQL search conditions to further restrict the scope. When a SPARQL query is compiled, each triple pattern is matched against the quad map patterns and the relevant ones are selected. There is sophisticated logic for pruning out joins that do not make sense.

```
from SYS_USERS as user from SYS_BLOGS as blog
where (^{blog.}^.OWNER_ID = ^{user.}^.U_ID)
```

A quad map value describes how to compose one of four fields of an RDF quad. It may be an RDF literal constant, an IRI constant or an IRI class with a list of columns of table aliases where SQL values come from. A special case of a value class is the identity class, which is simply marked by table alias and a column name.

Four quad map values (for `G`, `S`, `P` and `O`) form quad map pattern that specify how the column values of table aliases are combined into an RDF quad. The quad map pattern can also specify restrictions on column values that can be mapped. E.g., the following pattern will map a join of `SYS_USERS` and `SYS_BLOGS` into quads with `:homepage` predicate.

```
graph <http://myhost/users>
subject :user-iri (user.U_ID)
predicate :homepage
object :blog-home (blog.HOMEPAGE)
where (not ^{user.}^.U_ACCOUNT_DISABLED) .
```

Relational data is often mapped to RDF for purposes of integration. Typically, a single RDF quad may then originate with many different tables. The main task of the SPARQL to SQL translation is to avoid constructing unneeded unions of tables. For example, in ODS (OpenLink Data Spaces), we have a news reader and a blog application. Both have posts and comments. If one asked for all posts and comments from a given user's applications, including possibly multiple blogs and news readers, one should generate a union query that did not try to join between blog posts and news comments. This involves logic of considerable complexity in the SPARQL to SQL translator and requires careful design at the time of making the mappings. When a mapping is well declared, we can get a nearly 1:1 translation from SPARQL to SQL, with almost no penalty for the transformation, as the translation from SPARQL to SQL costs a small fraction of the time required by the SQL optimizer for finding the best join order.

No matter the complexity of a SPARQL query, it always produces a single SQL query. If this query refers to local tables or tables that are all located on the same remote database, the query is passed as a single statement to the database holding the data. This database does not have to be Virtuoso, since Virtuoso can attach tables from any other RDBMS through its SQL federation feature. Generating a single SQL query leaves all the optimization to the RDBMS, which is very important for performance, as the mapping layer cannot possibly have the statistics or knowledge of run time behavior the DBMS itself has. Also, message round trips between the mapping layer and DBMS are very expensive.

In the ODS application suite, there are blog posts, wiki articles, news items etc that are all mapped to the `sioc:Post` RDF type. Saying that something is a `sioc:Post` will pull in a union of these three tables if there is no extra information discriminating which kind of post is meant.

In pathological cases, one can end up with SQL statements of thousands of lines for a line of SPARQL. For example `{?s ?p ?o . ?o ?p ?o2}` would be a union of all columns of all tables joined to another such union. The mapping can prune out the pairs which obviously do not join but still the statement is impractical. Thus using variables in the predicate position is discouraged and specifying RDF types for variables is encouraged.

Using parametrized queries or stored procedures eliminates any mapping overheads.

21.7 Applications and Benchmarks

As of this writing, April 2009, the native Virtuoso triple store is available as a part of the Virtuoso open source and commercial offerings. The RDF Views system is part of the offering but access to remote relational data is limited to the commercial version.

Virtuoso has been used for hosting many of the data sets in the Linking Open Data Project [6], including DBpedia [2], MusicBrainz [23], Geonames [24], Freebase [20], PingTheSemanticWeb [25] and others. The largest databases are in the single billions of triples. Also the Neurocommons [12] and Bio2RDF data sets are hosted on Virtuoso.

Presently, we are operating the http://lod.openlinksw.com site with a large fraction of all published LOD data sets, 4.7 billion triples as of this writing. This will shortly be made available as a preloaded data set on Amazon EC2. In this way, anybody can rent their private copy of the world's linked data.

Web 2.0 Applications We can presently host many popular web 2.0 applications in Virtuoso, with Virtuoso serving as the DBMS and also optionally as the PHP web server.

We have presently mapped PHP BB, Mediawiki and Drupal into SIOC with RDF Views.

OpenLink Data Spaces (ODS) ODS is a web applications suite consisting of a blog, wiki, social network, news reader and other components. All the data managed by these applications is available for SPARQL querying as SIOC instance data. This is done through maintaining a copy of the relevant data as physical triples as well as through accessing the relational tables themselves via RDF Views.

Berlin SPARQL Benchmark Virtuoso was ranked the best performing triple store in the recent Berlin SPARQL benchmark. This compared representation as RDF triples, mapping of the equivalent relational data to RDF and pure relational solutions. In the relational section of this benchmark, Virtuoso also outperformed MySQL by a wide margin [5].

RDF load rates have been measured with the LUBM and various Linked Open Data data sets. Rates vary in function of the index scheme used, the presence of text indexing, the composition of the data set etc. On a single server with two Xeon 5410 CPUs running a cluster of 8 partitions, one per CPU core, the LUBM 8000 load rate, 2 indices, no text index, no materialized entailment is 110500 triples per second. The English Dbpedia 3.2 is loaded at a rate of 55700 triples per second, 4 indices. Counting full text indexing of all literals, the rate is 37400 triples/s. The rates scale linearly with the addition of machines. The amount of RAM across all the partitions is the decisive factor for load rate. These numbers were measured in a small 16 G space, with between 7.5 and 6 of 8 cores busy. If CPU utilization was under 100%, this was due to disk.

21.8 Future Directions

Clustering Future cluster work consists of adding parallel backward and forward chaining inference into the query engine. As Virtuoso has a highly parallel query platform, it is natural to exploit this for more complex operations. We can see backward chaining rules as a special case of a transitive subquery—each iteration makes more goals satisfied and/or completes variable bindings. The existing parallelization will work and since rule bodies will match data that is partitioned, the rule should be sent for matching to where the data resides.

On the forward chaining side, the whole database can be seen as a sort of RETE network. When a fact is added, it is matched to the database according to forward chaining rule heads. Each rule head is like a collection of stored queries that are evaluated with bindings from the incoming data. If there is a result, the rule body is instantiated, facts are added and the process repeats.

In this way, most RDF reasoning can be supported at the database level, with all the parallelism and scalability benefits this entails.

Federated query processing over multiple heterogeneous RDF end points faces many of the same problems as query evaluation on a cluster. The difference is that latencies are over two orders of magnitude longer and there is less flexibility in designing the message flow. We are planning to apply the cluster execution model to federated queries against arbitrary SPARQL end points.

A more traditional line of work is implementing a columnar representation for relational tables and further experimentation with compression. These would make Virtuoso a strong contender in the relational business intelligence arena.

Updating Relational Data by SPARUL Statements Many use cases of RDF involve relational-like repetitive structure. For these cases, up to an order of magnitude of gains may be had for storage size as well as retrieval performance by adopting a relational-like task specific data layout. On the query side, the relational to RDF mapping can be used for supporting this as is. The updating side requires however more work.

In many cases, an RDF view contains quad map patterns that map all columns of some table into triples in such a way that sets of triples made from different columns are "obviously" pairwise disjoint and invoked IRI classes are bijections. E.g., quad map patterns for RDF property tables usually satisfy these restrictions because different columns are for different predicates and column values are used unchanged as object literals. We are presently extending the SPARUL compiler and run-time in order to make such RDF views updatable [10].

21.9 Conclusion

With Virtuoso Cluster being operational at the time of this writing, we see that the greatest part of the RDF scalability issues is overcome. It remains the case that RDF, for all its flexibility, takes more space and is not as efficient as a task oriented relational representation. Advances in technology tend to benefit both RDF and relational models. For example, the clustering section applies 1:1 to relational workloads as well. Thus, for RDF to be equivalent to relational, it must accept some of the same restrictions, e.g., fixed graph, no variables in predicate position, strict enforcement of single value for cardinality one properties. If these are accepted, then mapping as discussed above can be used for application specific RDF representations that are essentially identical to the corresponding relational or the relational can be mapped to RDF, which are almost the same thing. The only difference is that a task specific RDF layout can still be typed at run time and use RDF data types like IRI's and typed literals. With these concessions, RDF is on a par with relational representations but does pay by embracing the same limitations.

How far one goes in the direction of application specific logical schema, indexes, materialized joins and the like is a function of the application. With Virtuoso Cluster, this is not a necessity at scales of billions and tens of billions of triples.

When relational databases replaced network databases, the argument in their favor was that one did not have to limit the set of possible queries when designing the database. Now, with RDF and linked data, the proposition is that one does not have to restrict what data can be joined with what other data when designing the database. Both represent a qualitative step in the direction of increased flexibility.

For a new technology to take hold, it must address a new class of problems: For the RDBMS, it was making the enterprise line of business applications around the database. For RDF, it is turning the Internet into a database. For the latter task, some of the flexibility for which RDF pays in 1:1 comparison against relational is necessary.

With Virtuoso, we address both sides of the matter: The generic storage of large volumes of RDF as well as exposing existing RDB's to the data web via SPARQL. Virtuoso does this with remarkable flexibility of scale, with a desktop version starting with a memory footprint of about 25 MB, small enough for mobile, going up to clusters with tens and hundreds of gigabytes of memory and terabytes of disk at the high end.

As of this writing, a W3C working group is preparing a new version of the SPARQL recommendation that will include the most important SPARQL extensions discussed in this paper. This goes a long way towards powerful interoperable querying of the web of data.

Further details on the SQL to RDF mapping and triple storage performance issues are found in separate papers on the http://virtuoso.openlinksw.com site. The Virtuoso blog http://virtuoso.openlinksw.com/blog is the most up-to-date information resource on the product.

References

1. Abadi, D.J., Marcus, A., Madden, S., Hollenbach, K.J.: Scalable Semantic Web data management using vertical partitioning. In: VLDB (2007)
2. Auer, S., Lehmann, J.: What have Innsbruck and Leipzig in common? In: Extracting Semantics from Wiki Content 4th European Semantic Web Conference. http://www.informatik.uni-leipzig.de/~auer/publication/ExtractingSemantics.pdf
3. Beckett, D.: Redland RDF Application Framework. http://librdf.org/
4. Bizer, C., Cyganiak, R., Garbers, J., Maresch, O.: D2RQ: Treating Non-RDF Databases as Virtual RDF Graphs. http://sites.wiwiss.fu-berlin.de/suhl/bizer/D2RQ/
5. Bizer, C., Schultz, A.: Berlin SPARQL Benchmark Results. http://www4.wiwiss.fu-berlin.de/bizer/BerlinSPARQLBenchmark/results/index.html
6. Bizer, C., Heath, T., Ayers, D., Raimond, Y.: Interlinking open data on the web. In: 4th European Semantic Web Conference. http://www.eswc2007.org/pdf/demo-pdf/LinkingOpenData.pdf
7. Chen, H., Wang, Y., Wang, H., et al.: Towards a Semantic Web of Relational Databases: a Practical Semantic Toolkit and an In-Use Case from Traditional Chinese Medicine. http://iswc2006.semanticweb.org/items/Chen2006kx.pdf
8. Erling, O.: ISWC 2008: Billion Triples Challenge. http://www.openlinksw.com/dataspace/oerling/weblog/Orri%20Erling's%20Blog/1478
9. Guo, Y., Pan, Z., Heflin, J.: LUBM: a benchmark for OWL knowledge base systems. J. Web Semant. **3**(2), 158–182 (2005). Available via http://www.websemanticsjournal.org/ps/pub/2005-16
10. Mikhailov, I.: Updating Relational Data Via SPARUL (Updatable RDF Views). http://esw.w3.org/topic/UpdatingRelationalDataViaSPARUL
11. Prudhommeaux, E.: SPASQL: SPARQL Support in MySQL. http://xtech06.usefulinc.com/schedule/paper/156
12. Ruttenberg, A.: Harnessing the Semantic Web to answer scientific questions. In: 16th International World Wide Web Conference. http://www.w3.org/2007/Talks/www2007-AnsweringScientificQuestions-Ruttenberg.pdf
13. Intellidimension RDF Gateway. http://www.intellidimension.com
14. Jena Semantic Web Framework. http://jena.sourceforge.net/
15. Northrop Grumman Corporation: Kowari Metastore. http://www.kowari.org/
16. Oracle and HP smash world record for TPC-H 10 TB data warehousing benchmark. http://dssresources.com/news/316.php
17. Oracle Real Application Clusters. http://www.oracle.com/database/rac_home.html
18. Oracle Semantic Technologies Center. http://www.oracle.com/technology/tech/semantic_technologies/index.html
19. Semantically-Interlinked Online Communities. http://sioc-project.org/
20. Getting Started with Freebase. http://www.freebase.com/view/guid/9202a8c04000641f8000000005b82619

21. Vertica—Column-store based DBMS. http://www.vertica.com/
22. Extensible Business Reporting Language (XBRL) 2.1. http://www.xbrl.org/Specification/XBRL-RECOMMENDATION-2003-12-31+Corrected-Errata-2006-12-18.rtf
23. About MusicBrainz. http://musicbrainz.org/doc/AboutMusicBrainz
24. About Geonames. http://www.geonames.org/about.html
25. Ping The Semantic Web. http://pingthesemanticweb.com/about.php

Chapter 22
Hera: Engineering Web Applications Using Semantic Web-based Models

Kees van der Sluijs, Geert-Jan Houben,
Erwin Leonardi, and Jan Hidders

Abstract In this chapter, we consider the contribution of models and model-driven approaches based on Semantic Web for the development of Web applications. The model-driven web engineering approach, that separates concerns on different abstraction level in the application design process, allows for more robust and structural design of web applications. This is illustrated by the use of Hera, an approach from the class of Web engineering methods that relies on models expressed using RDF(S) and an RDF(S) query language. It illustrates how models and in particular models that fit with the ideas and concepts from the Semantic Web allow to approach the design and engineering of modern, open and heterogeneous Web based systems. In the presented approach, adaptation and personalization are a main aspect and it is illustrated how they are expressed using semantic data models and languages. Also specific features of Hera are discussed, like interoperability between applications in user modeling, aspect orientation in Web design and graphical tool support for Web application design.

22.1 Introduction

The Web is *the* platform for ubiquitously accessible information and also offers numerous applications of any kind. However, even though the applications become increasingly complex, until recently most of the development process remained

K. van der Sluijs (✉)
Eindhoven University of Technology, P.O. Box 513, 5600 MB Eindhoven,
The Netherlands
e-mail: k.a.m.sluijs@tue.nl

G.-J. Houben · E. Leonardi · J. Hidders
Delft University of Technology, P.O. Box 5031, 2600 GA Delft, The Netherlands

G.-J. Houben
e-mail: g.j.p.m.houben@tudelft.nl

E. Leonardi
e-mail: e.leonardi@tudelft.nl

J. Hidders
e-mail: a.j.h.hidders@tudelft.nl

R. De Virgilio et al. (eds.), *Semantic Web Information Management*,
DOI 10.1007/978-3-642-04329-1_22,

ad-hoc. Mixing document markup languages like HTML with server-side scripting languages like PHP, ASP and Java Servlets typically allows the creation of the typical Web applications that you can find currently on the Web. However a large gap remains between current ad-hoc programming and disciplined development approaches that allow for a good separation of concerns, i.e., that can address the right issues at the right level of abstraction. The web poses unique requirements to applications in terms of usability, personalization, reusability and maintainability. As a result, many of the more complex web applications fail because of poor design and because its designers simply were not aware of the requirements to make their applications be accepted by the public. Model driven web engineering (MDWE) stands for a systematic approach for creating web applications, that allows the designer to manage the complexity and diversity that is inherent in such a task.

In the research field of Web Engineering, several MDWE methods have been proposed each with its own particular focus and its own strengths and weaknesses. Some of the most prominent methods include the Web Modeling Language (WebML) [4], Object-Oriented Hypermedia Design Model (OOHDM) [20], UML-based Web Engineering approach (UWE) [14] and the Object-Oriented Web Solutions Approach (OOWS) [11], which we will discuss in more detail in Sect. 22.6, while in this chapter we will focus on Hera [25]. What these methods share is that they dissect and describe web applications on the following levels (citing [21]):

1. data/information, with issues relating to data representation
2. navigation, with issues relating to navigation structure and behavior
3. functionality, with issues relating to application functionality beyond navigation
4. presentation/interface, with issues relating to interface and presentation design

This differs from traditional software engineering, which might typically place *functionality* as the core aspect of an application.

The first important notion is that of the subject matter of the application, i.e., what data or information is shown through the application. Most MDWE methods offer functionality for designing the information space of their application, e.g., via E/R-modeling (e.g., for data in relational databases), object-oriented approaches via UML or ORM, or using Semantic Web technology with languages like RDF. The information space is considered the basis of the application that is to be designed in most MDWE methods.

Second, MDWE allows designers to create the navigation behavior of their application. The navigation behavior is typically expressed in terms of the underlying data of the application. It defines the things being navigated and the structure of the navigation space. Designing the navigation space is based on the user requirements. This means that the navigation space must be tailored towards its user base, typically by differentiating between specific users with their specific context and preferences by means of personalization. Most MDWE methods support the navigation specification process by means of graphical tools. Moreover, the use of well-defined models allows model checking techniques to detect logical errors in the specification like dead ends (pages with no outgoing links) or unreachable pages.

Functional issues are built on top of the navigation structure. Functional behavior is basically all behavior that does not relate directly to the data navigation, even though it might influence it. The MDWE methods vary greatly in functional capabilities. One part of the application that is not about navigation is behavior within a navigation page. Since Web 2.0, web applications are no longer static pages where navigation is the only type of behavior, but they also interact with the user. Other examples of functional behavior are workflows and activities. Consider for instance a shopping cart where products can be bought and checked out. This is clearly behavior that is beyond navigation over the information set. Also, the use of Web services to get external information, or to do specific computations, is an example of the use of functional capabilities that a MDWE could support.

The web application will finally present its information to its user. Therefore, the MDWE also has to describe how it is presented. One issue that some MDWE address is platform adaptation. An application will be typically translated to HTML, but also translations to for instance Wireless Markup Language (WML) and Synchronized Multimedia Integration Language (SMIL) have been reported in literature [12] as alternative platforms. Another issue is that of device adaptation. There are quite some presentation related differences between an application for a regular Web browser and one for a mobile phone or PDA. MDWE methods typically have an abstract specification of the presentation. This allows applications to be browser independent and forward compatible by using updates of the MDWE implementing engine. It also allows designers to abstract from language specific issues and allows designers to design applications for specific devices and platforms without having knowledge of the actual technologies and languages.

In the rest of this chapter, we will focus on the particular MDWE design and engineering method called Hera. In Sect. 22.2, we explain how Hera differentiates from other methods and how its focus is on using Semantic Web techniques. We also explain Hera's architecture in the separation of three distinct phases, namely domain modeling, application design and presentation design. Then, in Sect. 22.3, we discuss a particular issue with user modeling (for personalization) in Hera, namely the cold start problem. We discuss our work to build a user modeling framework that facilitates the exchange of user models between applications. After that, we discuss aspect oriented issues in Sect. 22.4 and show how separate application aspects that influence the entire application can be separately defined and at runtime can be *weaved* into the code. In Sect. 22.5, we discuss how applications can be authored in the Hera system. We show that because of use of standard Semantic Web languages we can, besides our own authoring tools, reuse other authoring tools as well. Finally, in Sect. 22.6, we shortly discuss other main MDWE methods and we will point out their strengths and weaknesses and draw parallels with the Hera method.

22.2 Method

In this section, we discuss in more detail the Hera Web Modeling approach. Figure 22.1 shows an overview of Hera models. The starting point of building a Hera-based application is to define the Domain Model (DM) which captures the structure of content data. Based on the DM, the application designer creates an Application

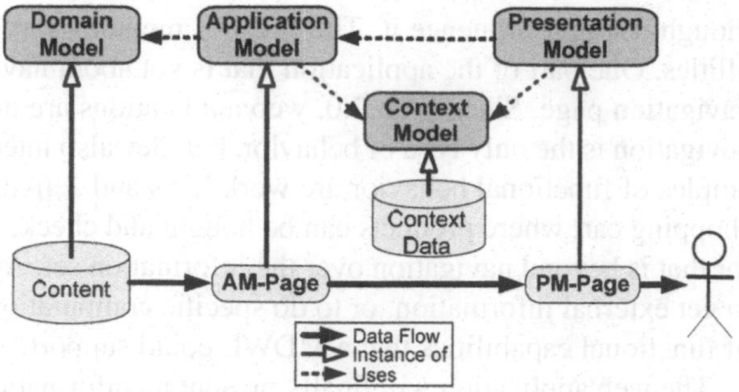

Fig. 22.1 The Hera models

Model (AM) that specifies a hypermedia-based navigation structure over the content. This navigation structure is devised for the sake of delivering and presenting the content to the user in a way that allows for a (semantically) effective access to the content. In order to support adaptation and personalization, the Context Model (CM) is maintained. This context data is dynamic, which means that it is typically updated based on the (inter)actions of the user as well as on external information. Based on the DM and the CM, the AM prescribes how the content is transformed into a navigational structure. To be more precise, instantiating the AM with concrete content results in AM (instance) pages (AMP). An AMP itself is not yet directly suitable for a browser, but can be transformed into a suitable presentation by a presentation generator, i.e., an engine that executes a specification, for example a Presentation Model (PM) of the concrete presentation design in terms of layout and other (browser-specific) presentation details.

22.2.1 Data Modeling

The first step in the Hera method is constructing the data models for the domain content (or content data) and the context of the user (or context data). RDF(S) is used for modeling the domain content. The primary objective of domain modeling is to capture the semantical structure of the domain content. With the Hera engine, the model is allowed to be an OWL ontology (without any restrictions). The Context Model (CM) is modeled and implemented in a similar fashion as the Domain Model (DM). The main difference is that the content data is meant to be presented to the user, while the context data is used for adaptation and personalization of the content data. Note that this distinction might not always be strict, but as it is only a conceptual distinction in Hera, the designer may separate content and context in whatever way he or she desires.

If we consider the role and function of the context data, then different aspects of the context data can be identified. In general, they are *session data*, *user data* and *global data*. Session data is data relevant to a certain session of a certain user. Data that is relevant to a particular user over different sessions is called user data. The user data can for example be used for personalization. Global data consists of aggregated information that gives information about groups of people.

In Hera, both the DM and CM data are stored in an RDF repository, specifically, a Sesame repository. Using Sesame brings some advantages. First, for CM, it allows the application to manage and update the context data. In addition, it offers the possibility for other processes to use and update (parts) of this information. This can be used for dynamic updates of the application, which can provide a hook for e.g., workflow processes on top of the Hera models. Furthermore, the application is able to combine several data sources (both content and context data) at the same time. Consequently, the designers can couple additional data sources to the already existing ones and can thus easily extend the domain content. Finally, it also makes it possible to exploit additional knowledge when performing search.

22.2.2 Application Modeling

The navigational structure of the Web Application is specified by the Application Model (AM). In the AM, it is specified what the AM page (AMP) will be that is shown to a user if he or she follows a certain navigation link or request a certain page. An AMP is an abstract description of a web page that defines which content and navigation links it contains and how these are organized, but explicitly does not describe how this is exactly formatted and presented to the user. The AM includes a specification of how this structure depends on the information present in the DM and CM at the moment the page is requested. This allows the navigational access to be personalized to a user and adapted for a specified context. In Hera, this is expressed by a language in RDF syntax that expresses the mapping from the user request, the DM and the CM to the resulting AMP. We will first present the part of this language that concerns itself with the basic constructs in the AMPs and then move on to the more advanced constructs. The language will be illustrated with examples from the movie domain.

22.2.2.1 Basic Constructs in Application Model

The fundamental notion in the Hera application model is that of *navigational unit* (or just *unit*) which describes a type of AMP or a fragment of an AMP, such as a page describing a movie, a page describing an actor or a fragment describing an actor on a movie page. An AMP then consists of a hierarchy of such units and this hierarchy describes its main structure. With a unit, we can associate attributes which represent a single piece of information that is shown to the user. The value of an attribute can be constant but typically these are literal values directly associated in the DM with the concept that is described by the unit. In the DM, of Hera these can be RDF literals such as strings but also Uniform Resource Identifiers (URIs) that point to other media. A special built-in media class `hera:Mime` is offered and can be used to specify an URL and the MIME-type of the object to which the URL points. This can be used if the media type is important during later processing.

Next to the unit's attributes, there can also be parameters specified. These identify the instance of a unit to which a user navigates, such as the identifier of the specific movie or actor that is shown. A full request for a page consists therefore not only of a unit but also of a set of parameters, i.e., variable names and their associated value.

As an illustration of a unit definition consider the following example:

```
:MovieUnit a am:NavigationUnit ;
   am:hasInput [
      am:variable [
         am:varName "M" ;
         am:varType imdb:Movie
      ]
   ] ;
   am:hasAttribute [
      rdfs:label "Title" ;
      am:hasQuery
         "SELECT ?T
         WHERE { ?M a imdb:Movie;
                   imdb:movieTitle ?T}
   ].
```

The example defines a very simple unit `MovieUnit` which displays information about a movie. The `am:hasInput` property defines here a single parameter `?M` which identifies the movie. As a consequence, we can use the variable `?M` in the remainder of this expression to refer to this movie. The `am:hasAttribute` property defines an attribute with name `Title`. The value of the attribute is defined by the property `am:hasQuery` which means that at the time an instance of this unit is requested the attribute value will be computed by the specified query which retrieves the title of `?M`. Note that in our examples we use the SPARQL (SPARQL Protocol and RDF Query Language) query language (cf. http://www.w3.org/TR/rdf-sparql-query/), but using other query languages is possible as well as long as the underlying datastore supports them. Any SPARQL query can be used to compute the value of an attribute, as long as it returns a single datatype property value.

With units, we can associate subunits to express the hierarchy. We can for example extend the unit `movieUnit` in the following way:

```
:MovieUnit a am:NavigationUnit ;
   am:hasInput [ am:variable [ am:varName "M";
                               am:varType imdb:Movie]] ;
   am:hasAttribute [ rdfs:label "Title" ; ... ] ;
   am:hasUnit [
      rdfs:label "LeadActor" ;
      am:refersTo :ActorUnit ;
      am:hasQuery
         "SELECT ?L
         WHERE {?M a imdb:Movie;
                   imdb:movieLeadActor ?L
                   a imdb:Actor}"
] .
```

Let us look closer at the important pieces of code in this example. The `hasUnit` property defines a nested unit. The `rdfs:label` property defines a label with which we can identify the position of this nested unit. The `am:refersTo` property indicates the type of the nested unit instance. The property `am:hasQuery` specifies a query that computes the parameters that are used to compute the instance of the nested unit. In this case, the query computes the lead actor of the movie identified by `?M`.

It is also possible to associate a navigation link with a unit, as is illustrated in the following example which defines the unit that describes an individual actor:

```
:ActorUnit a am:NavigationUnit ;
   am:hasInput [ am:variable [ am:varName "A" ;
                               am:varType imdb:Actor]] ;
   am:hasAttribute [
      rdfs:label "Name" ;
      am:hasQuery
         "SELECT ?N
          {WHERE ?A a imdb:Actor;
                 imdb:actor_name ?N" }] ;
   am:hasAttribute [
      rdfs:label "Photo" ;
      am:hasQuery
         "SELECT ?P
          WHERE {?A a imdb:Actor;
                 imdb:actorPhoto ?P"} ] ;
   am:hasNavigationRelationship [
      rdfs:label "Actor-Bio" ;
      am:refersTo :BioUnit ;
      am:hasQuery
         "SELECT ?B
          WHERE {?A a imdb:Actor;
                 imdb:actorBio ?B}"
   ] .
```

This unit specifies a parameter `?A` which is the name of the actor, two attributes `Name` and `Photo`, and with the `am:hasNavigationRelationship` property a navigation link to a `BioUnit` unit. This link will be followed if the user clicks on the representation of an instance of this unit on a page. Note that the parameters that are passed when this link is clicked will be computed by the specified SPARQL query which retrieves the `imdb:actorBio` of actor `?A` in the DM.

Next to nesting a single unit, it is also possible to nest a whole set of units. For example, we can redefine the unit `MovieUnit` such that it shows all actors in a movie:

```
:MovieUnit a am:NavigationUnit ;
   am:hasInput [ am:variable [ am:varName "M" ;
                               am:varType imdb:Movie]] ;
   am:hasAttribute [ rdfs:label "Title" ; ... ] ;
   am:hasSetUnit [
      rdfs:label "Cast";
      am:refersTo ActorUnit ;
      am:hasQuery
         "SELECT ?A
          WHERE {?M a imdb:Movie;
                 imdb:movieActor ?A}"
   ] .
```

The property `hasSetUnit` defines a special *set unit* which is nested in a `MovieUnit` and itself contains a set of unit instances of `ActorUnit`. This set is determined by the specified query: each binding in the result of the query is separately supplied as parameters to `ActorUnit` and defines a unit instance in the set unit.

The fact that values of attributes can be specified to be computed through queries over the DM and CM, already provides a limited form of adaptation. The same holds for navigation relationships and set units where the parameters and the set of units can also be determined through queries over the DM and CM. To also allow for personalization, i.e., adaptation to a specific user, a special role is given in these queries to the variable `?U` which identifies the user requesting the page. For example, assume that the CM contains information about the rating of actors by users. This can be represented by a multi-valued property `cm:actorRating` of users, which contains a set of ratings which have each a property `cm:stars` and `ratingOnActor` which represent the given number of stars and the actor to which the stars are given, respectively. We can then let the shown set of actors in a `MovieUnit` depend on the rating given by the user requesting the page as follows:

```
am:hasSetUnit [
   rdfs:label "Cast";
   am:refersTo ActorUnit ;
   am:hasQuery
      "SELECT ?A
       WHERE {?U cm:actorRating _:rating cm:stars ?V;
                 cm:ratingOnActor ?A imdb:playsIn ?M .
              FILTER (?V > 3) }"
] .
```

The expressive power of SPARQL and similar RDF query languages is relatively restricted such that they cannot express all types of desired adaptation. To improve this the adaptation language contains special if-then-else constructs that can be used to express adaptation that cannot be expressed in SPARQL. This is demonstrated in the following example:

```
:ActorUnit a am:NavigationUnit ;
   am:hasInput [ am:variable [ am:varName "A" ;
                               am:varType imdb:Actor]] ;
   ...
      am:hasSetUnit [
      rdfs:label "Movies Played In";
      am:refersTo MovieUnit ;
      am:hasConditionalQuery [
        am:if "SELECT *
               WHERE {?U cm:age ?G .
                      FILTER (?G > 17)}"
        am:then "SELECT ?M
                 WHERE {?A imdb:actorMovie ?M
                           a imdb:Movie}"
        am:else "SELECT ?M
                 WHERE {?A imdb:actorMovie ?M
                          a imdb:Movie;
                          imdb:mpaaRating ?R .
                    FILTER !regex(?R, "NC-17")}"
      ] ] .
```

The property `am:hasConditionalQuery` specifies a conditional query. It contains a `am:if` query that defines the condition such that a non-empty result represents *true* and an empty result represents *false*. Depending on this condition either the `am:then` query or the `am:else` query is executed when the AMP is constructed. In this case, this means that if the user is over 17 all movies of the actor are shown and otherwise only those that do not have the "NC-17" rating (No Children under 17 Admitted).

22.2.2.2 Other Constructs in the Application Model

An essential aspect of adaptive hypermedia is that it can adapt itself to the behavior of the user. To register the behavior of the user, the adaptation model of Hera allows the designer to associate update queries with certain events associated with a unit. These are the events `am:onLoad`, `am:onExit` and `am:onClick`. The first represents the event that the user navigates to the unit, the second that the user navigates away from the unit, and the last that the user clicks on the navigation link associated with the unit.

Another construct in the AM is frame based navigation. The basic structure of an AM page is a tree of units. The result of following a navigation link is usually that the current AM page shown to the user is completely replaced with the AM page that is the result of following the link. However, in frame-based web pages it is often the case that only a part of the current page is replaced with the result of the navigation, for example, when the link represents a menu item and only the body frame of the page is replaced with the page to which this menu item refers. To specify such behavior, the designer can define a `am:source` property with a navigation relationship, which indicates the part of the current AM page that is to be replaced with the result of the navigation. It can be either the label of a unit, or a relative reference such a `am:_self`, `am:_parent` or `am:_top`. These refer to the unit that is either the unit with which the navigation relationship is associated, its parent, or the root of the unit tree. Note that this frame behavior is not necessarily translated to e.g., HTML-frames, but that this behavior can also be simulated at the server side.

Hera also supports form-based input for more complex user interaction than only navigation links. For this, Hera provides the *form unit*. A form unit extends a normal unit with a collection of input elements that allow the user to input data into the form and an action that is executed when the form is submitted. In a form, a navigational relationship typically has a button that activates the submission.

Below, we give an example of a form that displays the text `Search Movie:` with one text input-field to let the user enter the movie he wants to browse to. If the user enters a value in this field, it is bound to the variable `movieName`. After submitting the form via a button with the text `Go`, the user navigates to the `MovieUnit` that will display the movie for which the name was entered in the input-field, which is specified in the query using the variable `$movieName`.

```
:MovieSearchForm a am:FormUnit ;
    am:hasAttribute [
        am:hasValue "Search Movie: "
    ];
    am:formElement [
        rdfs:label "Search Input";
        am:formType am:textInput;
        am:binding[
                    am:variable [am:varName "movieName" ;
                                    am:varType xsd:String ]]
    ];
    am:formElement [
        rdfs:label "Submit Button";
        am:formType am:button;
        am:buttonText "Go";
        am:hasNavigationRelationship [
            rdfs:label "Search Form-Movie" ;
            am:refersTo :MovieUnit ;
            am:hasQuery
                "SELECT ?M
                 WHERE {?M a imdb:Movie;
                             imdb:movieTitle ?X .
                        FILTER (X = $movieName)}"
        ]
    ].
```

Current Web applications offer users a wider range of client-side functionality by different kinds of scripting objects, like Javascript and VBscript, stylesheets, HTML + TIME timing objects etc. Even though MDWE methods like Hera concentrate more on the creation of a platform-independent hypermedia presentation over a data domain, and these scripts are often, but not always, browser/platform specific, Hera provides the designer a hook to insert these kind of scripting objects.

The designer can specify within a scripting object whatever code he or she wants, as this will be left untouched in generating the AMPs out of the AM. Furthermore, the designer can add an `am:hasTargetFormat` property to specify one or more target-formats for format-specific code, e.g., HTML or SMIL. This allows later in the process to filter out certain format-specific elements if these are not wanted for the current presentation. The scripting objects can use the variables that are defined within the scope of the units. Scripting objects can be defined as an element within any other element, i.e., units and attributes. Furthermore, it can be specified if the script should be an attribute of its super-element or not, e.g., similar to elements in HTML that have attributes and a body. The need to place some specific script on some specific place is of course decided by the designer.

An application designer might want to use additional functionality that cannot be realized by a client-side object, but involves the invocation of external server-side functionality. Therefore, Hera provides so-called service objects of type `am:serviceObject` to support Web services in the AM. The use of a service object and the reason to provide support for it is similar to that of scripting objects. The designer is responsible for correctness and usefulness of the service object. As an example, think of utilizing a Web service from a Web store selling DVDs in order to be able to show on a movie page an advertisement for buying its DVD. A service object needs three pieces of information: (1) a URL of the Web service one wants to use, (2) a SOAP message that contains the request to the Web service and (3) a definition of the result elements. A service object declaration can be embedded as a part of every other element. If a unit is navigated to, first the service objects will be executed. The results of the service object will either be directly integrated into the AM and treated as such, or the result can be bound to variables. Service objects can use unit variables in their calls.

22.2.3 Presentation Modeling

The objective of presentation modeling (PM) in Hera is to transform the logical level from the AM to the actual implementation. The structure of the information and functionality designed by the application designer are presented to the user by identifying navigational units and their relationships. The presentation specification of these navigational units (e.g., how they are displayed) is defined by the PM. By using this specification, the AMP is transformed into a corresponding Web presentation in a given output format, e.g., XHTML, cHTML, WML, etc. Let us now discuss the presentation specification of the PM.

The PM is defined by means of so-called regions and relationships between regions. Regions are abstractions for rectangular parts of the user display and thus they satisfy browsing platform constraints. They group AM elements in order of their presentation, and like navigation units, regions can be defined recursively. They are further specified by a layout manager, a style, and references to the navigational units that they aggregate. We note that the usage of layout managers was inspired by the AMACONT project's component-based document format [10], adopting its abstract layout manager concept in the Hera PM. This enables Hera to use external PM engines like AMACONT.

The specification of regions allows defining the application presentation in an implementation-independent way. However, to cope with different layout preferences and client devices, Hera also supports different kinds of adaptation in presentation design. As an example, based on the capabilities of the user's client device (screen size, supported document formats etc.), the spatial arrangement of regions can be adapted. Another adaptation target is the corporate design (the "look-and-feel") of the resulting Web pages. According to the preferences and/or visual impairments of users, style elements like background colors, fonts (size, color, type), or buttons can be varied.

Figure 22.2 depicts the presentation generation pipeline based on using AMACONT as an implementation. The first step is the transformation of AMPs to hierarchical AMACONT document component structures. Beginning at top-level document components and visiting their subcomponents recursively, the appropriate AMACONT layout descriptors (with adaptation variants) are added to each document component. This transformation can be performed in a straightforward way Then the automatically created AMACONT documents are processed by AMACONT's document generation pipeline. In AMACONT's document generation

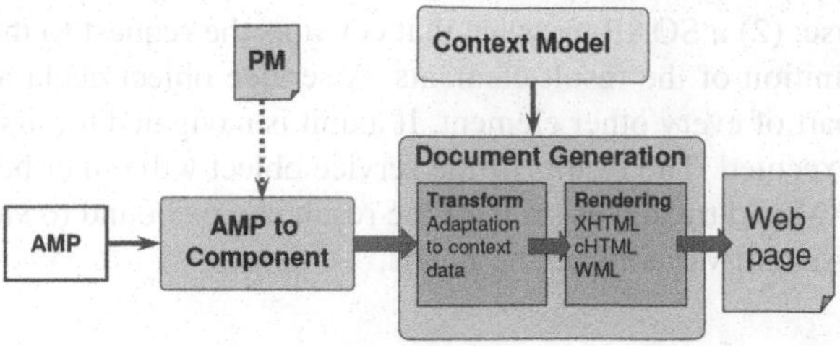

Fig. 22.2 The presentation generation with AMACONT

pipeline, first, all adaptation variants are resolved according to the current state of the context model. Then, a Web presentation in a given Web output format (e.g., XHTML, Compact HTML (cHTML), WML, etc.) is rendered and delivered to the client.

For a thorough elaboration of presentation layer adaptation, please refer to work by Fiala et al. [10].

22.3 User Modeling

In this section, we outline how the *cold start problem* is addressed in Hera. The cold start problem occurs when a system cannot perform personalization functionality due to lack of user information. Hera depends on user modeling for personalization and therefore needs up to date user models. However, often applications have been used only a limited time by the user or they are used by the user for the first time. This causes the applications to have insufficient information about the user. Consequently, they may not provide personalization properly and thus suffer from the cold start problem.

In Hera, we build a user modeling framework (UMF) that facilitates the exchange of user models between applications. This allows an application to use the user model of the same user from other applications in order to build up its own user model. We denote this process as *user model interoperability*. The main challenge of the user model interoperability is that we have to deal with *syntactic* and *semantic heterogeneity* of the user models in different applications. Observe that an application typically models the user information in a specific way which can be very different form the one of other applications. In addition, the user models from different applications rarely share the same terms and vocabularies.

Two approaches of addressing the *syntactic* and *semantic heterogeneity* of the user models are the *shared format* and the *conversion* approaches. In the shared format approaches, the applications are imposed to adopt a *lingua franca* as a common representation format which enables applications to exchange unified user models. That is, the applications have to use a shared syntax and semantics to represent user model data. Even though this approach offers no *syntactic* and *semantic heterogeneity* of the user models, this approach is impractical in open and dynamic environment such as the Web [15]. In the conversion approach, the applications do not need to use a *lingua franca*, instead, they have to convert the syntax and semantics of the user model data used in other systems to the ones they used. Of course, converting user models cannot be done perfectly as it may lead to the possibility of losing data during conversion process. It is also possible that the conversion cannot be made because the model is simply incompatible.

The UMF combines the benefits of those approaches and exploits the Semantic Web technology. It provides a user model storage facility for applications that want to use off the shelf UM technology, but it can also be used solely for applications that want to exchange some user model data. The Web applications that aim at exchanging user model data can "subscribe" to the UMF via a Webservices interface. The *UMF mapping engine* that is the core of the UMF performs translation and integration the instance data of one application to the instance data of another application. This transformation and subsequent integration form what we call an *instance mapping*. The instance mapping is generated from a *schema mapping* that needs to be provided by the designers of the applications. A schema mapping from a schema A to a schema B contains a specification of how all constructs in schema A are mapped to corresponding constructs in schema B. For example, application A has birthday information of a user U who also uses application B. In order to provide, for example, a list of movies that is restricted to the age of user U, application B has to convert the birthday information available in application A to the age information. The designer of application B can provide, for example, a mapping rule called *Birthday2Age* that contains a formula $Age = SystemTimeStamp - Birthdate$.

For some more elaborate description of the UMF, refer to some of our previous work [24]. Current research is looking at extending the UMF with mechanisms for things like access control, identity management and user model discovery.

22.4 Aspect Orientation

Within a Web application, there exist several adaptation concerns (e.g., device adaptation, security, adaptation to visual impaired users, etc.) that need to be taken into account in parallel. Some adaptation-concerns typically affect several parts of the underlying Web application. In other words, they cannot be localized to a particular module; instead, they are inherently distributed over the underlying Web application. Thus, such an adaptation concern can be considered as a *cross-cutting* concern. To weave some of these *cross-cutting* concerns at the modeling level would mean adapting all models.

In Hera, we concentrate on applying the concepts of Aspect-Oriented Programming [13] to Web application design. This allows different cross-cutting concerns to be specified in the aspect-oriented way by using an aspect-oriented adaptation specification. These concerns can be designed separately as *aspects* in the AM and are "weaved" into the code at runtime. Similar to the Aspect-Oriented Programming, we use the notion of *advice* and *pointcut*. An advice captures a particular transformation that consists of modifications to different navigational elements of the AM. Adding a single modification causes an addition of a single adaptation condition to certain navigational units or relationships in the form of a SPARQL query. A pointcut specifies an exact element to which a certain advice should be applied. By using advice/pointcut pairs, adaptation conditions can be injected to the elements of the AM. To exemplify this approach, consider the following example.

```
POINTCUT SET WITH PARENT cm:movie
ADVICE
     SELECT ?M
     WHERE {?M am:MPAA-rating ?R; a imdb:Movie .
              ?U cm:age ?G .
              FILTER (!regex(?R, 'NC-17')) || (?G > 17) }
```

The above pointcut-advice pair describes how an additional adaptation concern (e.g. age-group restriction) can be specified in an aspect-oriented way over an AM. Specifically, it restricts the visibility of all adult-rated (i.e., "NC-17"-rated) movies throughout the application, and only shows them if the user is older than 17 years old. Observe that the adaptation is not localized to one particular navigational unit, and is thus truly cross-cutting.

Furthermore, Hera also utilizes aspect-orientation to solve semantic granularity issues between the detail level of the user model and the desired adaptation. Let us illustrate this with an example. Suppose we want to select the language in which we present pages in our application, based on where a user lives. In this way, we could choose to give someone who lives, for example, in the Netherlands a Dutch version of the page, and other users the English version of the page. However, suppose we have a user model that contains the following location information about a user (in abbreviated TURTLE[1] syntax):

```
:userMary :livesin   :cityX
           a          :city;
           :cityname  "Delft" .
```

The above triples specify that a user named Mary lives in a city called Delft. The question is now where the application gets the knowledge from to understand that Delft is a city in the Netherlands; hence, it should display the Dutch version of the page to user Mary. One possible solution is to ask the user about this information. However, this would bother the user with additional questions while the country can be deduced from the city. Another possibility is to extend the adaptation query with an enumeration of all cities in the Netherlands. The main concern of this solution is that it is obviously not really viable as it would be extremely laborious to write such queries. In addition, it would make the query more complex and thus the performance would suffer significantly. Hera follows a more elegant solution by exploiting the knowledge of RDF and OWL ontologies to solve the semantic granularity problem. Many of such ontologies are freely available on the Web and can be

[1] Cf. http://www.w3.org/TeamSubmission/turtle/.

reused for this purposes. A good candidate for our case is the GeoNames Ontology.[2] This ontology simply provides us with additional knowledge:

```
geo:2757345    geo:name         "Delft" ;
               geo:inCountry    geo:NL .
```

These triples make a connection between Delft and the Netherlands. By using this information, the application is able to make the connection that if someone lives in Delft this also means he lives in the Netherlands. Therefore, Hera needs to be configured with a rule that specifies how it can infer the country of someone, knowing the city he lives in. An example of such a rule could be (simplified notation):

$$\left.\begin{array}{r} <?X\ \ :livesin\ \ ?Y> \\ <?Y\ \ rdf:type\ \ :city> \\ <?Y\ \ geo:inCountry\ \ ?Z> \end{array}\right\} \Rightarrow \left\{\begin{array}{l} <?X\ \ :livesin\ \ ?Z> \\ <?Z\ \ rdf:type\ \ :country> \end{array}\right.$$

These rules can be labeled and then referred to in the advice/pointcut rule by adding a "using" clause, enumerating which derivation rules to use. For more elaborate work on aspect orientation, refer to [5] and [18].

22.5 Tool Support

Authors that want to create web applications need to create the DM, UM, AM and PM models that where discussed in the previous sections. This can be done manually, but named structures are also suitable to be created graphically using authoring tools. The advantage of using Semantic Web languages is that tools to (graphically) create RDF structures can be used for authoring the structures in Hera as well, and quite some RDF editors are available nowadays. It also means that additional RDF tools can be used for several purposes as well, e.g., reasoners, visualizers, etc.

However, especially for the vocabulary used in the AM it is convenient to have some Hera specific tool support. The Hera graphical editor for DM and AM editing is called Hera Studio.

22.5.1 Hera Studio

In most RDF serializations, it can become difficult to see which structures belong together and what the general structure of the document is; especially if the documents get larger. This also applies to the Hera models and has the consequence

[2]Cf. http://www.geonames.org/ontology/.

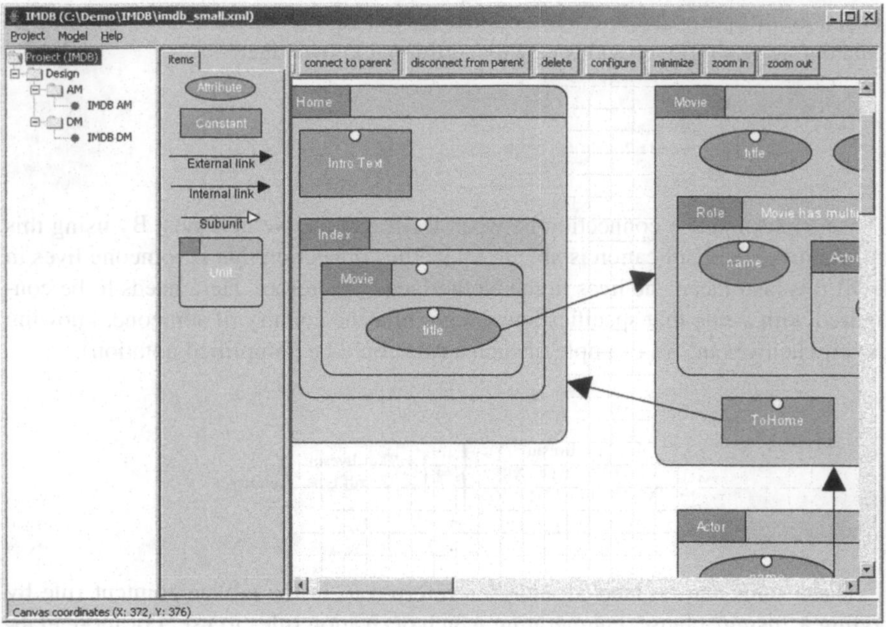

Fig. 22.3 The screenshot of Hera Studio

that manually creating them can become error-prone. It is therefore beneficial to offer Hera Studio for creating those models graphically. Hera Studio contains two model editors: *domain model editor* (DM editor) and *application model editor* (AM editor). By using these model editors, the designer is able to specify the models in a graphical way. The graphical representations of the models can be then exported to an RDF serialization which can be user by Hera. The screenshot of Hera Studio is show in Fig. 22.3. Note that Hera Studio is developed only for building models for Web application based on Hera. Hence, it is not a general purpose OWL or RDF(s)-editor.

The Web application designer can use the DM editor to define classes and object properties between those classes. For every class, a number of datatype properties can be given that have a specified media type (e.g., String, Image etc.). Moreover, the designer is able to denote the inheritance relations for classes and properties and to specify the instances of the classes and properties. Note that if more complex constructs are needed, the designer could also use a general purpose OWL/RDF editor like Protégé. Figure 22.4 depicts an example of DM. As such, the DM editor is a simplified RDF editor.

In AM-editor, the designer is able to graphically define an AM, in particular, to specify and organize the units and the relationships between them. Per unit, elements can be defined and displayed. Detailed information like queries is hidden in the graphical view, and can be configured by double-clicking the elements. The AM-

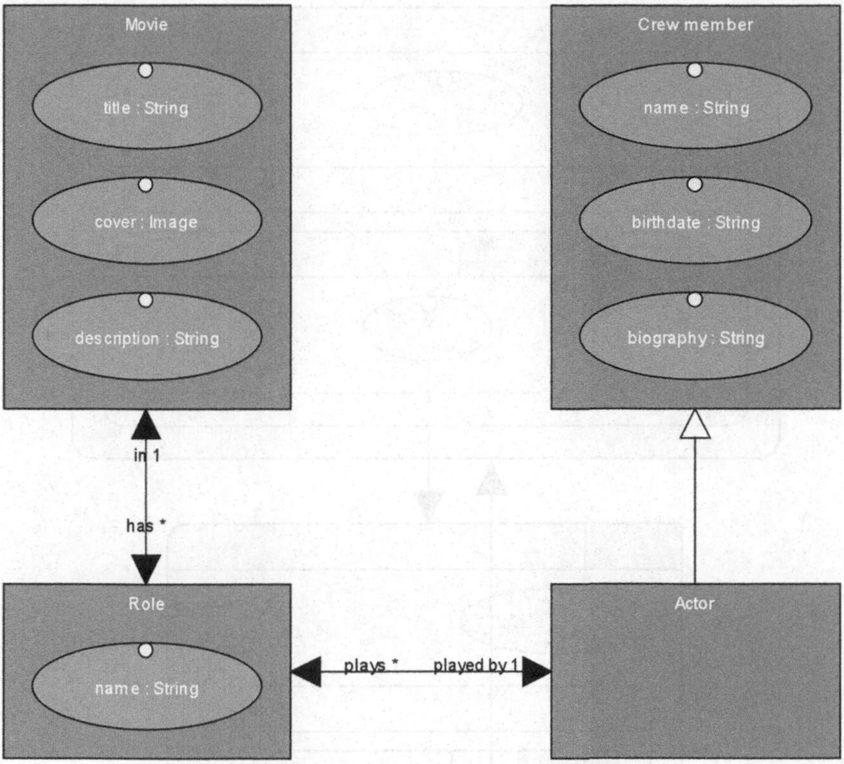

Fig. 22.4 DM example

editor provides direct help to the designer when he/she wants to define the simpler constructs. For example, when the designer defines a datatype property, the editor gives the designer a straightforward selection choice out of the (inherited) datatype properties of the underlying context and domain models. However, for the more complex constructs, the designer has the freedom to express his/her own queries and element-properties. In addition, the designer can control the level of detail of the model to get a better overview of the complete model. An example of AM is shown in Fig. 22.5

22.5.2 Other Tools

Besides Hera Studio, another specific tool for creating Hera models is available as well. This tool is called is the Hera Presentation Generator (HPG). HPG is classified into two different variants, namely, HPG-XSLT and HPG-Java. The HPG-XSLT implements the data transformation using XSLT stylesheets, and the HPG-Java uses Java for implementing the data transformation. Both tools are meant to showcase

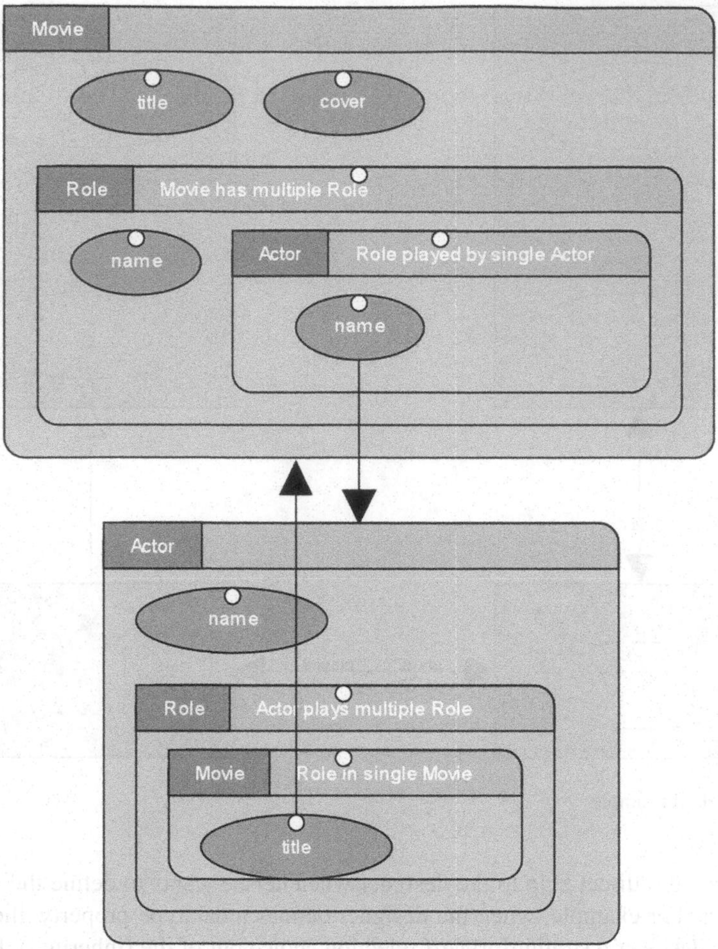

Fig. 22.5 AM example

specific strenghts of Hera, but they are both planned to be completely superseded by Hera studio. For more information on HPG-XSLT and HPG-Java, please refer to [12].

22.6 Related Work

In the previous sections, we specifically zoomed in on the Hera design and engineering method. In this section, we will shortly discuss some of the most well-known alternative methods, namely WebML in Sect. 22.6.1, OOHDM in Sect. 22.6.2, UWE in Sect. 22.6.3 and OOWS in Sect. 22.6.4. For a more comprehensive comparison between methods, please refer to [23].

22.6.1 WebML

WebML [4] is a mature web modeling language which has shown that MDWE methods can be commercially successful via its commercial tool implementation named WebRatio (cf. http://www.webratio.com). According to [8], WebML is a visual language for specifying the content structure of a Web application and the organization and presentation of such content in a hypertext. The WebML development process follows a repetitive cycle of requirements analysis, conceptual modeling of the application, implementation of the conceptual models and a testing and evaluation phase. Based on the outcome of these cycles, the web application will finally be deployed and maintained. In the conceptual modeling phase the abstract application is defined, which is done in two steps: Data Modeling and Hypertext Modeling. The information space is specified in the data modeling phase of WebML. The data is designed using well-known ER-modeling techniques. This is in contrast with Hera's use of Semantic Web languages. Both modeling choices are of course valid; it depends on the specific situation and wishes of the designer which approach is the most suitable for a specific application.

In the hypertext modeling phase, the conceptual application is defined. In WebML, the hypertext model defines the navigation structure between pages and page organization, but also functional specifications of e.g., services and content management operations, as well as presentation issues. WebML's hypertext model is a customized and particularly rich graphical language, which allows designers to add specific code bits on places where necessary. Hera's application model, in contrast, is written down in a RDF(S) vocabulary just like its data. Hera also has graphical builders for its application model, but these are not nearly as extensive as those of WebML. Where WebML is mostly focused on expressive graphical modeling, Hera is mostly focused on personalization and data selection and data reuse. WebML also does have an extension for context and user adaptation [6].

WebML's is extendable via model plugins. Throughout the years plugins for covering numerous issues have been added, e.g., with respect to context-awareness [7], services [16], workflows [3], Semantic Web [9] as well as rich internet applications [2].

22.6.2 OOHDM

OOHDM [20] is one of the earliest web modeling approaches. The OOHDM development process discerns 5 steps, namely requirements gathering, conceptual design, navigational design, abstract interface design and implementation.

In the requirements, gathering phase the stakeholders of the applications are identified and the tasks that they must performed. Based on this information, scenarios are collected which describe the use cases in the form of User Interaction Diagrams (UID). The diagrams represent the interaction of the user and the application during execution of a task.

In the conceptual design, the information space of the application is specified. OOHDM uses an extended version of UML to do that. The output of the requirements gathering phase serves as input for the conceptual design phase, i.e., the UIDs are used to initially derive a conceptual design (which can later be refined). Note that there is also a Semantic Web approach of OOHDM called SHDM [22] that, like Hera, is based on use of Semantic Web languages for the conceptual design.

The navigational design in OOHDM is considered to be a view on the conceptual design. This means that the objects (items) that the user navigates are not actually the conceptual objects, but other kinds of objects that are composed from one or more conceptual objects. The navigation objects are initially derived from tasks specified in the UIDs. Tasks in which a series of navigation objects needs to be visited are specified within in a certain context. In this way, the user can follow different context paths to fulfill particular tasks and the same concept can end up in different navigational objects, which are separately defined, such that the particular context determines how a concept is presented in that context.

In the abstract interface design phase, it is specified how the application is made perceptible to the user. The abstract interface in OOHDM focuses on the various types of functionality that can be played by interface elements with respect to the information exchange between the user and the application. The vocabulary used to define the abstract interface is established by an abstract widget ontology [17] and can be things like showing elements to the user, collecting mouse clicks and other events, and gathering user information via form elements.

The final implementation phase in OOHDM is typically the rewriting of the models obtained via the method, to corresponding code on some particular platform, so the models only support the thinking process of the designer. However, for the SHDM part there is an engine that can directly execute the models, which is called HyperDE.

22.6.3 UWE

UWE [14], which stands for UML-based Web Engineering, is a web engineering approach completely based on UML. The UWE development process consists of phases for requirements engineering, analysis, design, and implementation. It also discerns three layers of an application, namely content, navigation and presentation.

In the requirements phase, UWE considers two levels of granularity. First, a rough description of the functional behavior of the application is drawn up with UML use cases. Second, a more detailed description of this use case is developed with UML activity diagrams in which responsibilities and actions of the users of the system are modeled.

In the analysis phase, first a content model is described. This content model, expressed in a UML class diagram, captures the information space of the application. In a separate model, also the user model data is modeled.

Next, the navigation structure is specified in the design phase. The navigation structure is also specified in UML class-diagrams. In addition the navigation structure contains business logic rules. The classes in the diagram can be annotated with special semantic symbols to symbolize their function in the application, e.g., there are navigation classes, menus, access primitives and process classes. UWE provides a facility to derive a first version of the navigation structure based on the content model, which can be later refined.

The presentation is defined in classes that are associated with navigation classes in the navigation structure. Such a class is specified in terms of UI elements. The following UI elements are available in UWE: text, anchor, button, image, form and anchored collection.

A similarity that UWE shares with Hera is the use of aspect orientation [1]. UWE uses aspect orientation for adaptive link hiding, adaptive link annotation, and adaptive link generation. In order to use aspect orientation, the designer needs to (manually) put pointcuts in the model, where they want to integrate aspect considerations. The granularity of the considered aspects in UWE is thus different compared to the Hera approach. There we allow arbitrary adaptation actions and we do not require manual pointcuts, but use a generic querying mechanism to select the point to integrate aspect code.

22.6.4 OOWS

OOWS [11] is based on Model-Driven Architecture (MDA) as proposed by OMG (cf. http://www.omg.org/mda). OOWS is an extension of the OO-method [19], where the OO-method approaches web modeling as "classic" software development. OO-methods provide a Platform-Independent Model (PIM) that defines a structural model, a dynamic model and a functional model. The structural model captures the system structure (its classes, operations, and attributes) and its relationships in a class diagram. The dynamic model describes sequence diagrams that express the communication between objects. And finally, the functional model captures the semantics of state changes. OOWS extends the OO-method by providing a PIM for the user model, the navigation model and presentation model. Via automatic transformation, these PIMs are translated to Platform-Specific Models (PSM) and from PSMs to application code. The application code is generated via a three-tier architectural style, namely the presentational tier (containing user interface components), the application tier (which contains functionality like business logic) and the persistence tier (that manages the data stores used in the application).

OOWS extends the OO-method so that it can express complete web applications. It does that by providing a PIM for the user model, the navigation model and the presentation model. The user models describe the users in a hierarchical way. On the top level of this hierarchy, there are anonymous users, registered users and generic users. Navigation models are associated with users in the hierarchy and via inheritance this determines which users can access which part of the navigation. The navigation model specifies for each kind of user defined in the user model the view over the system in terms of classes, class attributes, class operations and class relationships. The presentation model depends on the links in the navigation model between system components and user types. For every such link, the presentation is specified in terms of patterns. The basic patterns are information paging (i.e., breaking instances into logical blocks), ordering criteria and information layout (e.g., tabular or tree layouts). In the automatic transformation process, these additional OOWS PIMs are orthogonally translated with the OO-method's PIMS to Platform-Specific Models (PSM) and from PSMs to the complete web application code.

The OOWS also includes some extensions to deal with some issues commonly encountered in modern web applications such as web requirements modeling. In this extension, structural and behavioral requirements have been extended with navigational requirements. This can be achieved via a task taxonomy that specifies the tasks users should achieve when interacting with the Web application, activity diagrams that describe these tasks in more detail and information templates that describe information that is exchanged in each interaction point. Another extension is business process modeling. OOWS allows the designer to express the business processes that drive the web application. For this, the designer needs to specify graphical user interfaces to launch and complete process activities, as well as the equivalent executable definition of the process. OOWS also implements an interface extension that allows interaction with Semantic Web tools. This interface is realized via two models. The first model specifies the system domain and the second model describes how external entities/agents should use the system functionality exposed in business settings.

22.7 Conclusion

In this chapter, we have discussed Model Driven Web Engineering, and more specifically Hera as an example approach. MDWE stands for a systematic approach for creating web applications, that allows the designer to manage the complexity and diversity that is inherent in such a task.

The Hera approach is characterized by a focus on adaptation in the navigation design and a number of the facilities are motivated by the goals of this adaptation support. The most characteristic element of the approach is the choice of RDF as the main language for expressing the domain and context data as well as the application model (AM) which defines the context-based navigation over and interaction with the content. Since the storage and retrieval of the RDF data involves the manipulation of RDF data, we have chosen to use SPARQL endpoints as an access mechanism over the data. As a consequence of this, we use SPARQL query expressions in the definition of the AM. With the RDF and SPARQL expressions, we have models that allow a more fine-grained specification of adaptation and context-dependency. Also we can exploit more extensively the interoperability of RDF data, for example when integrating data sources (e.g., for background knowledge), and interfering with the data processing independently from the navigation.

We have shown a user modeling approach that allows tackling the cold start problem. By using Semantic Web technology, we are able to bridge between user models of different applications. We have also shown the use of aspects to separate application wide concerns that are weaved in the code at run-time. Finally, we have shown the tool support that is available for building Hera applications. Either by using Hera custom tools, or by using existing tools on the Semantic Web.

We finally list some important benefits of using the MDWE approach to web engineering:

- better separation of concerns and as such simplifying the task of designing a complex web application,
- no coding, but modeling, which allows for logical validation of models, and forward compatibility for specific coding platforms,
- data-driven design methods allowing for rapid development of applications that present a view over the data to be presented to a user and
- support for personalization and adaptation to specific users and specific contexts.

References

1. Baumeister, H., Knapp, A., Koch, N., Zhang, G.: Modelling adaptivity with aspects. In: Proceedings of the 5th International Conference on Web Engineering (ICWE'05), pp. 406–416. Springer, Berlin (2005)
2. Bozzon, A., Comai, S., Fraternali, P., Carughi, G.T.: Conceptual modeling and code generation for rich internet applications. In: ICWE '06: Proceedings of the 6th International Conference on Web Engineering, pp. 353–360. ACM, New York (2006)
3. Brambilla, M., Celino, I., Ceri, S., Cerizza, D., Valle, E.D., Facca, F.M.: A software engineering approach to design and development of Semantic Web service applications. In: Proceedings of the 5th International Semantic Web Conference (ISWC'06), pp. 172–186. Springer, Berlin (2006)
4. Brambilla, M., Comai, S., Fraternali, P., Matera, M.: Designing web applications with WebML and WebRatio. In: Human-Computer Interaction Series, pp. 221–261. Springer, London (2008), Chap. 9
5. Casteleyn, S., van Woensel, W., van der Sluijs, K., Houben, G.J.: Aspect-oriented adaptation specification in web information systems: a semantics-based approach. New Rev. Hypermedia Multimed. **15**(1), 39–71 (2009)
6. Ceri, S., Daniel, F., Demaldé, V., Facca, F.M.: An approach to user-behavior-aware web applications. In: Proceedings of the 5th International Conference on Web Engineering (ICWE'05), pp. 417–428. Springer, Berlin (2005)
7. Ceri, S., Daniel, F., Matera, M., Facca, F.M.: Model-driven development of context-aware web applications. ACM Trans. Internet Technol. **7**(1) (2007)
8. Ceri, S., Fraternali, P., Bongio, A., Brambilla, M., Comai, S., Matera, M.: Designing Data-Intensive Web Applications. Morgan Kaufmann, San Mateo (2002)
9. Facca, F.M., Brambilla, M.: Extending webml towards Semantic Web. In: WWW '07: Proceedings of the 16th International Conference on World Wide Web, pp. 1235–1236. ACM, New York (2007)

10. Fiala, Z., Frasincar, F., Hinz, M., Houben, G.J., Barna, P., Meißner, K.: Engineering the presentation layer of adaptable web information systems. In: Web Engineering—4th International Conference, ICWE 2004, Munich, Germany, July 26–30, 2004, Proceedings. Lecture Notes in Computer Science, vol. 3140, pp. 459–472. Springer, Berlin (2004)
11. Fons, J., Pelechano, V., Pastor, O., Valderas, P., Torres, V.: Applying the OOWS model-driven approach for developing web applications. In: The Internet Movie Database Case Study. Human-Computer Interaction Series, pp. 65–108. Springer, London (2008), Chap. 5
12. Frasincar, F., Houben, G.J., Barna, P.: Hpg: The Hera presentation generator. J. Web Eng. **5**(2), 175–200 (2006)
13. Kiczales, G., Lamping, J., Mendhekar, A., Maeda, C., Lopes, C.V., Loingtier, J.M., Irwin, J.: Aspect-oriented programming. In: ECOOP, pp. 220–242 (1997)
14. Koch, N., Knapp, A., Zhang, G., Baumeister, H.: Uml-based web engineering: an approach based on standard. In: Human-Computer Interaction Series, pp. 157–191. Springer, London (2008), Chap. 7
15. Kuflik, T.: Semantically-enhanced user models mediation: Research agenda. In: Kuflik, T., Berkovsky, S., Heckmann, D., Krüger, A. (eds.) UbiqUM 2008: Theories and Applications of Ubiquitous User Modeling. International Conference on Intelligent User Interfaces. ACM, New York (2008)
16. Manolescu, I., Brambilla, M., Ceri, S., Comai, S., Fraternali, P.: Model-driven design and deployment of service-enabled web applications. ACM Trans. Internet Technol. **5**(3), 439–479 (2005)
17. de Moura, S.S., Schwabe, D.: Interface development for hypermedia applications in the Semantic Web. In: LA-WEBMEDIA '04: Proceedings of the WebMedia & LA-Web 2004 Joint Conference 10th Brazilian Symposium on Multimedia and the Web 2nd Latin American Web Congress, pp. 106–113. IEEE Computer Society, Los Alamitos (2004)
18. Niederhausen, M., van der Sluijs, K., Hidders, J., Leonardi, E., Houben, G.J., Meißner, K.: Harnessing the power of semantics-based, aspect-oriented adaptation for amacont. In: Ninth International Conference on Web Engineering (ICWE 2009). Lecture Notes in Computer Science. Springer, Berlin (2009)
19. Pastor, O., Gómez, J., Insfrán, E., Pelechano, V.: The oo-method approach for information systems modeling: from object-oriented conceptual modeling to automated programming. Inf. Syst. **26**(7), 507–534 (2001)
20. Rossi, G., Schwabe, D.: Modeling and implementing web applications with OOHDM. In: Human-Computer Interaction Series, pp. 109–155. Springer, London (2008), Chap. 6
21. Rossi, G., Schwabe, D., Olsina, L., Pastor, O.: Overview of design issues for web applications development. In: Human-Computer Interaction Series, pp. 49–63. Springer, London (2008), Chap. 4
22. Schwabe, D., Szundy, G., de Moura, S.S., Lima, F.: Design and implementation of Semantic Web applications. In: WWW Workshop on Application Design, Development and Implementation Issues in the Semantic Web (2004)
23. Schwinger, W., Retschitzegger, W., Schauerhuber, A., Kappel, G., Wimmer, M., Pröll, B., Castro, C.C., Casteleyn, S., Troyer, O.D., Fraternali, P., abd Franca Garzotto, I.G., Ginige, A., Houben, G.J., Koch, N., Moreno, N., Pastor, O., Paolini, P., Ferragud, V.P., Rossi, G., Schwabe, D., Tisi, M., Vallecillo, A., van der Sluijs, K., Zhang, G.: A survey on web modeling approaches for ubiquitous web applications. Int. J. Web Inf. Syst. **4**(3), 234–305 (2008)
24. van der Sluijs, K., Houben, G.J.: A generic component for exchanging user models between web-based systems. Int. J. Contin. Eng. Educ. Life-Long Learn. (IJCEELL) **16**(1/2), 64–76 (2006)
25. van der Sluijs, K., Houben, G.J., Broekstra, J., Casteleyn, S.: Hera-S—web design using sesame. In: Proceedings of the 6th International Conference on Web Engineering (ICWE'06), pp. 337–345. ACM, New York (2006)

Index

DOI 10.1007/978-3-642-04329-1, © Springer-Verlag Berlin Heidelberg 2010